Register Now f... ...s
to You. Book!

SPRINGER PUBLISHING COMPANY
CONNECT™

Your print purchase of *Assessment in Rehabilitation and Mental Health Counseling* **includes online access to the contents of your book**—increasing accessibility, portability, and searchability!

Access today at:

http://connect.springerpub.com/content/book/978-0-8261-6243-4 or scan the QR code at the right with your smartphone and enter the access code below.

X53S9AGH

Scan here for quick access.

SPRINGER PUBLISHING COMPANY
View all our products at springerpub.com

David R. Strauser, PhD, is a professor in the Department of Kinesiology and Community Health at the University of Illinois at Urbana–Champaign, where he also directs the Work and Disability Lab. He received his PhD in rehabilitation psychology from the University of Wisconsin–Madison in 1995. He is one of six members elected to the Sloan Family Institute section on work and disability. He has received the James Garrett Distinguished Career Research Award (2011) from the American Rehabilitation Counseling Association, the New Career Award (1997) and Researcher of the Year Award (2011) from the National Council on Rehabilitation Education, and multiple research awards from the American Rehabilitation Counseling Association and National Rehabilitation Association. In 2014, Dr. Strauser received the George N. Wright Varsity Award given to an outstanding alumnus of the Rehabilitation Psychology Program at the University of Wisconsin–Madison. His research focuses on the career and vocational development of young adults, including young adults with cancer. Dr. Strauser is the editor-in-chief of *Rehabilitation Research, Policy, and Education* and serves on multiple editorial boards of journals related to rehabilitation and persons with disabilities. He is the editor of the book *Career Development, Employment, and Disability in Rehabilitation: From Theory to Practice.* He has authored over 100 journal articles and book chapters and is consistently recognized as an international leader regarding the career and vocational development of people with disabilities and chronic health conditions.

Timothy N. Tansey, PhD, received his PhD in rehabilitation psychology from the University of Wisconsin–Madison. He is an associate professor in the Rehabilitation Counselor Education Program at the University of Wisconsin–Madison. Dr. Tansey has over 20 years' experience as a rehabilitation counselor, educator, and rehabilitation researcher. He has published over 50 peer-reviewed articles in the areas of evidence-based practices in vocational rehabilitation, self-regulation and self-determination, and applying novel technology in vocational rehabilitation and rehabilitation counselor education. Dr. Tansey has extensive experience in adapting technology and utilizing social media for knowledge translation and dissemination activities. He is currently the principal investigator, coprincipal investigator, or coinvestigator on five federally funded research or national technical assistance center grants from the U.S. Department of Education, U.S. Department of Labor, and U.S. Department of Health and Human Services (Social Security Administration and the National Institute on Disability, Independent Living, and Rehabilitation Research). These current projects, totaling over $50 million, seek to ascertain evidence-based practices in the vocational rehabilitation of youth with disabilities; identify employer practices in the recruitment, hiring, retention, and promotion of persons with disabilities; and provide technical assistance to state vocational rehabilitation programs to increase competitive, integrated employment of persons with disabilities living in areas of extreme poverty. Dr. Tansey serves as the coeditor of the *Rehabilitation Counseling Bulletin* and on the editorial boards for *Rehabilitation Research, Policy, and Education*, the *Journal of Vocational Rehabilitation*, and the *Australian Journal of Rehabilitation Counseling*, as well as an ad hoc reviewer to numerous other journals.

Fong Chan, PhD, CRC, is a professor emeritus in the Department of Rehabilitation Psychology and Special Education, University of Wisconsin–Madison. He is also the codirector of the Rehabilitation Research and Training Center on Evidence-Based Vocational Rehabilitation Practices. Before joining the faculty at the University of Wisconsin–Madison in 1992, he was on the faculty in the Department of Psychology at the Illinois Institute of Technology for 4 years and the Department of Rehabilitation Counseling Psychology at the University of Texas Southwestern Medical Center for 5 years. He is a certified rehabilitation counselor, a licensed psychologist, and a fellow in the American Psychological Association. Dr. Chan has more than 35 years of experience conducting applied rehabilitation research in the topical areas of neuropsychological assessment, psychosocial interventions, demand-side employment, transition and postsecondary education, evidence-based practice, and research methodologies. Dr. Chan has published over 300 refereed journal articles and book chapters. In addition, he is the editor of four textbooks: *Case Management for Rehabilitation Health Professionals*; *Counseling Theories and Techniques for Rehabilitation Health Professionals*; *Understanding Psychosocial Adjustment to Chronic Illness and Disability: A Handbook for Evidence-Based Practitioners in Rehabilitation*; and *Certified Rehabilitation Counselor Examination Preparation: A Concise Guide to the Foundations of Rehabilitation Counseling.*

ASSESSMENT IN REHABILITATION AND MENTAL HEALTH COUNSELING

David R. Strauser, PhD

Timothy N. Tansey, PhD

Fong Chan, PhD, CRC

Editors

SPRINGER PUBLISHING COMPANY

Springer Publishing Company, LLC
11 West 42nd Street
New York, NY 10036
www.springerpub.com
http://connect.springerpub.com

Acquisitions Editor: Rhonda Dearborn
Compositor: S4Carlisle Publishing Services

ISBN: 978-0-8261-6242-7
ebook ISBN: 978-0-8261-6243-4
Sample Syllabi ISBN: 978-0-8261-6244-1
Instructor's PowerPoints ISBN: 978-0-8261-6246-5
Instructor's Test Bank ISBN: 978-0-8261-6245-8
DOI: 10.1891/9780826162434

Instructor's Materials: Qualified instructors may request supplements by emailing textbook@springerpub.com.

21 22 / 5 4 3 2

The author and the publisher of this Work have made every effort to use sources believed to be reliable to provide information that is accurate and compatible with the standards generally accepted at the time of publication. The author and publisher shall not be liable for any special, consequential, or exemplary damages resulting, in whole or in part, from the readers' use of, or reliance on, the information contained in this book. The publisher has no responsibility for the persistence or accuracy of URLs for external or third-party Internet websites referred to in this publication and does not guarantee that any content on such websites is, or will remain, accurate or appropriate.

Library of Congress Cataloging-in-Publication Data
Names: Strauser, David R., author. | Tansey, Timothy N., author. | Chan,
  Fong, author.
Title: Assessment in rehabilitation and mental health counseling / David R.
  Strauser, PhD, Timothy N. Tansey, PhD, Fong Chan, PhD, CRC.
Description: New York : Springer Publishing, [2019] | Includes
  bibliographical references and index.
Identifiers: LCCN 2019020447 | ISBN 9780826162427 | ISBN 9780826162434 (ebook)
Subjects: LCSH: People with disabilities--Functional assessment. | Mental
  health counseling.
Classification: LCC RM930.8 .S77 2019 | DDC 362.2/04256--dc23
LC record available at https://lccn.loc.gov/2019020447

Contact us to receive discount rates on bulk purchases.
We can also customize our books to meet your needs.
For more information please contact: sales@springerpub.com

David R. Strauser: https://orcid.org/0000-0002-2359-8418
Timothy N. Tansey: https://orcid.org/0000-0001-6418-2163
Fong Chan: https://orcid.org/0000-0001-6254-6891

Printed in the United States of America.

CONTENTS

■ Section III. Applications

■ Section IV. Issues in Assessment

CONTRIBUTORS

Catherine A. Anderson, PhD, CRC   Researcher and Principal Investigator, Department of Rehabilitation Psychology and Special Education, University of Wisconsin–Madison, Madison, Wisconsin

Danielle Leigh Antol, MS   Doctoral Candidate, School of Rehabilitation, University of Texas Rio Grande Valley, Edinburg, Texas

Laura Avellone, PhD   Research Associate, Virginia Commonwealth University, Richmond, Virginia

Erin F. Barnes, PhD, CRC, NCC, LPC(TX)   Clinical Assistant Professor and Clinical Coordinator, Rehabilitation Counseling and Clinical Mental Health Counseling Programs, The University of Iowa, Iowa City, Iowa

Norman L. Berven, PhD   Professor Emeritus, Department of Rehabilitation Psychology and Special Education, University of Wisconsin–Madison, Madison, Wisconsin

Jill L. Bezyak, PhD   Professor, Department of Human Services, University of Northern Colorado, Greeley, Colorado

Emily A. Brinck, PhD   Assistant Professor, Rehabilitation Services, University of Maine at Farmington, Farmington, Maine

Antoinette Cambria, MEd, NCC   Doctoral Candidate, Department of Educational Psychology, Counseling, and Special Education, The Pennsylvania State University, State College, Pennsylvania

Fong Chan, PhD, CRC   Professor Emeritus, Department of Rehabilitation Psychology and Special Education, University of Wisconsin–Madison, Madison, Wisconsin

Xiangli Chen, MS   Doctoral Student, Department of Rehabilitation Psychology and Special Education, University of Wisconsin–Madison, Madison, Wisconsin

Jonique R. Childs, PhD, NCC   Assistant Professor, School Counselor Education Program, University of Massachusetts Amherst, Amherst, Massachusetts

Charles Edmund Degeneffe, PhD, MSSW, CRC   Professor, Department of Administration, Rehabilitation, and Postsecondary Education, San Diego State University, San Diego, California

Marc L. Espino, MA, LPC   Doctoral Student, Department of Rehabilitation Psychology and Special Education, University of Wisconsin–Madison, Madison, Wisconsin

Veronica Y. Estala-Gutierrez, MRC   Lecturer, Department of Rehabilitation Sciences, University of Texas at El Paso, El Paso, Texas

Julianne Frain, PhD, CRC   Diplomate, American Board of Vocational Experts, Rehab Pro Assessment and Consultation, Palm City, Florida

Michael Frain, PhD, CRC   Professor, Florida Atlantic University, Boca Raton, Florida

Beth H. Gilfillan, PhD   Assistant Professor, School of Counseling and Special Education, Bowling Green State University, Bowling Green, Ohio

Joy Gray, MEd, NCC   Counselor and Mental Health Professional, Blair Family Solutions, Altoona, Pennsylvania

Chelsea E. Greco, MA   Doctoral Candidate, Department of Kinesiology and Community Health, University of Illinois at Urbana–Champaign, Champaign, Illinois

Teresa Ann Grenawalt, MS, CRC   Doctoral Candidate, Department of Rehabilitation Psychology and Special Education, University of Wisconsin–Madison, Madison, Wisconsin

Whitney Ham, MS, CRC, BCBA, LBA   Autism Coordinator, Rehabilitation Research and Training Center, Virginia Commonwealth University, Richmond, Virginia

Michael T. Hartley, PhD, CRC   Associate Professor, Department of Disability and Psychoeducational Studies, University of Arizona, Tucson, Arizona

Jessica S. Henry, PhD, LPC, CRC   Assistant Clinical Professor, Rehabilitation and Human Services, The Pennsylvania State University, University Park, Pennsylvania

William T. Hoyt, PhD   Professor and Associate Dean, Department of Counseling Psychology, University of Wisconsin–Madison, Madison, Wisconsin

Kanako Iwanaga, PhD   Assistant Professor, Department of Rehabilitation Counseling, Virginia Commonwealth University, Richmond, Virginia

Beatrice Lee, MS   Doctoral Candidate, Department of Rehabilitation Psychology and Special Education, University of Wisconsin–Madison, Madison, Wisconsin

Mykal J. Leslie, PhD   Assistant Professor, Rehabilitation Counseling, College of Education, Health and Human Services, Kent State University, Kent, Ohio

Irmo Marini, PhD, CRC, CLCP, FVE   Professor, School of Rehabilitation, University of Texas Rio Grande Valley, Edinburg, Texas

Jennifer Todd McDonough, MS, CRC   Project Director, Virginia Commonwealth University, Henrico, Virginia

Elias Mpofu, PhD, DEd   Professor, Rehabilitation and Health Services, University of North Texas, Denton, Texas; Clinical and Rehabilitation Sciences, University of Sydney, Sydney, Australia; Educational Psychology, University of Johannesburg, Johannesburg, South Africa

Veronica Muller, PhD, CRC   Assistant Professor and Program Coordinator, Mental Health Counseling Program, Hunter College–City University of New York (CUNY), New York, New York

Joseph N. Ososkie, PhD   Professor and Department Chair, Department of Human Services, University of Northern Colorado, Greeley, Colorado

Deirdre O'Sullivan, PhD, CRC   Associate Professor, The Pennsylvania State University, University Park, Pennsylvania

Tanya Rutherford Owen, PhD, CRC, CLCP, CDMS, LPC   Adjunct Professor and Guest Lecturer, Department of Rehabilitation Education and Research, University of Arkansas, Fayetteville, Arkansas; Owner, Owen Vocational Services, Inc., Fayetteville, Arkansas

Rigel Macarena Pinon, MS   Doctoral Candidate, School of Rehabilitation, University of Rio Grande Valley, Edinburg, Texas

Phillip D. Rumrill, PhD, CRC   Professor, Kent State University, Munroe Falls, Ohio

Jennifer Sánchez, PhD, CRC   Assistant Professor and Program Coordinator, Rehabilitation Counseling and Clinical Mental Health Counseling Programs, The University of Iowa, Iowa City, Iowa

David R. Strauser, PhD   Professor, Department of Kinesiology and Community Health, University of Illinois at Urbana–Champaign, Champaign, Illinois

Timothy N. Tansey, PhD   Associate Professor, Department of Rehabilitation Psychology and Special Education, University of Wisconsin–Madison, Madison, Wisconsin

Jing Tao, PhD   Professor and Dean, School of Rehabilitation Medicine, Fujian University of Traditional Chinese Medicine, Fujian, China

Vilia M. Tarvydas, PhD   Professor Emerita, Department of Rehabilitation and Counselor Education, The University of Iowa, Iowa City, Iowa

Justin Watts, PhD, NCC, CRC   Assistant Professor, Rehabilitation and Health Services, University of North Texas, Denton, Texas

Paul Wehman, PhD   Professor of Physical Medicine and Rehabilitation; Chairman, Division of Rehabilitation Research; Director, Rehabilitation Research and Training Center, Virginia Commonwealth University, Richmond, Virginia

Holly Whittenburg, MAEd, MEd   Director of National Autism Research, Rehabilitation Research and Training Center, Virginia Commonwealth University, Richmond, Virginia

Jia-Rung Wu, PhD   Assistant Professor, Department of Counselor Education, Northeastern Illinois University, Chicago, Illinois

Rana Yaghmaian, PhD   Assistant Professor, Department of Counselor Education, Portland State University, Portland, Oregon

PREFACE

One of the historical pillars of rehabilitation counseling has been the use of assessment through-out the rehabilitation process. With this historical emphasis, it is not surprising that the focus on assessment and the methods and techniques used have changed and evolved. As a result, students, practitioners, and researchers are in a constant quest of updated and current information to guide and inform practice, policy, and research. This constant quest for updated and comprehensive information is directly relevant to the assessment of people typically served by rehabilitation and mental health practitioners and is the focus of this book. To date, there has not been a book that has been able to provide a comprehensive discussion of topics applicable to service delivery across both settings. This book attempts to fill this gap.

One factor that guided the development of this book was our goal to provide the foundational information necessary to understand and plan the assessment process and combine this material with information that is applicable to specific population and service delivery settings. To achieve this goal, each of the chapters is written by leaders in the field who have specialized knowledge regarding the chapter content. With contributions from our quality authors, this book provides relevant and easy-to-understand application of theory as it relates to assessment of people. The chapters are also written to support application to a variety of practice settings and provide prac-tical hands-on information that allows for easy incorporation of the material to rehabilitation and mental health practice. To further strengthen practical application, case studies and templates have been incorporated where applicable to highlight specific key aspects to promote application to service delivery.

Second, this is the first assessment book to be developed after the Council on Rehabilitation Education (CORE) and Council for Accreditation of Counseling and Related Educational Pro-grams (CACREP) merger. Postmerger, there is a need for textbooks to have a broader scope while still maintaining a focus on the important aspects of specific practice areas. This book addresses all the relevant CACREP standards as they relate to assessment and also is written to be applicable to both rehabilitation and mental health counseling settings and areas of research. This dual fo-cus and postmerger development make this book unique and should allow application for use in graduate rehabilitation and mental health programs and use by practitioners in the field who are looking for current and updated information regarding assessment.

Finally, we hope that the readers of this book can apply this information to enhance the overall quality of life of the clients they work with, especially people with disabilities. Through the quality contributions of many distinguished scholars in the field, I think that the readers will find this book to be a significant resource that can help them conceptualize assessment and its overall application to service delivery. As with many areas of rehabilitation and mental health practice, it is easy to lose sight of the importance of key concepts in the daily tedium of work. It is our hope that this book provides some recognition of the efforts of both students and service providers. **We also hope that instructors find the Sample Syllabi, PowerPoints, and Test Bank, which are available upon request by emailing textbook@springerpub.com, to be useful resources as they develop and teach this important information.**

FOUNDATION OF THE ASSESSMENT PROCESS

INTRODUCTION TO ASSESSMENT IN REHABILITATION

DAVID R. STRAUSER | CHELSEA E. GRECO

LEARNING OBJECTIVES

After reviewing this chapter, the reader should be able to:

- Describe the purpose of assessment in rehabilitation counseling and apply the problem-solving model.
- Describe the key terms and types of assessment typically used in rehabilitation counseling assessment.
- Define contemporary issues that have emerged regarding the use of assessment in rehabilitation counseling practice.

Introduction

Historically, assessment has been an important part of the rehabilitation process and has been viewed as critical service directed at enhancing rehabilitation outcomes of persons with all types of disability (Andrew, 1981; Chan, Reid, et al., 1997). The chapter introduces the role of assessment in contemporary rehabilitation counseling practice and describes a problem-solving process that can be employed by rehabilitation counselors to help guide the assessment process. Important terms are defined, and types of assessments that are relevant in rehabilitation counseling assessment are discussed. The chapter concludes with a discussion of the contemporary issues that have impacted and continue to have an impact on the use of assessment in rehabilitation counseling.

Purpose of Assessment in Rehabilitation Counseling

In an historical context, assessment has been viewed as the process of attempting to assess the client's aptitudes, achievement, intelligence, personality, interests, and behavior in an effort to determine potential goals and services needed to achieve desired rehabilitation outcomes (Andrew, 1981). In many environments, rehabilitation professionals are responsible for developing and implementing an evaluation strategy based on specific referral questions. A long-held view is that upon the completion of the assessment process, a rehabilitation counselor should obtain the following information that is relevant in developing an individualized rehabilitation plan: (a) the client's relevant levels of social, educational, psychological, and physiological functioning; (b) an estimate of the client's potential for behavior change; (c) the person's learning style; (d) specific education and training programs that might increase vocational potential; (e) jobs for which the client has the residual skills to perform without any additional training or skill development; (f) potentially feasible jobs for the client with additional training; and (g) community and auxiliary supports that can facilitate job acquisition and maintenance. Despite the ambitious expectation regarding the extent and quality of information gathered, it must be kept in mind that as with any good medical examination, information garnered from testing and evaluation is just one component of the assessment that should be used in planning and service provision (Strauser, Chan, Wang, Wu, & Rahimi, 2014).

The primary purpose of assessment in rehabilitation counseling is to help the rehabilitation counselor and consumers obtain important and relevant information to help achieve identified goals and outcomes. In addition, participation in the assessment process should be a therapeutic experience that assists the client in making sense of things that have happened in the past, understanding the present situation, and identifying the tasks and behaviors needed to achieve identifiable goals and directions for the future (Strauser et al., 2014). In rehabilitation counseling, the primary focus of the assessment process is typically diagnostic, with the goal of helping the client engage in productive self-evaluation, increased awareness and understanding, and monitoring progress toward goal attainment. According to Gregory (2011), testing as part of the assessment process has the following five major objectives: classification, diagnosis and treatment planning, client self-knowledge, program evaluation, and research to guide theory and technique development. However assessment is being used in the rehabilitation counseling process, it is important to include the client in all phases of the assessment process, clearly convey the purpose of the testing, and work with the client in identifying meaningful and achievable goals and outcomes. Simply stated, the assessment process should be part of the learning process, not something that is supplementary to the counseling process (Hays, 2013).

Because assessment in rehabilitation counseling is typically a diagnosis-based problem-solving process, it is beneficial for rehabilitation counselors to utilize a concrete and straightforward problem-solving–based approach to identify the issues that will guide the assessment process. Clients involved in the assessment process will have different problem-solving abilities, but the utilization of a tangible process will maximize problem identification, individual involvement, and the potential utilization of the information obtained from the assessment process. A five-step, basic problem-solving model can be used by rehabilitation counselors throughout the assessment process to identify and process information related to the client's potential outcomes (Chang, D'Zurilla, & Sanna, 2004; Hays, 2013). A description of each step follows:

> *Step 1: Problem Orientation*—In this step, the rehabilitation counselor assesses how the problem is being viewed and whether the client recognizes the problem. When both parties are aware of the problem, they can work together to approach the problem in a systematic fashion.

> *Step 2: Problem Identification*—In this step, both the rehabilitation counselor and the client work together to operationalize the problem in as much detail as possible. Research has found that clients are more likely to continue in the rehabilitation process if they have a clear understanding of the nature of the problem (Busseri & Tyler, 2004).

Identification of the problem also assists the rehabilitation counselor in communicating with other stakeholders such as referral sources, agency personnel, family, and other related professionals.

Step 3: *Generation of Alternatives*—Once the problem has been clearly identified, the rehabilitation counselor and the client can generate alternatives that can be used to help resolve the problem. In this step, the assessment process is used to help identify the client's personal strengths that can be leveraged to overcome difficulties and enhance individual development.

Step 4: *Decision-Making*—Once alternatives have been identified, the rehabilitation counselor and client can work together to anticipate the various consequences of the alternatives identified in step 3. In classical decision theory, choice can be conceptualized as the function of the probability of achieving success and the desirability of the outcome (Hays, 2013; Horan, 1979). According to this formula, the importance of assessing both the likelihood of success for the various alternatives and the attractiveness of those alternatives is emphasized with the understanding that clients will likely choose alternatives that maximize the likelihood of favorable outcomes (Hays, 2013).

Step 5: *Verification*—The final step of the decision-making process involves discussing with the client how both parties will be aware that the problem has been solved. This last step requires that the goals be clearly specified, that they be translated into specific behavioral objectives, and that the possibility for progress in accomplishing these goals be realistically viewed (Hays, 2013).

In addition to understanding how assessment can be used effectively in the rehabilitation counseling process, it is equally important to recognize the limitations of the assessment process. Tyler (1984) has provided an outline of the major limitations associated with the assessment process that can be applied to the rehabilitation counseling setting. First, tests do not measure unique characteristics but instead focus on common individual attributes. As a result, assessment and test results are not suitable for making group comparisons but only for approximating how well a person will function on the tested behavior in the culture for which the assessment is appropriate. Second, test scores do not exclusively measure specific human characteristics but instead note aspects of innate ability as influenced by the combination of cultural and environmental factors. Third, for many tests used in rehabilitation, a good score may mean the absence of disease or reduced functioning, rather than the possession of universal attributes to which most people aspire. Fourth, and perhaps most important, tests do not measure all traits and constructs equally, and test results are not necessarily indicative of the totality of a person's behaviors, attitudes, and skills (Hays, 2013).

Important Terms in Rehabilitation Counseling Assessment

In order for rehabilitation counselors to effectively use assessment and tests throughout the rehabilitation counseling process, they need to be aware of, and have command of, key terms that are used in the assessment process. In this section, the terms *assessment, tests, measurement,* and *variable* are defined. In addition, in rehabilitation counseling the term *consumer* and *client* is often used to refer to the person involved in the testing process. Also of note, the assessment process can take place in a variety of settings including, but not limited to, schools, community agencies, rehabilitation hospitals, mental health centers, colleges and universities, and vocational rehabilitation agencies. Brief descriptions of the four key terms follow.

Assessment—This all-encompassing term applies to the evaluation methods rehabilitation counselors use to measure characteristics of persons, places, and things (Hays, 2013). In addition, the terms *appraisal* and *evaluation* are often used interchangeably. The National Council on Measurement in Education (American Educational Research Association, American Psychological Association, and National Council on Measurement in Education, 1999) defines assessment as "any systematic method of obtaining information from tests or other sources used to draw inferences about the characteristics of people, objects, and programs" (p. 172). Two important aspects of this definition are important to consider. First, the definition implies that assessment utilizes a broad range of evaluation methods such as standardized tests, rating scales, observations, interviews, and record reviews as a means of obtaining information regarding the person being assessed. Second, the definition emphasizes the use of data derived from the assessment process to assist the rehabilitation counselor in understanding the person and the contextual issues impacting his or her specific situation. Overall, the term assessment is all encompassing in that it refers to the selection, administration, and interpretation of assessment results to develop hypotheses and specific questions related to the client's issues and possible approaches and services to promote insight, growth, and behavior change.

Test—Test refers to a specific instrument or technique used in the assessment process that obtains information in a systematic and often standardized manner to describe the behavior, feeling, attitude, thought, trait, or other constructs of interest. In rehabilitation counseling practice, tests are typically used to obtain data regarding an individual client's intelligence, ability, interests, personality, and physical and mental health functioning. In addition, tests can be considered *self-referenced* when the results are compared with the person's previous performance, *criterion referenced* when results are compared with a specific benchmark or standard, and *norm referenced* when results are compared with those of a standardized sample (Bolton & Parker, 2008; Drummond & Jones, 2010; Hays, 2013; Whiston, 2016).

Measurement—In rehabilitation counseling assessment, measurement refers to the process of operationalizing the variable of interest through the assignment of numerals or other appropriate units according to a set scale of measurement (i.e., nominal, ordinal, interval, and ratio; Bolton & Parker, 2008).

Variable—Variable refers to a "construct or concept that can take on more than one value" (Hays, 2013, p. 6). Categorical variables are qualitative in nature and often include groupings such as gender, ethnicity, and socioeconomic class. In contrast, continuous variables typically use quantitative units to measure across a spectrum and may include test scores, age, or rank. The terms *independent, dependent,* and *extraneous* designate specific types of variables that may be encountered indirectly in the assessment process. Consistent with how these variables are conceptualized in rehabilitation research, *independent* variable refers to a variable that is manipulated, *dependent* variable refers to outcome or response in relation to the independent variable, and *extraneous* (latent) variables often go unnoticed in the assessment process and can introduce error in the measurement process by impacting the dependent variable.

Types of Assessment Methods

In addition to being familiar with key terminology, rehabilitation counselors must be familiar with the major distinctions in assessments and any potential implications as they relate to the assessment process. In this section, individual versus group administration, standardized versus nonstandardized, and speed versus power tests are discussed. The assessment types such as rating scales, projective techniques, behavioral observations, interviews, biographical measures, and physiological measures also are introduced.

Group Versus Individual Assessment

Although some tests are designed specifically for individual administration only, numerous tests can be both individually and group administered. Group administration of a particular test allows for information to be obtained from multiple subjects over a relatively short period of time, which in turn increases efficiency and reduces cost. In turn, individual administration allows the rehabilitation counselor to be more sensitive to the client's needs and allows the examiner to be more flexible in identifying and implementing appropriate test modifications. For certain populations such as children and people with certain types of disabilities, it may be better to administer tests individually than in groups. One particular advantage of individual testing that is important in assessment regardless of the population is that individual administration allows for better observational data and behavioral observations.

Standardized Versus Nonstandardized Assessment

Standardized tests are considered to be the gold standard in overall assessment because they are considered the most reliable and valid. Specifically, when standardization is the key defining aspect of a specific test or assessment process, it implies that the particular test or assessment procedure must meet certain psychometric standards (reliability and validity), include uniform administration, utilize objective scoring, and apply to a representative normative group. Types of standardized tests used in rehabilitation assessment include, but are not limited to, intelligence, aptitude, achievement, personality, interest, and value inventories.

Nonstandardized measures also play an important role in rehabilitation counseling assessment and typically include assessment techniques such as rating scales, projective techniques, behavioral observations, and biographical techniques. Although nonstandardized tests are considered to be not as dependable as standardized approaches, they can produce valuable information regarding contextual issues that may not be addressed in standardized measures. When used in conjunction with standardized measures, nonstandardized approaches can provide needed depth and valuable information on topics that are not typically addressed or may be missed by standardized assessment procedures. The more flexible and qualitative-based approach can be incorporated easily into the overall counseling process and is extremely effective in promoting self-awareness. Nonstandardized techniques that may be beneficial to incorporate into rehabilitation counseling assessment include card sorts, project techniques, work simulation, and multi-domain behavioral observation.

Maximum Versus Typical Performance Tests

One way of differentiating tests is by categorizing them into tests that are designed to measure a person's maximum performance versus tests that are designed to measure how subjects typically perform. Tests of maximum performance can be further divided into tests of *power* and *speed*. The key characteristic of power tests is that they contain items of varying difficulty that most subjects taking the test are expected to complete within the specified time limit (Bolton & Parker, 2008). Specifically, according to Hays (2013), a test is considered a power test if 90% of the people for whom the test is designed can complete the test within the time limits. Although speed may be a factor for some people, speed is not considered to be a primary influence on the score. In contrast to power tests, speed-based tests place a heavy emphasis on the speed of the subject's response. Speed tests usually contain a group of easy-to-finish tasks based on a homogeneous construct that are designed to be completed quickly. Examples of speed tests include tests of finger dexterity (e.g., Purdue Pegboard), clerical speed, and a majority of the work samples (e.g., Valpar Work Sample Series). Finally, tests of typical performance measure how subjects typically perform and what they typically prefer. Sometimes these tests may be referred to as tests of preference. Tests falling into this category include career interest, value, and most personality measures.

Interviews

The interview is one of the most common forms of assessment used in the rehabilitation counseling process (Berven, 2008) and can be categorized as structured, semistructured, or unstructured. Structured interviews utilize a standardized set of questions to solicit information from the client. Structured interviews offer some form of standardization resulting in increased reliability and validity at the expense of flexibility or clinical judgment that can be used to probe deeper into issues or topics that may arise during the interview. Unstructured interviews provide the most flexibility, sacrificing reliability and validity, and allow the rehabilitation counselor to fully explore areas deemed to be important based on developments during the actual interview. A drawback of unstructured interviews is that rehabilitation counselors may run the risk of focusing too much on one topic while failing to gather necessary information. A hybrid approach and probably the most commonly used approach in rehabilitation counseling is the semistructured interview. In using a semistructured interview format, rehabilitation counselors are able to blend elements from both structured and unstructured formats, providing needed structure while allowing the rehabilitation counselor the freedom to explore areas of interest in more detail.

Biographical Data

Like interviews, the review of biographical or demographic data is a primary source of information for the rehabilitation counselor, especially early in the counseling process. Reviewing medical, demographic, work, and educational records provides valuable insight into the client and his or her level of functioning and past performance. As noted by Hays (2013), a key maxim regarding biographical data is that the "best predictor of future performance is past performance." Although the information obtained from record and file review may be robust, it can also be limited because of failure to consider or minimize contextual factors influencing performance and behavior.

Behavioral and Situational Assessments

Behavioral and situational assessments are used in rehabilitation counseling settings to observe people engaged in simulated or actual activities, typically involving work-related or social tasks or behaviors. To record observations, rating scales are used to provide subjective estimates of a person's behaviors or characteristics and typically include pre- and posttest evaluations. Because behavioral and situational assessments are subjectively based, they have a higher risk of incurring errors that may affect the findings. Three types of error are of particular concern and should be guarded against. The *halo effect* is seen when raters show a tendency to generalize findings in one area to other areas of the subject. For example, if the person undergoing assessment is viewed as friendly and easy to get along with, he or she may also be viewed positively in other areas as well such as being bright and having potential for being a good leader (Hays, 2013). The *error of central tendency* and the *leniency effect* are reciprocal versions of each other. With the *error of central tendency*, an observer tends to rate all behaviors or tasks as average. In contrast, the leniency effect is seen when an observer rates things more favorably than what they actually are. To combat these errors, Hays (2013) recommends that the following five strategies be implemented in assessments involving observations: (a) use raters who are familiar with the person being evaluated, (b) require multiple behavioral observations, (c) obtain ratings from more than one observer, (d) use characteristics that are publicly observable, and (e) identify behaviors for observation that are related to the characteristic in question.

Issues Regarding Assessment in Rehabilitation

As mentioned at the beginning of this chapter, the use of assessment as part of the rehabilitation counseling process has a long history. However, recently the use of assessment as part of rehabilitation counseling process has been questioned with expressed concerns regarding the utility and predictive value of the results. Issues regarding utility and applicability have been particularly voiced regarding people with severe disabilities. In this section, issues impacting the assessment process in rehabilitation are discussed addressing both the pros and cons, with an emphasis on the many benefits of using assessment in assisting rehabilitation professionals in determining the type and intensity of services needed to facilitate appropriate outcomes for people with disabilities.

Criticisms and Limitations

One of the primary philosophical underpinnings of assessment in rehabilitation counseling has been the focus on the individual client. With this focus, the primary goal has been to assist clients in obtaining information to facilitate a better understanding of themselves as individuals and to increase overall participation in society. A core value of the rehabilitation counseling–based approach to assessment is that when clients take an active role in the assessment process, they better understand the information generated and how the information is used to guide decisions about interventions and services for an optimal outcome. Ultimately, this should lead them to take a more active role in their own rehabilitation and self-development (Strauser, 2014). However, as with many medical and rehabilitation settings, involving the client in the process is often overlooked or minimized. The client then becomes an object of evaluation instead of a participant in the evaluation process—that is, an observer and consumer, rather than an active participant taking ownership and investing in the evaluation and rehabilitation process. As a result, some rehabilitation professionals have questioned the application of assessment in rehabilitation planning and have argued that assessment may be disempowering to clients participating in the rehabilitation process. Therefore, the perception of assessment is that it has limited utility in facilitating rehabilitation outcomes for people with severe disabilities (Bond & Dietzen, 1990).

Another criticism and more significant issue that has been levied against the use of assessment is that testing clients with disabilities lacks predictive value in determining viable rehabilitation outcomes (Szymanski & Parker, 2003). Specifically, researchers and practitioners who work with clients with severe cognitive and psychiatric disabilities and clients from diverse cultural backgrounds have been the most vocal in expressing this view of the perceived lack of efficacy regarding the use of traditional assessment. From the perspective of providers who work with people with severe disabilities, their argument appears to have some merit. For many who work with people with severe disabilities, the only potential use of any standardized assessment procedure may be, under certain circumstances, to provide relevant documentation in determining eligibility for benefits or services. It makes sense that for clients who have physical, cognitive, and affective symptoms that significantly limit functioning and ability to live and work independently without significant ongoing support, traditional assessment approaches might not be beneficial. However, for those with mild to moderate disabilities, by far the largest group of persons with disabilities, information obtained from assessment may provide important information to facilitate greater individual understanding, encourage exploration, and identify potential educational, social, interpersonal and employment opportunities that were not recognized previously.

Cultural and gender bias and discrimination have also been noted as limiting factors related to the use of assessment in rehabilitation counseling. Cultural limitations, especially those linguistic in nature, present a barrier to the use and productive nature of any evaluation, including interviews and ecologically and environmentally based evaluation. Cultural and linguistic factors must be considered in all phases of the rehabilitation process. Issues related to lack of representation of diverse groups during test construction and norming historically have been limiting factors negatively impacting the utility of many psychological instruments used in assessment. However, most evaluation instruments, including work samples, have attempted to address the limitations associated with gender and cultural limitations, and new instruments and procedures have been developed that take cultural issues into account (Strauser et al., 2014).

Finally, many rehabilitation practitioners and researchers have argued that using assessment to gauge ability significantly underestimates capacity to function from a skill perspective. Specifically, providers argue that aptitude and achievement levels are not relevant in determining employment skill in light of rehabilitation approaches such as supported and customized employment that provide wraparound services to people with severe disabilities to facilitate job acquisition and initial job maintenance. Instead, on-the-job training and the place and train approach may be the most relevant models to develop specific employment skills related to specific employment settings. Again, for people with severe disabilities, this is certainly true and would appear to be the most effective.

Advantages and Merits

Although the aforementioned criticisms have merit and apply to certain populations served by the rehabilitation community, those criticisms regarding the utility of assessment may not have broad application for a variety of important reasons. First, as previously noted, a majority of people with disabilities who are engaged in the rehabilitation process do not qualify as having a severe disability. Based on the concept of inclusion and empowerment that provides the basis of a rehabilitation counseling approach to assessment, clients should actively be involved in all phases of the evaluation process. The working alliance provides the foundation for the counseling approach to evaluation wherein the emphasis is on building a solid relationship with the individual, developing realistic and obtainable goals, and determining what tasks lead to goal accomplishment (Strauser, Lustig, & Donnell, 2004; Strauser et al., 2014). Considerable evidence has found that a well-developed working alliance leads to better rehabilitation outcomes for persons with disabilities (Chan, Shaw, McMahon, Koch, & Strauser, 1997; Donnell, Lustig, & Strauser, 2004; Lustig, Strauser, Weems, Donnell, & Smith, 2003; Strauser et al., 2014). When assessment is approached with the working alliance as a foundation, the focus should first be directed at developing a relationship with the individual that will contribute to accomplishing effective goals and tasks. This has particular application to persons who have disabilities but also have the residual ability to obtain and maintain rehabilitation outcomes with minimal or no on-site support.

Second, regarding the career development and employment of persons with disabilities, three primary factors are recognized (Conte, 1983; Strauser, O'Sullivan, & Wong, 2010; Szymanski & Hershenson, 2005). First, people with disabilities may not have had many career exploration experiences, and as a result they may have a narrow view of the world of work and available employment options. Second, people with disabilities may have fewer opportunities to develop effective career decision-making skills. The lack of such skills may in turn impair the development of the ability to identify and process information that is needed to make decisions and integrate relevant personal and contextual information. Third, people with disabilities may have a negative self-concept regarding career and employment because of negative societal attitudes toward those with disabilities, creating stigma and negative perceptions of employers. As a result, they may have a restricted view of viable career and employment options. When assessment is integrated into the overall rehabilitation counseling process, it can provide the client with the information necessary to engage in self-exploration regarding personal traits and how they relate to work and other areas of participation such as community, home, and social. Information obtained from assessment can provide a client with an opportunity to engage in the decision-making process with appropriate support and information, and increase self-confidence, concept, and efficacy as it relates to participating in career development and employment activities. When assessment results are used as part of the rehabilitation counseling process, they provide a framework or structure for examining and expanding rehabilitation options.

Third, research over the last 30 to 40 years has consistently shown that people with disabilities may not achieve appropriate rehabilitation outcomes for social, interpersonal, and contextual reasons, not from lack of skill or abilities (Wright, 1980). Therefore, there may be some logic in the criticism that skill-based assessment lacks predictive validity in determining appropriate goals and tasks related to achieving desired rehabilitation outcomes. However, assessment of personality, values, and interests may be particularly relevant in helping facilitate a client's development and identify appropriate and meaningful rehabilitation outcomes (Strauser, 2014). One common misperception of many practitioners is that the purpose of the assessment process is to diagnose a condition (e.g., depression) or determine a match between a client and a specific position or environment. Rehabilitation counselors should not endorse this view and instead should subscribe to an adjustment-based approach, which focuses on the dynamic, reciprocal, and continuous interaction between the person and the environment. Applying the principles of individual adjustment, one is concerned not only about initial diagnosis or match but about the person's ability to adjust to the changing demands of the environment and his or her own continued personal development and maturation (Strauser et al., 2014). Interests, personality, and values are critical components related to the ability to adjust to and meet the contextual demands of the environment. Evaluation of these constructs can provide the client with critical information that may not be readily available through introspection and self-analysis. In addition, assessment information can provide reinforcement of previously identified values, interests, and personality traits. Overall, obtaining this information is critical in facilitating effective individual adjustment.

Finally, research in the area of personality, values, and interests has provided empirical support that these constructs are significantly more robust predictors of career development and employment than ability for all people, including those with disabilities (Murdock & Rounds, 2014; O'Sullivan, 2014; Su & Rounds, 2014). When incorporated as part of the assessment and rehabilitation counseling process, information regarding these constructs should be used to facilitate self-exploration.

Conclusions

The primary purpose of this chapter was to introduce the role of assessment in contemporary rehabilitation counseling practice. A five-step, problem-solving approach consisting of *problem orientation, problem identification, generation of alternatives, decision-making,* and *verification* was introduced to help guide the rehabilitation assessment process. This chapter also introduced *assessment, test, measurement,* and *variable* as key terms that are relevant in rehabilitation counseling assessment and described the different types of assessment methods typically used. The chapter finished with a discussion of the contemporary issues that have emerged regarding the use of assessment in rehabilitation counseling. The introduction of these important issues and concepts related to assessment should provide rehabilitation counselors with the necessary basic understanding to be informed implementers and consumers of assessment in rehabilitation counseling. In addition, rehabilitation counselors who are familiar with the pros and cons associated with assessment in rehabilitation counseling will be more likely to use rehabilitation assessment to maximize individual outcomes.

References

American Educational Research Association, American Psychological Association, and National Council on Measurement in Education. (1999). *Standards for educational and psychological testing.* Washington, DC: Author.

Andrew, J. W. (1981). Evaluation of rehabilitation potential. In R. M. Parker & C. E. Hansen (Eds.), *Rehabilitation counseling: Foundations-consumers-service delivery* (pp. 205–226). Boston, MA: Allyn & Bacon.

Berven, N. L. (2008). Assessment interviewing. In B. Bolton & R. Parker (Eds.), *Handbook of measurement and evaluation in rehabilitation* (pp. 243–261). Austin, TX: Pro-Ed.

Bolton, B., & Parker, R. (Eds.). (2008). *Handbook of measurement and evaluation in rehabilitation.* Austin, TX: Pro-Ed.

Bond, G., & Dietzen, L. (1990). Predictive validity and vocational assessment: Reframing the question. In R. L. Glueckauf, L. Sechrest, G. Bond, & E. McDonel (Eds.), *Improving assessment in rehabilitation and health* (pp. 61–86). Newbury Park, CA: Sage.

Busseri, M. A., & Tyler, J. D. (2004). Client-therapist agreement on target problems, working alliance, and counseling outcome. *Psychotherapy Research, 14,* 77–88. doi:10.1093/ptr/kph005

Chan, F., Reid, C., Roldan, G., Kaskel, L., Rahimi, M., & Mpofu, E. (1997). Vocational assessment and evaluation of people with disabilities. *Physical Medicine and Rehabilitation Clinics of North America, 8*(2), 311–325. doi:10.1016/S1047-9651(18)30328-0

Chan, F., Shaw, L., McMahon, B. T., Koch, L., & Strauser, D. (1997). A model for enhancing consumer-counselor working relationships in rehabilitation. *Rehabilitation Counseling Bulletin, 41,* 122–137.

Chang, E. D., D'Zurilla, T. J., & Sanna, L. J. (2004). *Social problem solving: Theory, research, and training.* Washington, DC: American Psychological Association.

Conte, L. (1983). Vocational development theories and the disabled person: Oversight or deliberate omission? *Rehabilitation Counseling Bulletin, 26,* 316–328.

Donnell, C., Lustig, D. C., & Strauser, D. R. (2004). The working alliance: Rehabilitation outcomes for persons with severe mental illness. *Journal of Rehabilitation, 70*(2), 12–17.

Drummond, R. J., & Jones, K. D. (2010). *Assessment procedures for counselors and helping professionals* (7th ed.). Upper Saddle River, NJ: Pearson/Merrill Prentice Hall.

Gregory, R. (2011). *Psychological testing: History, principles, and applications* (6th ed.). Needham Heights, MA: Allyn & Bacon.

Hays, D. G. (2013). *Assessment in counseling: A guide to the use of psychological assessment procedures* (5th ed.). Alexandria, VA: American Counseling Association.

Horan, J. J. (1979). *Counseling for effective decision-making: A cognitive-behavioral perspective.* North Scituate, MA: Duxbury Press.

Lustig, D. C., Strauser, D. R., Weems, G. H., Donnell, C., & Smith, L. D. (2003). Traumatic brain injury and rehabilitation outcomes: Does working alliance make a difference? *Journal of Applied Rehabilitation Counseling, 34*(4), 30–37.

Murdock, C., & Rounds, J. (2014). Work values: Understanding and assessing motivation to work. In D. R. Strauser (Ed.), *Career development, employment, and disability in rehabilitation* (pp. 193–206). New York, NY: Springer Publishing Company.

O'Sullivan, D. (2014). Personality development, expression, and assessment for work adjustment considerations in rehabilitation contexts. In D. R. Strauser (Ed.), *Career development, employment, and disability in rehabilitation* (pp. 77–96). New York, NY: Springer Publishing Company.

Strauser, D. R. (2014). *Career development, employment and disability in rehabilitation: From theory to practice.* New York, NY: Springer Publishing Company.

Strauser, D. R., Chan, F., Wang, M., Wu, M., & Rahimi, M. (2014). Vocational evaluation in rehabilitation. In D. R. Strauser (Ed.), *Career development, employment, and disability in rehabilitation* (pp. 179–192). New York, NY: Springer Publishing Company.

Strauser, D. R., Lustig, D. C., & Donnell, C. (2004). The impact of the working alliance on therapeutic outcomes for individuals with mental retardation. *Rehabilitation Counseling Bulletin, 47,* 215–223. doi:10.1177/00343552040470040301

Strauser, D. R., O'Sullivan, D., & Wong, A. W. K. (2010). The relationship between contextual work behaviors self-efficacy and work personality: An exploratory analysis. *Disability and Rehabilitation, 32*(4), 1999–2008. doi:10.3109/09638281003797380

Su, R., & Rounds, J. (2014). Vocational interests. In D. R. Strauser (Ed.), *Career development, employment, and disability in rehabilitation* (pp. 207–222). New York, NY: Springer Publishing Company.

Szymanski, E. M., & Hershenson, D. B. (2005). An ecological approach to vocational behavior and career development of people with disabilities. In R. M. Parker, E. M. Szymanski, & J. B. Patterson (Eds.), *Rehabilitation counseling: Basics and beyond* (pp. 225–280). Austin, TX: Pro-Ed.

Szymanski, E. M., & Parker, R. M. (2003). Vocational assessment and disability. In E. M. Szymanski & R. M. Parker (Eds.), *Work and disability: Contexts and strategies in career development and job placement* (pp. 155–200). Austin, TX: Pro-Ed.

Tyler, L. E. (1984). Testing the test: What tests don't measure. *Journal of Counseling and Development, 63,* 48–50. doi:10.1002/j.1556-6676.1984.tb02682.x

Whiston, S. (2016). *Principles and applications of assessment in counseling* (5th ed.). Belmont, CA: Brooks/Cole.

Wright, G. N. (1980). *Total rehabilitation.* Boston, MA: Little, Brown.

THE WORLD HEALTH ORGANIZATION INTERNATIONAL CLASSIFICATION OF FUNCTIONING, DISABILITY AND HEALTH AS A FRAMEWORK FOR REHABILITATION ASSESSMENT

FONG CHAN | RANA YAGHMAIAN | XIANGLI CHEN | JIA-RUNG WU | BEATRICE LEE | KANAKO IWANAGA | JING TAO

LEARNING OBJECTIVES

After reviewing this chapter, the reader should be able to:

- Identify the components of the International Classification of Functioning, Disability and Health (ICF) model.
- Summarize the implications of assessing different components of the ICF model.
- Identify measures for ICF assessment.
- Summarize the use of ICF assessment in rehabilitation.

▒ Introduction

Work is central to the physical and psychological well-being of people with and without disabilities (Chan, Shaw, McMahon, Koch, & Strauser, 1997; Dutta, Gervey, Chan, Chou, & Ditchman, 2008). It is well documented that people who are unemployed are more likely to experience depressive symptoms, use alcohol more frequently, and report lower levels of self-esteem than people who are employed (Chan et al., 2018; Compton, Gfroerer, Conway, & Finger, 2014; Dooley, Catalano, & Hough, 1992; Dutta et al., 2008; McClelland, 2000; Mood & Jonsson, 2016; Zuelke et al., 2018). Unemployment is also associated with lower levels of physical and mental health, strained social relationships, and deterioration in living standards (Blustein, 2008; Durlauf, 2001; Dutta et al., 2008). Conversely, gainful employment significantly contributes to the health and well-being of individuals with chronic illness and disability (CID) and their families, and enables them to live with hope and dignity (Blustein, 2008; Hall, Kurth, & Hunt, 2013; Steinmetz, 2006; U.S. Census Bureau, 2003; Wang, 2005; Wolfensberger, 2002). It is for these reasons that the Office of the United Nations High Commissioner for Human Rights (OHCHR, n.d.) strongly advocates for the rights of people with CID to participate in competitive, integrated employment.

Despite the well-documented benefits of employment for people with and without CID, the employment rate for persons with disabilities is troublingly low at 18.7%, compared with 65.7% for those without disabilities (U.S. Department of Labor, 2018). Unsurprisingly, approximately 28% of working-age individuals with CID live below the poverty line (Federal Safety Net, 2015). The state–federal vocational rehabilitation (VR) program, which serves approximately 1 million persons with CID per year and spends more than $2.5 billion annually, has a long-standing history of helping people with disabilities achieve their independent living and employment goals (Martin, West-Evans, & Connelly, 2010; U.S. Government Accountability Office [GAO], 2005). The value of state VR services has been supported by disability employment research (e.g., Bolton, Bellini, & Brookings, 2000; Chan, Cheing, Chan, Rosenthal, & Chronister, 2006; Dutta et al., 2008; Gamble & Moore, 2003; O'Neill, Mamun, Potamites, Chan, & Cardoso, 2015; Wehman, Chan, Ditchman, & Kang, 2014). The employment rate of people with disabilities after receiving VR services is reported to be 55% (U.S. Department of Education, 2016), demonstrating the effectiveness of VR in enhancing psychosocial and vocational outcomes of people with CID.

Rehabilitation counselors play a significant role in promoting inclusion of people with CID in all aspects of society by helping them achieve employment, education, independent living, social functioning, and emotional and physical well-being goals through the assessment and counseling process (Chan, Tarvydas, Blalock, Strauser, & Atkins, 2009; Leahy et al., 2018). Emphasizing assets and strengths and contextual factors in both the person and the environment to promote psychosocial and vocational adjustment to disability is fundamental to the professional practice of rehabilitation counseling (Chou, Chan, Phillips, & Chan, 2013). This strengths-based rehabilitation counseling approach has been embraced by other rehabilitation health professionals worldwide, and is crucial to the development of the World Health Organization (WHO) International Classification of Functioning, Disability and Health (ICF; Chan & Ditchman, 2013; Chan, Sasson Gelman, Ditchman, Kim, & Chiu, 2009).

Specifically, the ICF paradigm is structured around three major components: (a) body functions and structure, (b) activities (related to tasks and actions by an individual) and participation (involvement in a life situation), and (c) person–environment contextual factors (Chan & Ditchman, 2013). Functioning and disability form a complex interaction between the health condition of the individual and person–environment contextual factors. The ICF model of disability is consistent with the holistic philosophy of VR and is well suited for conceptualizing rehabilitation and mental health counseling assessment of people with CID. The purpose of this chapter is to provide an overview of the ICF constructs related to VR and the ICF framework for evidence-based assessment practice in rehabilitation and mental health counseling.

▪ The ICF Model

The ICF model integrates all key concepts of the medical, functional, and social models of disability and provides the best potential for use as an integrative conceptual framework of disability (Chan & Ditchman, 2013). Specifically, the ICF model theorizes that the experience of disablement is connected to four separate but related constructs: body functions and structures,

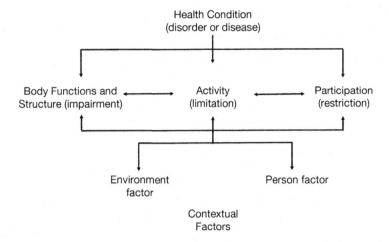

FIGURE 2.1 A graphical representation of the original International Classification of Functioning, Disability and Health (ICF) model.

activities and participation, environment factors, and person factors. The first two constructs, body functions and structures, and activities and participation, form Part 1 of the ICF and are directly related to health condition. The other two constructs (person–environment factors), which affect the Part 1 constructs, form Part 2 of the ICF. Part 1 constructs can be classified as components of health and disability, whereas Part 2 constructs can be classified as contextual factors. A graphical depiction of the ICF model is presented in Figure 2.1.

Body Functions and Structures

Body components comprise two major categories: body functions and body structures. Body functions refer to both the physical and psychological functions of body systems and include eight components:

1. Mental functions

2. Sensory functions and pain

3. Voice and speech functions

4. Functions of the cardiovascular, hematological, immunological, and respiratory systems

5. Functions of the digestive, metabolic, and endocrine systems

6. Genitourinary and reproductive functions

7. Neuromusculoskeletal and movement-related functions

8. Functions of the skin and related structures

Body structures parallel body functions and are associated with anatomical parts of the body such as organs, limbs, and their components. For example, mental function (body function) is related to structures of the nervous system (body structure). Specific components of body structures include:

1. Structures of the nervous system

2. The eye, ear, and related structures

3. Structures involved in voice and speech

4. Structures of the cardiovascular, immunological, and respiratory systems

5. Structures related to the digestive, metabolic, and endocrine systems

6. Structures related to the genitourinary and reproductive systems

7. Structures related to movement

8. Skin and related structures

In the ICF, significant permanent or temporary changes in body functions and structures, as compared to standards for the population, are defined as impairments (WHO, 2001).

Activities and Participation

Activities and participation represent the translation of differences in body functions and structures into changes in capacity and performance at the individual and community levels. Capacity describes an individual's ability to execute a task or action (e.g., gait velocity). Performance describes what people do in their current environment (e.g., difficulty ambulating at school) or what happens when a person with a particular health condition, impairment, or capacity limitation interacts with a particular set of environment factors. Additionally, the ICF model characterizes activities as basic tasks executed by an individual, while participation refers to engaging in life activities in the community (WHO, 2001). However, because even basic functional tasks (activities) occur or are performed within some environmental or societal context (participation), the ICF does not make a clear distinction between activities and participation (Fougeyrollas et al., 1998; Nordenfelt, 2003; Perenboom & Chorus, 2003). The ICF identifies the following nine domains for activities and participation:

1. Learning and applying knowledge (e.g., watching, listening, and solving problems)

2. General tasks and demand (e.g., single and multiple tasks)

3. Communication (e.g., receiving spoken messages and speaking)

4. Movement (e.g., lifting and carrying objects, walking, and using transportation)

5. Self-care (e.g., cleaning, eating, and dressing)

6. Domestic life areas (e.g., preparation of meals and doing housework)

7. Interpersonal interactions (e.g., relating with coworkers and intimate relationships)

8. Major life areas (e.g., informal education, school education, and employment)

9. Community, social, and civic life (e.g., recreation and leisure, religion and spirituality, and human rights)

Within the ICF schema, factors affecting activities and participation include functioning (current ability) and limitations regarding ability (WHO, 2001). Examples of functional abilities include mobility, communication, self-care, and other domains of ability. Limitations concerning ability include restriction in activities connected to emotional, physiological, and/or task-related demands. Generally, functional status refers to current abilities, whereas problems in body functions and structures are associated with limitations in activities or restrictions in participation (Bruyere, Van Looy, & Peterson, 2005; Scherer & Glueckauf, 2005). Participation can be conceptualized as an individual's involvement in life situations and roles, such as parenting, interpersonal relationships, academic pursuits, employment, recreation, worship, political expression, and volunteering (Scherer & Glueckauf, 2005). In addition, participation in life situations is influenced by person–environment interactions (Fougeyrollas et al., 1998).

Person and Environment Contextual Factors

Person factors are individual characteristics that can impact a person's performance in each component of the ICF model. Environment factors are external features of the physical, social, and attitudinal world that affect an individual's performance in each component of the ICF model (Chan, Sasson-Gelman, et al., 2009). The ICF includes person factors as one domain of health, to account for the individual differences across social classes and cultures (Peterson, 2005). Both personal and environment factors are important in the construction of disability, and together, they make up the two components of the ICF's contextual factors. Individual characteristics identified by ICF as contextual person factors include:

1. Gender
2. Age
3. Other health conditions
4. Coping style
5. Social background
6. Education
7. Profession
8. Past experience
9. Character style

Environment factors are external factors that make up the physical, social, and attitudinal environment of the community in which people with CID live and conduct their lives (Chan, Sasson-Gelman, et al., 2009). These environment factors form part of both the immediate and background environments and can serve as either facilitators or barriers to full inclusion of people with CID. For example, a performance problem in mobility would occur only in an inaccessible building for a person with capacity difficulties in walking ability is fine. The performance problem does not occur when the building is accessible. Negative societal attitudes toward disability can constrict the opportunity of people with CID to find and maintain employment in competitive integrated employment settings. Specific environment factors include:

1. *Products and technology:* the natural or human-made products or systems of products, equipment, and technology in an individual's immediate environment that are gathered, created, produced, or manufactured.
2. *Natural environment and human-made changes to the environment:* animate and inanimate elements of the natural or physical environment, and components of that environment that have been modified by people, as well as characteristics of human populations within that environment.

3. *Support and relationships:* people or animals that provide practical physical or emotional support, nurturing, protection, assistance, and relationships to other persons, in their home, place of work, school or at play, or in other aspects of their daily activities.

4. *Attitudes:* the attitudes of those people (external to the person whose situation is described) that are the observable consequences of customs, practices, ideologies, values, norms, factual beliefs, and religious beliefs.

5. *Services, systems, and policies:* services that are the provision of benefits, structured programs and operations; systems that are administrative control and monitoring mechanisms; and policies that are the rules, regulations, and standards.

Full inclusion and participation of people with CID in society is a generally accepted ideal. As mentioned, the ICF provides a useful framework for conceptualizing participation as an important health and rehabilitation outcome for people with CID.

The ICF Framework for Assessment

Assessment is central to the professional practice of rehabilitation counseling (Chan, Berven, & Thomas, 2015; Leahy, Chan, Sung, & Kim, 2013; Leahy et al., 2018). Assessment informs clinical decision-making, which is integral to effective VR service delivery. Rehabilitation counselors regularly make important and high-stakes decisions related to service eligibility, identification of needs, service provision, discharge/termination, and referral (Atkinson & Nixon-Cave, 2011; Strohmer & Leierer, 2000). According to Berven (2008), effective clinicians will construct a systematic "working model" or conceptualization of a client and then use that model as a foundation for making well-informed clinical decisions. These models, which are characterized by inductive and deductive reasoning, enable counselors to make inferences based on available information and to form/test hypotheses about the client to make predictions about his/her employment-related behavior and outcomes (Berven, 2008). In an ideal world, assessment and decision-making would be an objective process by which rehabilitation counselors conceptualize cases based on client and collateral input as well as evidence-based reasoning. However, in the "real world," counselors often make clinical decisions based on either very little information or large and complex amounts of information, requiring them to integrate past experiences with the information currently available to them (Strohmer & Leierer, 2000). This process can be highly subjective and quite problematic for a number of reasons; the field of rehabilitation counseling is in dire need of a strong conceptual system that will lead to greater uniformity in assessment and planning in VR agencies. While clinical reflection, reasoning, and case conceptualization are regarded as highly important parts of the assessment and planning process, there is a paucity of evidence-based structure currently available to guide rehabilitation counselors through the assessment and planning process. The ICF model provides a comprehensive, evidence-based, cross-cultural framework for this process.

While assessment occurs throughout the entire VR process, eligibility determination is one of the most important and influential assessment-based decisions a rehabilitation counselor makes. In the eligibility determination phase, rehabilitation counselors use assessment data to determine their clients' functional abilities related to preparing for, attaining, maintaining, or returning to employment (Ditchman et al., 2013). In addition, intelligence, achievement, personality, career interest, education, work history, employment opportunities, labor market analyses, and other pertinent data are evaluated to help determine the nature and scope of rehabilitation and counseling services needed to achieve disability employment goals (Ditchman et al., 2013; Leahy et al., 2018). As part of the data gathering process, rehabilitation counselors also appraise their clients' patterns of work behavior, ability to acquire occupational skills, and their capacity for successful job performance to determine their capability to perform satisfactorily in a work environment. Life skills such as home maintenance (e.g., cooking, cleaning, shopping, and childcare), finances (e.g., money management), housing, family, activities of daily living (ADLs), and instrumental ADLs (IADLs) are also assessed to determine independent living rehabilitation services that could be provided to ameliorate the adverse effect of chronic illnesses and disabilities on psychosocial, independent living, and employment outcomes (Chan, Sasson Gelman, et al., 2009).

The ICF constructs provide a meaningful framework for conceptualizing assessment and service needs of people with CID receiving rehabilitation and mental health services. Chan and associates (Iwanaga, Wu, et al., 2018; Kaya et al., 2018; Sanchez et al., 2016) have conducted extensive research to examine the structural relationships among ICF constructs and their relationships to community and participation and health-related quality of life. For example, Kaya et al. (2018) conducted a research study to evaluate the ICF framework as a participation model for cancer survivors in Turkey. Results from simultaneous regression analyses indicated that fatigue, perceived stress, role functioning, social functioning, core self-evaluations, social support, and autonomy support were significantly associated with participation. Sánchez, Rosenthal, Chan, Brooks, and Bezyak (2016) found that insight, self-care activity, social competency, and social support were significant predictors of community participation in a sample of people with severe mental illness. In addition, social competence, disability acceptance, family support, and social support were found to partially mediate the relationship between functional disability and quality of life (Sánchez et al., 2018). Pfaller (2016) tested a mediation model of community participation and found that core self-evaluations (self-esteem, emotional stability, generalized self-efficacy, and internal locus of control) and social skills mediated the relationship between functional disability and community participation. Lee et al. (2018) developed and validated an ICF environmental support scale for individuals with multiple sclerosis, and demonstrated that higher levels of health and mental health services; rehabilitation, social, and support services; and independent living supports are related to higher levels of community participation. Iwanaga, Wu, et al. (2018) investigated person–environment factors as potential mediators for the negative relationship between symptoms cluster (pain, stress, sleep problems, fatigue, cognitive deficits, and depression) and employment participation. Their findings demonstrated that higher levels of core self-evaluations and social support could lessen the negative effect of symptoms cluster on employment. Smedema et al. (2015) conducted a study to investigate the relationship between core self-evaluations and life satisfaction in a sample of college students with disabilities. They found that higher levels of core self-evaluations were associated with better life satisfaction because students with high core self-evaluations were better at coping with stress, maintaining a positive mood, and building social support than students with low core self-evaluations. Chen et al. (2019, under review) conducted a study to evaluate community participation as a mediator for the relationship between functional disability and life satisfaction. Results demonstrated that active community participation lessens the adverse effect of functional disability on quality of life of persons with fibromyalgia. Moser (2017) evaluated the effect of person–environment contextual factors on life satisfaction of young adults with epilepsy. Results indicated that environment factors such as family support and friend support contribute significantly to life satisfaction. In addition, person factors such as epilepsy self-efficacy, secure attachment, and core self-evaluations contributed significantly to life satisfaction. Sung (2012) evaluated ICF constructs as predictors of employment participation and found that vocational competencies and social support were significant predictors of employment participation. Yaghmaian and Smedema (2018) found that a model consisting of symptom severity, socioenvironmental factors, personal/psychological factors, and role functioning (participation) predicted 79% of the variance in subjective well-being in women with fibromyalgia.

Based on these research findings, Chan, Tarvydas, et al. (2009) recommend that the ICF should be adopted as a conceptual framework for assessment and counseling in clinical rehabilitation and mental health counseling practice. Furthermore, they contended that it is more relevant to use abbreviated and well-validated higher-order psychological measures to assess ICF factors and rehabilitation and mental health outcomes. The ICF approach is also consistent with the paradigm shift in rehabilitation and health services from biomedical parameters to the assessment of functioning, performance of daily activities, feelings and emotions, and clients' subjective evaluation of their physical and mental health in general (Stewart & Ware, 1992). A graphical depiction of the ICF model of assessment is presented in Figure 2.2.

In the ICF VR model, problems in body functions or structures will be assessed by evaluating the severity of symptoms commonly associated with chronic illnesses and disabilities (e.g., pain, stress, sleep problems, depression, fatigue, and cognitive impairment), functional limitations, and secondary health problems (Iwanaga, Wu, et al., 2018). Activity will be assessed in terms of activity restriction (i.e., functional disability). Participation will be assessed by evaluating the individual's ability to assume meaningful life roles (Wu et al., 2019). A strengths-based approach will be used to assess positive person–environment contextual factors (B. Lee et al., 2018). Lastly, participation and health-related quality of life are denoted as the main outcome variables in the assessment model (Chan, Keegan, et al., 2009).

There is strong evidence to indicate the adverse effects of disability-related symptom (symptoms cluster) on functional disability and the effect of both the symptoms cluster and functional disability on participation (including employment participation). There is also strong evidence that person–environment contextual variables (e.g., core self-evaluations and social support) can mediate the effect of functional disability on community participation. Person–environment contextual variables can also mediate the effect of community participation on quality of life. Based on these research findings, it is logical to assume that, at the practice level, rehabilitation and mental health counselors should systematically assess their clients' functioning/impairments (secondary

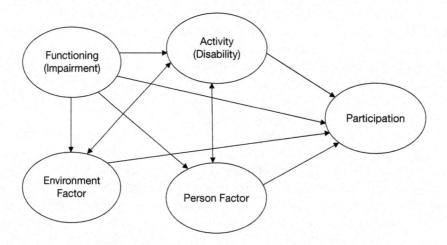

FIGURE 2.2 A graphical depiction of a modified International Classification of Functioning, Disability and Health (ICF) structural model for rehabilitation assessment.

health conditions, symptoms cluster, and functional limitations), disability, community participation, and health-related quality of life. Additionally, counselors should also assess positive person factors and environment factors that may mediate the adverse effects of impairment and disability on community participation and health-related quality of life. In the following section, we will provide a description of measures that can be used to assess these ICF-based variables.

A Comprehensive Taxonomy of ICF-Based Psychological Measures

Mermis (2005) advocated for the development of a clear and well-defined taxonomy in ICF-based measures for assessment in rehabilitation and mental health counseling. For example, assessment of functioning can help the counselor determine eligibility, as well as rehabilitation and mental health services that may be needed to improve the functioning of the applicant. To help counselors identify a battery of brief but psychometrically sound measures in the rehabilitation process, a comprehensive taxonomy of ICF-based psychological instruments can be organized around the major constructs of the ICF.

Impairment/Activity Limitations

Assessing functioning is an integral part of the eligibility determination and the order of selection process. Persons with multiple functional limitations often receive the highest priority to receive VR services (Ditchman et al., 2013). Traditionally, medical researchers have measured medical care outcomes through mortality rates and in terms of morbidity (i.e., the extent and severity of the pathological condition as measured by laboratory reports and pathologists). Today, researchers have shifted their emphasis from biomedical parameters to the assessment of functioning, performance of daily activities, feelings, and patients' subjective evaluation of their health in general (Stewart & Ware, 1992). In the VR process, rehabilitation counselors may purchase health intervention services for consumers with the goal of restoring, improving, and maintaining function of daily living. Therefore, a good way to assess functional outcomes is to use functional assessment measures.

PROMIS Health Measures

People with disabilities often report a range of symptoms including pain, perceived stress, sleep problem, fatigue, depression, and cognitive impairments that affect functioning (Patient-Reported Outcomes Measurement Information System [PROMIS], 2018). The PROMIS *Pain Intensity Scale* (Short Form 3a) comprises three items (e.g., "How intense was your pain at its worst?"). Each item is rated using a 5-point rating scale (1 = *Had no pain*, 2 = *Mild*, 3 = *Moderate*, 4 = *Severe*, 5 = *Very severe*). PROMIS *Sleep Disturbance Scale* (Short Form 6a) consists of six items (e.g., "My sleep was restless"). Each item is rated on a 5-point rating scale (1 = *Not at all*, 2 = *A little bit*, 3 = *Somewhat*, 4 = *Quite a bit*, 5 = *Very much*). PROMIS *Fatigue Scale* (Short Form 6a) is composed of six items (e.g., "I have trouble starting things because I am tired"). Each item is rated on a 5-point rating scale (1 = *Not at all*, 2 = *A little bit*, 3 = *Somewhat*, 4 = *Quite a bit*, 5 = *Very much*). PROMIS *Applied Cognition-General Concerns* (Short Form 6a) is composed of six items (e.g., "My brain was not working as well as usual"). Each item is rated on a 5-point rating scale (1 = *Never*, 2 = *Rarely*, 3 = *Sometimes*, 4 = *Often*, 5 = *Very often*). In a recent study, Quach et al. (2016) reported high internal consistency reliability coefficients (Cronbach's alpha) of between .86 and .96

for the anxiety, depression, fatigue, pain interference, physical function, and sleep disturbance measures. They also confirmed that these measures are sufficiently unidimensional. PROMIS health measures can be downloaded from the NIH PROMIS website (www.healthmeasures.net/explore-measurement-systems/promis).

Functional Independence Measure

The Functional Independence Measure (FIM; Uniform Data System for Medical Rehabilitation Group, 1996) is composed of 18 items and two domains: (a) motor domain (i.e., self-care, sphincter control, mobility, and locomotion) and (b) cognitive domain (i.e., communication, psychosocial adjustment, and cognitive function). Each item is rated on a 7-point Likert-type scale (1 = *complete dependence* to 7 = *complete independence*). Stineman et al. (1996) reported good internal consistency reliability for the FIM with the Cronbach's alpha coefficients ranging from .88 to .97 for the total FIM (18 items), from .86 to .97 for the motor-FIM, and from .86 to .95 for the cognitive-FIM.

Functional Assessment Inventory

The Functional Assessment Inventory (FAI; Crewe, Athelstan, & Meadows, 1975) is composed of 42 items including 30 behaviorally anchored rating items that assess clients' vocational capabilities and deficiencies, 10 items that identify unusual assets, and 2 global items that quantify severity of disability and probability of vocational success. There are seven subscales (Crewe & Dijkers, 1995): (a) adaptive behavior (e.g., "accurate perception of capabilities and limitations," "judgment," and "initiative"); (b) cognition (e.g., " ability to read and write in English"); (c) physical capacity (e.g., "endurance"); (d) motor functioning (e.g., "motor speed"); (e) communication (e.g., "speech and language functioning"); (f) vocational qualification (e.g., "work history"); and (g) vision. Each item is rated on a 4-point Likert-type scale (0 = *no impairment* to 3 = *severe impairment*). Crewe and Dijkers (1995) validated the seven-factor measurement structure of the FAI. Neath, Bellini, and Bolton (1997) also investigated the dimensionality of the FAI with 5,741 individuals representing five disability groups: (a) orthopedic/amputation, (b) chronic/physical condition, (c) mental illness, (d) mental retardation, and (e) learning disability. The six-factor measurement structure (adaptive behavior, cognition, physical capacity, motor function, communication, vocational qualifications) was similar to the seven-factor measurement structure of the FAI (Crewe & Dijkers, 1995). Neath et al. (1997) indicated that the FAI is highly valid as a measure of functional limitations for a range of primary disabilities.

Wisconsin Related Conditions Scale

The Wisconsin Related Conditions Scale (WRCS; Chen et al., 2018) is composed of seven secondary health conditions items identified by the Centers for Disease Control and Prevention (CDC) as related condition for people with CID (e.g., overweight and obesity). Each item is rated using a 4-point Likert-type scale (0 = *Not a problem*, 1 = *Mild or infrequent problem*, 2 = *Moderate problem*, 3 = *Significant problem*). Cronbach's alpha is reported to be .63 (Chen et al., 2018).

Patient Health Questionnaire

The Patient Health Questionnaire (PHQ-9; Kroenke, Spitzer, & Williams, 2001) is composed of nine items that incorporate *DSM-IV* diagnostic criteria for depression (e.g., "Little interest or pleasure in doing things"). Each item is rated on a 4-point Likert-type rating scale (0 = *Not at all*, 1 = *Several days*,

2 = *More than half the days*, and 3 = *Nearly every day*). The Cronbach's alpha coefficient of the PHQ-9 measure was reported to range between .86 and .89 (Kroenke et al., 2001).

Perceived Stress Scale-10

The Perceived Stress Scale-10 (PSS-10; Cohen & Williamson, 1988) is composed of 10 items (e.g., "In the last month, how often have you felt that you were unable to control the important things in your life?"). Each item is rated on a 5-point Likert-type scale (0 = *never* to 4 = *very often*). The PSS-10 Cronbach's alpha coefficients were reported to range from .78 to .91 (Lee, 2012).

WHODAS-12

The World Health Organization Disability Assessment Schedule II (WHODAS 2.0 item version) assesses the impact of a health condition or disability in terms of functioning, which is based on the ICF (Üstün, Kostanjsek, Chatterji, & Rehm, 2010). It is composed of 12 items, which cover six domains of common daily life activities: understanding and communicating with the world; moving and getting around; self-care; getting along with people; life activities; and participation in society. In each item, respondents estimate the impact of their disability (e.g., "how much have you been emotionally affected by your health problems?"). Each item is rated on a 5-point Likert-type scale (0 = *no difficulty* to 4 = *extreme difficulty/cannot do*). The Cronbach's alpha coefficients were reported to range from .77 to .98 (Garin et al., 2010).

Participation and Health-Related Quality of Life

Impact on Participation and Autonomy Questionnaire

The Impact on Participation and Autonomy Questionnaire (IPAQ; Cardol et al., 2001) assesses community participation and is composed of 32 items across five subdomains of perceived functioning and participation (autonomy indoors, autonomy outdoors, family role, social life, and work and education). Items include "My chances of getting around in my house when I want to are [. . .]" and "My chances of doing my paid or voluntary work the way I want to are [. . .]." Cronbach's alphas ranged from .81 to .91. The IPAQ was designed to measure participation according to terms laid out by the WHO and was originally developed with a Dutch sample (Magasi, Heinemann, & Whiteneck, 2008). For the English version, test–retest reliability ranged from .64 to .92 (Kersten et al., 2007).

Multiple Sclerosis Community Participation Scale

The Multiple Sclerosis Community Participation Scale (MSCPS; Wu et al., 2019) comprises 13 meaningful life role items: (a) employment (full-time), (b) employment (part-time), (c) volunteer work, (d) spouse, (e) parent, (f) children, (g) student, (h) recreation activities, (i) getting around, (j) live independently, (k) social life, (l) church member, and (m) engage in health-promoting activities. Each item is rated on a 6-point Likert-type scale anchored as follows: 0 (*not important*), 1 (*much lower than I would like to do*), 2 (*slightly lower than I would like to do*), 3 (*consistent with what I would like to do*), 4 (*better than I would like to do*), and 5 (*much better than I would like to do*). Each life role is also weighted by its relative importance score and summed to yield a total participation score ranging from 0 to 5. The Cronbach's alpha coefficient was reported to be .78 (Wu et al., 2019).

Short Form 12 Health Survey

The Short Form 12 Health Survey (SF-12; Ware, Kosinski, & Keller, 1996) assesses health-related quality of life and is composed of 12 items and eight major domains: (a) physical functioning, with two items (e.g., "moderate activities, such as moving a table, pushing a vacuum cleaner, bowling, or playing golf"); (b) role limitations due to physical problems, with two items (e.g., "accomplished less than you would like"); (c) bodily pain, with one item (e.g., "during the past 4 weeks, how much did pain interfere with your normal work [including both work outside the home and housework]?"); (d) general health, with one item (e.g., "in general, would you say your health is excellent/very good/good/fair/poor?"); (e) vitality, with one item (e.g., "did you have a lot of energy?"); (f) social functioning, with one item (e.g., "during the past 4 weeks, how much of the time has your physical health or emotional problems interfered with your social activities [like visiting with friends, relatives, etc.]?"), (g) role limitations due to emotional problems, with two items (e.g., "during the past 4 weeks, how much of the time have you had any of the following problems with your work or other regular daily activities as a result of any emotional problems [such as feeling depressed or anxious]?"); and (h) mental health, with two items (e.g., "have you felt calm and peaceful?"). Ten items (4, 5, 6, 7, 8, 9, 10, 11, 12) are rated on a 5-point Likert-type scale ranging from 1 (*excellent*) to 5 (*poor*). Two items (2, 3) are rated on a 3-point Likert-type scale ranging from 1 (*yes, limited a lot*) to 3 (*no, not limited at all*). The 12 items are summed as a physical component summary scale (PCS) and a mental component summary scale (MCS).

Satisfaction with Life Scale

The Satisfaction with Life Scale (SWLS; Diener, Emmons, Larsen & Giffin, 1985) is a subjective well-being measure composed of five items (e.g., "In most ways my life is close to my ideal" and "I am satisfied with my life"). Each item is rated on a 7-point Likert-type scale ranging from 1 (*strongly disagree*) to 7 (*strongly agree*), with total scores ranging from 5 to 35. Diener et al. (1985) reported good internal consistency estimates ranging from .61 to .81. The SWLS received validity support based on its correlations with other measures of subjective well-being, such as the *Self-Esteem Scale* (Rosenberg, 1965) and the *Affect Balance Scale* (Bradburn, 1969).

Person Factors

The ICF has identified several person factors (e.g., gender, age, race, secondary health and mental health conditions, coping style, social background, education, profession, work history, and character strength) as important for rehabilitation assessment. These factors can interact with functioning, activities, and the environment to affect participation outcomes including employment. In the ICF VR model, the focus is on positive human traits (character strengths) and positive communities. The following are descriptions of several measures that can be used to assess positive human traits.

Brief Resilience Scale

The Brief Resilience Scale (BRS; B. W. Smith et al., 2008) is composed of three positive valence items (e.g., "I tend to bounce back quickly after hard times") and three negative valence items (e.g., "It is hard for me to snap back when something bad happens"). Each item is rated on a 5-point Likert-type scale ranging from 1 (*strongly disagree*) to 5 (*strongly agree*). Negative valence items are reverse scored; the six items are summed so that high total scores indicate higher levels of resilience. Internal consistency reliability coefficients (Cronbach's alpha) of the BRS were reported to range from .80 to .91. Test–retest reliability coefficients for the scale were reported to range from .61 to .69 (B. W. Smith et al., 2008). In a study of people with CID receiving VR services, the Cronbach's alpha coefficient was computed to be .83 for negative valence items and .79 for the positive valence items (Tansey, Iwanaga, Bezyak, & Ditchman, 2017).

Life Orientation Test–Revised

The Life Orientation Test–Revised (LOT-R; Scheier, Carver, & Bridges, 1994) is a 10-item scale measuring optimism (e.g., "In uncertain times, I usually expect the best"). Each item is rated on a 5-point Likert-type scale ranging from 0 (*strongly disagree*) to 4 (*strongly agree*). Of the 10 items, four serve as distractor items. In prior research, Cronbach's alphas of the LOT-R have been reported to range from .67 to .78 (Scheier et al., 1994; A. R. Smith, Ebert, & Broman-Fulks, 2016). In a study with student veterans, the Cronbach's alpha coefficient was reported to be .86 (Umucu et al., 2018).

Trait Hope Scale

The Trait Hope Scale (THS; Snyder et al., 1991) is composed of 12 items and two subscales: (a) pathways thoughts (e.g., "I can think of many ways to get out of a jam") and agency thoughts (e.g., "I meet the goals that I set for myself"). Each item is rated on a 8-point Likert-type rating scale ranging from 1 (*definitely false*) to 8 (*definitely true*). The reported Cronbach's alpha coefficients ranged from .74 to .84 for total hope (Snyder et al., 1991). In a disability study, the Cronbach's alpha of the THS was computed to be .84 (Blake, Brooks, Greenbaum, & Chan, 2017).

Core Self-Evaluations Scale

The Core Self-Evaluations Scale (CSES; Judge, Erez, Bono, & Thoresen, 2003) is composed of 12 items (e.g., "I am confident I get the success I deserve in life"). Each item is rated on a 5-point Likert-type scale ranging from 1 (*strongly disagree*) to 5 (*strongly agree*). Scores range from 12 to 70. The test–retest reliability was reported to be .81, and the reported internal consistency reliability coefficients (Cronbach's alphas) range from .81 to .87 (Judge et al., 2003). In a study with people with spinal cord injury, the Cronbach's alpha coefficient was reported to be .89 (Smedema, Chan, & Phillips, 2014).

PERMA-Profiler

The PERMA-Profiler (PERMA-P; Butler & Kern, 2016) consists of 15 items and five subscales: (a) positive emotion (e.g., "In general, how often do you feel positive?"); (b) engagement (e.g., "How often do you become absorbed in what you are doing?"); (c) relationships (e.g., "To what extent do you receive help and support from others when you need it?"); (d) meaning (e.g., "To what extent do you lead a purposeful and meaningful life?"); and (e) accomplishment (e.g., "How much of the time do you feel you are making progress towards accomplishing your goals?"). Each item is rated on an 11-point Likert-type rating scale ranging from 0 (*never*) to 10 (*always*), or 0 (*not at all*) to 10 (*completely*). The reported internal consistency reliability coefficients (Cronbach's alpha) for the subscale scores range from .60 to .89 (Butler & Kern, 2016). In a study with student veterans, the internal consistency reliability coefficient was reported to be .91 for positive emotion, .57 for engagement, .85 for relationships, .92 for meaning, .81 for accomplishment, and .95 for overall well-being (Umucu et al., 2018).

Environment Factors

Oslo Social Support Scale

The Oslo Social Support Scale (OSSS-3; Dowrick et al., 1998) is composed of three items related to social support. The help from neighbor item ("How easy can you get help from neighbors if you should need it?") is rated using a 5-point rating scale (1 = *very easy*, 2 = *easy*, 3 = *possible*, 4 = *difficult*, 5 = *very difficult*). The people you can count on item ("How many people are so close to you that you can count on them if you have serious problems?") is quantified using four categories (none, 1–2, 3–5, 5+). The concern item "How much concern do people show in what you are doing?") is rated using a 5-point rating scale (1 = *a lot*, 2 = *some*, 3 = *uncertain*, 4 = *little*, 5 = *no*). The Cronbach's alpha coefficient was reported to be .64, which is considered satisfactory for a very brief scale (Kocalevent et al., 2018).

Multidimensional Scale of Perceived Social Support

The Multidimensional Scale of Perceived Social Support (MSPSS; Zimet, Dahlem, Zimet, & Farley, 1988) measures social support from multiple sources and is composed of 12 items and three domains: (a) family, with four items (e.g., "I can talk about my problems with my family"); (b) friends, with four items (e.g., "I can count on my friends when things go wrong"); and (c) significant others, with four items (e.g., "There is a special person who is around when I am in need"). Each item is rated on a 7-point type Likert-type scale ranging from 1 (*very strongly disagree*) to 7 (*very strongly agree*). Cronbach's alpha coefficients for the family, friends, and significant others were reported to be .87, .85, and .91, respectively. Construct validity was demonstrated by moderate correlations with symptoms of depression (Zimet et al., 1988).

Multiple Sclerosis Environmental Supports Scale

The Multiple Sclerosis Environmental Supports Scale (MSESS; Lee et al., 2018) is developed specifically for assessing the environmental support needs of people with MS based on a comprehensive review of the ICF model. It is composed of 17 items and three subscales: (a) health and mental health services (e.g., "I have access to good quality mental health services"); (b) rehabilitation, social, and support services (e.g., "I have access to good quality vocational rehabilitation services"); and (c) independent living supports (e.g., "I have access to transportation"). Each item is rated on a 5-point Likert-type agreement scale ranging from 1 (*strongly disagree*) to 5 (*strongly agree*). The Cronbach's alpha coefficients for the three subscales were reported to be .88, .72, and .64, respectively (B. Lee et al., 2018).

Person–Environment Measures for Vocational Rehabilitation

Person–environment contextual factors will be measured within this framework using the constructs of self-determination and self-efficacy (SDT/SET). These constructs will be denoted as predictors of VR engagement and readiness for employment. Following are descriptions of SDT/SET instruments that can be incorporated in the ICF VR assessment battery.

Behavioral Regulation in Work Questionnaire

The Behavioral Regulation in Work Questionnaire (BRWQ; Fitzgerald et al., 2015) was adapted from the *Behavioral Regulation in Exercise Questionnaire-2* (Markland & Tobin, 2004) by changing the referent from "exercise" to "work." It comprises 19 items and four subscales: (a) "amotivation" (e.g., "I can't see why I should bother with work"), (b) "external regulation" (e.g., "I work because other people say I should"), (c) "introjected regulation" (e.g., "I feel ashamed when I miss work"). and (d) "autonomous motivation" (e.g., "I enjoy my work"). Each item is rated on a 5-point Likert-type scale ranging from 1 (*not true*) to 5 (*very true for me*). The BRWQ has been validated in a sample of individuals with severe mental illness. It was found to have good factorial validity and Cronbach's alpha coefficients ranged from acceptable to good (Fitzgerald et al., 2015).

Vocational Outcome Expectancy Scale

The Vocational Outcome Expectancy Scale (VOES; Iwanaga et al., 2017) is an 11-item measure with two subscales: (a) positive outcome expectancy related to work, with six items; and (b) negative outcome expectancy related to work, with five items. Respondents are asked to rate their levels of agreement on 11 statements that begin with the stem: "Completing my vocational rehabilitation program will likely allow me to . . .". A sample item reflecting a positive outcome was: ". . . have a job with good pay and benefits," and a sample item reflecting a negative outcome was: ". . . experience increased stress." Each item is rated on a 5-point Likert-type scale ranging from 1 (*strongly disagree*) to 5 (*strongly agree*), and scores are computed by averaging ratings across the items of each subscale, with higher scores indicating higher outcome expectancy. Iwanaga et al. (2017) reported a Cronbach's alpha for the positive outcome expectancy related to work subscale as .79 and for the negative outcome expectancy related to work subscale as .79. Their study revealed moderate relationships between outcome expectancy subscales and SDT variables in the expected directions, providing additional support for the construct validity of the VOES (Iwanaga et al., 2017).

LSI-Vocational Competency Scale

The LSI-Vocational Competency Scale (LSI-VCS; Umucu et al., 2016) was originally developed to assess the vocational competency of people with mental illness (Umucu et al., 2016). Later, it was validated for other populations, including VR consumers (Tansey et al., 2017). It is a 15-item measure with two subscales: (a) job performance self-efficacy (e.g., "I know how to maintain regular work attendance on the job") with 11 items; and (b) job-seeking self-efficacy (e.g., "I know how to prepare a cover letter and resume") with four items. Each item is rated on a 5-point Likert-type scale ranging from 0 (*strongly disagree*) to 4 (*strongly agree*) and scores are calculated by averaging ratings across items, with higher scores indicating greater job performance self-efficacy or job-seeking self-efficacy. Umucu et al. (2016) found that both factors were correlated with other SDT constructs (i.e., autonomy support, autonomous motivation, relatedness, outcome expectancy, and stages of change for employment) in the expected directions. Umucu et al. (2016) reported Cronbach's alpha coefficients as .93 for job performance self-efficacy and .84 for job-seeking self-efficacy.

Working Alliance Inventory–Vocational Rehabilitation

The Working Alliance Inventory–Vocational Rehabilitation (WAI-VR; Chan, McMahon, Shaw, & Lee, 2004) scale is a modified version of the *Working Alliance Inventory* (WAI) that was developed by Tracey and Kokotovic (1989) to assess the goals, bond, and tasks dimensions of the working alliance. It is a 12-item measure with three subscales: (a) goal (e.g., "My client and I are working towards mutually agreed upon goals"); (b) bond (e.g., "My client and I are working towards mutually agreed upon goals"); and (c) tasks (e.g., "My client believes the way we are working with his/her problem is correct"). Each item is rated on a 7-point Likert-type scale ranging from

1 (*never*) to 7 (*always*) and scores are calculated by averaging ratings across the items with the higher score indicating a higher level of working alliance. Munder, Wilmers, Leonhart, Linster, and Barth (2010) reported Cronbach's alphas for bond (.82), task (.85), goal (.81), and total (.90). In addition, a Cronbach's alpha of .98 was found for the WAI-VR total scores in Tansey et al.'s (2017) study with VR consumers.

Vocational Rehabilitation Engagement Scale

The Vocational Rehabilitation Engagement Scale (VRES; Dutta et al., 2016) can be used to assess engagement of rehabilitation clients in VR services. It is a nine-item measure (e.g., "I strive to complete assignments and rehabilitation activities agreed upon with my rehabilitation counselor"). Each item is rated on a 5-point Likert-type scale ranging from 1 (*strongly disagree*) to 5 (*strongly agree*) and scores are calculated by averaging ratings across the items, with high scores indicating a higher level of engagement in VR services. Fitzgerald et al. (2016) validated the VRES with a sample of people with mental illness. Their study showed significant relationships between VR engagement and vocational self-efficacy and vocational outcome expectancy providing additional support for the construct validity of the VRES (Fitzgerald et al., 2016). These authors reported a Cronbach's alpha of .86. In addition, the Cronbach's alpha for the VRES with VR consumers was reported to be .92 (Tansey et al., 2017).

Stages of Change for Employment Scale

The 12-item Stages of Change for Employment Scale (SOCES; Tansey et al., 2017) was developed by researchers in the Rehabilitation Research and Training Center on Evidence-Based Practice in Vocational Rehabilitation (RRTC-EBP VR; Tansey et al., 2017) to assess VR clients' readiness for employment based on the stages of change theory (i.e., precontemplation, contemplation, preparation, action, and maintenance). Iwanaga et al. (2019, in review) further validated the SOCES and found four subscales: (a) precontemplation (e.g., "I am not thinking about finding a job"), (b) contemplation (e.g., "I am beginning to see the value of having a job"), (c) preparation (e.g., "I am currently applying and interviewing for jobs"), and (d) action (e.g., "I am performing well on my job"). Each item was rated on a 5-point Likert-type rating scale ranging from 1 (*strongly disagree*) to 5 (*strongly agree*), by averaging ratings across the items, with high scores of the each subscale indicating that the person is more likely to be in the stage of VR services. Tansey et al. (2017) reported Cronbach's alpha coefficients for precontemplation (.67), contemplation (.86), preparation (.63), and action (.85). Their study also showed moderate relationships between each subscale and SDT variables (i.e., job-seeking self-efficacy, job performance self-efficacy, positive outcome expectancy, and VR engagement) providing additional support for the construct validity of the SOCES (Tansey et al., 2017).

◼ Conclusion

The ICF framework for assessing biopsychosocial predictors of community participation and health-related quality of life is consistent with the values espoused by rehabilitation counselors. Rehabilitation counselors advocate for the dignity and worth of all people, for inclusion of people with disabilities in society to the fullest extent possible, and for advocacy to provide people with disabilities the best opportunity to maximize their independent functioning and community participation (Chan, Sasson Gelman, et al., 2009). The ICF model integrates all key concepts of the medical, functional, and social models of disability and provides the best potential for use as an integrative assessment framework for people with CID. Accordingly, in this chapter, we reviewed the key components of the ICF model, introduced the ICF VR framework, and supplied a battery of ICF VR measures to assist rehabilitation counselors in applying the ICF framework to real-world rehabilitation assessment practice.

References

Atkinson, H. L., & Nixon-Cave, K. (2011). A tool for clinical reasoning and reflection using the international classification of functioning, disability and health (ICF) framework and patient management model. *Physical Therapy, 91*(3), 416–430. doi:10.2522/ptj.20090226

Berven, N. L. (2008). Assessment interviewing. In B. Bolton & R. Parker (Eds.), *Handbook of measurement and evaluation in rehabilitation* (pp. 243–261). Austin, TX: Pro-Ed.

Blake, J., Brooks, J., Greenbaum, H., & Chan, F. (2017). Attachment and employment outcomes for people with spinal cord injury: The intermediary role of hope. *Rehabilitation Counseling Bulletin, 60*(2), 77–87. doi:10.1177/0034355215621036

Blustein, D. L. (2008). The role of work in psychological health and well-being: A conceptual, historical, and public policy perspective. *American Psychologist, 63*(4), 228–240. doi:10.1037/0003-066X .63.4.228

Bolton, B. F., Bellini, J. L., & Brookings, J. B. (2000). Predicting client employment outcomes from personal history, functional limitations, and rehabilitation services. *Rehabilitation Counseling Bulletin, 44*(1), 10–21. doi:10.1177/003435520004400103

Bradburn, N. M. (1969). *The structure of psychological well-being*. Chicago, IL: Aldine.

Bruyere, S. M., Van Looy, S. A., & Peterson, D. B. (2005). The international classification of functioning, disability and health: Contemporary literature overview. *Rehabilitation Psychology, 50*, 113–121. doi:10.1037/0090-5550.50.2.113

Butler, J., & Kern, M. L. (2016). The PERMA-Profiler: A brief multidimensional measure of flourishing. *International Journal of Wellbeing, 6*(3), 1–48. doi:10.5502/ijw.v6i3.526

Cardol, M., de Haan, R. J., de Jong B. A., van den Bos, G. A., & de Groot, I. J. (2001). Psychometric properties of the Impact on Participation and Autonomy Questionnaire. *Archives of Physical Medicine and Rehabilitation, 82*, 210–216.

Chan, F., Berven, N. L., & Thomas, K. R. (Eds.). (2015). *Counseling theories and techniques for rehabilitation and mental health professionals* (2nd ed.). New York, NY: Springer Publishing Company.

Chan, F., Cheing, G., Chan, J. Y. C., Rosenthal, D. A., & Chronister, J. (2006). Predicting employment outcomes of rehabilitation clients with orthopedic disabilities: A CHAID analysis. *Disability and Rehabilitation, 28*, 257–270. doi:10.1080/09638280500158307

Chan, F., & Ditchman, N. (2013). Applying the international classification of functioning, disability, and health to psychology practice [Review of the book ICF core sets: Manual for clinical practice]. *PsycCRITIQUES, 58*(13), 329–342. doi:10.1037/a0031605

Chan, F., Iwanaga, K., Umucu, E., Yaghmaian, R., Wu, J.-R., Bengtson, K., & Chen, X. (2018). Evidence-based practice and research utilization. In V. M. Tarvydas & M. T. Hartley (Eds.), *The professional practice of rehabilitation counseling* (2nd ed., pp. 359–380). New York, NY: Springer Publishing Company.

Chan, F., Keegan, J., Sung, C., Drout, M., Pai, C. H., Anderson, E., & McLain, N. (2009). The World Health Organization ICF Model as a framework for assessing vocational rehabilitation outcomes. *Journal of Rehabilitation Administration, 33*(2), 91–112.

Chan, F., McMahon, B. T., Shaw, L. R., & Lee, G. (2004). Psychometric validation of the expectations about rehabilitation counseling scale: A preliminary study. *Journal of Vocational Rehabilitation, 20*(2), 127–133.

Chan, F., Sasson Gelman, J., Ditchman, N., Kim, J.-H., & Chiu, C.-Y. (2009). The World Health Organization ICF model as a conceptual framework of disability. In F. Chan, E. Cardoso, & J. Chronister (Eds.), *Understanding psychosocial adjustment to chronic illness and disability: A handbook for evidence-based practitioners in rehabilitation* (pp. 23–74). New York, NY: Springer Publishing Company.

Chan, F., Shaw, L., McMahon, B. T., Koch, L., & Strauser, D. (1997). A model for enhancing consumer–counselor working relationships in rehabilitation. *Rehabilitation Counseling Bulletin, 41*, 122–137.

Chan, F., Tarvydas, V., Blalock, K., Strauser, D., & Atkins, B. (2009). Unifying and elevating rehabilitation counseling through model-driven, culturally-sensitive evidence-based practice. *Rehabilitation Counseling Bulletin, 52,* 114–119. doi:10.1177/0034355208323947

Chen, X., Muller, V., Lee, B., Wu, J. R., Iwanaga, K., Lee, D. K., & Chan, F. (under review). Community participation as both a mediator and moderator for the relationship between functional disability and life satisfaction for individuals with fibromyalgia. Manuscript submitted to Rehabilitation Research, Policy and Education (April, 2019).

Chen, X., Wu, J.R., Chan, F., & Tansey, T. N. (2018). *Wisconsin Related Condition Scale.* Madison, WI: Rehabilitation Research and Training Center for Evidence-Based Practice in Vocational Rehabilitation, University of Wisconsin-Madison.

Chou, C.C., Chan, F., Chan, Y.C., & Phillips, B. (2013). Introduction to positive psychology in rehabilitation. *Rehabilitation Research, Policy, and Education, 27,* 126–130. doi:10.1891/2168-6653.27.3.126

Cohen, S., & Williamson, G. (1988). Perceived stress in a probability sample of the US. In S. Spacapam & S. Oskamp (Eds.), *The social psychology of health: Claremont symposium on applied social psychology* (pp. 31–67). Thousand Oaks, CA: Sage.

Compton, W. M., Gfroerer, J., Conway, K. P., & Finger, M. S. (2014). Unemployment and substance outcomes in the United States 2002–2010. *Drug and Alcohol Dependence, 142,* 350–353. doi:10.1016/j.drugalcdep.2014.06.012

Crewe, N. M., Athelstan, G. T., & Meadows, G. K. (1975). Vocational diagnosis through assessment of functional limitations. *Archives of Physical Medicine and Rehabilitation, 56*(12), 513–516.

Crewe, N. M., & Dijkers, M. (1995). Functional assessment. In L. A. Cushman & M. J. Scherer (Eds.), *Psychological assessment in medical rehabilitation* (pp. 101–144). Washington, DC: American Psychological Association.

Diener, E., Emmons, R., Larsen, R., & Griffin, S. (1985). The satisfaction with life scale. *Journal of Personality Assessment, 49*(1), 71–75. doi:10.1207/s15327752jpa4901_13

Ditchman, N., Werner, S., Kosyluk, K., Jones, N., Elg, B., & Corrigan, P. W. (2013). Stigma and intellectual disability: Potential application of mental illness research. *Rehabilitation Psychology, 58*(2), 206–216. doi:10.1037/a0032466

Dooley, D., Catalano, R., & Hough, R. (1992). Unemployment and alcohol disorder in 1910 and 1990: Drift versus social causation. *Journal of Occupational and Organizational Psychology, 65*(4), 277–290. doi:10.1111/j.2044-8325.1992.tb00505.x

Dowrick, C., Casey, P., Dalgard, O., Hosman, C., Lehtinen, V., Vazquez-Barquero, J. L., & Wilkinson, G. (1998). Outcomes of Depression International Network (ODIN): Background, methods and field trials. *British Journal of Psychiatry, 172*(4), 359–363. doi:10.1192/bjp.172.4.359

Durlauf, S. N. (2001). A framework for the study of individual behavior and social interactions. *Sociological Methodology, 31*(1), 47–87. doi:10.1111/0081-1750.00089

Dutta, A., Chan, F., Kundu, M. M., Kaya, C., Brooks, J., Sánchez, J., & Tansey, T. N. (2016). Assessing vocational rehabilitation engagement of people with disabilities: A factor-analytic approach. *Rehabilitation Counseling Bulletin, 60*(3), 145–154. doi:10.1177/0034355215626698

Dutta, A., Gervey, R., Chan, F., Chou, C. C, & Ditchman, N. (2008). Vocational rehabilitation services and employment outcomes of people with disabilities: A United States study. *Journal of Occupation Rehabilitation, 18,* 326–334. doi:10.1007/s10926-008-9154-z

Federal Safety Net. (2015). *U.S. poverty statistics.* Retrieved from http://www.federalsafetynet.com/us-poverty-statistics.html

Fitzgerald, S., Chan, F., Deiches, J., Umucu, E., Hsu, S. T., Lee, H. L., . . . Iwanaga, K. (2015). Assessing work motivation in people with severe mental illness: A factor-analytic approach. *Australian Journal of Rehabilitation Counseling, 21,* 123–136. doi:10.1017/jrc.2015.12

Fitzgerald, S., Deiches, J., Umucu, E., Brooks, J., Muller, V., Wu, J. R., & Chan, F. (2016). Psychometric properties of the Vocational Rehabilitation Engagement Scale when used with people with mental illness in clubhouse settings. *Rehabilitation Research, Policy, and Education, 30*(3), 276–285. doi:10.1891/2168-6653.30.3.276

Fougeyrollas, P., Noreau, L., Bergeron, H., Cloutier, R., Dion, S.-A., & St. Michel, G. (1998). Social consequences of long-term impairments and disabilities: Conceptual approach and assessment of handicap. *International Journal of Rehabilitation Research, 21,* 127–141. doi:10.1097/00004356-199806000-00002

Gamble, D., & Moore, C. L. (2003). The relation between VR services and employment outcomes of individuals with traumatic brain injury. *Journal of Rehabilitation, 69*(3), 31–38.

Garin, O., Ayuso-Mateos, J. L., Almansa, J., Nieto, M., Chatterji, S., Vilagut, G., . . . Racca, V. (2010). Validation of the "World Health Organization Disability Assessment Schedule, WHODAS-2" in patients with chronic diseases. *Health and Quality of Life Outcomes, 8*(1), 51–66. doi:10.1186/1477-7525-8-51

Hall, J. P., Kurth, N. K., & Hunt, S. L. (2013). Employment as a health determinant for working-age, dually-eligible people with disabilities. *Disability and Health Journal, 6,* 100–106. doi:10.1016/j.dhjo.2012.11.001

Iwanaga, K., Rumrill, P., Miller, D., Wu, J. R., Chen, X., Lee, B., Tansey, T. N., & Chan, F. (in review). Assessing readiness for employment in vocational rehabilitation: An abbreviated measure. Manuscript submitted to *Journal of Rehabilitation* (April, 2019).

Iwanaga, K., Umucu, E., Wu, J. R., Yaghmaian, R., Lee, H. L., Fitzgerald, S., & Chan, F. (2017). Assessing vocational outcome expectancy in individuals with serious mental illness: A factor-analytic approach. *Journal of Mental Health,* 1–8. doi:10.1080/09638237.2017.1340603

Iwanaga, K., Wu, J. R., Chen, X., Lee, B., Reyes, A., Phillips, B., . . . Chan, F. (2018). Person-environment contextual factors as mediators for the relationship between symptoms cluster and employment outcome in multiple sclerosis. *Journal of Vocational Rehabilitation, 48,* 197–206. doi:10.3233/JVR-180930

Judge, T. A., Erez, A., Bono, J. E., & Thoresen, C. J. (2003). The core self-evaluations scale: Development of a measure. *Personnel Psychology, 56*(2), 303–331. doi:10.1111/j.1744-6570.2003.tb00152.x

Kaya, C., Chan, F., Tansey, T., Bezyak, J., Sercan, A., & Altundag, K. (2018). Evaluating the World Health Organization's international classification of functioning, disability and health framework as a participation model for cancer survivors in Turkey. *Rehabilitation Counseling Bulletin.* doi:10.1177/0034355218792900

Kocalevent, R. D., Berg, L., Beutel, M. E., Hinz, A., Zenger, M., Härter, M., ... Brähler, E. (2018). Social support in the general population: Standardization of the Oslo social support scale (OSSS-3). *BMC Psychology, 6*(1), 6–31. doi:10.1186/s40359-018-0249-9

Kroenke, K., Spitzer, R. L., & Williams, J. B. (2001). The PHQ-9: Validity of a brief depression severity measure. *Journal of General Internal Medicine, 16*(9), 606–613. doi:10.1046/j.1525-1497.2001.016009606.x

Leahy, M. J., Chan, F., Iwanaga, K., Umucu, E., Sung, C., Bishop, M., & Strauser, D. (2018). Test and item specifications for the certified rehabilitation counselor examination: An empirical validation study. *Rehabilitation Counseling Bulletin.* doi:10.1177/0034355218800842

Leahy, M. J., Chan, F., Sung, C., & Kim, M. (2013). Empirically derived test specifications for the certified rehabilitation counselor examination. *Rehabilitation Counseling Bulletin, 56*(4), 199–214. doi:10.1177/0034355212469839

Lee, B., Iwanaga, K., Pfaller, J., Chan, F., Chiu, C., Moser, E., & Rumrill, P. (2018). Psychometric validation of the multiple sclerosis environmental supports scale: A brief report. *Rehabilitation Counseling Bulletin, 61*(3), 187–191. doi:10.1177/0034355217734635

Lee, E. H. (2012). Review of the psychometric evidence of the perceived stress scale. *Asian Nursing Research, 6*(4), 121–127. doi:10.1016/j.anr.2012.08.004

Magasi, S. R., Heinemann, A. W., & Whiteneck, G. G. (2008). Participation following traumatic spinal cord injury: An evidence-based review for research. *Journal of Spinal Cord Medicine, 31*(2), 145–156.

Markland, D.A., & Tobin, V. (2004). A modification to the behavioural regulation in exercise questionnaire to include an assessment of amotivation. *Journal of Sport & Exercise Psychology, 26,* 191–196.

Martin, R., West-Evans, K., & Connelly, J. (2010). Vocational rehabilitation: Celebrating 90 years of careers and independence. *American Rehabilitation, 34*(1), 15–18.

McClelland, A. (2000). Effects of unemployment on the family. *The Economic and Labour Relations Review, 11,* 198–212. doi:10.1177/103530460001100204

Mermis, B. J. (2005). Developing a taxonomy for rehabilitation outcome measurement. *Rehabilitation Psychology, 50*(1), 15–23. doi:10.1037/0090-5550.50.1.15

Mood, C., & Jonsson, J. O. (2016). The social consequences of poverty: An empirical test on longitudinal data. *Social Indicators Research, 127*(2), 633–652. doi:10.1007/s11205-015-0983-9

Moser, E. N. (2017). *Person-environment contextual factors contribute to resilience in young adults with epilepsy* (Unpublished doctoral dissertation). University of Wisconsin, Madison.

Munder, T., Wilmers, F., Leonhart, R., Linster, H. W., & Barth, J. (2010). Working Alliance Inventory-Short Revised (WAI-SR): Psychometric properties in outpatients and inpatients. *Clinical Psychology and Psychotherapy: An International Journal of Theory and Practice, 17*(3), 231–239. doi:10.1002/cpp.658

Neath, J., Bellini, J., & Bolton, B. (1997). Dimensions of the functional assessment inventory for five disability groups. *Rehabilitation Psychology, 42*(3), 183–207. doi:10.1037/0090-5550.42.3.183

Nordenfelt, L. (2003). Action theory, disability, and ICF. *Disability and Rehabilitation, 25,* 1075–1079. doi:10.1080/0963828031000137748

Office of the United Nations High Commissioner for Human Rights. (n.d.). *Combating discrimination against persons with disabilities.* Retrieved from http://www.ohchr.org/EN/Issues/Discrimination/Pages/discrimination_disabilities.aspx

O'Neill, J., Mamun, A., Potamites, E., Chan, F., & Cardoso, E. (2015). Return to work of SSDI beneficiaries who do and don't access state vocational rehabilitation agency services: Case control study. *Journal of Disability Policy Studies, 26,* 111–123. doi:10.1177/1044207315583900

Patient-Reported Outcomes Measurement Information System. (2018). *Health measures.* Retrieved from http://www.healthmeasures.net/explore-measurement-systems/promis

Perenboom, R. J. M., & Chorus, A. M. J. (2003). Measuring participation according to the International Classification of Functioning, Disability and Health (ICF). *Disability and Rehabilitation, 25,* 577–587 doi:10.1080/0963828031000137081

Peterson, D. B. (2005). International classification of functioning, disability and health: An introduction for rehabilitation psychologists. *Rehabilitation Psychology, 50,* 105–112. doi:10.1037/0090-5550.50.2.105

Pfaller, J. S. (2016). *The World Health Organization International Classification of Functioning, Disability, and Health framework as a participation model for people with multiple sclerosis* (ProQuest Dissertations and Theses Global). Retrieved from https://search.proquest.com/docview/1814746528?accountid =12846

Quach, C. W., Langer, M. M., Chen, R. C., Thissen, D., Usinger, D. S., Emerson, M. A., & Reeve, B. B. (2016). Reliability and validity of PROMIS measures administered by telephone interview in a longitudinal localized prostate cancer study. *Quality of Life Research, 25*(11), 2811–2823. doi:10.1007/s11136-016-1325-3

Rosenberg, M. (1965). *Society and the adolescent self-image.* Princeton, NJ: Princeton University Press.

Sánchez, J., Muller, V., Chan, F. Brooks, J. M., Iwanaga, K., Tu. W.-M., . . . Crespo-Jones, M. (2018). Personal and environmental contextual factors as mediators between functional disability and quality of life in adults with serious mental illness: A cross-sectional analysis. *Quality of Life Research, 28,* 441–450 doi:10.1007/s11136-018-2006-1

Sánchez, J., Rosenthal, D., Chan, F., Brooks, J., & Bezyak, J. (2016). Relationships between World Health Organization ICF constructs and participation in adults with severe mental illness. *Rehabilitation Research, Policy, and Education, 30*(3), 286–304. doi:10.1891/2168-6653.30.3.286

Scheier, M. F., Carver, C. S., & Bridges, M. W. (1994). Distinguishing optimism from neuroticism (and trait anxiety, self-mastery, and self-esteem): A reevaluation of the life orientation test. *Journal of Personality and Social Psychology, 67*(6), 1063–1078. doi:10.1037/0022-3514.67.6.1063

Scherer, M. J., & Glueckauf, R. (2005). Assessing the benefits of assistive technologies for activities and participation. *Rehabilitation Psychology, 50,* 132–141. doi:10.1037/0090-5550.50.2.132

Smedema, S. M., Chan, J. Y., & Phillips, B. N. (2014). Core self-evaluations and Snyder's hope theory in persons with spinal cord injuries. *Rehabilitation Psychology, 59*(4), 399–406. doi:10.1037/rep0000015

Smedema, S. M., Pfaller, J. S., Yaghmaian, R. A., Weaver, H., da Silva Cardoso, E., & Chan, F. (2015). Core self-evaluations as a mediator between functional disability and life satisfaction in college students with disabilities majoring in science and technology. *Rehabilitation Research, Policy, and Education, 29*(1), 96–104. doi:10.1891/2168-6653.29.1.96

Smith, A. R., Ebert, E. E., & Broman-Fulks, J. J. (2016). The relationship between anxiety and risk taking is moderated by ambiguity. *Personality and Individual Differences, 95,* 40–44. doi:10.1016/j.paid.2016.02.018

Smith, B. W., Dalen, J., Wiggins, K., Tooley, E., Christopher, P., & Bernard, J. (2008). The brief resilience scale: Assessing the ability to bounce back. *International Journal of Behavioral Medicine, 15*(3), 194–200. doi:10.1080/10705500802222972

Snyder, C. R., Harris, C., Anderson, J. R., Holleran, S. A., Irving, L. M., Sigmon, S. T., ... Harney, P. (1991). The will and the ways: Development and validation of an individual-differences measure of hope. *Journal of Personality and Social Psychology, 60*(4), 570–585. doi:10.1037/0022-3514.60.4.570

Steinmetz, E. (2006). Americans with disabilities: 2002. *Current Population Reports, P70–107.* Washington, DC: U.S. Census Bureau.

Stewart, A. L., & Ware, J. E. (1992). *Measuring functioning and well-being: The medical outcomes study approach.* Durham, NC: Duke University Press.

Stineman, M. G., Shea, J. A., Jette, A., Tassoni, C. J., Ottenbacher, K. J., Fiedler, R., & Granger, C. V. (1996). The functional independence measure: Tests of scaling assumptions, structure, and reliability across 20 diverse impairment categories. *Archives of Physical Medicine and Rehabilitation, 77*(11), 1101-1108. doi:10.1016/S0003-9993(96)90130-6

Strohmer, D. C., & Leierer, S. J. (2000). Modeling rehabilitation counselor clinical judgment. *Rehabilitation Counseling Bulletin, 44*(1), 3-9. doi:10.1177/003435520004400102

Sung, Y. Y. (2012). *Evaluating the World Health Organization International Classification of Functioning, Disability and Health framework as an employment model for people with epilepsy* (Doctoral dissertation). Retrieved from https://depot.library.wisc.edu/repository/fedora/1711.dl:ATSBRBH4ZF5UZ84/datastreams/REF/content

Tansey, T. N., Iwanaga, K., Bezyak, J., & Ditchman, N. (2017). Testing an integrated self-determined work motivation model for people with disabilities: A path analysis. *Rehabilitation Psychology, 62*(4), 534–544. doi:10.1037/rep0000141

Umucu, E., Brooks, J., Lee, B., Iwanaga, K., Wu, J.-R., Chen, A., & Chan, F. (2018). Measuring dispositional optimism in student veterans: An item response theory analysis. *Military Psychology, 30*(6), 590–597. doi:10.1080/08995605.2018.1522161

Umucu, E., Iwanaga, K., Fitzgerald, S., Thompson, K., Moser, E., Sánchez, J., . . . Brooks. J. (2016). Assessing vocational competency of individuals with serious mental illness through self-report: A brief clinical measure. *Journal of Applied Rehabilitation Counseling, 47*(3), 22–28.

Uniform Data System for Medical Rehabilitation Group. (1996). *The guide for the uniform data set for medical rehabilitation (Adult FIM) (version 4.0).* Buffalo: State University of New York.

United Nations Human Rights Office of the High Commissioner. (2008). *Combating discrimination against persons with disabilities.* Retrieved from http://www.ohchr.org/EN/Issues/Discrimination/Pages/discrimination_disabilities.aspx

Üstün, T. B., Kostanjsek, N., Chatterji, S., & Rehm, J. (2010). Measuring health and disability: Manual for WHO Disability Assessment Schedule WHODAS 2.0. Geneva, Switzerland. Retrieved from https://apps.who.int/iris/bitstream/handle/10665/43974/9789241547598_eng.pdf;jsessionid=EFD52000AF262E9399FBA353E8338985?sequence=1

U.S. Census Bureau. (2003). *United States summary: 2000 summary social, economic, and housing characteristics.* Washington, DC: U.S. Government Printing Office.

U.S. Department of Education. (2016). *Annual report, fiscal year 2013, report on federal activities under the Rehabilitation Act.* Washington, DC: Office of Special Education and Rehabilitative Services, Rehabilitation Services Administration. Retrieved from https://www2.ed.gov/about/reports/annual/rsa/2013/rsa-2013-annual-report.pdf

U.S. Department of Labor. (2018). *Employment situation* [employment situation summary]. Retrieved from https://www.bls.gov/news.release/empsit.nr0.htm

U.S. Government Accountability Office. (2005). *Better measures and monitoring could improve the performance of the VR program.* Washington, DC: Author. Retrieved from http://www.gao.gov/products/GAO-05-865

Wang, J. (2005). *Disability and American families: 2000.* Washington, DC: U.S. Government Printing Office.

Ware, J., Kosinski, M., & Keller, S. (1996). A 12-item short-form health survey: Construction of scales and preliminary tests of reliability and validity. *Medical Care, 34*(3), 220–233. doi:10.1097/00005650-199603000-00003

Wehman, P., Chan, F., Ditchman, N., & Kang, H. J. (2014). Effect of supported employment on vocational rehabilitation outcomes of transition-age youth with intellectual and developmental disabilities: A case control study. *Intellectual and Developmental Disabilities, 52,* 296–310. doi:10.1352/1934-9556-52.4.296

Wolfensberger, W. (2002). Social role valorization and, or versus, "empowerment." *Mental Retardation, 40*(3), 252–258. doi:10.1352/0047-6765(2002)040<0252:SRVAOV>2.0.CO;2

World Health Organization. (2001). *International classification of functioning, disability and health: ICF.* Geneva, Switzerland: Author. Retrieved from http://www.who.int/classification/icf

Wu, J. R, Iwanaga, K., Chen, X, Lee, B., Umucu, E., Tao, J., . . . Chan, F. (2019). Psychometric validation of the brief multiple sclerosis community participation scale. *Journal of Vocational Rehabilitation, 51*(1), 33–39. doi:10.3233/JVR-191023

Yaghmaian, R. A., & Smedema, S. M. (2019). A feminist, biopsychosocial subjective well-being framework for women with fibromyalgia. *Rehabilitation Psychology, 64*(2), 154–166. doi:10.1037/rep0000226

Zimet, G., Dahlem, N., Zimet, S., & Farley, G. (1988). The multidimensional scale of perceived social support. *Journal of Personality Assessment, 52*(1), 30–41. doi:10.1207/s15327752jpa5201_2.

Zuelke, A. E., Luck, T., Schroeter, M. L., Witte, A. V., Hinz, A., Engel, C., . . . Villringer, A. (2018). The association between unemployment and depression—Results from the population-based LIFE-adult-study. *Journal of Affective Disorders, 235,* 399–406. doi:10.1016/j.jad.2018.04.073

BASIC PSYCHOMETRIC PRINCIPLES

WILLIAM T. HOYT | JIA-RUNG WU | KANAKO IWANAGA | FONG CHAN

LEARNING OBJECTIVES

After reviewing this chapter, the reader should be able to:

- Identify basic concepts related to reliability.
- Identify basic concepts of validity.
- Summarize the measurement of core self-evaluations.
- Summarize the research findings on reliability and validity for core self-evaluation measurement.

Introduction

Because most characteristics of interest to rehabilitation psychologists and rehabilitation counselors are not directly observable, they must be assessed indirectly, and an important question for research concerns the quality of the resulting scores. Many variables (here called *constructs*) of interest are either continuous or quantitative in nature, with the goal of measurement being to assign scores to the units under study (here assumed to be individual participants). *Psychometrics* refers to theory and techniques for assessing the adequacy of such quantitative scores, which is the subject of this chapter (Revelle, 2017).

By convention, psychometric theory conceptualizes measurement quality in terms of two related properties of scores (Nunnally & Bernstein, 1978). *Reliability* refers to the consistency of scores over replicated assessments. *Validity* refers to the extent to which differences in scores reflect actual differences in the characteristic (construct) of interest. In modern accounts, validity is defined in terms of the appropriateness of scores derived from a given measurement procedure for their intended use (e.g., unbiased selection of applicants for occupational or educational activities; testing of theoretical propositions by examining relations among scores representing various constructs of interest; Messick, 1998). Reliability (consistency) is important because it is a precondition for validity. Validity addresses the fundamental question of whether the scores provide information about the underlying constructs. In this chapter, we discuss basic concepts related to reliability and validity of measurement and provide examples derived from the growing literature on *core self-evaluations* (CSE), including empirical data derived from the most popular measure of this construct: the Core Self-Evaluation Scale (CSES; Judge, Locke, Durham, & Kluger, 1998).

▇ Reliability

Classical reliability theory proceeds from the assumption that scores derived from psychological assessment procedures are inherently imperfect. Each person's score is presumed to reflect in part the person's actual standing on the construct being measured and in part the effects of *measurement error*. Accordingly, variance in scores from multiple participants may be partitioned into *true score variance* (i.e., variance that is consistent over replicated assessments) and *error variance*. The *reliability coefficient* (usually notated r_{XX}) quantifies the proportion of variance in scores that is attributable to true scores (i.e., to true variation among participants in the construct of interest). The remaining proportion of variance (i.e., $1 - r_{XX}$) is attributed to measurement error.

Sources of Error

A potentially confusing feature of reliability theory is that measurement error comes in different types. It is not uncommon for researchers to report on multiple types of reliability coefficient, each yielding a different estimate of the proportion of variance in scores that is attributable to true score and error variance. For example, users of the CSES (Judge et al., 1998) may learn that Cronbach's alpha for the total scores in an initial validation sample (viz., sample 3 in Judge, Erez, Bono, & Thoresen, 2003) averaged $r_{XX} = .86$ over two time points, indicating that $1 - r_{XX} = 14\%$ of score variance is attributable to measurement error. However, this same study reported a test–retest reliability coefficient of $r_{XX} = .81$, which implies that $1 - r_{XX} = 19\%$ of score variance is attributable to measurement error. Which of these estimates is correct, and which should be reported as future investigators seek to provide psychometric evidence of the reliability of CSES scores?

Schmidt, Le, and Ilies (2003) addressed this question with a careful analysis of the meaning of different reliability coefficients. Cronbach's (1951) coefficient alpha is the most commonly reported reliability coefficient because it can (and should) be computed and reported any time a multi-item scale is administered to a sample of participants. Coefficient alpha is a coefficient of internal consistency reliability (sometimes referred to as a *coefficient of equivalence*, or CE; Cronbach, 1947): When alpha is reported, r_{XX} indicates the proportion of score variance that is consistent across items and $1 - r_{XX}$ indicates the proportion of score variance that is attributable to a combination of *specific factor error* (i.e., item variance that does not load on the general factor common to all items on the scale) and *random error* (Schmidt et al., 2003).

The test–retest reliability coefficient (or *coefficient of stability*; Cronbach, 1947) is a correlation between scores on the same measure administered to a group of participants at two different time points. When reporting a test–retest coefficient, r_{XX} indicates the proportion of variance in scores that is consistent (i.e., stable) across the two measurement occasions and $1 - r_{XX}$ indicates the proportion of score variance attributable to a combination of *transient error* and *random error* (Schmidt et al., 2003). Thus, it should not be surprising that different reliability coefficients yield different estimates of the proportion of true score variance. This difference reflects the fact that the two coefficients define measurement error differently.

As Schmidt et al. (2003) note, for most investigations in the behavioral sciences, both transient error and specific factor error have an effect on study findings, as described in the next section. Thus, it is normally relevant to report both coefficients of internal consistency and coefficients of stability in assessing quality of measurement in the behavioral sciences.

Effects of Measurement Error

Researchers should be concerned about reliability because measurement error biases estimates of effect sizes in psychological research. When we compute the correlation between scores on variables X and Y (known as the *observed correlation*), assumed to be measured with error, this is a biased estimate of the hypothetical correlation between true scores (i.e., between X_t and Y_t—the *true correlation* between X and Y). The observed correlation is always smaller in magnitude (i.e., closer to 0) than the true correlation—a phenomenon known as *attenuation*. The amount of attenuation depends on the reliabilities of the measures of both X and Y, as follows:

$$r_{xy} = r_{x_t y_t} (r_{xx} r_{yy})^{1/2} \tag{3.1}$$

where r_{xy} is the observed correlation, $r_{x_t y_t}$ is the true correlation, and r_{xx} and r_{yy} are the reliabilities of x and y, respectively. Using this formula, one can estimate the value of $r_{x_t y_t}$ from the observed correlation and the two reliability coefficients. This *disattenuated* correlation coefficient (Schmidt & Hunter, 1996) represents the best estimate of the true correlation, taking into account the effects of measurement error.

For example, Judge et al. (2003) published a table of correlation coefficients for the CSES, with measures of other related constructs in four samples, to summarize concurrent validity evidence for the CSES. For each correlation, they reported both the observed correlation (r) and the disattenuated (corrected) correlation (r_c)—the estimate of $r_{x_t y_t}$ from Equation 3.1. The correlation (r) between CSES and self-esteem in sample 1 was $r = .67$, indicating a very strong relationship (not surprising, as self-esteem is one of the constructs that serves as an indicator of CSE). The corrected correlation ($r_c = .80$) suggests a high level of overlap between these two measures. These correlations were even higher for other samples (e.g., in sample 4, $r = .79$ and $r_c = .92$, suggesting that CSES and self-esteem scores reflect nearly identical constructs in this sample), perhaps raising questions about discriminant validity, a topic discussed later.

Here, we return to the idea that measurement error comes in multiple forms and that each reliability coefficient captures some sources of measurement error but ignores others. Schmidt et al. (2003) showed that when disattenuated correlations are computed using Cronbach's alpha (CE), the error variance is somewhat underestimated, resulting in a corrected correlation coefficient that is still somewhat biased. Schmidt et al. (2003) show how to combine information from CE and CS (the coefficient of stability, or test–retest reliability) to form a CES (coefficient of equivalence and stability) that reflects the contribution of both forms of measurement error (specific factor error and transient error). Using the CES to disattenuate the correlations in Judge et al.'s Table 4 would take into account attenuation attributable to both of these types of measurement error and would yield estimates of the corrected correlations (r_c) that are even larger than those obtained by Judge et al. (2003).

Reliability Is a Property of Scores, Not Measures

Researchers should be aware that "Reliability is a property of the scores on a test for a particular population of examinees" (Wilkinson & American Psychological Association [APA] Task Force on Statistical Inference, 1999, p. 596); thus, reliability coefficients may fluctuate across test administrations (Vacha-Haase, 1998). A measure that yields highly reliable scores in the validation sample (e.g., in college students in the United States) could yield less reliable scores in samples drawn from other populations (e.g., high school students or older adults; lower socioeconomic status, or SES, populations). For this reason, it is important for researchers to select measures that have been shown to produce reliable scores in samples similar to those they intend to study and to report on the reliability (CE; and CS if longitudinal data are collected) of scores in their own samples.

For example, the CSES was developed and had mainly been utilized in the general population. When Smedema (2014) advocated applying this measure to survivors of spinal cord injury (SCI), she conducted a psychometric validation study to ascertain that factor structure and internal consistency (CE) reliability would be demonstrated for this population. Whereas Judge et al. (2003) reported internal consistency coefficients (CE) ranging from $r_{XX} = .81$ to .87 in four samples of working U.S. adults, Smedema et al. (2015) found a comparable level of reliability ($r_{XX} = .88$) for CSES scores in people with SCI ($N = 247$). Small variations (like this one) in reliability for studies with different samples may be attributable to sampling error, supporting the inference that the internal consistency of scores generalizes across samples. Larger variations in reliability between samples are less likely to be accounted for by sampling error and may reflect differences in item meaning or participant comprehension that affect score reliability.

The question of reliability generalization is especially pressing in cross-cultural research, which often requires that the scale be translated for use in different language communities. In such cases, there is the potential that item meanings and interitem correlations in the translated scale will differ from those in the original, so it is especially important for researchers to examine factor structure and scale (or subscale) reliability when using the translated version of the scale in research. For example, a German-language version of the CSES yielded internal consistency reliability (CE) of $r_{XX} = .86$ and test–retest reliability (CS) of $r_{XX} = .82$ over 2 months (Stumpp, Muck, Hülsheger, Judge, & Maier, 2010). A Korean version of the CSES estimated a CE of $r_{XX} = .77$ (Holt & Jung, 2008), and a Finnish-language version found CS of $r_{XX} = .83$ to .85 over three different time points in a longitudinal study (Mäkikangas, Kinnunen, Mauno, & Selenko, 2016). In each of these cases, the finding of a reliability coefficient not too different from the original English-language version indicates that score reliability was not substantially different for the new version of the scale than for the original. However, the finding that scores are reliable does not necessarily indicate that they are valid, and translated versions of existing measures should also be examined for evidence of validity, as described in the next section.

■ Validity

Validity refers to "the degree to which evidence and theory support the interpretation of test scores for the proposed uses of tests" (American Educational Research Association, APA, & National Council on Measurement in Education, 2014, p. 11). Validity theory addresses the critical question of whether scores derived from a measurement procedure reflect the intended construct (i.e., the latent trait, ability, or other characteristic of interest). Reliability is a necessary precondition for validity. If a measurement procedure does not produce replicable (reliable) variance, scores on this measure cannot be a valid measure of any construct. However, a very reliable measure may still have poor validity.

Relationship Between Reliability and Validity

Consider the case of two researchers wishing to develop a rater-based assessment of the working alliance in a counseling setting. Using recorded interactions between counselors and clients, the goal is for coders to watch these recordings and provide valid ratings of the affective *bond* (Bordin, 1981) between the counselor and the client.

- Researcher A focuses on discrete, observable behaviors that can serve as indicators of therapeutic bond and has coders break each session up into 1-minute segments and rate the degree of eye contact (0 = *none*, 1 = *some*, 2 = *predominant*) during each segment. These segment ratings can then be averaged over the length of the session to give a bond score for each session.

- Researcher B takes a different approach, providing coders with definitions of therapeutic bond derived from the literature and creating a scoring rubric that relies on holistic judgments from raters based on viewing the full session.

Each of these approaches has strengths and limitations. Researcher A will likely find that with a little training, coders can achieve high interrater reliability, as there is little room for subjectivity in the rating system. However, validity may be weak, as the microbehaviors that are the focus of this coding system do not capture the subtle cues that make up the alliance in counseling. Researcher B has designed a coding system that relies more on coder judgment, which leaves more room for subjectivity. Likely this will result in lower agreement between pairs of coders—however, by aggregating alliance ratings among multiple coders, one can generally arrive at reliable scores (Hoyt & Melby, 1999; Lakes & Hoyt, 2008). It may be that Researcher B's coding system, although it seems less rigorous at first glance, better captures the interpersonal import of the counselor's behaviors and thus results in scores that are more valid indicators of the alliance in the sessions observed.

To produce scores that are valid indicators of the construct of interest, a measurement procedure must necessarily produce reliable scores. Scores that demonstrate weak evidence of reliability are mostly error variance and so will also yield weak evidence of validity (as correlations with other measures will necessarily be greatly attenuated). But it is important to remember that not all reliable measures are valid. When the goal is to quantify internal states or nuanced relational dynamics, it may sometimes be that the most reliable measurement procedures, ironically, produce scores with the weakest construct validity.

There Are No Generic Validity Coefficients

Generic types of reliability (based on the sources of error discussed earlier) have long been recognized, with established procedures for computing coefficients of stability, internal consistency, and (where relevant) interrater reliability or agreement. Thus, the task of identifying and reporting evidence of score reliability may seem relatively straightforward.

In general, validity evidence is much more difficult to summarize succinctly, in part because construct validation is an ongoing process of assessing how measurement properties align with the theory of the underlying construct (Meehl, 1995) so that there is not a point at which cumulative validity evidence may be deemed conclusive. An additional complication in summarizing information relevant to validity is that relevant evidence comes in many forms. In the next section, we consider three common types of validity evidence, with illustrative examples drawn from the CSE literature.

Types of Evidence Relevant to Construct Validity

In reliability analyses, we partition score variance into replicable variance (historically referred to as *true score* variance) and nonreplicable variance (*error* variance). In validity analysis, we come to the further recognition that replicable variance in scores can be attributable to multiple factors, so does not all reflect the construct of interest. Messick (1995) noted that the two major threats to construct validity are *construct underrepresentation* and *construct-irrelevant variance*. Strong measurement development practices aim to maximize construct-relevant variance and minimize construct-irrelevant variance in scores. And construct validation investigations pose the fundamental question, "What constructs account for variance in test performance?" (Cronbach & Meehl, 1955). The goal of these investigations is to establish that test scores (i.e., scores derived from any standardized assessment procedure) largely reflect construct-relevant variance and also to understand the degree to which other sources, both systematic (construct-irrelevant variance) and random (measurement error), contribute to test scores.

Given that the goal of construct validation is to assure that test scores are well saturated with construct-relevant variance, it is critical for assessment developers to provide a clear definition of the construct of interest. In addition to a verbal definition, construct delineation involves specification of linkages to other established constructs, including antecedents (causes) and effects of the target construct. With a well-elaborated theory of the construct under study, future users will be able to make an appropriate evaluation of the evidence for construct validity. Three important sources of evidence are discussed in this section: test content, internal structure, and external validity (i.e., correlations with other measures).

Content Validity

An important step in the measurement development process is item generation and validation. (In some performance measures, the measurement procedures are conceptualized as *tasks* rather than items.) It is common to generate more items than will be used in the measure in the final form and to seek input from experts in the content area on whether each item seems relevant to the construct of interest and whether the items as a whole fully represent the content domain.

Content validation is relevant to Messick's (1995) threats to construct validity, as item format and content largely determine whether test scores will reflect construct-relevant variance and the extent to which construct-irrelevant variance will be present in test scores. Examples of construct-irrelevant variance are factors such as generic test–taking ability (for ability assessments; Messick, 1995) and self-presentation biases (for self-report measures of attitudes and traits; Tracey, 2016). These are personal characteristics that contribute to variance in test scores but are not relevant to the construct one is attempting to assess. This construct-irrelevant variance is a confound that complicates interpretation of both internal and external validity evidences, as discussed in the next two sections.

Judge (1997) defined CSE as a global tendency to evaluate the self positively that is consistent over time and across evaluative contexts. He postulated that CSE informs many value-laden self-reports, such as assessments of self-esteem and emotional stability, as well as assessments of capabilities such as global self-efficacy and locus of control. Judge postulated that CSE accounts for variance in outcomes of interest to organizational psychologists, including job satisfaction and perceptions of the work environment. The CSES (Judge et al., 1998) contains 12 items selected for their relevance to the four traits just mentioned. Questions regarding the content validity of the CSES have focused on the selection of the four traits (i.e., self-esteem, emotional stability, global self-efficacy, and locus of control) as the most important indicators of CSE. For example, CSE scores also correlate strongly with other personality traits, such as conscientiousness and extraversion (Chang, Ferris, Johnson, Rosen, & Tan, 2012). If CSES items were drawn from too narrow a pool, then these scores would not capture the full range of meaning of the CSE construct (Chen, 2012).

Internal Test Structure

Another source of evidence for construct validity relates to the factor structure of the scale. Factor analysis can support decisions about scoring and interpretation of measures. For example, sub-scale scores are generally justified by reference to factor analyses showing that the items on each subscale share variance and therefore constitute a meaningful dimension or facet of the under-lying construct. In a multidimensional scale, the decision to combine all items to produce a total score can be supported by showing that the subscale dimensions are well correlated or, better yet, that item variance is well modeled by a hierarchical factor structure, with subordinate dimensions (the subscales) loading on a superordinate factor (the latent construct).

Given that the CSES comprised items relevant to four interrelated personality traits, one might expect a hierarchical factor structure with a general factor and four specific factors (one for each of the constituent traits). However, support for this model is unclear. In a recent, comprehensive examination of the Finnish version of the CSES, Mäkikangas et al. (2016) reported adequate fit for a two-factor model, with the first factor comprising the positively worded CSES items (e.g., "When I try, I generally succeed") and the second factor comprising the negatively worded items (e.g., "There are times when things look pretty bleak and hopeless to me"). However, the authors did not test a model involving a third, higher order factor, nor did they report on the correlation between the two factors, leaving open the question of whether total scores on the CSES capture a unitary construct of CSE.

External Validity Evidence

Cronbach and Meehl (1955) described construct validation as an iterative process of examining correlations between scores on the measure of interest and scores on other measures to see whether they reflected the theoretically predicted relations—what Cronbach and Meehl referred to as the *nomological network* of the construct. This important source of evidence for construct validity is sometimes divided into subcategories of *concurrent validity* (correlations with other measures of conceptually related constructs) and *predictive validity* (correlations with theorized outcomes of the construct of interest, ideally in a longitudinal design where the outcome variables are assessed at a later time point). Mediator and moderator analyses may also serve to bolster judgments of construct validity if they provide support for theory-derived predictions about the focal construct.

The CSES was developed to operationalize a generalized self-regard that Judge (1997) predicted would be related to job satisfaction and other job perceptions. Chang et al. (2012) summarized ample evidence that CSES scores are related to scores on measures of job satisfaction (corrected $r = .44$) and even more strongly to global measures of life satisfaction (corrected $r = .57$), with weaker associations (although still in the predicted directions) with other work-related measures such as organizational commitment and task performance. Thus, there is support for several key theoretical propositions about the role of CSE in determining outcomes of interest in organizational behavior. In the next three sections, we describe common models for addressing more specific questions related to construct validity and consider their relevance to research uses of the CSES.

Discriminant Validity

The external validity analyses reviewed for the CSES earlier are of the type referred to as *convergent validity* analyses. Examination of correlations between CSES scores and scores on theoretically related measures aims to show that CSES scores *converge* with (or share variance with) scores on variables that are conceptually related to CSE. Also important in construct validation is the question of *discriminant validity*, encompassing evidence that the target measure captures unique variance beyond that assessed by existing measures of related constructs.

Often, measurement developers will examine correlations with measures of response biases (such as social desirability bias). The hope is that these correlations will not be too high, supporting the discriminant validity of scores on the target measure (That is, one hopes to find small or no overlap with measures of response bias, suggesting that most or all of the variance on the target measure is construct-relevant.). Tracey (2016) provided a thoughtful discussion of the complexities of interpreting such discriminant validity correlations, including concerns about the validity of scores on putative measures of social desirability bias.

Discriminant validity analyses can also be used to reassure ourselves that we are not inadvertently committing what Kelley (1927) referred to as the *jangle fallacy*—creating a measure that has a new name and unique item content but is empirically indistinguishable from an existing measure of a different construct. As we noted earlier, the high correlations between CSES scores and scores on measures of self-esteem (corrected rs in the .80–.90 range) raise concerns about discriminant validity. Although, in theory, self-esteem is just one of four proposed indicators of a broader underlying construct (CSE), in practice, it may be that the CSE displays nearly identical patterns of external correlation as existing self-esteem measures.

Incremental Validity

More sophisticated statistical analyses can address specific questions relevant to construct validity. *Incremental validity* addresses the ability of scores on the target measure to account for variance in outcomes over and above variance explained by other known predictors of these outcomes. For example, Lubinski (2004) reviews findings showing that measures of cognitive abilities account for variance in life outcomes (such as educational attainment and occupational prestige) when differences in SES are held constant. The implication of these findings is that, although scores on measures of cognitive ability are known to be confounded with SES, there is unique variance in these cognitive ability scores that accounts for variance in life outcomes, beyond what is predicted by SES.

Incremental validity analyses can be carried out using hierarchical regression models by entering one or more covariates (confounds) at step 1 in the analysis, followed by scores on the target measure at step 2. If there is a significant change in R^2 from step 1 to step 2, this supports the unique (*incremental*) contribution of the target construct to the prediction of the outcome variable. For example, to further probe discriminant validity between CSES scores and scores on self-esteem, one could include both constructs as predictors of important outcomes. If the CSES accounts for unique variance in the outcome variables after self-esteem has been statistically controlled, this suggests that despite considerable overlap, CSES does indeed capture unique and theoretically relevant variance in CSE, beyond that assessed by existing measures of related constructs.

Mediation and Moderation

Often, our theories about a target construct suggest (a) processes by which it has effects on key outcomes (mediator variables), (b) contextual or demographic variables that may alter the strength of its association with key outcomes (moderator variables), or (c) effects of the target construct on commonly studied relations among other variables in the research domain (target construct as a moderator of relations among these other variables). When there is clear theoretical support for mediator or moderator relations involving the target construct, tests of these mediator or moderator hypotheses can provide sophisticated evidence for construct validity of scores on the measure, further elaborating the nomological network for the construct under study.

Validity Generalization

As is the case with reliability, validity is a property of scores and not measures. Validity evidence may be affected by characteristics of the population under study, so that use of the measure in new populations calls for renewed investigation of validity for those populations. Messick (1995) noted that a critical dimension of validity appraisal is *consequential* in nature: The examination of the social consequences of particular uses of scores is a critical aspect of establishing construct validity for these uses.

To illustrate, there is evidence of statistically significant cultural differences in external validity of CSES scores for predicting job attitudes. Chang et al. (2012) found stronger relations between CSE and job satisfaction ($r_s = .44$ and $.32$, respectively) and between CSES and job performance ($r_s = .35$ and $.16$, respectively) among participants from collectivistic cultures, compared with those from individualistic cultures. Although the explanation for these differences is unclear (Chang et al. [2012] note that one might predict the opposite in theory, as CSE is likely to be valued in individualistic cultures), it highlights a consideration for validity generalization: We should not assume that external validity evidence obtained for one group will necessarily generalize when the measure is used in a different group.

As was the case with reliability generalization, this concern for validity generalization applies to researchers studying populations of interest in rehabilitation counseling. For example, CSES scores may show different patterns of correlation among participants who live with a disability than they do in the general population, so disability researchers should be cautious in assuming that validity findings will generalize to different disability groups and attend to the need to accumulate additional evidence of validity of CSES scores for particular uses in these populations.

▓ Conclusions

Reliability and validity are properties of scores and not tests (measures), and relevant findings from previous studies may be specific to populations examined in those studies. Thus, one consideration in selecting and justifying measures for a research project is whether evidence is available to support this use of scores in one's population of interest. Researchers developing and promulgating the use of new measures should give careful attention to what types of reliability are relevant and to nuanced construct definition and theoretical elaboration to allow for accumulation and evaluation of validity evidence. Establishing validity is a process, and each new investigation using an existing measurement procedure contributes to the evidentiary base for this measure as an operationalization of the construct of interest.

References

American Educational Research Association, American Psychological Association, & National Council on Measurement in Education. (2014). *Standards for educational and psychological testing.* Washington, DC: American Educational Research Association.

Bordin, E. S. (1981). A psychodynamic view of counseling psychology. *The Counseling Psychologist, 9*(1), 62–70. doi:10.1177/001100008000900114

Chang, C. H., Ferris, D. L., Johnson, R. E., Rosen, C. C., & Tan, J. A. (2012). Core self-evaluations: A review and evaluation of the literature. *Journal of Management, 38*(1), 81–128. doi:10.1177/0149206311419661

Chen, G. (2012). Evaluating the core: Critical assessment of core self-evaluations theory. *Journal of Organizational Behavior, 33*(2), 153–160. doi:10.1002/job.761

Cronbach, L. J. (1947). Test "reliability": Its meaning and determination. *Psychometrika, 12*(1), 1–16. doi:10.1007/bf02289289

Cronbach, L. J. (1951). Coefficient alpha and the internal structure of tests. *Psychometrika, 16*(3), 297–334. doi:10.4135/9781412961288.n54

Cronbach, L. J., & Meehl, P. E. (1955). Construct validity in psychological tests. *Psychological Bulletin, 52*(4), 281–309. doi:10.1037/h0040957

Holt, D. T., & Jung, H. H. (2008). Development of a Korean version of a core self-evaluations scale. *Psychological Reports, 103*(2), 415–425. doi:10.2466/pr0.103.6.415-425

Hoyt, W. T., & Melby, J. N. (1999). Dependability of measurement in counseling psychology: An introduction to generalizability theory. *The Counseling Psychologist, 27*(3), 325–352. doi:10.1177/0011000099273003

Judge, T. A. (1997). The dispositional causes of job satisfaction: A core evaluations approach. *Research in Organizational Behavior, 19*, 151–188. doi:10.1016/j.sbspro.2015.04.917

Judge, T. A., Erez, A., Bono, J. E., & Thoresen, C. J. (2003). The core self-evaluations scale: Development of a measure. *Personnel Psychology, 56*(2), 303–331. doi:10.1111/j.1744-6570.2003.tb00152.x

Judge, T. A., Locke, E. A., Durham, C. C., & Kluger, A. N. (1998). Dispositional effects on job and life satisfaction: The role of core evaluations. *Journal of Applied Psychology, 83*(1), 17–34. doi:10.1037//0021-9010.83.1.17

Kelley, T. L. (1927). *Interpretation of educational measurements.* Yonkers-on-Hudson, NY: World Book.

Lakes, K. D., & Hoyt, W. T. (2008). What sources contribute to variance in observer ratings? Using generalizability theory to assess construct validity of psychological measures. *Infant and Child Development: An International Journal of Research and Practice, 17*(3), 269–284. doi:10.1002/icd.551

Lubinski, D. (2004). Introduction to the special section on cognitive abilities: 100 years after Spearman's (1904). "General intelligence," objectively determined and measured. *Journal of Personality and Social Psychology, 86*(1), 96–111. doi:10.1037/0022-3514.86.1.96

Mäkikangas, A., Kinnunen, U., Mauno, S., & Selenko, E. (2016). Factor structure and longitudinal factorial validity of the *Core Self-Evaluation Scale*: Exploratory structural equation modeling. *European Journal of Psychological Assessment, 34*, 444–449. doi:10.1027/1015-5759/a000357

Messick, S. (1995). Validity of psychological assessment: Validation of inferences from persons' responses and performances as scientific inquiry into score meaning. *American Psychologist, 50*(9), 741–749. doi:10.1002/j.2333-8504.1994.tb01618.x

Messick, S. (1998). Test validity: A matter of consequence. *Social Indicators Research, 45*(1–3), 35–44.

Nunnally, J. C., & Bernstein, I. H. (1978). *Psychometric theory.* New York, NY: McGraw-Hill.

Revelle, W. (2017). *An introduction to psychometric theory with applications in R.* Retrieved from http://personality-project.org/r/book

Schmidt, F. L., & Hunter, J. E. (1996). Measurement error in psychological research: Lessons from 26 research scenarios. *Psychological Methods, 1*(2), 199–223. doi:10.1037//1082-989x.1.2.199

Schmidt, F. L., Le, H., & Ilies, R. (2003). Beyond alpha: An empirical examination of the effects of different sources of measurement error on reliability estimates for measures of individual-differences constructs. *Psychological Methods, 8*(2), 206–224. doi:10.1037/1082-989x.8.2.206

Smedema, S. M. (2014). Core self-evaluations and well-being in persons with disabilities. *Rehabilitation Psychology, 59*(4), 407–414. doi:10.1037/rep0000013

Smedema, S. M., Chan, F., Yaghmaian, R. A., Cardoso, E. D., Muller, V., Keegan, J., . . . Ebener, D. J. (2015). The relationship of core self-evaluations and life satisfaction in college students with disabilities: Evaluation of a mediator model. *Journal of Postsecondary Education and Disability, 28*(3), 341–358. Retrieved from http://www.ahead-archive.org/uploads/publications/JPED/jped28_3/ JPED28_3_Final.pdf

Stumpp, T., Muck, P. M., Hülsheger, U. R., Judge, T. A., & Maier, G. W. (2010). Core self-evaluations in Germany: Validation of a German measure and its relationships with career success. *Applied Psychology, 59*(4), 674–700. doi:10.1111/j.1464-0597.2010.00422.x

Tracey, W. R. (2016). *The human resources glossary: The complete desk reference for HR executives, managers, and practitioners*. Boca Raton, FL: CRC Press.

Vacha-Haase, T. (1998). Reliability generalization: Exploring variance in measurement error affecting score reliability across studies. *Educational and Psychological Measurement, 58*(1), 6–20. doi:10.4135/9781412985789.n13

Wilkinson, L., & APA Task Force on Statistical Inference. (1999). Statistical methods in psychology journals: Guidelines and explanations. *American Psychologist, 54*, 594–604. doi:10.1037/0003-066x .54.8.594

PLANNING THE ASSESSMENT PROCESS

DAVID R. STRAUSER | CHELSEA E. GRECO

▓ Introduction

Planning assessment as part of the rehabilitation counseling process is an important step in providing critical information that can be used to establish relevant goals, achieve outcomes, and promote self-exploration. In this chapter, the important elements of the planning process are discussed with an underlying assumption that assessment is part of the overall rehabilitation counseling process. With this assumption as a basis, this chapter begins with a brief discussion on how the International Classification of Functioning, Disability and Health (ICF) can be used to provide a structure to plan assessment and how process variables such as *stages of change* (SOC), *motivational interviewing* (MI), and *working alliance* (WA) can be used to help clients engage in the assessment process. After briefly outlining the theoretical orientation issues related to test selection, evaluating tests, test administration, interpretation of findings, and communicating test results are discussed.

▓ Theoretical Foundations Related to Planning Rehabilitation Counseling Assessment

The primary goal of testing and evaluation in rehabilitation counseling is to determine the type and intensity of rehabilitation services needed to facilitate the goals and objectives of people with disabilities. One of the primary philosophical underpinnings of the assessment process in rehabilitation is the focus on the person. When the primary focus of testing and evaluation is on the person, the primary goal is to assist these people in obtaining information to facilitate a better understanding of themselves and their place in the world to achieve desired outcomes. A core value in the rehabilitation counseling profession is that the assessment process is synonymous with the counseling process and that the client must be actively involved throughout the assessment process. As Hays (2013) noted, the assessment process involves a continued dialogue that focuses on identifying the presenting and underlying issues to gain a fuller understanding of the attributes that may assist clients in achieving their desired goals. One strategy that has been proposed for use in rehabilitation counseling has been to identify the client's *assets, limitations,* and *preferences* (Berven, 2008). To be effective in implementing testing and evaluation as part of the assessment process, rehabilitation counselors need to start the process with an awareness of the types of tools that are available for use, determine how they can effectively communicate with the client, and understand the client's level of motivation to participate in the assessment process.

Like other areas of counseling, theories related to behavioral change provide rehabilitation counselors with guidelines to help their clients engage in and benefit from assessment in rehabilitation counseling (Strauser, O'Sullivan, & Wong, 2018). A strong grasp of behavioral change theory allows rehabilitation counselors to work more effectively with clients and their families to promote self-determination and independence. Given the demands and life changes that accompany disability, ongoing support and guidance of the client are needed in managing the pursuit of desired outcomes. Research in rehabilitation counseling notes the importance of reducing premature termination and increasing active participation through increasing the client's motivation to change (Chan, Miller, Lee, Pruett, & Chou, 2004). The sustainment of the client and rehabilitation counselor relationship is central for successful changes to occur. During the rehabilitation assessment process, preparing the client for change is of great significance (Chou, Ditchman, Pruett, Chan, & Hunter, 2009) and requires considerable time and long-term commitment. Research has found that rehabilitation counselors who incorporate evidence-based practice approaches, such as SOC, MI, and WA, are more likely to bring about effective behavioral change (Bordin, 1979; Chan et al., 2004; Miller & Rollnick, 1991; Wagner & McMahon, 2004). These theoretical approaches can be conceptualized as *process variables*, and to augment their discussion here, the reader is referred to a more detailed description of each approach in a recent chapter by Strauser, Greco, and O'Sullivan (2018). However, before briefly describing the process variables, this section reviews the ICF, which provides the *structure* that guides rehabilitation counseling assessment.

Structure

International Classification of Functioning, Disability and Health

The ICF (Bruyère, Van Looy, & Peterson, 2005) provides the structural foundation that guides rehabilitation counseling assessment and is based on important concepts of the medical, functional, and social models of disability to provide an integrative conceptual framework (Chan & Ditchman, 2013). The ICF model posits that chronic health conditions and disability are associated with four separate but related constructs: *body functions and structures, activities and participation, environment factors,* and *person factors.* However, given recent research in rehabilitation counseling, Chan et al. (2004) have advocated for the use of a modified version of the ICF to guide rehabilitation counseling assessment. A graphical depiction of the modified ICF model of assessment is

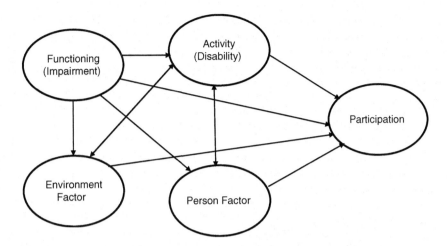

FIGURE 4.1 A modified International Classification of Functioning, Disability and Health (ICF) structural model for rehabilitation assessment.

presented in Figure 4.1, and more detailed discussion regarding the ICF and its application to rehabilitation counseling assessment is offered in Chapter 3, Basic Psychometric Principles, of this text.

Process Variables

In rehabilitation counseling assessment, process variables can be conceptualized as constructs that rehabilitation counselors can use to engage their clients and help them move through the assessment process. SOC, MI, and WA are considered to be major process variables for use during the rehabilitation counseling assessment process.

Stages of Change Model

The SOC model provides a comprehensive framework with which to understand and describe the change process of the person (Chou et al., 2009). The SOC model has a strong theoretical and empirical base and thus is applicable to diverse populations as a general model of change with practical applications in the field of rehabilitation counseling (Chan et al., 2004).

According to the SOC model, people move through the following five distinct stages (Prochaska & DiClemente, 1983): (a) *precontemplation* (the person is not intending to take action and may be unaware or in denial that his or her behavior is problematic), (b) *contemplation* (the person is starting to recognize that his or her behavior is problematic and is considering change), (c) *preparation* (the person starts to increase his or her commitment to change and may begin taking small [initial] steps to change behavior), (d) *action* (changing behavior by making specific overt modifications in altering his or her problem behavior), and (e) *maintenance* (sustaining the new behavior and working to prevent relapses). It is expected that a person will circle back between stages or remain at a particular stage for some time. The first stage a person currently occupies determines the degree of readiness he or she has to make the necessary changes for successful transition.

Motivational Interviewing

MI is a client-centered counseling approach designed to strengthen a client's motivation by focusing on his or her experiences, values, goals, and plans while promoting individual choice and responsibility in implementing change (Miller & Rollnick, 1991). MI consists of four basic principles: (a) *express empathy*, (b) *roll with resistance*, (c) *develop discrepancy*, and (d) *support self-efficacy*. The first principle, express empathy, allows the rehabilitation counselor to, through nonjudgmental listening, understand the client's impressions, perceptions, feelings, desires, concerns, and hopes and validate his or her point of view by creating an environment where the client can explore and consider multiple options (Chou et al., 2009; Wagner & McMahon, 2004). In the second phase, roll with resistance, resistance to change happens when there are direct confrontations or threats to personal choice. Adherence to change can be enhanced by choice, and exploration of issues and competing motivations of the client is more likely to occur if the counselor realizes and accepts, instead of fighting against, the reality that the client will have these competing motivations (Wagner & McMahon, 2004). Exploration of issues (change) is more likely if, instead of getting defensive when the client has differing or even undesirable viewpoints, the rehabilitation counselor remains in harmony with the client (Miller, Benefield, & Tonigan, 1993). In the third phase, develop discrepancy, to create change, the client needs to be able to explore discrepancies between current behavior and core values. The rehabilitation counselor's job is to gently direct this exploration so that the client, in turn, will benefit from exploring how his or her current behavior may be preventing him or her from reaching his or her desired goals and how the process of change may increase his or her future satisfaction (Wagner & McMahon, 2004). In the fourth phase, support self-efficacy, creating an environment that encourages hope and optimism, the rehabilitation counselor helps the client gain confidence about making changes and achieving goals. People may not make the effort to change, even if they desire to, if there is no hope for success (Wagner & McMahon, 2004). It is the counselor's job to promote this likelihood for success by reinforcing successive approximations, affirming success (even small ones), and reframing failures as intermediate success (Bandura, 1997). Developing a strong WA can help the rehabilitation counselor create an environment where a client can experience being accepted.

Working Alliance

WA is a collaboration between the client and rehabilitation counselor in which each makes equal contributions to the relationship based on the development of a bond that leads to a shared commitment to the goals and tasks of counseling (Bordin, 1979). Research has suggested that clients who experienced high levels of WA with their vocational rehabilitation (VR) counselor had greater satisfaction with their rehabilitation services and experienced better vocational outcomes (Lustig, Strauser, Weems, Donnell, & Smith, 2003). A good counseling relationship is based on the fundamental principles of the WA: (a) developing a strong relationship with the client, (b) identifying reasonable and obtainable goals, and (c) determining the tasks need to achieve the identified goals (Donnell, Lustig, & Strauser, 2004; Strauser, Lustig, & Donnell, 2004). Bonds form between the rehabilitation counselor and client through trust and confidence that the tasks will lead to achieving the goals. Having a feeling of common purpose and understanding can be a way of expressing a bond (Bordin, 1979; 1994). Goals are the outcome of the rehabilitation counseling process and are what the client hopes to achieve or gain. Developing goals can assist in the counselor–individual bond. Tasks that are needed to achieve the goals are agreed upon and engaged in by both the rehabilitation counselor and the client during the provision of rehabilitation counseling services. WA between both of them is imperative. The WA is the core element to facilitate change in clients and is often referred to as the glue that holds all strategies to facilitate change together.

■ Core Elements of Planning the Rehabilitation Counseling Assessment Process

Utilizing the theoretical approach outlined earlier, it is important for rehabilitation counselors to take the necessary steps to plan the assessment process. In this section, the core elements involved in planning the assessment process are introduced.

Part 1—Test Selection

The process of selecting the assessment strategies, test instruments, and evaluation processes that will be used to address the questions being asked is an important part of the overall assessment. To guide the identification and selection of appropriate test instruments, rehabilitation counselors must have a good understanding of the structure and process variables discussed earlier and be able to utilize decision-making strategies that are based on fundamental assessment principles to determine appropriate assessment strategies. A three-step process initially developed by Drummond (2004) has been modified for rehabilitation counselors to use in guiding the decision-making process regarding what tests to include in the rehabilitation assessment process.

Step 1—Identifying What Information Is Needed

The first step of the process is for rehabilitation counselors to determine what actual information is needed and would be useful in the rehabilitation counseling process. An assessment tool is helpful only if it provides information that is useful and relevant to the rehabilitation counselor and the person being served and addresses the specific questions being asked. In Step 1, it is important to remember that the specific information not only will focus on the client but may also be needed by the organization for which the rehabilitation counselor is working.

Step 2—Identifying Specific Strategies to Obtain the Needed Information

After identifying the specific information that is needed, the second step is to identify what specific strategies should be used to obtain the information. This step requires the rehabilitation counselor to analyze existing individual information such as records that are part of the case file, intake forms and interviews, academic transcripts, prior testing results and reports, and medical information. By engaging in this important step, rehabilitation counselors avoid wasting time and duplicating existing information. A primary decision for the rehabilitation counselor at this point is to determine whether the information needed can be obtained through formal or informal techniques or a combination of both. Often, the combination of both informal and formal assessment techniques has been found to be effective because the strengths of one technique complement the other, and together they can provide in-depth information about the client (Drummond, 2004). Finally, when choosing what assessment techniques are going to be used, rehabilitation counselors must have a good understanding of the person being evaluated and his or her specific qualities and characteristics.

Step 3—Identifying Appropriate Tests

Once the information needed has been identified and the assessment strategies have been determined, the next step is to review existing test information to select the specific tests or instruments that will be used in the evaluation. When possible, the client, who is part of the assessment process, should be involved in this selection. This does not mean that the rehabilitation counselor should defer to the client completely or provide in-depth psychometric information regarding specific instruments under consideration. Instead, the rehabilitation counselor should briefly discuss possible tests and their potential strengths and weaknesses. Because there are so many different tests and evaluation instruments, it is impossible for rehabilitation counselors to know all of the published and unpublished instruments that are available. Therefore, rehabilitation counselors need to rely on multiple sources of information that have been developed to provide up-to-date information regarding specific tests and instruments. Table 4.1 describes several commonly used sources of information about assessment procedures.

Part 2—Evaluating Tests

Once the rehabilitation counselor has identified possible instruments and informal strategies that may be used in the assessment process, a comprehensive evaluation will determine the most appropriate assessment method for the specific situation and questions being addressed. Some of the initial information that should be evaluated is available from secondary sources such as those identified in Table 4.1 or by talking to colleagues and other professionals who are familiar with tools and instruments under consideration. However, a complete evaluation of an instrument usually involves a careful examination of the instructor's manual. With this in mind, several important aspects of each test under consideration should be evaluated.

The first step in determining whether an instrument is appropriate is to evaluate the stated purpose of the test and the constructs that it purports to measure and decide if they are consistent with the behaviors and constructs under consideration (Drummond, 2004). A review of the test manual will determine the purpose of the test and the behavior it measures. After reviewing the manual, reading the specific test booklet and test protocol will determine whether the test items appear to be measuring the traits, objectives, or behaviors that are to be assessed (Mpofu & Mpofu, 2018; Whiston, 2016).

The second step in evaluating a test is to determine whether the test has an appropriate norming group and adequate psychometrics (Drummond, 2004; Drummond & Jones, 2010). For a norm-referenced test, the analysis of the normative group is critical when deciding whether the instrument is appropriate. Evaluating the normative group in terms of age, gender, ethnicity, socioeconomic representation, educational level, and geographic location are all important factors to consider (Mpofu & Mpofu, 2018). Although there are no specific guidelines to determine an appropriate normative group, normative groups usually involve larger samples, are drawn in systematic manner, and tend to garner the most confidence (Bolton & Parker, 2008). For criterion-referenced tests, the procedures the test developers used to determine the criterion must be considered. This is especially relevant to rehabilitation counselors who typically work with clients who may need some type of accommodation or modification when completing the assessment process.

The third step in evaluating a test is to determine whether the test material provides sufficient information for the rehabilitation counselor to provide a meaningful interpretation of the test results (Drummond, 2004). In other words, does the test material provide the information and

TABLE 4.1 Sources of Information About Assessment Procedures Used in Rehabilitation Counseling

SOURCE OF INFORMATION	DESCRIPTION
Mental Measurement Yearbook (MMY)	The MMY, now in its 18th edition (Spies, Carlson, & Geisinger, 2010), is considered the best general source of information regarding commercially available tests. The MMY provides access to information and reviews including a reference list for each test. First published in 1938, the MMY is revised every few years and has been available online since 1985. For a test to be included in a new edition, it must be new or revised since the previous edition.
Tests in Print (TIP)	TIP was originally published in 1961 and is currently in the 8th edition (Spies, Murphy, Geisinger, & Carlson, 2011). TIP is a comprehensive index of all the tests in the Buros system including those published in the prior issues of the MMY. For all tests in print, including those commercially available, TIP provides information regarding the purpose, acronyms, in-print status, cost, publisher, author information, and publication date.
Tests	*Tests* is a concise reference that provides test descriptions for a majority of the tests used in psychology, education, and business. It is updated annually and provides identifying information for each test. No psychometric or review information is provided.
Test Critiques	*Test Critiques* is designed as a supplement to *Tests* and provides more extensive test descriptions and test reviews. Information is also provided regarding the testing process.
ETSTestLink www.etes.org/test_link/about	Posted by the Educational Testing Services (ETS), this site lists 25,000 tests published since 1990 with approximately 1,000 tests that are available for purchase directly from ETS.
Buros Test Review Online http://unl.edu/buros/	Posts test reviews from the MMY, 9th edition, to the present.
Directory of Unpublished Experimental Mental Measure	Information on noncommercial psychological measures used for research in the fields of education, psychology, and sociology.
Counselors Guide to Career Assessment Instruments	Provides a description and publisher information of over 300 career assessment instruments.
Rehabilitation counseling–related professional journals	*Measurement and Evaluation in Counseling, Rehabilitation Counseling Bulletin, Journal of Rehabilitation, Rehabilitation Research, Policy and Education, Rehabilitation Psychology, Journal of Occupational Rehabilitation Career Development Quarterly, Psychological Assessment, Disability and Rehabilitation,* and *Journal of Career Assessment.*

resources necessary to make a proper and meaningful interpretation of the specific test results? For example, does the test manual and scoring protocol effectively describe how raw scores should be translated to standard scores and how those standard scores should be interpreted? Relative to the interpretation of scoring, how are test results conveyed to the examinee and other relevant parties? Is the exam computer administered and scored with immediate feedback provided, or does that test require a rehabilitation counseling professional to score and interpret test results? Consistent with the view that testing is part of the counseling process, self-interpretation must never take the place of the individual communication between the examiner and the examinee and explanation of test results. Instead, self-interpretation reports or materials should be viewed as supplemental materials that can aid the rehabilitation counselor during the interpretation process (Hays, 2013).

The fourth step in evaluating a test is to determine whether it is appropriate for the client being tested (Drummond & Jones, 2010; Mpofu & Mpofu, 2018). One consideration is the reading level of the actual test. If the reading level is too difficult, it will compromise the integrity of the test results and may also risk discouraging the client, who may become less motivated or may begin to question the relevance of the information obtained during the evaluation process (Hays, 2013). In addition to reading level, the format, layout, print size, and visual presentation of the test itself are important factors. Relative to the test format, how is the client required to respond to the specific test questions? Are item responses recorded in writing, on the test directly, or on a separate answer sheet? Does the client respond verbally to the examiner? Does the examiner observe the client performing certain tasks and then record the behavior observations (Drummond, 2004)? Also, is the test free from bias? Traditionally, focus regarding bias has been primarily on gender and culture, but in rehabilitation counseling, tests must be reviewed for implications related to disability and any stigma associated with having a disability or coming from a socioeconomically marginalized population (Bolton & Parker, 2008; Whiston, 2016).

Finally, when evaluating a test to determine whether it is appropriate, the counselor must consider what competencies the evaluator will need to have and whether the test is practical to administer. Tests require different levels of preparation and training to administer. A commonly used framework for detailing the level of training and preparation is a grading system that classifies test instruments based on certain user qualifications (Table 4.2). Although this grading scheme is commonly used and accepted, it is incumbent on the rehabilitation counselor to check the category and system used by each specific test publisher because of the variations. In addition, rehabilitation counselors must be familiar with the Commission on Rehabilitation Counselor Certification (CRCC) and American Counseling Association (ACA; 2009) code of ethics, as it applies to assessment and testing. In addition to qualifications, what is the test length, how much time does it take to administer the test, and can it be administered in a group or individually? Also, is the test a practical selection in terms of cost and usage? Can the test protocols be reused, or are they designed for a one-time use? Can the test be computer administered or scored, or does scoring need to be done directly by the evaluator?

Part 3—Test Administration

After appropriate test instruments have been identified, rehabilitation counselors need to engage in appropriate test administration. Test administration will vary on the questions being asked and specific test instruments that have been chosen to be part of the evaluation process. The *Standards for Educational and Psychological Testing* (American Educational Research Association [AERA], American Psychological Association [APA], & National Council on Measurement in Education [NCME], 1999) and the counselor code of ethics provide specific standards related to test administration. For rehabilitation counselors, the CRCC and the ACA code of ethics apply and can be used to guide the test administration process. State licensure requirements and standards will also serve to guide rehabilitation counselors as it relates to test administration. In addition to adherence to ethical and professional standards, the following three-phase test administration process

TABLE 4.2 Requirement by Category for Educational and Psychological Testing

CATEGORY	REQUIREMENTS
A	No requirements for Category A
B	*Required Degree:* Bachelor degree *Acceptable Fields of Study:* Psychology, counseling, related field *Course Work:* Test interpretation, psychometrics, and measurement theory; educational statistics; or closely related area. An individual has an option of using a license or certification from an agency/organization that requires appropriate training and experience in the ethical and competent use of psychological tests if he or she does not have the required course work.
C	*Required Degree:* Advanced professional degree that provides appropriate training in the administration and interpretation of psychological tests and all of the level B qualifications. An individual has an option of using a license or certification from an agency that requires appropriate training and experience in the ethical and competent use of psychological tests if he or she does not have the required coursework.
S	*Required Degree:* Degree, certificate, or license to practice in a physical or mental healthcare profession or occupation. *Additional Training:* Training and expertise in the ethical administration, scoring, and interpretation of clinical behavioral assessment instruments.

can be applied to guide rehabilitation counselors through the entire test administration process (Drummond, 2004; Drummond & Jones, 2010).

Phase 1—Preadministration

In Phase 1, rehabilitation counselors need to make sure that not only do they adhere to specific ethical guidelines but that they are also aware of how to administer and score the specific tests that will be used. The counselor should know how the test instrument can be modified, how the testing environment can be altered to accommodate people with disabilities (Bolton & Parker, 2008), and how any modifications impact the test results and the reliability and validity of the findings (Strauser, Chan, Wang, Wu, & Rahimi, 2013). Engaging in practice test administration and examining the test materials are essential steps in this phase, especially if the rehabilitation counselor is using a specific test or assessment method for the first time.

Examining the specific testing environment and paying attention to the specific room setup will help the overall administration process and is critical in maximizing the integrity of the test results. The rehabilitation counselor should allow appropriate time for the subject to be able to travel to the test setting and settle in prior to the start of the evaluation process. Securing appropriate test space at office, school, or community center well ahead of the evaluation and ensuring that the space is well-lit, quiet, free from distraction, and accessible are necessary steps in the assessment process, along with ensuring that during the evaluation, there are appropriate writing utensils and necessary testing supplies (e.g., timer; Drummond, 2004; Drummond & Jones, 2010). Finally, determining the specific order of the tests for administration and determining how the data will be collected are critical steps that all need to be completed prior to the start of the actual testing.

Phase 2—Administration of Tests

After the first phase has been completed, the actual administration of the tests takes place. A key point during this phase is compliance and adherence to the standardized test procedures. According to the *Standards for Educational and Psychological Testing* (AERA, APA & NCME, 1999), the usefulness and interpretability of the test scores require that the test be administered according to the test development standards outlined in the instructor's manual. As indicated earlier, the rehabilitation counselor must be familiar with the test manual and engage in practice administrations to maximize adherence to standardization, time requirements, and methods for gathering and reporting item responses. The rehabilitation counselor must also establish good rapport with the subject being tested to maximize comfort in the testing environment and maximize the validity of the test results (Hays, 2013). During test administration, any test modifications or accommodations should be noted in addition to the subject's behavior during the evaluation process (Bolton & Parker, 2008). To assist in behavioral observation during the testing process, it may be beneficial to utilize one of the many behavior rating forms that focus on physical reactions, test behavior, social behavior, and observable verbal characteristics during the testing process. As part of observation during the evaluation process, counselors need to be aware of the expectancy or Rosenthal effect, which is the premise that data sometimes can be affected by the expectations of the administrator (Hays, 2013).

Related to the Rosenthal effect is the issue of examiner bias and its impact on the overall evaluation process (Whiston, 2016). There are six major forms in which examiner bias can affect the evaluation process, with each one being equally important. The first form of examiner bias is the ethnicity and gender of the examiner. Research has found that dominant culture counselors may contribute to anxiety, fears, strained and unnatural reactions, insecurity, and latent prejudice, all of which may contribute to diminished or reduced test results. In addition, research has found that female administrators are more favorable than their male counterparts (Hays, 2013). The second form of examiner bias involves verbal and nonverbal language used by the evaluator and contributes to problems in communication and misunderstanding. Attitudes and expectations of the examiner are the third form of bias. An examiner who presents as warm, open, and empathetic, and displays genuine demeanor will likely create a warm testing environment where the subject feels more comfortable during the evaluation. The fourth type of bias affecting the evaluation process is the competence and experience of the rehabilitation counselor (Mpofu & Mpofu, 2018). Evaluators who are poorly prepared or inexperienced may express uncertainty, creating tension in the test environment. In addition, lack of preparation or inexperience may contribute to difficulty in providing appropriate test accommodations or limit proper test administration with diverse groups of people. Finally, the examiner's familiarity with and adherence to the code of ethics outlined earlier will affect the overall testing environment. A key component of the CRCC and ACA code of ethics is the fundamental belief in the dignity and worth of the person and the commitment to work in the best interest of the person (CRCC & ACA, 2009).

Phase 3—Postadministration

At the end of the test administration and the overall assessment process, the overall effectiveness of the process is evaluated. The overarching question guiding the postadministration evaluation is, Did the testing and assessment process achieve the intended purpose by providing information and insight into the questions asked (Drummond, 2004)? Basically, did the client gain needed and important information that allows him or her to move forward in achieving the goals outlined as part of the counseling process? In evaluating outcomes strategies, the techniques should take into account the client's developmental level, the specific goals, and questions addressed during the process, and should be sensitive enough to show individual change (Whiston, 2016). When feasible, the evaluation process should include feedback from multiple perspectives (e.g., client, counselor, evaluator, family members) and focus on multiple outcomes, such as knowledge gained, increased introspection and understanding, and behavior change. Outcomes should also take into account immediate, intermediate, and overall long-term goals and utilize data from multiple points in time. Despite the depth of information desired, the outcome evaluation process should be efficient, brief, easy to administer and score, and cost-effective (Drummond, 2004; Drummond & Jones, 2010). Typical techniques used in outcome evaluations include satisfaction forms, self-report scales, individual interviews, and rating scales (Hays, 2013). Finally, to obtain information regarding the overall administration process, it is recommended that clients be asked the following questions (Drummond, 2004):

1. How would you rate the physical test environment?
2. How would you rate the performance of the administrator?
3. Was the orientation to the testing process helpful?
4. Did you feel that you had enough time to finish all of the tests without feeling rushed?

Test Interpretation and Communication of Findings

The process of interpreting assessment results including data collected from a variety of sources and methods involves more than scoring the actual test. When assessment is viewed as part of the counseling process, rehabilitation counselors are able to incorporate the interpretation test results into the overall rehabilitation counseling process. Infusing interpretation in the counseling process increases the therapeutic value and impact of the assessment results and is more likely to bring about effective behavioral change. The manner in which the test results are interpreted and conveyed to the client by the rehabilitation counselor can significantly impact the level of self-awareness, insight, and decision making that client will experience.

The actual communication of the assessment process can occur during and after the test results have been scored. Communication and discussion of the test results and the implications for the client can occur informally, either in a counseling interaction or, more formally, in the form of an assessment report (Hays, 2013). Whether test results are presented and discussed individually or as part of a group, the rehabilitation counselor should also evaluate if further assessment is needed. Sometimes additional assessment is needed because of the client gaining insight and developing new questions or requesting additional information based on the analysis and synthesis of the assessment results.

Regarding the actual scoring of the tests, there are several things that rehabilitation counselors should be aware of and consider (Bolton & Parker, 2008; Drummond, 2004; Drummond & Jones, 2010). First, it is important for rehabilitation counselors to have a basic, but good, understanding of psychometric concepts such as reliability and validity and how they impact the generation of specific test scores. Second, tests can be scored either by hand or by the computer, and in many cases, both types of scoring are options. When tests are scored by hand, they typically involve the use of a scoring template or coded scoring system that is embedded into the assessment instrument. In addition, tests or assessments that allow for a self-scoring option are usually scored by hand. An important issue to address with hand scoring is error that may jeopardize the validity of the test results. To reduce this potential for error during hand scoring, rehabilitation counselors can take extra precautions, such as having each test double scored either by oneself or ideally using a colleague (Hays, 2013). Computer scoring is usually much faster and much more accurate than hand scoring. Despite the high level of accuracy, rehabilitation counselors should also be on guard for any unusual or questionable scores. If any results appear to be questionable, the test protocols and scoring should be checked immediately.

Because conveying the actual test results to the client is an important part of the assessment and rehabilitation counseling process, there are several things that rehabilitation counselors should keep in mind during the process.

- First, as mentioned throughout this chapter, it is critically important the rehabilitation counselors be knowledgeable about the information contained in the manual and how to score and interpret the test results. An important part of this process is to have good understanding of the specific tests strengths and weaknesses (Drummond, 2004; Drummond & Jones, 2010).

- Second, interpretation of test results is part of the counseling process, so attention should be paid to important counseling variables such as the counseling relationship and how the counselor and client interact. To strengthen the counseling relationship during the assessment process, it is important to prepare the client to receive the test feedback (Hays, 2013).

- Third, rehabilitation counselors should have multiple strategies for conveying the test results to the client. This is particularly important because when using the manual to score and interpret test results, the results are usually presented in standard scores and standard deviations and are based on the normal curve. For most clients, understanding standardized scores can be a difficult and confusing process. To offset the lack of individual understanding, rehabilitation counselors should be prepared to use more descriptive terms and visual methods to present test results. Whenever possible, test results should be provided to the client in descriptive terms rather than numerical scores and as probabilities instead of absolute certainties (Hays, 2013; Mpofu & Mpofu, 2018).

- When presenting test scores in terms of probabilities, research suggests that it is better to use numerical descriptions (e.g., there is a 95% chance) rather than verbal ones (e.g., there is a high probability) to convey precise information and promote better individual understanding (Hays, 2013).

- When discussing the test results with the client, the description of the test results should be tied to the specific reason for the testing (Strauser et al., 2013). Contextualizing the test results using other relevant individual information allows for the interpretive process to maximize the integration of diverse individual information and promote an integrated comprehensive understanding of the client.

- Consistent with the counseling approach to assessment, clients should be involved in the interpretation process so that they can address any questions that they may have regarding test results or the evaluation (Hays, 2013). This also allows the evaluator to observe the client's behaviors and reactions to the test results and seek feedback from the client. Asking the client to provide his or her reactions to the assessment process lays the foundation for an interactional interpretation.

- The rehabilitation counselors should discuss any limitations with the testing process in nontechnical terms. In a rehabilitation setting, it is important that any discussion of test limitations take into consideration the client's level of cognitive, affective, and executive functioning (Bolton & Parker, 2008). Any culture, gender, or socioeconomic factors should be fully discussed in practical terms with the client being encouraged to ask questions throughout the whole assessment process (Whiston, 2016).

■ To end the interpretation process and maximize outcomes, it is helpful for the rehabilitation counselor to provide a summary of the test results and restate and stress important points. Summarization allows time for the client to ask additional questions and ask for clarification. Clients should not leave the testing process confused or with misinformation that could create significant stress (Hays, 2013; Strauser et al., 2013).

The Assessment Report

In rehabilitation settings, one of the primary means of conveying test results to the client and other related parties is through an assessment report. This is particularly relevant when a person has been referred for an evaluation and a battery of tests has been completed. An evaluation report completed by a rehabilitation counselor can be provide a wealth of relevant clinical information and will typically include the following eight sections: (a) identifying information, (b) reason for referral, (c) background information, (d) behavioral observation, (e) results and interpretation, (f) recommendations, (g) summary of findings, and (h) signature (Drummond, 2004; Drummond & Jones, 2010; Hays, 2013).

Identifying Information

This section provides relevant demographic information and typically includes the client's name, date of examination, date of birth, age, date of report completion, examiner's name, and a list of the tests administered.

Reason for Referral

The information typically included in this section are the name of the person or organization making the referral; the reason for the referral or specific questions that should be addressed; a brief summary of the symptoms, behaviors, or functioning; and circumstances that led to the referral. This section provides the rationale for the selection of the instruments or procedures utilized and directly connects them to the specific questions being addressed.

Background Information

This section provides an overview of relevant information about the client so that the reader of the report can gain an understanding of current issues and concerns. The specific focus on the background information may vary depending on the reason for the assessment but will typically include educational, medical, and work history. This information is usually obtained from record reviews, prior test results, and information obtained from related people, such as parents or significant others.

Behavioral Observations

This part of the report allows the examiner to describe what was observed during the assessment process. The behavioral observation section of the report should include a brief description of the client's physical appearance, comments, and reactions to testing; behaviors and mannerisms; pain and discomfort during the evaluation; and any other behavior observed. If inferences are being made about the client's behavior, those inferences should be accompanied by descriptions of the behavior supporting the inferences. For example, if the evaluator indicates that the client displayed low back pain behaviors during the evaluation, he or she may want to indicate how many times the client had to stand up, if any breaks were taken, any facial expressions observed, and the client's actual report of pain.

Results and Clinical Interpretation

This section is arguably the most important part and usually the longest part of the rehabilitation assessment report. Typically covered in this section are the assessment findings, the meaning of the results, and the clinical and diagnostic interpretations. When discussing the assessment findings, the precise scores on every test may not be necessary. Instead, the focus should be on the pertinent findings and interpreting rather than simply reporting the results. This section should include enough detail so that the reader who may be unfamiliar with the specifics of the instrument can understand the meaning of the results. To help report interpretation, it is usually helpful to provide the specific names of the instruments and descriptions of the scores and scales. The interpretation should include a description of the client's strengths and limitations and a discussion of both consistent and inconsistent test results. The evaluator may also use this section to provide possible hypotheses and explanations of notable or important test results.

Recommendations

In the recommendation section, the evaluator should extend the material and findings in the report into future actions that will be beneficial to the client in achieving meaningful and important rehabilitation outcomes. The support and rationale for the recommendations should be based on the information presented in the prior sections of the report. The recommendations should be realistic and take into consideration the client's specific resources and situation. Sufficient detail should also be provided so that the recommendations can be fully implemented.

Summary

The summary section provides a succinct recap of the entire assessment report with a focus on the results and interpretation. The summary should not exceed two paragraphs but should briefly touch on all the major aspects of the report.

Signature

The signature should include the evaluator's name, degree, and professional title with the evaluator signing his or her name above the typewritten name.

Conclusion

The primary focus of this chapter was to introduce the role of planning the assessment as an important part of the rehabilitation counseling process. The goal of planning in the assessment process is to provide the client with critical information that can be used to establish relevant goals, achieve outcomes, and promote self-exploration. An underlying assumption outlined in this chapter is that assessment is part of the overall rehabilitation counseling process. With this assumption, the ICF was used to provide a structure to plan assessment, and the process variables of SOC, MI, and WA were introduced as important variables that assist the client in engaging in the assessment process. After discussing the theoretical orientation to rehabilitation assessment, issues related to test selection, evaluating tests, test administration, interpretation of findings, and communicating test results were presented.

References

American Educational Research Association, American Psychological Association, & National Council on Measurement in Education. (1999). *Standards for educational and psychological testing.* Washington, DC: Authors.

Bandura, A. (1997). *Self-efficacy: The exercise of control.* New York, NY: W. H. Freeman.

Berven, N. L. (2008). Assessment interviewing. In B. Bolton & R. Parker (Eds.), *Handbook of measurement and evaluation in rehabilitation* (pp. 243–261). Austin, TX: Pro-Ed.

Bolton, B., & Parker, R. (Eds.). (2008). *Handbook of measurement and evaluation in rehabilitation.* Austin, TX: Pro-Ed.

Bordin, E. (1979). The generalizability of the psychoanalytic concept of the working alliance. *Psychotherapy, 16,* 252–260.

Bordin, E. (1994). Theory and research on the therapeutic working alliance: New directions. In A. Horvath & L. Greenberg (Eds.), *The working alliance: Theory, research and practice* (pp. 13–37). New York, NY: Wiley.

Bruyère, S. M., Van Looy, S. A., & Peterson, D. B. (2005). The international classification of functioning, disability and health: Contemporary literature overview. *Rehabilitation Psychology, 50*(2), 113–121. doi:10.1037/0090-5550.50.2.113

Chan, F., & Ditchman, N. (2013). Applying the International Classification of Functioning, Disability, and Health to Psychology Practice. *Psyccritiques, 58*(13). doi:10.1037/a0031605

Chan, F., Miller, S. M., Lee, G., Pruett, S. R., & Chou, C. C. (2004). Research. In T. F. Rigger & D. R. Maki (Eds.), *Handbook of rehabilitation counseling* (pp. 159–170). New York, NY: Springer Publishing Company.

Chou, C. C., Ditchman, N., Pruett, S. R., Chan, F., & Hunter, C. (2009). Application of self-efficacy related theories in psychosocial interventions. In F. Chan, E. Cardoso, & J. Chronister (Eds.), *Understanding psychosocial adjustment to chronic illness and disability* (pp. 243–276). New York, NY: Springer Publishing Company.

Commission on Rehabilitation Counselor Certification, American Rehabilitation Counseling Association. (2009). *Code of professional ethics for rehabilitation counselors.* Retrieved from https://www.crccertification.com/code-of-ethics-4

Donnell, C., Lustig, D. C., & Strauser, D. R. (2004). The working alliance: Rehabilitation outcomes for persons with severe mental illness. *Journal of Rehabilitation, 70*(2), 12–17.

Drummond, R. J. (2004). *Appraisal procedures for counselors and helping professionals* (5th ed.). Upper Saddle River, NJ: Pearson.

Drummond, R. J., & Jones, K. D. (2010). *Assessment procedures for counselors and helping professionals* (7th ed.). Upper Saddle River, NJ: Pearson/Merrill Prentice Hall.

Hays, D. G. (2013). *Assessment in counseling: A guide to the use of psychological assessment procedures* (5th ed.). Alexandria, VA: American Counseling Association.

Lustig, D. C., Strauser, D. R., Weems, G. H., Donnell, C., & Smith, L. D. (2003). Traumatic brain injury and rehabilitation outcomes: Does working alliance make a difference. *Journal of Applied Rehabilitation Counseling, 34*(4), 30–37.

Miller, W. R., Benefield, R. G., & Tonigan, J. S. (1993). Enhancing motivation for change in problem drinking: A controlled comparison of two therapist styles. *Journal of Consulting Clinical Psychology, 61,* 455–461. doi:10.1037//0022-006x.61.3.455

Miller, W. R., & Rollnick, S. (1991). *Motivational interview.* New York, NY: Guilford Press.

Mpofu, E., & Mpofu, N. (2018). Assessment. In V. M. Tarvydas & M. T. Hartley (Eds.), *The professional practice of rehabilitation counseling* (pp. 201–220). New York, NY: Springer Publishing Company.

Prochaska, J. O., & DiClemente, C. C. (1983). Stages and processes of self-change in smoking: Toward an integrative model of change. *Journal of Consulting and Clinical Psychology, 51,* 390–395. doi:10.1037//0022-006x.51.3.390

Spies, R. A., Carlson, J. F., & Geisinger, K. F. (Eds.). (2010). *The eighteenth mental measurements yearbook.* Buros Institute of Mental Measurements.

Spies, R. A., Murphy, L. L., Geisinger, K. F., & Carlson, J. F. (2011). *Tests in print VIII.* Buros Center for Testing.

Strauser, D. R., Chan, F., Wang, M., Wu, M., & Rahimi, M. (2013). Vocational evaluation in rehabilitation. In D. R. Strauser (Ed.), *Career development, employment, and disability in rehabilitation* (pp. 179–192). New York, NY: Springer Publishing Company.

Strauser, D. R., Greco, C., & O'Sullivan, D. (2018). Career and lifestyle planning in vocational rehabilitation settings. In D. Capuzzi & M. D. Stauffer (Eds.), *Career counseling: Foundations, perspectives, and applications* (3rd ed.). London, UK: Routledge.

Strauser, D. R., Lustig, D. C., & Donnell, C. (2004). The impact of the working alliance on therapeutic outcomes for individuals with mental retardation. *Rehabilitation Counseling Bulletin, 47,* 215–223.

Strauser, D. R., O'Sullivan, D., & Wong, A. W. (2018). Career development and employment of people with disabilities. In V. M. Tarvydas & M. T. Hartley (Eds.), *The professional practice of rehabilitation counseling* (pp. 273–296). New York, NY: Springer Publishing Company.

Wagner, C. C., & McMahon, B. T. (2004). Motivational interviewing and rehabilitation counseling practice. *Rehabilitation Counseling Bulletin, 47,* 152–161. doi:10.1177/00343552040470030401

Whiston, S. (2016). *Principles and applications of assessment in counseling* (5th ed.). Belmont, CA: Brooks/Cole.

II

ASSESSMENT INSTRUMENTS AND TECHNIQUES

TESTS OF ABILITY

TIMOTHY N. TANSEY | EMILY A. BRINCK | JIA-RUNG WU |
VERONICA Y. ESTALA-GUTIERREZ | MARC L. ESPINO

LEARNING OBJECTIVES

After reviewing this chapter, the reader should be able to:

- Identify issues that affect the reliability and validity of tests of ability.
- Identify a basic framework for conceptualizing intellectual ability.
- Identify measures of general abilities and their corresponding indexes and subfactors.
- Classify different types of specific abilities.
- Identify measures of specific abilities and metrics used to assess these abilities.

▒ Introduction

The assessment of cognitive capacity, aptitudes, and current knowledge has been used throughout history to label individual capacity and distinguish among participants. With limited resources available for training a qualified workforce, assessments focused on understanding individual capacity and readiness have been used to identify individual capacity under the auspices of efficient use of resources and maximizing benefit to society (Power, 2000). Thus, a primary role of tests of ability and current skills has been to classify and categorize people into different groups for inclusion or exclusion in certain activities. Central to the use of instruments to identify individual abilities and knowledge are the concerns over the extent that measures of ability are distinct and differentiated from the effects of experience (Anastasi, 1988). Despite the numerous theories of abilities, the methods used to delineate functioning of general cognition or other aptitudes are routinely criticized for the contamination of the results due to the potential effects of experience inherent in the mechanisms used in assessing those domains (Dana, 2008; Helms, 1997). As a result, concerns also abound of the effects that experience may have on the identification of persons' abilities in the forecasting of future outcomes, as those predictions would be at least partially biased on those persons' experiences in areas related to the outcome prediction (Parker, 2008). To this end, when considering performance on tests of ability, examiners should acknowledge the potential interference of past experience on the obtained results as part of the overall context of the evaluation and in the interpretation of findings. Failure to identify experiences, whether life experiences or the effect of previous testing, will likely result in underestimation of individual capacity and subsequent erroneous conclusions of potential (Parker, 2008).

In addition to the potential interference experience has on measures of ability, a related concern is the recognition that assessments of ability may obtain variable results as a function of membership in diverse racial and cultural backgrounds. That is, findings in the available research suggest that persons from nonmajority groups score differently on certain measurements, but that those differences may not reflect an inferior score (Erickson, 2004). Rather, the variation in scores may be a function of an interaction between culture and the methods of measuring ability, affecting the validity of the measure (Delpit, 1995). The Culturally Different model has been proposed as a mechanism for understanding the variability in observed scores among persons from diverse racial and cultural backgrounds (Sue, Arredondo, & McDavis, 1992). The central premise of this model is that variation in scores is not an indication of inferior capacity, cultural deprivation, or other deficits. Rather, the difference on measures of ability is a product of the cultural differences between persons of diverse racial and cultural backgrounds and persons who identify as whites (Sue et al., 1992) and that diverse people have untested qualities and strengths that, if evaluated properly, would ultimately require examiners to adopt a broader approach in the evaluation of abilities (Washington, Malone, Briggs, & Reed, 2016).

As a result, as with concerns over the effect of experience on tests of ability, caution should be taken when assessments of abilities are used as the primary predictor of capacity or the likelihood of a specific outcome, as these assessments may underestimate the functioning of persons from certain groups (Anastasi & Urbina, 1997; Leong & Park, 2016). Further, credentialing organizations such as the Commission on Rehabilitation Counselor Certification (CRCC) and professional bodies such as the American Counseling Association (ACA) recognize the importance of considering a broad range of diversity in the selection, administration, and interpretation of assessments (see Box 5.1).

Although further exploration of this concern is provided in another section of this textbook, a brief summary of four key points to promote fairness in testing is provided here, given the potential impact on the provision of services and foreclosure of certain opportunities. The four points,

---

BOX 5.1

COMMISSION ON REHABILITATION COUNSELOR CERTIFICATION (CRCC) AND AMERICAN COUNSELING ASSOCIATION (ACA) CODES OF ETHICS STATEMENTS REGARDING DIVERSITY IN ASSESSMENT

G.7.B. Diversity Issues in Assessment.

Rehabilitation counselors use caution when interpreting results normed on populations other than that of the client. Rehabilitation counselors recognize the potential effects of disability, culture, or other factors that may result in potential bias and/or misinterpretation of data (CRCC, 2017, p. 22).

E.8. Multicultural Issues/Diversity in Assessment

Counselors select and use with caution assessment techniques normed on populations other than that of the client. Counselors recognize the effects of age, color, culture, disability, ethnic group, gender, race, language preference, religion, spirituality, sexual orientation, and socioeconomic status on test administration and interpretation, and they place test results in proper perspective with other relevant factors (ACA, 2014, p. 12).

SOURCES: Commission on Rehabilitation Counselor Certification. (2017). *Code of professional ethics for rehabilitation counselors.* Schaumburg, IL: Author; American Counseling Association. (2014). *ACA code of ethics.* Alexandria, VA: Author.

described in the *Standards for Educational and Psychological Testing* (American Educational Research Association, American Psychological Association, & National Council on Measurement in Education, 2014), evaluators should strive for, to the greatest extent possible, are as follows:

1. Evaluators should avoid use of tests that produce different results or that have different meaning across different racial or cultural groups.

2. Evaluators should provide all examinees an equal opportunity to demonstrate their standing on the construct the test is measuring.

3. Examinees who perform equally well on a test should have an equal chance of being chosen, regardless of group membership.

4. Examinees being evaluated must have had equal opportunity to learn or achieve the construct being measured.

As access to quality education, cultural differences in the review and response to specific content, and cultural influences or interference on test administration can affect outcomes on tests, evaluators should consider the impact of this variability when interpreting findings of tests of abilities and making recommendations for opportunities, supports, or services based on those findings.

In identifying the potential effects of experience and diverse racial and cultural background on test performance, Figure 5.1 provides a basic illustration of tests of ability and current skills and a theoretical relationship between those evaluation methods and the concerns identified previously.

As noted in Figure 5.1, measures of nonverbal abilities, such as the Raven's Standard Progressive Matrices (SPM), are relatively protected from the benefits of a priori experience and consequences of diverse group membership. Alternatively, tests of current skills are likely to be the most vulnerable to variations in experience and racial and cultural diversity based on their underlying theoretical bases and test construction.

A third, and more pragmatic consideration of tests of abilities is the qualification requirements to purchase and, potentially more important, be recognized as competent in the administration, scoring, and interpretation of the assessments. For example, two of the many publishers of tests of abilities, Pearson (www.pearsonclinical.com) and Western Psychological Services

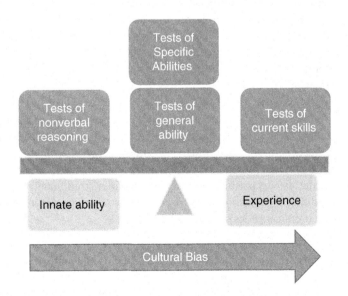

FIGURE 5.1 Relationship of assessments of ability to experiences.

TABLE 5.1 Qualification Levels to Purchase Testing Materials

PEARSON CLINICAL	DESCRIPTION[a]	WESTERN PSYCHOLOGICAL SERVICES
Level A	No degree or other specified requirements	Level A
	BA (schoolteacher); a bachelor's degree (BA, BS) in psychology, school counseling, occupational therapy, speech–language pathology, social work, education, special education, or related field	Level B
Level B	A master's degree (MA, MS, MSW, CAGS) in psychology, school counseling, occupational therapy, speech–language pathology, social work, education, special education, or related field	Level C
Level C	A doctoral degree (PhD, PsyD, MD) in psychology or related field	Level N

[a] Descriptions provided are abbreviated versions of requirements. Persons interested in the full descriptions, including other qualifications, should review the requirements found on the publishers' websites.

SOURCES: *Qualifications.* (n.d.). Retrieved from https://www.pearsonclinical.com/psychology/qualifications.html; Western Psychological Services. (2018). *Qualification guidelines.* Retrieved from https://www.wpspublish.com/store/Qualification_Guidelines%20V3.pdf.

(www.wpspublish.com), have identified educational standards for the purchase of assessments (see Table 5.1; "Qualifications", n.d.; Western Psychological Services, 2018).

These qualifications serve several functions. First, by limiting purchases to qualified consumers, it provides a basic level of test security that helps maintain the integrity of the evaluation process by reducing the capacity of persons to review the methods and questions on assessments and artificially increase their observed performance. Both the CRCC and the ACA identify test security as an ethical responsibility for purposes of both test integrity and legal issues regarding copyright of instruments through standards found in their respective codes of ethics (see Box 5.2).

A second purpose of limiting purchases to qualified consumers relates to the competency to administer, score, and interpret outcomes of tests of ability and other metrics. As identified earlier in this chapter, tests of ability have been used extensively to categorize persons to identify eligibility and potential benefit of opportunities, supports, and services. Untrained or unqualified use of assessment instruments potentially magnifies the validity issues identified with experience and diversity while also decreasing the reliability of administration and scoring. As a result, professional or accrediting organizations require competency in all professional areas, including evaluation, within their ethical codes of conduct (see Box 5.3).

Tests of Abilities

In considering the measurement of abilities, the common taxonomy is to separate this broad group of instruments into two divisions: (a) tests of general abilities and (b) tests of specific abilities. *Tests*

BOX 5.2

COMMISSION ON REHABILITATION COUNSELOR CERTIFICATION (CRCC) AND AMERICAN COUNSELING ASSOCIATION (ACA) CODES OF ETHICS STATEMENT REGARDING TEST INTEGRITY AND SECURITY

. . . counselors maintain the integrity and security of tests/instruments consistent with legal and contractual obligations. Rehabilitation counselors do not appropriate, reproduce, or modify published tests/instruments or parts thereof without the acknowledgment and permission of the publisher.

SOURCES: Commission on Rehabilitation Counselor Certification. (2017). *Code of professional ethics for rehabilitation counselors* (p. 22). Schaumburg, IL: Author; American Counseling Association. (2014). *ACA code of ethics* (p. 11). Alexandria, VA: Author.

BOX 5.3

COMMISSION ON REHABILITATION COUNSELOR CERTIFICATION (CRCC) AND AMERICAN COUNSELING ASSOCIATION (ACA) CODES OF ETHICS STATEMENTS REGARDING PROFESSIONAL COMPETENCE

D.1.a. Professional Competence: Boundaries of Competence

Rehabilitation counselors practice only within the boundaries of their competence, based on their education, training, supervised experience, professional credentials, and appropriate professional experience. Rehabilitation counselors do not misrepresent their competence to clients or others (CRCC, 2017, p. 13).

C.2.a. Professional Competence: Boundaries of Competence

Counselors practice only within the boundaries of their competence, based on their education, training, supervised experience, state and national professional credentials, and appropriate professional experience. Whereas multicultural counseling competency is required across all counseling specialties, counselors gain knowledge, personal awareness, sensitivity, dispositions, and skills pertinent to being a culturally competent counselor in working with a diverse client population (ACA, 2014, p. 8).

SOURCES: Commission on Rehabilitation Counselor Certification. (2017). *Code of professional ethics for rehabilitation counselors*. Schaumburg, IL: Author; American Counseling Association. (2014). *ACA code of ethics*. Alexandria, VA: Author.

of general ability attempt to measure *g*, a construct identified as overall intelligence and linked to the capacity to understand, integrate, and utilize information and to identify, analyze, and problem solve. *Tests of specific abilities*, commonly referred to as aptitudes, provide an assessment of particular strength in specific domains (Groth-Marnat, 1990). Despite there being overlap in many of the constructs incorporated into the construct of *g* or global intelligence and aptitudes in that both evaluate problem-solving, reasoning, and processing of information or situations, test of specific abilities are often represented as discrete abilities rather than a comprehensive single metric of intellectual capacity. Likewise, the utility of an IQ score derived from a test of general ability has limited predictive value in identifying capacity to work or succeed in training environments (Duckworth & Seligman, 2005; White & Weiner, 2004). Therefore, selecting the correct measurement depends largely on the specific referral questions and the corresponding rationale for conducting the assessment.

Tests of General Ability

Tests of general ability, as indicated in the preceding section, are generally focused on the measurement of individual intelligence, ultimately arriving at a quantification of *g*. Arriving at an agreed-upon definition of intelligence, much less how to define the construct *g*, has been an elusive achievement. Since Francis Galton first published his text, *Hereditary Genius*, in 1869, and many theorists and researchers investigating this construct since, consensus has been difficult to achieve on whether *g* is a unitary construct or, if there are multiple forms of *g*, the cognitive subfactors that combine to represent the construct, or even the construct validity and reliability of measures of the subfactors (Thorndike, 1997; Kaufman, 1990).

Wechsler (1944) defined intelligence as "the aggregate or global capacity of the individual to act purposefully, to think rationally and to deal effectively with his environment" (p. 3). This definition has influenced subsequent definitions and theories of intelligence, including a modern model of intelligence, the Cattell-Horn-Carroll (CHC) model (Schneider & McGrew, 2018). The CHC model is a hierarchical model of intelligence that expands on the previous Gf-Gc theory proposed by Cattel and Horn (McGrew, 1997). The model identifies eight subfactors or secondary order abilities that serve as a composite to the overall general intellectual ability, or *g* (Horn & Noll, 1997). The eight CHC subfactors include crystallized intelligence (Gc), fluid intelligence (Gf), quantitative reasoning (Gq), reading and writing ability (Grw) short-term memory (Gsm), long-term storage and retrieval (Glr), auditory processing (Ga), visual–spatial ability (Gv), and cognitive processing speed (Gs; see Figure 5.2; Schneider & McGrew, 2018). Although the CHC model defines eight secondary factors contributing to the overall intelligence, a comprehensive measure that incorporates assessment of all factors is not currently available. Instead, the two most widely used measures of intelligence, as least for adults, the Wechsler Adult Intelligence Scale, Fourth Edition (WAIS-IV) and the Stanford-Binet Intelligence Scales, Fifth Edition (SB5), measure select subfactors and develop a composite IQ score as an estimation of *g*.

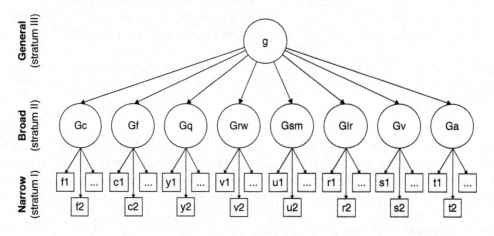

FIGURE 5.2 The Cattell-Horn-Carroll model of intelligence: overview of cognitive abilities.

Wechsler Adult Intelligence Scale, Fourth Edition

The WAIS-IV (2008) is published by Pearson and is classified as a Class C instrument. It is based on David Wechsler's early work on the Wechsler-Bellevue Intelligence Scale that was published in 1939 and his subsequent development of the WAIS in 1955 (WAIS-IV, 2008). Wechsler viewed intelligence as "the global capacity to act purposefully, to think rationally, and to deal effectively with [one's] environment" (Wechsler, 1939, p. 229). The modern version of the measure, the WAIS-IV, provides an overall full-scale IQ score as well as four indexes of intellectual functioning: verbal comprehension, perceptual reasoning, working memory, and processing speed. Identifying the full-scale IQ and the four indexes requires the completion of a core battery of 10 subtests (see Table 5.2).

The WAIS-IV includes five supplemental subtests that provide additional information on functioning within each index or can be used as a replacement for core subtests under certain conditions (Lichtenberger & Kaufman, 2009). The supplemental subtests are not required to calculate the full-scale IQ or the four indexes. Administration time for the 10 core subtests requires approximately 1 hour and 30 minutes without breaks between the subtests. The WAIS-IV is administered individually and is not available for group administration (Lichtenberger, Kaufman, & Kaufman, 2008). The normative sample of the WAIS-IV is based on data from 2,200 adults with stratification across gender, age, race, and other factors to maximize reliability of the results for different groups. The standardized scores for the WAIS-IV full-scale IQ and index scores are based on a standard score of 100 with a standard deviation of 15; the subtest scores have a mean of 10 with a standard deviation of 2.5 (Lichtenberger & Kaufman, 2009). To support the evaluation of clinical diagnoses and cognitive functioning, the WAIS-IV technical manual provides data on 13 special group studies on specific clinical populations. These clinical populations provide a comparison profile in considering certain diagnoses as well as demonstrate clinical significance of cognitive differences observed between different clinical populations (WAIS-IV, 2008).

Stanford-Binet Intelligence Scales, Fifth Edition

The SB5 is a Class C test published by Western Psychological Services (Roid, 2018). Using the Binet-Simon scale developed by Alfred Binet and Theodore Simon in 1905, a psychologist at Stanford University, Lewis Terman, revised the test in 1916 to create the Stanford-Binet Intelligence

TABLE 5.2 Wechsler Adult Intelligence Scale, Fourth Edition: Indexes, Core Subtests, and Supplemental Subtests

	VERBAL COMPREHENSION SCALE	PERCEPTUAL REASONING SCALE	WORKING MEMORY SCALE	PROCESSING SPEED SCALE
Core subtests	Similarities	Block design	Digit span	Symbol search
	Vocabulary	Matrix reasoning	Arithmetic	Coding
	Information	Visual puzzles		
Supplemental subtests	Comprehension	Picture completion	Letter–number sequencing	Cancellation
		Figure weights		

TABLE 5.3 Stanford-Binet Intelligence Scales, Fifth Edition: Verbal IQ, Nonverbal IQ, Cognitive Subfactors, and Subtests

COGNITIVE FACTOR	VERBAL IQ SUBTESTS	NONVERBAL IQ SUBTESTS
Fluid Reasoning	Early Reasoning/Verbal Absurdities and Verbal Analogies	Object Series/ Matrices
Knowledge	Vocabulary	Procedural Knowledge/Picture Absurdities
Quantitative Reasoning	Verbal Quantitative Reasoning	Nonverbal Quantitative Reasoning
Visual–Spatial Reasoning	Innovative New Position and Direction	Form Board/Form Patterns
Working Memory	Memory for Sentences/Last Word	Delayed Response

SOURCE: Roid, G. H., & Barram, R. A. (2004). *Essentials of Stanford-Binet Intelligence Scales (SB5) assessment.* Hoboken, NJ: Wiley & Sons.

Scale. In its fifth edition, the SB5 provides full-scale IQ score and outcomes with two cognitive domains, Verbal IQ and Nonverbal IQ, and five cognitive subfactors: Knowledge, Working Memory, Fluid Reasoning, Quantitative, and Visual–Spatial (Roid & Barram, 2004). Table 5.3 provides a list of the subtests corresponding to Verbal IQ and Nonverbal IQ and the cognitive subfactors.

The SB5 can be used with a larger age range than the WAIS-IV and can be administered to subjects from 2 to 85+ years old. Administration of the SB5 requires approximately 55 minutes, although this duration will vary depending on individual response patterns on the test. The structure of the individual subtests, as well as the normative sample of the SB5 of 4,800 subjects, supports the use of the test on persons with hearing impairments, persons with limited English proficiency, those with autism spectrum disorders, and several other clinical populations. The standardized scores for the SB5 full-scale IQ and index scores are based on a standard score of 100 with a standard deviation of 16 (Roid & Barram, 2004).

Raven's Standard Progressive Matrices

First published in 1938, the Raven's SPM (n.d.). is a Class B test published by Pearson. Unlike the WAIS-IV or SB5, the SPM is not intended to provide an approximation of *g*. Rather, it is one of the more widely used measures of fluid intelligence (Gf) as it is a nonverbal test that can readily be administered to persons from a broad range of geographic and linguistic diversity. The SPM evaluates capacity of observation skills and clear thinking ability through a series of five-item sets consisting of 12 items per set. Items on the SPM consist of diagrammatic puzzles. Each puzzle has a part missing, and the examinee has to select the missing piece from options provided in a multiple-choice format (Raven's SPM, n.d.). Although the average time to complete the SPM is approximately 30 minutes, examinees proceed at their own pace, as there is no time limit and length of administration will vary depending on the skill level and persistence of the subject. The SPM provides a single raw score with corresponding percentile rank to indicate fluid reasoning ability. Of the measures described under tests of general ability, the SPM is the least influenced by prior experience and cultural performance issues identified previously in this chapter (Raven's SPM, n.d.). Table 5.4 provides a comparison of the three measures described under tests of general ability and corresponding CHC model cognitive domains.

TABLE 5.4 Comparison of Cognitive Domains Assessed by the Wechsler Adult Intelligence Scale, Fourth Edition (WAIS-IV), the Stanford-Binet Intelligence Scales, Fifth Edition (SB-V), and Raven's Standard Progressive Matrices (SPM)

COGNITIVE DOMAIN	WAIS-IV	SB-V	SPM
g	✓	✓	
Gc	✓	✓	
Gf	✓	✓	✓
Gq		✓	
Grw			
Gsm	✓	✓	
Glr			
Gv	✓	✓	
Ga			
Gs	✓		

Tests of Specific Abilities

In contrast to tests of general disabilities, tests of specific or developed abilities are those measures focused on the assessment of skills and abilities as they relate to aptitudes associated with select occupations or success in certain training programs. Aptitude testing has routinely been used in career counseling to identify abilities in specific areas toward developing vocational rehabilitation and career development plans (Power, 2000).

According to Aiken (2002), measures of aptitude tests have a significant overlap with measures of achievement to such an extent that there is little difference between the two types of tests. As such, the measurement of aptitudes and the evaluation of performance on aptitude test must consider past relevant experiences that may have served to prepare someone for the tasks on the test. In general, *aptitudes* refer to the capacity to learn in a specific cognitive domain or to demonstrate a certain skill. In considering the over 13,000 types of employment identified by the U.S. Department of Labor (USDOL, 1991), job analysts identified 11 vocationally relevant aptitudes. These aptitudes represent the skills and abilities in specific domains that are vocationally relevant. Table 5.5 provides an overview of the aptitudes and their relevant descriptions from the USDOL O*Net website (www.onetcenter.org; USDOL, Employment and Training Administration, 2018).

It is important to note that although there is conceptual overlap between the cognitive domains of intelligence and the aptitudes identified by the U.S. government, there are distinct differences in the methodologies of these two sets of instruments and the theoretical models guiding these two areas of evaluation are substantially different. Nonetheless, it is far too common an event when performance on an aptitude measure is misinterpreted as a measure of overall intellectual ability or cognitive ability in select indices.

TABLE 5.5 Overview of the U.S. Department of Labor's Vocationally Relevant Aptitudes

APTITUDE CODE	APTITUDE LABEL	APTITUDE DESCRIPTION
G	General	Understanding instruction, facts, and underlying reasoning. Being able to reason and make judgments. Closely related to school achievement.
V	Verbal	Understanding meanings of words and ideas. Using them to present information or ideas clearly.
N	Numerical	Doing arithmetic operations quickly and correctly.
S	Spatial	Looking at flat drawings or pictures of objects. Forming mental images of them in three dimensions—height, width, and depth.
P	Form perception	Observing detail in objects or drawings. Noticing differences in shapes or shading.
Q	Clerical perception	Observing details and recognizing errors in numbers, spelling and punctuation in written materials, charts, and tables. Avoiding errors when copying materials.
K	Motor coordination	Moving the eyes and hands or fingers together to perform a task rapidly and correctly.
F	Finger dexterity	Moving the fingers to work with small objects rapidly and correctly.
M	Manual dexterity	Moving the hands with ease and skill. Working with the hands in placing and turning motions.
E	Eye-hand-foot coordination	Moving the hands and feet together in response to visual signals or observations.
C	Color discrimination	Seeing likenesses or differences in colors or shades. Identifying or matching certain colors. Selecting colors that go well together.

SOURCE: U.S. Department of Labor, Employment and Training Administration. (2018). *O*Net ability profiler administration manual*. Retrieved from https://www.onetcenter.org/AP.html#administration

Another important consideration of aptitude tests is the differentiation, or lack thereof, between aptitudes and achievement as well as the tests of those constructs. While aptitude tests, in concept, are designed to measure capacity in a specific area, achievement tests are intended to evaluate what persons have learned from through experiences, such as formal education, employment, and leisure activities (Parker, 2008). Consider a measure of verbal aptitude and the differentiation between this measure and that of a measure of achievement in reading. Measures of verbal achievement often use items focused on reading, grammar, and spelling. Likewise, measures of verbal aptitude often rely on making use of an attained level of verbal information, such as vocabulary. Differentiating between the benefits of past experience and capacity is problematic and can give the false impression of limited capacity as the aptitude measure is being affected by limited experience (Anastasi, 1988; Parker, 2008). In considering the content and construct overlap between aptitude and achievement, evaluators should consider the relational representation provided in Figure 5.1. That is, aptitudes are a measure to evaluate performance along a continuum that is dependent on experience and cultural representativeness, with tests of general abilities (e.g., intelligence) and tests of achievement (e.g., reading, math, spelling) representing polar ends of the continuum owing to their respective constructs and the clearly identified impact of culture and experience on those measures.

O*NET Ability Profiler

The O*NET Ability Profiler (O*Net AP) was developed by the USDOL as a replacement to the General Aptitude Test Battery (GATB; USDOL, Employment and Training Administration, 2018). The GATB, first published in 1947, was widely used as a measure of aptitudes in identifying candidates for hire. Although it demonstrated validity in predicting job performance (Kirnan & Geisinger, 1990), the GATB was also associated with differential impact-related to scores and poor predictive utility for African-American applicants (Sackett & Wilk, 1994). To address the concerns of disparate impact and improve other aspects of the GATB, the USDOL revised and replaced the GATB with the O*Net AP. In response to federal requirements under the Workforce Investment Act, the USDOL sought to increase the reliability and validity of the GATB while retaining the multiple aptitude evaluation system in support of vocational assessment and placement (USDOL, Employment and Training Administration, 2018). To this end, relative to the GATB, the O*Net AP has fewer subtests and few items on those subtests to decrease concerns regarding response burden and overall test fatigue. In addition, to broaden the applicability of the O*Net AP to a more diverse population, the administration instructions and testing materials were revised to better communicate test-taking strategies for individual subtests and to enhance the visual presentation of test items. Another enhancement on the O*Net AP is the ability for evaluators to administer the measure without including the apparatus tests to evaluate motor coordination, manual dexterity, or finger dexterity. The flexibility in administration allows evaluators more control than available with the GATB in focusing evaluation to those areas pertinent to the vocational assessment. An added benefit is the efficiency in administration. It is feasible to evaluate up to 10 people in a group setting with the paper-and-pencil sections of the test, as compared to the apparatus tests that set a limit of five people for administration with a single evaluator (USDOL, Employment and Training Administration, 2018). Beyond the revisions specific to the administration of the O*Net AP, the USDOL also developed a scoring program, the O*NET Ability Profiler Score Report, that can be cross-walked to Standard Occupation Classification codes of jobs that have equivalent aptitude profiles.

Of the 11 aptitudes identified by the USDOL, the full version of the O*Net AP provides aptitude scores in nine areas: Verbal Ability, Arithmetic Reasoning, Computation, Spatial Ability, Form Perception, Clerical Perception, Motor Coordination, Manual Dexterity, and Finger Dexterity (USDOL, Employment and Training Administration, 2018). The test requires a sixth-grade reading level and is intended for working age persons (ages 16–65 years). See Table 5.6 for a list of the aptitudes and their corresponding O*Net AP measures.

The time required to administer the O*Net AP will vary depending on whether the complete measure is used or only the paper-and-pencil sections are administered. The complete test requires approximately 2.5 hours to administer.

TABLE 5.6 Aptitude Score Areas and Corresponding O*NET Ability Profiler (AP) Measures

APTITUDE	O*NET AP MEASURE
Verbal ability	Vocabulary
Arithmetic reasoning	Arithmetic reasoning
Computation	Computation
Spatial ability	Three-dimensional space
Form perception	Object matching
Clerical perception	Name comparison
Motor coordination[a]	Mark making
Manual dexterity[a]	Place and turn
Finger dexterity[a]	Assemble and disassemble

[a] Subtest requires the O*Net AP apparatus kits to administer.

SOURCE: U.S. Department of Labor, Employment and Training Administration (2018). *O*Net Ability Profiler administration manual*. Retrieved from https://www.onetcenter.org/AP.html#administration

Differential Aptitude Test for Personnel and Career Assessment

The Differential Aptitude Test (DAT; n.d.) is published by Pearson and, to purchase, requires persons to be approved through a select Talent Assessment process. The DAT includes tests that assess six aptitudes: Verbal Reasoning, Numerical Reasoning, Abstract Reasoning, Mechanical Reasoning, Space Relations, and Language Usage. The information about relative strengths and weaknesses in these six areas assesses job seekers and young adults concerning their abilities associated with capacity to succeed in different educational programs and careers. The six tests included in the DAT are intended to be relevant to certain types of training programs and occupations (DAT, n.d.).

Verbal Reasoning

The Verbal Reasoning test measures the ability to see relationships among words, to understand ideas expressed in words, and to think and reason with words. The test consists of analogies, each of which has two words missing—the first word in the first relationship and the second word in the second relationship. The Verbal Reasoning test may be useful in helping to predict capacity in a broad range of occupations as it is associated with the general verbal ability required for many areas of work.

Numerical Reasoning

The Numerical Reasoning test measures the ability to perform mathematical reasoning tasks and make use of numerical information. Numerical reasoning is associated with capacity in many occupations, including accounting, laboratory sciences, carpentry, and other construction trades.

Abstract Reasoning

The Abstract Reasoning test is a nonverbal measure intended to assess how well a person can reason using geometric patterns and figures. The test requires the subject to infer the rule(s) operating and to predict the figure that would be the next in a series based on those rules. The capacity for abstract reasoning is associated with aptitude in such occupations as computer programming, science, and architecture.

Mechanical Reasoning

The Mechanical Reasoning test measures the ability to understand basic mechanical principles of motion, machinery, and tools. Items represent simple principles that involve reasoning rather than special knowledge. The capacity for mechanical reasoning is associated with aptitude for such professions as engineering, mechanics, and construction trades.

Space Relations

The Space Relations test measures the ability to visualize a three-dimensional object from a two-dimensional image as well as the capacity to visualize objects if rotated in space. The capacity for spatial relations is associated with aptitudes for such occupations as art, medicine, and engineering.

Language Usage

The Language Usage test measures the ability to identify errors in punctuation, capitalization, and grammar. The test items involve reviewing sentences and identifying if a section of the sentence has an error or it is correct as written. The capacity for language usage is generally required for success in postsecondary education and for careers in journalism, writing, and law.

Summary

Tests of ability, either general or specific, can have a profound effect on many lives. Because these tests are used to determine educational services, vocational rehabilitation plans, and eligibility for a range of other life activities, evaluators should take great care in interpretation of findings. When interpreting assessments of ability, those determinations cannot be done without consideration of the context of the evaluation, the referral questions, and ultimately, the limitations of the validity of these assessments regarding the impact of the environment and compensatory strategies that subjects may utilize to overcome "tested" limitations in real-world environments. To that end, findings of tests of abilities should be interpreted using available contextual information derived from interviews with subjects and persons familiar with their abilities, assessment information focused on other areas of functioning and behavior, and most important, ecological evaluation of those abilities in the actual school or work environments. The purpose of expanding the focus of assessment is to incorporate the larger context of daily living and the environments where subjects will ultimately be tasked to demonstrate their abilities.

References

Aiken, L. R. (2002). *Psychological testing and assessment* (11th ed.). Boston, MA: Allyn & Bacon.
American Counseling Association. (2014). *ACA code of ethics.* Alexandria, VA: Author.
American Educational Research Association, American Psychological Association, & National Council on Measurement in Education. (2014). *Standards for educational and psychological testing.* Washington, DC: American Educational Research Association.

Anastasi, A. (1988). *Psychological testing* (6th ed.). New York, NY: Macmillan.

Anastasi, A., & Urbina, S. (1997). *Psychological testing* (7th ed.). Upper Saddle River, NJ: Prentice Hall.

Commission on Rehabilitation Counselor Certification. (2017). *Code of professional ethics for rehabilitation counselors.* Schaumburg, IL: Author.

Dana, R. H. (2008). Multicultural issues in assessment. In B. Bolton & R. Parker (Eds.), *Handbook of measurement and evaluation in rehabilitation* (4th ed., pp. 569–594). Austin, TX: Pro-Ed.

Delpit, L. (1995). *Other people's children: Cultural conflict in the classroom.* New York, NY: New Press.

Differential Aptitude Test for Personnel and Career Assessment. (n.d.). Hoboken, NJ: Pearson. Retrieved from https://www.pearsonclinical.com/talent/products/100000364/differential-aptitude-tests-for-personnel-and-career-assessment-dat-dat.html

Duckworth, A. L., & Seligman, M. E. P. (2005). Self-discipline outdoes IQ in predicting academic performance of adolescents. *Psychological Science, 16,* 939–944. doi:10.1111/j.1467-9280.2005.01641.x

Erickson, F. (2004). Culture in society and in educational practices. In J. A. Banks & C. A. M. Banks (Eds.), *Multicultural education: Issues and perspectives* (5th ed., pp. 31–55). Hoboken, NJ: John Wiley & Sons.

Groth-Marnat, G. (1990). *Handbook of psychological assessment* (2nd ed.). New York, NY: John Wiley & Sons.

Helms, J. E. (1997). The triple quandary of race, culture, and social class in standardized cognitive ability testing. In D. Flanagan, J. Genshaft, & P. Harrsion (Eds.), *Contemporary intellectual assessment: Theories, tests, and issues* (pp. 517–532). New York, NY: Guilford Press.

Horn, J. L., & Noll, J. (1997). Human cognitive capabilities: Gf-Gc theory. In D. Flanagan, J. Genshaft, & P. Harrsion (Eds.), *Contemporary intellectual assessment: Theories, tests, and issues* (pp. 53–91). New York, NY: Guilford Press.

Kaufman, A. S. (1990). *Assessing adolescent and adult intelligence.* Boston, MA: Allyn & Bacon.

Kirnan, J. P., & Geisinger, K. F. (1990). General aptitude test battery. In J. Hogan & R. Hogan (Eds.), *Business and industry testing: Current practices and test reviews.* Austin, TX: Pro-Ed.

Leong, F. T., & Park, Y. S. (2016). Introduction. In F. Leong & Y. Park (Eds.), *Testing and assessment with persons and communities of color* (pp. 1–2). Washington, DC: American Psychological Association.

Lichtenberger, E. O., & Kaufman, A. S. (2009). *Essentials of WAIS-IV assessment.* Hoboken, NJ: Wiley & Sons.

Lichtenberger, E. O., Kaufman, J. C., & Kaufman, A. S. (2008). Intelligence testing. In B. Bolton & R. Parker (Eds.), *Handbook of measurement and evaluation in rehabilitation* (4th ed., pp. 91–120). Austin, TX: Pro-Ed.

McGrew, K. S. (1997). Analysis of the major intelligence batteries according to a proposed comprehensive Gf-Gc framework. In D. Flanagan, J. Genshaft, & P. Harrsion (Eds.), *Contemporary intellectual assessment: Theories, tests, and issues* (pp. 151–180). New York, NY: Guilford Press.

Parker, R. (2008). Aptitude testing. In B. Bolton & R. Parker (Eds.), *Handbook of measurement and evaluation in rehabilitation* (4th ed., pp. 121–150). Austin, TX: Pro-Ed.

Power, P. W. (2000). *A guide to vocational assessment* (3rd ed.). Austin, TX: Pro-Ed.

Qualifications. (n.d.). Retrieved from https://www.pearsonclinical.com/psychology/qualifications.html

Raven's Standard Progressive Matrices (SPM) and Raven's Standard Progressive Matrices Plus (SPM Plus). (n.d.). Hoboken, NJ: Pearson. Retrieved from https://www.pearsonclinical.com/psychology/products/100000504/ravens-standard-progressive-matrices.html

Roid, G. (2018). *(SB-5) Stanford-Binet Intelligence Scales, Fifth Edition.* Retrieved from https://www.wpspublish.com/store/p/2951/sb-5-stanford-binet-intelligence-scales-fifth-edition

Roid, G. H., & Barram, R. A. (2004). *Essentials of Stanford-Binet Intelligence Scales (SB5) assessment.* Hoboken, NJ: Wiley & Sons.

Sackett, P. R., & Wilk, S. L. (1994). Within-group norming and other forms of score adjustment in pre-employment testing. *American Psychologist, 49,* 929–954. doi:10.1037//0003-066x.49.11.929

Schneider, W. J., & McGrew, K. S. (2018). The Cattell–Horn–Carroll theory of cognitive abilities. In D. P. Flanagan & E. M. McDonough (Eds.), *Contemporary intellectual assessment: Theories, tests, and issues* (pp. 73–163). New York, NY: Guilford Press.

Sue, D. W., Arredondo, P., & McDavis, R. J. (1992). Multicultural counseling competencies and standards: A call to the profession. *Journal of Counseling and Development, 70,* 477–483. doi:10.1002/j.1556-6676.1992.tb01642.x

Thorndike, R. M. (1997). The early history of intelligence testing. In D. Flanagan, J. Genshaft, & P. Harrsion (Eds.), *Contemporary intellectual assessment: Theories, tests, and issues* (pp. 3–16). New York, NY: Guilford Press.

U.S. Department of Labor. (1991). *Dictionary of occupational titles*. Retrieved from https://www.oalj.dol.gov/LIBDOT.HTM

U.S. Department of Labor, Employment and Training Administration. (2018). *O*Net Ability Profiler administration manual*. Retrieved from https://www.onetcenter.org/AP.html#administration

Washington, K., Malone, C., Briggs, C., & Reed, G. (2016). Testing and African-Americans. In F. Leong & Y. Park (Eds.), *Testing and assessment with persons and communities of color* (pp. 3–11). Washington, DC: American Psychological Association.

Wechsler, D. (1939). *The measurement of adult intelligence*. Baltimore, MD: Williams & Wilkins.

Wechsler, D. (1944). *The measurement of adult intelligence* (3rd ed.). Baltimore, MD: Williams & Wilkins.

Wechsler Adult Intelligence Scale, Fourth Edition (WAIS-IV). (2008). Upper Saddle River, NJ: Pearson. Retrieved from https://www.pearsonclinical.com/psychology/products/100000392/wechsler-adult-intelligence-scalefourth-edition-wais-iv.html?origsearchtext=wais%20iv

Western Psychological Services. (2018). *Qualification guidelines*. Retrieved from https://www.wpspublish.com/store/Qualification_Guidelines%20V3.pdf

White, J., & Weiner, J. S. (2004). Influence of least restrictive environment and community based training on integrated employment outcomes for transitioning students with severe disabilities. *Journal of Vocational Rehabilitation, 21,* 149–156. Retrieved from https://content.iospress.com/articles/journal-of-vocational-rehabilitation/jvr00263

PERSONALITY ASSESSMENT IN CLINICAL REHABILITATION AND MENTAL HEALTH SETTINGS

DEIRDRE O'SULLIVAN | BETH H. GILFILLAN | JESSICA S. HENRY

LEARNING OBJECTIVES

After reviewing this chapter, the reader should be able to:

- Understand the construct of personality presented from a synthesis of several theoretical perspectives.

- Recognize how personality traits are assessed, including identification of major objective and projective assessments.

- Understand how personality relates to life domains, including health, relationships, and work.

- Understand how clinical and nonclinical personality expression fits into the International Classification of Functioning, Disability and Health (ICF) model of client conceptualization.

- Recommend assessments related to personality based on their purpose, psychometric properties, and other attributes relevant to clinical rehabilitation and mental health interventions.

Introduction

More than any other commonly assessed attribute, personality is understood as the essence of who we are. For this reason, counselors must be sensitive to how clients interpret the words we use to describe personality traits. Personality traits, although descriptive of many personal attributes, are not synonymous with identity. Rather, personality traits are expressions of our tendencies. There are many other aspects of the self that are not reflected in our personality traits, such as our values, our intelligence, and our achievements. Our identity is how we define ourselves and may have parts that are subconsciously unknown to us; our personality is how that identity is expressed in the external world and can be observed. If we understand personality from this perspective, we can see that personality is malleable and can be assessed in terms of our tendencies for expression. As counselors, we know that tendencies can change, and with appropriate intervention and support, lasting change is possible. Although significant changes in personality are not likely or expected, small modifications in expression can lead to improvements in a range of life outcomes, including work, health maintenance, and relationships. Personality is perceived by observers as mostly congruent with the subject's self-perception, although significant incongruity between observed and self-perceived traits is possible. These incongruences can lead to a range of life problems, including difficulty in maintaining and sustaining work and conflicts in relationships with others and with the self. By assessing for personality traits, clinical rehabilitation and mental health counselors can identify incongruences, which may be contributing to negative life outcomes. Both clinical and nonclinical personality assessment will inform holistic client conceptualization using the International Classification of Functioning, Disability and Health (ICF; World Health Organization [WHO], 2001) model.

Theoretical Foundations of Personality Development

Personality develops across the life span and emerges as a result of how our genes and our environment interact. Any counseling theories textbook will provide an overview of the major theoretical explanations for the development, structure, functioning, and disorder of personality. Although not all theories emphasize in equal measure the importance of early childhood experiences on personality, all do acknowledge that early childhood events are influential and that consideration of all human developmental stages is necessary (Neukrug, 2011; Sharf, 2000). We must consider the entire life span and how each developmental stage presents opportunities for people to express personality traits, receive feedback for the expression, and subsequently reinforce that expression or adjust accordingly. Facets of a personality can be observed very early in the life span as babies express their inherited temperamental traits, receive feedback from caretakers and other consistent providers in their environment, and continue to express similarly or adjust, dependent on the feedback and reaction received. Early-life exchanges with parents and siblings illustrate the dynamic processes known as personality–relationship transactions, which explain parallels of thoughts and behavior between people (Neyer, Mund, Zimmerman, & Wrzus, 2014). Even at very young ages, children observe how others receive feedback, which also influences the expression-feedback-response cycle. Figure 6.1, in showing the expression-feedback process, roughly depicts the bioenvironmental process of personality–relationship transaction, in which traits are expressed to outsiders, and the response and feedback contribute to either reinforcement of the expressed trait or adjusted expression. The dotted lines indicate the adjustment process of personality trait expression based on environmental feedback, whereas the solid line represents the reinforcement of expressed traits.

According to behavioral genetic studies in humans, both genetic and environmental factors influence personality traits in men and women about equally (Bouchard & Loehlin, 2001; Caspi & Shiner, 2005; Emde & Hewitt, 2001). Research on personality, genes, and the environment reveals that environmental experiences tend to account for differences among siblings who grow up in the same family-of-origin household and share similar temperaments (Caspi & Shiner, 2005). The environment is a significant moderator of inherent personality trait expression. From this,

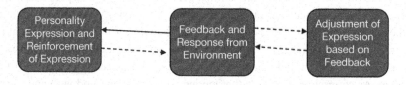

FIGURE 6.1 Bioenvironmental process of personality–relationship transaction.

we can infer that general temperamental factors are common among families mainly because of genetic contributions, but environmental influences have a large impact on the development and expression of the nuanced differences observed in families. As our personality traits propel us toward a certain environmental stimulus, we are rewarded by an experience of person–environment fit and thus, perceived positively, reinforcing this tendency. Most will seek out this kind of reward over and over so that it becomes increasingly difficult to disentangle the influence of nature and nurture. For most of us, we cannot easily trace the origins of trait reinforcement over time. There are exceptions, of course, most notably people who survive trauma. Chaotic and traumatic environments can alter one's biology, including how facets of our personality are expressed as they relate to anxiety, depression, emotion regulation, anger, and trust (Evans & Wachs, 2010; Ford & Courtois, 2014). Two psychosocial theories, and one established model, are outlined in more detail, including specific assessments that align with each theory or model.

Attachment Theory

Attachment theory (Ainsworth, 1989; Bowlby, 1988) has contributed tremendously to our understanding of how early caregiver–child bonding contributes to our experience of the world and subsequent expression of those experiences in the form of coping strategies, self-identity, ease of entering and navigating relationships, and development of personality traits. In sum, attachment theory explains the evolutionary origins of children's attachment to caregivers (Cassidy & Shaver, 1999). In order to survive, children communicate hunger, safety, and comfort needs to caregivers. Children who remained "attached" to their caregivers (usually the mother) had much higher survival rates compared to those who did not remain attached (Cassidy & Shaver, 1999). The caregivers respond (i.e., feedback) in ways that either promote optimal attachment or not. Based on responses from caregivers, the child will either be reinforced to continue the typical expressions or make adjustments. The nature of the bonding at young ages is indicative of later personality development, including emotional stability, social interactions, and exploration tendencies, all of which can be observed as personality traits (Ainsworth & Bowlby, 1991). The intense emotional bonding that occurs in infancy between child and caretaker predicts long-term psychological adjustment with impressive robustness. The child–caretaker attachment process will result in lasting security if this bonding occurs without disruption and in lovingly secure ways. Alternatively, variations of insecure attachment result when the child must balance the evolutionary drive to maintain closeness with the caretaker, while psychologically protecting himself or herself from the disrupted bond. Scenarios of disrupted bonding include repeated threat of disruption, separation from caretaker, either physical or psychological, or neglectful attention. A child who grows up under this type of attachment system is at risk for developing avoidant or ambivalent attachment tendencies in adulthood, which can lead to further disruptions in relationships, reinforcing this maladjusted component of the personality (Cassidy & Shaver, 1999).

Insecure and negative attachment experiences in early childhood, middle childhood, or emerging adolescence can contribute to negative adult personality development. Disrupted or insufficient attachment can manifest in a range of personality expression from the pervasively disordered personality on the extreme end to contained and specific facet expressions of anxiety, anger, vulnerability, trust, straightforwardness, openness, and sociability, among others, all of which will be expressed differently in each person depending on the unique bonding experiences and other environmental factors present, in conjunction with inherent personality traits.

The *Trauma and Attachment Belief Scale* (TABS; Pearlman, 2003) is one assessment recommended when insecure attachment and suspected trauma are present. The TABS is an 84-item assessment with 10 scales related to how prior trauma impacted facets of personality related to trust, self-concept, safety, control, and intimacy. This scale uses T-scores, has validity checks to screen for false information, and has a range of clinical uses. Internal and test–retest reliability estimates are adequate to good (.75–.96), with evidence of construct and criterion validity. For more information about this scale, see Table 6.1.

TABLE 6.1 Summary of Personality Assessments

INSTRUMENT	PURPOSE	POPULATION	STRENGTHS	WEAKNESSES
House-Tree-Person (HTP)	Projective assessment test	Age 3+ years	Can be used with a wide range of ages; useful for children and people who are nonverbal. No instrument is administered. Client is asked to draw a house, a tree, and a person.	More research is needed to establish validity and reliability; additional training required for interpretation.
Measures of Psychosocial Development	Assesses the degree to which people resolve developmental stages	Age 16+ years	Covers each stage in the life span; has strong psychometric properties.	Duration to self-administer is approximately 30 minutes, risking fatigue.
Myers-Briggs Type Indicator (MBTI)	Determines personality type using Jungian categories	Age 14+ years (7th-grade reading level)	Most widely used for nonclinical samples; counselors with a master's degree can administer; relatively quick to administer.	Categorical rather than dimensional. People are divided into 16 types—can be too general. Reliability is strong, but validity is weaker.
Millon Index of Personality Styles–Revised (MIPS-R)	Assesses personality styles for people experiencing difficulties in relationships, also for assessing disordered personality	Age 18+ years (8th-grade reading level)	Also has an adolescent version (MAPI); counselors with a master's degree can administer MIPS.	MAPI requires advanced and specific training to administer and interpret. Measures clinical personality; not suitable for nonclinical samples.
Minnesota Multiphasic Personality Inventory (MMPI-2)	Used to assess psychological disorders	Age 18+ years (5th-grade reading level)	Also has an adolescent version (MMPI-A) and short version (MMPI-2-RF).	MMPI requires advanced training to administer; takes a lot of time to administer and score.

(continued)

TABLE 6.1 Summary of Personality Assessments (*continued*)

INSTRUMENT	PURPOSE	POPULATION	STRENGTHS	WEAKNESSES
NEO-FFM	Nonclinical personality assessment; objective	Late adolescent to adult	Strong validity and reliability; normed by gender using T-scores; validated across diverse samples; one of the most widely used; short and long versions available; dimensional rather than categorical; "Big Five" traits correlate to life domains.	The factors did not emerge from theory, but rather from empirical studies. The "Big Five" may not be comprehensive for personality conceptualization.
Rorschach Inkblot Test	Projective assessment test	Age 5+ years	Can identify latent defense mechanisms when used correctly.	Requires advanced training to administer; takes a long time to administer and score.
Sixteen Personality Factor, Fifth Edition (16PF)	Assesses normal personality	Age 16+ years (5th-grade reading level); norm group ranges in age from 16 to 82 years	Counselors with a master's degree can administer 16PF; also has high school and children's versions.	Assessment is fairly long, contributing to test fatigue.
Washington University Sentence Completion Test (WUSCT)	Projective assessment test; measures ego development and self-concept	Age 18+ years (6th-grade reading level)	Child and adolescent version (SCT-Y) available.	Reliability estimates range from inadequate (.67) to adequate (.80). Usefulness is limited.

FFM, Five-Factor Model of Personality; MAPI, Millon Adolescent Personality Inventory; SCT-Y, Sentence Completion Test for Children and Youth.

Erik Erikson's Developmental Theory

Using Erik Erikson's psychosocial framework for identity development, we can trace the common life milestones that shape our identity and thus our external personality trait expression. According to Erikson, most people develop along the life course during eight distinct stages that present crises or conflicts (Erikson, 1968). How a person resolves a given crisis will contribute to the progression to the next stage and overall personality development. If a person is able to resolve the major conflict during a developmental stage, he or she is thought to carry that resolution throughout the life span as it is folded into the other stage resolutions (Erikson, 1963, 1968). Erikson used the term "crisis" or "conflict" because in his view, each stage presents the person with life circumstances that have not yet been navigated, which creates a sense of vulnerability. Counselors can explore how each stage was navigated and resolved and provide supports for optimal resolution for current developmental stage. Findings specific to developmental stages and personality changes point to the importance of transitional stages (from adolescence through adulthood) due to the many new and diverse roles (partner, employee, parent, and caretaker) that present during those stages. Personality continues to change throughout adulthood, but only modestly after around age 50 (Caspi & Shiner, 2005).

Erikson's theory explains that resolution of prior stages influences the resolution of future stages, so that more negative resolution will likely lead to negative future resolution. Although this sounds bleak, Erikson was optimistic in his view and believed that negative stage resolution could be revisited through therapeutic support at any time in the life span with the intention of reaching a more positive resolution. Each stage of Erikson's model is outlined briefly in the following paragraphs (Erikson, 1959; O'Sullivan, 2014), with examples of how the environment contributes to the expression-feedback-reinforcement/adjustment process. Keep in mind that most people do not resolve stages in an "absolute" sense, meaning that people tend to experience each stage with a mixture of positive and negative encounters. The sum of these experiences as either mostly negative or mostly positive is how we convey the resolution into our self-concept and future resolutions. Attachment theory has particular salience in the earliest stages, with less relevance in late adolescence and adulthood.

The *Measures of Psychosocial Development* (MPD; Hawley, 1988) scale is recommended to assess for personality development based on Erikson's 8-item stage model and is appropriate to use with adolescents and adults. The inventory contains 112 items using a Likert-type scale to indicate the degree of resolution for each stage. Adequate to strong internal and test–retest reliability scores have been observed, and strong convergent validity is evidenced by high or low resolutions, with positive scale resolutions correlating with each other (.75–.85) and negative scales correlating with each other (.67–.89). For more information, see Table 6.1.

Trust Versus Mistrust

In this first stage (infancy to 18 months) children communicate needs first by crying and then by smiling, reaching, and gazing. The caretakers' responses to the child's attempts to communicate will facilitate a sense of safety or not. A crying infant in need of comfort or food will cry out, and consistently attending to these needs in loving ways contributes to the feeling of safety. Inconsistent or unloving attention to the child's needs contributes to the feeling of an unsafe and unpredictable world where needs are not necessarily met and attempts at communication are unwelcome or misunderstood.

Autonomy Versus Shame and Doubt

As a toddler (18 months to 3 years) a child is able to explore the world first through crawling and grasping and then through walking. A child learning to explore his or her world learns to be self-sufficient and independent when caretakers lovingly encourage supervised exploration and provide comfort when needed, and reinforcement for successful exploration. A child who is not consistently encouraged to explore safely is more likely to feel insecure and thus more inclined to rely on others for exploration needs. This child is more likely to express feelings of dependence and insecurity rather than independence.

Initiative Versus Guilt

In early childhood (ages 3 to 6) a child is walking, speaking, and constantly seeking stimulus in order to make sense of the world. Children tend to experiment with both people and objects in order to observe outcomes. Lovingly attentive caretakers encourage this type of experimentation by reinforcing the positive outcomes, tolerating negative outcomes, and supporting a child when unexpected outcomes occur. A child with caretakers such as these will likely develop a sense of enjoyment from such experiments and start to see himself or herself as having governance over outcomes as she or he tries new behaviors. This facilitates a sense of initiative. Children who are not encouraged to explore and experiment in this way are less likely to appreciate their own sense of governance in the world and are more likely to feel confused or overwhelmed by trying new behaviors.

Industry Versus Inferiority

Children in this stage (middle childhood, grade school years) are slowly learning to take on more responsibility as they attend school, are assigned homework and chores, and interact with peers on the playground and in other extracurricular activities. Children who are provided clear guidelines for what is expected of them regarding school attendance and tasks, behavior at home, and on the playground will learn the joy of accomplishment and satisfaction when completing tasks that are appropriate to their level of capacity. It is important that tasks be developmentally appropriate and that expectations are consistently communicated by parents and teachers. Children who are not provided clear guidelines for behavioral task completion at home and school are more likely to develop low confidence in their abilities. Inconsistent feedback regarding behavioral tasks completion or unreliable or meaningless feedback can also contribute to low confidence regarding their contributions.

Identity Versus Identity Confusion

During adolescence teenagers and young adults in this stage are completing their education and are exploring the roles they want to occupy as they discover how they may best contribute to the world. Caretakers, teachers, school counselors, and coaches, among others, provide feedback about how skills and talents are received. Helping young adults to accurately and realistically appraise their abilities and limitations and appreciate their strengths is important for positive resolution in this stage. Appreciation for strengths can be applied in work settings, relationship settings, and recreational settings. Teens and young adults who are not appreciated by caretakers and role models for their talents are at risk of feeling uncertain about the roles they can occupy.

Intimacy Versus Isolation

Young adults (mid-20s to 40s) in this phase of life are usually actively seeking friends and potential partners with whom they can share life goals. Casual dating with low commitment levels will continue for those who are not confident that they can provide support and love to another person as they maintain their own sense of self. Adults who feel confident that they can navigate the risks involved with commitment are more likely to resolve this stage positively.

Generativity Versus Stagnation

Adults in this stage of middle adulthood are confronted with the realities of their legacy on the world as they transition from establishing themselves in their careers and family lives, into a phase fulfilling personal goals at work and home. Adults who successfully resolve this stage are able to shift their focus away from role fulfillment obligations to personal rewards that provide satisfaction derived from mentoring and working toward lasting positive impact in work and personal settings. Adults who have low confidence in their ability to give back to a younger generation are more likely to feel as though they have failed. A sense of regret for not pursuing meaningful goals that highlighted their unique gifts may be experienced.

Integrity Versus Despair

Adults in this stage (late adulthood) feel confident that they lived their life well, have few regrets, and accept their past mistakes, past hurts, and the inevitability of death without excessive anxiety. Adults who resolve this crisis negatively are more inclined to repeatedly review their past mistakes, have difficulty accepting the past, and experience excessive fear regarding their inevitable death.

The Five-Factor Model of Personality

The Five-Factor Model of Personality (FFM) framework respects the underlying assumption that all people express degrees of traits consistent across cultures. The FFM has been employed in rigorous research and demonstrated impressive structure integrity pertaining to the five factors of *neuroticism, extroversion, openness, agreeableness,* and *conscientiousness* (McCrae & Costa, 2010). These five factors have held up across diverse demographic groups repeatedly over substantial periods of time. Each of us expresses our thoughts, feelings, and behaviors on a continuum of these five factors as we navigate multiple life domains. Although these five factors are not necessarily the only appropriate and valid personality traits appropriate to humans, they are the ones that have demonstrated impressive validity and reliability. From a long list of descriptors relevant to multiple cultures, five distinct factors emerged after a series of analyses, and these factors have been replicated numerous times and correlate with other personality frameworks and assessments (McCrae & Costa, 2010). The five factors are normed according to gender differences, but other group differences are less well established at this time.

When investigating the degree of changes at the factor and facet levels over time, patterns emerge for large samples of the population. Specifically, people tend to become more agreeable in later adulthood (ages 50–60) and only more conscientious as they develop in adulthood to middle adulthood. Neuroticism shows the greatest decrease in young adulthood, whereas dominance (a facet of extroversion) increased from adolescence to middle-age, and sociability (another extroversion facet) first increases in adolescence and young adulthood, before decreasing along certain points in adulthood and late adulthood (Roberts, Walton, Bogg, & Caspi, 2006). Facets of openness increase in adolescence and young adulthood, with a steady decline in adulthood to late adulthood (Caspi & Shiner, 2005; Fraley & Roberts, 2005). Overall, longitudinal research results reveal young adulthood as a vibrant stage of personality development, with more changes than other life stages (Roberts et al., 2006). From ages 20 to 40, life provides ample opportunities for personality shifts as people strive to adapt to their environments and important relationships and as people occupy multiple social, family, and occupational roles. The expression-feedback process continues at all stages in the life span. Again, it is important to emphasize that major changes in personality are not realistic, nor are they necessary for people to experience benefits. Small modifications in how we express our personality can enhance our relationships, our work, and our health. Counselors can identify specific facets that may be contributing to reduced life outcomes with the intention of helping clients make modifications to support counseling goals.

The *NEO-PI-R* (McCrae & Costa, 2010) measures the five factors of personality, as well as the facets within each factor. This instrument has been validated using large, culturally diverse samples, and factors are normed by gender using T-scores. The internal consistency of NEO-PI-3 ranges from .89 to .93 for five domains and .54 to .83 for each of the 30 facets. For more information, see Table 6.1.

One major criticism of this model is the weak theoretical underpinnings of the five factors. Despite multiple replication and consistency of factors across time and culture, the factors emerged empirically and were not derived from one unified theory of personality (Erford, 2007). Within each factor is a set of related traits called "facets." Personality factors explain the broad temperament expression (largely genetic), whereas facets explain the nuanced mechanisms for trait expression (moderated by environment). High and low scores on the factors are not necessarily indicative of positive or negative personality expression. Rather, the environments in which we operate influence trait expression. Some contexts are conducive to low expression of a given trait, whereas high expression of the same trait may be valued in a different setting. For instance, high extroversion is a trait valued more in Western cultures and certainly more so in certain professions that require leadership and entrepreneurship, compared to professions that do not require these traits. Each factor is briefly summarized in the following paragraphs (McCrae & Costa, 2010; O'Sullivan, 2014).

Neuroticism

Persons who express high neuroticism (N) are said to express a tendency to experience the world as a distressing place, which may include feelings of anxiety, fear, general negative affect, hostility, and self-reproach. Conversely, persons generally low in their expression of "N" are perceived as being emotionally stable, relaxed, and able to handle stressful situations with ease. When examined more closely, the neuroticism factor is made up of six facets: *anxiety, anger, depression, self-consciousness, impulsiveness,* and *vulnerability.*

Extroversion

Persons who express high extroversion (E) are likely to express sociability, positive affect, exuberance, and optimism. Conversely, those who express low "E" are reserved in their demeanor and tend to be independent, but not necessarily socially anxious or pessimistic. The six facets of extroversion are *warmth, gregariousness, assertiveness, activity, excitement seeking,* and *positive emotions.*

Openness

Persons who express high openness (O) are described as imaginative, intellectually curious, attentive to their inner feelings, and unconventional. Persons low in their expression of "O" are said to prefer conventions and traditions, less likely to seek out intellectual and artistic pursuits, and prefer the familiar to the new and novel. The facets of openness include *imaginative, aesthetic appreciation, being receptive to feelings, willingness to try new activities,* and *intellectual curiosity.*

Conscientiousness

Persons who express high conscientiousness (C) are said to be purposeful, dutiful, determined, reliable, and achievement oriented. Conversely, persons who express low conscientiousness are described as being disorganized and impulsive. These are not necessarily negative traits, as some contexts value a person who can function in environments where order is not predictable, and reacting on impulse may be needed. The facets of conscientiousness include *competence, order, dutifulness, achievement, self-discipline,* and *deliberation.*

Agreeableness

Persons who express high agreeableness (A) are described as being prosocial, altruistic, polite, sympathetic, and eager to help others, as they generally believe that others would be likely to help them. Conversely, persons who express low "A" are more inclined to be skeptical of others, self-focused, and competitive rather than cooperative. The agreeableness facets include *trust, altruism, compliance, modesty, straightforwardness,* and *tender-mindedness.*

■ Personality Assessment

The World Health Organization's ICF (WHO, 2001) is an ecological framework for holistic and comprehensive client conceptualization (for discussion of ICF model, see Chapter 2, The World Health Organization International Classification of Functioning, Disability and Health as a Framework for Rehabilitation Assessment). This model serves as a tool to informally assess for factors related to health and functioning, personal, and environment. This framework helps organize life factors that may be worsening the presenting problem or providing support that can be leveraged. For instance, personality is known to relate to health, work, and relationships in significant ways, and as such, assessment of personality traits is recommended for comprehensive assessment using the ICF framework. Clinical personality trait expression, such as disordered personalities, should be noted in Part 1 of the ICF when appropriate, because disordered personalities are believed to result from differences in brain functioning and directly impact functioning in multiple life domains (American Psychiatric Association, 2013). Normal, nonclinical personality trait expression, when included as part of ICF personal factors, can help the client understand how personality trait expression relates to broad life outcomes, such as work, health, and relationships.

Modest modifications in personality trait expression can lead to significant changes in life outcomes related to work, health, and relationships (O'Sullivan, 2014; Roberts, Kuncel, Shiner, Caspi, & Goldberg, 2007). For instance, small-to-moderate increases in conscientious behavior can lead to improved health and wellness, as well as improved work productivity and even relationship satisfaction (Holland & Roisman, 2008; Roberts, 2006; Roberts et al., 2007). Counselors can help clients develop plans to enhance conscientiousness or other personality trait expression as one way to facilitate changes in life outcomes aligned with client's goals. We caution counselors about their expectations related to changes in personality. Counselors should not, and need not, expect large shifts in personality expression in order for significant changes related to life goals to occur. Personality should be explored sensitively with clients and with an awareness that many clients are unaware of how they are perceived by others, including, at times, people closest to them.

Personality and Work

For decades, scholars have designated personality as a substantial contributor to intrinsic and extrinsic career success and job satisfaction (e.g., Judge, Higgins, Thoresen, & Barrick, 1999; Seibert & Kraimer, 2001). The Big Five factors of conscientiousness, neuroticism, extroversion, agreeableness, and openness (outlined in a previous section of this chapter) are recognized as factors that predict predispositions of behaviors and are recognized as valid across diverse cultures. When considering personality traits, studies suggest that three of the five factors—*neuroticism, extroversion,* and *conscientiousness*—are most relevant to career success (Judge et al., 1999). Specifically, indicators of personality highlight that people with higher neuroticism dislike careers that induce stress or are considered highly complex (Seibert & Kraimer, 2001). People scoring high on extroversion are characterized as more proactive in addressing stressful situations related to work through the expressed facet of *assertion*. Likewise, a person with high levels of conscientiousness thrives in a range of careers by exhibiting characteristics including dependability, self-control, and orderliness (Judge et al., 1999). In a multiphase study of junior high and high school students investigating academic effort, achievement, efficacy, and personality, the trait of conscientiousness was found to predict academic effort across a range of subjects more than other variables such as efficacy and achievement (Trautwein, Lüdtke, Roberts, Schnyder, & Niggli, 2009). Given the importance of academic results to many work and career opportunities, this is an important consideration for early intervention.

Personality and Health

Personality is a salient factor in health as well. Preventable deaths in the United States are largely due to illnesses such as diabetes, cardiac disease, lung disease, and liver failure; car accidents; overdoses; and shootings, all of which are clearly connected to behaviors including poor diet, low physical activity, smoking, drug and alcohol use, and risky and impulsive behaviors (Bogg & Roberts, 2004). People who are high on conscientiousness are significantly less likely to report these behaviors, greatly reducing their risk for certain chronic diseases and early death. Further, low agreeableness is known to amplify stress, causing a higher risk for inflammation, eventually triggering somatic responses to physical health among people with conditions such as multiple sclerosis (MS; Mohr, 2007; Robles, Glaser & Kiecolt-Glaser, 2005). Notably, the impact of personality on health outcomes can vary across health domains (i.e., physical and mental health; Strickhouser, Zell, & Krizan, 2017). People with levels of neuroticism are more likely to develop psychopathology as well as demonstrate negative responses to stress that perpetuate moodiness, overeating substance use, and anxiety disorders. Research on personality and health behaviors suggests that conscientiousness is associated with health-promoting lifestyles whereas factors such as high extroversion and openness are connected to certain harmful health behaviors such as cigarette smoking, alcohol use/binge drinking, and increased sexual partners with decreased condom use (Raynor & Levine, 2009). People with higher levels of agreeableness and extroversion are more likely to have strong social support systems, an important environmental factor to consider in client assessment.

Personality and Relationships

Traits such as agreeableness, neuroticism, and conscientiousness have all predicted relationship quality. Extroversion predicts popularity and social support, which can moderate both health and work outcomes. High neuroticism and low agreeableness predict relationship dissatisfaction, abuse, conflict, and eventual termination (Ozer & Benet-Martinez, 2006). When looking at self and partner reports of personality in dating, engaged, and married couples, neuroticism was the best predictor of relationship satisfaction for all three groups. As such, results on personality impacts of romantic relationship characteristics determined that through meditation, persons with higher conscientiousness had better quality relationships as well as positively impacted social control (Cotter & Kerschner, 2018). Relationship quality and satisfaction have proved to be higher if persons have lower levels of negative traits such as neuroticism. High agreeableness protects relationship status, whereas people with lower scores in agreeableness are likely to demonstrate selfishness and little concern for others, clear barriers to relationship maintenance (Hussain, Abbas, Shahzad, & Bukhari, 2012).

▦ Commonly Used Personality Assessments

There are dozens of available assessments for clinicians to use as tools to better understand their clients' tendencies, preferences, and expressions. Results from personality assessments can enhance clients' self-awareness as well as provide information about overall health and functioning in life domains as explained earlier. It is important for counselors to stress that personality expression varies considerably and that the degree to which specific traits are expressed can depend on environmental factors. Again, we remind counselors to be sensitive to how our clients might interpret our words as we describe personality and work to educate clients about the construct of personality. The following section briefly describes other personality assessments that may be useful in clinical practice. Table 6.1 summarizes the psychometric properties, strengths, and weaknesses of each.

House-Tree-Person

The House-Tree-Person (HTP) was developed by John Buck in 1948. It is a projective test, meaning that it is somewhat unstructured and responses are more open-ended, leaving subjective interpretation to the clinician. For this assessment, the client is given blank sheets of paper and is told to draw a house, a tree, and a person, with each figure representing facets of personality, ego, and defense mechanisms. For instance, a house with few or no windows may indicate that at person is not "open" to others. A person who is floating can be interpreted as "not grounded." Next, the client is asked to explain the drawings, and the counselor interprets the drawings and responses. Although manuals exist to help with interpretation, one major criticism of the HTP is that there is not a large base of research to analyze the validity and reliability.

Myers-Briggs Type Indicator

The Myers-Briggs Type Indicator (MBTI) was based on Jung's theory and developed by Katharine Briggs and Isabel Myers and originally published in 1962. The assessment includes dichotomies in four areas: attitudes (extroversion and introversion), lifestyle preferences (judging and perceiving), and two sets of functions (sensing and intuition as well as thinking and feeling). There are two forms of the MBTI; Form M has 93 items and is appropriate for ages 14 and older, whereas Form Q has 144 items and is appropriate for ages 18 and older. Clients respond to the forced-choice items and are then given 1 of 16 possible types based on their responses. Form Q has internal consistency reliability ranging from .56 to .82; Form M has internal consistency reliability above .90. The test–retest reliability ranges from .44 to .88. Master's level counselors can administer the MBTI.

Millon Index of Personality Styles–Revised

The Millon Index of Personality Styles (MIPS) was developed by Theodore Millon in 1994. It was revised in 2003. The MIPS is used to measure three dimensions of personality: motivating styles, thinking styles, and behaving styles. It includes 180 true/false items, and scores range from 0 to 100. A score of 50 is prevalent in the general population. Counselors use the MIPS with people experiencing difficulties in relationships and to assess for disordered personality. It has an internal consistency reliability of .82 for adults and .77 for students. There is also an adolescent version available (Millon Adolescent Personality Inventory, or MAPI)—appropriate for ages 13 to 18, for which at least a sixth-grade reading level is needed. Although a master's level counselor can administer the MIPS, the MAPI requires advanced training.

Minnesota Multiphasic Personality Inventory 2

The Minnesota Multiphasic Personality Inventory (MMPI) was developed by Starke Hathaway and J.C. McKinley in 1942. The latest update (MMPI-2) was in 2009. The MMPI-2 is used to assess psychological disorders. The latest version has 567 true/false items, including validity, clinical, and content scales. Raw scores are converted to T-scores, and scores of 65 and above are considered clinically significant. It has internal consistency reliability from .34 to .85 for males and .37 to .87 for females. The test–retest reliability scores are .54 to .92 for females and .63 to .93 for males. There is an adolescent version available (MMPI-A), which is appropriate for ages 14 to 18. There is also a shorter version available, which contains 338 items (MMPI-2-RF). All versions require advanced training to administer.

Rorschach Inkblot Test

The Rorschach was developed by Hermann Rorschach in 1921. It is the most widely used projective personality assessment. The test consists of 10 bilaterally symmetrical inkblots (5 are black and white; 2 are black, white, and red; and 3 are a variety of colors). The counselor asks the client to describe what he or she sees in each ink blot. It takes about 45 minutes, then about 2 hours to score. To score the responses, the counselor uses a manual; the most commonly used scoring manual is Exner's Comprehensive System (CS). The CS scoring is based on over 100 characteristics in three categories: content, location, and determinants. The CS is known for reliable scoring and strong test–retest reliability. Specialized training is required before a counselor can administer the test.

Sixteen Personality Factor, Fifth Edition

The Sixteen Personality Factor, Fifth Edition (16PF) was originally developed by Raymond B. Cattell and colleagues. It is an assessment of normal personality. The 16PF contains 185 items that are based on a list of adjectives, including 16 primary factors of personality: warmth, reasoning, emotional stability, dominancy, liveliness, rule-consciousness, social boldness, sensitivity, vigilance, abstractedness, privateness, apprehension, openness to change, self-reliance, perfectionism, and tension. It also explores global factors of extroversion, anxiety, tough-mindedness, independence, and self-control. The scores range from 1 to 10 for each area. Standard scores have a mean of 5.5 and a standard deviation of 2.0. Scores above 7 are considered high, whereas scores below 4 are considered low. It has internal consistency reliability from .68 to .87. The test–retest reliability scores are from .65 to .80. Master's level counselors can administer the 16PF. There are also a High School Personality Questionnaire (appropriate for ages 12–18) and a Children's Personality Questionnaire (appropriate for ages 8–12).

Washington University Sentence Completion Test

The Washington University Sentence Completion Test (WUSCT) was developed by Jane Loevinger in 1970. It is a projective test that is used to measure ego development and assess self-concept. It is semistructured; 36 sentence stems are given to the client, who is asked to complete each sentence. A manual is provided for scoring. It has internal consistency reliability from above .80. The test–retest reliability scores are from .67 to .76. There is also a child and adolescent form (Sentence Completion Test for Children and Youth [SCT-Y]) that includes 32 sentence stems and is appropriate for ages 8 to 18.

▇ Conclusion

In this chapter, the construct of personality was presented, synthesizing several theoretical perspectives, and it discussed how personality traits are assessed, including identification of major objective and projective assessments. An important feature, the chapter also discussed how personality relates to life domains including health, relationships, and work and how clinical and nonclinical personality expression fits into the ICF model of client conceptualization. The chapter concluded with the recommendation of assessments that are related to personality based on their purpose, psychometric properties, and other attributes relevant to clinical rehabilitation and mental health interventions.

▇ References

Ainsworth, M. S. (1989). Attachments beyond infancy. *American Psychologist, 44*(4), 709–716. doi:10.1037//0003-066x.44.4.709

Ainsworth, M. S., & Bowlby, J. (1991). An ethological approach to personality development. *American Psychologist, 46*(4), 333–341. doi:10.1037//0003-066x.46.4.333

American Psychiatric Association. (2013). *Diagnostic and statistical manual of mental disorders* (5th ed.). Arlington, VA: American Psychiatric Publishing.

Bogg, T. & Roberts, B. (2004) Conscientiousness and health-related behaviors: A meta-analysis of the leading behavioral contributors to mortality. *Psychological Bulletin, 130*(6), 887–919. doi:10.1037/0033-2909.130.6.887

Bouchard, T. J., & Loehlin, J. C. (2001). Genes, evolution, and personality. *Behavior Genetics, 31*(3), 243–273. doi:10.1023/a:1012294324713

Bowlby, J. (1988). *A secure base: Parent-child attachment and healthy human development*. New York, NY: Basic Books.

Caspi, A., & Shiner, R. L. (2005). Personality development. *Annual Review of Psychology, 56*, 453–484. doi:10.1146/annurev.psych.55.090902.141913

Cassidy, J., & Shaver, P. R. (Eds.). (1999). *Handbook of attachment: Theory, research, and clinical application*. New York, NY: Guilford Press.

Cotter, K. A., & Kerschner, B. J. (2018). Personality and health: Impacts of romantic relationship characteristics. *Personality and Individual Differences, 120*, 40–46. doi:10.1016/j.paid.2017.08.023

Emde, R. N., & Hewitt, J. K. (Eds.). (2001). *Infancy to early childhood: Genetic and environmental influences on development change*. New York, NY: Oxford University Press.

Erford, B. (2007). *Assessment for Counselors*. Belmont, CA: Cengage Learning.

Erikson, E. H. (1959). *Identity and the life cycle; Selected papers with a historical introduction by David Rapaport*. New York, NY: International University Press.

Erikson, E. H. (1963). *Childhood and society*. New York, NY: W.W. Norton.

Erikson, E. H (1968). *Identity: Youth and crisis*. New York, NY: W.W. Norton.

Evans, G. W., & Wachs, T. D. (Eds.). (2010). *Decade of behavior (science conference). Chaos and its influence on children's development: An ecological perspective*. Washington, DC: American Psychological Association.

Ford, J. D., & Courtois, C. A. (2014). Complex PTSD, affect dysregulation, and borderline personality disorder. *Borderline Personality Disorder and Emotion Dysregulation, 1*, 9. doi:10.1186/2051-6673-1-9

Fraley, R. C., & Roberts, B. W. (2005). Patterns of continuity: A dynamic model for conceptualizing the stability of individual differences in psychological constructs across the life course. *Psychological Review, 112*(1), 60. doi:10.1037/0033-295x.112.1.60

Hawley, G. A. (1988). *The measures of psychosocial development (MPD)*. Odessa, FL: Psychological Assessment Resources.

Holland, A. S., & Roisman, G. I. (2008). Big five personality traits and relationship quality: Self-reported, observational, and physiological evidence. *Journal of Social and Personal Relationships, 25*(5), 811–829. doi:10.1177/0265407508096697

Hussain, S., Abbas, M., Shahzad, K., & Bukhari, S. A. (2012). Personality and career choices. *African Journal of Business Management, 6*(6), 2255–2260. doi:10.5897/ajbm11.2064

Judge, T. A., Higgins, C. A., Thoresen, C. J., & Barrick, M. R. (1999). The big five personality traits, general mental ability, and career success across the life span. *Personal Psychology, 52*, 621–652. doi:10.1111/j.1744-6570.1999.tb00174.x

McCrae, R. R., & Costa, P. T. (2010). *NEO inventories for the NEO personality inventory-3 (NEO-PI-3), NEO five-factor inventory-3 (NEO-FFI-3), NEO personality inventory-revised (NEO PI-R): Professional manual*. Lutz, FL: Psychological Assessment Resources.

Mohr, D. C. (2007). Stress and multiple sclerosis. *Journal of Neurology, 254*(2), 1165–1168. doi:10.1007/s00415-007-2015-4

Neukrug, E. S. (2011). *Counseling theory and practice*. Boston, MA: Brooks/Cole.

Neyer, F. J., Mund, M., Zimmerman, J., & Wrzus, C. (2014). Personality-relationship transactions revisited. *Journal of Personality, 82*(6), 539–550. doi:10.1111/jopy.12063

O'Sullivan, D. (2014). Personality development, expression, and assessment for work adjustment considerations in rehabilitation contexts. In D. Strauser (Ed.), *Career development, employment and disability in rehabilitation: From theory to practice* (pp. 77–96). New York, NY: Springer Publishing Company.

Ozer, D. J., & Benet-Martinez, V. (2006). Personality and the prediction of consequential outcomes. *Annual Review of Psychology, 57*, 401–421. doi:10.1146/annurev.psych.57.102904.190127

Pearlman, L. A. (2003). *Trauma and Attachment Belief Scale*. Los Angeles, CA: Western Psychological Services.

Raynor, D. A., & Levine, H. (2009). Associations between the Five-Factor model of personality and health behaviors among college students. *Journal of American College Health, 58*(1), 73–82. doi:10.3200/jach.58.1.73-82

Roberts, B. W. (2006). Personality development and organizational behavior. *Research in Organizational Behavior, 27*, 1–40. doi:10.1016/s0191-3085(06)27001-1

Roberts, B. W., Kuncel, N. R., Shiner, R., Caspi, A., & Goldberg, L. R. (2007). The power of personality: The comparative validity of personality traits, socioeconomic status, and cognitive ability for predicting important life outcomes. *Perspectives on Psychological Science, 2*(4), 313–345. doi:10.1111/j.1745-6916.2007.00047.x

Roberts, B. W., Walton, K., Bogg, T., & Caspi, A. (2006). De-investment in work and non-normative personality trait change in young adulthood. *European Journal of Personality, 20*(6), 461–474. doi:10.1002/per.607

Robles, T. F., Glaser, R., & Kiecolt-Glaser, J. K. (2005). Out of balance: A new look at chronic stress, depression, and immunity. *Current Directions in Psychological Science, 14*, 111–115. doi:10.1111/j.0963-7214.2005.00345.x

Seibert, S. E., & Kraimer, M. L. (2001). The Five-Factor model of personality and career success. *Journal of Vocational Behavior, 58*, 1–21. doi:10.1006/jvbe.2000.1757

Sharf, R. S. (2000). *The theories of psychotherapy and counseling* (2nd ed.). Belmont, CA: Brooks/Cole.

Strickhouser, J. E., Zell, E., & Krizan, Z. (2017). Does personality predict health and well-being? A metasynthesis. *Health Psychology, 36*(8), 797–810. doi:10.1037/hea0000475

Trautwein, U., Lüdtke, O., Roberts, B. W., Schnyder, I., & Niggli, A. (2009). Different forces, same consequence: Conscientiousness and competence beliefs are independent predictors of academic effort and achievement. *Journal of Personality and Social Psychology, 97*(6), 1115–1128. doi:10.1037/a0017048

World Health Organization. (2001). *International Classification of Functioning, Disability and Health*. Geneva, Switzerland: Author.

ASSESSMENT OF PSYCHOPATHOLOGY

JENNIFER SÁNCHEZ | VERONICA MULLER | ERIN F. BARNES | JONIQUE R. CHILDS

LEARNING OBJECTIVES

After reviewing this chapter, the reader should be able to:

- Identify key terms related to the assessment of psychopathology.
- Summarize the models of assessment.
- Describe a conceptual framework for assessing psychopathology.
- Summarize measures that can be used to assess for psychopathology.
- Explain how data collected from tests can be used to formulate a diagnosis and case conceptualization.

▩ Introduction

Assessment of psychopathology, an important aspect in rehabilitation and mental health counseling, has a long history. The earliest formal assessments began centuries ago and were geared toward philosophical understanding and life planning (Mpofu, Oakland, Herbert, & O'Donnell, 2010). As psychological counseling gained popularity during the past century, clinicians recognized the need for practical methods of understanding their clients' problems, goals, and capabilities. One main consideration to keep in mind is that assessment and testing are not synonymous. *Testing* can be defined as a method for determining or examining the presence of some phenomenon (VandenBos, 2007). Thus, testing is one part of assessment, whereas assessment refers to a broader range of procedures.

Assessment is a process that counselors use to gather, evaluate, and integrate the information they need to form a comprehensive view about their clients and guide their decision-making regarding diagnosis, case conceptualization, treatment planning, measuring of client outcomes, and evaluating the efficacy of the counseling treatment. *Psychopathology* is the expression of mental impairment, characterized by psychological signs and symptoms. Psychological assessment is the "systematic measurement of a person's behavior" (Haynes, Richard, & Kubany, 1995, p. 238). Therefore, counselors conduct psychological assessments in order to determine the presence (or absence) of psychopathology.

Models of Assessment

Clients may be referred to treatment for various problems. As a result, different models have been established in attempts to conceptualize these problems. A *model* forms the basis for appropriate assessment and service delivery, is less than a theory, and operates at an intermediate level of conceptualization.

Functional Models

There are two main types of functional models. Their main difference is related to their definition of the term *function*, which is rooted in the field in which they arose. In the rehabilitation literature, the term *function* has been defined as "a set of skills necessary to perform roles and/or age-appropriate activities that are required for daily living in typical environments" (Gilson, DePoy, & Cramer, 2001, p. 423) or capacity. In the behavior analysis literature, however, the term *function* has been used in two ways: (a) "the purpose the behavior serves for an individual" and (b) as "a relation between two variables . . . in which one varies given the presence or absence of the other" (Hanley, Iwata, & McCord, 2003, p. 148). Therefore, we can differentiate the functional models as functional capacity (rehabilitation) and functional behavior (behavior analysis).

Functional Capacity Model

In functional capacity models, a person's level of functioning influences the definition of the disability (e.g., psychopathology). A *functional limitation* (FL) represents an "inability to meet a standard of an anatomical, physiological, psychological, or mental nature (impairment)" due to a health condition (Granger, 1984, p. 16), whereas *functional capacity* (FC) represents the "ability to perform a specific role or task which is expected of an individual within a social environment" (Indices, 1979, p. 7), or the residual physical, cognitive, or behavioral capabilities of a person in his or her task performance and environment negotiation. FC can refer to a person's ability to complete activities of daily living (ADLs) and/or instrumental activities of daily living (IADLs). ADLs are more basic activities (e.g., bathing, eating), whereas IADLs include more complex ones (e.g., budgeting, driving).

Functional Behavior Model

In functional behavior models, the behaviors and sets of behaviors are assessed and then classified or organized by the functional processes that produced and maintained them (Hayes, Wilson, Gifford, Follette, & Strosahl, 1996). By examining functional behaviors, we seek to identify the function of the behavior and/or the functional relationship between the behavior and its consequences. There are four main functions that maintain behaviors—specifically a person behaves in a certain way because it feels good to him or her (*sensory stimulation*); in order to get out of doing something she or he does not want to do (*escape or avoidance*); in order to get focused attention from a person of interest (e.g., peer) or other people who are around him or her (*attention seeking*); or in order to get a preferred item or participate in an enjoyable activity (*seeking access to tangibles*; Durand & Crimmins, 1988).

Biopsychosocial Models

The biopsychosocial model posits that clinicians simultaneously attend to the biological, psychological, and social dimensions of illness (Engel, 1977). In this model, health and illness are the product of biological characteristics (e.g., genes), psychological or behavioral factors (e.g., coping style), and social or environmental conditions (e.g., cultural influences). The World Health Organization (WHO)'s *International Classification of Functioning, Disability and Health* (ICF) model assumes that biological, environmental, and personal factors together define a person's health or disability status (Chan, Gelman, Ditchman, Kim, & Chiu, 2009; Peterson, 2005) and is thus a biopsychosocial model. The ICF comprises three major components: (a) body functions and structures, (b) activities (related to tasks and actions by an individual) and participation (involvement in a life situation), and (c) contextual personal and environmental factors (Chan et al., 2009; Smart & Smart, 2006; WHO, 2001). A main asset is that it provides a paradigm shift in which health, rather than illness, is the focus (WHO, 2001). However, biopsychosocial models are not easily applied to problems of classification and could potentially make problems even more difficult by limiting the usefulness of etiology and pathogenesis to classify syndromes (Paris, 2010).

Classification Models

Classification models divide a given set of objects (e.g., mental disorders) into subclasses based on hierarchical groupings. The most commonly used classification models are categorical and dimensional. Mental health clinicians have traditionally divided mental disorders into subclasses (or categories), which should be mutually exclusive and jointly exhaustive (Hempel, 1959); however, dimensional classification could be used to record symptom profiles and etiological contributions and include a full range of relevant types and extents (Stein, 2012).

Categorical Classification Model

Within categorical classification models, "a diagnosis is seen as a discrete entity" (Simonsen, 2010, p. 350), and a clinician is required to determine whether (or not) a client meets the diagnostic criteria for a specific disorder. Determination (i.e., diagnosis) is based on a specified number of descriptive "yes/no" criteria from a larger set from which clients are diagnosed as having a disorder (e.g., psychopathology), if appropriate. The two primary categorical classification models used in medical and behavioral healthcare are the WHO's *International Classification of Diseases,* 11th edition (*ICD-11*; WHO, 2018) and the American Psychiatric Association (APA)'s *Diagnostic and Statistical Manual of Mental Disorders,* 5th edition (*DSM-5*; APA, 2013).

Dimensional Classification Model

In dimensional classification models, the client being evaluated "may match the description of the ideal type or prototype to a greater or lesser extent" (Simonsen, 2010, p. 351), and a clinician has the flexibility to conceptualize and assess psychiatric syndromes and symptoms on a continuum (Stein, 2012). Although the *ICD* and *DSM* systems are primarily based on categorical classification models, they also incorporate severity (of a disorder, often ranging from mild to severe), which is representative of dimensional classification models. The *ICD-11* and the *DSM-5* allow a clinician more latitude to assess the severity of a condition rather than imposing a definitive threshold between disorder (i.e., psychopathology) and nondisorder (APA, 2013; WHO, 2018).

DSM-5 Conceptual Framework

A *conceptual framework* is a synthesis of the literature (i.e., research) on how to explain a phenomenon. Psychopathology (i.e., the phenomenon) is assessed based on empirical evidence in order to reach an appropriate diagnosis. *Diagnosis* has been defined as the identification of the nature and cause of a certain phenomenon; the act of identifying a disease from its signs and symptoms; and the investigation or analysis of the cause or nature of a condition, situation, or problem. The *ICD* and the *DSM* are the most common conceptual frameworks used to diagnose disorders. The *ICD-11* is the global diagnostic classification standard for diseases, disorders, injuries, and other related health conditions (WHO, 2018) and is currently used in more than 100 countries. The *DSM-5* is the diagnostic classification standard for mental disorders used by mental health professionals in the United States (APA, 2013); its main advantages are that it focuses solely on mental disorders, has better-defined diagnostic criteria, and is more user-friendly.

The *DSM* was designed to help mental health professionals working with clients who were experiencing mental distress by providing guidelines for assessment and case conceptualization. Previous editions of the *DSM* used a syndromal approach, which focused on the classification and treatment of behaviors according to their topographical characteristics (i.e., associated signs and symptoms). Changes to the *DSM-5* include revisions to definitions of diagnoses and symptoms, proposed diagnostic categories, dimensional assessment (including crosscutting), and a renewed emphasis on severity specifiers (Buckley, 2014) to assist clinicians in making a diagnosis. In the *DSM-5*, diagnostic criteria "are offered as guidelines for making diagnoses, and their use should be informed by clinical judgment" (APA, 2013, p. 21).

The *DSM-5* has three major components: diagnostic classification, diagnostic criteria sets, and descriptive text. The diagnostic classification is a list of all mental disorders, with corresponding codes (typically used for billing) for each disorder (APA, 2013). For each disorder, a set of diagnostic criteria indicates the (minimum number of) symptoms that must be present (and for how long), as well as other symptoms, disorders, and conditions that must be ruled out in order to qualify for that diagnosis. The descriptive text provides information about each disorder (e.g., associated features supporting diagnosis, prevalence, development and course, risk and prognostic factors, culture-related diagnostic issues, gender-related diagnostic issues, suicide risk, functional consequences, differential diagnosis, and comorbidity).

The *DSM-5* underwent major reorganization from previous editions. It uses a developmental and life-span framework to organize disorders beginning with those that are typically diagnosed during childhood and adolescence (e.g., neurodevelopmental disorders), followed by those that are more relevant to adulthood, and then those that appear later in life (e.g., neurocognitive disorders). Chapters (i.e., disorders) are grouped (and ordered) according to epidemiological and neurobiological relatedness (schizophrenia spectrum and other psychotic, bipolar and related, and depressive disorders), similar symptom characteristics (anxiety, obsessive-compulsive and related, trauma- and stressor-related, dissociative, and somatic symptom and related disorders), and prominent physical manifestations (feeding and eating, elimination, and sleep–wake disorders, and sexual dysfunctions; Clark, Cuthbert, Lewis-Fernández, Narrow, & Reed, 2017). A clustering framework is also used to differentiate disorders associated with "internalizing" (depressive, anxiety, and somatic) factors from those with "externalizing" (disruptive, impulsive, and addictive) behaviors. The *DSM-5* reflects current knowledge and understanding of underlying vulnerabilities and symptom characteristics of disorders, making it more a hybrid of functional, biopsychosocial, and classification models.

Using the *DSM-5* to Assess for Psychopathology

The *DSM-5* does not make diagnoses—clinicians (e.g., counselors) do. Counselors should make diagnoses only following systematic and objective assessment procedures. In order to accurately assess for (and diagnose) psychopathology, clinicians need to gather "evidence" (data) from numerous sources. Data can be *descriptive* (a summary), *cross-sectional* (from one time point), or *longitudinal* (from multiple time points). Counselors can utilize various methods to acquire the necessary data, including (un)structured interviews, behavioral observations, self-report inventories, psychological testing, historical/medical record review, functional assessment, and clinical judgment (Benson, 2010). *Clinical judgment* (i.e., the process used to determine what data to collect, interpret the data, and arrive at a diagnosis) is complex; requires problem-solving, decision-making, and critical thinking skills; and is only "developed through practice, experience, knowledge and continuous critical analysis" (Kienle & Kiene, 2011, p. 621).

Counselors must have the requisite knowledge, skills, and abilities to conduct assessments with their clients. The Council for Accreditation of Counseling and Related Educational Programs (CACREP, 2015) requires that all CACREP-accredited counseling programs train students in assessment and testing, including appropriate selection, administration, and interpretation of diagnostic tests. Specifically, clinical rehabilitation and mental health counseling programs must train students in the diagnostic process, including differential diagnosis and the use of current diagnostic classification systems, including the *DSM-5*. Moreover, various professional and credentialing organizations specific to rehabilitation and mental health counseling have established ethical codes (see Table 7.1) pertaining to informed consent; instrument selection, administration, and interpretation; reporting and releasing of assessment results; and competence, cultural sensitivity, and historical and social prejudices in the diagnosis of pathology, to guide the assessment process (American Counseling Association [ACA], 2014; American Mental Health Counselors Association [AMHCA], 2015; Commission on Rehabilitation Counselor Certification [CRCC], 2015; National Board for Certified Counselors [NBCC], 2016). Thus, it is imperative that counselors are not only well versed in the diverse tools used in assessment, but also able to determine the appropriateness of those tools for use with the diverse client populations they serve (e.g., individuals from racial/ethnic minority groups, people with disabilities).

TABLE 7.1 Rehabilitation and Mental Health Counseling Organization Codes of Ethics

ORGANIZATION	ASSESSMENT-RELATED CODES
ACA	A.2.b. Types of Information Needed for Informed Consent in Counseling Relationships E: Evaluation, Assessment, and Interpretation (all of E1–E11, E13)
AMHCA	I.B.2.a. Necessary Information Provided for Informed Consent in Counseling Process, Keeping Commitment to Clients I.D. Assessment and Diagnosis (all of D1–D4)
CRCC	A.1.b. Rehabilitation Counseling Plans Promote the Welfare of Those Served in Counseling Relationships B.2. Exceptions in Confidentiality, Privileged Communication, and Privacy Pertaining to: b. Contagious, Life-Threatening Diseases, and c. Court-Ordered Disclosure G: Assessment and Evaluation (all of G1–G9)
NBCC	Prevent harm: 16; Qualified: 25; Promote welfare: 33–37; Communicate truthfully: 48–50; Encourage active participation: 79–80; Accountable: 91–92

ACA, American Counseling Association; AMHCA, American Mental Health Counselors Association; CRCC, Commission on Rehabilitation Counselor Certification; NBCC, National Board for Certified Counselors.

Measures for Constructs in Model

Constructs are mental abstractions (e.g., theoretical concepts) used to express the things we are interested in (e.g., phenomena). Psychopathology-spectrum constructs organize broad domains of psychological factors (e.g., internalizing and externalizing) based on theoretical evidence (Krueger & Markon, 2008). Counselors can use constructs (e.g., [neuro]biological function, psychological adaptation, sociocultural factors) in the *DSM-5* (conceptual framework) to explain how and why certain phenomena (i.e., psychopathological disorders) behave the way that they do. In order to do so, however, abstract constructs (which are not measurable) need to be translated to concrete (i.e., measurable) variables (e.g., psychological distress). Therefore, we use psychological tests (e.g., psychiatric symptom questionnaires) to measure psychopathology.

Numerous psychological instruments have been developed to assess for psychopathology by measuring cognitive functioning, emotional functioning, substance abuse, risk potential, and psychopathological symptoms. Instrumentation ranges from global to specific. Counselors should select empirically sound (i.e., reliable and valid) instruments in order to achieve accurate results. Although reliability and validity are often used interchangeably, they refer to different aspects of measurement and are independent of each other. *Reliability* refers to the consistency of an instrument over time (test–retest reliability), across items (internal consistency), and across different clinicians/administrators/researchers (inter-rater reliability). *Validity* refers to the extent to which the instrument measures what it is supposed to measure. Content (or face) validity is based on the appropriateness of the items; criterion validity is determined by comparing (correlating) the instrument with current (concurrent validity) or future (predictive validity) expected variables. Construct validity is an ongoing process based on theory to assess whether the instrument correlates highly with variables it should correlate with (convergent validity) or if it does not significantly correlate with variables from which it should differ (divergent validity).

General Instruments

Some instruments can be used to assess for numerous (including co-occurring) disorders and to assist with differential diagnosis. These instruments are more comprehensive and can provide counselors with rich information to assist with treatment recommendations. Descriptions of some commonly used instruments are provided in the subsequent paragraphs.

Structured Clinical Interview for *DSM*

The Structured Clinical Interview for *DSM-5* (SCID-5), derived from its predecessors (first developed for use with the *DSM-III*; Spitzer & Williams, 1984), is a semistructured interview guide for making *DSM-5* diagnoses in adults (aged 18 years or older). Multiple versions of the SCID-5 include clinician (SCID-5-CV; First, Williams, Karg, & Spitzer, 2016), research (SCID-5-RV; First, Williams, Karg, & Spitzer, 2015b), and clinical trials (SCID-5-CT; First, Williams, Karg, & Spitzer, 2015a) versions for diagnosing the major *DSM-5* disorders, as well as traditional (SCID-5-PD; First, Williams, Benjamin, & Spitzer, 2016) and alternative model (SCID-5-AMPD III; First, Skodol, Bender, & Oldham, 2018) versions for diagnosing personality disorders. The SCID-5 also contains the Social and Occupational Functioning Assessment Scale (SOFAS; APA, 1994; Goldman, Skodol, & Lave, 1992). Clinicians who opt to use the SOFAS rate their client's social and occupational functioning/impairment due to physical and mental capacity/limitations on a 100-point continuum. Although rating anchors for functioning are provided in deciles, from grossly impaired (1–10 = *persistent inability to function without considerable external support*) to excellent (91–100 = *superior functioning*), clinicians are encouraged to use intermediary rating codes (e.g., 45, 68, 72) when appropriate; there is a separate option if more information is needed (0 = *inadequate information*).

The SCID-5-CV (First, Williams, Karg, & Spitzer, 2016) provides a step-by-step guide through the *DSM-5* diagnostic process, covering 10 major *DSM-5* diagnoses (e.g., schizophrenia spectrum disorders, bipolar disorders, depressive disorders, anxiety disorders, substance use disorders) and can be used as a screening tool for 17 additional ones (e.g., specific phobia, hoarding disorder, anorexia and bulimia nervosa, gambling disorder). The interview begins with an open-ended overview of the presenting problem (and any previous episodes of psychopathology), which should provide the clinician with enough information to formulate a list of tentative diagnoses to be explored with the modules; therefore, the SCID-5-CV should be administered only by trained clinicians who also have knowledge of the *DSM-5*. Following the overview, the clinician proceeds to the structured interview portion and reads the questions exactly as they appear (in the first of the three columns). The questions are grouped by diagnosis (individual modules) and criteria (i.e., each question coincides with its respective *DSM-5* criterion), which aids the clinician in rating each criterion as either present or absent (in the second column). Client responses are recorded and rated (in the third column) as "?" (*insufficient information*), "1" (*absent or false*), "2" (*subthreshold*), or "3" (*threshold or true*), and a minimum number of symptoms (which differs by diagnosis) must be present to meet diagnostic criteria. The SCID-5-CV encourages the clinician to repeat or ask probing questions, challenge client responses, and ask for clarification as needed to determine symptom presence/absence. Each module also provides guidelines on when to skip the remaining questions for that diagnosis (e.g., if a certain criterion or set of criteria are not met). Administration time can vary significantly (from 30 to 120 minutes) based on numerous factors, such as the number of disorders being assessed, the diagnostic complexity of the client, the client's (in)ability to describe his or her history and symptoms, and the clinician's level of experience (First, Williams, Karg, & Spitzer, 2016). After completing the interview, the clinician fills out the score sheet, including the *DSM-5* diagnosis with corresponding code(s). Currently, reliability and validity data for the SCID-5 are very limited. One study used the SCID-5-RV with adults from the community and clinics and found good internal consistency (all Cronbach's alphas >.80), test–retest reliability, and concurrent and predictive validity (Shankman, Funkhouser, Lerner, & Hee, 2018). The various SCID-5 versions can be purchased from APA Publishing (www.appi.org).

Millon Clinical Multiaxial Inventory

The Millon Clinical Multiaxial Inventory (MCMI)-IV (Millon, Grossman, & Millon, 2015), fourth revision (the first version corresponded with the *DSM-III*; Millon, 1977), is a self-report instrument designed to measure personality and psychopathology, including specific psychiatric disorders in the *DSM-5*, in adults (18 years or older). It contains a total of 30 subscales: 15 personality scales (12 clinical personality patterns and 3 severe personality pathology scales); 10 clinical syndrome scales (7 clinical syndromes and 3 severe clinical syndromes); and 5 validity scales (2 random response indicators and 3 modifying indices). Seven of the 12 clinical personality patterns (i.e., Schizoid, Avoidant, Dependent, Histrionic, Narcissistic, Antisocial, and Compulsive) and the 3 severe personality pathology (i.e., Schizotypal, Borderline, and Paranoid) scales correspond with the 10 personality disorders in the *DSM-5*. The 7 clinical syndromes (i.e., Generalized Anxiety, Somatic Symptom, Bipolar Disorder, Persistent Depression, Alcohol Use, Drug Use, and Post-Traumatic Stress) and 3 severe clinical syndromes (i.e., Schizophrenic Spectrum, Major Depression, and Delusional) correspond with clinical disorders in the *DSM-5*, which aids clinicians in making appropriate diagnostic decisions. The MCMI-IV also added the Grossman Facet Scales to improve the clinical utility of the test. There are 3 facet scales for each of the personality and syndrome scales, 45 in total (Millon et al., 2015). The 2 random response indicators assist in determining the validity (Validity Scale) and interpretability (Inconsistency Scale) of a client's test responses. The 3 modifying indices provide information about the client's response style, such as whether the client was open about details of his or her history during the assessment (Disclosure Scale) and whether the client presented herself or himself in a positive (Desirability Scale) or negative (Debasement Scale) light.

The MCMI-IV is based on Millon's (2011) personality theory, consists of 195 true/false items, and takes 25 to 30 minutes to complete. Once the client completes the MCMI-IV, the clinician needs to score and determine the validity of the test before attempting to interpret the personality and syndrome scales. The clinician should review (a) the Validity Scale, in which endorsement of an improbability item indicates the test is likely invalid (if invalid, stop; if valid, proceed); (b) the number of inconsistent responses (20 or above = do not interpret, stop; 9–19 = questionable, proceed with caution; fewer than 9 = okay to interpret, proceed) on the Inconsistency Scale; (c) Disclosure Scale scores (115 or above/<6, invalid, stop; 61–114/6–20, probably over/ underreporting, proceed with caution; 21–60, adequate reporting, proceed); and (d) the Desirability Scale scores (above 75, may be faking good) and the Debasement Scale scores (75–84, may be a cry for help, proceed with caution; 85 and over, invalid, stop). Next, the clinician should review the personality scales, first checking the 3 "severe" personality scales to determine whether any are elevated. Personality (and syndrome) raw scores are converted to base rate (BR) scores on a scale of 1 to 115, where 60 is the median. BR scores of 75 to 84 indicate the presence of a personality trait (or syndrome), while scores of 85 or more indicate the persistence of a personality trait (or clinical syndrome; Millon et al., 2015). The clinician should then review the facet scales (evaluate differences in symptom presentations between clients with elevated scores on the same personality scale). Next, the clinician should review the syndromes, first checking the scores for 3 "severe" syndromes to determine whether any are elevated. Finally, the clinician should integrate the MCMI-IV results with client history and other relevant data. The MCMI-IV has good psychometric properties with internal consistency median values for the personality and syndrome scales of .84 and .83, respectively; test–retest reliability ranging from .73 (Delusional) to .93 (Histrionic), with most scales above .80; and correlations between the MCMI-IV (personality and syndrome scales) and the Minnesota Multiphasic Personality Inventory-2–Restructured Form (MMPI-2-RF; clinical and specific problem scales) were low to moderate and moderate to high, respectively (Millon et al., 2015). The MCMI-IV is available for purchase from Pearson (www.pearsonclinical.com).

Symptom Checklist

The Symptom Checklist (SCL)-90-R (Derogatis, 1983), a 90-item revision of the Hopkins Symptom Checklist (HSCL; Derogatis, Lipman, Rickels, Uhlenhuth, & Covi, 1974), is designed to screen for type, quantity, and severity of self-reported psychological symptoms in clients at least 13 years of age. It reflects 9 primary symptom dimensions (i.e., Somatization, Obsessive-Compulsive, Interpersonal Sensitivity, Depression, Anxiety, Hostility, Phobic Anxiety, Paranoid Ideation, and Psychoticism), as well as 3 global indices of distress: Global Severity Index (GSI; overall psychological distress), Positive Symptom Distress Index (PSDI; symptom intensity), and Positive Symptom Total (PST; number of self-reported symptoms). Clients are asked to rate their level of distress (during the past 7 days) for each item on a 5-point Likert-type scale (0 = *not at all*, 1 = *a little bit*, 2 = *moderately*, 3 = *quite a bit*, 4 = *extremely*), with higher scores indicating greater symptom severity. The SCL-90-R can be completed in 12 to 15 minutes. Scores for the symptom dimensions and global indices are calculated, transformed to standard T-scores (range = 30–80; mean [M] = 50; standard deviation [SD] = +/-10), and plotted on the profile sheet. A T-score above 63 (normal range = 40–60) on the GSI (or on at least two symptom dimensions) indicates the presence of significant psychological distress. The SCL-90-R is a well-established instrument with more than 1,000 independent studies conducted for internal consistency (coefficients ranged from .77 for psychoticism to .90 for depression), test–retest reliability (coefficients ranged from .78 for hostility to .90 for phobic anxiety after 1-week interval), and criterion validity (all 9 dimension subscales correlated with MMPI clinical scales), supporting its reliability and validity (Derogatis & Fitzpatrick, 2004). The SCL-90-R can also be used to measure client progress and treatment outcomes. Abbreviated, 53-item (Brief Symptom Inventory [BSI]; Derogatis, 1993) and 18-item (BSI-18; Derogatis, 2001) versions of the HSCL are also available. The SCL-90-R, BSI, and BSI-18 can be purchased from Pearson (www.pearsonclinical.com).

Specific Instruments

One of the barriers to using longer tests is the time required to administer, score, and interpret them. Depending on the situation, setting, and client, such instruments may be inappropriate or unnecessary. In those instances, focused (or specific) instruments may be more appropriate. These measures can assist with assessing specific disorders and, in some instances, with differentiating between similar disorders. Brief descriptions of some of the more common psychiatric disorders seen by rehabilitation and mental health counselors are presented next, followed by some of the instruments commonly used to assist with diagnosing them.

Schizophrenia Spectrum and Other Psychotic Disorders

Schizophrenia spectrum and other psychotic disorders, in the *DSM-5*, comprise schizophrenia, schizophreniform, and schizoaffective disorders; other psychotic disorders; and schizotypal (personality) disorder (APA, 2013). Characteristic features include symptoms from at least one of the following five domains: (a) *delusions* (untrue beliefs that are maintained despite being presented with contradicting evidence); (b) *hallucinations* (perceptions that occur in the absence of external stimuli); (c) *disorganized thinking* (e.g., switching from one topic to another, responding to questions with completely unrelated answers); (d) *grossly disorganized or abnormal motor behavior* (e.g., childlike "silliness," unpredictable agitation, catatonia); and (e) *negative symptoms* (e.g., diminished emotional expression, avolition, anhedonia). Disorders exist on a psychopathological continuum, and diagnostic criteria differ based on the number (and type) of required symptoms, duration of disturbance, existence and level (or lack) of functional impairment, required concurrence with (or exclusion of) other disorders or symptoms, and presumed etiology.

Positive and Negative Syndrome Scale

The Positive and Negative Syndrome Scale (PANSS; Kay, Fiszbein, & Opler, 1987) is a semistructured interview to assess the severity of symptoms associated with schizophrenia. Each of the 30 items is rated on a 7-point Likert-type scale (1 = *absent*, 2 = *minimal*, 3 = *mild*, 4 = *moderate*, 5 = *moderate severe*, 6 = *severe*, 7 = *extreme*), which form 3 distinct subscales: Positive (e.g., hallucinations, delusions; 7 items), Negative (e.g., blunted affect, emotional withdrawal; 7 items), and General Psychopathology (e.g., anxiety, depression; 16 items). Possible scores for the PANSS range from 30 to 210, specifically from 7 to 49 for the Positive and Negative scales and from 16 to 112 for the General Psychopathology scale (Kay et al., 1987). Internal consistency for the subscales ranged from .62 to .74 (Positive), .69 to .92 (Negative), and .55 to .79 (General Psychopathology). Test–retest reliability estimates for the subscales were .80 (Positive), .68 (Negative), and .60 (General Psychopathology). Construct validity was determined by inverse (−.23) and nonsignificant (.09) correlations between the Positive and Negative scales, and concurrent validity was established by correlations with the Positive and Negative scales and the Scale for the Assessment of Positive Symptoms (SAPS; .70) and the Scale for the Assessment of Negative Symptoms (SANS; .81), respectively (Bell, Milstein, Beam-Goulet, Lysaker, & Cicchetti, 1992; Kay et al., 1987; Peralta & Cuesta, 1994). The PANSS can be purchased from Multi-Health Systems Inc. (MHS; www.mhs.com).

Brief Psychiatric Rating Scale

The Brief Psychiatric Rating Scale (BPRS), available in 16-item (Overall & Gorham, 1962), 18-item (Overall, Hollister, & Pichot, 1967), and two 24-item versions (24-item; Lukoff, Nuechterlein, & Ventura, 1986; and version 4.0; Ventura et al., 1993), is one of the most widely used instruments for assessing the presence and severity of psychiatric symptoms. Version 4.0 provides administration instructions for a more detailed semistructured interview with probe questions for each symptom, as well as better defined rules (for anchor points 2–7) for rating. Clinicians follow the rules to rate the client responses to items (1 = *not present*, 2 = *very mild*, 3 = *mild*, 4 = *moderate*, 5 = *moderately severe*, 6 = *severe*, 7 = *extremely severe*, or as *not assessed*); possible scores can range from 24 to 168, with higher scores indicating greater psychopathology severity (Ventura et al., 1993). Intra-class correlation was .78, test–retest reliability was .92 (18-week interval), and validity was determined by correlation with the degree of severity (.66; Andersen et al., 1986).

Bipolar and Related Disorders

Bipolar and related disorders are considered to be a bridge between schizophrenia spectrum and other psychotic disorders and depressive disorders; they include bipolar I and II, cyclothymic, and related disorders (APA, 2013). The distinguishing feature is "mania," as evidenced by a *manic episode* (a distinct period of abnormal and persistent elevated, expansive, or irritable mood, and abnormal and persistent increased activity or energy lasting at least 1 week and present for most of the day, nearly every day [or any duration if hospitalization required]), a *hypomanic episode* (shorter duration [i.e., lasting at least 4 consecutive days, but less than 1 week] and less severe [i.e., no hospitalization] than a manic episode), or *hypomanic symptoms* (e.g., inflated self-esteem, decreased need for sleep, pressured speech, flight of ideas, distractibility, psychomotor agitation, engagement in risky activities).

Bipolar Spectrum Diagnostic Scale

The Bipolar Spectrum Diagnostic Scale (BSDS; Ghaemi et al., 2005), originally developed by Ronald Pies (C. J. Miller, Ghaemi, Klugman, Berv, & Pies, 2002), is a self-report screening instrument for bipolar spectrum disorders. It has two scored portions. Clients are instructed to read the narrative (consisting of 19 sentences that describe features or symptoms that may occur in people with bipolar spectrum disorders) without filling in any blanks. After they read the entire passage, they are asked whether "This story": *fits me very well or almost perfectly* (6 points), *fits me fairly well* (4 points), *fits me to some degree, but not in most respects* (2 points), or *does not really describe me at all* (0 points). Then, they are instructed to place a checkmark after each sentence that *definitely describes* them (1 point each). The clinician then sums up the scores. Possible scores range from 0 to 25, indicating the likelihood of having bipolar disorder as highly unlikely (0–6), low probability (7–12), moderate probability (13–19), or high probability (20–25), with a score of 13 or more indicating the presence of bipolar disorder. *Sensitivity* (percentage accurately diagnosed) of the BSDS ranged from 76% to 81%, approximately equal in clients with bipolar I (75%–77%) and bipolar II (77%–79%) disorders, and *specificity* (percentage of clients with unipolar depression correctly identified as not having bipolar spectrum disorder) ranged from 85% (using a cutoff of 12) to 93% (using a cutoff of 13; Ghaemi et al., 2005; C. J. Miller et al., 2002).

General Behavior Inventory

The General Behavior Inventory (GBI) is a 73-item self-report measure of mood (manic and depressive) symptomatology to screen for bipolar (Depue et al., 1981) and depressive (Depue, Krauss, Spoont, & Arbisi, 1989) disorders. Clients rate their symptom intensity, duration, and frequency on a 4-point Likert-type scale (1 = *never or hardly ever*, 2 = *sometimes*, 3 = *often*, 4 = *very often or almost constantly*); however, the items are scored dichotomously (i.e., scores of 1 and 2 = 0; scores of 3 and 4 = 1). To identify those with bipolar disorders, a cutoff of at least 27 is recommended, and to rule out bipolar disorder, a cutoff of a maximum of 14 is recommended (Depue et al., 1981). The GBI demonstrated good sensitivity ranging from 73% to 88%, specifically among clients with cyclothymia (100%), dysthymia (92%), bipolar (76%–78%), and unipolar depressive (72%–76%) disorders. It also displayed an excellent specificity ranging from 96% to 97%, performing well among those with nonaffective psychiatric disorders (87%) and equal among those with bipolar (99%) and unipolar depressive (99%) disorders (Depue et al., 1989; Klein, Dickstein, Taylor, & Harding, 1989; Mallon, Klein, Bornstein, & Slater, 1986). In addition, it exhibits excellent internal consistency (.94), test–retest reliability (.73 after 15 weeks), and construct validity (cyclothymia is dimensional to bipolar disorders), supporting its reliability and validity (Depue et al., 1981) as a useful screening tool. There is an abbreviated version (14 items) of the GBI, the 7 Up 7 Down Inventory (7U7D; Youngstrom, Murray, Johnson, & Findling, 2016). It has also been adapted for use as a 73-item parent-report measure of mood (P-GBI; Youngstrom, Findling, Danielson, & Calabrese, 2001) and a 10-item parent-report measure of mania (P-GBI-10-M; Youngstrom, Frazier, Demeter, Calabrese, & Findling, 2008) in children and adolescents.

Depressive Disorders

The *DSM-5* section on depressive disorders consists of all unipolar (i.e., not bipolar or related) depressive disorders that share the common features of "sad, empty, or irritable mood, accompanied by somatic and cognitive changes that significantly affect the individual's capacity to function," differing only in "duration, timing, or presumed etiology" (APA, 2013, p. 155).

Beck Depression Inventory

The Beck Depression Inventory (BDI; A. T. Beck, Ward, Mendelson, Mock, & Erbaugh, 1961), currently in its third revision (BDI-II; A. T. Beck, Steer, & Brown, 1996), is the most widely used measure of depression and aligns with the *DSM-IV-TR* (APA, 2000). The 21-item self-report instrument uses a multiple-choice, 3-point (0 = *not present* to 3 = *severe*) Likert-type format, yields two factors (Cognitive-Affective and Somatic-Vegetative; A. T. Beck et al., 1996), and can be completed in 5 to 10 minutes. Clients (aged 13 years or older) are instructed to respond based on how they felt (e.g., sadness, agitation, loss of interest) over the previous 2 weeks. Scores are summed and interpreted as no or minimal (0–13), mild (14–19), moderate (20–28), or severe (29–63) depression, with the most severe cases of depression scoring between 40 and 50 and scores below 4 indicating possible denial of depression (A. T. Beck et al., 1996). The BDI-II can be used to assess for suicidality, with a score of 2 or 3 on Item 2 (pessimism) or 9 (suicidal thoughts or wishes).

Internal consistency ranged from .90 to .94, test–retest reliability was .93 (1-week interval); con- tent validity was established through its alignment with the *DSM*, and concurrent validity was determined by correlations with the Hamilton Psychiatric Rating Scale for Depression (.71) and the SCL-90-R Depression dimension (.89; Arnau, Meagher, Norris, & Bramson, 2001; A. T. Beck et al., 1996; Steer, Ball, Ranieri, & Beck, 1999; Steer, Rissmiller, & Beck, 2000). Discriminant valid- ity was established with weaker correlations to the Hamilton Rating Scale for Anxiety (.47 vs. .89) and the SCL-90-R Anxiety dimension (.71 vs. .89) than to their respective depression scales. There are BDI versions specifically for youth (BYI-2 Depression scale; J. S. Beck, Beck, Jolly, & Steer, 2005) and medical patients (BDI-FS; A. T. Beck, Steer, & Brown, 2000). The Beck invento- ries can be purchased from Pearson (www.pearsonclinical.com).

Patient Health Questionnaire

The Patient Health Questionnaire (PHQ)-9 is the depression subscale from the PHQ (Spitzer, Kroenke, & Williams, 1999; originally PRIME-MD; Spitzer et al., 1994). It is a self-report mea- sure designed to screen for depression in primary care settings. Clients are instructed to rate the frequency of their distress (0 = *not at all*, 1 = *several days*, 2 = *more than half the days*, 3 = *nearly every day*) for the nine *DSM-IV-TR* (APA, 2000) symptom criteria for major depressive disorder over the previous 2 weeks. If any problem was indicated (a supplementary question), clients are to rate their level of difficulty (*not difficult at all, somewhat difficult, very difficult,* or *extremely dif- ficult*) in completing tasks in major life areas (e.g., work, home, relationships). The PHQ-9 aligns with *DSM-5* criteria for a major depressive episode. It can usually be completed within 3 min- utes. Scores are summed and used to interpret levels of depression as minimal (0–4), mild (5–9), moderate (10–14), moderately severe (15–19), or severe (20–27), with sensitivity and specificity ranging from 68% (≥15) to 95% (≥9) and from 84% (≥9) to 95% (≥15), respectively, based on the cutoff score used (Kroenke, Spitzer, & Williams, 2001). Internal consistency ranged from .86 to .89, and test–retest reliability was .84 (48-hour interval). Concurrent validity was determined by correlations with the Medical Outcomes Study Short Form General Health Survey (SF-20) domains of mental health (.73), general health (.55), social functioning (.52), role functioning (.43), physical functioning (.37), and bodily pain (.33; Kroenke et al., 2001). The PHQ-9, PHQ, and other variations are available for no cost from Pfizer (www.phqscreeners.com).

Anxiety Disorders

The *DSM-5* anxiety disorders include anxiety, panic, and phobic disorders whose core fea- tures consist of "excessive fear and anxiety and related behavioral disturbances" (APA, 2013, p. 189). Despite the obvious overlap, there are distinct differences among the features. *Fear* is an unpleasant emotion in response to perceived (real or imagined) imminent threat, which often triggers the fight-flight-freeze response. *Anxiety* is a feeling of unease, worry, or nervousness in anticipation of an imminent event, threat, or unknown outcome, which often results in muscle tension and (hyper)vigilance. Lastly, a *panic attack* is the abrupt onset of fear, without the pres- ence of real danger, which usually subsides within 10 minutes. The disorders are arranged devel- opmentally (according to typical age at onset) and differ based on the types of objects or situations that cause the distress, as well as their associated cognitive ideation.

State-Trait Anxiety Inventory

The State-Trait Anxiety Inventory (STAI) has been through several iterations since its develop- ment (Form X; Spielberger, Gorsuch, & Lushene, 1970) to its current format (Form Y/STAI-AD;

Spielberger, Gorsuch, Lushene, Vagg, & Jacobs, 1983) and is the most widely used measure to distinguish anxiety from depression in clients aged 16 years and older. It takes approximately 10 minutes to complete the 40-item self-report instrument. The STAI-AD is made up of two (20-item) scales: the State Anxiety Scale (S-Anxiety) assesses how a person is feeling at the moment (transitory emotional state), whereas the Trait Anxiety Scale (T-Anxiety) assesses a person's general feeling (personality trait). The S-Anxiety has 10 anxiety-present and 10 anxiety-absent statements that clients rate on a 4-point Likert-type scale based on how they feel "right now" (1 = *not at all*, 2 = *somewhat*, 3 = *moderately so*, 4 = *very much so*), with higher scores indicating greater anxiety. On the other hand, the T-Anxiety has 11 anxiety-present and 9 anxiety-absent statements that are rated on a 4-point Likert-type scale based on how clients "generally" feel (1 = *almost never*, 2 = *sometimes*, 3 = *often*, 4 = *almost always*), with higher scores indicating greater anxiety. Anxiety-absent items are reverse-scored, and scores for the S-Anxiety and T-Anxiety can range from 20 to 80, with recommendations for gender- and age-normed cutoffs to detect clinically significant symptoms (Knight, Waal-Manning, & Spears, 1983). The S-Anxiety and T-Anxiety exhibit good psychometric properties; internal consistency median coefficients for the scales have ranged from .86 to .94 and .87 to .91, respectively, and test–retest reliability coefficients have ranged from .34 to .62 and .71 to .86 (intervals from 20–60 days), respectively. Concurrent validity for the S-Anxiety and T-Anxiety was determined by correlations with the Beck Anxiety Inventory (BAI; .52 and .44, respectively; Kabacoff, Segal, Hersen, & van Hasselt, 1997; Knight et al., 1983; Spielberger et al., 1983). There are also a child version of the STAI (STAI-CH; Spielberger, 1973) and an abbreviated (6-item) version of the S-Anxiety (STAI-6; Marteau & Bekker, 1992). The STAI versions are available for purchase from Mind Garden (www.mindgarden.com).

Generalized Anxiety Disorder

The Generalized Anxiety Disorder (GAD)-7 (Spitzer, Kroenke, Williams, & Löwe, 2006) scale is a 7-item self-report measure of anxiety modeled after the PHQ-9 (Spitzer et al., 1999) and aligned with the *DSM-IV-TR* (APA, 2000). Clients rate the frequency of their distress "over the past 2 weeks" on a 4-point Likert-type scale (0 = *not at all*, 1 = *several days*, 2 = *more than half the days*, 3 = *nearly every day*) and can usually complete it within 2 to 5 minutes. Scores are summed and used to interpret level of anxiety severity as minimal (0–4), mild (5–9), moderate (10–14), or severe (15–21). Sensitivity and specificity range from 48% ($\geq$15) to 92% ($\geq$9) and from 76% ($\geq$9) to 95% ($\geq$15), respectively, based on the cutoff score used (Spitzer et al., 2006). The GAD-7 scale is a good screening tool for (generalized and other) anxiety disorders (with a recommended cutoff score of 10) as well as panic disorder, social phobia, and posttraumatic stress disorder (PTSD; with a recommended cutoff score of 8; Kroenke, Spitzer, Williams, Monahan, & Löwe, 2007). Internal consistency was .92, test–retest reliability was .83 (1-week interval), and convergent validity was determined by correlations with the BAI (.72) and the anxiety subscale of the SCL-90 (.74; Spitzer et al., 2006). An abbreviated (2-item) version of the GAD scale is also available (GAD-2; Kroenke et al., 2007). The GAD-7 scale and other PHQ screeners are available at no cost from Pfizer (www.phqscreeners.com).

Substance-Related and Addictive Disorders

The *DSM-5* substance-related and addictive disorders chapter is concerned with substance use, substance-induced (e.g., intoxication, withdrawal, other substance/medication-induced mental disorders), and gambling disorders (APA, 2013). The essential features are continued substance use despite significant substance-related problems (*substance use disorder*), reversible substance-specific symptomatology (*substance-induced disorder*), and continued gambling despite significant gambling-related problems (*gambling disorder*). The *DSM-5* includes 10 main drug types or categories: alcohol; caffeine; cannabis; hallucinogens (including phencyclidine); inhalants; opioids; sedatives, hypnotics, and anxiolytics; stimulants; tobacco; and other (or unknown) substances.

Substance Abuse Subtle Screening Inventory

The Substance Abuse Subtle Screening Inventory (SASSI; G. A. Miller, 1985), currently in its fourth revision (SASSI-4; Lazowski, Kimmell, & Baker, 2016), is a self-report screening measure for substance use disorders. There are 105 items, which can be completed in approximately 15 minutes and form 11 scales: Face-Valid Alcohol and Face-Valid Other Drug scales (assess frequency of alcohol/other drug-related consequences), Symptoms scale (assesses symptoms related to alcohol/other drug use), Obvious and Subtle Attributes scales (assess insight/lack of insight regarding substance use disorders and treatment), Defensiveness and Supplemental Addiction Measure scales (assess minimization/identify individuals with/without substance use disorders), Family vs. Control Subjects scale (identifies individuals who have family members with substance use disorders), Correctional scale (assesses for risk of legal problems), Random Answering Pattern scale (assesses validity in response pattern), and Prescription Drug Abuse scale (assesses for misuse of prescription medications). The 74 statements (Side 1) reflecting feelings, thoughts, and behaviors are rated as *true* or *false*, whereas the 31 questions (Side 2) reflecting frequency and consequences of alcohol (13 items) and other drug (18 items) use are rated on a 4-point Likert-type scale (0 = *never*, 1 = *once or twice*, 2 = *several times*, 3 = *repeatedly*) over a clinician-specified time period (e.g., lifetime, past 6/12 months, 6 months before/after [specific date]). Clients record their responses on a scantron-like form, which the clinician then uses to score and plot on a profile sheet. The SASSI-4 sensitivity and specificity ranged from 93% to 94% and from 88% to 90%, respectively; internal consistency was .97, and test–retest reliability ranged from .78 to .99 (8–60-day intervals; Lazowski & Geary, 2019; Lazowski et al., 2016). There are SASSI versions specifically for adolescents (SASSI-A2; F. G. Miller & Lazowski, 2001), vocational rehabilitation clients (SAVR-S2; Winningham & Lazowski, 2010), and clients who communicate in American Sign Language (SAS-ASL; Winningham & Lazowski, 2012). The SASSI-4, SASSI-A2, SAVR-S2, and SAS-ASL can be purchased from the SASSI Institute (www.sassi.com).

Addiction Severity Index

The Addiction Severity Index (ASI; McLellan, Luborsky, Woody, & O'Brien, 1980) is a structured clinical interview used to screen for problems associated with substance use disorders. Currently in its sixth revision (ASI-6; McLellan, Cacciola, Alterman, Rikoon, & Carise, 2006), the ASI-6 consists of 165 questions in 7 domains. The ASI-6 is more structured and comprehensive yet remains brief (can be completed within 1 hour) by adding screening questions with instructions for "skip-outs" and should be used only by clinicians with specified training (McLellan et al., 2006). The problem areas assess for type, duration, and frequency of medical health/problems and service utilization (Medical, 11 items); employment status/capacity/barriers, income/debt, and homelessness (Employment/Support, 23 items); recent alcohol/drug use/problems and service utilization (Alcohol/Drugs, 45 items); recent illegal activities/interactions with criminal justice system (Legal, 16 items); adult relationship problems/support, parent–child problems/needs, domestic violence/trauma, and leisure activities (Family/Social, 49 items); and presence/absence of psychiatric symptoms/distress/impairment related to (or independent of) substance use and service utilization (Psychiatric,

21 items) over the lifetime and past 30 days (Cacciola, Alterman, Habing, & McLellan, 2011; Denis, Cacciola, & Alterman, 2013). Clients are asked to rate how much they are distressed on a 5-point Likert-type scale (0 = *not at all*, 1 = *slightly*, 2 = *moderately*, 3 = *considerably*, 4 = *extremely*), and the clinician rates the client's severity and need for treatment from 0 to 10 (0–1 = *no real problem, treatment not indicated*; 2–3 = *slight problem, treatment probably not necessary*; 4–5 = *moderate problem, some treatment indicated*; 6–7 = *considerable problem, treatment necessary*; 8–9 = *extreme problem, treatment absolutely necessary*) for each domain. This score can be used for treatment planning and to assess treatment outcomes (Samet, Waxman, Hatzenbuehler, & Hasin, 2007). Intra-class correlations for the ASI-6 ranged from .71 (Family/Social Problems) to .94 (Drug); test–retest reliability for the ASI (among substance abuse counselors) ranged from .79 (Alcohol) to .91 (Psychiatric), with .84 overall (3-day interval); and concurrent validity was determined by correlations with the ASI-Employment and Social Adjustment Scale–Self-Report (SAS)-work factor (.39), ASI-Legal and number of days engaged in illegal activities for profit (.43), ASI-Psychiatric and BDI (.51), and with the corresponding ASI-5 Medical (.73), Employment/Support (.50), Alcohol (.77), Drug (.84), Legal (.39), Family/Social (.38), and Psychiatric (.70) domains (Cacciola et al., 2011; Denis et al., 2013; Kosten, Rounsaville, & Kleber, 1983; McLellan et al., 1985).

Standards for Testing

Many of the psychological tests used in clinical practice are available only from commercial publishers. The current *Standards for Educational and Psychological Testing* (2014) were jointly established and published by the American Educational Research Association (AERA), the American Psychological Association (APA), and the National Council on Measurement in Education (NCME) to provide "definitive technical, professional and operational standards for all forms of assessments that are professionally developed and used in a variety of settings" (Camara, 2014). Licensed counselors often meet the required criteria for the highest qualification levels of the major clinical test publishers in the United States. Specifically, MHS (n.d.), Psychological Assessment Resources Inc. (PAR; 2018), Pearson (2018), and Western Psychological Services (WPS; 2018) adhere to these professional standards and require practitioners to meet established qualification levels (see Table 7.2) in order to legally purchase or use their tests. Requisite education and/

TABLE 7.2 Qualification Levels for Use of Psychological Tests From Professional Publishers

USER QUALIFYING CRITERIA	LEVEL	PUBLISHER	SAMPLE
No specific qualifications.	A	MHS	NA
		PAR	
		Pearson	
		WPS	
Degree, certificate, or license in healthcare field, plus appropriate training and/or experience in ethical administration, scoring, and interpretation of clinical assessments.	S	PAR	MAQ

(continued)

TABLE 7.2 Qualification Levels for Use of Psychological Tests From Professional Publishers (*continued*)

USER QUALIFYING CRITERIA	LEVEL	PUBLISHER	SAMPLE
License or certification that requires appropriate training and experience in ethical administration, scoring, and interpretation of clinical assessments.	B	PAR	DAPS
		Pearson	BSI
Bachelor's degree in counseling/psychology.	B	WPS	PDSQ
Bachelor's degree in counseling/psychology, plus course work in testing and measurement.	B	PAR	CDS
Bachelor's degree in counseling/psychology, plus license or certification that requires training and experience in assessment.	C	WPS	RHRSD
Graduate-level courses in testing and measurement, or documented equivalent.	B	MHS	PANSS
Master's degree in counseling/psychology, plus formal training in ethical administration, scoring, and interpretation of clinical assessments.	B	Pearson	SCL-90-R
	C	WPS	BORRTI
Master's degree in counseling/psychology, plus at least a weekend workshop on neuropsychological assessment.	N	WPS	TOMM
Advanced professional degree (e.g., psychology), plus training and/or experience in ethical administration, scoring, and interpretation of psychological assessments.	C	MHS	MCCB
		PAR	SASSI-4
		Pearson	Rorschach
	N	WPS	MPS
License or certification from an agency that requires appropriate training and experience in the ethical and competent use of psychological tests.	C	PAR	TAT
		Pearson	MCMI-IV
Only for use in a law enforcement agency setting.	M	MHS	M-PULSE

BORRTI, Bell Object Relations and Reality Testing Inventory; BSI, Brief Symptom Inventory; CDS, Cognitive Distortion Scales; DAPS, Detailed Assessment of Posttraumatic Stress; MAQ, Multidimensional Anxiety Questionnaire; MCCB, MATRICS Consensus Cognitive Battery; MCMI-IV, Millon Clinical Multiaxial Inventory-IV; MHS, Multi-Health Systems Inc.; MPS, Malingering Probability Scale; M-PULSE, Matrix-Predictive Uniform Law Enforcement Selection Evaluation Inventory; PANSS, Positive and Negative Syndrome Scale; PAR, Psychological Assessment Resources Inc.; PDSQ, Psychiatric Diagnostic Screening Questionnaire; RHRSD, Revised Hamilton Rating Scale for Depression; Rorschach, Rorschach Technique; SASSI-4, Adult Substance Abuse Subtle Screening Inventory-4; SCL-90-R, Symptom Checklist-90–Revised; TAT, Thematic Apperception Test; TOMM, Test of Memory Malingering; WPS, Western Psychological Services.

or training experience to qualify for the varied levels generally range from none to an advanced degree in a specific field, specialized training, and licensed to practice independently. Specifically, tests used in the assessment of psychopathology overwhelmingly require (at least) a master's degree, licensure, or certification.

▒ Diagnosis and Case Conceptualization

Just as the *DSM* does not diagnose clients, neither do the tests. The tests provide objective data and help identify ("screen" for) areas to explore further. Rehabilitation and mental health counselors must use clinical judgment in order to diagnose their clients. Making an accurate diagnosis is an important initial step in the larger assessment process. Counselors should view diagnosis as "a tool for *describing* client needs," case conceptualization as "a tool for *understanding* these needs," and treatment planning as "a tool for *addressing* these needs to bring about change" (Schwitzer & Rubin, 2012, p. 28). The treatment plan is formulated from the case conceptualization, which is informed by the counselor's diagnostic impression. Thus, making an accurate diagnosis is necessary to lay a solid foundation from which the treatment is ultimately built. Unfortunately, for clients with psychiatric disorders, being misdiagnosed is quite common, with over half (51%) having to wait 5 years or more to be accurately diagnosed (Hirschfeld, Lewis, & Vornik, 2003).

With an estimated one in five adults experiencing a mental illness (18.3%; Ahrnsbrak, Bose, Hedden, Lipari, & Park-Lee, 2017), or disability (22.2%; Courtney-Long et al., 2015), in a given year, it is likely that many will be referred to, or seek services from, rehabilitation and mental health counselors. In the United States, 12-month and lifetime prevalence rates for some of the most common mental disorders were estimated to be 19.1% and 31.2% for anxiety disorders (using *DSM-IV-TR* criteria, includes PTSD and obsessive-compulsive disorder), 6.8% and 16.9% for major depressive disorders, and 2.8% and 4.4% for bipolar disorders (Harvard Medical School, 2007a, 2007b). Among subjects aged 12 years and older, 12-month prevalence rates for specific substance use disorders were estimated to be 5.6% for alcohol, 1.5% for cannabis, .8% for opioids (prescription pain relievers and heroin), and .8% for stimulants (methamphetamine, cocaine, and prescription stimulants); among adults aged 18 years or older, the 12-month prevalence rate for co-occurring mental and substance use disorders was estimated to be 3.4% (Ahrnsbrak et al., 2017). Many of these disorders are also those most often misdiagnosed.

Specifically, rates of misdiagnosis have ranged from 62% to 93% for bipolar disorders, 32% to 66% for depressive disorders, 50% to 98% for anxiety disorders, and 35% to 57% for co-occurring depressive and anxiety disorders (Altamura et al., 2015; Hirschfeld et al., 2003; Mitchell, Vaze, & Rao, 2009; Ormel, Koeter, van den Brink, & van de Willige, 1991; Vermani, Marcus, & Katzman, 2011; Wittchen et al., 2002). Misdiagnosis can occur for various reasons and have numerous culprits, including clinicians who fail to conduct a comprehensive assessment, lack experience with the particular disorder, or submit to cognitive bias and over-rely on a previous diagnosis; clients who provide inaccurate information or fail to authorize the release of their medical records; and restrictive mental health parameters that rely on psychiatric symptomatology and utilize classification models to diagnose mental disorders. However, psychiatric symptoms can be shared (or overlap) across mental disorder groups. For example, generalized anxiety disorder, major depressive disorder, and bipolar disorder share many of the same symptoms (see Table 7.3). Coincidentally, incorrect diagnoses given instead of bipolar disorder were depression (9%–71%), anxiety (7%–26%), schizophrenia (15%–21%), delusion disorder (18%), personality (e.g., borderline, antisocial) disorders (2%–17%), obsessive-compulsive disorder (15%), alcohol or substance abuse/dependence (14%), and schizoaffective disorder (11%–14%; Altamura et al., 2015; Hirschfeld et al., 2003; Shen et al., 2018). The similar psychiatric symptoms shared across disorders can make reaching an accurate diagnosis more difficult.

Consequences of misdiagnosis include the establishment of inappropriate goals, provision of inadequate services, and decreased likelihood of successful rehabilitation, which can subsequently negatively impact the therapeutic relationship and diminish the client's hope. More concerning, however, is that misdiagnosis followed by inaccurate (e.g., contraindicated) treatment can exacerbate

TABLE 7.3 Overlapping *DSM-5* Diagnostic Criteria Across GAD, MDD, and BP

SYMPTOM/CRITERION	GAD	MDD (MDE)	BP (ME)
Difficulty concentrating	C3	A8	B5
Thought processes	B	A9	B4
Irritable mood	C4	A1	A
Energy level	C2	A6	A
Psychomotor behavior	C1	A5	B6
Sleep disturbance	C6	A4	B2
Impairment in functioning	D	B	C

BP, bipolar disorder; GAD, generalized anxiety disorder; MDD, major depressive disorder; MDE, major depressive episode; ME, manic episode.

psychiatric symptoms, impair psychosocial functioning, and require psychiatric hospitalization. When compared with their accurately diagnosed peers, misdiagnosed clients were found to require more outpatient (74%–80%), emergency department (106%–147%), and inpatient (82%–206%) psychiatric treatment services (Schultz, Stensland, & Frytak, 2008; Stensland, Schultz, & Frytak, 2010).

Diagnosis

To improve diagnostic accuracy, thus limiting misdiagnosis, counselors should employ effective strategies. The process for *DSM-5* diagnosis can be broken down into six basic steps: (1) ruling out malingering and factitious disorder; (2) ruling out a substance etiology; (3) ruling out an etiological medical condition; (4) determining the specific primary disorder(s); (5) differentiating adjustment disorder from the residual other specified and unspecified conditions; and (6) establishing the boundary with no mental disorder (First, 2014). The first few steps (1–3) are used to rule out other reasons/causes for psychiatric symptoms, while the last few steps (4–6) are used to identify the correct disorder (i.e., differential diagnosis). At each step, the counselor must review information and make a determination that influences the next step (see Table 7.4).

In order to rule out alternative causes for the client's clinical presentation, there are some determinations the counselor must make. First (Step 1), the counselor must determine whether the client is being honest about the nature and severity of his or her presenting symptoms (First, 2014). Although most clients are forthcoming, some resort to feigning symptoms to either obtain (e.g., disability compensation) or avoid (e.g., criminal conviction) a foreseeable outcome (*malingering*), or for no obvious external reward (*factitious disorder*). Next (Step 2), the counselor decides whether the client's symptoms are due to the effects of a substance. If substance use is established, the clinician needs to determine what, when, and how much was taken and if it could mimic the presenting symptoms (First, 2014). Similarly (Step 3), the counselor determines whether the client's symptoms are due to the effects of a general medical condition, and if so, the clinician needs to examine its etiological relationship to the psychiatric symptoms to determine whether the general medical condition caused the psychiatric symptoms, the psychiatric symptoms caused the general medical condition, or the psychiatric symptoms and the general medical condition are coincidental (First, 2014).

TABLE 7.4 *DSM-5* Diagnostic Step Process: Rationale, Information to Review, and Determination

STEP	CONSIDER	RATIONALE	INFORMATION	DETERMINE
1	First	+ If the client is being dishonest, the clinician's ability to reach an accurate diagnosis is severely compromised.	+ Reason/referral + MCMI-IV Validity Scales	Validity
2	Always	+ Substances can produce almost any psychiatric symptom(s). + One of the most common diagnostic errors is missing a substance etiology.	+ Reason/referral + MCMI-IV Alcohol Use and Drug Use Scales + SASSI-4 + ASI	Rule-out
3	Always	+ General medical conditions often produce psychiatric symptoms. + Psychiatric symptoms often have an underlying general medical condition.	+ Reason/referral + Medical records	Rule-out
4	After rule-outs	+ Psychiatric disorders are arranged by diagnostic groupings.	+ Reason/referral + SCID-5 + SCL-90-R	Differential diagnosis
5	If NO primary diagnosis	+ Psychiatric disorders do not always conform to particular diagnostic patterns.	+ Reason/referral + Specific Instruments (e.g., PHQ-9, GAD-7)	Differential diagnosis
6	If NO diagnosis	+ Not all psychiatric symptoms warrant a mental disorder diagnosis.	+ Reason/referral + Client goals	V and/or Z codes

ASI, Addiction Severity Index; GAD-7, Generalized Anxiety Disorder Questionnaire; MCMI-IV, Millon Clinical Multiaxial Inventory-IV; PHQ-9, Public Health Questionnaire-Depression scale; SASSI-4, Adult Substance Abuse Subtle Screening Inventory-4; *SCID-5*, Structured Clinical Interview for *DSM-5*; SCL-90-R, Symptom Checklist-90-Revised.

In Step 4, the clinician must determine which of the *DSM-5* primary mental disorders best account for the client's presenting symptoms (First, 2014). The counselor would then conduct a differential diagnosis to ensure all potential disorders have been considered and ruled out in order to choose the correct diagnosis. If the client's clinical presentation (e.g., symptom pattern, severity, or duration) does not meet criteria for a specific *DSM-5* diagnosis, but includes clinically significant impairment in functioning, the clinician must determine (Step 5) whether the symptoms developed as a maladaptive response to (an *adjustment disorder*), or independent of (an *other specified* or *unspecified disorder*), a psychosocial stressor (First, 2014). If the clinician is able (or unable) to specify the reason(s) the clinical presentation does not meet criteria for a specific *DSM-5* disorder within a group (e.g., depressive disorders), a diagnosis of other specified (or unspecified) disorder is used. However, if the client does not meet criteria for an adjustment, other specified, or unspecified disorder, the clinician must determine (Step 6) whether the client even has a mental disorder (First, 2014). The *DSM-5* has a criterion requiring "clinically significant" distress/impairment for a diagnosis but fails to define clinical significance; counselors must use clinical judgment to make that determination.

Differential Diagnosis

Psychiatric disorders are mainly identified by their symptomatology. However, symptoms overlap across mental disorder groups. For example, psychotic symptoms can be found in schizophrenia spectrum and other psychotic, bipolar and related, and depressive disorders. Depressive symptoms can be found in depressive, bipolar and related, and schizophrenia spectrum and other psychotic disorders; and anxiety symptoms can be found in anxiety, depressive, and bipolar and related disorders. With a superficial review, they may look identical (see Table 7.3); however, upon closer investigation, they can be distinguishable (see Table 7.5).

In the *DSM-5*, grouped mental disorders tend to share psychiatric symptoms, while distinguishing them from other disorders. For example, schizophrenia spectrum and other psychotic

TABLE 7.5 Differentiating Symptoms Common to GAD, MDD, and BP Disorders Based on *DSM-5* Criteria

SYMPTOM	GAD	MDD (MDE)	BP (ME)
Difficulty concentrating	Difficulty concentrating (mind goes blank) (C3)	Diminished ability to think or concentrate (indecisiveness) (A8)	Easily distracted (difficulty focusing on one task) (B5)
Thought processes	Excessive anxiety and worry (apprehensive expectation) about a number of events or activities (e.g., work or school performance) (A)	Recurrent thoughts of death (not just fear of dying) or recurrent suicidal ideation (A9)	Thoughts race faster than they can be verbally expressed, or accelerated speech with abrupt shifts between topics (B4)
Irritable mood	Can be irritable (C4)	Can be irritable, though more depressed (A1)	Extremely irritable or euphoric (A)
Energy level	Tires easily (C2)	Constant fatigue or loss of energy (A6)	Subjective feeling of increased energy (A)
Psychomotor behavior	Seems more keyed up (C1)	Seems more withdrawn (A5)	Increase in risky behavior (B7)
Sleep disturbance	Insomnia (mostly difficulty falling asleep) (C6)	Hypersomnia or insomnia (more likely waking up too early) (A4)	Decreased need for sleep (energetic after sleeping 2–4 hours) (B2)
Impairment in functioning	Caused by anxiety, worry, or physical symptoms (D)	Caused by depressive symptoms (B)	Caused by manic mood disturbance (C)

BP, bipolar disorder; GAD, generalized anxiety disorder; MDD, major depressive disorder; MDE, major depressive episode; ME, manic episode.

SOURCE: Adapted from Singh, T., & Williams, K. (2006). Is it anxiety, depression, or bipolar disorder? *Current Psychiatry, 5*(8), 103, Table 2.

disorders share psychotic (e.g., delusions, hallucinations) features, bipolar and related disorders share manic (e.g., elevated/expansive mood and increased activity/energy) features, and depressive disorders share depressive (e.g., feelings of sadness, emptiness, or irritability) features. The similar psychiatric symptoms shared among and across disorders can make reaching an accurate diagnosis difficult. Therefore, counselors should perform a differential diagnosis (see Table 7.6) to determine which disorder is most appropriate.

TABLE 7.6 Differentiation Among and Across Psychiatric Disorders With Similar Symptomatology

PRIMARY DISORDER VS. POTENTIAL DISORDERS	DIFFERENTIATION	MAIN FEATURES OF PRIMARY DISORDER / MAIN FEATURES OF POTENTIAL DISORDERS
SCHIZOPHRENIA SPECTRUM AND PSYCHOTIC DISORDERS		
Schizophrenia vs.	NA	**Disturbance lasts at least 6 months (with at least 1 month of active-phase psychotic symptoms) and significant functional impairment in at least 1 major life area (e.g., work, interpersonal relations, self-care).**
Schizophreniform disorder	**Duration Functioning**	Equivalent symptomatic presentation (to schizophrenia) except for duration (<6 months) and no requirement of functional impairment/decline.
Schizoaffective disorder	**Concurrence**	Mood (i.e., manic or major depressive) episode and active-phase psychotic symptoms (i.e., schizophrenia) occur together (and preceded/followed by at least 2 weeks of delusions or hallucinations sans mood episode).
Substance/ medication-induced psychotic disorder	**Cause**	Delusions or hallucinations are a direct physiological consequence (intoxication or withdrawal) of substance (e.g., illicit drug, medication) use (or toxin exposure) and cease after removal of the agent.
Bipolar I disorder with psychotic features	**Concurrence**	Delusions or hallucinations occur exclusively during manic episode.
Major depressive disorder with psychotic features	**Concurrence**	Delusions or hallucinations occur exclusively during major depressive episode.
BIPOLAR AND RELATED DISORDERS		
Bipolar I disorder vs.	NA	**At least 1 manic episode (i.e., symptoms last at least 1 week) and significant impairment in social or occupational functioning, requiring hospitalization, or with psychotic features.**
Bipolar II disorder	**Duration Concurrence Exclusion**	Both (at least 1) hypomanic (i.e., symptoms last at least 4 consecutive days) and (at least 1) major depressive episodes, and no manic episodes.

(continued)

TABLE 7.6 Differentiation Among and Across Psychiatric Disorders With Similar Symptomatology (*continued*)

PRIMARY DISORDER VS. POTENTIAL DISORDERS	DIFFERENTIATION	MAIN FEATURES OF PRIMARY DISORDER / MAIN FEATURES OF POTENTIAL DISORDERS
Cyclothymic disorder	Duration Concurrence Exclusion	Numerous periods of both hypomanic and depressive symptoms for at least 2 years (with both hypomanic and depressive periods present at least 1 year and not symptom free for more than 2 months at a time), and no manic, hypomanic, or major depressive episodes.
Substance/medication-induced bipolar disorder	Cause	Mood disturbance (i.e., elevated, expansive, or irritable mood, with or without depressed mood) is a direct physiological consequence (intoxication or withdrawal) of substance (e.g., illicit drug, medication) use.
Major depressive disorder	Nonconcurrence	At least 1 major depressive episode, significant distress or impairment in social, occupational, or other area of functioning, and no manic episodes.
Schizoaffective disorder	Concurrence Nonconcurrence	Mood (i.e., manic or major depressive) episode and active-phase psychotic symptoms (i.e., schizophrenia) occur together (and preceded/followed by at least 2 weeks of delusions or hallucinations sans mood episode).
DEPRESSIVE DISORDERS		
Major depressive disorder vs.	NA	At least 1 major depressive episode, significant distress or impairment in social, occupational, or other area of functioning, and no manic or hypomanic episodes.
Persistent depressive disorder (dysthymia)	Duration	Depressed mood for most of the day, for more days than not, for at least 2 years (not symptom free for >2 months at a time), significant distress or impairment in social, occupational, or other area of functioning, and no manic or hypomanic episodes.
Substance/medication-induced depressive disorder	Cause	Mood disturbance (i.e., depressed mood or markedly diminished interest/pleasure in most/all activities) is a direct physiological consequence (intoxication or withdrawal) of substance (e.g., illicit drug, medication) use.
Bipolar II disorder	Concurrence	Both (at least 1) hypomanic (i.e., symptoms last at least 4 consecutive days) and (at least 1) major depressive episodes, and no manic episodes.
Cyclothymic disorder	Duration Concurrence Exclusion	Numerous periods of both hypomanic and depressive symptoms for at least 2 years (with both hypomanic and depressive periods present at least 1 year and not symptom free for more than 2 months at a time), and no manic, hypomanic, or major depressive episodes.
Schizoaffective disorder	Concurrence Nonconcurrence	Mood (i.e., manic or major depressive) episode and active-phase psychotic symptoms (i.e., schizophrenia) occur together (and preceded/followed by at least 2 weeks of delusions or hallucinations sans mood episode).

NOTE: This list is neither exhaustive nor comprehensive, but simply representative.

Some of the *DSM-5* diagnoses include subtypes, specifiers, and/or severity ratings in order to improve diagnostic utility, provide greater homogeneity of subgroupings, and communicate relevant treatment information. While *subtypes* are mutually exclusive and jointly exhaustive sub-groupings within a diagnosis, *specifiers* are not; *severity* ratings are used to indicate the intensity, frequency, and duration of a disorder (APA, 2013). Similarly, clinicians are instructed to "*Specify whether*" (i.e., pick one subtype), "*Specify*" or "*Specify if*" (i.e., pick as many specifiers as appropriate), and "*Specify* current severity" (i.e., pick the most appropriate level) in the criteria set. For example, for a diagnosis of schizoaffective disorder, the clinician would *Specify* whether: bipolar or depressive type; *Specify* if: with catatonia; and *Specify* current severity: of primary psychotic symptoms from 0 (*not present*) to 4 (*present and severe*).

Comorbidity

Differential diagnosis assumes that diagnoses are mutually exclusive, which *DSM-5* diagnoses (i.e., psychiatric disorders) are not; thus, more than one diagnosis can (and should) be given to clients, if (and when) appropriate. Although population estimates of co-occurring (i.e., comorbid) disorders is relatively low (<5%), estimates in clinical settings are much higher, usually closer to 50%. Among adults receiving treatment for a substance use disorder, more than half (53.5%) also have a mental disorder (Mericle, Ta, Holck, & Arria, 2012). Specifically, lifetime prevalence rates for co-occurring mental disorders for clients with substance use disorders range from 18% to 36% for mood disorders, 16% to 40% for anxiety disorders, 18% to 28% for schizophrenia, and 30% to 42% for personality disorders (Mericle et al., 2012; Rush & Koegl, 2008). However, comorbidity does not necessarily indicate causality. The possible relationships between the comorbid disorders ("A" and "B") fall into a few broad categories: (a) there is a *direct causal relationship* (e.g., A causes B, B causes A, or reciprocal causation); (b) they share *common factors* (e.g., an underlying condition "C" causes both A and B); (c) they are *alternate forms* of the same disorder (e.g., A and B belong to a syndrome that can be artificially split; they are different manifestations of a single disorder, actually A_1 and A_2 or B_1 and B_2; not comorbidity); (d) they are *artifactually enhanced by definitional overlap* (e.g., A and B have the same defining symptoms; if comorbidity remains after deleting overlapping symptoms, can reject artifactual comorbidity; the converse is not necessarily true—deleting symptoms changes definitions of the disorders); or (e) they co-occur by *chance* (First, 2014; Pennington, Willcutt, & Rhee, 2005). If more than one diagnosis is appropriate, they should be ordered based on the need of clinical attention (APA, 2013). The primary diagnosis would be the reason for the client's visit or the main focus of the treatment, followed by the secondary diagnosis, and any additional diagnoses.

Case Conceptualization

The diagnosis describes *what* happened, and the case conceptualization (or formulation) explains *why* it happened. A case conceptualization is a "clinician's collective understanding of the client's presenting problems as viewed through a particular theoretical orientation; as defined by the biological, psychological, and social contexts of the client; and as supported by a body of research and practice that links a set of co-occurring symptoms to a diagnosis and, ultimately, a treatment plan" (John & Segal, 2015, p. 448). It should identify the "5 Ps" (see Table 7.7): (a) *presenting* problems, (b) *predisposing* factors, (c) *precipitating* factors, (d) *perpetuating* factors, and (e) *protective* factors (Macneil, Hasty, Conus, & Berk, 2012), by incorporating biological, psychological, and social theories to help explain the relationships between the client's history and presentation (Kuyken, Padesky, & Dudley, 2009).

TABLE 7.7 The 5 Ps: Biopsychosocial Case Conceptualization/Formulation Matrix

"P" FACTORS	BIOLOGICAL FACTORS	PSYCHOLOGICAL FACTORS	SOCIAL FACTORS
Presenting Problems – What problems does the client identify?	Symptoms	Distress	Functional impairment
Predisposing Factors – What factors (i.e., over the course of the client's lifetime) contributed to the development of the problem?	Genetic Birth trauma Brain injury Illness Medication Drugs/alcohol Pain	Personality Defenses (unconscious) Coping strategies Self-esteem Body image Cognition Trauma	Socioeconomic status Culture Religion Spirituality
Precipitating Factors – Why now (i.e., what triggers or events exacerbated the problem)?	Medication Drugs/alcohol Trauma Acute illness Pain	Stage of life Loss/grief Treatment Stressors	Work Finances Connections Relationships
Perpetuating Factors – What factors (i.e., if not addressed) are likely to maintain (or worsen) the problem?	Any factors from above that are continuing	Any factors from above that are continuing	Any factors from above that are continuing
Protective Factors – What client strengths, social supports, or community resources can be drawn upon?	Physical health	Engagement Insight Adherence Coping strategies Intelligence	Group belonging and affiliations Family and social relationships

SOURCE: Adapted from Selzer, R., & Ellen, S. (2010). *Psych-Lite: Psychiatry that's easy to read.* (p. 22, Table 4.1). Sydney, Australia: McGraw-Hill.

The 5 Ps are time-oriented, representing different eras (i.e., *past*, *present*, and *future*). Presenting problems are identified through descriptive data (Kuyken et al., 2009) and include the diagnosis and client- and clinician-identified issues (*present*) as well as which difficulties should be included in the treatment (*future*) plan (Macneil et al., 2012). Relevant *DSM-5* information to consider are diagnostic and associated features, prevalence, culture- and gender-related diagnostic issues, suicide risk, differential diagnosis, and comorbidity (Gintner, 2015). The predisposing factors are assessed via longitudinal data (Kuyken et al., 2009) and comprise biological (e.g., genetic vulnerabilities), psychological (e.g., personality), and social (including cultural and environmental) factors (*past*) that may increase a person's risk of developing a specific mental disorder (Macneil et al., 2012). *DSM-5* information on development and course, risk and prognostic factors, and culture- and gender-related diagnostic issues should also be reviewed (Gintner, 2015). The precipitating factors are derived from cross-sectional data (Kuyken et al., 2009) and include significant biological (e.g., substance use), psychological (e.g., maladaptive coping strategies), and social (e.g., occupational stressors) events that preceded the onset (*past* or *present*) of the disorder (Macneil et al., 2012). Relevant *DSM-5* information to consider includes culture- and gender-related diagnostic issues (Gintner, 2015).

The perpetuating factors are identified through cross-sectional data (Kuyken et al., 2009) and comprise biological (e.g., ongoing substance use), psychological (e.g., repeating behavioral patterns), and social (e.g., enduring financial stressors) factors (*present*) that are likely to maintain (*future*) the current difficulties (Macneil et al., 2012). *DSM-5* information on development and course, risk and prognostic factors, culture- and gender-related diagnostic issues, functional consequences, and comorbidity should be reviewed (Gintner, 2015). The protective factors are identified through longitudinal data (Kuyken et al., 2009) and include biological (e.g., physical health), psychological (e.g., treatment engagement), and social (e.g., social support) strengths (*past* and *present*) that may buffer or mitigate (*present* and *future*) the negative impacts of the disorder (Macneil et al., 2012). Information on the *DSM-5* disorder pertaining to development and course, risk and prognostic factors, and culture- and gender-related diagnostic issues should also be considered (Gintner, 2015). Including protective factors in treatment plans can help reduce symptoms, increase resilience, foster optimism, and establish a positive therapeutic relationship (Kuyken et al., 2009; Macneil et al., 2012).

Treatment Plans and Interventions

Once rehabilitation and mental health counselors have completed the diagnosis and case conceptualization, they should have a hypothesized picture of the etiological and maintaining factors (see 5 Ps), which will inform treatment planning. The treatment plan should seek to address, reduce, manage, or resolve the client's issues. It should be individualized, developed with the client, and incorporate information from the assessment including client symptoms as well as the relevant history, age, gender, cultural identity, general health, coping and defensive factors, social environment, potential risk factors, and needs and goals. The treatment plan should also describe the type of therapy (e.g., cognitive behavioral therapy, interpersonal therapy) or interventions (e.g., individual therapy, family therapy), frequency (e.g., weekly, monthly) and duration (e.g., 3 sessions, 12 weeks) of visits, and referral for any adjunctive treatments (e.g., pharmacotherapy, 12-step program) recommended or indicate if no treatment is recommended. This will require thoughtful, comprehensive, and insightful efforts to ensure successful outcomes (Zuckerman, 2010). Given the shift toward accountability in mental healthcare, outcome measures should be incorporated into the treatment plan to demonstrate treatment effectiveness and revise the treatment plan as needed.

As counselors work to formulate the interventions, they should consider their client's strengths, resources, and motivation for engaging in treatment. The case conceptualization serves as a link for selecting specific interventions to address each presenting concern (Sperry, 2005). Selected interventions should be based on research evidence, tracked and evaluated with appropriate assessment measures, and updated as needed. Two clients (P and R) both diagnosed with major depressive disorder may be prescribed different psychotherapeutic interventions based on what caused their depression. For example, P's depression was caused and exacerbated by disturbed personal relationships, while R's depression reflects chronic unhappiness; P would benefit from interpersonal therapy (de Mello, de Jesus Mari, Bacaltchuk, Verdeli, & Neugebauer, 2005), while R would be a better candidate for mindfulness-based cognitive therapy (MBCT; Segal, Williams, & Teasdale, 2002). When client disorders are effectively treated, benefits can be tremendous. For example, persons with attention deficit/hyperactivity disorder (ADHD) who received stimulant treatment were less likely to develop a subsequent substance use disorder (Wilens, Faraone, Biederman, & Gunawardene, 2003).

Treatment plans and their associated interventions can also provide information that may be used to modify or change a diagnosis. For example, a client diagnosed with depression may be prescribed antidepressants by his or her physician, which usually works well for unipolar depression; however, if a client with bipolar disorder is treated with antidepressants, it can result in manic episodes and trigger rapid cycling (Ghaemi, Boiman, & Goodwin, 2000). Unfortunately, those who are prescribed treatments based on an incorrect diagnosis have less chance that their treatment will be successful. An effective treatment for borderline personality disorder is dialectical behavior therapy (DBT; Linehan et al., 2006), but for bipolar disorder, treatment is with lithium, which is not recommended to treat borderline personality disorder (Binks et al., 2006); thus, non-response could indicate a misdiagnosis. However, clients with bipolar disorder who had at least four depressive (or 12 manic) episodes were also less likely to respond to lithium (Swann, Bowden, Calabrese, Dilsaver, & Morris, 2000). Psychotherapy has even been found to be contraindicated for some client populations. Persons with bipolar disorder who had more than 12 episodes actually got worse with cognitive behavioral therapy (Scott et al., 2006). Similarly, critical incident stress management (CISM), when used to treat PTSD and anxiety symptoms in people who experienced extreme stress, resulted in an increase in trauma and anxiety scores (Bledsoe, 2003).

One way to reduce the possibility of negative psychotherapy effects is to screen for them during the assessment and prescribe a "trial of psychotherapy" if there is doubt (Crown, 1983). Counselors can create effective treatment goals using the SMART or SMARTER format. SMART goals are *specific* (e.g., clearly define what will be achieved), *measurable* (e.g., indicate criteria needed for goal achievement), *action-oriented* (e.g., identify actions needed to achieve goal), *realistic* (e.g., potential for achieving goal is reasonable), and *time-bound* (e.g., estimate timeline for achieving goal, including benchmarks). Similarly, SMARTER goals are *specific, measurable, action-oriented, realistic, time-bound, evaluated* (e.g., goal achievement, including progress, is regularly assessed), and *readjusted* (e.g., modifications to treatment plan are made as needed). Without the establishment of SMART/SMARTER goals, counselors may set goals that are not achievable, cannot be measured, or are not based in evidence, thereby opening themselves and their clients to potential ethical, safety, or legal issues; however, with their implementation, counselors can monitor client progress, make amends as needed, and share these milestones with their clients.

▪ Conclusion

In conducting psychological assessments to identify psychopathology, it is essential that clinicians continue to engage in activities that help them remain current on the state of the science. As demonstrated in this chapter, the models to conceptualize psychopathology, the diagnostic criteria, and the instruments used to inform clinicians in arriving at diagnoses and treatment plans continue to evolve. The assessment of psychopathology is rooted in knowledge of the empirical evidence of the diagnostic criteria, and a lack of current information of the empirical evidence can lead to faulty application of assessments or incorrect conclusions regarding diagnoses.

As stated earlier in this chapter, the *DSM-5* does not make diagnoses. Rather, diagnoses are rendered by competent clinicians who implement systematic and objective assessment procedures—processes that are based on evidence from numerous sources but ultimately arranged by the clinician to support or rule out specific diagnoses. Interviews, behavioral observations, self-report inventories, psychological testing, historical/medical record review, functional assessment, and clinical judgment are all necessary in the formation of a diagnostic picture that provides an accurate depiction of clients' current issues and the selection of interventions that are likely to be the most effective.

References

Ahrnsbrak, R., Bose, J., Hedden, S. L., Lipari, R. N., & Park-Lee, E. (2017). *Key substance use and mental health indicators in the United States: Results from the 2016 National Survey on Drug Use and Health.* Retrieved from https://www.samhsa.gov/data/sites/default/files/NSDUH-FFR1-2016/NSDUH -FFR1-2016.htm

Altamura, A. C., Buoli, M., Caldiroli, A., Caron, L., Cumerlato Melter, C., Dobrea, C., . . . Zanelli Quarantini, F. (2015). Misdiagnosis, duration of untreated illness (DUI) and outcome in bipolar patients with psychotic symptoms: A naturalistic study. *Journal of Affective Disorders, 182,* 70–75. doi:10.1016/j.jad.2015.04.024

American Counseling Association. (2014). *2014 ACA code of ethics.* Alexandria, VA: Author.

American Educational Research Association, American Psychological Association, National Council on Measurement in Education, Joint Committee on Standards for Educational, & Psychological Testing (US). (2014). *Standards for educational and psychological testing* (7th ed.). Washington, DC: American Educational Research Association.

American Mental Health Counselors Association. (2015). *AMHCA code of ethics: Revised October 2015.* Alexandria, VA: Author.

American Psychiatric Association. (1994). Social and Occupational Functioning Assessment Scale (SOFAS). In *Diagnostic and statistical manual of mental disorders* (4th ed., pp. 760–761). Washington, DC: Author.

American Psychiatric Association. (2000). *Diagnostic and statistical manual of mental disorders* (4th ed., text rev.). Washington, DC: Author.

American Psychiatric Association. (2013). *Diagnostic and statistical manual of mental disorders* (5th ed.). Arlington, VA: Author.

Andersen, J., Larsen, J. K., Kørner, A., Nielsen, B. M., Schultz, V., Behnke, K., & Bjørum, N. (1986). The Brief Psychiatric Rating Scale: Schizophrenia, reliability and validity studies. *Nordisk Psykiatrisk Tidsskrift, 40,* 135–138. doi:10.3109/08039488609096456

Arnau, R. C., Meagher, M. W., Norris, M. P., & Bramson, R. (2001). Psychometric evaluation of the Beck Depression Inventory-II with primary care medical patients. *Health Psychology, 20,* 112–119. doi:10.1037//0278-6133.20.2.112

Beck, A. T., Steer, R. A., & Brown, G. K. (1996). *BDI-II manual.* San Antonio, TX: Psychological Corporation.

Beck, A. T., Steer, R. A., & Brown, G. K. (2000). *BDI-Fast Screen for Medical Patients: Manual.* San Antonio, TX: Psychological Corporation.

Beck, A. T., Ward, C. H., Mendelson, M., Mock, J., & Erbaugh, J. (1961). An inventory for measuring depression. *Archives of General Psychiatry, 4,* 561–571.

Beck, J. S., Beck, A. T., Jolly, J. B., & Steer, R. A. (2005). *Beck Youth Inventories-Second Edition for Children and Adolescents manual.* San Antonio, TX: PsychCorp.

Bell, M., Milstein, R., Beam-Goulet, J., Lysaker, P., & Cicchetti, D. (1992). The positive and negative syndrome scale and the brief psychiatric rating scale: Reliability, comparability, and predictive validity. *The Journal of Nervous and Mental Disease, 180,* 723–728. doi:10.1097/ 00005053-199211000-00007

Benson, N. (2010). Types of tests and assessments. In E. Mpofu & T. Oakland (Eds.), *Assessment in rehabilitation and health* (pp. 72–90). Upper Saddle River, NJ: Merrill.

Binks, C. A., Fenton, M., McCarthy, L., Lee, T., Adams, C. E., & Duggan, C. (2006). Pharmacological interventions for people with borderline personality disorder. *Cochrane Database Systematic Review, 25*(1), CD005653. doi:10.1002/14651858.cd005653

Bledsoe, B. E. (2003). Critical incident stress management (CISM): Benefit or risk for emergency services? *Prehospital Emergency Care, 7,* 272–279. doi:10.1080/10903120390936941

Buckley, M. R. (2014). Back to basics: Using the DSM-5 to benefit clients. *The Professional Counselor, 4,* 159–165. doi:10.15241/mrb.4.3.159

Cacciola, J. S., Alterman, A. I., Habing, B., & McLellan, A. T. (2011). Recent status scores for version 6 of the Addiction Severity Index (ASI-6). *Addiction, 106,* 1588–1602. doi:10.1111/j.1360-0443.2011.03482.x

Camara, W. (2014, September 12). *Standards for educational and psychological testing: Historical notes.* Paper presented at the Capitol Hill Briefing: Standards for Educational and Psychological Testing.

Washington, DC: American Educational Research Association, American Psychological Association, National Council on Measurement in Education. Retrieved from http://www.aera.net/Portals/38/docs/Outreach/Standards_Hill_Briefing_Slides_FINAL.pdf?timestamp=1410876719244

Chan, F., Gelman, J. S., Ditchman, N., Kim, J.-H., & Chiu, C.-Y. (2009). The World Health Organization ICF model as a conceptual framework of disability. In F. Chan, E. D. Cardoso, & J. A. Chronister (Eds.), *Understanding psychosocial adjustment to chronic illness and disability: A handbook for evidence-based practitioners in rehabilitation* (pp. 23–50). New York, NY: Springer Publishing Company.

Clark, L. A., Cuthbert, B., Lewis-Fernández, R., Narrow, W. E., & Reed, G. M. (2017). Three approaches to understanding and classifying mental disorder: ICD-11, DSM-5, and the National Institute of Mental Health's Research Domain Criteria (RDoC). *Psychological Science in the Public Interest, 18*(2), 72–145. doi:10.1177/1529100617727266

Commission on Rehabilitation Counselor Certification. (2015). *Code of professional ethics for rehabilitation counselors.* Schaumburg, IL: Author.

Council for Accreditation of Counseling and Related Educational Programs. (2015). *2016 CACREP standards.* Alexandria, VA: Author.

Courtney-Long, E. A., Carroll, D. D., Zhang, Q. C., Stevens, A. C., Griffin-Blake, S., Armour, B. S., & Campbell, V. A. (2015). Prevalence of disability and disability type among adults—United States, 2013. *Morbidity and Mortality Weekly Report, 64*, 777–783. doi:10.15585/mmwr.MM6429a2

Crown, S. (1983). Contraindications and dangers of psychotherapy. *British Journal of Psychiatry, 143*, 436–441. doi:10.1192/bjp.143.5.436

de Mello, M. F., de Jesus Mari, J., Bacaltchuk, J., Verdeli, H., & Neugebauer, R. (2005). A systematic review of research findings on the efficacy of interpersonal therapy for depressive disorders. *European Archives of Psychiatry and Clinical Neuroscience, 255*, 75–82. doi:10.1007/s00406-004-0542-x

Denis, C. M., Cacciola, J. S., & Alterman, A. I. (2013). Addiction Severity Index (ASI) summary scores: Comparison of the recent status scores of the ASI-6 and the composite scores of the ASI-5. *Journal of Substance Abuse Treatment, 45*, 444–450. doi:10.1080/10550490500528316

Depue, R. A., Krauss, S., Spoont, M. R., & Arbisi, P. (1989). General behavior inventory identification of unipolar and bipolar affective conditions in a nonclinical university population. *Journal of Abnormal Psychology, 98*, 117–126. doi:10.1037//0021-843x.98.2.117

Depue, R. A., Slater, J. F., Wolfstetter-Kausch, H., Klein, D., Goplerud, E., & Farr. D. (1981). A behavioral paradigm for identifying persons at risk for bipolar depressive disorder: A conceptual framework and five validation studies. *Journal of Abnormal Psychology, 90*, 381–437. doi:10.1037/0021-843x.90.5.381

Derogatis, L. R. (1983). *SCL-90-R: Administration, scoring, and procedures manual-II for the R(evised) version and other instruments of the Psychopathology Rating Scale series.* Towson, MD: Clinical Psychometric Research.

Derogatis, L. R. (1993). *Brief Symptom Inventory (BSI): Administration, scoring, and procedures manual* (3rd ed.). Minneapolis, MN: National Computer Systems.

Derogatis, L. R. (2001). *Brief Symptom Inventory-18 (BSI-18): Administration, scoring, and procedures manual.* Minneapolis, MN: NCS Pearson.

Derogatis, L. R., & Fitzpatrick, M. (2004). The SCL-90-R, the Brief Symptom Inventory (BSI), and the BSI-18. In M. E. Maruish (Ed.), *The use of psychological testing for treatment planning and outcome assessment* (3rd ed., pp. 1–41). Mahwah, NJ: Lawrence Erlbaum Associates.

Derogatis, L. R., Lipman, R. S., Rickels, K., Uhlenhuth, E. H., & Covi, L. (1974). The Hopkins Symptom Checklist (HSCL): A self-report symptom inventory. *Behavioral Scientist, 19*, 1–15. doi:10.1002/bs.3830190102

Durand, V. M., & Crimmins, D. B. (1988). *The Motivation Assessment Scale (MAS) administration guide.* Topeka, KS: Monaco & Associates.

Engel, G. (1977). The need for a new medical model: A challenge for biomedicine. *Science, 196*, 129–136.

First, M. B. (2014). *DSM-5 handbook of differential diagnosis.* Arlington, VA: American Psychiatric Association.

First, M. B., Skodol, A. E., Bender, D. S., & Oldham, J. M. (2018). *Structured Clinical Interview for the DSM-5® Alternative Model for Personality Disorders (SCID-5-AMPD) module III: Personality Disorders (including personality disorder-trait specified).* Arlington, VA: American Psychiatric Association.

First, M. B., Williams, J. B. W., Benjamin, L. S., & Spitzer, R. L. (2016). *Structured Clinical Interview for DSM-5® Personality Disorders (SCID-5-PD).* Arlington, VA: American Psychiatric Association.

First, M. B., Williams, J. B. W., Karg, R. S., & Spitzer, R. L. (2015a). *Structured Clinical Interview for DSM-5® Disorders—Clinical Trials version (SCID-5-CT)*. Arlington, VA: American Psychiatric Association.

First, M. B., Williams, J. B. W., Karg, R. S., & Spitzer, R. L. (2015b). *Structured Clinical Interview for DSM-5® Disorders—Research Version (SCID-5-RV)*. Arlington, VA: American Psychiatric Association.

First, M. B., Williams, J. B. W., Karg, R. S., & Spitzer, R. L. (2016). *Structured Clinical Interview for DSM-5® Disorders—Clinician Version (SCID-5-CV)*. Arlington, VA: American Psychiatric Association.

Ghaemi, S. N., Boiman, E. E., & Goodwin, F. K. (2000). Diagnosing bipolar disorder and the effect of antidepressants: A naturalistic study. *Journal of Clinical Psychiatry, 61,* 804–808. doi:10.4088/jcp.v61n1013

Ghaemi, S. N., Miller, C. J., Berv, D. A., Klugman, J., Rosenquist, K. J., & Pies, R. W. (2005). Sensitivity and specificity of a new bipolar spectrum diagnostic scale. *Journal of Affective Disorders, 84,* 273–277. doi:10.1016/S0165-0327(03)00196-4

Gilson, S. F., DePoy, E., & Cramer, E. P. (2001). Linking the assessment of self-reported functional capacity with abuse experiences of women with disabilities. *Violence Against Women, 7,* 418–431. doi:10.1177/10778010122182532

Gintner, G. G. (2015, July). *Case formulation using DSM-5.* Paper presented at the annual conference of the American Mental Health Counselors Association, Philadelphia, PA.

Goldman, H. H., Skodol, A. E., & Lave, T. R. (1992). Revising Axis V for DSM-IV: A review of measures of social functioning. *American Journal of Psychiatry, 149,* 1148–1156. doi:10.1176/ajp.149.9.1148

Granger, C. V. (1984). A conceptual model for functional assessment. In C. V. Granger & G. E. Gresham (Eds.), *Functional assessment in rehabilitation medicine* (pp. 14–25). Baltimore, MD: Williams & Wilkins.

Hanley, G. P., Iwata, B. A., & McCord, B. E. (2003). Functional analysis of problem behavior: A review. *Journal of Applied Behavior Analysis, 36,* 147–185. doi:10.1901/jaba.2003.36-147

Harvard Medical School. (2007a). [Table 1. Lifetime prevalence of DSM-IV/WMH-CIDI disorders by sex and cohort1 (n = 9282) July 19, 2007]. *National Comorbidity Survey (NCS).* Retrieved from https://www.hcp.med.harvard.edu/ncs/ftpdir/NCS-R_Lifetime_Prevalence_Estimates.pdf

Harvard Medical School. (2007b). [Table 2. 12-month prevalence of DSM-IV/WMH-CIDI disorders by sex and cohort1 (n = 9282) July 19, 2007]. *National Comorbidity Survey (NCS).* Retrieved from https://www.hcp.med.harvard.edu/ncs/ftpdir/NCS-R_12-month_Prevalence_Estimates.pdf

Hayes, S. C., Wilson, K. G., Gifford, E. V., Follette, V. M., & Strosahl, K. (1996). Experiential avoidance and behavioral disorders: A functional dimensional approach to diagnosis and treatment. *Journal of Consulting and Clinical Psychology, 64,* 1152–1168. doi:10.1037/0022-006x.64.6.1152

Haynes, S. N., Richard, D. C. S., & Kubany, E. S. (1995). Content validity in psychological assessment: A functional approach to concepts and methods. *Psychological Assessment, 7,* 238–247. doi:10.1037/1040-3590.7.3.238

Hempel, C. G. (1959). Some problems of taxonomy. In *American Psychopathological Association: Report of work conference on problems of field studies in mental disorders.* New York, NY: Grune & Stratton.

Hirschfeld, R. M. A., Lewis, L., & Vornik, L. A. (2003). Perceptions and impact of bipolar disorder: How far have we really come? Results of the National Depressive and Manic-Depressive Association 2000 Survey of Individuals with Bipolar Disorder. *Journal of Clinical Psychiatry, 64,* 161–174. doi:10.4088/jcp.v64n0209

Indices. (1979). *Functional limitations: A state of the art review.* Falls Church, VA: Author.

John, S., & Segal, D. L. (2015). Case conceptualization. In R. L. Cautin & S. O. Lilienfeld (Eds.), *The encyclopedia of clinical psychology* (Vol. 1, pp. 448–452). Hoboken, NJ: John Wiley & Sons. doi:10.1002/9781118625392.wbecp106

Kabacoff, R. I., Segal, D. L., Hersen, M., & van Hasselt, V. B. (1997). Psychometric properties and diagnostic utility of the Beck Anxiety Inventory and the State-Trait Anxiety Inventory with older adult psychiatric outpatients. *Journal of Anxiety Disorders, 11,* 33–47.

Kay, S. R., Fiszbein, A., & Opler, L. A. (1987). The Positive and Negative Syndrome Scale (PANSS) for schizophrenia. *Schizophrenia Bulletin, 13,* 261–276. doi:10.1093/schbul/13.2.261

Kienle, G. S., & Kiene, H. (2011). Clinical judgement and the medical profession. *Journal of Evaluation in Clinical Practice, 17,* 621–627. doi:10.1111/j.1365-2753.2010.01560.x

Klein, D. N., Dickstein, S., Taylor, E. B., & Harding, K. (1989). Identifying chronic affective disorders in out-patients: Validation of the General Behavior Inventory. *Journal of Consulting and Clinical Psychology, 57,* 106–111. doi:10.1037//0022-006x.57.1.106

Knight, R. G., Waal-Manning, H. J., & Spears, G. F. (1983). Some norms and reliability data for the State-Trait Anxiety Inventory and the Zung Self-Rating Depression scale. *British Journal of Clinical Psychology, 22*, 245–249. doi:10.1111/j.2044-8260.1983.tb00610.x

Kosten, T. R., Rounsaville, B. J., & Kleber, H. D. (1983). Concurrent validity of the Addiction Severity Index. *Journal of Nervous and Mental Disease, 171*, 606–610. doi:10.1097/00005053-198310000-00003

Kroenke, K., Spitzer, R. L., & Williams, J. B. W. (2001). The PHQ-9: Validity of a brief depression severity measure. *Journal of General Internal Medicine, 16*, 606–613. doi:10.1046/j.1525-1497.2001.016009606.x

Kroenke, K., Spitzer, R. L., Williams, J. B. W., Monahan, P. O., & Löwe, B. (2007). Anxiety disorders in primary care: Prevalence, impairment, comorbidity, and detection. *Archives of Internal Medicine, 146*, 317–325. doi:10.7326/0003-4819-146-5-200703060-00004

Krueger, R. F., & Markon, K. E. (2008). Understanding psychopathology: Melding behavior genetics, personality, and quantitative psychology to develop an empirically based model. *Current Directions in Psychological Science, 15*(3), 113–117. doi:10.1111/j.0963-7214.2006.00418.x

Kuyken, W., Padesky, C. A., & Dudley, R. (2009). *Collaborative case conceptualization: Working effectively with clients in cognitive-behavioral therapy.* New York, NY: Guilford Publications.

Lazowski, L. E., & Geary, B. B. (2019). Validation of the adult Substance Abuse Subtle Screening Inventory-4 (SASSI-4). *European Journal of Psychological Assessment, 35*, 86–97. doi:10.1027/1015-5759/a000359

Lazowski, L. E., Kimmell, K. S., & Baker, S. L. (2016). *The Adult Substance Abuse Subtle Screening Inventory-4 (SASSI-4) user guide & manual.* Springville, IN: The SASSI Institute.

Linehan, M. M., Comtois, K. A., Murray, A. M., Brown, M. Z., Gallop, R. J., Heard, H. L., … Lindenboim, N. (2006). Two-year randomized controlled trial and follow-up of dialectical behavior therapy vs therapy by experts for suicidal behaviors and borderline personality disorder. *Archives of General Psychiatry, 63*, 757–766. doi:10.1001/archpsyc.63.7.757

Lukoff, D., Nuechterlein, K. H., & Ventura, J. (1986). Manual for expanded Brief Psychiatric Rating Scale. *Schizophrenia Bulletin, 12*, 594–602.

Macneil, C. A., Hasty, M. K., Conus, P., & Berk, M. (2012). Is diagnosis enough to guide interventions in mental health? Using case formulation in clinical practice. *BMC Medicine, 10*(111), 1–3. doi:10.1186/1741-7015-10-111

Mallon, J. C., Klein, D. N., Bornstein, R. F., & Slater, J. F. (1986). Discriminant validity of the General Behavior Inventory: An outpatient study. *Journal of Personality Assessment, 50*, 568–577. doi:10.1207/s15327752jpa5004_4

Marteau, T. M., & Bekker, H. (1992). The development of a six-item short-form of the state scale of the Spielberger State—Trait Anxiety Inventory (STAI). *British Journal of Clinical Psychology, 31*, 310–306. doi:10.1111/j.2044-8260.1992.tb00997.x

McLellan, A. T., Cacciola, J. C., Alterman, A. I., Rikoon, S. H., & Carise, D. (2006). The Addiction Severity Index at 25: Origins, contributions and transitions. *American Journal on Addictions, 15*, 113–124. doi:10.1080/10550490500528316

McLellan, A. T., Luborsky, L., Cacciola, J., Griffith, J., Evans, F., Barr, H. L., & O'Brien, C. P. (1985). New data from the Addiction Severity Index: Reliability and validity in three centers. *Journal of Nervous and Mental Disease, 173*, 412–423. doi:10.1097/00005053-198507000-00005

McLellan, A. T., Luborsky, L., Woody, G. E., & O'Brien, C. P. (1980). An improved diagnostic evaluation instrument for substance abuse patients: The Addiction Severity Index. *Journal of Nervous and Mental Disease, 168*, 26–33. doi:10.1097/00005053-198001000-00006

Mericle, A. A., Ta, V. M., Holck, P., & Arria, A. M. (2012). Prevalence, patterns, and correlates of co-occurring substance use and mental disorders in the US: Variations by race/ethnicity. *Comprehensive Psychiatry, 53*, 657–665. doi:10.1016/j.comppsych.2011.10.002

Miller, C. J., Ghaemi, S. N., Klugman, J., Berv, D. A., & Pies, R. W. (2002, May). *Utility of Mood Disorder Questionnaire and Bipolar Spectrum Diagnostic Scale.* Poster presented at the 155th annual meeting of the American Psychiatric Association, Philadelphia, PA.

Miller, F. G., & Lazowski, L. E. (2001). *The Adolescent Substance Abuse Subtle Screening Inventory-A2 (SASSI-A2) manual.* Springville, IN: The SASSI Institute.

Miller, G. A. (1985). *The Substance Abuse Subtle Screening Inventory (SASSI) manual.* Springville, IN: The SASSI Institute.

Millon, T. (1977). *Millon Clinical Multiaxial Inventory Manual.* Minneapolis, MN: National Computer Systems.

Millon, T. (2011). *Disorders of personality: Introducing a DSM/ICD spectrum from normal to abnormal.* Hoboken, NJ: Wiley.

Millon, T., Grossman, S., & Millon, C. (2015). *Millon Clinical Multiaxial Inventory-IV (MCMI-IV): Manual.* Bloomington, MN: NCS Pearson.

Mitchell, A. J., Vaze, A., & Rao, S. (2009). Clinical diagnosis of depression in primary care: A meta-analysis. *The Lancet, 374,* 609–619. doi:10.1016/S0140-6736(09)60879-5

Mpofu, E., Oakland, T., Herbert, J. T., & O'Donnell, P. J. (2010). Testing and assessment: History, current context, and prevailing issues. In E. Mpofu & T. Oakland (Eds.), *Assessment in rehabilitation and health* (pp. 3–21). Upper Saddle River, NJ: Merrill.

Multi-Health Systems. (n.d.). *Qualification criteria & who can order.* Retrieved from https://www.mhs .com/support/qual-criteria

National Board for Certified Counselors. (2016). *National Board for Certified Counselors (NBCC) code of ethics.* Greensboro, NC: Author.

Ormel, J., Koeter, M. W. J., van den Brink, W., & van de Willige, G. (1991). Management, and course of anxiety and depression in general practice. *Archives of General Psychiatry, 48,* 700–706. doi:10.1001/ archpsyc.1991.01810320024004

Overall, J. E., & Gorham, D. R. (1962). The Brief Psychiatric Rating Scale. *Psychological Reports, 10,* 799–812. doi:10.2466/pr0.1962.10.3.799

Overall, J. E, Hollister, L. E, & Pichot, P. (1967). Major psychiatric disorders: A four-dimensional model. *Archives of General Psychiatry, 16,* 146–151. doi:10.1001/archpsyc.1967.01730200014003

Paris, J. (2010). Biopsychosocial models and psychiatric diagnosis. In T. Millon, R. F. Krueger, & E. Simonsen (Eds.), *Contemporary directions in psychopathology: Scientific foundations of the DSM-V and ICD-11* (pp. 473–482). New York, NY: Guilford Press.

Pearson. (2018). *Clinical assessment: Qualifications policy.* Retrieved from https://www.pearsonclinical .com/qualifications.html

Pennington, B. F., Willcutt, E., & Rhee, S. H. (2005). Analyzing comorbidity. *Advances in Child Development Behavior, 33,* 263–304. doi:10.1016/S0065-2407(05)80010-2

Peralta, V., & Cuesta, M. J. (1994). Psychometric properties of the Positive and Negative Syndrome Scale (PANSS) in schizophrenia. *Psychiatry Research, 53,* 31–40. doi:10.1016/0165-1781(94)90093-0

Peterson, D. B. (2005). International Classification of Functioning, Disability and Health: An introduction for rehabilitation psychologists. *Rehabilitation Psychology, 50,* 105–112. doi:10.1037 /0090-5550.50.2.105

Psychological Assessment Resources. (2018). *Qualification levels.* Retrieved from https://www.parinc .com/Support/Qualification-Levels

Rush, B., & Koegl, C. J. (2008). Prevalence and profile of people with co-occurring mental and substance use disorders within a comprehensive mental health system. *Canadian Journal of Psychiatry, 53,* 810–821. doi:10.1177/070674370805301207

Samet, S., Waxman, R., Hatzenbuehler, M., & Hasin, D. S. (2007). Assessing addiction: Concepts and instruments. *Addiction Science and Clinical Practice, 4,* 19–31. doi:10.1151/ascp074119

Schultz, J. S., Stensland, M. D., & Frytak, J. R. (2008). Diagnoses of unipolar depression following initial identification of bipolar disorder: A common and costly misdiagnosis. *Journal of Clinical Psychiatry, 69,* 749–758. doi:10.4088/jcp.v69n0508

Schwitzer, A. M., & Rubin, L. C. (2012). Clinical thinking skills: Diagnosis, case conceptualization, and treatment planning. In *Diagnosis and treatment planning skills for mental health professionals: A popular culture casebook approach* (pp. 27–40). Thousand Oaks, CA: Sage.

Scott, J., Paykel, E., Morriss, R., Bentall, R., Kinderman, P., Johnson, T., . . . Hayhurst, H. (2006). Cognitive-behavioural therapy for severe and recurrent bipolar disorders: Randomised controlled trial. *British Journal of Psychiatry, 188,* 313–320. doi:10.1192/bjp.188.4.313

Segal, Z. V., Williams, J. M. G., & Teasdale, J. D. (2002). *Mindfulness-based cognitive therapy for depression: A new approach to preventing relapse.* New York, NY: Guilford Press.

Selzer, R., & Ellen, S. (2010). *Psych-Lite: Psychiatry that's easy to read.* Sydney, Australia: McGraw-Hill.

Shankman, S. A., Funkhouser, C. J., Lerner, D., & Hee, D. (2018). Reliability and validity of severity dimensions of psychopathology assessed using the Structured Clinical Interview for DSM-5 (SCID). *International Journal Methods of Psychiatric Research, 27*(e1590), 1–12. doi:10.1002/mpr.1590

Shen, H., Zhang, L., Xu, C., Zhu, J., Chen, M., & Fang, Y. (2018). Analysis of misdiagnosis of bipolar disorder in an outpatient setting. *Shanghai Archives of Psychiatry, 30,* 93–101. doi:10.11919/j.issn .1002-0829.217080

Simonsen, E. (2010). The integration of categorical and dimensional approaches to psychopathology. In T. Millon, R. F. Krueger, & E. Simonsen (Eds.), *Contemporary directions in psychopathology: Scientific foundations of the DSM-V and ICD-11* (pp. 350–361). New York, NY: Guilford Press.

Singh, T., & Williams, K. (2006). Is it anxiety, depression, or bipolar disorder? *Current Psychiatry, 5*(8), 95–104.

Smart, J. F., & Smart, D. W. (2006). Models of disability: Implications for the counseling profession. *Journal of Counseling & Development, 84,* 29–40. doi:10.1002/j.1556-6678.2006.tb00377.x

Sperry, L. (2005). Case conceptualizations: The missing link between theory and practice. *The Family Journal, 13,* 71–76. doi:10.1177/1066480704270104

Spielberger, C. D. (1973). *The State-Trait Anxiety Inventory for Children: Preliminary manual.* Palo Alto, CA: Consulting Psychologists Press.

Spielberger, C. D., Gorsuch, R. L., & Lushene, R.E. (1970). *Test manual for the State-Trait Anxiety Inventory.* Palo Alto, CA: Consulting Psychologists Press.

Spielberger, C. D., Gorsuch, R. L., Lushene, R., Vagg, P. R., & Jacobs, G. A. (1983). *Manual for the State-Trait Anxiety Inventory.* Palo Alto, CA: Consulting Psychologists Press.

Spitzer, R. L., Kroenke, K., & Williams, J. B. W. (1999). Validation and utility of a self-report version of PRIME-MD: The PHQ primary care study. *Journal of the American Medical Association, 282,* 1737–1744. doi:10.1001/jama.282.18.1737

Spitzer, R. L., Kroenke, K., Williams, J. B. W., & Löwe, B. (2006). A brief measure for assessing generalized anxiety disorder. *Archives of Internal Medicine, 166,* 1092–1097. doi:10.1001/archinte.166.10.1092

Spitzer, R. L., & Williams, J. B. (1984). *Structured Clinical Interview for DSM-III disorders.* New York: Biometrics Research Development, New York State Psychiatric Institute.

Spitzer, R. L., Williams, J. B., Kroenke, K., Linzer, M., deGruy, F. V., 3rd, Hahn, S. R., . . . Johnson, J. G. (1994). Utility of a new procedure for diagnosing mental disorders in primary care: The PRIME-MD 1000 study. *Journal of the American Medical Association, 272,* 1749–1756. doi:10.1001/jama.272.22.1749

Steer, R. A., Ball, R., Ranieri, W. F., & Beck, A. T. (1999). Dimensions of the Beck Depression Inventory-II in clinically depressed outpatients. *Journal of Clinical Psychology, 55,* 117–118. doi:10.1002/(SICI) 1097-4679(199901)55:1<117::AID-JCLP12>3.0.CO;2-A

Steer, R. A., Rissmiller, D. J., & Beck, A. T. (2000). Use of the Beck Depression Inventory-II with depressed geriatric inpatients. *Behaviour Research and Therapy, 38,* 311–318. doi:10.1016/s0005-7967(99)00068-6

Stein, D. J. (2012). Dimensional or categorical: Different classifications and measures of anxiety and depression. *Medicographia, 34,* 270–275. Retrieved from https://www.medicographia.com/2013/01/ dimensional-or-categorical-different-classifications-and-measures-of-anxietyand-depression/

Stensland, M. D., Schultz. J. S., & Frytak, J. R. (2010). Depression diagnoses following the identification of bipolar disorder: Costly incongruent diagnoses. *BMC Psychiatry, 10*(39), 1–8. doi:10.1186/1471-244X-10-39

Swann, A. C., Bowden, C. L., Calabrese, J. R., Dilsaver, S. C., & Morris, D. D. (2000). Mania: Differential effects of previous depressive and manic episodes on response to treatment. *Acta Scandinavica Psychiatrica, 101,* 444–451.

VandenBos, G. R. (Ed.). (2007). *APA dictionary of psychology.* Washington, DC: American Psychological Association.

Ventura, J., Lukoff, D., Nuechterlein, K. H., Liberman, R. P., Green, M., & Shaner, A. (1993). A manual for the expanded Brief Psychiatric Rating Scale. *International Journal of Methods in Psychiatric Research, 3,* 227–244.

Vermani, M., Marcus, M., & Katzman, M. A. (2011). Rates of detection of mood and anxiety disorders in primary care: A descriptive, cross-sectional study. *Primary Care Companion CNS Disorders, 13*(2), e1–e10. doi:10.4088/PCC.10m01013

Western Psychological Services. (2018). *Qualification guidelines.* Retrieved from https://www .wpspublish.com/app/HelpWithShopping/PurchasingQualifications

Wilens, T. E., Faraone, S. V., Biederman, J., & Gunawardene, S. (2003). Does stimulant therapy of attention-deficit/hyperactivity disorder beget later substance abuse? A meta-analytic review of the literature. *Pediatrics, 111,* 179–185. doi:10.1542/peds.111.1.179

Winningham, N., & Lazowski, L. E. (2010). *The Substance Abuse in Vocational Rehabilitation-Screener2 (SAVR-S2) user's guide*. Springville, IN: SASSI Institute.

Winningham, N., & Lazowski, L. E. (2012). *The Substance Abuse Screener in American Sign Language (SAS-ASL) user's guide*. Springville, IN: SASSI Institute.

Wittchen, H.-U., Kessler, R. C., Beesdo, K., Krause, P., Höfler, M., & Hoyer, J. (2002). Generalized anxiety and depression in primary care: Prevalence, recognition, and management. *Journal of Clinical Psychiatry, 63*(Suppl. 8), 24–34.

World Health Organization. (2001). *International classification of functioning, disability, and health: ICF*. Geneva, Switzerland: Author. Retrieved from http://www.who.int/classification/icf

World Health Organization. (2018). *Classifications: ICD-11 is here!* Retrieved from http://www.who.int/classifications/icd/en

Youngstrom, E. A., Findling, R. L., Danielson, C. K., & Calabrese, J. R. (2001). Discriminative validity of parent report of hypomanic and depressive symptoms on the General Behavior Inventory. *Psychological Assessment, 13*, 267–276. doi:10.1037//1040-3590.13.2.267

Youngstrom, E. A., Frazier, T. W., Demeter, C., Calabrese, J. R., & Findling, R. L. (2008). Developing a 10-item mania scale from the Parent General Behavior Inventory for children and adolescents. *Journal of Clinical Psychiatry, 69*, 831–839. doi:10.4088/jcp.v69n0517

Youngstrom, E. A., Murray, G., Johnson, S. L., & Findling, R. L. (2016). The 7 Up 7 Down Inventory: A 14-item measure of manic and depressive tendencies carved from the General Behavior Inventory. *Psychological Assessment, 25*, 1377–1383. doi:10.1037/a0033975

Zuckerman, E. L. (2010). *Clinician's thesaurus: The guide to conducting interviews and writing psychological reports* (7th ed.). New York, NY: Guilford Press.

CAREER ASSESSMENT IN REHABILITATION

DAVID R. STRAUSER | CHELSEA E. GRECO

LEARNING OBJECTIVES

After reviewing this chapter, the reader should be able to:

- Define the centrality of work and describe the major benefits derived from engaging in productive work–related activities.

- Identify common barriers to the career development of people with disabilities and describe how the Illinois Work and Well-Being Model (IW^{2}M) can be used to guide the career assessment process.

- Identify and describe the commonly used career assessments used in contemporary rehabilitation counseling practice.

Introduction

One of the primary focuses of rehabilitation counseling is the career development, employment, and vocational behavior of people with disabilities (Strauser, 2013; Strauser, Greco, & O'Sullivan, 2018). Career assessment plays a very large role in the conceptualization of career-related issues and the delivery of appropriate career and employment services to people with disabilities. The goal of this chapter is to provide rehabilitation counselors with the necessary information for understanding the concepts and career assessments that affect the career development and employment of people with disabilities. This chapter begins with an overview of the importance of work and the benefits derived from engaging in productive work–related activities. Understanding the centrality of work is critical because it equips the rehabilitation counselor with the foundation for conceptualizing issues that have an impact on career and vocational behavior. Building on the centrality of work, the chapter briefly discusses the factors recognized to affect the career development and employment of people with disabilities and introduces the Illinois Work and Well-Being Model (IW^{2}M) as a conceptual framework that can be used to guide career assessment. The chapter concludes with a description and overview of commonly used career measures used in rehabilitation counseling setting.

▨ Centrality of Work

The idea that work is a fundamental source of defining one's identity in society is the core philosophy that drives rehabilitation counseling (Blustein, 2008; Strauser, 2013). Work provides opportunities for economic participation and advancement, social support, self-expression, and self-determination and has been linked to increased physical and psychological health (Blustein, 2008). The benefits derived from work can be therapeutic for all people, but may be of particular value for persons with disabilities, for whom greater social isolation, stigma, and increased risks associated with poverty are both more common and more pronounced than for people without disabilities (Blustein, 2008; Strauser, O'Sullivan, & Wong, 2010). Research has consistently found that people who experience chronic ill health and disability often become socially isolated and undergo a decrease in self-esteem and overall psychological well-being in the workplace. A congruent work environment can offset these drawbacks by providing opportunities for increased income, social interaction, and support and broadening one's social role (Wolfensberger, 2002). According to Neff (1985), most work spaces provide social environments within which a person can interact with others, perform rituals and customs that are meaningful, participate in opportunities for growth, and derive direct and indirect social support necessary for sustaining and increasing mental health (Blustein, 2008). Employment can also lead to improved access to better housing, health care, nutrition, neighborhoods, and school districts, as well as crime-free communities and better family relationships (Blustein, 2008).

Despite the large amount of research highlighting the positive mental health impact of work, there are times when participating in work can have negative implications and contribute to decreased physical and psychological health and well-being. As an example, increased levels of stress and depression can be caused by an incongruent person–environment fit and lack of vocational identity (O'Sullivan & Strauser, 2010; Strauser, Greco, & O'Sullivan, 2018). An incongruent fit is one in which the person's personal work style and value system do not fit well with the work environment (Strauser, 2013). Low-level and unskilled positions (e.g., service sector positions) that are common employment sites for people with disabilities typically involve chaotic, noisy, or dirty environments; require long hours; and are emotionally taxing, all likely to lead to increased stress levels (Szymanski & Parker, 2010). Job role ambiguity, lack of control or input, lack of support in high-responsibility jobs, and very low pay are other factors that contribute to reduction in psychological well-being (Strauser et al., 2010; Strauser, Greco, & O'Sullivan, 2018). For people with disabilities, the relationship between the job and work stress is complex, with the presence of a disability or chronic health condition further complicates the ability to manage contextual factors in the workplace that contribute to or exacerbate stress.

Work and Human Needs

Because work is central to people's lives and is particularly related to improved health, participating in work is the primary means by which people meet the following three basic human needs: (1) survival and power, (2) social connection, and (3) self-determination and well-being (Blustein 2008; Blustein, Kenna, Gill, & DeVoy, 2008). Each basic human need is briefly described next.

Survival and Power

Work provides a means for people with disabilities to derive psychological, economic, and social power that is closely tied to meeting basic survival needs (Blustein et al., 2008). Ideally, through competitive employment, people with disabilities should be able to generate enough income and benefits to meet their most basic needs. However, research continuously has found that those with disabilities are employed at a much lower rate than their counterparts without disabilities, are likely to be employed in positions with no real career path and no benefits, are underemployed, and, when employed, occupy low-paying positions (Lustig & Strauser, 2007). A reciprocal relationship between disability and poverty has been established and is exacerbated by high rates of unemployment and underemployment for people with disabilities and provides evidence regarding the importance of providing quality vocational rehabilitation services (Lustig & Strauser, 2007). As a result, many people with disabilities are unable to meet their most basic human needs independently—often creating a state of dependence with no real promise for achieving higher states of vocational or career functioning. One of the primary goals of rehabilitation counseling should be to provide purpose and relevance within the broader environment. Those who are working assume a greater social role that ultimately increases their ability to derive psychological, social, and economic power (Wolfensberger, 2002).

Social Connection

Humans are social beings who need to be connected with society as a whole and develop strong interpersonal relationships (Blustein, 2006). Participation in work-related activities provides an opportunity for people with disabilities to connect with others and their broader social and cultural environments (Blustein, 2008). Ideally, through work, people develop positive relationships that supply the support needed to manage work-related stress and foster identity development (Blustein, 2008). In contrast, in a negative work environment, in which a person feels isolated, disconnected, and under stress, job performance and work adjustment will most likely be negatively affected. Finally, working provides a mechanism for people with disabilities to develop a sense of connection with their broader social world through contributing to the larger economic structure of society (Blustein, 2006).

Self-Determination and Well-Being

People search for environments that promote self-determination, self-expression, and well-being. A primary goal of rehabilitation counseling is to conceptualize and facilitate work environments that promote physical and psychological well-being of people with disabilities. Ideally, the work environment provides opportunities for self-determination, self-expression, and individual well-being through participation in work that is consistent with the worker's skills and interests. However, very few people with disabilities have the opportunity to participate in work-related activities that correspond to their personal skills and interests, and they often pursue employment for extrinsic reasons such as income (Blustein, 2008; Strauser, 2013). Research has suggested that promoting *autonomy*, *relatedness*, and *competence* in relation to work that is initially pursued for extrinsic reasons can increase the person's level of self-determination and well-being related to work (Ryan & Deci, 2000).

■ Factors Impacting the Career Development and Employment of People With Disabilities

In conceptualizing the problems associated with the career development process and low employment rates of persons with disabilities in the United States, a wide variety of factors contribute to this issue at the individual, societal, and policy levels. At the individual level, research has found that persons with disabilities are typically not provided with the necessary opportunities to learn and develop self-advocacy skills and self-understanding of their individualized needs. Frequency of interpersonal experiences and participation in the classroom in the formative years have been found to be less for those with disabilities than for those without disabilities (Eriksson, Welander, & Granlund, 2007). Research suggests that such experiences in the formative years can serve as the foundation for later vocational identity development. In a study of young adult cancer survivors, Wong and Strauser (2013) found that the younger the age of onset of disability, the greater the difficulties associated with vocational identity later in life. Furthermore, Strauser, Wagner, Wong, and O'Sullivan (2013) found that people with onset of central nervous system (CNS) cancer between the ages of 6 and 12 experience higher degree of career indecision-making later in life as compared to those who experience onset of cancer before or after this time period in childhood.

At the societal level, disability continues to carry a stigma despite its high and growing prevalence. As a consequence, employees with disabilities may not choose to disclose their disability and associated functional limitations out of fear of being viewed by their employers as unmotivated, irresponsible, and incompetent. Companies are increasingly viewing the importance of reaching out to qualified applicants with disabilities as a part of their diversity recruiting practices; however, research has also suggested that human resources (HR) departments and hiring managers were not overly enthusiastic about people with disabilities as reliable and productive employees (Chan et al., 2010).

At the policy level, for some people, hesitancy in obtaining employment may be due to fear of losing disability benefits (Kregel & O'Mara, 2011), as they do not believe that the system supports their ability to be meaningfully employed, and the impact of losing disability benefits due to employment has greater negative consequences than being unemployed. Furthermore, employees with disabilities, particularly those with nonvisible disabilities, still experience significant reservations in the decision on whether to disclose their disability status to their employer despite the existence of the Americans with Disabilities Act (ADA, 1990). This may be due to the lack of understanding of one's rights under the ADA (Kim & Williams, 2012), as well as fear of differential treatment as a result of disability disclosure (Madaus, 2008).

Illinois Work and Well-Being Model

To maximize the effectiveness of career assessment in rehabilitation counseling practice, it is important for rehabilitation counselors to have a conceptual framework to guide the career assessment process. The IW^{2}M (Figure 8.1) identifies the interaction of contextual, employment development, and participation domains as key elements in explaining how personal, environmental, chronic health, treatment-related, educational, and potential interventions serve as facilitators or barriers related to overall societal participation. The framework is grounded in the major tenets of the International Classification of Functioning, Disability and Health (ICF) framework and theory-driven research related to the career development and employment of people with disabilities. The framework has three major domains with an intervention component that facilitates the interaction between the contextual and career development domains and conceptually has both direct and indirect effects on the participation domain. The type and focus of interventions are not specified, and no theoretical orientation is preferred. Conceptually, the three domains and the intervention component of the framework provide a structure to

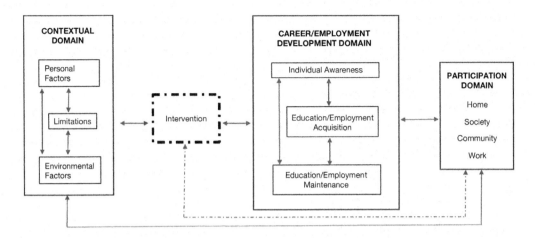

FIGURE 8.1 The Illinois Work and Well-Being Model.

operationalize how career development and employment are related to the overall participation of persons with disabilities.

The IW^{2}M is not designed to replace specific theories that attempt to explain or describe important career and employment constructs, such as decision-making, motivation, interest, value, or personality development. Instead, with the application of the IW^{2}M, these constructs and theories are viewed as important process-oriented factors that are inherent and embedded in the framework. In addition, like the framework's domains and factors, these process factors should be points of relevant and valuable career development and employment assessment.

Illinois Work and Well-Being Domains

The IW^{2}M consists of Contextual, Career Development, and Participation domains that interact to provide a structure for understanding the career and employment development of young adult cancer survivors. The Career Interventions component is purposefully situated between the Contextual and Career Development domains. Accordingly, the model implies that career interventions directly and indirectly influence both the Contextual and the Career Development domains and have an indirect effect on the Participation domain. Each domain consists of factors that allow for analysis at both the individual domain and the factor level. As a result, domains and factors can be conceptualized as both independent and interdependent in nature. All arrows between domains and factors are bidirectional, indicating a reciprocal effect between the model components. Relationships between domains, factors, and interventions can be positive, negative, or neutral, implying that the value of the directional impact is determined by the situational specific activities, expressions, and reactions to both specific and broad stimuli. A detailed discussion regarding the IW^{2}M can be found in chapters by Strauser, Greco, and O'Sullivan (2018) and Strauser, O'Sullivan, and Wong (2018).

The *Contextual* domain applies the ICF framework as a guide to operationalize how personal and environmental factors interact with people with disabilities and treatment-related limitations and restrictions. The bidirectional arrow between the domain factors implies a reciprocal relationship, implying that growth or change in one factor can directly or indirectly impact the growth or change in the other factors. The solid bidirectional arrow between the Contextual and

Career Development domains indicates a direct reciprocal connection between these two major domains independent of any intervention, implying a mutual interdependent developmental process. The solid bidirectional arrow along the bottom of the model between the Contextual and Participation domains implies a reciprocal relationship independent of the Career Development domain and any career interventions.

The *Career Development* domain is based on career and employment research related to people with disabilities. The domain consists of the following three factors: Individual Awareness, Educational and Employment Acquisition, and Educational and Employment Maintenance. Specifically, *awareness* is developmentally mediated with the individual becoming aware of how he or she relates to the world and in which activities he or she may choose to participate. The Individual Awareness factor theoretically provides the foundation for the acquisition and maintenance factors, although, as implied by the bidirectional arrow, all factors have a reciprocal impact influencing each factor's continual development. The Education and Employment *Acquisition* factor addresses the process in which people go about acquiring access to educational and employment-related activities. From an educational perspective, acquisition includes, but is not limited to, the process and activities associated with applying for appropriate educational-related activities, including trade and 2-year and 4-year training programs. The Employment and Educational Acquisition factor provides the foundation for the Maintenance Factor–related activities and has a reciprocal impact on individual awareness. The Educational and Employment *Maintenance* factor addresses the activities and behaviors associated with maintaining engagement and participation in educational and occupational–related activities. Although Maintenance occurs after Acquisition and is typically conceptualized as an outcome, it too has a reciprocal effect on the preceding factors.

The *Participation* domain utilizes the ICF framework as a guide to identify meaningful and broad-based participation in major life areas. In this conceptual model, the life areas of home, society, community, and work have been identified and can serve as outcomes of interest. Although the work area may seem an obvious focal area for those working to improve career development and employment outcomes for persons with chronic health conditions, the model stresses the interconnectivity of all participation areas. A fundamental tenet guiding the model is that increased positive participation will lead to an overall increase in a person's well-being and overall quality of life.

According to the conceptual model, the intervention component is situated between the Contextual and Career Development domains. This placement suggests that the primary goal of career, educational, and employment interventions is to facilitate and maximize the direct interaction between the Contextual and Career domains, which will, in turn, indirectly impact the Participation domain. By pulling the intervention component outside the Career Development domain and placing it between the Contextual and Career Development domains, the model implies that interventions should focus on the correspondence between the two respective domains. Effective interventions should focus on minimizing the personal, environmental, and disability-related limitations for greatest impact on the Career Development domain and specific Career Development domain factors. Another way to think about the various domain factors is in context of the most frequently utilized vocational rehabilitation services. Table 8.1 provides an overview of those services and indicates which domains these services could potentially impact.

TABLE 8.1 Services Provided by State VR Agencies Within the Work and Well-Being Model

TYPE OF SERVICE AND DESCRIPTION	CONTEXTUAL DOMAIN			CAREER DOMAIN		
	Personal	Environmental	Limitation	Awareness	Acquisition	Maintenance
ELIGIBILITY						
Assessment: Services provided and activities performed to determine a client's eligibility for VR services, to assign an individual priority category of a state VR agency that operates under an order of selection, and/or to determine the nature and scope of VR services to be included in the IPE.	✓	✓	✓			
Diagnosis of Treatment of Impairments: Surgery, prosthetics and orthotics, nursing services, dentistry, occupational therapy, physical therapy, speech therapy, and drugs and supplies; also diagnosis and treatment of mental and emotional disorders.	✓		✓			
COUNSELING AND GUIDANCE						
Vocational Rehabilitation Counseling and Guidance: Discrete therapeutic counseling and guidance services necessary for a client to achieve an employment outcome, including personal adjustment counseling; counseling that addresses medical, family, or social issues; vocational counseling; and any other form of counseling and guidance necessary for a person with a disability to achieve an employment outcome; this service is distinct from the general counseling and guidance relationship that exists between the counselor and the client during the entire rehabilitation process.	✓	✓		✓	✓	✓

(continued)

TABLE 8.1 Services Provided by State VR Agencies Within the Work and Well-Being Model (*continued*)

TYPE OF SERVICE AND DESCRIPTION	CONTEXTUAL DOMAIN			CAREER DOMAIN		
	Personal	Environmental	Limitation	Awareness	Acquisition	Maintenance
TRAINING						
College or University Training: Full-time or part-time academic training above the high school level that leads to a degree (associate, baccalaureate, graduate, or professional), a certificate, or other recognized educational credential; such training may be provided by a 4-year college or university, community college, junior college, or technical college.				✓	✓	
Occupational/Vocational Training: Occupational, vocational, or job skill training provided by a community college and/or a business, vocational/trade, or technical school to prepare students for gainful employment in a recognized occupation; this training does not lead to an academic degree or certification.				✓	✓	
On-the-Job Training: Training in specific job skills by prospective employer; generally, the person is paid during this training and will remain in the same or a similar job upon successful completion; this category also includes apprenticeship training programs conducted or sponsored by an employer, a group of employers, or a joint apprenticeship committee representing both employers and a union.					✓	✓

(*continued*)

TABLE 8.1 Services Provided by State VR Agencies Within the Work and Well-Being Model (*continued*)

TYPE OF SERVICE AND DESCRIPTION	CONTEXTUAL DOMAIN			CAREER DOMAIN		
	Personal	Environmental	Limitation	Awareness	Acquisition	Maintenance
Basic Academic Remedial or Literacy Training: Literacy training or training provided to remediate basic academic skills needed to function on the job in the competitive labor market.				✓	✓	✓
Job Readiness Training: Training to prepare a client for the world of work (e.g., appropriate work behaviors, methods for getting to work on time, appropriate dress and grooming, methods for increasing productivity).				✓	✓	
Disability-Related, Augmentative Skills Training: Service includes, but is not limited to, orientation and mobility, rehabilitation teaching, training in the use of low-vision aids, Braille, speech reading, sign language, and cognitive training/retraining.	✓	✓	✓			
Miscellaneous Training: Any training not recorded in one of the other categories listed, including GED or high school training leading to a diploma.				✓	✓	
JOB PLACEMENT						
Job Search Assistance: Job search activities that support and assist a consumer in searching for an appropriate job; may include help in preparing résumés, identifying appropriate job opportunities, and developing interview skills; and may include making contacts with companies on behalf of the consumer.					✓	

(continued)

TABLE 8.1 Services Provided by State VR Agencies Within the Work and Well-Being Model (*continued*)

TYPE OF SERVICE AND DESCRIPTION	CONTEXTUAL DOMAIN			CAREER DOMAIN		
	Personal	Environmental	Limitation	Awareness	Acquisition	Maintenance
Job Placement Assistance: A referral to a specific job resulting in an interview, whether or not the client obtained the job.					✓	
SUPPORTIVE MODALITIES						
On-the-Job Supports: Support services to a client who has been placed in employment in order to stabilize the placement and enhance job retention; such support includes job coaching, follow-up and follow-along, and job retention services.						✓
Transportation Services: Travel and related expenses necessary to enable an applicant or eligible client to participate in VR service; includes adequate training in the use of public transportation vehicles and systems.					✓	✓
Rehabilitation Technology: The systematic application of technologies, engineering methodologies, or scientific principles to meet needs of and address the barriers confronted by persons with disabilities in areas that include education, rehabilitation, employment, transportation, independent living, and recreation; includes rehabilitation engineering services, assistive technology devices, and assistive technology services.	✓	✓	✓	✓	✓	✓

(continued)

TABLE 8.1 Services Provided by State VR Agencies Within the Work and Well-Being Model (*continued*)

TYPE OF SERVICE AND DESCRIPTION	CONTEXTUAL DOMAIN			CAREER DOMAIN		
	Personal	Environmental	Limitation	Awareness	Acquisition	Maintenance
Reader Services: Services for people who cannot read print because of blindness or other disability; includes reading aloud and transcribing printed information into Braille or sound recordings if requested by the client; generally are offered to those who are blind or deaf-blind but may also be offered to clients unable to read because of serious neurological disorders, specific learning disabilities, or other physical or mental impairments.			✓			
Interpreter Services: Sign language or oral interpretation services performed by specifically trained persons for persons who are deaf or hard of hearing, and tactile interpretation services for those who are deaf-blind; includes real-time captioning services; does not include language interpretation.			✓			
Personal Attendant Services: Those personal services that an attendant performs for a person with a disability, such as bathing, feeding, dressing, and providing mobility and transportation.		✓	✓			

(continued)

TABLE 8.1 Services Provided by State VR Agencies Within the Work and Well-Being Model (*continued*)

TYPE OF SERVICE AND DESCRIPTION	CONTEXTUAL DOMAIN			CAREER DOMAIN		
	Personal	Environmental	Limitation	Awareness	Acquisition	Maintenance
Technical Assistance Services: Technical assistance and other consultation services provided to conduct market analyses, to develop business plans, and to provide resources to clients in the pursuit of self-employment, telecommuting, and small business operation outcomes.				✓	✓	✓
Information and Referral Services: Services provided to persons who need assistance from other agencies (through cooperative agreements) not available through the VR program.	✓	✓	✓	✓	✓	✓
Other Services: All other VR services that cannot be recorded elsewhere; included here are occupational licenses, tools and equipment, initial stocks and supplies, and medical care for acute conditions arising during rehabilitation and constituting a barrier to the achievement of an employment outcome.	✓	✓	✓	✓	✓	✓

GED, General Education Development; IPE, Individualized Plan for Employment; VR, vocational rehabilitation.

■ Areas of Career Assessment

As mentioned previously, one of the primary emphasis of rehabilitation counseling has been the career development, vocational behavior, and employment of people with disabilities. This emphasis has led rehabilitation counselors to focus on individual aspects of the career development and employment process by identifying personal traits and attributes that contribute to career and employment success. With this focus on the individual and personal traits and attributes came the use of different assessment techniques to measure or operationalize these constructs of interest. With the application of the IW^{2}M, all the instruments covered in this section address the *Awareness* factor of the *Career Development* domain and introduce the most commonly used career and vocational assessment tools used in rehabilitation counseling settings. Specifically, the most commonly used tests are classified according to the following categories: *interests, values/ needs, decision-making, career maturity and development,* and *career thoughts.*

Career Interests

Measures of career and vocational interest were initially developed in 1927 and were used in the secondary schools and colleges based on the assumption that people choose occupations in which they are interested in the required activities (Tang, 2018). Two major types of interest scales are used in rehabilitation counseling settings. Basic interest scales measure the strength of the person's interests in broad areas, such as art, music, and sports, and are considered to be homogeneous in nature because they refer to one type of activity (Hays, 2013). Basic interest measures are constructed using a rationale process with the items designed to logically fit together. Examples of basic interest measures are the Occupational Theme and Basic Interest Scales of the Strong Interest Inventory (SII; Hays, 2013).

Occupational interest scales assess the similarity of the person's interest pattern to that of people in specific occupations or positions. Items that make up occupational scales are designed to differentiate people, and the items are selected for inclusion in the scale based on empirical analysis, not theoretical or logical considerations. The Occupational Scales (OS) on the Strong and the Campbell Interest and Skill Survey are examples of empirically derived scales (Hays, 2013).

Overall, both types of scales can contribute to the career and vocational counseling processes in rehabilitation settings. Interest scores can be used to help subjects explore, discover, and become aware of new career, educational, or vocational opportunities; facilitate decisions; and confirm prior choices. When using career interest tests in rehabilitation counseling settings, several things should be kept in mind. First, interest inventories measure likes and dislikes, not abilities. Second, general interest inventories are not helpful when people must make fine distinctions. Third, a person who has decreased emotional functioning or is managing stress is more likely to interpret the test questions in a negative manner and potentially endorse more passive interests when compared to others (Hays, 2013). Finally, as mentioned, people with disabilities are more likely to have limited career experiences, and as a result, it is likely that interest inventory results may change. Therefore, it is important to retest the subject, especially as he or she gains access to more educational and career experiences (Hays, 2013; Strauser, 2013).

The following are examples of commonly used career interest inventories.

Strong Interest Inventory (SII): The SII is designed to measure a subject's interests in a broad range of occupations, work activities, and leisure interests. The most recent version published in 2004 reduced the number of items from 317 to 291 (Donnay, Thompson, Morris, & Schaubhut, 2004). Scores are profiled across six General Occupational Scales (GOT) based on Holland's typology; 30 Basic Scales (BIS) that measure clusters of interests related to the GOT; 244 OS; and five Personality Scales (Learning Style, Work Environment, Leadership Style, Risk Taking, and Team Orientation). Because the SII is frequently updated, the instrument reflects the current status of the workforce. The newest development of the SII is the use in conjunction with the Skills Confidence Inventory developed by Betz, Borgen, and Harmon (2005) that provides confidence levels for each of the six GOTs. A major strength of the SII is the outstanding psychometrics. However, the length does present a significant barrier for use with people with certain types of disabilities. More information regarding the SII can be found at www.cpp.com/products/strong/index.aspx.

Self-Directed Search (SDS; Holland, Fritzsche, & Powell, 1994): The SDS measures a subject's interests according to Holland's typology theory, which consists of the following six vocational personality types: *Realistic, Investigative, Artistic, Social, Enterprising,* and *Conventional.* The fundamental assumption guiding the use of the SDS is that people and jobs can be categorized according to the same six categories. The SDS is easy to administer and can be self-scored and self-interpreted. However, it is important to note that more advanced interpretation is available and can provide significant insight into overall vocational identity and overall development. The SDS comes in the following four versions that have been created for different populations: Regular Form (R) for high school and college students and adults, Easy Form (E) for high school students and adults with limited reading ability, Career Planning Form (CP) for career transition or persons seeking upper level positions, and the SDS Career Explorer for middle school students. The SDS can be used in conjunction with the Occupation or Education Opportunities Finder, and Holland recommends using the My Vocational Situation to supplement interpretation of the SDS. More details regarding the SDS can be found at the Psychological Assessment Resources (PAR) website at www4.parinc.com/Products/Product.aspx?ProductID=SDS_R.

Kuder Career Interest Assessment (KCIA-32): The KCIA contains 32 triads of interest items that the subject ranks by preference from most preferred to third most preferred. The KCIA-32 provides two sets of scores; one presents the occupational scales of the 16 career clusters and pathways, and the other presents the scores according to Holland's typology (Realistic, Investigative, Artistic, Social, Enterprising, Conventional [RIASEC]). The six Holland areas of interest can be used in conjunction with the O*NET occupations and 16 national career clusters (Harris-Bowlsbey, Niles, Zytowski, Rayman, & Trusty, 2013). The KCIA-32 is part of the larger Kuder Career Planning System that was developed for use with students and adults involved in career counseling and planning. One advantage of the Kuder System is that it is easily accessible (Internet-based assessment) and the results are immediately available. More details regarding the Kuder System can be found at www.kuder.com.

*O*NET Interest Profiler:* The O*NET Interest Profiler was developed by the U.S. Department of Labor, Employment and Training Administration as part of the O*NET database (National Center for O*NET Development, n.d.). The Interest Profiler is a self-administered and self-scored assessment of one's work-related interests. It can be administered in the paper–pencil form or on the computer and is easy and accessible to use (Crockett, 2013). The Interest Profiler is organized using Holland's typology (RIASEC), with the highest code among the six codes being viewed as the primary interest area. More information regarding the O*NET Interest Profiler can be found at www.onetcenter.org/overview.html?p=3.

Suggestions for Interpreting Interest Results

When interpreting interest test results, there are several things that rehabilitation counselors can do to get the client more involved and promote greater growth and development. The following are several recommendations that the rehabilitation counselors may find helpful (Hays, 2013; Strauser, 2013):

- Make certain the client has answered all or a majority of the items and confirm that he or she understood the directions.

- To continue individual involvement, ask how the client felt about the test and if she or he had any questions or concerns.

- Pay attention to the number of *like, dislike,* or *indifferent* responses. If the response pattern consists of an unusually high or low percentage of either *likes* or *dislikes*, give the most consideration to the highest scores.

- If available, be sure to use appropriate sex-based norms when interpreting scores.

- Emphasize that the interest test scores reflect interests, not abilities.

- Do not overinterpret small differences. As a guide, Hays (2013) recommends that *T*-score differences of less than 10 points should not be viewed as significant.

- Relate scores to other information concerning the client, such as work experience, educational background, stated interests, and career plans.

- Use other career resources to expand occupational considerations.

Work Values

Values are an important construct that has significant implications for motivation and satisfaction (Hays, 2013; Super, 1990; Tang, 2018). Work values are a subcategory of values and specifically address personal motivation and satisfaction with the work environment (Murdock & Rounds, 2013). Work values inventories assess values that pertain to work situations by measuring objectives that can be satisfied by the work itself (intrinsic) or through work as a means to an end (extrinsic). Creativity, mental challenges, and achievement are considered intrinsic values, whereas money, prestige, and working conditions are considered extrinsic. When evaluating work values, it is important to consider both intrinsic and extrinsic values because they play an important role in worker satisfaction (Hays, 2013; Murdock & Rounds, 2013; Strauser, 2013).

The following are examples of commonly used work value inventories.

Minnesota Importance Questionnaire (MIQ): The MIQ (Rounds, Henley, Dawis, Lofquist, & Weiss, 1981) is based on the Minnesota Theory of Work Adjustment, which suggests that a person's needs affects his or her choice of work environment and the degree in which the work environment meets those needs directly impacts the person's satisfaction with the work environment. The MIQ measures the subject's needs, values, and occupational preferences across the following six scales: Achievement, Comfort, Status, Altruism, Safety, and Autonomy. With each of the scales measuring needs, the hierarchical taxonomy of the MIQ allows the results be used with people at different stages of the career development process from general exploration to specific decisions on career choice or transition (Rounds & Jin, 2013). Originally developed in 1981, the MIQ was updated for inclusion in the O*NET system. More information regarding the MIQ can be found at www.psych.umn.edu/psylabs/vpr/miqinf.htm.

*O*NET Work Importance Profiler (WIP):* The WIP is a computer-based instrument that has an equivalent paper-and-pencil version known as the Work Importance Locator (WIL-P&P). The WIP is part of the O*NET system and can be accessed through the O*NET website. The WIP provides rankings for the six core values of achievement, independence, recognition, relationships, support, and working conditions. Subjects are instructed to rank the items in comparison with each other as a means to determine which values are the most important to them.

The Value Scale: The Value Scale (Nevill & Super, 1986) was based on Super's Lifespan Career Development theory and measures one's occupational value including ability, utilization, economic security, personal development, economic rewards, lifestyle, altruism, social relations, working conditions, advancement, creativity, aesthetics, autonomy, prestige, cultural identity, social interactions, authority, variety, physical activity, risk, and physical prowess (Tang, 2018). The focus of the instrument is to assess one's general values that can be satisfied through various life roles, including work and career.

Kuder Work Values Assessment (KWVA): The KWVA was formerly known as Super's Work Values (SWVI) and consists of the following subscales: workplace, innovation, accomplishment, income, and prestige. The KWVA is now part of the Kuder Career Planning System, which is an Internet-based assessment and was most recently updated in 2012 (Harris-Bowlsbey et al., 2013). More details regarding the KWVA can be found at www .kuder.com/solutions/kuder-career-planning-system.

Suggestions for Interpreting Work Values

When reviewing and interpreting the results from value inventories, the following are several recommendations that rehabilitation counselors may find helpful (Hays, 2013);

- Utilize both measures of value and interest to help gain an understanding of the client's motivation for work.

- When interpreting work values, it is also important to consider the person's other values and how together they may impact overall life planning.

- It is important to consider how the client's overall contextual factors impact his or her work values. It may be particularly important to consider cultural factors and issues related to disability and stigma.

- It is important to remember that a person's values may change with time and life experiences. As basic needs are met, a person will likely focus on higher-order needs, potentially leading to a change or reexamination of values.

Career Decision-Making, Maturity, and Readiness

In rehabilitation counseling settings, the career development process involves the client assessing how his or her contextual factors (e.g., personal, environmental, and functioning) interact with the career development factors (e.g., awareness, acquisition, and maintenance) to process information related to making meaningful and effective career decisions that facilitate appropriate education and employment outcomes (Strauser, Greco, & O'Sullivan, 2018). Good career development is predicated on gaining increased self-awareness and self-understanding by exploring not only one's interest and values but also one's career maturity, readiness, decision making, and thoughts. The career instruments covered in this section differ from measures that address interest and values because the instruments address the constructs and processes that clients need to engage with to make effective and meaningful career decisions. It is important for rehabilitation counselors to understand that many times clients find it difficult to make career and employment decisions, not because they lack an understanding regarding their interest or values but because they lack the skills or abilities needed to make effective career and employment decisions. In this section, instruments commonly used to measure level of maturity, readiness, beliefs, and decision-making are covered.

Career Decision-Making

Career Decision Scale (CDS): The CDS consists of two subscales, one measuring indecision (16 items) and the other measuring certainty (three items), with the certainty subscale primarily acting as a validity check (Osipow & Winer, 1996). Originally developed by Samuel H. Osipow, the most recent version is published by Psychological Assessment Resources (Osipow, 1987).

My Vocational Situation (MVS): The MVS was primarily developed to assess career planning concerns by measuring vocational identity and assessing the subject's perception regarding occupational information and career barriers (Holland, Daiger, & Power, 1980). The first subscale measures vocational identity (VI) and consists of 18 true/false items. The two remaining subscales, Occupational Information (OI) and Barriers (B), consist of one question with four parts. The OI subscale provides data concerning the subject's perceived need for occupational information, whereas the Barrier (B) identifies perceived barriers negatively impacting the career development process. The MVS has been the most widely used career assessment tool for both research and practice and is recommended to be used with both the SDS and the Career Thoughts Inventory (Strauser, 2013).

Career Decision-Making Self-Efficacy Scale (CDSES): The CDSES consists of 50 items making up the following five subscales: self-appraisal, occupational information, goal setting, planning, and problem solving (Betz, Klein, & Taylor, 1996). The CDSES also comes in a short form consisting of 25 items making up the same five subscales (Betz & Taylor, 2001). The CDSES is widely used in research and has been used in cross-cultural settings as well (Creed, Patton, & Watson, 2002; Luzzo, 1993; Zhang-Hampton, 2005).

Career Maturity

Career Development Inventory (CDI): The CDI measures the subject's readiness to make vocational and educational decisions across the following five subscales: career planning, career exploration, decision making, knowledge of the world of work, and knowledge of preferred occupations. According to Glavin (2013), the preferred occupations subscale is not recommended for use with those who have not completed the 11th grade. Originally developed in 1981 by Super, Thompson, Lindeman, Jordaan, and Meyers, it has been suggested that there is a need to update the scale (Pietrzak, 2013). The instrument is available for free at vocopher.com.

Career Maturity Inventory (CMI): The CMI was designed to be used by 6th to 12th graders and may have application for transition-age youth. The primary aim of the scale is to measure how ready a person is to make career decisions. Designed by Crites and Savickas (1996), the revised version of the CMI has been greatly enhanced and is helpful in teaching students career decision making and promoting insight into career maturity (McDivitt, 2002). The CMI can be found for free at vocopher.com.

Career Beliefs and Thoughts

Career Beliefs Inventory (CBI): Developed by John Krumboltz (1991), the CBI is designed to identify beliefs that may hamper accomplishment. It contains 96 items across 25 subscales. Given the limited psychometric properties of the CBI, it has been recommended that it be used primarily for discussion purposes and has been found an effective aid in the career interview.

Career Thoughts Inventory (CTI): The CTI was designed to assess dysfunctional thinking, problem-solving, and decision-making in high school and college students and adults (Sampson, Peterson, Lenz, Reardon, & Saunders, 1996). Utilizing Cognitive Information Processing as the theoretical basis, the CTI consists of 48 items that measure misperceptions across the following three subscales: Decision-Making Confusion, Commitment Anxiety, and External Conflict. In addition to the CTI protocol, additional career resources are available to guide career counseling (Tang, 2018). The CTI is published by Psychological Assessment Resources (PAR).

Suggestions for Interpreting Career Measures

When reviewing and interpreting the results from career assessment inventories, rehabilitation counselors may find the following recommendations helpful:

- Determine the intensity of the career intervention based on the client's level of career planning readiness. Persons with low readiness will need more intense and long-term counseling, whereas persons with increased levels of readiness may only need short and less intense interventions (Strauser, 2013).

- Help clients identify and challenge distorted career thoughts and help them identify contextual factors that may be contributing to the perpetuation of dysfunctional career thoughts. For example, does the client's perception of disability, cultural background, or personal factor negatively impact his or her career readiness?

- When planning career interventions, it is important to factor in complexity of the client's contextual factors, such as family, socioeconomic status, and organizational factors.

- When planning intervention, it is important to consider the client's capability to make appropriate career choices and external factors that may act as barriers or supports (Sampson, Peterson, Reardon, & Lenz, 2000).

- To monitor progress and help the client gain an understanding of career growth and development, it may be beneficial to administer career assessments on multiple occasions.

▪ Conclusion

The primary goal of this chapter was to introduce rehabilitation counselors to the necessary information and concepts related to career assessments that impact the career development and employment of people with disabilities. The importance of work and the benefits derived from engaging in productive work–related activities was outlined and provide the foundation for sound career and vocational assessment. Building on the centrality of work, factors that impact the career development and employment of people with disabilities were identified. As highlighted, individual, societal, and policy factors were briefly described, and the implications for career development were discussed. The IW^2M was introduced as a conceptual framework that can be used to guide career assessment process. The IW^2M consists of contextual, career development, and participation domains that are made up of factors that can be points of analysis and assessment. For the purposes of this chapter, the instruments introduced primarily focus on the career awareness factor of the career development domain. Finally, career measures most commonly used in the rehabilitation counseling setting were described, with Table 8.1 including a more comprehensive list of career assessment instruments. Along with instrument descriptions, recommendations to guide the interpretation process were provided to help rehabilitation counselors process and incorporate assessment information into effective rehabilitation planning.

■ References

Americans with Disabilities Act. Pub. L. No. 101-336, 104 Stat. 328 (1990). Retrieved from www.ada.gov/pubs/ada.htm

Betz, N. E., Borgen, F. H., & Harmon, L. (2005). *Skills confidence inventory applications and technical guide* (2nd ed.). Palo Alto, CA: Consulting Psychologists Press.

Betz, N. E., Klein, K. L., & Taylor, K. M. (1996). Evaluation of a short form of the Career Decision-Making Self-Efficacy Scale. *Journal of Career Assessment, 4,* 413–428. doi:10.1177/106907279600400103

Betz, N. E., & Taylor, K. M. (2001). *Career decision self-efficacy scale: Technical manual.* Worthington, OH: Author.

Blustein, D. L. (2006). *The psychology of working: A new perspective for career development, counseling, and public policy.* Mahwah, NJ: Lawrence Erlbaum.

Blustein, D. L. (2008). The role of work in psychological health and well-being. *American Psychologist, 63*(4), 228–240. doi:10.1037/0003-66X.63.4.228

Blustein, D. L., Kenna, A. C., Gill, N., & DeVoy, J. E. (2008). The psychology of working: A new model for counseling practice and public policy. *The Career Development Quarterly, 56,* 294–308. doi:10.1002/j.2161-0045.2008.tb00095.x

Chan, F., Strauser, D., Maher, P., Lee, E., Jones, R., & Johnson, E. (2010). Demand-side factors related to employment of people with disabilities: A survey of employers in the midwest region of the United States. *Journal of Occupational Rehabilitation, 20*(4), 412–419. doi:10.1007/s10926-010-9252-6

Creed, P. A., Patton, W., & Watson, M. B. (2002). Cross-cultural equivalence of the Career Decision-Making Self-Efficacy Scale and career commitment: An Australian and South African comparison. *Journal of Career Assessment, 10,* 327–342. doi:10.1177/10672702010003004

Crites, J. O., & Savickas, M. L. (1996). Revision of the Career Maturity Inventory. *Journal of Career Assessment, 4*(2), 131–138.

Crockett, S. A. (2013). O*Net interest profiler and computerized O*Net interest profiler. In C. Wood & D. G. Hays (Eds.), *A counselor's guide to career assessment instruments* (6th ed., pp. 262–267). Broken Arrow, OK: National Career Development Association.

Donnay, D. A. C., Thompson, R. C., Morris, M. L., & Schaubhut, N. A. (2004). *Technical brief for the newly revised STRONG INTEREST INVENTORY© ASSESSMENT: Content, reliability, and validity.* Retrieved from https://www.cpp.com/Pdfs/StrongTechnicalBrief.pdf

Eriksson, L., Welander, J., & Granlund, M. (2007). Participation in everyday school activities for children with and without disabilities. *Journal of Physical and Developmental Disabilities, 19,* 485–502. doi:10.1007/s10882-007-9065-5

Glavin, K. (2013). Career development inventory. In C. Wood & D. G. Hays (Eds.), *A counselor's guide to career assessment instruments* (6th ed., p. 319). Broken Arrow, OK: National Career Development Association.

Harris-Bowlsbey, J., Niles, S., Zytowski, D., Rayman, J., & Trusty, J. (2013). Kuder career planning system: Kuder career interest assessment, Kuder skills confidence assessment, and Kuder work values assessment. In C. Wood & D. G. Hays (Eds.), *A counselor's guide to career assessment instruments* (6th ed., pp. 203–208). Broken Arrow, OK: National Career Development Association.

Hays, D. G. (2013). *Assessment in counseling: A guide to the use of psychological assessment procedures* (5th ed.). Alexandria, VA: American Counseling Association.

Holland, J. L., Daiger, D. C., & Power, G. (1980). *My vocational situation.* Palo Alto, CA: Consulting Psychologists Press.

Holland, J. L., Fritzsche, B., & Powell, A. (1994). *Self-directed search: Technical manual.* Odessa, FL: Psychological Assessment Resources.

Kim, M. M., & Williams, B. C. (2012). Lived employment experiences of college students and graduates with physical disabilities in the United States. *Disability & Society, 27,* 837–852. doi:10.1080/09687599.2012.673081

Kregel, J., & O'Mara, S. (2011). Work incentive counseling as a workplace support. *Journal of Vocational Rehabilitation, 35*(2), 73–83. doi:10.1177/003435520004300205

Krumboltz, J. D. (1991). *Career beliefs inventory.* Palo Alto, CA: Consulting Psychologists Press.

Lustig, D. C., & Strauser, D. R. (2007). Causal relationships between poverty and disability. *Rehabilitation Counseling Bulletin, 50*(4), 194–202. doi:10.1177/00343552070500040101

Luzzo, D. A. (1993). Reliability and validity testing of the career decision-making self-efficacy scale. *Measurement and Evaluation in Counseling and Development, 26,* 137–142.

Madaus, J. W. (2008). Employment self-disclosure rates and rationales of university graduates with learning disabilities. *Journal of Learning Disabilities, 41,* 291–299. doi:10.1177/0022219407313805

McDivitt, J. (2002). Review of the career maturity inventory. In J. T. Kapes & E. A. Whitfield (Eds.), *A counselor's guide to career assessment instruments* (4th ed., pp. 336–342). Alexandria, VA: National Career Development Association.

Murdock, C., & Rounds, J. (2013). Work values: Understanding and assessing motivation to work. In D. R. Strauser (Ed.), *Career development, employment, and disability in rehabilitation* (pp. 193–206). New York, NY: Springer Publishing Company.

National Center for O*NET Development. (n.d.). *O*NET OnLine.* Retrieved from https://www.onetonline.org

Neff, W. S. (1985). *Work and human behavior.* New York, NY: Aldine.

Nevill, D. D., & Super, D. E. (1986). *The value scale: Theory, application, and research (manual).* Palo Alto, CA: Consulting Psychologists Press.

Osipow, S. H. (1987). *Manual for the career decision scale.* Odessa, FL: Psychological Assessment Resources.

Osipow, S. H., & Winer, J. L. (1996). The use of the Career Decision Scale in career assessment. *Journal of Career Assessment, 4,* 117–130. doi:10.1177/106907279600400201

O'Sullivan, D., & Strauser, D. (2010). Validation of the developmental work personality model and scale. *Rehabilitation Counseling Bulletin, 54*(1), 46–56. doi:10.1177/0034355210378045

Pietrzak, D. (2013). Career development inventory. In C. Wood & D. G. Hays (Eds.), *A counselor's guide to career assessment instruments* (6th ed., pp. 320–323). Broken Arrow, OK: National Career Development Association.

Rounds, J. B., Henley, G. A., Dawis, R. V., Lofquist, L. H., & Weiss, D. J. (1981). Manual for the Minnesota Importance Questionnaire: A measure of vocational needs and values. Minneapolis: University of Minnesota, Department of Psychology.

Rounds, J., & Jin, J. (2013). Nature, importance and assessment of needs and values. In S. D. Brown & R. W. Lent (Eds.), *Career development and counseling: Putting theory and research to work* (2nd ed., pp. 417–447). Hoboken, NJ: Wiley.

Ryan, R. M., & Deci, E. L. (2000). Self-determination theory and the facilitation of intrinsic motivation, social development, and well-being. *American Psychologist, 55,* 68–78. doi:10.1037//0003-066x.55.1.68

Sampson, J. P., Jr., Peterson, G. W., Lenz, J. G., Reardon, R. C., & Saunders, D. E. (1996). *Career thoughts inventory (CTI). Professional manual.* Odessa, FL: Psychological Assessment Resources.

Sampson, J. P., Jr., Peterson, G. W., Reardon, R. C., & Lenz, J. G. (2000). Using readiness assessment to improve career services: A cognitive information processing approach. *The Career Development Quarterly, 49,* 146–174. doi:10.1002/j.2161-0045.2000.tb00556.x

Strauser, D. R. (2013). *Career development, employment and disability in rehabilitation: From theory to practice.* New York, NY: Springer Publishing Company.

Strauser, D. R., Greco, C., & O'Sullivan, D. (2018). Career and lifestyle planning in vocational rehabilitation settings. In D. Capuzzi & M. D. Stauffer (Eds.), *Career counseling: Foundations, perspectives, and applications* (3rd ed., pp. 429–426). London, UK: Routledge.

Strauser, D. R., O'Sullivan, D., & Wong, A. W. K. (2010). The relationship between contextual work behaviors self-efficacy and work personality: An exploratory analysis. *Disability and Rehabilitation, 32*(24), 1999–2008. doi:10.3109/09638281003797380

Strauser, D. R., O'Sullivan, D., & Wong, A. W. (2018). Career development and employment of people with disabilities. In V. M. Tarvydas & M. T. Hartley (Eds.), *The professional practice of rehabilitation counseling* (pp. 273–296). New York, NY: Springer Publishing Company.

Strauser, D. R., Wagner, S., Wong, W. K., & O'Sullivan, D. (2013). Career readiness, developmental work personality and age of onset in young adult CNS survivors. *Journal of Disability and Rehabilitation, 35*(7), 543–550.

Super, D. E., Thompson, A. S., Lindeman, R. H., Jordaan, J. P., & Myers, R. A. (1981). *The career development inventory.* Palo Alto, CA: Consulting Psychologists Press

Super, D. E. (1990). A life-span, life-space approach to career development. In D. Brown & L. Brooks (Eds.), *Career choice and development: Applying contemporary theories to practice* (2nd ed., pp. 197–261). San Francisco, CA: Jossey-Bass.

Szymanski, E. M., & Parker, R. M. (2010). Work and disability: Basic concepts. In E. M. Szymanski & R. M. Parker (Eds.), *Work and disability: Contexts, issues, and strategies for enhancing employment outcomes for people wtih disabilities* (pp. 1–15). Austin, TX: Pro-Ed.

Tang, M. (2018). *Career development and counseling: Theory and practice in a multicultural world.* Los Angeles, CA: Sage.

Wolfensberger, W. (2002). Social role valorization and, or versus, "empowerment." *Mental Retardation, 40*(3), 252–258. doi:10.1352/0047-6765(2002)040<0252:srvaov>2.0.co;2

Wong, A. W. K., & Strauser, D. R. (2013, November 19). *Measuring workplace outcomes using the ICF model in adult survivors of childhood cancer.* Presented at the 3rd Annual Postdoctoral Research Symposium, Urbana, IL.

Zhang-Hampton, N. Z. (2005). Testing for the structure of the Career Decision Self-Efficacy Scale-Short Form among Chinese college students. *Journal of Career Assessment, 13,* 98–113. doi:10.1177/1069072704270298.

ADAPTIVE BEHAVIOR ASSESSMENT: CONCEPTUAL, TECHNICAL, AND PRACTICAL APPLICATIONS

CHARLES EDMUND DEGENEFFE | TERESA ANN GRENAWALT

LEARNING OBJECTIVES

After reviewing this chapter, the reader should be able to:

- Understand the purpose of assessing adaptive behavior when diagnosing and determining support needs with persons with intellectual disabilities.

- Gain awareness of available standardized measures for assessing adaptive behavior.

- Apply the practice of adaptive behavior assessment to contemporary rehabilitation practice with persons with intellectual disabilities.

▦ Introduction

With its traditional focus on employment, career development, and vocational rehabilitation (Power, 2013), the rehabilitation counseling profession provides much less attention to the practice of adaptive behavior. The likely reason concerns the focus on adaptive behavior assessment, which largely attends to how clients meet the demands of independent living in school and home environments (Shapiro, 1987). This shortcoming in awareness is unfortunate, however, as adaptive behavior can inform diagnostic and treatment planning purposes for populations including persons with intellectual disabilities (IDs; Woolf, Woolf, & Oakland, 2010), autism (Charman, Howlin, Berry, & Prince, 2004), neurological disorders (Tarazi, Mahone, & Zabel, 2007), and learning disabilities (Weller, Watteyne, Herbert, & Crelly, 1994). Further, adaptive behavior is an important correlate for predicting employment versus unemployment outcomes (Su, Lin, Wu, & Chen, 2008).

Professional understanding of adaptive behavior is strongly influenced by the American Association on Intellectual and Developmental Disabilities (AAIDD). In 2002, the AAIDD (Schalock et al., 2010) published its 11th iteration of its diagnostic criteria of ID, wherein it established that adaptive behavior is best understood with the domains of conceptual, social, and practical skills.

The establishment of these domains guides the development (Tassé, Schalock, et al., 2016) of adaptive behavior instruments, research, and assessment practices (Obi et al., 2011) and reflects a developmental progression on understanding the adaptive behavior construct since the AAIDD first established diagnostic criteria for ID in 1959 (Tassé et al., 2012). A client's ability to meet the conceptual, social, and practical demands of independent living is best understood as fluid and contextually grounded, as one's cultural environment largely dictates what is required of its members for successful function (Sattler & Levin, 2014).

Consistent with professional reliance on the AAIDD for understanding adaptive behavior, professional attention on adaptive behavior primarily focuses on the diagnosis of ID (Dixon, 2007). This is not surprising. Adaptive behavior has been a key component of ID diagnostic systems (Schalock et al., 2010) including (since 1959) criteria set by the AAIDD and (since 1968) the American Psychiatric Association's *Diagnostic and Statistical Manual of Mental Disorders* (*DSM*). The diagnosis of ID is an important public policy issue in areas such as service eligibility (Schalock et al., 2010), Supplemental Security Income benefits (Livermore, Bardos, & Katz, 2017), determination of criminal culpability (Tassé, 2009), access to K-12 (Center for Parent Information and Resources, 2017), and postsecondary accommodations (Stodden & Whelley, 2004). Hence, the assessment of ID (and, by definition, adaptive behavior assessment) presents high-stakes implications.

This chapter presents a review of adaptive behavior assessment from conceptual, technical, and practical perspectives. Although adaptive behavior is a construct with relevance across multiple disability populations served by rehabilitation professionals, its greatest relevance concerns persons with ID. Therefore, this chapter presents adaptive behavior assessment within an ID context. The chapter begins by describing the population of persons with ID and how they are defined through federal legislation and professional associations. Specific focus is placed on the growing importance of adaptive behavior in the process of identifying persons with this disability. The chapter then presents a review of standardized and informal approaches to adaptive behavior assessment, used for both diagnostic and service planning purposes. To illustrate its professional importance and use of best-practice approaches, the chapter then addresses three practice areas in which adaptive behavior assessment plays a key role in contemporary practice with persons with ID, including death penalty evaluations, community-based habilitation, and culturally responsive assessment.

■ Intellectual Disability Assessment and Development of the Adaptive Behavior Construct

ID is a common disability in the United States. Recent estimates propose that 12 in 1,000 persons share the characteristics associated with ID (Maenner et al., 2016). Given their challenges in meeting the demands of work and independent living, persons with ID often require lifelong and, at times, extensive assistance from a variety of rehabilitation and medical professionals. In FY 2011, it was estimated that $56.65 billion was spent to support the needs of persons with ID and other developmental disabilities (DD) in the United States (The Arc, 2014).

In the United States, ID is defined by both legislative and professional standards. Legislatively, the federal definition of ID was first established in the early 1960s through federal legislation and the establishment of the President's Panel on Mental Retardation (Administration for Community Living, 2017). Presently, ID is defined on the federal level through the Developmental Disabilities Assistance and Bill of Rights Act of 2000 (DD Act), in which ID is part of the more expansive DD category, which relies on identifying multiple areas (see Box 9.1) of adaptive behavior limitation.

BOX 9.1

FEDERAL DEVELOPMENTAL DISABILITY CRITERIA

REQUIRED ELEMENTS

- Attributable to a mental or physical impairment or combination of mental and physical impairments
- Manifested before the person attains age 22
- Likely to continue indefinitely
- Reflects the person's need for a combination and sequence of special, interdisciplinary, or generic services; individualized supports; or other forms of assistance that are of lifelong or extended duration and are individually planned and coordinated
- Results in substantial functional limitations in three or more of the following areas of major life activities, including:
  - ○ Self-care
  - ○ Receptive and expressive language
  - ○ Learning
  - ○ Mobility
  - ○ Self-direction
  - ○ Capacity for independent living
  - ○ Economic self-sufficiency

From these criteria, states establish their own DD definition (Degeneffe, 2000). Further adding to a lack of uniformity on ID, states differ on defining ID in the ID/DD service, special education, and criminal justice systems. As part of these discrepancies, states contrast on their use of adaptive behavior assessment as part of their ID diagnostic criteria. In the special education system, for example, Bergeron, Floyd, and Shands (2008) examined how all 50 states plus the District of Columbia defined ID for special education service eligibility. With regard to determining what constitutes an adaptive behavior deficit, 77% of states did not establish any criteria, while 16% required deficits of at least 2 standard deviations below the mean. Another 2% use a 1.5 standard deviation below the mean.

Although there is a lack of ID assessment consistency in public systems, alternatively, there is a high degree of uniformity in the practice of psychological assessment. For almost 60 years, the professional approach toward ID assessment in the United States has been driven by the AAIDD (Obi et al., 2011). In 1959, the AAIDD (then known as the American Association on Mental Deficiency, or AAMD) defined ID (then referred to as "mental retardation") as follows: "Mental retardation refers to subaverage general intellectual functioning that originates during the developmental period and is associated with impairment in one or more of the following: (a) maturation, (b) learning, (c) social adjustment" (Heber, 1959, p. 3). The other source of established ID assessment standards in the United States is the *Diagnostic and Statistical Manual of Mental Disorders (DSM)*, starting with the *DSM-II* in 1968. Like the 1959

AAIDD definition, the *DSM-II* (American Psychiatric Association [APA], 1968) indicated that "Mental retardation refers to subnormal general intellectual functioning that originates during the developmental period and is associated with impairment of either learning and social adjustment or maturation, or both" (p. 14). Historically, ID diagnostic criteria between the *DSM* and AAIID have been consistent (Schalock et al., 2010). Internationally, ID is likewise understood through consideration of intelligence, adaptive behavior, and age of onset, as reflected in *International Classification of Disease*, 10th edition (*ICD-10*) criteria (World Health Organization, 1992).

Current diagnostic criteria for ID remain remarkably similar to these early systems, although important changes were made with how the developmental period, subaverage intellectual functioning, and adaptive behavior limitation domains are now defined. Currently, the AAIDD (Schalock et al., 2010) defines each domain with the following criteria:

1. *Developmental period*: Before the age of 18 years

2. *Intellectual functioning*: Approximately 2 standard deviations below the mean using standardized assessment instruments

3. *Adaptive behavior*: Approximately 2 standard deviations below the mean on an overall assessment of conceptual, social, and practical adaptive behavior skills, or in any one of these three areas, using standardized assessment instruments

The AAIDD now conceptualizes adaptive behavior into three domains: (a) practical skills, (b) conceptual skills, and (c) social skills. These domains were identified through a series of factor analytic studies (Schalock et al., 2010; Tassé et al., 2012), wherein adaptive behavior consistently coalesced around this three-pronged (i.e., conceptual, social, and practical skills) construct. The AAIDD's three-domain system of adaptive behavior reflects a refinement of the AAIDD's 1992 ID diagnostic criteria (Luckasson et al., 1992), in which adaptive behavior limitations were required in any 2 or more of 10 possible areas of adaptive behavior limitation. The AAIDD's current operational definition of each adaptive behavior (Tassé et al., 2012, p. 293) includes domains for practical (e.g., use of money), conceptual (e.g., reading), and social skills (e.g., social problem-solving).

Professional understanding of ID increasingly reflects an appreciation of adaptive behavior measurement, which is a departure from the historical reliance (Meins & Süssmann, 1993; Tassé et al., 2012) on IQ scores for diagnosing ID. One reason for this shift concerns the importance of adaptive behavior assessment for determining support needs involved with vocational participation, independent living, and overall community participation. Professionals find adaptive behavior information more useful in planning supports instead of simple reliance on IQ. Reflective of this point, the AAIDD (Schalock et al., 2010) and *DSM-5* (APA, 2013) ID diagnostic systems both describe levels of ID (*DSM-5*—mild, moderate, severe, profound; AAIDD—intermittent, limited, extensive, pervasive) based on adaptive behavior information and not IQ. Second, professionals increasingly recognize adaptive behavior as a distinct and equally important factor alongside IQ when diagnosing ID instead of assuming that adaptive behavior limitation is the result of low IQ (Tassé, Luckasson, & Schalock, 2016). Tassé and associates stated, "There are no published studies supporting the notion of a causal link between intelligence and adaptive behavior" (p. 387). In making this point, they critique the following statement in the *DSM-5* that directly links adaptive behavior to IQ. The *DSM-5* states, "to meet diagnostic criteria for intellectual disability, the deficits in adaptive functioning must be directly related to the intellectual impairments described in Criterion A" (APA, 2013, p. 38).

Standardized Versus Informal Approaches to Adaptive Behavior Assessment

Hangauer, Worcester, and Armstrong (2013) stressed that the key reason for performing adaptive behavior assessment "is to develop supports and services to meet the needs of the individual. To accomplish this, it becomes essential to identify the individual's functional strengths and needs in relation to their family, culture, and community expectations" (p. 652). Rehabilitation counselors and other professionals supporting persons with ID/DD are presented with both formal (i.e., standardized assessment) and informal approaches to accomplish these central assessment goals. With regard to formal, or standardized, assessment, like other areas of rehabilitation assessment (Power, 2013), there are many valid and reliable psychometric instruments to measure adaptive behavior for both diagnostic and support planning purposes.

Rehabilitation counselors should acknowledge the limitations of only relying on standardized instruments given their inherent weaknesses. Standardized instrument information may be limited to general descriptions of adaptive behavior instead of generating more client-specific information (Harrison & Boney, 2002). Standardized adaptive behavior instruments may lack relevance to a client's culture and ethnicity (Allen-Meares, 2008). Also, most adaptive behavior standardized instrument items are answered by informants and not clients themselves. Informants are typically parents, family members, close friends, colleagues, or anyone who is in a position to know firsthand the adaptive behavior skills possessed by the client (Tassé et al., 2012). The relationships informants hold with clients calls into question the ability of informants to be truly objective. Ratings "may reflect their own expectations and standards for adaptive skills, and the expectations may differ between respondents and between settings" (Harrison & Boney, 2002, p. 1173). Informants may be influenced by their own self-interest in the outcome of the assessment (Tassé et al., 2012). Informants sometimes rate adaptive behaviors differently based on the context in which they know the client, which is why, for example, parents and teachers can rate a child's adaptive behavior skills inconsistently. Informants can also hold different perspectives on adaptive behaviors compared to a client's views (Sattler & Levin, 2014).

Informal Approaches to Adaptive Behavior Assessment

While standardized assessment of adaptive behavior skills is based on retrospective informant responses, informal methods of adaptive behavior skills instead involve gathering information on the basis of observing actual, real-life settings and activities (Shapiro, 1987). The value of an informal approach is that it avoids the shortcomings of standardized assessments and presents a high degree of ecological validity, because the actual behaviors needed for different work and independent living environments can be directly observed. Rehabilitation counselors are presented with a variety of approaches to perform informal adaptive behavior assessments. Sattler and Levin (2014) described informal adaptive behavior assessment with the use of case histories, interviews, daily diaries or checklists, teacher–parent communication, home and school observations, task analysis, systematic observations, controlled teaching trials, and life skills evaluations.

Specific to a rehabilitation counseling context, two informal adaptive behavior assessment approaches with particular relevance are situational assessments and ecological assessment. Situational assessment "is based on an effort to simulate actual working conditions with an orientation toward work behavior in general" (Strauser, Chan, Wang, Wu, & Rahimi, 2013, p. 189). Strauser and associates noted this form of assessment focuses on adaptive behaviors involved with employability, such as punctuality, safety, and relationships with supervisors, by observing these adaptive behaviors in actual work environments.

As an informal approach toward adaptive behavior assessment, rehabilitation counselors possess considerable flexibility in assessing work behaviors in a situational assessment environment. Situational assessment though requires a means to assess the client's adaptive behavior skills systematically and comprehensively. When considering clients with ID, supported employment is a vocational approach particularly helpful, given the practice of providing support to meet the needs of the client (i.e., the place and train placement model) rather than requiring clients to demonstrate vocational independence prior to job placement (Degeneffe, 2000).

Situational assessments fit well with supported employment, given the challenges many clients with ID experience in most standardized vocational evaluation applications. Moon, Inge, Wehman, Brooke, and Barcus (1990) offered an approach toward gathering adaptive behavior information in a supported employment-related situational assessment. They presented the idea of gathering information from 30 different adaptive behavior domains in three situational assessment placements. For each of the 30 areas, persons completing the forms are instructed to describe the activity or behavior and, when applicable, its environment (i.e., antecedent, consequences, people, location) and frequency. For each adaptive behavior domain, the form provides prompts and criteria for describing the behavior or activity. For example, with "Time Awareness," options to describe this skill include "unaware of time and clock function," "identifies breaks/lunch," "can tell time to the hour," or "can tell time in hours/minutes." Also, for "Independent Work Rate" (no prompts), response choices include "slow pace," "steady/average pace," "above average," "sometimes fast," or "continual fast pace." The value of this information is that it provides rehabilitation counselors specific information on the type (e.g., job modifications, vocational training) and intensity of support (e.g., hours of weekly job coaching) the client with ID needs for workplace success (Degeneffe, 2000).

Ecological assessment is another form of assessment that incorporates an understanding of the adaptive behavior skills of the client. Ecological assessment involves matching the environmental characteristics of potential workplaces to maximize the fit of learning styles and abilities of the client (Strauser et al., 2013). It is an approach with particular utility for persons with ID in supported employment environments, because it involves a qualitative matching of person to environment (Degeneffe, 2000) involved in place and train job placement approaches (Strauser et al., 2013). Ecological assessment could, for example, evaluate how an adaptive behavior, like a client's social skills, fits the employer's expectations for social contact with customers, supervisors, and other employees, as well as available natural supports to reinforce expected social behaviors (Parker, Szymanski, & Hanley-Maxwell, 1989).

Standardized Adaptive Behavior Assessment

Although informal assessment approaches present several advantages, most assessment of adaptive behavior among persons with ID, however, relies on standardized testing (Boan & Harrison, 1997). Because of the high number of persons evaluated annually for ID and the importance of ID diagnosis for public policy and service funding, professionals rely on standardized assessment approaches that facilitate normative comparisons of adaptive behavior to the general population. The following review presents commonly used standardized assessment instruments used for both diagnostic and service planning purposes.

Standardized Adaptive Behavior Instruments: Diagnostic

According to Tassé and associates (2012), there are four standardized adaptive behavior instruments that were developed specifically for the diagnosis of ID. Each of the four measures is considered to be representative of the general population of the United States and determined to be psychometrically sound for the purpose of ID diagnostic assessment. These four instruments are summarized in Table 9.1. A fifth measure (Tassé, Schalock, et al., 2016), the Diagnostic Adaptive Behavior Scale (DABS), is also reviewed, given it was specifically designed for the diagnosis of ID. Although these measures are presented as sharing a primary diagnostic purpose, all five likewise provide useful information for planning supports and interventions.

Vineland Adaptive Behavior Scales, Third Edition (Vineland-3)

The Vineland-3 represents the third iteration of the Vineland Adaptive Behavior Scales (Sparrow, Cicchetti, & Saulnier, 2016). The Vineland-3 is an individual assessment of adaptive behavior. It has wide applicability across different disability populations faced with adaptive behavior limitation, including persons with ID. The Vineland-3's domains measuring communication, daily living skills, and socialization match the three areas of adaptive behavior assessment addressed in the AAIDD (Schalock et al., 2010) and *DSM-5* (APA, 2013) ID assessment systems. The Vineland-3 (PsychCorp, 2016) has three ways to measure adaptive behavior:

1. *The Interview Form*: Semistructured interview, which gathers information from a parent or caregiver. Normed to ages 0 to 90+ years.

2. *The Parent/Caregiver Form*: Questionnaire that requires respondents to provide adaptive behavior in a home and family-life context. Normed to ages 0 to 90+ years.

3. *The Teacher Form*: Gathers information from teacher perspective in a school or daycare context. Normed to ages 3 to 21 years.

The Vineland-3 (PsychCorp, 2016; Sparrow et al., 2016) assesses five domains (each with subdomains) of adaptive behavior: *communication* (receptive, expressive, and written), *daily living skills* (personal, domestic, and community), *socialization* (interpersonal relationships, play and leisure, and coping skills). These first three domains are required in the Vineland-3's administration. The remaining two domains, which are optional measures, are *motor skills* (fine motor and gross motor) and *maladaptive behavior* (internalizing, externalizing, and critical items). Each item present a specific adaptive behavior rated on the frequently in which it is performed. The majority of items are answered with a 2 (*behavior is usually performed*), a 1 (*behavior is sometimes performed*), or a 0 (*behavior is never performed*). Several questions are rated 2 for *Yes* or 0 for *No*. The Vineland-3 can be given online through Q-global or in a paper-and-pencil format (PsychCorp, 2016; Sparrow et al., 2016).

Each form of the Vineland-3 is based on separate normative samples (Sparrow et al., 2016). To facilitate representation of the instrument to the U.S. population, norm groups were matched to population demographics for gender, education level, race/ethnicity, and geographic region (Northeast, North Central, South, and West). Norm sample information was obtained in 2014 and 2015. The Vineland-3's total sample size is 6,535 persons, with 2,456 persons each for the Interview and Parent/Caregiver Forms and 1,415 for the Teacher form.

TABLE 9.1 Diagnostic Standardized Adaptive Behavior Assessments

ASSESSMENT AND PURPOSE	DEVELOPERS	DOMAINS	ADMINISTRATION	NORMATIVE DATA
Vineland Adaptive Behavior Scales, Third Edition (Vineland-3): an individual assessment of adaptive behavior.	Sparrow, Cicchetti, & Saulnier (2016)	■ Communication ■ Daily living skills ■ Socialization ■ Motor skills (optional) ■ Maladaptive behavior (optional)	Three forms may be administered through Q-global or paper-and-pencil format: 1. *The Interview Form*: Semistructured interview, which gathers information from a parent or caregiver. Normed to ages 0 to 90+ years. 2. *The Parent/Caregiver Form*: Questionnaire that requires respondents to provide adaptive behavior in a home and family-life context. Normed to ages 0 to 90+ years. 3. *The Teacher Form*: Gathers information from a teacher perspective in a school or day-care context. Normed to ages 3 to 21 years.	Norm groups were matched to population demographics for gender, education level, race/ethnicity, and geographic region in the United States. Normative data were collected in 2014 and 2015. The Vineland-3's total sample size is 6,535 persons, with 2,456 persons each for the Interview and Parent/Caregiver Forms and 1,415 for the Teacher form.
Adaptive Behavior Scale-School, Second Edition (ABS-S:2): can be used to diagnose ID in children, assess adaptive behavior skills of children with autism spectrum disorders, and determine appropriate educational placements.	Nihira, Leland, & Lambert, 1993	Part I: ■ Independent functioning ■ Physical development ■ Economic activity ■ Language development ■ Numbers and time ■ Prevocational and vocational activity ■ Self-direction ■ Responsibility ■ Socialization	The ABS-S:2 is a paper-and-pencil–administered assessment. It can be completed by an informant familiar with the child being assessed or by an examiner answering the items by interviewing the informant.	Norm comparisons for persons aged 3 to 21 years and includes samples of persons with and without ID. The ID sample includes 2,074 persons, whereas the non-ID group is composed of 1,254 sample members. Norm group members collectively came from 40 states and stratified on several demographic factors to match the school-aged population in the United States.

(continued)

TABLE 9.1 Diagnostic Standardized Adaptive Behavior Assessments *(continued)*

ASSESSMENT AND PURPOSE	DEVELOPERS	DOMAINS	ADMINISTRATION	NORMATIVE DATA
		Part II: ■ Social behavior ■ Conformity ■ Trustworthiness ■ Stereotyped and hyperactive behavior ■ Self-abusive behavior ■ Social engagement ■ Disturbing interpersonal behavior		
Adaptive Behavior Assessment System, Third Edition (ABAS-3): provides a comprehensive assessment of adaptive skills and is used in the diagnosis of ID.	Harrison & Oakland (2015b)	■ Conceptual skills ■ Practical skills ■ Social skills	Five forms may be administered through online or paper-and-pencil format: 1. *Parent/Primary Caregiver Form* (ages 0–5 years) 2. *Teacher/Day-care Provider Form* (ages 2–5 years) 3. *Parent Form* (ages 5–21 years) 4. *Teacher Form* (ages 5–21 years) 5. *Adult Form* (ages 16–89 years)	The ABAS-3 is based on a representative sample reflecting the U.S. population. It is an instrument with utility for those with ID as well as other types of neurodevelopmental disability.
Scales of Independent Behavior–Revised (SIB-R): helps professionals plan support, supervision, and resources needs into one of six possible levels of support: pervasive, extensive, frequent, limited, intermittent, and infrequent or no support.	Bruininks, Bradley, Weatherman, Woodcock, & Hill (1996)	Full Scale: ■ Motor skills ■ Social interaction ■ Communication skills ■ Community living Problem Behavior Scale: ■ Internalized maladaptive behavior ■ Asocial maladaptive behavior ■ Externalized maladaptive behavior	The SIB-R is usually completed by an informant familiar with the adaptive behavior of the client, such as a caregiver or teacher. Typically, it is administered through a structured interview with the informant, but clients themselves are allowed to provide the information needed to complete the SIB-R.	There were a total of 2,182 persons in the norm population, with most (1,817) between 3 months and 19 years old. The remaining 365 persons composed the portion of the norm group 20 to 90 years old.

(continued)

TABLE 9.1 Diagnostic Standardized Adaptive Behavior Assessments (*continued*)

ASSESSMENT AND PURPOSE	DEVELOPERS	DOMAINS	ADMINISTRATION	NORMATIVE DATA
Diagnostic Adaptive Behavior Scale (DABS): created specifically to facilitate the diagnosis of ID of persons aged 4–21 years.	Tassé, Schalock, et al. (2016)	▪ Conceptual skills ▪ Social skills ▪ Practical skills	Administration is completed through a semistructured interview with an adult respondent familiar with the client (e.g., family, friends, teachers, employers, or direct care support staff). Clients are not permitted to provide responses for themselves. Interviewers should possess at least a bachelor's degree with assessment experience and direct work experience with persons with ID or related developmental disabilities.	The standardization sample consisted of 474 people from 36 states in the United States. The sample was representative of males and females ranging in age from 4 to 21 years. Approximately one-quarter of the sample had a diagnosis related to ID.

ID, intellectual disability.

Adaptive Behavior Scale-School, Second Edition

The Adaptive Behavior Scales-School (ABS-S:2) is the second version of an instrument first developed by the AAMD (now referred to as AAIDD) in 1975 (Nihira, Leland, & Lambert, 1993; Sattler & Levin, 2014). The ABS-S:2 can be used to diagnose ID in children, assess adaptive behavior skills of children with autism spectrum disorders, and determine appropriate educational placements. The ABS-S:2 comes in two parts.

Part I examines personal independence and evaluates a client's coping skills needed for managing the challenges of independent living. It measures nine domains of behavior: (a) independent functioning, (b) physical development, (c) economic activity, (d) language development, (e) numbers and time, (f) prevocational/vocational activity, (g) self-direction, (h) responsibility, and (i) socialization. Part I coalesces around three factors: personal self-sufficiency, community self-sufficiency, and personal–social responsibility (Sattler & Levin, 2014). Part II addresses a client's maladaptive behaviors in seven domains: (a) social behavior, (b) conformity, (c) trustworthiness, (d) stereotyped and hyperactive behavior, (e) self-abusive behavior, (f) social engagement, and (g) disturbing interpersonal behavior (Nihira et al., 1993). These Part II factors coalesce around two factors of adaptive behavior: social adjustment and personal adjustment (Sattler & Levin, 2014).

The ABS-S:2 is a paper-and-pencil–administered assessment (Nihira et al., 1993). It can be completed by an informant familiar with the child being assessed or by an examiner answering the items by interviewing the informant (Sattler & Levin, 2014). The ABS-S:2 provides norm comparisons for persons aged 3 to 21 years and includes samples of persons with and without ID. The ID sample includes 2,074 persons, whereas the non-ID group is composed of 1,254 sample members. Norm group members collectively came from 40 states and stratified on several demographic factors to match the school-aged population in the United States (Sattler & Levin, 2014).

Adaptive Behavior Assessment System, Third Edition

The Adaptive Behavior Assessment System, Third Edition (ABAS-3) is a revised version of the 2008 Adaptive Behavior Assessment System-II (ABAS-2; Harrison & Oakland, 2015b). The ABAS-2 was included by Tassé and associates (2012) as one of four adaptive behavior instruments specifically designed for ID diagnoses. The ABAS-3 is included in the present review of ID-specific diagnostic instruments, given that it is a revision and not a replacement for the ABAS-2. Also, it maintains its utility for ID diagnostic purposes (Harrison & Oakland, 2015a). The ABAS-3 provides a comprehensive assessment of adaptive skills. It addresses adaptive behavior across the life span, given its norm comparisons start at birth and extend to 89 years, 11 months (Harrison & Oakland, 2015b).

The ABAS-3 addresses three adaptive behavior domains, measuring conceptual, social, and practical skills (Harrison & Oakland, 2015a), areas consistent with the AAIDD (Schalock et al., 2010) and *DSM-5* (APA, 2013) ID diagnostic systems. Within these three areas, 11 adaptive skill areas are assessed (Harrison & Oakland, 2015a). Like the ABAS-2, the ABAS-3 is based on representative sample reflecting the U.S. population. It is an instrument with utility for those with ID as well as other types of neurodevelopmental disability. In addition to ID diagnoses, it can also be used for educational and treatment planning and in program evaluation and research (Harrison & Oakland, 2015b).

The ABAS-3 can be administered through online and paper-and-pencil administration (Harrison & Oakland, 2015a). It consists of five assessments developed by those who are aware of the daily activities and skills of the client. The intended rater and the age group addressed (Harrison & Oakland, 2015a) for assessment are as follows:

1. Parent/Primary Caregiver Form: for ages 0 to 5 years

2. Teacher/Day-care Provider Form: for ages 2 to 5 years

3. Parent Form: for ages 5 to 21 years

4. Teacher Form: for ages 5 to 21 years

5. Adult Form: for ages 16 to 89 years

Scales of Independent Behavior-Revised

The Scales of Independent Behavior-Revised (SIB-R) is a second edition of the original instrument (Bruininks, Bradley, Weatherman, Woodcock, & Hill, 1996). It measures four adaptive behavior areas (i.e., the Full Scale) and three areas of problem behavior (i.e., Problem Behavior Scale). Adaptive behaviors assessed are (a) motor skills, (b) social interaction and communication skills, (c) personal living skills, and (d) community living skills. The three problem behavior areas measured are (a) internalized maladaptive behavior, (b) asocial maladaptive behavior, and (c) externalized maladaptive behavior (Sattler & Levin, 2014). In most cases, the SIB-R is completed by an informant familiar with the adaptive behavior of the client, such as a caregiver or teacher. Typically, it is administered through a structured interview with the informant, but clients themselves are allowed to provide the information needed to complete the SIB-R. The SIB-R can be computer scored (Sattler & Levin, 2014).

The SIB-R helps professionals plan support, supervision, and resources needs into one of six possible levels of support: pervasive, extensive, frequent, limited, intermittent, and infrequent or no support (Bruininks et al., 1996). These support levels are consistent with the ID levels of support that are part of the AAIDD (Schalock et al., 2010) and *DSM-5* (APA, 2013) ID classification systems of disability severity.

There were a total of 2,182 persons in the SIB-R norm population, with most (1,817) between 3 months and 19 years old. The remaining 365 persons were in the portion of the norm group 20 to 90 years old (Sattler & Levin, 2014). Sattler and Levin commented that, although the publishers of the SIB-R attempted to create a norm sample representative of the U.S. population (i.e., 1990 Census data), the sample was in fact not proportional to the numbers of persons residing in the four U.S. census regions. In addition to the Full Scale and Problem Scale, the SIB-R also includes alternative formats. The Short-Form includes 40 items for clients at any level of development. The Early Development Scale likewise includes 40 items for infants through approximately 6 years of age. The Early Development Scale can also be administered to those with age 8 years or younger level of development (Bruininks et al., 1996; Sattler & Levin, 2014).

Diagnostic Adaptive Behavior Scale

The AAIDD's DABS (Tassé, Schalock, et al., 2016; Tassé et al., 2017) is a comprehensive standardized assessment of adaptive behavior focused on diagnostic information, developed through item response theory methodology. The DABS was created specifically to facilitate the diagnosis of ID of persons aged 4 to 21 years. It assesses three areas of adaptive behavior consistent with the AAIDD (Schalock et al., 2010), *DSM-5* (APA, 2013), and the *ICD-11* (World Health Organization, 2018). Tassé, Schalock, and associates (2016) summarized the domains and subdomains of adaptive behavior of the DABS:

1. *Conceptual skills* (literacy; self-direction; and concepts of number, money, and time);

2. *Social skills* (interpersonal skills, social responsibility, self-esteem, gullibility, naïveté, social problem-solving, following rules, obeying laws, and avoiding being victimized);

3. *Practical skills* (activities of daily living, occupational skills, use of money, safety, health care, travel/transportation, schedules/routines, and use of the telephone; p. 80).

The DABS consists of a total of 75 items, with 25 items in each domain. Summary scores are generated for each of the three areas of adaptive behavior in addition to an overall DABS score. Administration is completed through a semistructured interview with an adult respondent familiar with the client, such as "family, friends, teachers, employers, or direct care support staff (if appropriate)" (Tassé, Schalock, et al., 2016, p. 82). Clients are not permitted to provide responses for themselves. To administer the DABS, it is suggested interviewers possess at least a baccalaureate degree with assessment experience and direct work experience with persons with ID or related DD (between 4 and 21 years of age). The DABS allows for interviewers who lack a bachelor's degree to administer the instrument if they possess "extensive professional experience and knowledge of behavioral assessment or psychological testing" (Tassé, Schalock, et al., 2016, p. 82).

The standardization sample consisted of 474 individuals from 36 states in the United States. The sample was representative of males and females ranging in age from 4 to 21 years. Approximately one-quarter of the sample had a diagnosis related to ID (Tassé, Schalock, et al., 2016).

Standardized Adaptive Behavior Instruments: Additional Measures

Six additional measures are also reviewed that were not included in the list of adaptive behavior instruments identified by Tassé and associates (2012) specific to ID diagnostic assessment (see Table 9.2). These instruments, however, provide rehabilitation counselors and other professionals useful information for better understanding the adaptive behavior skills of persons with ID and other DD applicable to vocational rehabilitation, independent living, and community integration.

Adaptive Behavior Evaluation Scale, Third Edition

The Adaptive Behavior Evaluation Scale, Third Edition (ABES-3) uses teacher and parent/caregiver ratings of observed adaptive behavior (McCarney & House, 2017a). It is a revision to the ABES-2. The ABES-3 measures adaptive behavior of persons with ID, students with ID, as well as those with behavior disorders, learning disability, visual impairment, hearing impairment, or physical disability. The ABES-3 measures 10 adaptive skills areas, which are grouped into the conceptual (communication, functional academics), social (social, leisure, self-direction), and practical (self-care, home living, community use, health and safety, work) skills consistent with the AAIDD (Schalock et al., 2010) and *DSM-5* (American Psychiatric Association, 2013) ID diagnostic criteria. ABES-3 items are rated on a six-point scale and answered by those familiar with the client's adaptive behavior in school or home environments. The ABES-3 (McCarney & House, 2017a) is administered in one of the following four formats:

1. *The ABES-3: 4-12 School Version*: Adaptive behaviors expressed in the school environment. Normed to children 4 to 12 years old.

2. *The ABES-3: 4-12 Home Version*: Adaptive behaviors expressed in the home environment. Normed to children 4 to 12 years old.

3. *The ABES-3: 13-18 School Version*: Adaptive behaviors expressed in the school environment. Normed to adolescents 13 to 18 years old.

4. *The ABES-3: 13-18 Home Version*: Adaptive behaviors expressed in the home environment. Normed to children 13 to 18 years old.

TABLE 9.2 Additional Standardized Adaptive Behavior Assessments

ASSESSMENT AND PURPOSE	DEVELOPERS	DOMAINS	ADMINISTRATION	NORMATIVE DATA
Adaptive Behavior Evaluation Scale, Third Edition (ABES-3): measures adaptive behavior of persons with ID, as well as those with behavior disorders, learning disability, visual impairment, hearing impairment, or physical disability.	McCarney & House (2017a)	■ Conceptual skills ■ Practical skills ■ Social skills	ABES-3 items are rated on a 6-point scale and answered by persons familiar with the client's adaptive behavior in school or home environments. It is administered in one of the following four formats: 1. *The ABES-3: 4–12 School Version: Adaptive behaviors* expressed in the school environment (ages 4–12 years old). 2. *The ABES-3: 4–12 Home Version: Adaptive behaviors* expressed in the home environment (ages 4–12 years old). 3. *The ABES-3: 13-18 School Version: Adaptive* behaviors expressed in the school environment (ages 3–18 years old). 4. *The ABES-3: 13-18 Home Version: Adaptive behaviors* expressed in the home environment (ages 3–18 years old).	The ABES-3 standardization sample population for the age group 4–12 years was 2,012 persons for the School and 1,518 for the Home Versions. For the age group 13–18 years, the sample numbers were 672 persons for the School and 381 for the Home Versions. For all sample groups, efforts were made to match national population demographics for gender, residence, geographic area, parent occupation, and race.
Inventory for Client and Agency Planning (ICAP): assesses adaptive behavior and maladaptive behaviors to identify the level of care, supervisor, or training a client requires.	Bruininks, Hill, Weatherman, & Woodcock (1986)	Adaptive behavior: ■ Motor skills ■ Social and commu-nication skills ■ Personal living skills ■ Community living skills, ■ Maladaptive behaviors	ICAP items are rated on a 1–9 scale. A total of 77 questions correspond to adaptive behavior, whereas 24 questions address maladaptive behaviors. Raters familiar with the client rate the ICAP adaptive behavior domains through informal observation.	The standardization sample included 1,764 persons without disabilities, aged 1–82 years.

(continued)

TABLE 9.2 Additional Standardized Adaptive Behavior Assessments *(continued)*

ASSESSMENT AND PURPOSE	DEVELOPERS	DOMAINS	ADMINISTRATION	NORMATIVE DATA
Adaptive Behavior Scale–Residential and Community, Second Edition (ABS-RC:2): evaluates personal independence, responsibility, and social behaviors and is the counterpart to the ABS-S:2.	Nihira, Leland, & Lambert (1993)	Part I: ■ Personal self-sufficiency ■ Community self-sufficiency ■ Personal–social responsibility Part II: ■ Social adjustment ■ Personal adjustment	Like the ABS-S:2, the ABS-RC:2 can be completed by an interview of the informant or by informants themselves answering the items.	The ABS-RC:2 is normed on a sample of 4,103 persons with ID between the ages of 18 and 74 years residing in community settings or residential facilities in 46 states. The standardization sample was stratified on multiple demographic variables to represent the U.S. population. Because no members of the norm sample group are from the general population, Dixon (2007) warns against its use for ID diagnostic purposes.
Supports Intensity Scale–Adult Version (SIS-A) and Supports Intensity Scale–Children's Version (SIS-C): addresses support needs information for adults aged 16 years and older (SIS-A) and children aged 5–16 years (SIS-C).	Thompson et al. (2015, 2016)	SIS-A: ■ Home living ■ Community living ■ Lifelong learning ■ Employment ■ Health and safety ■ Social activities ■ Protection and advocacy SIS-C Part I: ■ Medical conditions ■ Behavioral concerns	The SIS-A is administered through interviews with the client and those who are familiar with the client's support needs. AAIDD (n.d.) recommends SIS-A administrators hold at least a bachelor's degree, and in unique circumstances, those without this level of education could administer the instrument if they have extensive assessment experience.	The standardization sample of the SIS-A is based on data (collected from 1998 to 2003) from over 1,300 persons with ID and other developmental disabilities aged 16–72 in 33 states plus two Canadian provinces (AAIDD, n.d.).

(continued)

TABLE 9.2 Additional Standardized Adaptive Behavior Assessments (*continued*)

ASSESSMENT AND PURPOSE	DEVELOPERS	DOMAINS	ADMINISTRATION	NORMATIVE DATA
		SIS-C Part II: ■ Home living activities ■ Community and neighborhood activities ■ School participation activities ■ School learning activities ■ Health and safety activities ■ Social activities ■ Advocacy activities		
Street Survival Skills Questionnaire (SSSQ): determines readiness of persons with ID for community employment and community living.	Linkenhoker and McCarron (1993)	■ Basic concepts ■ Functional signs ■ Tools ■ Domestic management ■ Health, safety, and first aid ■ Public services ■ Time ■ Money ■ Measurements	Administration is completed by an evaluator involving a set of picture plates and takes approximately 30–45 minutes.	The SSSQ is normed on 200 7th- to 12th-grade general population students from two schools in the United States.

ID, intellectual disability.

The ABES-3 standardization sample population for the age group 4 to 12 years was 2,012 persons for the School and 1,518 for the Home Versions (McCarney & House, 2017b). For the age group 13 to 18 years, the sample numbers were 672 persons for the School and 381 for the Home Versions (McCarney & House, 2017c). For all sample groups, efforts were made to match national population demographics for gender, residence, geographic area, parent occupation, and race (McCarney & House, 2017b, 2017c).

Inventory for Client and Agency Planning

The Inventory for Client and Agency Planning (ICAP; Bruininks, Hill, Weatherman, & Woodcock, 1986) assesses adaptive behavior in five domains, including motor skills, social and communication skills, personal living skills, community living skills, and maladaptive behaviors. Eight areas of maladaptive behaviors are assessed to generate internalized, asocial, externalized, and general maladaptive indexes (Rose, White, Conroy, & Smith, 1993). In addition to these domains, the ICAP combines adaptive behavior and maladaptive scores to create a "Service Level Profile," which, as Harries, Guscia, Kirby, Nettelbeck, and Taplin (2005) noted, indicates "the overall level of care, supervision, or training an individual requires" (p. 395).

ICAP items are rated on a 1 to 9 scale. A total of 77 questions correspond to adaptive behavior, whereas 24 questions address maladaptive behaviors (Agosta, Vazquez, Kidney, Taylor, & Mendoza, 2016). Raters familiar with the client rate the ICAP adaptive behavior domains through informal observation. The ICAP was described by Rose and associates (1993) as "simple to complete" and "requires minimal training to administer" (p. 150). The standardization sample included 1,764 persons without disabilities, aged 1 to 82 years. One key weakness of the ICAP is that is has not been updated since its 1986 publication (Agosta et al., 2016). Regarding its influence in research, Dixon (2007) shared, "The majority of studies using the ICAP have focused on the effects of community integration" (p. 105).

Adaptive Behavior Scale-Residential and Community, Second Edition

As noted with the ABS-S:2, its counterpart, the Adaptive Behavior Scale-Residential and Community, Second Edition (ABS-RC:2) is the second version of an instrument first developed in 1969 by the AAMD (now referred to as the AAIDD; Nihira et al., 1993; Sattler & Levin, 2014). The ABS-RC:2 evaluates personal independence, responsibility, and social behavior (Sattler & Levin, 2014). It shares the same two-part structure with ABS-S:2, wherein Part I includes the domains of personal self-sufficiency, community self-sufficiency, and personal–social responsibility, whereas Part I is composed of social adjustment and personal adjustment. It also contains the same subdomains of adaptive behavior within each of the primary Part I and Part II adaptive behavior domains (Sattler & Levin, 2014). The ABS-RC:2 is normed on a sample of 4,103 persons with ID between the ages of 18 and 74 years residing in community settings or residential facilities in 46 states. The standardization sample was stratified on multiple demographic variables to represent the U.S. population (Boan & Harrison, 1997). Because no members of the norm sample group are from the general population (Boan & Harrison, 1997; Zimbelman, 2005), Dixon (2007) warns against its use for ID diagnostic purposes. Like the ABS-S:2, the ABS-RC:2 can be completed by an interview of the informant or by informants themselves answering the items (Sattler & Levin, 2014).

Supports Intensity Scale-Adult Version and Supports Intensity Scale-Children's Version

The Supports Intensity Scales are published by the AAIDD and available in Adult (SIS-A, Thompson et al., 2015) and Child (SIS-C, Thompson et al., 2016) Versions. The SIS-A provides support need information for persons with ID aged 16 years and older. The standardization sample of the SIS-A is based on data (collected from 1998 to 2003) from over 1,300 persons with ID and other DD aged 16 to 72 in 33 states plus two Canadian provinces (AAIDD, n.d.) The SIS-A assesses support needs in 57 life activity and 28 behavioral and medical areas. The SIS-A adaptive behavior domain areas include home living, community living, lifelong learning, employment, health and safety, social activities, and protection and advocacy. These areas are rated with regard to frequency (i.e., none, at least once a month), amount (i.e., none, less than 30 minutes), and type of support (i.e., monitoring, verbal gesturing; Thompson et al., 2015). The AAIDD (n.d.) recommends the SIS-A administrators hold at least a baccalaureate degree, and in unique circumstances, those without this level of education could administer the instrument if they have extensive assessment experience. The SIS-A is administered through interviews with the client and those who are familiar with the client's support needs.

The SIS-C addresses support needs information for children with ID and other DD aged 5 to 16 years. It includes a total of 363 items measuring needs in two parts. Part I examines support needs related to specific medical conditions and behavioral concerns. Part I questions are rated with regard to the intensity of support needed on a 3-point scale (i.e., no support needed, some support needed, extensive support needed). Part II items address support needs in the domains of home living activities, community and neighborhood activities, school participation activities, school learning activities, health and safety activities, social activities, and advocacy activities. Part II items are rated with regard to frequency (i.e., how often is extraordinary support needed?), time (i.e., how much time by another person is needed to provide extraordinary support?), and type (i.e., what is the nature of the extraordinary support that is provided) of support needed (Thompson et al., 2016).

Street Survival Skills Questionnaire

The Street Survival Skills Questionnaire (SSSQ) was developed by Linkenhoker and McCarron (1993) to determine the readiness of persons with ID for community employment and community living. It is also effective for evaluating the outcomes of a client's gains in training or curriculum activities (McCarron-Dial Systems, n.d.). The SSSQ is not appropriate for use in diagnosing ID, given its specific focus on the practical dimensions of adaptive behavior, its narrow standardization sample population, and its intended use for persons with severe levels of ID (Denkowski & Denkowski, 2008). In their review of the SSSQ manual, Denkowski and Denkowski (2008) pointed out that the instrument is normed on only 200 7th- to 12th-grade general population students from just two schools in the United States. The SSSQ addresses nine domains of adaptive behavior: (a) basic concepts; (b) functional signs; (c) tools; (d) domestic management; (e) health, safety, and first aid; (f) public services; (g) time; (h) money; and (i) measurements. SSSQ administration involves a set of picture plates and takes approximately 30 to 45 minutes to administer (McCarron-Dial Systems, n.d.). The SSSQ is one of several measures included in the McCarron-Dial Evaluation System (Denkowski & Denkowski, 2008).

■ Special Issues With Adaptive Behavior Assessment

Beyond serving a diagnostic and service planning role, adaptive behavior assessment with clients with ID presents implications for public policy and psychological assessment for rehabilitation counselors and other professionals supporting persons with ID. In this final section, three areas are reviewed to explicate the importance of adaptive behavior assessment and the use of best-practice approaches in the practice and application of adaptive behavior assessment. Areas reviewed in the role of adaptive behavior assessment are death penalty evaluations, the benefits of community integration, and the need for culturally responsive assessment.

Death Penalty Evaluations

In 2002, in *Atkins v. Virginia*, the U.S. Supreme Court ruled that persons diagnosed with ID could not be subject to the death penalty, because it would be considered "cruel and unusual punishment, a violation of the Eighth Amendment of the United States Constitution" (Tassé, 2009, p. 114). Fabian, Thompson, and Lazarus' (2011) review highlighted that (as of 2007) only 11 of the 35 states with the death penalty made determinations of ID using accepted professional standards. Fabian and associates noted, for example, that many of the remaining 24 states failed to define the meaning of an adaptive behavior limitation. The result of the inconsistency was that theoretically defendants with identical intelligence and adaptive behavior skills could be subject to the death penalty in one state, while being safe from execution in another state.

The 2002 *Atkins v. Virginia* decision resulted in increased focus on the role of adaptive behavior and its proper measurement in the criminal justice system. Prior to the *Atkins* decision, professional discussion was already occurring on the role of adaptive behavior assessment to understand criminal culpability among defendants with ID. For example, in a 1991 *Mental Retardation* article, Dr. George S. Baroff, a Professor of Psychology at the University of North Carolina-Chapel Hill and an expert witness in criminal cases involving defendants suspected of having ID, discussed challenges with addressing adaptive behavior assessment in death penalty cases. Baroff noted the difficulty in determining whether a defendant's participation in criminal activity is itself evidence of adaptive behavior limitation. Also, he argued adaptive behavior scores in the normative range "places relatively little weight on the issue of greatest interest to the courts—the defendant's capacity to weigh the consequences of his or her actions" (p. 349).

Because of the high-stakes nature of ID assessment in capital cases, Doane and Salekin (2009) discussed the possibility that criminal defendants in capital cases might try to fake adaptive behavior limitations to obtain an ID diagnosis. They conducted a study with 224 Psychology 101 students enrolled at the University of Alabama to determine whether they could provide responses consistent with a level of adaptive behavior limitation to constitute ID. Doane and Salkein created three experimental groups (and one control group), with each group assigned to fake mild, moderate, or severe levels of ID. Experimental group members were provided professional definitions (i.e., IQ and adaptive behavior) for each level of ID. Sample group members took the ABAS-II and the SIB-R. Doane and Salekin found that experimental group members were able to successfully fake believable ID-level adaptive behavior scores with the ABAS-II, whereas their faking of adaptive behavior deficits was detected on the SIB-R.

Because of these inherent problems with adaptive behavior assessment in the criminal justice system, several authors have suggested best-practice solutions in capital case–related ID assessment, which also present implications for the general practice of adaptive behavior assessment. Tassé (2009) stressed the need for multiple sources of information, when standardized assessment can be compared to information from informants who know the defendant's adaptive behavior functioning in different environments over an extended period. Tassé further recommended that previous psychological assessments and other records be carefully evaluated. These recommendations are especially important, given that, in most cases, defendants will be evaluated for ID many years removed from the developmental period (i.e., before the age of 18 years).

Stevens and Price (2006) argued that current adaptive behavior instruments with adult versions (e.g., ABAS-2 and SIB-R) should incorporate norm groups applicable to an incarcerated population. They suggested the need to conduct psychometric research on the suitability of commonly used adaptive behavior instruments specific to death penalty cases. Stevens and Price also conveyed the need to develop alternative means of evaluating adaptive behavior (other than standardized adaptive behavior measures), such as direct assessments of adaptive behavior and the use of neuropsychological tests to determine a defendant's capacities for logical reasoning and abstract thinking. Finally, Stevens and Price recommended the need to develop systematic clinical guidelines to reduce the subjectivity of evaluating adaptive behavior in criminal cases, and as Tassé (2009) stressed, adaptive behavior evaluations should be based on an integration of multiple data sources.

Benefits of Community Integration

Only recently have persons with ID enjoyed access to community life and integration. Degeneffe (2000) noted that prior to the 1960s, the primary public support provided to persons with ID in the United States were large-scale public institutions, which often featured a high degree of social isolation and inhuman living conditions. As public officials and advocates recognized the need for change, the 1950s through 1970s brought large-scale reductions in institutional populations and enhanced opportunities for persons with ID to live and work in community settings (Bradley & Knoll, 1990). The movement of persons with ID out of institutions and into community settings was likely a key motivator for professionals to establish measures of adaptive behavior, so limitations in adaptive skills for community participation could be identified and addressed. To this point, in explaining their reasons for measuring adaptive behavior skills among residents of Parsons State Hospital and Training Center in Parsons, Kansas, Nihira and Shellhaas (1970) shared, "systematic knowledge about the retardate's resources and limitations, as well as the environmental demands and conditions he encounters, is an essential prerequisite for the development of effective rehabilitation programs" (p. 15).

Since the deinstitutionalization period, many studies document the positive benefits of community life among persons with ID through the means of adaptive behavior assessment. With its focus on assessing a client's ability to meet the needs of the surrounding environment, the use of adaptive behavior measurement is an appropriate evaluation tool, given the demands placed on persons with ID in community living for skills not taught and not needed in the restrictive living environments of institutions. The emergence of adaptive behavior in this context was likely a key reason for its enhanced importance in ID diagnostic systems and for its common use in planning systems of support for persons with ID.

From the 1970s to the current time, numerous studies document specific instances in which community living presents positive gains for persons with ID. For example, Rose and associates (1993) examined extended benefits of community placement among seven adults with ID who had moved 1 year earlier from a congregate setting to a community-based apartment setting. Participants included four males and three females, with an average age of 19.6 years. On average, participant IQ was 60 points. Compared to measurement of adaptive behavior skills prior to the move, participants demonstrated statistically significant gains (as measured by ICAP scores) in social/communication and community living skills. These gains were likely the result of learning experiences available in their community living arrangements.

Two recent comprehensive reviews document the collective positive adaptive behavior outcomes of deinstitutionalization. Hamelin, Frijters, Griffiths, Condillac, and Owen (2011) conducted a meta-analysis involving 23 studies that examined adaptive behavior outcomes for persons with ID who moved from an institutional to community residence. The analysis was based on studies published from 1976 to 2006 on 2,083 persons with ID. Hamelin and associates determined that moderate gains were found in 75% of the adaptive behavior domains evaluated across the 23 studies. Larson, Lakin, and Hill (2012) reviewed 43 studies (published between 1977 and 2010) on persons with ID/DD who moved from institutional to community-based settings. Larson and associates (2012) developed a coding process to document adaptive behavior outcomes in eight domains and challenging behaviors in three domains. Among their findings was that statistically significant adaptive behavior gains were found in 15 of the 27 studies employing a longitudinal design. Also, of the eight studies reporting statistically significant changes in challenging behavior, five studies reported improved outcomes.

Beyond the economic, civil rights, and quality-of-life implications of deinstitutionalization, the use of adaptive behavior assessment remains an important metric, given the continued use of congregate living arrangements for persons with ID. Between June 30, 2009, and June 30, 2010, four states housed more than 2,000 persons with ID/DD in institutional settings, including Texas (4,207 persons), New Jersey (2,703 persons), Illinois (2,111 persons), and California (2,070 persons). An additional eight states had institutional populations of 1,000 to 1,999 persons (Larson, Salmi, Smith, Wuourio, & Webster, 2012, p. iii). The need for enhanced community participation among persons with ID will continue to be an important advocacy initiative for rehabilitation counselors and other disability professionals.

Culturally Responsive Assessment

A long-standing issue in special education is the overrepresentation of children from racial and ethnic minority populations in special education, including the disproportionate identification of African American children as having ID (Allen-Meares, 2008). A key aspect of these findings regards the inherent bias of standardized tests that reflects "a White, middle-class perspective" (Allen-Meares, 2008, p. 313). This presents an ethical challenge for rehabilitation counselors. The *Code of Professional Ethics for Rehabilitation Counselors* established in Section G (Assessment and Evaluation), Part B (Diversity Issues in Assessment), that rehabilitation counselors "recognize the potential effects of disability, culture, or other factors that may result in potential bias and/or misinterpretation of data" (Commission on Rehabilitation Counselor Certification, 2017, p. 22). Much of this discussion has focused on the improper use of IQ instruments. A number of lawsuits established the problems involved with relying on IQ scores as the primary means of determining ID given the inherent bias IQ instruments present for African American clients, as established, for example, in the seminal *Larry P. v. Riles* case (Boan & Harrison, 1997). In 1979, the Northern District of California heard the case of Larry P., an African American child placed in an "educable mentally retarded classroom" on the basis of IQ testing in the San Francisco Unified School District. Advocates for Larry P. brought legal action against Wilson Riles, the Superintendent of Education for the State of California for unfair testing practices, which resulted in an inferior educational setting for Larry P. (Wade, 1980).

In favor of Larry P., "the judge ruled that intelligence tests were culturally biased, resulting in the overrepresentation of minorities in special education classes for mental retardation and banned the use of such instruments with African-Americans" (Boan & Harrison, 1997, p. 34). The court also ruled that California school officials could ask the court for permission to administer IQ tests to African American students (Wade, 1980), a step Wade acknowledged as not realistic. In addition to banning the use of IQ tests for California African American students in ID assessment, the court also ordered that all California school districts re-evaluate African American students previously identified as "educable mentally retarded" on the basis of IQ testing (Foster, 1984). Reflective of a perspective that adaptive behavior assessment represented a more culturally fair form of assessment, the court ruled that adaptive behavior should be part of ID determinations for African American students when making special education placement decisions (Boan & Harrison, 1997).

Today, there is increased recognition on the importance of addressing a client's contextual background in psychological assessment, especially given the increasing diversity of the U.S. population (Allen-Meares, 2008). Litigation such as *Larry P. v. Riles* has likely played a role in moving assessment practices in this direction. Because of professional and legal recognition of the culturally responsive shortcomings of relying on IQ as the sole factor in ID assessment, adaptive behavior assessment has emerged as a required diagnostic element. Boan and Harrison (1997) argued that incorporating adaptive behavior assessment facilitates an ID diagnostic process that "helps ensures a multifactored, nonbiased assessment," "is believed to be a means of decreasing the overrepresentation of individuals from minority groups in programs for mental retardation," and "provides a more comprehensive means of assessing an individual's level of functioning in the community" (p. 35).

◼ Conclusion

Adaptive behavior evaluation plays an important role in culturally responsive assessment, service planning, advocacy, disability diagnosis, criminal justice, and public policy. It is imperative that rehabilitation counselors become proficient on the use of adaptive behavior instruments and assessment options given its varied and high-stakes purposes.

To this end, this chapter provides a comprehensive review of state-of-the-art adaptive behavior assessment approaches. Rehabilitation counselors should receive enhanced training in adaptive behavior assessment practices during their preservice and continuing education to meet the complex demands of contemporary practice. In the 2017 curricula standards submitted to the Council for Accreditation of Counseling and Related Educational Programs, the Council on Rehabilitation Education (2017) underscored this point by specifically mentioning the need for rehabilitation counselors to receive training on how to assess the adaptive skills of clients in the *Practice* domain of its standards, as identified through its role and function research. The present chapter supports the rehabilitation counseling profession in this pursuit.

◼ References

Administration for Community Living. (2017). *History of the DD Act*. Retrieved from https://www.acl.gov/about-acl/history-dd-act

Agosta, J., Vazquez, A., Kidney, C., Taylor, B., & Mendoza, G. (2016). *Description of the inventory for client and agency planning*. Retrieved from https://static1.squarespace.com/static/57f2fcef15d5dbffa426be06/t/581fa49ce58c62bd098730a6/1478468802375/HSRI+ICAP+summary+2016-11-02.pdf

Allen-Meares, P. (2008). Assessing the adaptive behavior of youths: Multicultural responsivity. *Social Work, 53*(4), 307–316. doi:10.1093/sw/53.4.307

American Association on Intellectual and Developmental Disabilities. (n.d.). *SIS: Product information*. Retrieved from http://aaidd.org/sis/product-information#.WYzuj8mQz-Y

American Psychiatric Association. (1968). *Diagnostic and statistical manual of mental disorders* (2nd ed.). Washington, DC: Author.

American Psychiatric Association. (2013). *Diagnostic and statistical manual of mental disorders* (5th ed.). Arlington, VA: American Psychiatric Publishing.

The Arc. (2014). *State of the states in developmental disabilities project: Overview*. Retrieved from https://www.thearc.org/document.doc?id=4645

Baroff, G. S. (1991). Establishing mental retardation in capital cases: A potential matter of life and death. *Mental Retardation, 29*(6), 343–349. doi:10.1352/0047-6765(2003)41<198:emricc>2.0.co;2

Bergeron, R., Floyd, R. G., & Shands, E. I. (2008). States' eligibility guidelines for mental retardation: An update and consideration of part scores and unreliability of IQs. *Education and Training in Developmental Disabilities, 43*(1), 123–131.

Boan, C. H., & Harrison, P. L. (1997). Adaptive behavior assessment and individuals with mental retardation. In R. L Taylor (Ed.), *Assessment of individuals with mental retardation* (pp. 33–53). San Diego, CA: Singular.

Bradley, V., & Knoll, J. (1990). *Shifting paradigms in services to people with developmental disabilities.* Cambridge, MA: Human Services Research Institute.

Bruininks, R. H., Bradley, H. K., Weatherman, R. F., Woodcock, R. W, & Hill, B. K. (1996). *Scale of Independent Behavior–Revised.* Rolling Meadows, IL: Riverside.

Bruininks, R. H., Hill, B. K., Weatherman, R. F., & Woodcock, R. W. (1986). *Inventory for client and agency planning.* Allen, TX: DLM Teaching Resources.

Center for Parent Information and Resources. (2017). *Categories of disability under IDEA.* Retrieved from http://www.parentcenterhub.org/categories

Charman, T., Howlin, P., Berry, B., & Prince, E. (2004). Measuring developmental progress of children with autism spectrum disorder on school entry using parent report. *Autism, 8*(1), 89–100. doi:10.1177/1362361304040641

Commission on Rehabilitation Counselor Certification. (2017). *Code of Professional Ethics for Rehabilitation Counselors.* Retrieved from https://www.crccertification.com/filebin/pdf/ethics/CodeOfEthics_01-01-2017.pdf

Council on Rehabilitation Education. (2017). *CORE standards: May 2017.* Schaumburg, IL: Author.

Degeneffe, C. E. (2000). Supported employment for persons with developmental disabilities: Unmet promises and future challenges for rehabilitation counselors. *Journal of Applied Rehabilitation Counseling, 31*(2), 41–47.

Denkowski, G. C., & Denkowski, K. M. (2008). Misuse of the Street Survival Skills Questionnaire (SSSQ) for evaluating the adult adaptive behavior of criminal defendants with intellectual disability claims. *Intellectual and Developmental Disabilities, 46*(2), 144–149. doi:10.1352/0047-6765(2008)46[144:motsss]2.0.co;2

Developmental Disabilities Assistance and Bill of Rights Act of 2000, 42 U.S.C. §§ 101–401 (2000).

Dixon, D. R. (2007). Adaptive behavior scales. *International Review of Research in Mental Retardation, 34,* 99–140. doi:10.1016/s0074-7750(07)34003-2

Doane, B. M., & Salekin, K. L. (2009). Susceptibility of current adaptive behavior measures to feigned deficits. *Law and Human Behavior, 33*(4), 329–343. doi:10.1007/s10979-008-9157-5

Fabian, J. M., Thompson, W. W., IV, & Lazarus, J. B. (2011). Life, death, and IQ: It's much more than just a score: Understanding and utilizing forensic psychological and neuropsychological evaluations in Atkins intellectual disability/mental retardation cases. *Cleveland State Law Review, 59,* 399. Retrieved from https://engagedscholarship.csuohio.edu/clevstlrev/vol59/iss3/7/

Foster, S. G. (1984). *Court finds IQ tests to be racially biased for black pupils' placement.* Retrieved from http://www.edweek.org/ew/articles/1984/02/08/05320018.h03.html

Hamelin, J. P., Frijters, J., Griffiths, D., Condillac, R., & Owen, F. (2011). Meta-analysis of deinstitutionalisation adaptive behaviour outcomes: Research and clinical implications. *Journal of Intellectual and Developmental Disability, 36*(1), 61–72. doi:10.1080/13668250.2010.544034

Hangauer, J., Worcester, J., & Armstrong, K. (2013). Models and methods of assessing adaptive behavior. In D. H. Saklofske, C. R. Reynolds, & V. Schwean (Eds.), *The Oxford handbook of child psychological assessment.* New York, NY: Oxford University Press. Retrieved from http://www.oxfordhandbooks.com/view/10.1093/oxfordhb/9780199796304.001.0001/oxfordhb-9780199796304-e-027

Harries, J., Guscia, R., Kirby, N., Nettelbeck, T., & Taplin, J. (2005). Support needs and adaptive behaviors. *American Journal on Mental Retardation, 110*(5), 393–404. doi:10.1352/0895-8017(2005)110[393:snaab]2.0.co;2

Harrison, P. L., & Boney, T. L. (2002). Best practices in the assessment of adaptive behavior. In A. Thomas & J. Grimes (Eds.), *Best practices in school psychology* (4th ed., pp. 1167–1179). Bethesda, MD: National Association of School Psychologists.

Harrison, P. L., & Oakland, T. (2015a). *(ABAS-3) Adaptive behavior assessment system* (3rd ed.). Retrieved from https://www.wpspublish.com/store/p/3234/adaptive-behavior-assessment-system-third-edition-abas-3#description

Harrison, P. L., & Oakland, T. (2015b). *Adaptive behavior assessment system* (3rd ed.). Bloomington, MN: Pearson.

Heber, R. (1959). A manual on terminology and classification in mental retardation [Monograph Supplement]. *American Journal of Mental Deficiency, 64,* 1–111.

Larson, S., Lakin, C., & Hill, S. (2012). Behavioral outcomes of moving from institutional to community living for people with intellectual and developmental disabilities: US studies from 1977 to 2010. *Research and Practice for Persons with Severe Disabilities, 37*(4), 235–246. doi:10.2511/027494813805327287

Larson, S., Salmi, P., Smith, D., Wuourio, A., & Webster, A. (2012). *Residential services for persons with developmental disabilities: Status and trends through 2010.* Minneapolis: University of Minnesota, Institute on Community Integration, Research and Training Center on Community Living.

Linkenhoker, D., & McCarron, L. (1993). *Adaptive behavior: The Street Survival Skills Questionnaire.* Dallas, TX: McCarron-Dial System.

Livermore, G. A., Bardos, M., & Katz, K. (2017). Supplemental security income and social security disability insurance beneficiaries with intellectual disabilities. *Social Security Bulletin, 77*(1), 17–40. doi:10.1093/oxfordhb/9780199838509.013.026

Luckasson, R., Coulter, D. L., Polloway, E. A., Reiss, S., Schalock, R. L., Snell, M. E., . . . Stark, J. A. (1992). *Mental retardation: Definition, classification, and systems of supports* (9th ed.). Washington, DC: American Association on Mental Retardation.

Maenner, M. J., Blumberg, S. J., Koban, M. D., Christensen, D., Yeargin-Allsopp, M., & Schieve, L. A. (2016). Prevalence of cerebral palsy and intellectual disability among children identified in two U.S. National Surveys, 2011–2013. *Annals of Epidemiology, 26,* 222–226. doi:10.1016/j.annepidem.2016.01.001

McCarney, S. B., & House, S. N. (2017a). *Adaptive Behavior Evaluation Scale* (3rd ed.). Columbia, MO: Hawthorne.

McCarney, S. B., & House, S. N. (2017b). *Adaptive Behavior Evaluation Scale: Third edition: 4-12 years.* Retrieved from https://www.hawthorne-ed.com/images/adaptive%20behavior/samples/h01850sb.pdf

McCarney, S. B., & House, S. N. (2017c). *Adaptive Behavior Evaluation Scale: Third edition: 13-18 years.* Retrieved from https://www.hawthorne-ed.com/images/adaptive%20behavior/samples/h01950sb.pdf

McCarron-Dial Systems. (n.d.). *Adaptive behavior: Street Survival Skills Questionnaire.* Retrieved from http://www.mccarrondial.com/SSSQinfo.pdf

Meins, W., & Süssmann, D. (1993). Evaluation of an adaptive behaviour classification for mentally retarded adults. *Social Psychiatry and Psychiatric Epidemiology, 28*(4), 201–205. doi:10.1007/bf00797324

Moon, M. S., Inge, K. J., Wehman, P., Brooke, V., & Barcus, M. (1990). *Helping persons with severe disabilities get and keep employment: Supported employment issues and outcomes.* Baltimore, MD: Paul H. Brookes.

Nihira, K., Leland, H., & Lambert, N. (1993). *AAMR Adaptive Behavior Scale–Residential and Community Version* (2nd ed.). Austin, TX: Pro-Ed.

Nihira, K., & Shellhaas, M. (1970). Study of adaptive behavior: Its rationale, method and implication in rehabilitation programs. *Mental Retardation, 8*(5), 11–16.

Obi, O., Van Naarden Braun, K., Baio, J., Drews-Botsch, C., Devine, O., & Yeargin-Allsopp, M. (2011). Effect of incorporating adaptive functioning scores on the prevalence of intellectual disability. *American Journal on Intellectual and Developmental Disabilities, 116*(5), 360–370. doi:10.1352/1944-7558-116.5.360

Parker, R. M., Szymanski, E. M., & Hanley-Maxwell, C. (1989). Ecological assessment in supported employment. *Journal of Applied Rehabilitation Counseling, 20*(3), 26–33.

Power, P. (2013). *A guide to vocational assessment* (5th ed.). Austin, TX: Pro-Ed.

PsychCorp. (2016). *Vineland-3: The adaptive behavior assessment you know and trust.* Retrieved from http://images.pearsonclinical.com/images/Assets/vineland-3/Vineland-3-Flyer.pdf

Rose, K. C., White, J. A., Conroy, J., & Smith, D. M. (1993). Following the course of change: A study of adaptive and maladaptive behaviors in young adults living in the community. *Education and Training in Mental Retardation, 28,* 149–154.

Sattler, J. M., & Levin, E. (2014). Adaptive behavior. In J. M. Sattler (Ed.), *Foundations of behavioral, social, and clinical assessment of children* (6th ed., pp. 375–394). San Diego, CA: Jerome M. Sattler.

Schalock, R. L., Borthwick-Duffy, S. A., Bradley, V. J., Buntinx, W. H. E., Coulter, D. L., Craig, E. M., . . . Yeager, M. H. (2010). *Intellectual disability: Diagnosis, classification, and systems of supports* (11th ed.). Washington, DC: American Association on Intellectual and Developmental Disabilities.

Shapiro, E. S. (1987). Assessing adaptive behavior. In *Behavioral assessment in school psychology* (pp. 147–182). Hillsdale, NJ: Lawrence Erlbaum Associates.

Sparrow, S. S., Cicchetti, D. V., & Saulnier, C. A. (2016). *Vineland adaptive behavior scales* (3rd ed.). Bloomington, MN: Pearson.

Stevens, K. B., & Price, J. R. (2006). Adaptive behavior, mental retardation, and the death penalty. *Journal of Forensic Psychology Practice, 6*(3), 1–29. doi:10.1300/j158v06n03_01

Stodden, R. A., & Whelley, T. (2004). Postsecondary education and persons with intellectual disabilities: An introduction. *Education and Training in Developmental Disabilities, 39*(1), 6–15.

Strauser, D., Chan, F., Wang, M. H., Wu, M., & Rahimi, M. (2013). Vocational evaluation in rehabilitation. In D. Strauser (Ed.), *Career development, employment, and disability in rehabilitation: From theory to practice* (pp. 179–192). New York, NY: Springer Publishing Company.

Su, C. Y, Lin, Y. H., Wu, Y. Y., & Chen, C. C. (2008). The role of cognition and adaptive behavior in employment of people with mental retardation. *Research in Developmental Disabilities, 29,* 83–95. doi:10.1016/j.ridd.2006.12.001

Tarazi, R. A., Mahone, E. M., & Zabel, T. A. (2007). Self-care independence in children with neurological disorders: An interactional model of adaptive demands and executive dysfunction. *Rehabilitation Psychology, 52*(2), 196–205. doi:10.1037/0090-5550.52.2.196

Tassé, M. J. (2009). Adaptive behavior assessment and the diagnosis of mental retardation in capital cases. *Applied Neuropsychology, 16*(2), 114–123. doi:10.1080/09084280902864451

Tassé, M. J., Luckasson, R., & Schalock, R. L. (2016). The relation between intellectual functioning and adaptive behavior in the diagnosis of intellectual disability. *Intellectual and Developmental Disabilities, 54*(6), 381–390. doi:10.1352/1934-9556-54.6.381

Tassé, M. J., Schalock, R. L., Balboni, G., Bersani H., Jr., Borthwick-Duffy, S. A., Spreat, S., . . . Zhang, D. (2012). The construct of adaptive behavior: Its conceptualization, measurement, and use in the field of intellectual disability. *American Journal on Intellectual and Developmental Disabilities, 117*(4), 291–303. doi:10.1352/1944-7558-117.4.291

Tassé, M. J., Schalock, R. L., Thissen, D., Balboni, G., Bersani, H., Jr., Borthwick-Duffy, S. A., . . . Navas, P. (2016). Development and standardization of the Diagnostic Adaptive Behavior Scale: Application of item response theory to the assessment of adaptive behavior. *American Journal on Intellectual and Developmental Disabilities, 121*(2), 79–94. doi:10.1352/1944-7558-121.2.79

Tassé, M. J., Schalock, R. L., Balboni, G., Bersani, H., Jr., Borthwick-Duffy, S. A., Spreat, S. . . . Zhang, D. (2017). *Diagnostic adaptive behavior scale: User's manual.* Washington, DC: American Association on Intellectual and Developmental Disabilities.

Thompson, J. R., Bryant, B., Schalock, R. L., Shogren, K. A., Tassé, M.J., Wehmeyer, M. L., . . . Rotholz, D. A. (2015). *Supports Intensity Scale—Adult Version: User's manual.* Washington, DC: American Association on Intellectual and Developmental Disabilities.

Thompson, J. R., Wehmeyer, M. L., Hughes, C., Shogren, K. A., Little, T. D., Seo, H., . . . Tassé, M. J. (2016). *Supports Intensity Scale–Children's Version user's manual. Washington,* DC: American Association on Intellectual and Developmental Disabilities.

Wade, D. (1980). Racial discrimination in IQ testing: *Larry P. v. Riles. DePaul Law Review, 29*(4), 1193–1214.

Weller, C., Watteyne, L., Herbert, M., & Crelly, C. (1994). Adaptive behavior of adults and young adults with learning disabilities. *Learning Disability Quarterly, 17*(4), 282–295. doi:10.2307/1511125

Woolf, S., Woolf, C. M., & Oakland, T. (2010). Adaptive behavior among adults with intellectual disabilities and its relationship to community independence. *Intellectual and Developmental Disabilities, 48*(3), 209–215. doi:10.1352/1944-7558-48.3.209

World Health Organization. (1992). *The ICD-10 classification of mental and behavioural disorders: Clinical descriptions and diagnostic guidelines* (Vol. 1). Geneva, Switzerland: Author.

World Health Organization. (2018). *International statistical classification of diseases and related health problems* (11th Revision). Retrieved from https://icd.who.int/browse11/l-m/en

Zimbelman, K. (2005). Instruments for assessing behavioural problems. In J. Hogg & A. Langa (Eds.), *Assessing adults with intellectual disabilities: A service providers' guide* (pp. 179–191). Malden, MA: Blackwell.

ASSESSMENT OF SUBSTANCE USE DISORDERS FROM AN ECOLOGICAL AND TRAUMA-INFORMED LENS

DEIRDRE O'SULLIVAN | ANTOINETTE CAMBRIA | JOY GRAY | JUSTIN WATTS

LEARNING OBJECTIVES

After reviewing this chapter, the reader should be able to:

- Conceptualize people living with substance use disorders (SUDs) from a holistic, ecological, and trauma-informed perspective.

- Recognize diagnostic criteria for SUD, including assessment for severity of disorder.

- Understand the prevalence of this disorder, including its comorbidity with other chronic health conditions.

- Identify a range of risk factors and protective factors relevant to assessment of SUD.

- Identify important personal and environmental factors known to contribute to worsening of symptoms and understand the complication of treatment interventions, including trauma.

- Distinguish among terms related to SUD and trauma.

- Identify appropriate psychometrically sound assessments for use among populations at risk for SUD or currently in treatment for SUD, including trauma assessments.

- Identify emerging trends related to assessment practices in populations struggling with SUD and recovery.

Introduction

Substance use disorders (SUDs) are complex health conditions, which are frequently remitting and relapsing disorders. They can impact many domains of life and require comprehensive knowledge in order to assess in a meaningful way. This chapter first outlines ways to broadly assess clients at risk for SUD or currently struggling with SUD using an ecological model, as well as provides specific assessments for use in clinical settings. Because SUDs are complex and impact many life domains, we include discussion of health and disability, risk factors, protective factors, and assessments for commonly co-occurring life features, such as trauma, as part of comprehensive SUD assessment practice. This approach aligns with the International Classification of Health, Disability and Functioning (ICF) model of inclusion of personal and environmental factors known to impact functioning, health, and rehabilitation and recovery efforts. As counselors, we are often faced with the presenting problem, the underlying problem(s), and the perception or misperceptions of the problems. Accurate use of formal and informal methods of assessment helps both the client and the counselor understand the complications that our clients are facing and helps us identify underlying or related problems both known and unknown to clients. Understanding severity levels can help both the client and the counselor understand if our perception of the problem is accurate, overestimated, or underestimated.

■ Introduction to SUDs From an Ecological Perspective

According to the National Institute of Mental Health (n.d.), it is estimated that 20.2 million adults (8.4% of the total U.S. population) are living with an SUD and 7.9 million people have a co-occurring mental health diagnosis. SUDs affect people from all age groups, races, socioeconomic status (SES), and gender identity (National Institute on Alcohol Abuse and Alcoholism [NIAAA], 2017; SAMHSA, 2019a). For persons with a physical, sensory, and/or psychiatric disability, the rate of SUD is considerably higher than the rate for those without. Within the population of those who have a developmental disability, 12% to 14% of them have been found to have SUD; persons with psychiatric disabilities reported an SUD rate between 15% and 40%; and persons who experience a disability resulting from a traumatic injury reported the presence of SUD in approximately 50% of cases (O'Sullivan, Xiao, & Watts, 2017; West, Graham, & Cifu, 2009). For these reasons, clinical rehabilitation and mental health counselors are very likely to work with clients struggling with these disorders and should be knowledgeable about assessment procedures and best practices to identify symptoms of SUD as well as important life conditions known to accompany SUDs. This chapter outlines helpful ways to assess clients using an ecological model for holistic and comprehensive assessment, and it specifies valid and reliable instruments to use in clinical settings when an SUD is present or suspected. SUDs are among the most complex disorders as they have the potential to negatively impact a person's biology, neurology, emotional health, learning and education, vocation, social relationships, self-esteem, and legal standing, among other factors, both acutely and over time (American Psychiatric Association [APA], 2013; Richmond-Rakerd et al., 2016; Roll, Rawson, Ling, & Shoptaw, 2009; Verweij et al., 2009). Each of these life outcomes may also be a contributing factor to the development or maintenance of SUD. For these reasons, it is important for rehabilitation and mental health counselors to understand the complex ecological factors that both contribute to and are outcomes frequently targeted in clinical rehabilitation counseling contexts. SUDs are often called "biopsychosocial" disorders because of the biological, psychological, and environmental risk factors involved. The biopsychosocial model is useful, but an even more comprehensive ecological model developed by the World Health Organization (WHO, 2001) helps counselors and clients understand not only the individual and environmental factors, but how these factors interact with each other.

The WHO's ICF (WHO, 2001) is an ecological framework for holistic and comprehensive client conceptualization (for more information on ICF, see Chapter 2, The World Health

Organization International Classification of Functioning, Disability and Health as a Framework for Rehabilitation Assessment). This model serves as a tool to informally assess for factors related to health and functioning, personal and environmental factors, and how these factors influence capacity and performance related to activities, goals, and social roles. This framework helps organize life factors that may be worsening the presenting problem or providing support that can be leveraged. For instance, the social support in a person's life can be instrumental in either enabling an SUD or making significant life changes that support recovery from an SUD. Using a systems approach makes it easier to perceive how the environmental factors at various levels interact and impact each other as well as the client (Magasi et al., 2015). Understanding global risk and protective factors is an important first step in evaluating individual client risk and resiliency. Ongoing assessment of risk and protective factors is recommended as part of best practice with the goal of reducing risks and enhancing protective factors when possible. Additionally, clinicians need to assess for level of severity in order to understand appropriate interventions. A combination of formal and informal assessments, including semistructured interviews that are guided by the bioecological ICF framework, is recommended for best assessment practice. Counselors can use individual items on a particular formal assessment or screening tool to prompt further discussion with clients.

Protective Factors

Some common protective factors include positive coping skills, economic resources, and social supports. Skills that can help clients with an SUD may include interpersonal communication, impulse control, and academic skills (National Institute on Drug Abuse [NIDA], 2003). Strengths are experiences on a personal level, within a familial system, at school, with social support, and in the community. The presence of support across these factors will increase a person's protective factors and decrease immediate risks. Clients who have greater access to resources are also at an advantage; therefore, those in rural communities, with lower SES, and no insurance would have a harder time accessing these necessary resources. Clients with a strong social support network are more likely to use those supports to decrease imminent risks.

Risk Factors

Important risk factors known to enhance onset and maintenance of SUD include access to substances, family history of SUD and other psychiatric disorders, early onset of engaging in risky behaviors (e.g., unsafe sex, skipping school), unsafe living environments, personal or parental legal history, lack of supervision, poverty, young age of initial use, child maltreatment, and trauma (NIDA, 2003; WHO, 2009). Clinical rehabilitation and mental health counselors can work with clients to teach adaptive coping, increase the number and quality of social supports, and connect clients and families to important community and financial resources to offset risk factors.

Terminology Related to SUD

Addiction, abuse, dependence, problem use, and *binge use* are all terms that may describe client issues related to drug and alcohol use. An important clinical skill for counselors to possess is accurate assessment of severity of the clinical concern. Drug use can be considered normal or nonclinical, meaning that someone drinks alcohol in moderation (typically defined as 1–2 drinks a day or less), with no legal, health, social, or vocational concerns. Others can be physically and emotionally dependent on a drug to the point of using daily, increasing use over time, experiencing painful withdrawal when the drug is not available, and suffering social, financial, legal, educational, or vocational consequences as a result. The terms *substance abuse* and *substance dependence* are former diagnostic terms that have since been replaced with new diagnostic criteria (see next section). Both were considered clinically relevant, but the main distinction pertained to physical dependence on a substance, as evidenced by withdrawal symptoms, whereas abuse signified problems related to social, vocational, or health outcomes. The term *binge use* is technically defined as four or more drinks for women and five or more for men, within a 2-hour time frame, resulting in peak blood alcohol content of .08 (NIAAA, 2018). A drink is defined as 1.5 oz. of liquor, one 5-oz. glass of wine, or one 12-oz. beer. *Binge* was originally a clinical description of problematic alcohol use immediately followed by a period of abstinence. The limitation with this term is that the time frame is not specified, and although gender is important for metabolic reasons, this term is usually best regarded as a "rule of thumb" rather than diagnostic or reflective of drug use patterns observed in clinical settings. *Addiction* is a term that implies physical and emotional dependence on a substance, but can also include behaviors, or process addictions, such as gambling, online gaming, spending, sex, or pornography. This chapter does not include a discussion of how to assess for process addictions, and it should be noted that there is debate about the validity of some process addictions among experts.

Diagnostic Criteria

The use of the *Diagnostic and Statistical Manual of Mental Disorders*, fifth edition (*DSM-5*; APA, 2013) provides criteria and timeline for determining the presence of SUD. The *DSM-5* assesses persons within a 12-month period in order to determine whether criteria for diagnosis are met. If a person is abstinent from substance use for at least 3 months, then an early remission criterion is met. After 12 months of not meeting SUD criteria, a person is considered in sustained remission (APA, 2013). There are a myriad of symptoms and combinations that can accumulate to one of the three levels for severity. The range of severity can impact a person's life in specific ways and should be considered in the context of the ecological model, including other health conditions, as well as risk and protective factors specific to SUDs for comprehensive diagnostic assessment and treatment planning. *A mild classification is suggested when two to three of the symptom criteria are met; a moderate severity means four to five symptoms are present; and severe indicates that an individual meets six or more of the criteria for diagnosis. The criteria for diagnosis include the following:*

- Continuing to use a substance despite negative personal consequences
- Repeatedly unable to carry out major obligations at work, school, or home because of substance use
- Recurrent substance use in physically hazardous situations
- Continued use despite persistent or recurring social or interpersonal problems caused or made worse by substance use
- Tolerance, as defined by a need for either markedly increased amounts to achieve desired effect or markedly diminished effect with continued use of the same amount
- Withdrawal manifesting as either characteristic syndrome or the substance is used to avoid withdrawal symptoms

- Using greater amounts or using over a longer period of time than intended

- Persistent desire, or unsuccessful efforts, to cut down or control use

- Spending a lot of time obtaining drugs, using drugs, or recovering from drug use

- Stopping or reducing important social, occupational, or recreational activities because of substance use

- Consistent substance use, despite acknowledgment of persistent or recurrent physical or psychological difficulties from using

- Craving or a strong desire to use

The APA (2013) denotes 10 classes of drugs: alcohol; caffeine; hallucinogens; opioids; cannabis; inhalants; sedatives, hypnotics, and anxiolytics; stimulants (such as amphetamine-type products, cocaine, and others); tobacco; and other, or unknown, substances. Each of these classes have a corresponding *DSM-5* diagnosis—with the exception of caffeine, which cannot be diagnosed as an SUD. The International Statistical Classification of Diseases and Related Health Problems (*ICD*) also has corresponding diagnostic codes. The use of *DSM-5* or *ICD* diagnoses may depend on the type of service provider setting.

Continuum of Care

Depending on the severity of the SUD, clients may benefit from varying levels of care. The level of treatment depends on severity of use and consideration of the client's current level of resources, which can range from psychoeducation, counseling targeted at addressing substance use, outpatient services, intensive outpatient services, and medically monitored detoxification services to residential intensive inpatient treatment (American Society of Addiction Medicine [ASAM], 2018). SAMHSA (2019b) recommends four levels to specifically address the spectrum of needs that depend on substance use severity: (a) promotion (strategies and environmental conditions intended to advance support of comprehensive behavioral health and one's ability to successfully navigate challenges related to health), (b) prevention (often psychoeducational in nature, which is delivered prior to developing a diagnosable condition that is intended to reduce health-related risks), (c) treatment (services offered to persons with SUDs), and (d) recovery (continued supports that assist with recovery efforts).

ASAM (2018) has developed a set of guidelines that provide a framework to manage the continuum of care for persons with SUDs (Table 10.1). Assessment regarding a person's needs in each of these dimensions should dictate the recommendation concerning the level of care that he or she needs. It is important to note that recent research has emphasized the chronic nature of SUDs, emphasizing the importance of continued post-treatment supports and aftercare (Longo, Volkow, Koob, & McLellan, 2016; NIDA, 2018). Specifically, recovery from SUDs does not entail a singular event; rather, it is a complex process that involves multiple life domains, each of which require varying levels of support.

Biological and Neurological Outcomes Associated With Drug Use

Assessment of chronic illness and disability (CID) is recommended for many people living with SUD. Psychiatric disorders are the most commonly reported co-occurring disorder for those seeking treatment for SUD (SAMHSA, 2018). Acute substance use can contribute to CID through overdose,

TABLE 10.1 American Society of Addiction Medicine's Criteria: Elements of Multidimensional Assessment

DIMENSION	DESCRIPTION	FOCUS
Dimension 1	Acute intoxication and/or withdrawal potential	Person's present substance use and substance use history, instances of withdrawal
Dimension 2	Biomedical conditions and complications	Person's present physical condition, comprehensive health history
Dimension 3	Emotional, behavioral, or cognitive conditions and complications	Mental health concerns, exploration of thoughts and emotions
Dimension 4	Readiness to change	Person's motivation to change
Dimension 5	Relapse, continued use, or continued problem potential	Consideration of relapse potential and issues with sustained use of substances
Dimension 6	Recovery and living environment	Social and environmental aspects of the person's recovery process

accidents, and/or injury. Chronic substance use further contributes to CID by altering biological and neurological functioning (Abadinsky, 2008). Drug types differ with regard to the effects they have within the body, though many different substances disrupt biological functioning in a way that nutrient deficiencies occur when substances are used chronically, leading to a range of health conditions (Abadinsky, 2008). Stimulants such as cocaine and methamphetamines affect the sympathetic branch of the nervous system, increasing heart rate and blood pressure, decreasing appetite, and changing blood sugar regulation (Abadinsky, 2008). Stimulants ingested chronically put the heart muscles under increased pressure for prolonged periods of time, thus increasing the risk for myocardial infarction and heart failure. Heroin interferes with the homeostatic processes, such as temperature, digestion, and blood vessel dilation. This causes a rise in body temperature, flushed skin, and constipation (Abadinsky, 2008; McKim, 2007). Chronic alcohol abuse damages the liver to the extent that it is scarred and unable to function, a condition called cirrhosis of the liver, as well as being the cause of several types of cancer, such as cancers of the liver, mouth, and throat (McKim, 2007). Additionally, chronic alcohol abuse can result in neurological disorders and alcohol-associated brain damage. Seizure disorder and Wernicke-Korsakoff syndrome are two possible results of chronic alcohol use on the brain. Intravenous drug use increases the risk for infectious conditions such as hepatitis C, HIV, and AIDS (Centers for Disease Control and Prevention [CDC], 2013). All psychoactive drugs affect neurobiology to some degree; it is, therefore, believed that chronic drug use contributes to a range of psychiatric disorders. Neurotransmitter functioning often continues to be negatively impacting for a long period of time after the cessation of drug use, such that mood, impulsivity, aggression, and sleep cycles continue to be dysregulated (Roll et al., 2009).

CID Is a Significant Risk Factor for SUD

The health outcomes associated with SUD are largely explained by biological theories as explained above. The reverse relationship between CID and substance abuse is best explained from a psychological–environmental perspective. Substance abuse is reported at higher rates among persons with a disability when compared to nondisabled persons (Glazier & Kling, 2013). Within the disability community, persons with an acquired disability report SUD at a higher rate than those whose disability is congenital (NAADD, 2013). It is important to note that estimates as high as over 50% of people seeking clinical help for SUD report psychiatric disabilities, primarily anxiety, and depression (Drake, Becker, & Bond, 2003; Donnell, Mizelle, & Zheng, 2009; National Alliance on Mental Illness, 2019). The use of substances is often a maladaptive coping mechanism for persons living with a disability. This is particularly problematic for persons who are prescribed narcotics to assist with chronic pain and who become dependent on the highly addictive substances. Additionally, social isolation and stigma resulting from the presence of a disability may contribute to the higher rates of SUD. As a result of the bidirectional relationship between CID and SUD, it is recommended that health assessments are included as a part of general practice when working with persons with SUD. CID is both a significant risk factor for development and maintenance of SUD, as well as a likely outcome for many living with SUDs. Specific tools for general health assessments or specific health conditions are beyond the scope of the current chapter, but we recommend Chapter 2, The World Health Organization International Classification of Functioning, Disability and Health as a Framework for Rehabilitation Assessment, in this text for more information.

■ Trauma

Estimates as high as 70% to 80% of inpatient clients seeking help for SUD reported at least one form of trauma, with most reporting multiple forms of childhood traumas and adversities (Ford & Courtois, 2014). Trauma-informed SUD practice begins with an understanding of trauma types as well as implications and with knowledge and application of trauma screening and assessments so that targeted interventions are included in comprehensive treatment planning. Additionally, in order to prevent intergenerational transmission of childhood trauma, assessment for prior trauma is a necessary first step for those in treatment who are parents. *Trauma* is defined as an emotional reaction to highly distressing or threatening event that can encompass a single event (a sexual assault, house fire, or natural disaster) or can be chronic (living with a domestically violent partner or parent, or living in a combat zone; APA, 2018; Foa, Keane, Friedman, & Cohen, 2009). *Traumatic events* can be experienced at any time in the life span. These experiences can lead to posttraumatic stress disorder (PTSD) or SUD. Although not all who are exposed to trauma develop PTSD or SUD, many do, particularly those with fewer protective factors in place. Additionally, people with disabilities experience increased risk for trauma exposure (Fisher, Hodapp, & Dykens, 2008; Hibbard & Desch, 2007). Children with disabilities, particularly those with developmental disabilities, are at highest risk for child maltreatment, a known risk factor for SUD (Fisher et al., 2008). Both trauma and disability are risk factors enhancing the likelihood for developing and/or maintaining SUD. For these reasons, trauma-informed clinical rehabilitation and mental health counselors should incorporate trauma screening for *all* clients seeking help for SUD, or when working with people at high risk for SUD, including many living with CID. As part of holistic client assessment using the ICF model, screening for types of trauma for those at highest risk (children with disabilities, persons seeking clinical treatment for SUD) is recommended. Trauma is an important personal factor impacting multiple life domains, including health and maintenance of SUD. People who seek treatment for SUD are very likely to have trauma histories as well. Many also live with a CID. For these reasons, *simultaneous treatment* of SUD, trauma symptoms, and CID is often required.

The terms *adversity*, *trauma*, and *child maltreatment* are frequently used interchangeably, and although they frequently co-occur, it is important to understand the distinctions. *Child maltreatment*, as it is most often operationalized and measured, encompasses interpersonal forms of violence, neglect, or exploitation, including sexual abuse, physical abuse, emotional abuse, emotional neglect, and physical neglect and typically refers to events that occurred at home between a caretaker and child (CDC, 2019; WHO and International Society for Prevention of Child Abuse and Neglect, 2006). Childhood maltreatment, particularly chronic and severe maltreatment and maltreatment at young ages, is connected to significant reductions in health, learning, and cognitive functioning, as well as employment and social relationships (Gilbert et al., 2009). Each of these life reductions poses significant risk for SUD. *Childhood adversities* include not only some types of maltreatment but also distinct conditions such as chronic poverty; witnessing domestic violence; living with a parent or caretaker who is mentally ill, abusing substances, and/or incarcerated; or death of a parent or caretaker, particularly in the absence of a loving and supportive system (Felitti et al., 1998). Exposure to four or more adversities in childhood strongly predicts a range of negative health conditions, including SUDs, among others (Dube, Anda, Felitti, Edwards, & Croft, 2002; Felitti et al., 1998).

■ Specific Assessments and Screening Tools for Clinical Use

Instruments designed to assess for substance use differ greatly in length, comprehensiveness, and purpose. Some are intended to be the first line of screening during a clinical interview that addresses substance use or trauma and indicate to the clinician whether or not it is an area worth exploring in greater detail. In contrast, others provide more detailed information to give a more accurate description of the substance use that can aid in providing an accurate diagnosis. Both rely on the judgment of the clinician in administering the assessment and interpreting the results. One thing that experts can agree on is that assessments of substance use and co-occurring mental health concerns are integral to effective treatment planning (Brooks & McHenry, 2015; Flynn & Brown, 2008; Nidecker, DiClemente, Bennett, & Bellack, 2008). These assessments may differentiate between levels of severity of use, which basic screenings may not. Most assessments are provided during a clinical interview, and the setting in which the interview is taking place may in part dictate the type of assessment that is appropriate. For example, the Fast Alcohol Screening Test (FAST) was designed to screen for alcohol use in under a minute, making it ideal to use as a routine screening in any intake procedure when time is limited (Hodgson, Alwyn, John, Thom, & Smith, 2002).

Interviews may be structured, semistructured, or unstructured, and the type of interview used may also influence the assessment used; those that are semistructured or unstructured have the ability to follow up on preliminary screenings and ask the client to expand on their reported substance use, whereas structured interviews may benefit from incorporating assessments that give a large amount of detailed data from specific lines of questioning. Assessments also vary in the type of substances addressed; many are created to test for alcohol use alone and may not be valid if they are altered to assess for other substances by the clinician. It is important to keep the individuality of the client in mind when administering an assessment; age, culture, and geographic location may mean that some assessments are inappropriate if they have not been normed on a similar population. For example, the drinking habits normed on adolescents, young adults, and older adults may vary a great deal.

Assessing for SUD should be done with sensitivity. Owing to the stigma associated with substance use, it is important for clinicians to explore patterns of drug and alcohol use with clients in a way that conveys nonjudgmental acceptance of past and current behaviors. Many people initiate and maintain drug use to cope with chronic pain or the effects of trauma. Use of drugs and alcohol are maladaptive coping strategies to deal with physical and/or psychological pain. When clients and counselors explore this reality, with the intention of learning how to replace maladaptive coping with adaptive coping, clients feel understood by their counselors and are more likely to have hope for their sober lives. Persons with substance-related issues often experience greater levels of societal stigma when compared to those with other related issues (mental illness, psychiatric disabilities, or other disabilities). In many cases, they internalize these societal beliefs in the form of self-stigma, which can result in negative stereotypes and attitudes toward self (Corrigan, Kuwabara, & O'Shaugnessy, 2009). This often generates shame and guilt related to substance-related behaviors, which can translate to denial and underreporting of use. Therefore, it is essential to address these concerns with clients prior to engaging in the assessment process in order to gain an accurate understanding of the client's substance use history. The manner in which the counselor gathers information is an essential skill to develop. It might be helpful to describe the assessments to clients and help them to understand that they are intended to measure behaviors related to substance use and are not a reflection of their character. Helping clients to understand the role and function of specific assessments and explicitly explaining confidentiality of this information (such as who has access to this information and where is the information kept) can be helpful in addressing these sorts of concerns. Being transparent during substance use screening and taking the mystery out of the process often results in more accurate information.

The CAGE

This questionnaire was developed by Dr. John Ewing (1984). The CAGE is the briefest of all the instruments used for assessment, with each letter of "CAGE" representing one item. This can be used very quickly to gather initial information on alcohol use only as a screening tool rather than a diagnostic one and can be self-administered or administered by a clinician (O'Brien, 2008; Williams, 2014). Of the following four questions, two or more responses of "yes" are clinically significant and indicate that a concern with alcohol use may be present that the clinician can follow up on.

- Have you ever felt a need to Cut down on your drinking?
- Have people Annoyed you by criticizing your drinking?
  - This question may indicate the presence of denial about the extent of the drinking.
- Have you ever felt Guilty about drinking?
- Have you ever felt you needed a drink first thing in the morning (Eye-opener) to steady your nerves?
  - This question can be considered the most important, as it indicates that the client may be experiencing withdrawal symptoms (Williams, 2014).

Psychometric Properties

The CAGE has a reported sensitivity of 93% and 76% specificity for the identification of excessive drinking and 91% sensitivity and 77% specificity for the identification of alcoholism, respectively. These rates decreased when alcohol use is discussed prior to the administration of the CAGE (Williams, 2014). Despite this, clinicians can be reasonably confident of detecting the presence of problem drinking when it exists, while maintaining a relatively low rate for false negatives. The reliability of the CAGE is less strong, and in a review of studies on the CAGE, the median internal consistency reliability was .74, with a range of .52 to .90 (Shields & Caruso, 2004). Overall, the reliability, validity, sensitivity, and specificity evidence for the CAGE support the use of this as a reliable and efficient screening instrument.

Strengths and Limitations

The CAGE is simple and easy to read, and its most attractive strength is its brevity, though the corresponding payoff is the limited amount of information obtained. Though reproduction of the questionnaire requires permission from the *Journal of the American Medical Association*, it is free to use and can be accessed online. The CAGE is, therefore, used as a screening instrument to assess possible substance use during an intake interview rather than to gather detailed information. It may not be clear to the client, but the questions pertain to the entirety of the client's life and not the circumstances that have led to the current assessment (Williams, 2014). The CAGE also takes into account a person's experience of drinking, rather than asking for an estimate of the number of drinks a day, which usually leads to lower reports. It can only be used for alcohol use, though a variation (CAGE-AID) has been created to substitute "drink or drugs" into each of the questions, which reports a sensitivity of .70 and a specificity of .85 when two positive responses are given (Williams, 2014).

The Alcohol Use Disorders Identification Test

The Alcohol Use Disorders Identification Test (AUDIT) was developed in an extensive WHO study over two decades and in six different countries and was designed to specifically identify current hazardous, harmful, or dependent alcohol use in primary health settings (Hodgson et al., 2002; Saunders, Aasland, Babor, de le Fuente, & Grant, 1993). The AUDIT can not only be administered in a clinical setting but also be taken by anyone online for free on the auditscreen.org website. When administered by a clinician, it can be taken as a self-report questionnaire or through an oral interview. The online version asks the subject to select "male" or "female" and then lists the 10 AUDIT questions. After these are completed, the results of the assessment and the level of alcohol use identified are explained. The AUDIT has a manual of guidelines for use, which can also be accessed and reproduced for free online (Babor, Higgins-Biddle, Saunders, & Monteiro, 2001).

Psychometric Properties

Research using the AUDIT reflects strong validity and reliability. It was initially validated during its creation in six different countries, with a sensitivity ranging from the mid-.80s to the mid-.90s across those countries (Babor et al., 2001). The AUDIT's test–retest reliability over a 6-week period has been found to be .88 (Daeppen, Yersin, Landry, Pecoud, & Decrey, 2000), and its internal consistency to be .94 (Meneses-Gaya et al., 2010). Daeppen and colleagues (2000) examined discriminant validity against at-risk drinking and alcohol dependence. Results indicated a strong validity with a Spearman's correlation coefficient of .88 ($p < .001$).

Strengths and Limitations

The AUDIT has undergone a long and extensive developmental process to create a measure that provides an accurate assessment across gender, age, and cultures. The AUDIT is brief to administer and provides results quickly, which are clear and easy to understand. The AUDIT is free to download or take online and is available in 28 different languages and is the only screening test designed specifically for international use (Babor et al., 2001). The AUDIT comes with a comprehensive manual to guide use that is also available online for free. However, it is important to note that the AUDIT does not produce separate assessments for hazardous use, harmful use, and alcohol dependence and that further assessment is needed following a high score on the AUDIT to differentiate the diagnoses. Based on numerous research studies, the cutoff scores were developed to indicate problem drinking and the need for additional tests. The AUDIT assesses for current use, so it is not appropriate to assess for future behaviors, such as the likelihood of a relapse.

The Drug Use Disorder Identification Test

The Drug Use Disorder Identification Test (DUDIT) was developed to parallel the AUDIT instrument in order to identify those with drug-related problems (Berman, Bergman, Palmstierna, &Schlyter, 2003). The DUDIT is an 11-item screening tool used to help identify patterns of problem drug use. It is appropriate for use in a clinical setting and can be administered as a self-report or interview-style screener. The DUDIT was developed for use in groups in which the prevalence of drug use is lower than in the typical population: schools, social services, and employee assistance. The scoring for the DUDIT assigns 0, 1, 2, 3, or 4 points for the first nine items, and 0, 2, or 4 points for items 10 and 11. The maximum score is 44 points, and the cutoff scores are expected to be 6 or more points for men and 2 or more points for women (Berman et al., 2003). For high-prevalence groups, the cutoff score for drug dependence is 25 points, with a 90% sensitivity to the *DSM* and *ICD* diagnoses. The specificity of the DUDIT in relation to the *DSM* and *ICD* were 78% and 88%, respectively.

Psychometric Properties

Berman and colleagues (2003) found moderately strong reliability, with a Cronbach's alpha coefficient of .80.

Strengths and Limitations

The DUDIT is a quick and easy-to-use screening tool that can be administered in a wide variety of clinical settings. It can be completed as a self-report tool or completed during a clinical interview. Because it has only 11 items, a typical administration time is approximately 5 minutes. The DUDIT is a screening tool and is not valid for a sole identification of an SUD. DUDIT can be utilized in order to rule out interactions among various prescription drugs and illicit substance use (Berman et al., 2003). Hildebrand (2015) examined the DUDIT via meta-analysis and found limited information about the validity of the DUDIT, including an inadequate factorial structure analysis. More research is suggested in order to assess convergent and divergent validity, factor analysis, and test–retest reliability.

The Fast Alcohol Screening Test

The FAST was developed using the AUDIT as a "gold standard," under the premise that an even shorter questionnaire than the AUDIT would be beneficial in medical settings where time pressure is incredibly high, such as emergency departments. Hodgson et al. (2002) theorized that if alcohol misuse could be identified in under a minute, then screenings and subsequent interventions are more likely to become part of routine medical, mental health, and social services. They condensed the AUDIT down to its highest loading items and modified them to be relevant only for use within the last year. If a score of 3 or more is reached on the FAST, the rest of the AUDIT may then be completed.

Psychometric Properties

As one might expect, the AUDIT and the FAST have a high correlation index of .93, providing evidence for convergent validity. The FAST has a test–retest reliability of .82 after a 15-day time interval and an internal consistency of .87, indicating strong reliability (Meneses-Gaya et al., 2010). However, the individual-item test–retest reliability exhibited a variable range of moderate (.50) to substantial (.73). The FAST was found to have a near-perfect inter-rater reliability correlation as whole, and the individual-item analysis yielded high values for all above .97 (Meneses-Gaya et al., 2010).

Strengths and Limitations

Consistent with the premise of its creation, the FAST is simple to use and very quick to administer. It is available for free online and has clear instructions including images of alcohol units to aid in administering and completing it and the four FAST questions. Using only the most heavily weighted items for alcohol use, one of its strengths is that the single first item successfully identifies hazardous and nonhazardous use for over half of all samples (Hodgson et al., 2002). If a score of 3 or more is reached on the FAST questions, the remaining AUDIT questions are also listed below the FAST. One limitation of the FAST is that the language used to describe drinks differs slightly between cultures, so it is imperative to give the correct version of the test and be clear in the instructions. For example, the original test created in the United Kingdom uses units of alcohol such as pint, whereas a U.S. version asks for the number of drinks, which could give vastly different responses. Because of its brevity, the amount of information gained is not particularly detailed.

The Substance Abuse Subtle Screening Inventory-3

The Substance Abuse Subtle Screening Inventory, Third Edition (SASSI-3) is a self-reported questionnaire that has an adolescent and adult version. It was developed to help clinicians identify persons who have a higher probability of having an SUD and to determine a need for further examination (Sadeghi, Najafi, Rostami, & Ghorbani, 2010). One unique quality of the SASSI-3 is the idea of assessing a person's risk of an SUD, regardless of their willingness, or ability, to acknowledge or identify relevant symptoms. The SASSI-3 includes 93 items and 10 separate scales, 8 of which are true/false responses, and 2 of which utilize Likert-type scales (Sadeghi et al., 2010).

Psychometric Properties

The SASSI-3 was examined against the Addiction Admission Scale to determine convergent validity, and results indicated a strong correlation of .697 ($p < .01$; Sadeghi et al., 2010). Convergent validity was also found between the subscales and the SASSI-3 as a single phenomenon. The SASSI-3 was shown to have strong convergent validity with the Minnesota Multiphasic Personality Inventory (MMPI). Discriminant validity was examined through a multivariate analysis of variance (MANOVA) between a sample group of students and a group of persons with identified addictions of .97 (Sadeghi et al., 2010).

Strengths and Limitations

The SASSI-3 takes at least 15 minutes to administer, which is relatively long for a screening. There are audio versions available for subjects with reading, visual, or cognitive impairments. There is a Spanish version to provide greater administration opportunities. There is excellent customer service support for the SASSI and a manual for ease of use. This allows counselors to review the manual in between administrations to ensure proper use. The SASSI is less valid for persons with traumatic brain injuries (TBIs; Arenth, Bogner, Corrigan, & Schmidt, 2001). Sadeghi et al. (2010) found that the SASSI-3 is not a reliable tool for assessing clients with dual diagnosis; therefore, supplemental measures for other mental health concerns will be needed.

The Drug Use Screening Inventory–Revised

The Drug Use Screening Inventory (DUSI) is a multidimensional instrument to quantify substance use and psychosocial concerns (Tarter, Laird, Bukstein, & Kaminer, 1992). The screening consists of 149 items, covering 10 domains of assessment such as substance use, behavioral problems, health, psychiatric disorder, social skills, family system, school, work, peer relationships, and leisure and recreation. The items are "yes/no" responses, which indicate a problem density index from 0% to 100% (Tarter et al., 1992).

Psychometric Properties

Kirisci, Mezzich, and Tarter (1995) examined the norms and sensitivity of the DUSI with the adolescent population. Results indicated that the screening correctly classified approximately 95% of the normal sample and 81% compared to those with a diagnosis for substance use. Tarter and colleagues (1992) found significant results for 8 of the 10 subscales ($p < .05$), but the highest was for the substance use scale at $p < .001$. This indicates a high level of content validity for the DUSI; however, the sample size was modest for the study.

Strengths and Limitations

There are adult and adolescent versions of the DUSI-R, which allows for greater generalizability of use. Although the multiple versions indicate higher generalizability, research is limited by modest sample sizes to indicate a broader generalizability of the DUSI. The length of the screening may be a deterrent for some subjects, as the number of items may fatigue participants. This may be especially true for the adolescent population, persons with disabilities, or those who are actively using substances (Table 10.2).

Trauma Assessments

The Traumatic Life Events Questionnaire

The Traumatic Life Events Questionnaire (TLEQ) was created to assess the re-experiencing of symptoms associated with trauma, frequency, and the aftermath of a traumatic episode, such as intense fear, helplessness, and horror (Deady, 2009). The TLEQ consists of 23 items regarding the trauma event itself and the fear and hopelessness associated with it. The initial item asks participants if they have experienced a specific type of traumatic event, and if a "yes" is indicated, participants will score the frequency in which it occurred. Scores range from "never" to "more than five times." Some of the categories of events include accidents, physical abuse, sexual assault, other threats (which contains sexual harassment and stalking), and other (Pierce, Burke, Stoller, Neufeld, & Brooner, 2009). The last question requests identification of the event that "causes you the most distress" (Deady, 2009, p. 85). There are two versions: a self-report and interview-style.

TABLE 10.2 Overview of Substance Use Disorders Assessments

INSTRUMENT	PURPOSE	POPULATION	STRENGTHS	WEAKNESSES
AUDIT	Screens for multiple alcohol use disorder severity	Recommended for age 16+ years	Brief; free; easy to administer; offered in 28 languages; only screening available for international use; valid; reliable	Follow-up assessments and differential diagnoses required to determine hazardous and dependent use; future use indicators are poor
CAGE	Screens for possible alcohol use disorder	All ages	Brief; free; high sensitivity; easy to administer	Low reliability; lower specificity; due to brevity, follow-up assessments are recommended; need to adapt for PWD
DUDIT	Screens for problem drug use	Adults	Brief; free; high sensitivity; available in English, Norwegian, Portuguese, and Swedish	Long format; potential testing fatigue; moderate generalizability to population
DUSI	Screens for SUD and health and psychosocial concerns	Adult and adolescent versions available	Comprehensive; three formats for variety of use: pencil/paper self-administration, clinical interview, and computer administration	Long format; potential testing fatigue; cost for use; requires a minimum of 5th-grade reading level for self-administration
FAST	Quick screening for possible SUD	Recommended for age 16+ years	Brief; free; beneficial to time-sensitive settings; identifies hazardous use	Variable-item test–retest reliability; clarification for drink sizing needed depending on culture/language; lacks detailed information
SASSI	Screen for SUD severity levels	Adult and adolescent versions available	Has audio version for those who cannot read; Spanish-language version available	Long format; counselors will need additional assessments for mental health in dual diagnoses

AUDIT, Alcohol Use Disorders Identification Test; DUDIT, Drug Use Disorder Identification Test; DUSI, Drug Use Screening Inventory; FAST, Fast Alcohol Screening Test; PWD, people with disabilities; SASSI, Substance Abuse Subtle Screening Inventory; SUD, substance use disorder.

Psychometric Properties

Kubany et al. (2000) found that the TLEQ had good construct validity, as it was based on expert review. There was adequate sensitivity and specificity overall, with average test–retest reliability of .83; however, it was low for specific items (Kubany et al., 2000). The TLEQ was found to have good convergent validity with the Traumatic Life Events Interview (TLEI), with correlation coefficients averaging .80 (Read, Bollinger, & Sharkansky, 2003). The diagnostic rate of PTSD increased from 25% from a structured interview to 33% when using the TLEQ assessment (Pierce et al., 2009). A gender difference among the type of traumatic events experienced was found: Men were more likely to report traumatic accidents, and women were more likely to report childhood sexual assault. This was highly correlated with the structured interview, which indicated men reporting accidents as highly traumatic, but women reporting young adult sexual assaults (Pierce et al., 2009).

Strengths and Limitations

The TLEQ is a thorough, but quick assessment for traumatic event identification, typically requiring 10 to 15 minutes to administer. The assessment is available through *Western Psychological Services* publishing for approximately $150 for 25 forms. There is an additional cost in order to obtain the training manual and DVD for administration. Pierce and colleagues (2009) found that the TLEQ identified nine times more traumatic event experiences of participants than a structured interview. This could help practitioners identify more clients who may be at risk of developing an SUD or a PTSD diagnosis. There is no normative data to support use for specific populations; however, the TLEQ does display strong validity and reliability ratings.

The Childhood Trauma Questionnaire

The Childhood Trauma Questionnaire (CTQ) is a 28-item self-report screening instrument to detect a history of child maltreatment in adults as well as assess the frequency and severity of maltreatment across five categories: *emotional abuse, physical abuse, sexual abuse, emotional neglect,* and *physical neglect* (Bernstein & Fink, 1998). Three items are used as validity checks. Responses on the instrument involve a 5-point Likert-type scale, which ranges from "never true" to "very often true." Possible scores on the CTQ range from 25 to 125, aligning with severity levels from "none" to "extreme."

Psychometric Properties

The items on the CTQ have a good internal consistency (Waldinger, Schulz, Barsky, & Ahern, 2006), with the maltreatment cutoff score demonstrating good convergence with clinician ratings of child maltreatment (Bernstein et al., 2003). Several research studies (Driessen, Schroeder, Widmann, von Schoenfeld, & Schneider, 2006; Waldinger et al., 2006) have used an overall composite score for the CTQ, demonstrating sufficient levels of internal consistency reliability. Normative data were collected from 231 patients engaged in substance abuse treatment from two Veterans Affairs hospitals in New York City (Bernstein & Fink, 1998). Within the sample Latino and African American clients were overrepresented. The aforementioned factor items resulted in high levels of internal consistently reliability as Cronbach's alpha coefficients ranged from .79 to .94; the entire scale resulted in a Cronbach's alpha coefficient of .95. Test–retest reliability was also high for the instrument ($r = .88$) for clients ($N = 40$) who were asked to complete the CTQ again after 3.6 months. The CTQ sexual abuse ($r = .58$), physical abuse ($r = .42$), and emotional abuse ($r = .51$) scores were highly correlated with corresponding factors on the Childhood Trauma

Interview, indicating a high degree of convergent validity. Also, discriminant validity for the CTQ was established using measures of verbal intelligence ($r = .10$) and social desirability ($r = .10$); no significant correlations were found between these measures and the CTQ.

Strengths and Limitations

The CTQ is a quick and easy-to-use measurement for assessing child maltreatment. The questionnaire can be completed in approximately 5 minutes, yet it thoroughly examines five different types of childhood trauma. The CTQ is available to purchase through *Pearson Education* and costs approximately $180 for the CTQ complete kit, which includes a manual, 25 questionnaires, and scoring documents. The CTQ is assigned a level B qualification assessment; therefore, only clinicians with a master's degree or license may administer the measure. Knowledge and experience with child maltreatment and trauma are recommended before administering the CTQ because of the sensitive nature of the content and population.

The Adverse Childhood Experiences-Abuse Short Form

The Adverse Childhood Experiences (ACE) Questionnaire is one of the most widely used instruments to assess child abuse exposure (CDC, n.d.). The ACE comprises 10 domains that measure emotional, physical, and sexual abuse; neglect; violence; and other various household dysfunctions (Meinck, Cosma, Mikton, & Baban, 2017). The ACE-ASF is a short form of the ACE, comprising eight items that are solely focused on abuse in adolescents and adults; household dysfunction was removed in the short form. Rothman, Edwards, Heeran, and Hingson (2008) examined the impacts of ACE on age of first substance use. Results indicated a significant difference between those who experienced an ACE (first use age is <14 years) and those who did not (age >21 years). Additionally, the study found that persons who experience multiple ACEs were more likely to report using substances as a means for coping. The most common ACE was parental separation/divorce (41.3%), followed by living with a household member who was considered a "problem drinker" (28/7%), mental illness (24.8%), and sexual abuse (19.1%; Rothman et al., 2008).

Psychometric Properties

There are minimal research studies that examine the reliability and validity of the ACE-ASF. Meinck and colleagues were the first to examine its psychometric properties for this short form. They assessed adolescents with a mean age of 15 years, with a 56.2% female sample. Results indicated that 39.7% of the sample experienced emotional abuse, 32.2% reported physical abuse, and 13.1% experienced sexual abuse (Meinck et al., 2017). Factor loadings were high for physical/emotional abuse and sexual abuse, .902 and .961, respectively. Internal consistency was measured using a Cronbach's alpha and demonstrated a variation among items: .57 for physical and emotional abuse subscale, .83 for the sexual abuse subscale, and an overall alpha of .71 for the total ACE-ASF scale (Meinck et al., 2017). Concurrent criterion validity was measured using factor scores of the physical/emotional abuse and sexual abuse items and other relationships: Physical/emotional abuse was associated with reduced quality of life ($\beta = -.508$, $p < .001$), perceived health ($\beta = -.247$, $p < .001$), and life satisfaction ($\beta = -.269$, $p < .001$; Meinck et al., 2017). Sexual abuse was associated with increased bullying perpetration ($\beta = .225$, $p < .001$), externalizing behavior including substance use ($\beta = .354$, $p < .001$), and health complaints ($\beta = .237, p < .001$).

Meinck and colleagues (2017) found lower levels of impact on those who reported sexual abuse than on those who identified physical and emotional abuse.

Strengths and Limitations

The ACE-ASF is mainly used in the United States and other high-income countries (Meinck et al., 2017). Rothman and colleagues (2008) examined a large, diverse sample to assess ACEs in relation to substance use, controlling for demographic information; results indicated a higher generalizability to the population of the United States. There is limited research on the reliability and validity of the short form, but initial studies indicate a high concurrent validity and moderate reliability. The ACE-ASF is brief and free to use, but is recommended to use in conjunction with other measures or interviews in order to gain understanding into a subject's experience with childhood adverse experiences.

The Adult Adolescent Parenting Inventory-2

The Adult Adolescent Parenting Inventory (AAPI) was developed in 1979 in order to assess for potential maltreatment or neglect through child-rearing beliefs of abusive parental practices (Conners, Whiteside-Mansell, Deere, Ledet, & Edwards, 2006). The AAPI-2 consists of 40 items and takes approximately 20 minutes to administer. Each item is presented as a 5-point Likert-type scale (1 = *strongly agree*, 2 = *agree*, 3 = *disagree*, 4 = *strongly disagree*, 5 = *uncertain*). Factor analysis revealed five factors/subscales, including expectations of children, use of corporal punishment, parental empathy toward child's needs, parent–child family roles, and children's power and independence (Conner et al., 2006).

Psychometric Properties

Factor analysis was completed to assess the five subscales. Cronbach's alpha was used to assess reliability for the AAPI-2 and found an overall alpha of .85, equal alphas for the lack of empathy and corporal punishment subscales of .79, and a low internal consistency for oppressing children's power and independence with an alpha of .50 (Conners et al., 2006). For internal validity, three of the subscales (inappropriate expectations, lack of empathy, and corporal punishment) correlated significantly with the full scale, using alpha $<.05$ as the criterion (Conners et al., 2006). In order to assess for discriminant validity, the Home Observation Measurement of the Environment (HOME) interview was used and found a small correlation with the lack of empathy scale (.22, $p < .01$). The directionality of the correlation indicates that a higher level of empathy is positively correlated with the presence of nurturing and responsivity on the HOME and negatively to the harsh parenting style. Adolescents with a history of being abused are more likely to express abusive parenting attitudes than their peers ($p < .001$). Males, both adolescents and adults, were more likely to endorse abusive parenting attitudes than the female participants ($p < .001$). Results indicated a correlation between participants who endorsed corporal punishment and those who abuse their children, an indication for diagnostic and discriminant validity (Conners et al., 2006).

Strengths and Limitations

The AAIP-2 is available for purchase through *Family Development Resources*. It typically takes about 10 to 15 minutes to administer and requires a fifth-grade reading level to complete. For subjects who are unable to read, the administrator may read the items aloud. The AAIP-2 is a valid instrument to assess for abusive and neglectful parenting attitudes but demonstrates moderate reliability and may be supplemented with alternative information gathered from clients. The AAIP-2 is available in multiple languages and two norming populations (English-speaking and Spanish-speaking) and is in the process of developing expanded use for various populations.

The Clinician-Administered PTSD Scale

The Clinician-Administered PTSD Scale (CAPS) was developed to assess children's and adolescents' traumatic symptoms (Strand, Sarmiento, & Pasquale, 2005). The initial assessment was used with adults to measure children's symptoms, ages 16 and older. However, the CAPS for Children and Adolescents (CAPS-CA) was developed to specifically target children ages 8 to 15 years (Strand et al., 2005). The CAPS-CA is a semistructured clinical interview that evaluates a child's frequency and intensity of traumatic symptoms and how they impact functioning. The assessment reviews each of the 17 symptoms of a PTSD diagnosis and examines the impact over 1 month. The CAPS-CA can take between 30 minutes and 2 hours to complete the entire interview depending on the participant's engagement.

Psychometric Properties

The CAPS and CAPS-CA are widely used to assess clients' symptomatology. The CAPS is considered the "gold standard" and demonstrates a .82 sensitivity and .64 specificity (Kok et al., 2013). In order to assess for inter-rater reliability, researchers compared a separate rater for seven interviews: Excellent agreement was found, with reliability coefficients ranging from .92 to .99 (Weathers, Keane, & Davidson, 2001). Additionally, raters found perfect agreement with diagnoses of PTSD. Convergent reliability was measured against the Mississippi Scale for combat veterans at .70 and the Keane PTSD scale (PK) scale of the MMPI at .84 (Weathers et al., 2001). The CAPS was measured for discriminant validity against depression and anxiety scales, and results indicate correlations of .61 to .75 and .66 to .76, respectively. The CAPS-CA was examined for reliability and results indicated a total scale Cronbach's alpha of .86 in the age group of 13 to 18 years (Diehle, de Roos, Boer, & Lindauer, 2013). Convergent validity correlations between the CAPS-CA and the Children's Revised Impact of Events Scale (CRIES) were medium to strong dependent on the cluster examined: The total scale comparisons were highest, whereas cluster C displayed the lowest relationship (Diehle et al., 2013). The CAPS-CA was found to be more reliable for older children than for younger children, likely given the avoidant nature of the cluster A. Children had significantly lower scores on the CAPS-CA after receiving trauma therapy treatment, indicating a likelihood to measure treatment effects (Diehle et al., 2013).

Strengths and Limitations

The CAPS and CAPS-CA need to be administered by an experienced clinician with a level 3 qualification. The CAPS and CAPS-CA may be used with some flexibility, and an administrator may choose to assess criteria A-F only or just specific symptoms during a time frame. Because both the CAPS and the CAPS-CA are sensitive to clinical changes, they can be used to monitor and track treatment progress. The CAPS indicates both reliability and validity for use in adults, children, and adolescent populations. The instruments are available for purchase through *Western Psychological Services* for approximately $150, which includes an interviewer's guide, technical manual, and interview booklets. The administration time may vary, but typically it takes 25 to 45 minutes for the CAPS and 45 minutes for the CAPS-CA (Table 10.3).

TABLE 10.3 Summary Overview of Trauma Assessments

INSTRUMENT	PURPOSE	POPULATION	STRENGTHS	WEAKNESSES
AAPI-2	Screens for parental practices that could be abusive	Parents and parents-to-be	Assesses the parents; translated into Spanish, Creole, and Arabic; normed in English and Spanish; two forms to assess pre- and post-parenting attitudes	Long form; potential testing fatigue; cost to administer; 5th-grade reading level required
ACE-ASF	Screens for ACE on 10 domains	Adolescents and adults	Brief; free; strong concurrent validity; comprehensive for adversity	Typically used in higher income countries; moderate reliability; further research needed on more diverse populations; dichotomous responses
CAPS CAPS-CA	Screening for PTSD symptoms and can supplement diagnosis	Children and adolescents (CAPS-CA); adolescents and adults (CAPS)	Flexibility; can be used for screening and diagnosis; available in Italian; established validity and reliability	Long, structured format; cost to use; requires a level 3 qualification for administration
CTQ	Screens for five categories of child maltreatment: sexual abuse, physical abuse, physical neglect, emotional abuse, and emotional neglect	Adolescents and adults	Considered the "gold standard"; established reliability and validity; easy to score and interpret; relatively brief	Cost; because of sensitive nature of items, counselors should be knowledgeable about maltreatment and discuss with clients; no current versions available in other languages or for PWD

AAPI, Adult Adolescent Parenting Inventory; ACE, adverse childhood experiences; ACE-ASF, Adverse Childhood Experiences-Abuse Short Form; CAPS, Clinician-Administered PTSD Scale; CAPS-CA, Clinician-Administered PTSD Scale for Children and Adolescents; CTQ, Childhood Trauma Questionnaire; PTSD, posttraumatic stress disorder; PWD, people with disabilities.

■ Emerging Trends and Future Directions for Clinical Assessment in SUD Populations

This section briefly outlines factors to assess in clinical treatment planning, such as determination of recovery stage and appropriate peer support community referral for relapse prevention. Working with clients who are currently using and considering recovery is distinct from working with those currently in stable recovery from SUD; however, both groups present unique clinical challenges that are important to recognize. Clinical rehabilitation counselors and traditional vocational rehabilitation (VR) counselors are likely to work with people in stable recovery because of the high comorbidity rate of SUD and CID (NAADD, 2013; West et al., 2009), making them eligible to receive VR services and other individual counseling services to support adjustment to disability. Clinical mental health and substance abuse counselors are likely to work with those wishing to make changes in their drug and alcohol use or who are re-entering treatment after relapse. Recovery from SUD occurs in stages, with specific treatment goals recommended depending on the stage. Recovery from addiction is a developmental process that progresses from a singular focus on abstinence in the earliest stage, to an eventual focus on individual growth in the later stages (Flores, 2001; Gorski, 1989). Sustained, long-term recovery is more likely when clients in recovery are focused on appropriate goals and supported accordingly. An understanding of the factors related to sustained recovery efforts in different stages is important for comprehensive treatment planning purposes and relapse prevention. For instance, early recovery is focused on sobriety and establishing sober networks and peer supports, such as connecting to a sponsor through Alcoholics Anonymous (AA). Knowledge of the various peer support groups helps counselors identify the support network most likely aligned with the client's beliefs about recovery.

Recovery Stages

Recovery is a developmental process. Stage models include active use, detoxification (for some), through early, middle, and late recovery (Brooks & McHenry, 2015; Brown, 1985; Gorski, 1989). The stages are not necessarily linear, and exact timelines are not established. Relapse risk is highest in the earliest stage and reduces significantly as people progress and continue to connect to appropriate sober networks. Counselors can support clients progressing through stages of recovery as they gain confidence and strive toward new goals designed to support recovery efforts. Early recovery is focused almost exclusively on maintaining sobriety and finding and connecting to a sober network to support these early efforts. This stage typically spans the time from initial sober-focused intentions and behaviors until a minimum of about 3 months, when relapse risk reduces considerably (APA, 2013; NIDA, 2018). The focus during this time is learning to avoid triggers, establishing a sober support system, and working to avoid or reduce relapse risk. Once some level of stability in a sober network has been established and sober behaviors are practiced with consistency, clients shift their focus to the next stage.

Middle recovery is characterized by more stability and less focus on sober behaviors and networks. Counselors working with those in middle recovery should support ongoing sober networking and active participation in peer support groups, but the counseling goals at this stage can begin to shift to relationships, employment, and other life goals relevant to the client. Middle recovery is often conceptualized as the period beginning no earlier than about 90 days of sequential sobriety and can last several years (Laudet & White, 2008; NIDA, 2003; White, 2009). Those in later stages of recovery are likely focused on quality of life and goals that support self-fulfillment. In order to maintain long-term sobriety, the client must find life to be compelling and rewarding without drugs and alcohol (Flores, 2001). Those in late recovery have demonstrated stability, are far less focused on sobriety, are likely still actively engaged in sober networks and peer support groups, but likely to a lesser degree. People in this stage are actively pursuing ways to maintain their recovery lifestyle; many do this by advocating for others struggling to maintain sobriety by sponsoring others in 12-step fellowships, or pursuing life goals that lead to high levels of personal satisfaction (O'Sullivan et al., 2017). There is no valid measure for the determination of recovery stage as the research on recovery stages is not well established. However, we recommend basic informal assessment of recovery stage for clients by asking questions pertaining to timeline and focus of their efforts. Although relapse is possible at any stage, the risk greatly reduces with advancing stage and reduces more if the counseling goals are aligned with the client's recovery stage (Dennis & Scott, 2007; Hser, Hoffman, Grella, & Anglin, 2001).

Peer Support

Peer support is one of the most important protective factors against relapse (Kelly, Stout, Magill, Tonigan, & Pagano, 2010; Moos, 2007; Project Match Research Group, 1998). Peer support groups provide a recovery-oriented and social network primarily focused on supporting members' goals related to achieving and maintaining sobriety. Reduction in peer support involvement is connected to higher relapse rates (Bond, Kaskutas, & Weisner, 2003). Peer support groups provide a recovery-focused network consisting of others facing similar struggles. Peer support groups are free, available in most communities, provide regular and consistent contact with others working on similar goals, and provide opportunities for safe sharing, connecting, and learning. Rigorous research supports the efficacy of peer support by outlining the social learning that occurs as a result of committed membership (Kelly, Stout, & Slaymaker, 2013). A range of peer support networks is available in most communities around the globe, with some communities offering online meetings for those who cannot access space due to disability, geography, or limited availability. The most prominent and well-known peer support model is the 12-step model, such as AA and Narcotics Anonymous (NA). Twelve-step groups are widely available, with millions of members worldwide, and multiple meetings are held in most communities. The 12-step models outline a philosophy of drug dependence as a medical and spiritual disease based on the following premises: (a) persons with SUD cannot manage their lives; (b) persons with SUD cannot stop on their own; (c) surrender to a higher power is necessary; and (d) following the 12 steps outlined in the "big book" facilitates sobriety (AA World Services, 1939; Ferri, Amato, & Davoli, 2006). Members are encouraged to connect with a sponsor, or sober-mentor, and milestones related to recovery stages are celebrated. Many people attribute their sober lives to 12-step membership. People who struggle to identify with a "higher power" have reported lower satisfaction and success with 12-step programs (O'Sullivan, Blum, Watts, & Bates, 2015). Alternative options should be explored for those who do not connect with the philosophy of the 12 steps.

An alternative peer support model, based on Cognitive and Behavioral Theory (CBT), Rational-Emotional Behavioral Therapy (REBT), and Motivational Interviewing (MI), is Self-Management And Recovery Training (SMART), which was founded as a purposeful alternative to those seeking support in recovery using self-empowered strategies, rather than higher power strategies. SMART Recovery groups are available in many communities globally, including online formats. One distinguishing feature of SMART Recovery is that the meetings are led by trained facilitators who rely on theory-based curriculum, rather than member-led story sharing in 12-step meetings. SMART Recovery and 12-step groups are distinct in their beliefs about how to best support recovery efforts, but both communities provide free, regular, and consistent social support and connections with others working on recovery from SUD. There is no existing validated instrument to assess for the suitability of various peer support communities based on client characteristics and preferences. Informal assessments designed to inquire about client's spirituality and philosophical beliefs of how SUD is perceived and best managed, in the context of explaining the distinctions of various recovery models, will likely lead to identification of suitable peer support community. We encourage and recommend that practitioners be informed of the various peer support models available and work to help identify the peer network best suited to their clients.

Conclusion

This chapter conceptualized people living with SUDs from a holistic, ecological, and trauma-informed perspective and discussed the diagnostic criteria for SUD, including assessment for severity of disorder. The prevalence of this disorder, including its comorbidity with other chronic health conditions, was discussed along with identifying a range of risk factors and protective factors relevant to assessment of SUD. Important personal and environmental factors known to contribute to worsening of symptoms, and complication of treatment interventions including trauma, were reviewed along with distinguishing among terms related to SUD and trauma. Appropriate psychometrically sound assessments for use among populations at risk for SUD or currently in treatment for SUD, including trauma assessments, were identified, and emerging trends related to assessment practices in populations struggling with SUD and recovery were discussed.

References

Abadinsky, H. (2008). *Drug use and abuse: A comprehensive introduction* (6th ed.). Belmont, CA: Thomson Wadsworth.

Alcoholics Anonymous World Services. (1939). *Alcoholics anonymous—Big book*. New York, NY: Author.

American Psychiatric Association. (2013). *Diagnostic and statistical manual of mental disorders* (5th ed.). Arlington, VA: American Psychiatric Publishing.

American Psychological Association. (2018). *Trauma*. Retrieved from https://www.apa.org/topics/trauma/

American Society of Addiction Medicine. (2018). *The ASAM criteria*. Retrieved from https://www.asam.org/resources/the-asam-criteria

Arenth, P. M., Bogner, J. A., Corrigan, J. D., & Schmidt, L. (2001). The utility of the Substance Abuse Subtle Screening Inventory-3 for use with individuals with brain injury. *Brain Injury, 15,* 499–510. doi:10.1080/02699050117045

Babor T. F, Higgins-Biddle J. C., Saunders J. B., & Monteiro, M. (2001). *AUDIT: The alcohol use disorders identification test: Guidelines for use in primary care* (2nd ed.). Geneva, Switzerland: World Health Organization.

Berman, A. H., Bergman, H., Palmstierna, T., & Schlyter, F. (2003). *DUDIT: The drug use disorders identification test manual*. Stockholm, Sweden: Karolinska Institute, Department of Clinical Neuroscience. Retrieved from https://www.paihdelinkki.fi/sites/default/files/duditmanual.pdf

Bernstein, D. P., & Fink, L. (1998). *Child trauma questionnaire: A retrospective self-report: Manual*. San Diego, CA: Harcourt Brace.

Bernstein, D. P., Stein, J. A., Newcomb, M. D., Walker, E., Pogge, D., Ahluvalia, T., . . . Zule, W. (2003). Development and validation of a brief screening version of the childhood trauma questionnaire. *Child Abuse & Neglect, 27*(2), 169–190. doi:10.1016/s0145-2134(02)00541-0

Bond, J., Kaskutas, L. A., & Weisner, C. (2003). The persistent influence of social networks and Alcoholics Anonymous on abstinence. *Journal of Studies on Alcohol, 64,* 579–588. doi:10.15288/jsa.2003.64.579

Brooks, F., & McHenry, B. (2015). *A contemporary approach to substance use disorders and addiction counseling* (2nd ed.). Alexandria, VA: American Counseling Association.

Brown, S. (1985). *Treating the alcoholic: A developmental model of recovery*. New York, NY: John Wiley & Sons.

Centers for Disease Control and Prevention. (n.d.). Adverse Childhood Experiences (ACE) Study. Child maltreatment violence prevention injury center. Retrieved from http://www.cdc.gov/violenceprevention/acestudy

Centers for Disease Control and Prevention. (2013). *Alcohol and public health: Alcohol-Related Disease Impact (ARDI)*. Retrieved from https://nccd.cdc.gov/DPH_ARDI/default/default.aspx

Center for Disease Control and Prevention. (2019). *Essentials for childhood: Steps to create safe, stable, nurturing relationships and environments*. Retrieved from https://www.cdc.gov/violenceprevention/childabuseandneglect/essentials.html

Conners, N. A., Whiteside-Mansell, L, Deere, D., Ledet, T., & Edwards, M. C. (2006). Measuring the potential for child maltreatment: The reliability and validity of the adult Adolescent Parenting Inventory-2. *Child Abuse and Neglect, 30,* 39–53. doi:10.1016/j.chiabu.2005.08.011

Corrigan, P. W., Kuwabara, S. A., & O'Shaughnessy, J. (2009). The public stigma of mental illness and drug addiction: Findings from a stratified random sample. *Journal of Social Work, 9*(2), 139–147. doi:10.1177/1468017308101818

Daeppen, J. B., Yersin, B., Landry, U., Pecoud, A., & Decrey, H. (2000). Reliability and validity of the Alcohol Use Disorders Identification Test (AUDIT) imbedded within a general health risk questionnaire: Results of a survey in 332 primary care patients. *Alcoholism: Clinical and Experimental Research, 24,* 659–665. doi:10.1097/00000374-200005000-00010

Deady, M. (2009). *A review of screening, assessment and outcome measures for drugs and alcohol settings.* Retrieved from https://www.drugsandalcohol.ie/18266/1/NADA_A_Review_of_Screening,_Assessment_and_Outcome_Measures_for_Drug_and_Alcohol_Settings.pdf

Dennis, M., & Scott, C. K. (2007). Managing addiction as a chronic condition. *Addiction Science and Clinical Practice, 4,* 45–55.

Diehle, J., de Roos, C., Boer, F., & Lindauer, R. J. L. (2013). A cross-cultural validation of the clinician-administered PTSD scale for children and adolescents in a Dutch population. *European Journal of Pscyhotraumatology, 4.* doi:10.3402/ejpt.v4i0.19896

Donnell, C. M., Mizelle, N. D., & Zheng, Y. (2009). Consumers of vocational rehabilitation services diagnosed with psychiatric and substance use disorders. *Journal of Rehabilitation, 75*(3), 41–49.

Drake, R. E., Becker, D. R., & Bond, G. R. (2003). Recent research on vocational rehabilitation for persons with severe mental illness. *Current Opinion in Psychiatry, 16*(4), 451–455. doi:10.1097/01.yco.0000079209.36371.84

Driessen, M., Schroeder, T., Widmann, B., von Schoenfeld, C., & Schneider, F. (2006). Childhood trauma, psychiatric disorders, and criminal behavior in prisoners in Germany: A comparative study in incarcerated women and men. *Journal of Clinical Psychiatry, 67,* 1486–1492. doi:10.4088/jcp.v67n1001

Dube, S. R., Anda, R. F., Felitti, V. J., Edwards, V. J., & Croft, J. B. (2002). Adverse childhood experiences and personal alcohol abuse as an adult. *Addictive Behaviors, 27*(5), 713–725. doi:10.1016/s0306-4603(01)00204-0

Ewing, J. A. (1984). Detecting alcoholism: The CAGE questionnaire. *Journal of the American Medical Association, 252,* 1905–1907. doi:10.1001/jama.1984.03350140051025

Felitti, V. J., Anda, R. F., Nordenberg, D., Williamsnon, D. F., Spitz, A. M., Edwards, V., … Marks, J. S. (1998). Relationship of childhood abuse and household dysfunction to many of the leading causes of death in adults: The adverse childhood experiences (ACE) study. *American Journal of Preventive Medicine, 14*(4), 245–258. doi:10.1016/j.amepre.2019.04.001

Ferri, M., D'Amato, L., & Davoli, M. (2006). Alcoholics Anonymous and other 12-step programmes for alcohol dependence. *Cochrane Database of Systematic Reviews,* (3), CD005032. doi:10.1002/14651858.CD005032.pub2

Fisher, M. H., Hodapp, R. M., & Dykens, E. M. (2008). Child abuse among children with disabilities: What we know and what we need to know. *International Review of Research in Mental Retardation, 35,* 251–289. doi:10.1016/s0074-7750(07)35007-6

Flores, P. J. (2001). Addiction as an attachment disorder: Implications for group therapy. *International Journal of Group Psychotherapy, 51,* 63–81. doi:10.1521/ijgp.51.1.63.49730

Flynn, P. M., & Brown, B. S. (2008). Co-occurring disorders in substance abuse treatment: Issues and prospects. *Journal of Substance Abuse Treatment, 34,* 36–47. doi:10.1016/j.jsat.2006.11.013

Foa, E. B., Keane, T. M., Friedman, M. J., & Cohen, J. A. (Eds.). (2009). *Effective treatments for PTSD: Practice guidelines from the International Society for Traumatic Stress Studies* (2nd ed.). New York, NY: Guilford Press.

Ford, J. D., & Courtois, C. A. (2014). Complex PTSD, affect dysregulation, and borderline personality disorder. *Borderline Personality Disorder and Emotional Dysregulation, 1,* 9. doi:10.1186/2051-6673-1-9

Gilbert, R., Widom, C. S., Browne, K., Fergusson, D., Webb, E., & Janson, S. (2009). Burden and consequences of child maltreatment in high-income countries. *The Lancet, 373*(9657), 68–81. doi:10.1016/s0140-6736(08)61706-7

Glazier, R. E., & Kling, R. N. (2013). Recent trends in substance abuse among persons with disabilities compared to that of persons without disabilities. *Journal of Disability Health, 6*, 107–115. doi:10.1016/j.dhjo.2013.01.007

Gorski, T. T. (1989). The CENAPS Model of Relapse Prevention Planning. In D. C. Daley (Ed.), *Relapse: Conceptual, Research and Clinical Perspectives* (pp. 153–170). Binghamton, NY: Haworth Press.

Hibbard, R. A., & Desch, L. W. (2007). Maltreatment of children with disabilities. *Pediatrics, 119*(5), 1018–1025. doi:10.1542/peds.2007-0565

Hildebrand, M. (2015). The psychometric properties of the Drug Use Disorder Identification Test (DUDIT): A review of recent research. *Journal of Substance Abuse Treatment, 53*, 52–59. doi:10.1016/j.jsat.2015.01.008

Hodgson, R., Alwyn, T., John, B., Thom, B., & Smith, A. (2002). The FAST alcohol screening test. *Alcohol and Alcoholism, 37*(1), 61–66. doi:10.1093/alcalc/37.1.61

Hser, Y. I., Hoffman, V., Grella, C. E., & Anglin, M. D. (2001). A 33-year follow-up of narcotics addicts. *Archives of General Psychiatry, 58*, 503–508. doi:10.1001/archpsyc.58.5.503

Kelly, J. F., Stout, R. L., Magill, M., Tonigan, S. J., & Pagano, M. E. (2010). Mechanisms of behavior change in alcoholics anonymous: Does alcoholic anonymous lead to better alcohol use outcomes by reducing depression symptoms? *Addiction, 105*, 626–636. doi:10.1111/j.1360-0443.2009.02820.x

Kelly, J. F., Stout, R. L., & Slaymaker, V. (2013). Emerging adults' treatment outcomes in relation to 12-step mutual-help attendance and active involvement. *Drug and Alcohol Dependence, 129*, 151–157. doi:10.1016/j.drugalcdep.2012.10.005

Kirisci, L., Mezzich, A., & Tarter, R. (1995). Norms and sensitivity of the adolescent version of the drug use screening inventory. *Addiction Behaviors, 20*, 149–157.

Kok, T., de Haan, H. A., van der Velden, H. J. W., van der Meer, M., Najavits, L. M., & de Jong, C. A. J. (2013). Validation of two screening instruments for PTSD in Dutch substance use disorder inpatients. *Addictive Behaviors, 38*, 1726–1731. doi:10.1016/jaddbeh.2012.10.011

Kubany, E. S., Haynes, S. N., Leisen, M. B., Owens, J. A., Kaplan, A. S., Watson, S. B., & Burns, K. (2000). Development and preliminary validation of a brief broad-spectrum measure of trauma exposure: The Traumatic Life Events Questionnaire. *Psychological Assessment, 12*, 210–224. doi:10.1037/1040-3590.12.2.210

Laudet, A. B., & White, W. L. (2008). Recovery capital as prospective predictor of sustained recovery, life satisfaction and stress among former poly-substance users. *Substance Use and Misuse, 43*, 27–54. doi:10.1080/10826080701681473

Longo, D. L., Volkow, N. D., Koob, G. F., & McLellan, A. T. (2016). Neurobiologic advances from the brain disease model of addiction. *The New England Journal of Medicine, 374*(4), 363–371. doi:10.1056/nejmra1511480

Magasi, S., Wong, A., Gray, D. B., Hammel, J., Baum, C., Wang, C. C., & Heinemann, A. W. (2015). Theoretical foundations for the measurement of environmental factors and their impact on participation among people with disabilities. *American Journal of Physical Medicine and Rehabilitation, 96*, 569–577. doi:10.1016/j.apmr.2014.12.002

McKim, W. (2007). *Drugs and behaviour: An introduction to behavioural pharmacology* (6th ed.). Upper Saddle River, NJ: Prentice Hall.

Meinck, F., Cosma, A. P., Mikton, C., & Baban, A. (2017). Psychometric properties of the Adverse Childhood Experiences Abuse Short Form (ACE-ASF) among Romanian high school students. *Child Abuse and Neglect, 72*, 326–337. doi:10.1016/j.chiabu.2017.08.016

Meneses-Gaya, C., Crippa, J. A. S., Zuardi, A. W., Loureiro, S. R., Hallak, J. E. C., Trzesniak, C., . . . Martín-Santos, R. (2010). The fast alcohol screening test (FAST) is as good as the AUDIT to screen alcohol use disorders. *Substance Use & Misuse, 45*(10), 1542–1557. doi:10.3109/10826081003682206

Moos, R. H. (2007). Theory-based active ingredients of effective treatments for substance use disorders. *Drug and Alcohol Dependency, 88*, 109–1221. doi:10.1016/j.drugalcdep.2006.10.010

National Alliance on Mental Illness. (2019). *Mental health by the numbers*. Retrieved from https://www.nami.org/Learn-More/Mental-Health-By-the-Numbers

National Institute on Alcohol Abuse and Alcoholism. (2018). Alcohol facts and statistics. Retrieved from https://www.niaaa.nih.gov/alcohol-health/overview-alcohol-consumption/alcohol-facts-and-statistics

National Institute on Drug Abuse. (2003). *Preventing drug use among children and adolescent (in brief): What are risk factors and protective factors?* Retrieved from https://www.drugabuse.gov/publications/preventing-drug-abuse-among-children-adolescents/chapter-1-risk-factors-protective-factors/what-are-risk-factors

National Institute on Drug Abuse. (2018). *The science of drug abuse and addiction: The basics.* Retrieved from https://www.drugabuse.gov/publications/media-guide/science-drug-abuse-addiction-basics

National Institute of Mental Health. (n.d.). *Substance use and mental health.* Retrieved from https://www.nimh.nih.gov/health/topics/substance-use-and-mental-health/index.shtml

Nidecker, M., DiClemente, C. C., Bennett, M. E., & Bellack, A. S. (2008). Application of the transtheoretical model of change: Psychometric properties of leading measures in patients with co-occurring drug abuse and severe mental illness. *Addictive Behaviors, 33,* 1021–1030. doi:10.1016/j.addbeh.2008.03.012

O'Brien, C. P. (2008). The CAGE questionnaire for detection of alcoholism: A remarkably useful but simple tool. *Journal of the American Medical Association, 300*(17), 2054–2056. doi:10.1001/jama.2008.570

O'Sullivan, D., Blum, J. B., Watts, J., & Bates, J. K. (2015). SMART recovery: Continuing care considerings for rehabilitation counselors. *Rehabilitation Counseling Bulletin, 58*(4), 1–14. doi:10.1177/0034355214544971

O'Sullivan, D., Xiao, Y., & Watts, J. R. (2017, September). Recovery capital and quality of life in stable recovery from addiction. *Rehabilitation Counseling Bulletin.* doi:10.1177/0034355217730395

Pierce, J. M., Burke, C. K., Stoller, K. B., Neufeld, K. J., & Brooner, R. K. (2009). Assessing traumatic event exposure: Comparing the traumatic life events questionnaire to the structured clinical interview for the *DSM-IC. Psychological Assessment, 21,* 210–218. doi:10.1037/a0015578

Project Match Research Group. (1998). *Project MATCH hypotheses: Results and casual chain analyses.* Retrieved from https://pubs.niaaa.nih.gov/publications/projectmatch/match08.pdf

Read, J. P., Bollinger, A. R., & Sharkansky, E. (2003). Assessment of comorbid substance use disorder and posttraumatic stress disorder. In P. Ouimette & P. J. Brown (Eds.), *Trauma and substance abuse: Causes, consequences, and treatment of comorbid disorders* (pp. 111–125). Washington, DC: American Psychological Association.

Richmond-Rakerd, L. S., Slutske, W. S., Lynskey, M. T., Agrawal, A., Madden, P. A. F., Bucholz, K. K., . . . Statham, D. J. (2016). Age at first use and late substance use disorder: Shared genetic environmental pathways for nicotine, alcohol, and cannabis. *Journal of Abnormal Psychology, 125,* 946–959. doi:10.1037/abno0000191

Roll, J. M., Rawson, R. A., Ling, W., & Shoptaw, S. (2009). *Methamphetamine addiction: From basic science to treatment.* New York, NY: Guilford Press.

Rothman, E. F., Edwards, E. M., Heeran, T., & Hingson, R. W. (2008). Adverse childhood experiences predict earlier age of drinking onset: Results from a representative US sample of current or former drinkers. *American Academy of Pediatrics, 122,* e298–304. doi:10.1542/peds.2007-3412

Sadeghi, V., Najafi, S., Rostami, R., & Ghorbani, N. (2010). The evaluation of validity and reliability of substance abuse subtle screening inventory (SASSI-3). *Social and Behavioral Sciences, 5,* 1129–1134. doi:10.1016/j.sbspro.2010.07.248

Saunders, J. B., Aasland, O. G., Babor, T. F., de le Fuente, J. R., & Grant, M. (1993). Development of the alcohol use disorders identification test (AUDIT). WHO collaborative project on early detection of persons with harmful alcohol consumption—II. *Addiction, 88,* 791–804. doi:10.1111/j.1360-0443.1993.tb02093.x

Shields, A. L., & Caruso, J. C. (2004). A reliability induction and reliability generalization study of the cage questionnaire. *Educational and Psychological Measurement, 64*(2), 254–270. doi:10.1177/0013164403261814

Strand, V. C., Sarmiento, T. L., & Pasquale, L. E. (2005). Assessment and screening tools for trauma in children and adolescents: A review. *Trauma, Violence, & Abuse, 6,* 55–78. doi:10.1177/1524838004272559

Substance Abuse and Mental Health Services Administration. (2018). *Age- and gender-based populations.* Retrieved from https://www.mentalhealthce.com/courses/contentCACS/ACS-Alcoholism-Age-and-Gender-Based-Populations.pdf

Substance Abuse and Mental Health Services Administration. (2019a). *Mental health and substance use disorders.* Retrieved from https://www.mentalhealthce.com/courses/contentCACS/ACS-Alcoholism-Age-and-Gender-Based-Populations.pdf

Substance Abuse and Mental Health Services Administration. (2019b). *Substance abuse and mental illness prevention*. Retrieved from https://www.samhsa.gov/prevention

Tarter, R. E., Laird, S. B., Bukstein, O., & Kaminer, Y. (1992). Validation of the adolescent drug use screening inventory: Preliminary findings. *Psychology of Addictive Behaviors, 6*, 233–236. doi:10.1037/h0080632

Verweij, K. J. H., Zeitsch, B. P., Lynskey, M. T., Medland, S. E., Neale, M. C., Martin, N. G., . . . Vink, J. M. (2009). Genetic and environmental influences on cannabis use initiation and problematic use: A meta-analysis of twin studies. *Addiction, 105*, 417–430. doi:10.1111/j.1360-0443.2009.02831

Waldinger, R. J., Schulz, M. S., Barsky, A. J., & Ahern, D. K. (2006). Mapping the road from childhood trauma to adult somatization: The role of attachment. *Psychosomatic Medicine, 68*, 129–135. doi:10.1097/01.psy.0000195834.37094.a4

Weathers, F. W., Keane, T. M., & Davidson, J. R. T. (2001). Clinician-Administered PTSD Scale: A review of the first ten years of research. *Depression and Anxiety, 13*, 132–156. doi:10.1002/da.1029

West, S. L., Graham, C. W., & Cifu, D. X. (2009). Rates of persons with disabilities in alcohol/other drug treatment in Canada. *Alcoholism Treatment Quarterly, 27*(3), 253–264. doi:10.1080/07347320903008158

Williams, N. (2014). The CAGE questionnaire. *Occupational Medicine, 64*(6), 473–474. doi:10.1093/occmed/kqu058

World Health Organization. (2001). *International classification of functioning, disability, and health: ICF*. Geneva, Switzerland: Author.

World Health Organization. (2009). *Global health risks: Mortality and burden of disease attributable to selected major risks*. Geneva, Switzerland: Author.

World Health Organization and International Society for Prevention of Child Abuse and Neglect. (2006). *Preventing child maltreatment: A guide to taking action and generating evidence*. Retrieved from https://apps.who.int/iris/bitstream/handle/10665/43499/9241594365_eng.pdf;sequence=1

ASSESSMENT INTERVIEWING

JILL L. BEZYAK | NORMAN L. BERVEN | JOSEPH N. OSOSKIE

Introduction

Assessment in counseling informs practitioners to assist in making clinical decisions, diagnoses, treatment interventions, and in the evaluation of services provided (Whiston, 2016). Individual areas of assessment include personality, intelligence, achievement and aptitude, physical and intellectual disability, employability, and readiness for counseling to mention some major areas of appraisal (Berven, 2008). Overall, the information obtained about clients by practitioners has the added benefit of enhancing the therapeutic relationship (Whiston, 2016). Assessment in counseling is integral in all aspects of the therapeutic process from defining the problem to measuring the effectiveness of the treatment strategy (Spiegler, 2013). In essence, understanding where the client is and where the client wants to be cannot be determined effectively without the inclusion of assessment throughout the process of assisting clients in making changes.

Assessment interviewing often takes place during the early stages of helping, which includes obtaining information about the client related to the client's problem or area of change desired (Cormier, Nurius, & Osborn, 2017). During this stage of helping, the counselor is involved in "conceptualization or formulation" (Cormier et al., 2017, p.178) of the problem within counseling sessions or specifically within the assessment interview. Interviewing to assess entails a focus on all aspects of clinical concern, including physiology, cognition, behavior, duration, severity, relationships, and context (Cormier et al., 2017). A detailed and thorough assessment interview that clarifies the problem holistically leads not only to accurate assessment but also, in later stages of helping, to amelioration. As a result, assessment interviewing is viewed as the foundation of the therapeutic, counseling, and/or rehabilitation process.

The focus of the present chapter is on the assessment interview. Types and formats of assessment interviews are covered. This overview is intended to orient the reader to the importance of depth, detail, and thoroughness within the assessment interview.

Types of Interviews Used in Assessment

When initially considering assessment, psychological and vocational tests are identified as the primary tools of practitioners. Despite this assumption, interviews are the most common and frequently used assessment method in rehabilitation and related disciplines (Berven, 2008; Groth-Marnat, 2003). Psychometric tests typically use a series of questions to elicit responses from the client. These responses are then scored to provide normative descriptions of the individual. Clinical interviews differ from this traditional format of assessing using verbal and nonverbal responses to the practitioner's probes in order to gain information from the client. This information is then integrated with other client material to make clinical decisions and interpretations (Berven, 2008).

Practitioners may depend on the interview to collect information about an individual and establish a foundation for treatment. At other times, it may be necessary to supplement the interview with other forms of standardized testing and assessment, which would be integrated with information and observations from interviews and other sources, including family, acquaintances, and other professionals (Berven, 2008). Regardless of the combination of strategies used to collect information, specific types of interviews are used to generate key assessment data, such as initial interviews and diagnostic screening interviews.

Structured, Semistructured, and Unstructured Interviews

Assessment interviews not only vary in terms of content, but they also vary in terms of structure with a continuum from highly structured to unstructured (Machado, Beutler, Harwood, Mohr, & Lenore, 2011). Structured interviews include fixed questions, which are presented in a specific sequence, and in many cases, practitioners are unable to deviate from this structure. Semistructured interviews are similar in that many topics and questions are clearly established as part of the instrument, but practitioners are often able to vary the order of topics and questions, along with the extent and type of follow-up questions. Unstructured interviews are highly flexible, and practitioners are able to make all decisions related to content, order, and follow-up inquiries.

In order to develop an effective and useful structured interview, clear and concise criteria need to be established regarding the behavior of interest (Groth-Marnat & Wright, 2016). Once developed, structured interviews are more easily standardized, which allows practitioners to reach similar conclusions when assessing a specific client (Berven, 2008). In addition, by meeting psychometric standards, structured interviews can be used to study groups of individuals in order to improve assessment and treatment options (Machado et al., 2011). However, practitioners often report that highly structured interviews are highly constraining and time-consuming (Machado et al., 2011). In order to explore each client's unique situation, respond to specific client statements using clinical judgment, and more easily develop rapport with a client, less structured interviews are often implemented. Reduced structure allows counselors to communicate specific skills and style while facilitating open communication and a positive client–counselor relationship (Whiston, 2016).

Initial Interviews

Practitioners in rehabilitation settings often use an initial interview to begin service with a client. The interview typically begins with obtaining basic client information and providing necessary information regarding available services (Saladin, Parker, & Bolton, 2013). The initial interview also provides the opportunity to begin relationship building and pulling together information of the client's culture, values, experiences, needs, and goals, which will lay the foundation for effective ongoing treatment delivery (Saladin et al., 2013). Three goals can be used to direct the process of an initial interview: (a) provide information to the client regarding available services, client and practitioner responsibilities, and informed consent; (b) beginning the process of assessment; and (c) establishing rapport with the client for future treatment provision (Berven, 2008; Koch & Rumrill, 2005; Power, 2013). By accomplishing these three tasks, clients and practitioners are well positioned for future assessment and treatment success.

The initial interview provides a prime opportunity for clients to "tell their story" to the counselor. This process involves not only explaining the presenting problem or concern but also sharing relevant contextual and historical information. Practitioners in rehabilitation settings also facilitate the discussion of client strengths, limitations, and preferences, along with information on significant others and their impact on the presenting concern. Practitioners are also able to observe clients, which may facilitate information regarding physical appearance, affect, thought process, and interpersonal skills (Berven, 2008).

Initial interviews guide specific decisions and determinations that must be made as the treatment process unfolds. One of the primary decisions includes the ability to benefit from treatment or service, which is influenced by the client's problems and/or disabilities and the counselor's clinical judgment regarding the likelihood of client success with treatment or services. A second decision in rehabilitation settings involves identifying specific vocational and career objectives, which align with the client's strengths, limitations, and preferences, in order to promote successful employment. A third decision includes the selection of specific services and treatment strategies to sufficiently address the client's problems, concerns, and barriers to employment and/or other goals. Although much of this information may be collected throughout the assessment process, the initial interview provides a useful starting point for obtaining information for these decisions and determinations (Berven, 2008).

The structure of initial interviews also varies significantly, and agencies and programs often define the structure and information that must be obtained during the interview. Initial interviews are often the method for collecting information on eligibility criteria, fees, services provided, and various other factors, and as a result, the structure of the interview ensures that all necessary information is collected (Berven, 2008). Organizations and programs may also use computer applications or forms to collect this type of information prior to the interview, and the practitioner may then use the collected information as a guide to allow clients to elaborate on important areas.

Along with initial interview formats required by specific organizations and programs, many published resources provide guides for initial interviews or topics to explore with the client (Drummond, Sheperis, Jones, 2016; Groth-Marnat & Wright, 2016; Sommers-Flanagan & Sommers-Flanagan, 2013), and interview guides exist specifically for use in rehabilitation settings. One specific interview guide provides interview topics and questions in the following areas: (a) physical factors, including factors related to disability; (b) psychosocial factors, including adjustment to disability, interpersonal relationships, and social support; (c) educational–vocational factors, including education and work history; and (d) economic factors, including income, debts, and insurance (Farley & Rubin, 2006). Power (2013) provides a second example of an initial interview guide specific to rehabilitation settings. Power provides a list of key information to obtain and a suggested format for organizing information in the interview. Topics of information include aspects of client functioning (e.g., mood and affect, coping resources, strengths, interests, work history), along with approaches to connect each category of information to training or employment. Practitioners may choose to use interview guides, such as those described earlier, to provide the structure and format for initial interviews, or these guides may serve as a tool to identify topic areas of importance and/or approaches for collecting specific information, which promotes flexibility for the practitioner regarding how the interview is conducted and how information is obtained.

Diagnostic and Screening Interviews

Interviews may also serve specific purposes, including interview protocols resulting in diagnosis or screening, which focus on even more specific needs (Rogers, 2001). Diagnostic interviews are often designed according to criteria for psychiatric disorders as defined in the *DSM-5*, or *Diagnostic and Statistical Manual of Mental Disorders*, fifth edition (American Psychiatric Association, 2013). An example of a commonly used diagnostic interview protocol following the criteria of the *DSM-5* is the Structured Clinical Interview for the DSM-5 (SCID-5; First, Williams, Karg, & Spitzer, 2015), which guides practitioners through interview questions designed to reach a *DSM-5* diagnosis. The SCID-5 includes versions adaptable for clinical uses, as well as for research purposes. Clinical versions of the SCID-5 include interviews focusing on the traditional Axis I diagnoses and separate protocols for assessing personality disorders. All versions are able to be modified to meet specific needs of the client and/or practitioner (First et al., 2015).

The mental status examination is another type of diagnostic interview and can be used to assess psychopathology and/or cognitive functioning (Groth-Marnat & Wright, 2016). Aspects of functioning typically assessed in a mental status examination include physical appearance, behavior, thought content, attention, memory, insight, social judgment, and perceptual disorders (i.e., hallucinations; Groth-Marnat & Wright, 2016). The structure used in administering a mental status examination varies widely with unstructured approaches using the mental status examination as a mere guideline for the interview. More highly structured approaches include the North Carolina Mental Status Examination, which provides ratings of 33 items on a three-point scale (1 = *not present*, 2 = *slight or occasional*, 3 = *marked or repeated*) to cover all clinical dimensions (Ruegg, Ekstrom, Evans, & Golden, 1990). One of the most commonly used mental status examination is the Mini-Mental State Examination, which includes 11 items and assesses areas of orientation, registration, attention, calculation, and language (Folstein, Folstein, & McHugh, 1975).

A review of the literature points to several additional sources for conducting interviews for diagnostic purposes (Groth-Marnat & Wright, 2016; Rogers, 2001; Sommers-Flanagan & Sommers-Flanagan, 2013). Training required for administration varies significantly among interview protocols. For example, training required to administer the SCID-5 varies depending on the version being used and the experience of the practitioner. Specific training materials for all versions of the SCID-5 are currently under development.

Diagnostic interviews are also used to assess vocational capacity in a variety of rehabilitation settings. Many rehabilitation professionals provide expert testimony in various legal proceedings, including employment implications for personal injury cases and workers' compensation litigation (Choppa & Schaffer, 1992; Lynch & Lynch, 1998). The vocational diagnostic interview is often the initial procedure used and provides an opportunity to assess the individual's perception of history of the disability, treatment, strengths, limitations, goals related to employment, educational and training history, work history, and social history (Berven, 2008; Toppino & Boyd, 1996). This interview is accompanied by various other pieces of assessment information, including review of medical records, physical capacity and medical evaluations, and various standardized tests to measure aptitudes, strengths, barriers, and labor market surveys to identify potential occupations (Lynch & Lynch, 1998).

Additional interview protocols have been developed to screen for specific problems that may not be easily recognized, including suicide risk and alcohol or drug use. These types of protocols provide specific indicators that are the focus of the interview, along with scoring procedures that provide a quantifiable indication of risk and suggested recommendations (Berven, 2008). The SAD PERSONS Scale is an interview protocol designed to assess risk for suicide with attention on risk factors, including age, gender, affect, alcohol use, social support, history of past suicide attempts, and scoring criteria, and to provide recommended clinical actions (Patterson, Dohn, Bird, & Patterson, 1983). The CAGE questionnaire is an interview protocol designed to assess problems associated with alcohol use (W. R. Miller, 1976). The interview consists of four questions (representing the acronym CAGE): investigations of the need to *C*ut down on alcohol use, *A*nnoyance with others who criticize your alcohol use, *G*uilt associated with alcohol use, and the need for alcohol to serve as an *E*ye opener (Ewing, 1984). A response of "Yes" on two or more items is considered clinically significant, whereas a response of "Yes" on one item should be further assessed in order to more easily identify individuals with substance use problems (Berven, 2008). Interview protocols assessing specific problems such as suicide risk and alcohol use allow practitioners to identify concerns that may be overlooked and are in need of additional attention.

▓ Psychometric Characteristics of Interviews

All forms of assessment, including standardized tests and procedures, are subject to scrutiny in terms of reliability and validity, and although the interview provides useful flexibility for practitioners, it is subject to the same type of examination. Reliability and validity estimates are often less than optimal for traditional standardized assessment procedures, and interviews experience additional limitations in the pursuit of reliable and valid information. A thorough review of the research on reliability and validity of assessment interviews is beyond the scope of this chapter, but an examination of some of the foundational issues and general conclusions on this topic is provided.

Reliability

Reliability can be understood as consistency in measurement, and instruments with strong reliability estimates are increasingly free from measurement error. Traditionally, measurement error results from two main sources, the behavior of the client and the situational context. The client being assessed may be impacted by fatigue, mood, difficulties related to attention and concentration, and additional variability in clarity of thought, and all of these factors may vary by location or time of observation. The situational context may also impact the client and result in measurement error due to factors such as temperature, noise level, and behaviors of others in the environment. The interview is subject to an additional layer of measurement error, which results from the practitioner. The behavior of the practitioner may vary across clients, situations, or time, resulting in further measurement error (Berven, 2008).

Highly structured interviews typically produce higher reliability estimates, but this increased structure removes the flexibility, which practitioners often find valuable when collecting initial information from a client (Groth-Marnat & Wright, 2016). With semistructured and unstructured interviews, practitioners are able to vary the topics, questions, and overall organization of the interview, which impacts the client's responses and ultimately leads to measurement error. When using a structured interview format, practitioners will vary in how questions are asked, along with accompanying verbal and nonverbal behavior, which will influence the information and observations produced by the client. Regardless of the interview structure, practitioners will differ in their interpretation of identical client responses or behavior. The variability present in the practitioner leads to various sources of measurement error and impacts reliability estimates, even if assessment is completed on the same client at the same point in time.

In order to provide the most accurate reliability estimate for an interview, which is impacted by the behavior of the practitioner, interrater reliability estimates are often used. This may be accomplished by asking multiple practitioners to view a video of a client interview. Practitioners may vary in their clinical judgment and interpretation of the information and behavior presented, which would be accounted for by the interrater reliability estimate. However, consideration would not be given to variation in the topics, questions, or organizations of the interview format, which may yield inflated reliability estimates (Berven, 2008). Consideration to measurement error influenced by the practitioner, client, and situational context can be obtained by using interrater and test–retest reliability estimates. In order to account for all of these sources of measurement error, different practitioners may interview the same clients at different points in time, which will indicate consistency across each possible area of measurement error.

With consideration to the several possible areas of measurement error present in an interview, the reliability of information and observations presented may be expected to be quite poor. A review of the literature suggests significant variability in interrater reliability estimates of interviews (Avery & Campion, 1982; Groth-Marnat & Wright, 2016; Ulrich & Trumbo, 1965). Interviews focused on a more specific topic, such as the likelihood of suicidal behavior, tend to have increased interrater reliability, while broad topics yield reduced estimates of interrater reliability (Groth-Marnat & Wright, 2016). As a result, it is difficult to reach a consensus regarding the reliability of the assessment interview, as different methods are used to estimate reliability, which may fail to account for all variability in measurement. Traditional standardized tests and procedures are typically not subject to the variability present in the interview format, but the flexibility provided by an interview may allow the client to disclose information or behavior that would be otherwise overlooked.

Validity

Validity refers to the ability of an instrument to measure what it is designed to measure. For example, a practitioner may use an interview to assess a client's interpersonal skills for employment purposes. The interview would be considered reliable if different practitioners drew consistent conclusions regarding the client's interpersonal skills. The interview would be considered valid if the information and observations collected as part of the interview were relevant to interpersonal skills needed in the workplace. Alternatively, the interview serves as a prediction of the client's ability to relate well to coworkers and supervisors on the job.

Using the previous example, the two stages of documenting validity in clinical assessment can be more easily examined. According to Foster and Cone (1995), the initial stage of documenting validity focuses on whether the information being collected through the interview actually represents the construct being measured, which, in this case, is interpersonal skills. Traditionally, evidence that indicates the assessment instrument is measuring what it is intended to measure is referred to as construct-related evidence, and Foster and Cone (1995) refer to it as definitional validity. In the second stage, the purpose is to use the information collected through the interview to make inferences regarding behavior, which may mean understanding behavior, predicting behavior, or determining effective treatment interventions (Berven, 2008; Foster & Cone, 1995). For example, using assessment information to predict an individual's ability to relate well to coworkers in the workplace is an example of this type of evidence, which is traditionally referred to as criterion-related evidence, and Foster and Cone (1995) describe it as elaborative validity.

Measurement error that threatens the reliability of an interview (i.e., client behavior, situational context, and practitioner behavior) also threatens the validity of an interview, since reliability is essential to validity. In addition, sources of systematic error, rather than random error, may also impact the validity of an interview. Systematic error may stem from clients who intentionally distort information, perhaps by presenting an overly favorable view of themselves (Groth-Marnat & Wright, 2016). When providing retrospective information, clients may fail to be completely accurate. Henry, Moffitt, Caspi, Langley, and Silva (1994) found that retrospective information is less accurate when reporting psychosocial information, such as family conflict or onset of psychiatric symptoms, as compared to variables such as height, weight, or place of residence. Practitioner behavior also contributes to inaccuracy of information collected in the interview process. Similar to other interactions in the counseling process, the behavior of the practitioner may influence client behavior, which could potentially impact the accuracy of information collected (Berven, 2008).

Additional systematic error related to practitioner behavior can contribute to inaccuracy of information provided during an interview. Cognitive heuristics, which include representativeness, availability, anchoring and adjustment, and past behavior heuristics, are rules that describe how judgments are made (Kahneman, Slovic, & Tversky, 1982). For example, if a practitioner recently completed a training on the prevalence of personality disorders among clients of child abuse, the practitioner may employ the availability heuristic when interviewing a client and interpret client information as indicative of a personality disorder, although that may not be accurate. Practitioners may also exhibit confirmatory bias, in which an initial inference regarding a client is made and information is then collected in a way to confirm that inference. Information may also be discounted by the practitioner if it does not support the initial inference (Groth-Marnat & Wright, 2016). Similarly, a practitioner's theoretical orientation may cause interpretations of client information to be made that align well with a specific theory. Additionally, knowledge structures regarding problems and pathology, along with stereotypes, prototypes, and scripts, may cause practitioners to misinterpret or misrepresent client information (Lopez, 1989). A racial stereotype held by a practitioner may lead to inaccurate information regarding educational or vocational ability, for example (Rosenthal & Berven, 1999). All of these examples of client and practitioner behavior can threaten the validity of the assessment interview.

Sources of systematic error resulting from client or practitioner behavior significantly threaten the validity of the assessment interview. Previous research points to problems using clinical judgment to diagnosis psychopathology, determine appropriate treatment planning, and predict future behavior, and multiple sources of assessment information may guard against some of the limitation inherent in clinical judgment (Garb, 2005, 2007). As previously noted, highly structured interviews are typically more reliable and valid, as compared to semistructured or unstructured interview formats (Groth-Marnat & Wright, 2016). Unstructured interviews, which are flexible, and as a result useful for many practitioners, experience various threats to validity and are highly dependent on the skills of the practitioner (Machado et al., 2011).

■ Interview Strategies and Techniques

As discussed earlier, the reliability and validity of assessment interviews vary significantly. Both are dependent on the accuracy of information and observations obtained from the client and the validity of clinical judgments made by the practitioner when interpreting the information and behavior. In addition, the reliability and validity of assessment interviews vary, depending on the structure of the interview. Highly structured interviews are often standardized, and as a result, they yield increasingly reliable and valid information. On the contrary, less structured interviews provide flexibility for the practitioner to acquire information in a format and time frame that can be modified to meet the needs of individual clients and allow practitioners to make adjustments as needed. Assessment interviews using less structure depend highly on the skills of the practitioner to elicit information from the client, along with skills needed to process and interpret the information accurately.

Elicitation of Information

A wide variety of textbooks have been published covering interviewing and counseling techniques, which are often used during the assessment interview. It is beyond the scope of this chapter to review all related strategies and techniques, but further information is available in various sources (Berven & Bezyak, 2015; Cormier et al., 2017; Ivey, Ivey, & Zalaquitt, 2014). This chapter reviews the three major components of assessment interviews: (a) the context in which the interview is conducted; (b) the content of the interview; and (c) the format and techniques used by the practitioner during the interview (Machado et al., 2011).

The *context of the interview* refers to the physical environment where the assessment takes place. Typically, this is an office or similar setting that can be used to facilitate professionalism, warmth, safety, organization, and calmness. The physical environment includes things such as furniture, lighting, seating arrangements, general decor, and items displayed on the desk or walls (Berven, 2008). An environment that is neat and well organized conveys a sense of responsibility and care, which is essential in a counseling environment. Seating arrangements should promote eye contact between the client and the practitioner, and soft lighting and comfortable furniture can promote a sense of calmness and relaxation, although this may not be ideal for an extended formal assessment (Machado et al., 2011). The context of the interview also extends beyond the practitioner's office, as the registration area should also set the tone for a welcoming, organized, and safe environment. Although a thorough review is beyond the scope of this chapter, it is important to note that cultural differences exist regarding client perceptions of the physical environment (Cormier et al., 2017; Ivey et al., 2014).

Comfort and organization can also be communicated in the initial interactions between the client and the practitioner. It may be necessary to explain necessary paperwork, clinic procedures, and answer-related questions. Clarifying the client's right to refuse assessment or treatment and the confidentiality of information provided during the interview, including the limits on confidentiality, will also promote a sense of safety and trust in the practitioner (Machado et al., 2011).

The content of the interview includes and verbal and nonverbal information conveyed by the client following the practitioner's inquiries (Machado et al., 2011). It is often useful to identify the specific topics of the interview in advance, and grounding these topics in empirical evidence will enhance the validity of the assessment interview (Berven, 2008). For example, an interview designed to assess interpersonal skills must investigate factors that contribute to interpersonal skills according to the current research. Structured interviews are often accompanied with guides or manuals that carefully determine the interview content, but less structured interviews may not include this information. Prior to the interview, practitioners may be well served to review recent research and determine specific topics for the assessment. Semistructured interviews still allow great flexibility in the format and order of the interview, which allows practitioners to further inquire about specific topics as needed. Information can also be collected in advance of the interview through questionnaires, which may highlight important topics for the interview.

The interview format and techniques will be used to explore the specific content determined by the practitioner with accurate and comprehensive responses provided by the client. Establishing rapport with the client is a necessary initial step to conduct a successful interview assessment. Although a full discussion of a positive client–practitioner relationship will not be provided, a few key details will be emphasized. For example, allowing clients to understand and verify the practitioner's expertise, respect, credibility, trustworthiness, and interpersonal skills will promote a positive client–practitioner relationship and open, ongoing communication. Additional behaviors that enhance client's perceptions of a practitioner include eye contact, body language, openness, honesty, lack of judgment, and use of thoughtful, open-ended questions (Berven & Bezyak, 2015; Cormier et al., 2017). Communication of the three facilitative conditions, as initially outlined by Rogers (1957), of empathy, genuineness, and unconditional positive regard will also enhance the client–practitioner relationship and promote open communication.

Specific techniques can also be used to promote a comprehensive and open dialogue between the client and the practitioner throughout the interview. These techniques are particularly important in less structured interviews. As the practitioner uses open probes about specific topics, the client is allowed to determine what information is provided and how that information is communicated to the practitioner. As a result, techniques that facilitate this communication will yield more thorough and accurate information. Techniques used to facilitate the interview include open-ended questions, minimal encouragers, paraphrases, reflections of feeling, and summarizations (Ivey et al., 2014). Skilled use of these techniques will allow the client to discuss a topic in greater depth, which will promote the development of effective treatment plans and strategies. All of these techniques can be explored in greater depth, and the following example provides some direction as to how these techniques can be refined. The example illustrates problems with closed-ended questions when eliciting information from a client during the interview ("P" is used to designate practitioner and "C" to designate client).

P: What types of jobs have you had in the past?
C: I worked in a factory for a few years before trying out construction.
P: Which job did you enjoy?
C: I guess I prefer the construction work.

Using open-ended questions may invite the client to provide more in-depth responses and possibly explore new alternative with the practitioner.

P: Tell me about what you enjoyed in your most recent job?
C: I was working in construction, and I loved being outside and working with my hands. I always felt accomplished at the end of the day.
P: How would you explain accomplished?
C: I feel accomplished when I build something. When I can touch the final product with my hands and realize that I created it, that makes my job worth doing.

The use of open-ended questions in this example highlighted the individualized benefits of employment for this client, which could allow the practitioner to focus remaining interview questions and eventually obtain increasingly valid assessment information.

Clinical Judgment

Despite the amount of structure used in an assessment interview, clinical judgment is an essential part of the process. Following each client response, a practitioner uses clinical judgment to determine the practitioner's next response. This process involves interpreting both verbal and nonverbal information throughout the assessment interview, and clinical judgment is an essential part of eliciting information throughout the interview (Berven, 2008).

Clinical judgment allows a practitioner to interpret information collected from interviews and other sources, which promotes clinical decision making and determinations. Practitioners integrate and examine all of the information in an attempt to identify themes and inferences, which will assist clients in goal development, maintenance, and future skill acquisition. One organizational strategy that allows practitioners to more easily make sense of all the information is to organize all the material obtained in the interview under the headings of client assets, limitations, and preferences (Berven, 2008). Information about the individual and the environmental context can be organized using these headings, which may prove useful to the practitioner and client in making clinical decisions.

As discussed earlier, clinical judgment contributes to problems with the validity of the assessment interview. In fact, previous research indicates that clinicians often fail to fully inquire about all symptoms a client may be experiencing, and as a result, interviews are not fully comprehensive (P. R. Miller, Dasher, Griffiths, Collins, & Brown, 2001). In order to improve clinical judgment, Garb (2005) provides several recommendations: (a) attend to empirical research results over clinical experience when interpreting assessment information; (b) increase awareness of cultural biases and attempt to counteract biases; (c) attend to client strengths rather than focusing only on problems and pathology; (d) be aware of tasks requiring clinical judgment and the related problems with reliability and validity; (e) be systematic and comprehensive when conducting interviews; (f) use psychological tests and behavioral assessments to compliment the interview and improve reliability and validity; and (g) use de-biasing strategies to improve clinical judgments.

Unlike standardized tests, which often come ready with clear administration and scoring instructions, gaining client information through an interview is not nearly as straightforward. While it might be intuitive to think that clinical judgment, as used in the assessment interview, improves with experience and training, the literature on this topic is not clear. Historically, several researchers suggest there is no association between experience and skills in clinical judgment (Faust, 1994; Garb, 1998), highlighting a lack of data to support such a conclusion. A meta-analysis completed by Spengler et al. (2009) sought to use quantitative data to determine whether there is a clear relationship between educational and clinical experience and clinical judgment. Results found a small and homogeneous ($d = .12$) effect, indicating that clinical experience is positively associated with accuracy in clinical judgment. As a result, training and experience are not only necessary to improve interviewing skills, but they also contribute to improvements in clinical judgment.

Computer-Based Assessment Interviews

Online technology provides various alternatives to face-to-face communication and can be used throughout the counseling process, including assessment interviews. Interviews may be conducted using microphones and speakers and/or video technology, and the online technology offers benefit over face-to-face communication. According to Barak (2010), assessment interviews conducted online allow individuals access to services that are at a distance; practitioners are easily able to record interviews, which may improve clinical judgment and decision making; and cost is typically quite low. As a result, practitioners may benefit from advanced training in conducting online interviews, along with other assessment procedures.

Online interviews may be less structured and guided by the practitioner or more highly structured. Diagnostic and screening interviews conducted online or using a computer have been used for various purposes, including assessing psychiatric disorders, suicide risk, and alcohol or drug use (Barak, 2010; Berven, 2008). One example of an online diagnostic interview tool is the automated, web-based version of the SCID-5, which is based on the *DSM-5* diagnoses and symptoms (American Psychiatric Association, 2013). The web-based version of the SCID-5 allows practitioners to customize the interview, while automating relevant questions and tracking diagnoses. Research indicates the web-based version of the SCID-5 is valid and quicker and easier to administer for most practitioners (Brodey et al., 2016). Additional computer-based assessment interviews may be used in rehabilitation settings and may be combined with traditional face-to-face interviews. For example, computer-based programs may be used to assess interpersonal skills or behavior when part of a larger group, which provides useful information when assisting an individual with employment-related goals (Barak, 2010).

Although computer-based assessments may seem unusual when compared to the traditional format, this technology has several advantages (Barak, 2010; Berven, 2008; Emmelkamp, 2005). Computers can be programmed easily to ask all required questions, and as previously mentioned, all responses can be recorded, eliminating problems with practitioners' memory and/or note-taking skills. Computers can also use decision rules to ask follow-up questions, which is a feature present in the web-based version of the SCID-5 (Brodey et al., 2016). Clients may also be more likely to disclose personal information using a computer, as opposed to a face-to-face communication, and may be more comfortable, which would improve the validity of the interview (Barak, 2010). With the growth of online counseling, conducting assessment, including interviews, using online and other computer-based technology will undoubtedly expand in the coming years.

Conclusions

Assessment interviewing is an important piece of the overall process of clinical assessment, and it acknowledges the dynamic change process from presenting concern to successful intervention. When using and applying results of the assessment interview, the practitioner must always be aware of client change in order to determine effective treatment, alter treatment plans and modalities, engender client trust, recognize crisis and urgency, and complete referral and treatment. Owing to the nature of the client concern, the practitioner should also be cognizant of the appropriate assessment interview to be conducted and whether the interview is structured or unstructured. The practitioner must be knowledgeable in the validity and reliability of it, especially because diagnoses, interventions, and treatment referrals are the result of the interview. In other words, the client's well-being is of utmost importance. Ethically, clinical decisions must be made with confidence in the assessment information utilized to make such determinations.

Practitioners have many decisions to make about clients and also need to facilitate the decision making of clients. It is prudent that they have the proper information about clients obtained through appropriate and effective assessment interviews.

■ References

American Psychiatric Association. (2013). *Diagnostic and statistical manual of mental disorders* (5th ed.). Arlington, VA: American Psychiatric Publishing.

Avery, R. D., & Campion, J. E. (1982). The employment interview: A summary and review of recent research. *Personnel Psychology, 35,* 281–322. doi:10.1111/j.1744-6570.1982.tb02197.x

Barak, A. (2010). Internet-based psychological testing and assessment. In. R. Krause, G. Stricker, & C. Speyer (Eds.), *Online counseling: A handbook for mental health professionals* (2nd ed., pp. 225–246). San Diego, CA: Academic Press.

Berven, N. L. (2008). Assessment interviewing. In B. F. Bolton & R. M. Parker (Eds.), *Handbook of measurement and evaluation in rehabilitation* (4th ed., pp. 241–261). Austin, TX: Pro-Ed.

Berven, N. L., & Bezyak, J. L. (2015). Basic counseling skills. In F. Chan, N. L. Berven, & K. R. Thomas (Eds.), *Counseling theories and techniques for rehabilitation and mental health professionals* (2nd ed., pp. 227–246). New York, NY: Springer Publishing Company.

Brodey, B. B., First, M., Linthicum, J., Haman, K., Sasiels, J. W., & Ayer, D. (2016). Validation of the NetSCID: An automated web-based adaptive version of the SCID. *Comprehensive Psychiatry, 66,* 67–70. doi:10.1016/j.comppsych.2015.10.005

Choppa, A. J., & Schaffer, K. (1992). Introduction to personal injury and expert witness work. In J. M. Siefker (Ed.), *Vocational evaluation in private sector rehabilitation* (pp. 135–168). Menomonie: University of Wisconsin-Stout, Stout Vocational Rehabilitation Institute.

Cormier, S., Nurius, P. S., & Osborn, C. J. (2017). *Interviewing and change strategies for helpers* (7th ed.). Belmont, CA: Brooks/Cole.

Drummond, R. J., Sheperis, C. J., & Jones, K. D. (2016). *Assessment procedures for counselors and helping professionals* (8th ed.). Upper Saddle River, NJ: Pearson.

Emmelkamp, P. M. G. (2005). Technological innovations in clinical assessment and psychotherapy. *Psychotherapy and Psychosomatics, 74,* 336–343. doi:10.1159/000087780

Ewing, J. A. (1984). Detecting alcoholism: The CAGE questionnaire. *Journal of the American Medical Association, 252*(14), 1905–1907. doi:10.1001/jama.252.14.1905

Farley, R. C., & Rubin, S. E. (2006). The intake interview. In R. Roessler & S. E. Runbin (Eds.), *Case management and rehabilitation counseling: Procedures and techniques* (4th ed., pp. 51–74). Austin, TX: Pro-Ed.

Faust, D. (1994). Are there sufficient foundations for mental health experts to testify in court? No. In S. A. Kirk & S. D. Einbinder (Eds.), *Controversial issues in mental health* (pp. 196–201). Boston, MA: Allyn & Bacon.

First, M. B., Williams, J. B., Karg, R. S., & Spitzer, R. L. (2015). *Structured clinical interview for DSM-5 disorder: Clinical version.* Washington DC: American Psychiatric Association.

Folstein, M. F., Folstein, S. E., & McHugh, P. R. (1975). "Mini mental state". A practical method for grading the cognitive state of patients for the clinician. *Journal of Psychiatric Research, 12*(3), 189–198.

Foster, S. L., & Cone, J. D. (1995). Validity issues in clinical assessment. *Psychological Assessment, 7,* 248–260. doi:10.1037/1040-3590.7.3.248

Garb, H. N. (1998). *Studying the clinician: Judgment research and psychological assessment.* Washington, DC: American Psychological Association.

Garb, H. N. (2005). Clinical judgement and decision-making. *Annual Review of Clinical Psychology, 1,* 67–89. doi:10.1146/annurev.clinpsy.1.102803.143810

Garb, H. N. (2007). Computer-administered interviews and rating scales. *Psychological Assessment, 19,* 4–13. doi:10.1037/1040-3590.19.1.4

Groth-Marnat, G. (2003). *Handbook of psychological assessment* (4th ed.). New York, NY: Wiley.

Groth-Marnat, G., & Wright, J. (2016). *Handbook of psychological assessment* (6th ed.). New York, NY: Wiley.

Henry, B., Moffitt, T. A., Caspi, A., Langley, J., & Silva, P. A. (1994). "On the remembrance of things past": A longitudinal evaluation of the retrospective method. *Psychological Assessment, 6,* 92–101. doi:10.1037/1040-3590.6.2.92

Ivey, A. E., Ivey, M. B., & Zalaquitt, C. P. (2014). *Intentional interviewing and counseling: Facilitating client development in a multicultural society* (8th ed.). Belmont, CA: Brooks/Cole.

Kahneman, D., Slovic, P., & Tversky, A. (1982). *Judgment under uncertainty: Heuristics and biases.* New York, NY: Cambridge University Press.

Koch, L. C., & Rumrill, P. D. (2005). Interpersonal communication skills for case managers. In F. Chan, M. J. Leahy, & J. L. Saunders (Eds.), *Case management for rehabilitation health professionals* (2nd ed., Vol. 1, pp. 122–143). Osage Beach, MO: Aspen Professional Services.

Lopez, S. R. (1989). Patient variable biases in clinical judgment: Conceptual overview and methodological information. *Psychological Bulletin, 106,* 184–203.

Lynch, R. K., & Lynch, R. T. (1998). Rehabilitation counseling in the private sector. In R. M. Parker & E. M. Szymanski (Eds.), *Rehabilitation counseling: Basics and beyond* (3rd ed., pp. 71–105). Austin, TX: Pro-Ed.

Machado, P., Beutler, L. E., Harwood, T. M., Mohr, D., & Lenore, S. (2011). The integrative clinical interview. In T. M. Harwood, L. E. Beutler, G. Groth-Marnat (Eds.), *Integrative assessment of adult personality* (3rd ed., pp. 80–118). New York, NY: Guilford.

Miller, P. R., Dasher, R., Griffiths, R., Collins, P., & Brown, F. (2001). Inpatient diagnostic assessments: 1. Accuracy of unstructured vs. structured interviews. *Psychiatry Research, 105*(3), 255–264. doi:10.1016/s0165-1781(01)00317-1

Miller, W. R. (1976). Alcoholism scales and objective assessment methods: A review. *Psychological Bulletin, 83,* 649–674. doi:10.1037/0033-2909.83.4.649

Patterson, W. M., Dohn, H. H., Bird, J., & Patterson, G. A. (1983). Evaluation of suicidal patients: The SAD Persons scale. *Psychosomatics, 24*(4), 343–345. doi:10.1016/s0033-3182(83)73213-5

Power, P. W. (2013). *A guide to vocational assessment* (5th ed.). Austin, TX: Pro-Ed.

Rogers, C. R. (1957). The necessary and sufficient conditions of therapeutic personality change. *Journal of Consulting Psychology, 21,* 95–103. doi:10.1037/h0045357

Rogers, R. (2001). Diagnostic interview schedule. In. R. Rogers (Ed.), *Handbook of diagnostic and structured interviewing* (pp. 61–83). New York, NY: Guilford Press.

Rosenthal, D. A., & Berven, N. L. (1999). Effects of client race on clinical judgment. *Rehabilitation Counseling Bulletin, 42,* 243–264.

Ruegg, R. G., Ekstrom, D., Evans, D. L., & Golden, R. N. (1990). Introduction of standardized report form improves the quality of mental status examination reports by psychiatry residents. *Academic Psychiatry, 14*(3), 157–163. doi:10.1007/bf03341289

Saladin, S., Parker, R. M., & Bolton, B. (2013). Assessment in rehabilitation counseling. In R. M. Parker & J. B. Patterson (Eds.), *Rehabilitation counseling: Basics and beyond* (4th ed., pp. 285–306). Austin, TX: Pro-Ed.

Sommers-Flanagan, J., & Sommers-Flanagan, R. (2013) *Clinical interviewing* (4th ed.). Hoboken, NJ: John Wiley & Sons.

Spengler, P. W., White, M. J., Aegisdottir, S., Maugherman, A. S., Anderson, L. A., Cook, R. S . . . Rush, J. D. (2009). The meta-analysis of clinical judgement project. *The Counseling Psychologist, 37*(3), 350–399. doi:10.1177/0011000006295149

Spiegler, M. D. (2013). Behavior therapy I. Traditional behavior therapy. In J. Few & M. D. Spiegler (Eds.), *Contemporary psychotherapies for a diverse world* (pp. 259–300). New York, NY: Taylor & Francis.

Toppino, D. C., & Boyd, D. (1996). Wage loss analysis: Vocational expert foundation and methodology. *American Rehabilitation Economics Association Journal, 1*(1), 1–12.

Ulrich, L., & Trumbo, D. (1965). The selection interview since 1949. *Psychological Bulletin, 63*(2), 100–116. doi:10.1037/h0021696

Whiston, S. C. (2016). *Principles and applications of assessment in counseling* (5th ed.). Belmont, CA: Brooks/Cole.

III

APPLICATIONS

12

VOCATIONAL ASSESSMENT AND EVALUATION

DAVID R. STRAUSER | JULIANNE FRAIN | MICHAEL FRAIN | TIMOTHY N. TANSEY

LEARNING OBJECTIVES

After reviewing this chapter, the reader should be able to:

- Understand the role of vocational evaluation in the vocational rehabilitation process.
- Understand the theoretical frameworks for vocational evaluation.
- Understand the different levels of vocational evaluation.
- Understand the basic approaches utilized in vocational evaluation.

▓ Introduction

In the provision of vocational rehabilitation services, the predominant goal is to support clients with disabilities in obtaining and maintaining employment. To identify those occupations that they have the capacity to succeed in, vocational assessment is used to ascertain their abilities, personality traits, vocational interests, and academic skills (e.g., reading, math). Although vocational assessment can provide useful information on clients' abilities as they relate to meeting functional capacity requirements necessary for specific occupations, it is limited in its efficacy to identify the primary concerns related to maintaining employment: vocationally relevant "soft skills" and clients' interactions with the work environment. The capacity of vocational assessment to recognize the unique interaction between clients and the work environment is limited because of the connection between the task on these assessments and the actual experience of work. A broader, more holistic approach to understand clients' capacity to both obtain and *retain* work is that of vocational evaluation (Patterson, 2008). Whereas vocational assessment is useful in developing an understanding of work skills and knowledge, vocational evaluation often incorporates many of those assessments as part of a larger focus to identify work-related soft skills and appreciate the work behaviors that clients exhibit in work environments (for examples of soft skills, see Box 12.1). It provides an overall assessment of clients' health conditions (e.g., physical or psychological impairments), personal factors (e.g., educational attainment, work history, culture), and environmental factors (e.g., social stigma, built environment, labor market factors) (Appendices 12.1 to 12.4).

BOX 12.1

OVERVIEW OF SOFT SKILLS

Soft skills are the interpersonal skills necessary to interact effectively with supervisors, coworkers, and others encountered in the work environment (e.g., customers). These are distinguished from "hard skills," which are those skills central to performing the tasks of a job that are generally learned through training and education in specific work tasks or job-specific content. Whereas hard skills are more amenable to proficiency testing (e.g., work sample evaluation, formal assessments), development and evaluation of soft skills generally require observation of people in real-world environments such as work settings.

Employers are interested in potential hires who have soft skills at application or have the capacity to develop these skills through on-the-job training. Some common soft skills of interest to employers include:

Communication – Capacity to communicate with others to receive and share information

Attitude – Capacity to engage others in a positive manner so that others enjoy being around them in the workplace

Leadership – Capacity to make decisions and manage situations or people toward a specific outcome or performance target

Networking – Capacity to develop professional relationships with others, both within and outside the workplace

Resilience – Capacity to respond proactively to difficult situations or other forms of adversity and maintain a positive demeanor

Problem-Solving and Critical Thinking – Capacity to analyze situations, develop options, and select a course of action based on available information

Professionalism – Capacity to be at work when scheduled to be there, complete assigned tasks with limited need for oversight, and stay on task until the work is finished

Teamwork – Capacity to work effectively with coworkers

Vocational evaluation is useful in understanding the vocational readiness and social capacity of persons with disabilities to enter the workforce and retain jobs toward developing a career trajectory (Patterson, 2008). As such, vocational evaluation is inclusive of vocational assessment but is more expansive in nature based on the overall goals and the methodologies implemented in developing an overall picture of individual capacity to obtain and retain employment (Figure 12.1).

■ Theoretical Frameworks

Because of the complexity and difficulty of assessing the states and traits associated with the vocational development of persons with disabilities, vocational evaluators need to have a comprehensive understanding of both the dynamics of the world of work and the impact of disability on work and on human behavior (Chan, Reid, et al., 1997). It is imperative for the vocational

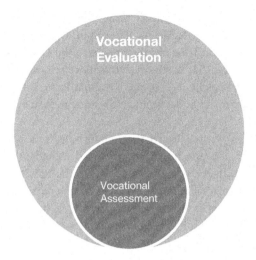

FIGURE 12.1 Vocational assessment and vocational evaluation.

evaluation professional to have an integrated theoretical framework to guide the evaluation process and organize information regarding the traits and factors associated with work performance. The Minnesota Theory of Work Adjustment (MTWA) provides a comprehensive framework for conceptualizing how individual and environmental variables interact to facilitate work role behavior, task performance, and overall satisfaction.

Minnesota Theory of Work Adjustment

The MTWA was originally developed through the support of a federal-funded rehabilitation research program to address how persons being evaluated in the vocational rehabilitation program adjusted to work (Lofquist & Dawis, 1969). The MTWA was initially influenced by research related to the job placement of people with physical disabilities. The foundation of the theory is based on person–environment theories emphasizing the correspondence between the person's work personality and environment, leading to job satisfaction and satisfactoriness (Dawis, 2000, 2005). From a theoretical perspective, work adjustment is defined as the process by which a person achieves and maintains correspondence with the work environment (Lofquist & Dawis, 1969). According to this model, skills and needs are constructs that are used to describe the person's work personality, and the terms "reinforcers" and "skill requirements" are used to describe the work environment. The correspondence between the requirements of the work environment and the person's skills determines satisfactoriness (i.e., the extent to which the person is capable of performing the specific job). The correspondence between the reinforcers offered by the work environment and the person's specific needs is what determines the person's satisfaction with the specific job. Satisfaction and satisfactoriness interact to determine how long the employee will hold a job. This is referred to as "tenure" and is the principal indicator of work adjustment (Lofquist & Dawis, 1969). Work adjustment is defined as "the continuous and dynamic process by which the individual seeks to achieve and maintain correspondence with the work environment" (Lofquist & Dawis, 1969, p. 46).

To facilitate correspondence with the work environment, the vocational evaluation process should provide information regarding factors related to satisfaction, such as obtaining information regarding the person's needs, values, interests, and personality traits. This information is needed so that the person is able to identify work environments that match and correspond to these key constructs. This information is also important in providing the person with a clear understanding of these constructs as they relate to the facilitation of the necessary and continuous adjustment process that is required to achieve tenure. It is important to note that this information cannot only be obtained through standardized instruments but should also be obtained through multidimensional data-gathering strategies, such as interviews and behavioral observation.

Although assessing the abovementioned traits contributes to a person's overall satisfaction with the work environment, it is also important to consider factors that contribute to the work environment's satisfaction with the person. According to the MTWA, this is termed "satisfactoriness." Employability and placeability are two factors that contribute to satisfactoriness. Employability can be conceptualized as the person's ability to meet the specific demands of the work environment. One step in determining employability is to assess specific skills, achievement level, and physical functioning, as they relate to meeting the specific skill requirements and demands of particular work environments. As noted earlier, these constructs may have limited predictive value. Instead, assessing employability by general work personality, a construct that includes, but is not limited to, behaviors such as personal hygiene, attendance, punctuality, safety, consciousness, relationships with coworkers and supervisors, frustration tolerance, and work stamina, may provide more robust information (Chan, Reid, et al., 1997). Research suggests that these factors may be more critical in establishing initial congruence between the person and work environment and facilitating continuous adjustment.

The likelihood that the person is perceived as attractive to a potential work environment, the person's degree of sophistication in obtaining employment, and the overall ability to actually be hired is referred to as "placeability." Placeabilty has little to do with the person's employability or ability to meet the specific skill and contextual demands of the work environment. However, it is a critical factor in determining whether the person has the skills and resources needed to obtain employment. Job-seeking behaviors are typically evaluated in terms of the person's resourcefulness, motivation, resume writing skills, ability to employ appropriate impression management techniques, and overall interview behavior. During the vocational evaluation, all job satisfaction and satisfactoriness factors should be considered simultaneously to maximize career and vocational development. Additional factors that impact career development and employment such as legislation, current economic conditions, technology, demand-side factors, and potential job accommodations should also be examined.

▪ Levels of Vocational Evaluation

The primary goal of vocational evaluation is to assess and predict a client's ability to meet the task and contextual demands of the work environment. Depending on the referral questions of interest, achieving this goal may take several forms that require different amounts of individual and professional time. The length and levels of client involvement in the evaluation process have long been discussed in relation to the career and vocational evaluation of clients with disabilities (Chan, Reid, et al. 1997; IRI, 2003). As early as 1975, the Vocational Evaluation and Work Adjustment Association (VEWAA) Task Force (1975) described three levels of evaluation that still have application to today's vocational evaluation process. Based on the VEWAA Task Force, the factors to consider in determining the level of vocational assessment are purpose, length of contact time with the client, background data gathered and analyzed, and tools typically used in the evaluation

FIGURE 12.2 Levels of vocational evaluation from the Vocational Evaluation and Work Adjustment Association (VEWAA) Task Force.

process (IRI, 2003). The following description of the three levels of evaluation provides a basic framework for understanding the evaluation continuum (Figure 12.2).

Level 1 (Screening)

Level 1 evaluation can be conceptualized as basic evaluation or screening and is designed to obtain necessary information in a quick, efficient, reliable, and valid manner. In most cases, screening is the appropriate level of evaluation needed to obtain relevant and appropriate information related to vocational planning. This is especially true, as evaluation should focus less on ability and more on personality, interests, and values. Screening is essentially similar to the career testing completed in high schools across the United States and typically involves one or two interviews with the client and then 2 to 3 hours of testing. The client's vocational needs are derived on the basis of subjective and objective evaluation of work values, interests, personality, and work-related skills and abilities. Interview data regarding work background, education, and residual capacity are used to supplement the evaluation and psychometric data obtained.

Level 2 (Clinical Case Study)

Level 2 evaluation is primarily diagnostic in nature with the goal of providing information that can be used in the rehabilitation plan development. The primary focus is on the client's past behaviors, education background, and work history with the goal of predicting the person's current level of functioning. In addition to the methods used in Level 1 evaluation, this level involves obtaining a detailed psychosocial and vocational history and synthesizing information from other professionals (e.g., medical specialists, social workers, psychologists, educators). In many cases, a full range of psychometric tests and procedures will be utilized along with several hours of in-depth personal interviews. This level of evaluation usually involves conducting a transferable skills analysis to address job placement and possible vocational training.

Level 3 (Vocational Evaluation)

Level 3 evaluation is the most comprehensive and time-consuming and may be the most appropriate for persons with limited educational and work backgrounds. Consistent with Level 2, the primary focus is diagnostic in nature with the goal of identifying the client's vocational assets, limitations, and preferences (Chan, Reid, et al., 1997). This information is then used to facilitate appropriate career development and employment options by developing suggestions for possible job placement, vocational training, and appropriate career goals. This level extends the use of the interviews and psychometric tests to include strategies such as job analysis, work samples, situational evaluation, job tryouts, and actual observation of work behavior in community-based evaluation. Multiple factors should be considered at this level, such as personal characteristics, local job prospects and labor market information, community resources, family environment, assistive technology, external supports, and access to appropriate medical services. This level of evaluation is the lengthiest and usually requires between 1 and 2 weeks to complete.

With the passage of the Rehabilitation Act Amendments of 1973, state vocational rehabilitation agencies are required to provide services to persons with severe disabilities. In addition, subsequent amendments have also identified alternative appropriate outcomes such as independent living and supported employment. For those with more severe disabilities, alternative approaches that include multiple points of evaluation may be the most appropriate. As with all levels of disability, taking an individualized approach and considering the unique factors associated with each person are important. For example, when evaluating those with severe traumatic brain injury, mental retardation, and psychiatric conditions, it is important to consider how their condition, especially cognitive and psychosocial issues, may be manifested in the work setting (Stergiou-Kita, Dawson, & Rappolt, 2011, 2012). These behaviors may not be exclusively evaluated within the controlled evaluation setting, and it may be important to supplement with information from the larger environmental context. Therefore, expanding evaluation to include a more ecological approach may be the most appropriate. In addition, periodic reevaluation may be appropriate to monitor and document individual progress and gain an understanding of the situational factors that may be impacting the person's vocational functioning.

■ Basic Approaches to Vocational Evaluation

Vocational evaluation is a comprehensive process that focuses on maximizing the work adjustment process. To achieve this goal, the vocational evaluation can employ a variety of systematic approaches that utilize work, real or simulated, as the focal point for evaluation and vocational exploration with the goal of aiding the client's career and vocational development. Medical, psychological, social, vocational, educational, cultural, and economic information is incorporated into the vocational evaluation process to identify specific goals of the vocational evaluation.

The following four major approaches can be used in the vocational evaluation process: (a) standardized testing, (b) job analysis, (c) work samples, and (d) situational evaluation (Figure 12.3). Each is unique, has assets and limitations, and has a role in measuring vocational behaviors. In addition, a community-based approach can be used to expand the traditional vocational evaluation process (Figure 12.4).

Clinical Interview

Although a more in-depth overview of interviews of an assessment tool is provided in Chapter 7, Assessment of Psychopathology, it is important to note the importance of this method of assessment in vocational evaluation. The clinical interview is the most commonly used method in vocational evaluation and provides a context to conceptualize and integrate findings toward developing an

FIGURE 12.3 Components of vocational evaluation.

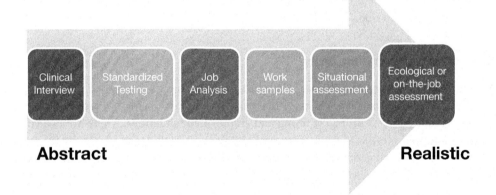

FIGURE 12.4 Application of different methods to the work environment.

overall picture of clients and their capacity for employment (Berven, 2008). In the absence of a clinical interview, the assessment information obtained through standardized testing and other methods will lack the necessary perspective required to integrate those findings into a comprehensive picture of vocational aptitude and readiness (Groth-Marnat, 2003). Initially, the interview provides evaluators the opportunity to establish rapport with clients toward increasing the reliability of subsequent testing by increasing their comfort with the testing process. Apart from being a progenitor of connection between the evaluator and the client, the clinical interview is used to gather information regarding the eligibility of clients for services, diagnostic screening, and the identification of needs and barriers that will influence retention in services or attaining desired outcomes (Berven, 2008).

Clinical interviews are generally classified as structured, semistructured, or unstructured depending on the amount of structure or flexibility allowed in the questions evaluators ask during the interview (Berven, 2008). The level of structure will vary depending on the evaluator's objectives for a clinical interview. Intake or eligibility screening interviews tend to be structured as evaluators attempt to gather specific information necessary for preliminary decision-making, initial diagnosis, or collecting data regarding the population being served by an agency. Semistructured or unstructured interviews are used to develop an understanding of clients' treatment goals, conditions that have contributed to the current situation, or the barriers specific to the client that will affect outcomes or limit the benefit of services.

Standardized Testing

In vocational evaluation, psychological testing can be used to evaluate behavior, mental abilities, and personal characteristics in order to assist in making judgments, predictions, and decisions about work potential of people with disabilities (Berven, 1979). Psychological testing has several advantages as an assessment tool in rehabilitation. It is brief, quick, and relatively inexpensive and can be used early in the evaluation process to obtain baseline information about the client and to provide direction for subsequent assessment efforts (Berven, 1979; Chan, Reid, et al., 1997). Standardized testing may be particularly appropriate for people with mild and moderate disabilities but less useful for people with severe disabilities because of its strong emphasis on speed, brevity, abstract thinking, and motivation and concentration. Berven (1979) classified psychometric assessment into four major categories: (a) test of ability, (b) test of current skills, (c) vocational inventories, and (d) personality assessment.

Test of Ability (or Aptitude Tests)

Aptitude tests can be used to answer the same kinds of questions as work samples, except in paper-and-pencil formats. They are designed to measure a client's potential to master the skills required in vocational training and employment situations. There are two subcategories of aptitude tests: (a) tests of general ability (i.e., intelligence tests) and (b) tests of specific abilities. Intelligence tests are used to assess general learning ability, reasoning, and the ability to adapt to new and different situations. They are most effective for predicting performance in school. In vocational evaluation, intelligence test results can provide information about the client's ability to learn new tasks and adapt to new situations in training or employment settings. The *Wechsler Adult Intelligence Scale–Fourth Edition* (*WAIS-IV*) is an individually administered intelligence test, and the *Beta III* is a nonverbal measure of cognitive abilities commonly used in rehabilitation settings. Conversely, tests of specific abilities provide measures of several different abilities. The *Ability Profiler*, a measurement system developed by the U.S. Department of Labor as a replacement for the General Aptitudes Test Battery, provides assessment of nine separate aptitudes in cognitive, perceptual, and motor areas and is used to answer questions about potential for a range of occupations. The *Bennett Mechanical Comprehension Test* and the *General Clerical Test–Revised* are examples of tests of specific aptitudes in the mechanical and clerical areas. The *Purdue Pegboard*, the *Crawford Small Parts Dexterity Test*, and the *Hand Tool Dexterity Test* are examples of tests of motor aptitudes commonly used in vocational evaluation.

Test of Current Skills (Achievement Tests)

Instead of assessing the potential to learn, the purpose of achievement tests is to assess the effects of past learning (e.g., verbal, numerical, or reading skills). Achievement test results are useful for identifying academic skill deficits that may need to be remediated (e.g., passing the General Educational Development [GED] test) or accommodated prior to academic training or job training (Berven, 1979). The *Wide Range Achievement Test 4* (WRAT4), the *Adult Basic Learning Examination, Second Edition* (ABLE), and the *Peabody Individual Achievement Test–Revised-Normative Update* are among the most recommended achievement tests.

Interest Inventories

Interest inventories assess interests and values related to career choice. Typically, interest inventories asked questions about preferences for various job titles, work activities, leisure activities, school subjects, types of people with whom to associate, or for various sources of satisfaction that might be derived from work (Berven, 1979). The assumption is that people whose preferences are consistent with satisfied workers in a particular occupation are more likely to find that occupation satisfying. Many of the interest inventories are developed based on the Holland's theory of work preferences and personality type (i.e., Realistic, Investigative, Artistic, Social, Enterprising, and Conventional personality types). The *Strong Interest Inventory*, *Career Assessment Inventory – The Enhanced Version*, and *Self-Directed Search* are examples of interest inventories using Holland's career choice theory.

Personality Assessment

Personality assessment is a very broad category and typically includes assessment of attitudes, needs and values, or temperaments, and more specific attributes, such as anxiety, depression, or motivation. Personality inventories can be administered to answer questions related to psychosocial adjustment factors (e.g., depression) that can affect work performance and potential personality conflicts with coworkers and supervisors. Some of the popular personality inventories used in rehabilitation settings include the *16PF Fifth Edition*, the *Minnesota Multiphasic Personality Inventory-2–Restructured Form* (MMPI-2-RF), and the *Beck Depression Inventory*.

Job Analysis

The emphasis of job analysis is on the description of work to be performed (Chan, Reid, et al., 1997). In vocational evaluation, job analyses enable the vocational evaluator to better understand the realistic demands of a job in the workplace. It allows the evaluator to better correlate the vocational evaluation data with the demand of particular occupations in the workplace. It is similar to on-the-job evaluation without the client. By focusing on the nature of the task to be performed, the evaluator can better match the client to appropriate jobs and to determine the job modification and accommodation needs of the client in the real world. In addition, by conducting job analyses of demand occupations in the community, the vocational evaluator will be able to develop work samples and other assessment procedures that are realistic, in demand, and responsive to local employment opportunities.

The process of job analysis can help vocational rehabilitation and risk management personnel to better understand the specific physical demands of a particular job. During the course of a job analysis, the vocational evaluator observes the worker in a particular workplace for an entire workday to assist in appropriately logging the amount of time spent sitting, standing, bending, lifting, stooping, and so on, all of which can, in turn, help to determine whether or not a person with an injury would require a workplace accommodation and whether or not that workplace accommodation may be afforded reasonably (for an example of job analysis documentation, see Box 12.2).

BOX 12.2

EXAMPLE OF THE JOB ANALYSIS DOCUMENTING PROCESS

JOB ANALYSIS

Employer:	**Johnny's Bar**
	21497 Seaside Blvd.
	Honolulu, HI
Phone:	**808-555-1239**
Position:	**Server & Hawaiian Entertainment Performer**
Date of Analysis:	**October 10, 2012**
Supervisor:	**Janet Arrg**

Essential job features:

The essential features of a Hawaiian dancer call for the use of full body on an elevated platform in order to demonstrate to customers a form of dancing in a barroom/restaurant setting and serving food and drinks to patrons.

Essential features include:

Ability to stand and move about constantly while keeping balance.
Ability to multitask Hawaiian dances and food and beverage service constantly.
Good eye contact with broad smile.

Predominant physical positions:

Sitting: 10%, Occasional
Walking: 80%, Constant
Standing: 10%, Occasional

Physical demands:

Note: In terms of an 8-hour workday.

Occasionally = 1%–33% or 0–3 hours
Frequently = 34%–66% or 3–6 hours
Continuously = 67%–100% or 6–8 hours

(continued)

BOX 12.2 (continued)

STANDING: *To maintain entire body in erect posture without change in location*
Worker occasionally stands and smiles while shaking arms and body.
Total hours per day: 1
Type of surface(s): Wood floor
Work performed: Stand and entertain restaurant guests with Hawaiian dancing

WALKING: *To move entire body for some distance using heel/toe gait*
Constant
Total hours per day: 7
Type of surface(s): Wood floor
Work performed: Walks across wood floor and dances to music.

KNEELING: *Perform task while on knees*
Occasional

CRAWLING: *To move entire body along a surface with hip/knee flexion and arm flexion/ extension*
Occasional

USE OF HANDS: *Requiring simple grasping, carrying lightweight objects, other forms of hand dexterity*
Constant
Total hours per day: 8
Type of surface(s): Stands on wood floor, or holds various entertainment goods
Worked performed while using hands: Shakes hands and performs different dance moves

USE OF FEET (*other than standing/walking*): *To flex and extend the foot*
Constant

SITTING: *To rest weight on the lower part of the body*
Occasional
Total hours per day: 1–2
Type of surface(s): Seat, Wood
Work performed: Dances from seated position

LIFTING: *To exert physical strength necessary to move objects from one level to another*
Constant lifting of tips, occasional lifting of other entertainment torches or Hawaiian decor, rare lifting of food and drinks to assist with other wait staff.

(*continued*)

BOX 12.2 (continued)

Total hours per day: 8
Weight: Less than one ounce
Size/type of objects: 3" × 4"
Type of surface(s): Wood floor
Work performed: Collect tips

BENDING: *To move forward from the neck or waist, or to flex the elbow, knee, wrist, or other body parts*
Constant
Total hours per day: 8
Degree: 189°–200°
Type of surface(s): Wood floor
Work performed: Use bending as part of dance routine

TWISTING: *To rotate the upper trunk to right or left from neutral position while sitting or standing*
Constant
Total hours per day: 8
Body Part(s): Waist
Work Performed: Twist and bend at waist

PUSHING, PULLING, AND DRAGGING: *To exert force toward or against an object to move it away*
Occasional pulling of customers on stage

CLIMBING: *To ascend or descend ladders, scaffolding, stairs, poles, inclined surfaces*
Occasional climbing of four steps to stage
Total hours per day: ½
Height: 9"
Type of surface(s): Wood steps
Work performed: Climb to stage

Psychological requirements:
Must be friendly, conversational, good motor coordination, good balance, manual/finger dexterity, eye–hand–foot coordination

Hours of work:
7 p.m. to 3 a.m.

Working conditions:
Indoors, noisy, constant music, ability to deal with large crowds and distractions

Safety equipment/tools used:
Occasional use of kitchen equipment such as fryer and pots and pans as needed when filling in for prep cooks.
ANALYSIS PREPARED BY: Vocational Evaluator

Work Samples

The work sample is used frequently in traditional vocational evaluation programs. It is a generic term used to describe any sample of work, either real or simulated, irrespective of its purpose or use (Pruitt, 1986). A work sample may involve the simulation or mock-up of a job or an instrument for measuring a work trait. It must be developed based on an analysis of job tasks related to a specific occupation or a cluster of occupations and is designed to assess a representative sample of realistic competitive worker traits/skills related to the specific area of work (Pruitt, 1986). Work samples can be grouped into trait-oriented and work-oriented instruments (Menchetti & Flynn, 1990). Trait-oriented work samples are similar to multiple aptitude batteries in that they are designed to measure a number of traits inherent in a job or a variety of jobs. The major differences between trait-oriented work samples and aptitude tests are that (a) work samples tend to focus on measuring motor responses through the use of complex and more expensive devices; (b) there is less focus on general intellectual and academic abilities in the work samples; and (c) many work samples are designed to be used independently and need not be administered as part of a larger battery (Menchetti & Flynn, 1990). In contrast, work-oriented work samples utilize simulated work, such as drill press operation and electronic assembly, to measure performance on specific tasks. These work samples have higher face validity because they approximate real work activity. In general, work samples focus on assessing work potential for skilled, semiskilled, and unskilled jobs. Some of the most popular work sample systems include the Valpar Pro3000 and the McCarron-Dial Evaluation System.

Situational Assessment

Whereas standardized testing, job analysis, and work samples tend to emphasize specific employability skills, situational assessment focuses on general employability skills and adaptive work behaviors (Neff, 1985). Certain employability skills (e.g., intelligence, aptitudes, achievement, temperament, physical capacity) are job specific and vary from one job class to another. Behavior and skills specific to employability are important in predicting job performance behavior. Conversely, general employability skills are not job specific. General employability skills, also known as general work personality, are said to be required in every job. Examples of these behaviors include grooming and hygiene, attendance, punctuality, safety consciousness, relationships with coworkers and supervisors, frustration tolerance, work stamina, production rate, and so on. Behavior and skills in general employability are important for predicting job maintenance behavior.

Situational assessment is based on an effort to simulate actual working conditions with an orientation toward work behavior in general. The vocational evaluator uses different means to structure the work environment so that general work behavior can be observed. Information obtained from situational assessment is designed to help the vocational evaluator answer questions such as, "Can the worker work at all? Can he or she conform to customary work rules? Can he or she respond appropriately to supervision? Can he or she produce at an acceptable rate both in terms of quality and quantity?" Situational assessment is the most appropriate method for answering these questions while also assessing potential behavioral problems in the real work environment (Chan, Reid, et al., 1997).

In order to achieve answers to these questions, vocational evaluators must establish relationships with community employment venues close to the vocational rehabilitation consumer so that they can facilitate a simulated work environment, which could eventually lead to a successful job placement for that consumer. The locations where situational assessments take place may also be known as worksites. For example, the vocational evaluator (or facility with whom they are employed) may harvest friendships with local grocery or department store managers so that there is a mutual understanding that the situational assessment that takes place at the facility may result in a successful job placement of the disabled client. These venues then become worksites. Activities that occur at each worksite may include tasks such as sorting, stocking, sizing, or bagging groceries. More sophisticated tasks may also take place, such as categorizing inventory or placing items in line for shipping or receiving, all of which are contingent on the level of functioning of the consumer. It is the responsibility of the vocational evaluator to first identify the specific needs and goals of the vocational rehabilitation consumer in advance of the situational assessment so that the assessment process can be appropriately catered to the individual client. These specific needs and goals can be identified through the process of vocational evaluation and then applied to the specific worksite location. Contingent on the skills, knowledge, and resources of the vocational evaluator, situational assessments can range from unskilled worksites to skilled worksites.

Ecological Vocational Evaluation

As mentioned previously, the traditional vocational evaluation approach has many limitations for assessing career choice, job skills, and workplace support needs of people with severe disabilities. It is not useful for matching people to vocational interventions, such as supported employment, that use a place–train approach. An ecological vocational evaluation can fill the need for assessment in the work environment and the gap in evaluation technology for vocational evaluation in the workplace. An ecological systems approach views behavior from a person–environment interaction perspective involving the client, family, school, occupation, and society (Davidson & Rappaport, 1983). It has a focus on assets instead of limitations. It also assesses the conditions under which learning is maximized for an individual in a place–train work environment in order to gain knowledge about the person and the work environment in order to improve instruction and ecological supports (Langford & Lawson, 1994). Ecological vocational evaluation incorporates the principles of relativity, diversity, and person–environment fit as an operational philosophy toward persons with severe disabilities. As such, ecological assessment strives to identify the strengths of the person and base recommendations on the best utilization of assets. The focus of the evaluation is on systems beyond an individual level (such as the family, community, and society) as influencing factors both during and after the evaluation process. It emphasizes the use of environmental measures such as job analysis, labor market surveys, or on-site assessment to increase the chance of work adjustment between a rehabilitation client and the work setting. Ecological vocational evaluation also recognizes the dynamic nature of the workforce and the workplace and advocates that strategies must continuously be adapted to environmental changes and as a result will require frequent reappraisal. Ecological evaluation relies heavily on environmental measurement, such as the social climate or ecology of the workplace (Menchetti & Flynn, 1990). Menchetti and Flynn (1990) delineated several dimensions that should be considered when measuring the ecology of the work environment: (a) the physical ecology, (b) the social ecology, and (c) the organization ecology. Other dimensions, such as transportation requirements, family support, work disincentives (e.g., Supplemental Security Income [SSI] or Social Security Disability Insurance [SSDI] benefits), and the availability of external incentives (e.g., targeted jobs tax credits) must also be considered. The assessment of these dimensions allows evaluators to determine the adaptability of the environment to meet the needs of the client. The adaptability of the environment can be compared with the client's abilities to determine the degree of person–environment fit. Decisions about the client's work potential in that environment can be made in terms of accepting the person for employment, accepting the person for employment with support, or recommending a specific alternative (Menchetti & Flynn, 1990).

Vocational Evaluation Within Life Care Planning

The technique of life care planning is commonly used in a litigated context wherein a person becomes injured and there is a question as to the extent of financial damages that person will accrue into his or her future as a direct result of that injury. Vocational rehabilitation professionals can be cross-trained in how to act as both a vocational rehabilitation counselor and a life care planner within litigated contexts and can implement the process of vocational evaluation into the life care plan. In the context of life care planning, the process of vocational evaluation is focused on different outcomes than those it is typically focused on in other venues. For example, instead of the vocational evaluation assessing skills, abilities, and interests to derive prospective job placement options, in the life care planning process, the outcome of the life care plan is directed toward putting a numeric value on the future loss of earning capacity a person has suffered as a result of injury. In other words, if evidence of the facts presented to the life care planner suggests the person's injury has resulted in industrial impairment, the question is, How much less is that injured person now able to earn per hour, week, year, or the rest of his or her life?

When afforded an opportunity to meet with the injured person, the life care planner will embark on a very similar (and in some cases identical) vocational evaluation process to that which is used in other, more traditional venues: clinical interviewing, vocational testing, transferable skills analysis, and labor market assessment. The file review in the life care planning venue tends to be much more expansive as the life care planner must incorporate medical records from before and after the accident and review pay stubs, tax returns or financial documents, and other legal documents that may be provided, such as depositions or affidavits. The report writing process concludes differently as well, as there is an emphasis on the future loss of earning capacity and methodology for such calculation.

CASE STUDY 12.1   JUAN: AN EXAMPLE OF VOCATIONAL EVALUATION AND CALCULATING FUTURE LOSS OF EARNING CAPACITY

Juan is a 43-year-old Hispanic man with less than high school education who had a documented history of working full time as a roofer up until a disabling motor vehicle accident in 2017. At the time of the accident, he was earning $17.00 per hour. The motor vehicle accident resulted in him sustaining several disc herniations in both his cervical and lumbar spine. Juan has since undergone a cervical fusion and has a subsequent lumbar fusion pending. His permanent work restrictions are yet to be known, but medical evidence reviewed has made it clear that Juan can no longer safely or competitively perform within his former occupation as a roofer or in any other labor-intensive work.

In this case, a vocational evaluation was performed during the course of the life care planning process to assess Juan's residual earning capacity and calculate future loss of earning capacity. The vocational evaluation consisted of an interview of Juan followed by vocational testing, including intelligence testing, academic achievement testing, computer skills test, and vocational interest testing. These tests were used to determine whether Juan had the capabilities of successfully completing a GED or alternative retraining program and to assess what his level of transferability would be into different occupations.

(continued)

CASE STUDY 12.1   (*continued*)

Vocational testing results showed that Juan possessed a borderline IQ of 70, and his academic skills were all in the lower extreme for word reading, spelling, math computation, and sentence comprehension. Similarly, Juan's computer skills were limited with little-to-no knowledge of basic computer applications and slow typing speed. He did demonstrate social work personality type and interest in working with people outside his general interests in construction and labor work during vocational interest testing. These results were not surprising for a man with Juan's educational background and history of work exclusive to roofing and point toward Juan being an unlikely candidate for retraining.

From the results, the following scenarios were concluded:

In the best-case scenario, Juan would be able to find entry-level, unskilled work in a sedentary or light duty capacity that does not require a high school education or additional training and would allow Juan accommodations as needed to leave work for medical appointments and switch positions for pain relief related to his back injuries. Within his local economy, these potential job opportunities were identified as ticket taker, gate attendant, information clerk, lobby attendant, or order taker, all of which are anticipated to grow at least 8% per year. A local labor market survey revealed that these jobs most commonly pay minimum wage ($8.25 per hour). This would leave Juan with a minimum deficit of $8.75 per hour (preexisting wages of $17.00 minus $8.25 future earning capacity), not including inflation and his potential for raises, benefits, or overtime.

In the worst-case (and seemingly most likely) scenario, Juan would find it very difficult to succeed in job retention of any sort because of his lack of placeability, limited skill set, academic and intellectual weaknesses, and work history exclusive to labor-intensive work. In this scenario, Juan may suffer up to $17.00 per hour in future loss of earning capacity. This future loss of earning capacity is substantiated by Juan's medical history, functional limitations, performance on vocational testing, work history, and the demands of the local labor market.

This case study provides a very simple example of how a vocational evaluation can play a role in the life care planning process. However, many cases present complexities that exceed what is mentioned previously and may require additional vocational testing, retesting, or utility of more labor market resources, statistics, and preplacement services.

■ Conclusions

Vocational evaluation historically has played a critical part in the vocational rehabilitation process. Research related to personality, interests, and values lends significant support for the continued need and importance of vocational evaluation in the contemporary practice of vocational rehabilitation. In addition, the counseling approach to vocational evaluation, with an emphasis on building a strong working alliance, provides additional support for incorporating vocational evaluation into vocational rehabilitation service delivery. Vocational evaluation has a strong theoretical framework that guides the evaluation process, and rehabilitation providers have a variety of levels and approaches that can be utilized to facilitate the career development and the employment of persons with disabilities. As vocational testing continues to advance, inclusion of new testing instruments to improve the quality of the evaluation process should be considered frequently. Similarly, commonly relied upon tools necessary for labor market research and obtaining labor market statistics during the vocational evaluation process change from year to year. Continued training and research related to all resources and techniques used during the vocational evaluation process would appear to be important and should be a focus for both rehabilitation practitioners and researchers.

References

Berven, N. L. (1979). Psychometric assessment in rehabilitation. In B. Bolton (Ed.), *Rehabilitation client assessment* (pp. 46–64). Baltimore, MD: University Park Press.

Berven, N. L. (2008). Assessment interviewing. In B. Bolton & R. Parker (Eds.), *Handbook of measurement and evaluation in rehabilitation* (pp. 241–262). Austin, TX: Pro-Ed.

Chan, F., Reid, C., Roldan, G., Kaskel, L., Rahimi, M., & Mpofu, E. (1997). Vocational assessment and evaluation of people with disabilities. *Physical Medicine and Rehabilitation Clinics of North America, 8*(2), 311–325. doi:10.1016/s1047-9651(18)30328-0

Davidson, W., & Rappaport, J. (1983). Advocacy and community psychology. In G. Webber & G. McCall (Eds.), *Social scientists as advocates* (pp. 67–97). Beverly Hills, CA: Sage

Dawis, R. V. (2000). The person-environment tradition in counseling psychology. In W. E. Martin, Jr., & J. L. Swartz-Kulstad (Eds.), *Person-environment psychology and mental health* (pp. 91–111). Mahwah, NJ: Erlbaum.

Dawis, R. V. (2005). The Minnesota theory of work adjustment. In S. D. Brown & R. W. Lent (Eds.), *Career development and counseling: Putting theory and research to work* (pp. 3–23). Edison, NJ: John Wiley & Sons.

Groth-Marnat, G. (2003). *Handbook of psychological measurement* (4th ed.). New York, NY: Wiley.

Institute on Rehabilitation Issues. (2003). *A new paradigm for vocational evaluation* (30th Institute on Rehabilitation Issues ed.). Washington, DC: Rehabilitation Services Administration, U.S. Department of Education.

Langford, G., & Lawson, S. (1994). Changes in assessment procedures for supported employment. *Assessment in Rehabilitation and Exceptionality, 1*, 307–322.

Lofquist, L. H., & Dawis, R. V. (1969). *Adjustment to work: A psychological view of man's problems in a work-oriented society.* New York, NY: Appleton-Century-Crofts.

Menchetti, B. M., & Flynn, C. C. (1990). Vocational evaluation. In F. R. Rusch (Ed.), *Supported employment: Models, methods, and issues* (pp. 111–130). Sycamore, IL: Sycamore Publishing Company.

Neff, W. S. (1985). *Work and human behavior.* New York, NY: Aldine.

Patterson, J. (2008). Assessment of work behavior. In B. Bolton and R. Parker (Eds.), *Handbook of measurement and evaluation in rehabilitation* (pp. 309–336). Austin, TX: Pro-Ed.

Pruitt, W. A. (1986). *Vocational evaluation.* Menomonie, WI: Walt Pruitt Associates.

Stergiou-Kita, M., Dawson, D. R, & Rappolt, S. G. (2011). An integrated review of the processes and factors relevant to vocational evaluation following traumatic brain injury. *Journal of Occupational Rehabilitation, 21,* 374–394. doi:10.1007/s10926-010-9282-0

Stergiou-Kita, M., Dawson, D. R, & Rappolt, S. G. (2012). Inter-professional clinical practice guideline for vocational evaluation following traumatic brain injury: A systematic and evidence-based approach. *Journal of Occupational Rehabilitation, 22,* 166–181. doi:10.1007/s10926-011-9332-2

Vocational Evaluation and Work Adjustment Association. (1975). Vocational evaluation project final report, reprint no. 12. *Vocational Evaluation and Work Adjustment Bulletin, 8* (Special Edition).

COMPREHENSIVE VOCATIONAL EVALUATION TEMPLATE

Client's Name	
Parent/Guardian Name (if applicable)	
Date of Birth/Age	
Address	
Employment Status	
Diagnoses	
Prominent Limitations or Restrictions	
Educational Recommendations	
Employment Recommendations	
Evaluation Date(s)	
Report Date	
Evaluator(s)	

PURPOSE AND SOURCE OF REFERRAL

_____
_____
_____
_____
_____
_____

SCHEDULING PROCESS AND PUNCTUALITY

_____
_____
_____
_____
_____
_____

DOCUMENTS CONSIDERED

▦ BACKGROUND

GENERAL INFORMATION

Current Living Situation: _____

_____

Family History and Marital Status: _____

_____

_____

Current Employment Status: _____

Military Experience: _____

Purpose for Entering Vocational Rehabilitation: _____

_____

_____

MEDICAL CONDITIONS

Primary Diagnoses: _____

Co-occurring Conditions Include: _____

_____

Symptoms: _____

_____

Functional Limitations and Impact on Work or School: _____

_____

_____

Health Insurance: _____

_____

MEDICATIONS AND TREATMENT

Current Treatment Regimen (Including Frequency of Visits to Physician): _____

_____

_____

Current Medication: _____

_____

_____

_____

Current Medical Concerns: _____

Pending Surgeries: _____

EDUCATIONAL HISTORY

School History: _____

_____

_____

_____

Learning Accommodations: _____

_____

Grade Point Average: _____

_____

Educational Goals: _____

_____

VOCATIONAL HISTORY

Competitive Work Experience: _____

_____

_____

_____

_____

_____

_____

_____

_____

_____

_____

_____

_____

_____

Volunteer Work Experience: _____

_____

VOCATIONAL GOALS

Voiced Goals or Desired Outcomes: _____

_____

_____

ACTIVITIES OF DAILY LIVING

(Independent, Assistance Needed, Depends on Others)

Hygiene: _____

Dressing: _____

Homemaking: _____

Home Maintenance: _____

Community/Leisure: _____

Self-Management: _____

Summary of Independence in the Home: _____

FINANCIAL INFORMATION

Current Income/Wages: _____

_____

_____

_____

Prior Wage Earning: _____

_____

Desired Wage Earning: _____

CRIMINAL HISTORY

History of Arrests: _____

BEHAVIORAL OBSERVATIONS

Attitude Toward Testing: _____

_____

_____

_____

Attention: _____

_____

Affect/Mood: _____

Appearance: _____

■ VOCATIONAL TESTING

Tests that were administered to assess vocational functioning are listed as follows:

1.   Academic Achievement

2.   Vocational Interest Testing

3. Life Skills

4. Computer Skills

5. Motivation

6. Aptitude Testing

ACADEMIC ACHIEVEMENT

The Test of Adult Basic Education (TABE) was administered to assess the client's performance on an extended test of Academic Achievement. This test is occasionally used as a screening tool for admission into postsecondary training certificate programs. The client's performance on this test is outlined as follows:

SUBTEST	GRADE EQUIVALENCY
Reading	
Math Computation	
Applied Math	
Language	
Total Math	
Total Battery	

Summary of Performance:

_____
_____
_____
_____

VOCATIONAL INTERESTS

_____
_____
_____
_____
_____
_____
_____

_____
_____
_____
_____
_____
_____
_____
_____
_____
_____
_____
_____
_____

LIFE SKILLS

_____
_____
_____
_____
_____
_____
_____

COMPUTER SKILLS

Typing Speed: _____

_____
_____

E-mail Access: _____

_____
_____

MOTIVATION

_____
_____
_____
_____
_____

APTITUDE TESTING

Numerical Reasoning: _____
_____
_____
_____

Abstract Reasoning: _____
_____
_____
_____
_____

Verbal Reasoning: _____
_____
_____
_____
_____

Mechanical Reasoning: _____
_____
_____
_____
_____

■ SUMMARY

SUMMARY OF VOCATIONAL TESTING RESULTS

Strengths: _____
_____
_____
_____
_____

Weaknesses: _____
_____

SUMMARY OF OTHER STRENGTHS AND WEAKNESS

Strengths: _____
_____
_____
_____
_____

Weaknesses: _____
_____

FEASIBILITY

How realistic are the client's goals in relation to the evaluation results and labor market demands?

EMPLOYMENT RECOMMENDATIONS

Title 1: _____

_____

Title 2: _____

_____

Title 3: _____

_____

Title 4: _____

_____

Title 5: _____

_____

LABOR MARKET INFORMATION (Taken from O*NET)

_____

_____

_____

_____

_____

_____

_____

_____

_____

_____

_____

_____

_____

_____

_____

GENERAL OBSERVATIONS, RECOMMENDATIONS, AND CONCLUSIONS

Summary of Client: _____

_____

_____

_____

_____

Performance on Testing: _____
_____
_____
_____
_____

Academic Recommendations: _____
_____
_____
_____
_____

Employment Recommendations: _____
_____
_____
_____
_____

Medical/Psychological Recommendations: _____
_____
_____

Additional Services:

Respectfully Submitted,

Evaluator's Signature

Encl: Current Job Postings

EXAMPLE COMPREHENSIVE VOCATIONAL EVALUATION

▓ COMPREHENSIVE VOCATIONAL EVALUATION

VR Client Name	Client Example
Date of Birth/Age	October 5, 1956/60
Address	1234 A Street, Madison, WI
Employment Status	Unemployed
Primary Limitations/Restrictions	Herniated intervertebral disc Left knee replacement Inability to perform work past light duty
Educational Recommendations	No postsecondary training recommended
Employment Recommendations	Direct job placement in part-time, sedentary work
Job Titles	Dispatcher, Order Clerk, Receptionist, Call Center Representative, Customer Service Representative
Evaluation Date(s)	May 20, 2017
Report Date	June 2, 2017
Evaluator(s)	Evaluator Joe, MS, CRC

PURPOSE AND SOURCE OF REFERRAL

Mrs. Client Example was referred for a Comprehensive Vocational Evaluation at the request of her Vocational Rehabilitation Counselor, Mr. John Black. The purpose of the Vocational Evaluation was to assess the Vocational Rehabilitation Client's performance on interest and aptitude testing in efforts to appropriately assist in creating an Individual Plan for Employment. The client's ability to obtain work and/or the necessity for retraining was also considered.

SCHEDULING AND PUNCTUALITY

The Vocational Evaluation took place at the vocational evaluator's office, located at 50 State Street in Madison, WI, at 9 a.m. on Saturday, May 20, 2017. The evaluation appointment was scheduled through Mrs. Example directly. The client arrived on time and independent to the appointment. Upon initiation of the evaluation, the purpose of the evaluation was discussed with the client.

DOCUMENTS CONSIDERED

Rehab Pro Assessment and Consultation received the following documents from Vocational Rehabilitation upon the time of the referral:

- Referral form from Vocational Rehabilitation outlining the following questions, for which respective answers are provided:

  - What is the client's Academic Achievement level?

    - According to Mrs. Example's performance on the TABE, she functions within an average range in areas of academic performance with strength in Applied Math and Reading.

  - What is the vocational interest of the client?

    - Mrs. Example presented with an open mind and motivation to work in any area that can accommodate her need to change positions as needed and avoid heavy lifting.

  - Can this client return to work at prior occupation?

    - Mrs. Example is unable to return to her former employment because of the physical nature of the jobs she previously held and was paid competitively for. For example, her former career of truck driving is one she cannot return to, and since sustaining her injuries, it has been hard for her to find occupations that can accommodate her. Her job search now must be directed to sedentary employment where she can sit/stand as needed and change positions.

  - Does this client possess transferable skills?

    - Mrs. Example possesses transferable skills in communicating with customers, coworkers, supervisors, and other staff as well as multitasking and group management. She has also previously trained on database symptoms for various employers and has an ability to train on computer or data entry systems.

  - Is the client ready for direct job placement?

    - Mrs. Example presents as ready to work and motivated to obtain employment.

  - Can this client endure or tolerate a full workday?

    - Mrs. Example may have difficulty sustaining an 8-hour workday and is recommended for part-time employment with shifts up to 4 hours.

  - Is the client employable in full-time or part-time work?

    - Mrs. Example is recommended for part-time employment because of her disability as well as her SSDI benefits.

  - What are the client's physical/motor skills?

    - Mrs. Example has physician-diagnosed work restrictions of no squatting, stooping, kneeling, bending, climbing, or lifting over 50 lb. She has difficulty staying in one position for an extended period of time. Her motor skills are intact.

    - She uses a cane sometimes because of her legs giving out.

  - Does the client stay on task?

    - Mrs. Example was capable of staying on task throughout the evaluation process.

GENERAL INFORMATION

Current Living Situation: Mrs. Example currently resides in a single-family house with her husband in Madison, WI.

Family History and Marital Status: Mrs. Example is a 60-year-old married female of Caucasian descent. She has been married for over 25 years. She has three grown children, who are 46, 35, and 32 years old. She reported having a strong support system and a good relationship with her family.

Current Employment Status: Mrs. Example is not employed at this time.

Military Experience: Mrs. Example has no military experience.

Purpose for Entering Vocational Rehabilitation: Per Mrs. Example, she is diagnosed with herniated intervertebral disc and a left knee replacement. Mrs. Example is seeking assistance to determine if she is eligible to work and/or receive vocational support or accommodations.

MEDICAL CONDITIONS

Primary Diagnoses: She has a herniated intervertebral disc.

Secondary Diagnoses: She has a left knee replacement.

Other Diagnoses: Co-occurring conditions include hypertension, hyperlipidemia, and depression.

Functional Limitations/Symptoms and Impact on Work or School: Mrs. Example is unable to stand, sit, and walk for a long period of time. Also, she is unable to squat, stoop, kneel, bend, climb, or lift over 50 lb.

She uses a cane sometimes because of her legs giving out.

Health Insurance: Mrs. Example has Blue Cross and Blue Shield insurance through her husband's employer.

MEDICATIONS AND TREATMENT

Current Treatment Regimen (Including Frequency of Visits to Physician): Mrs. Example is not receiving any treatment. Her primary care physician is Dr. Stone, with whom she makes follow-up visits every 2 to 3 months.

Current Medication: Mrs. Example is currently taking five medications, which are amlodipine besylate (hypertension), losartan (hypertension), potassium citrate, sertraline (depression), and simvastatin (hyperlipidemia). She also mentioned tramadol, which has unpleasant side effects, but is needed for pain.

Current Medical Concerns: There were no pressing medical concerns reported.

Pending Surgeries: She has no scheduled or pending surgeries.

EDUCATIONAL HISTORY

School History: Mrs. Example reported graduating from Bangor Area High School in 1974 in Pennsylvania with a standard diploma. When asked about her grades, she reported being a student with mostly all C's and a few B's. In 2006, she received an AS degree in Business Management from Lehigh Valley College, which is located in Pennsylvania.

Learning Accommodations: Mrs. Example reported having no accommodations provided to her in school or college.

Grade Point Average: Mrs. Example stated she did not remember her GPA in high school. She mentioned having a 3.5 GPA from college.

Educational Goals: Mrs. Example is not interested in going back to college due to the difficulties adjusting to a college teaching style and her age.

VOCATIONAL HISTORY

Competitive Work Experience: Mrs. Example has not been employed since March 2015. Her last job was with Walmart in Jacksonville, Florida, as a cashier from October 2014 to March 2015. Her job duties being a cashier were to greet customers, scan orders, deal with money, process credit cards, and bag items. Her job ended because it was a seasonal position. She worked 4 hours a day with a 15-minute break. She requested a chair or stool; however, no special accommodations were given to her. Prior to that job, she was employed at J. B. Hunt Transportation in Pennsylvania as an operational supervisor from October 2013 to September 2014. She left this job to relocate to Florida. Her job duties were to manage over 100 drivers, comply with regulations, process bill of lading forms, assign truck loads to drivers, and hiring/firing of employees. She reported that she liked this job because she was not confined or stationed in one area all day. She had freedom to move around. Prior to that job, she was employed at Split Rock Lodge in Pennsylvania as a house-keeper inspector from 2008 to 2013. Her job duties were hiring/firing, overseeing associates for training, visually inspecting guest rooms, training associates, and operating storage chemicals. Other jobs were as warehouse worker, forklift operator, auditor, driver, and travel agent. Her longest jobs were as a truck driver for 13 years and housekeeping administrator for 9 years.

Volunteer Work Experience: There was no volunteer experience reported.

VOCATIONAL GOALS

Mrs. Example is interested in obtaining a full-time or part-time job. She is mainly interested in jobs that allow her to have accommodations and not feel discriminated against.

ACTIVITIES OF DAILY LIVING

(Independent, Assistance Needed, Depends on Others)

Hygiene: Independent

Dressing: Independent

Homemaking: Independent

Home Maintenance: Independent

Community/Leisure: Independent

Self-Management: Independent

Summary of Independence in the Home: Mrs. Example reported being completely independent in all activities of daily living. Mrs. Example has a driver's license and owns a vehicle.

FINANCIAL INFORMATION

Current Income/Wages: Mrs. Example is receiving Social Security disability benefits of $1,049 per month. Her husband earns $4,500 per month with his employer as truck driver. She reported being fearful of her husband losing his job because of his back injury. She pays the electric, cell phone, water, and car bills. Her husband pays the rest of the bills.

Prior Wage Earning: Mrs. Example's last job earned her $8.50 an hour. Prior to that job, she was earning $22.14 an hour.

Desired Wage Earning: Mrs. Example stated she would like to make at least $12.00 an hour.

CRIMINAL HISTORY

History of Arrests: There was no arrest history provided.

BEHAVIORAL OBSERVATIONS

Attitude Toward Testing: Mrs. Example was very cooperative and friendly throughout the testing time. She was dressed casually, wearing a blouse and pair of slacks. After completing the test, she appeared to have some difficulties while getting out of the chair. She stated that her legs get stiff after sitting for a long period of time.

Attention: Mrs. Example was very focused during testing and did not take any breaks. She also completed the test in a fairly good time.

Affect/Mood: Mrs. Example remained cooperative and friendly throughout the appointment.

■ VOCATIONAL TESTING

In order to conduct an appropriate vocational evaluation, Mrs. Example's educational and vocational histories and relevant medical status were discussed. Tests that were administered to assess Mrs. Example's vocational functioning are listed as follows:

1. TABE

2. Holland Code Quiz

3. Life Skills Inventory (LSI)

4. Computer Skills—Typing Speed Test and E-mail Proficiency

5. Motivational Inventory

6. Job Observation and Behavior Scale: Opportunity for Self-Determination (JOBS:OSD)

ACADEMIC ACHIEVEMENT

The TABE was administered to assess the client's performance on an extended test of Academic Achievement. This test is occasionally used as a screening tool for admission into postsecondary training certificate programs. The client's performance on this test is outlined as follows:

SUBTEST	GRADE EQUIVALENCY
Reading	12.4
Math Computation	8.9
Applied Math	12.9+
Language	9.8
Total Math	11.6
Total Battery	11.2

Mrs. Example's performance on this test is within the average range with consideration of her age. She demonstrates some strength in reading and applied mathematics and some weakness in math computation, but overall is within the average range in each area tested.

VOCATIONAL INTERESTS

The Picture Interest Career Survey (PICS) was used to assess the client's areas of vocational interest. This test is administered on a computer and the client is provided with three pictures on each screen and asked to choose which picture most aligns with her interests. The results on this assessment demonstrate Mrs. Example is mostly Social, Investigative, Artistic, Enterprising, Conventional, and Realistic.

R—Realistic

Score: **13**
People interested in this area usually like to work with things, use tools and machines, and prefer physical and mechanical work. They are often described as persistent and practical. They are most comfortable in a structured and stable work environment. Workers with high realistic interest are typically found in construction and skilled trades, production and manufacturing, applied technologies, agriculture, transportation and logistics, textiles, hospitality and recreation, food service, and natural resources.

I—Investigative

Score: **15**
People interested in this area usually like to work with ideas and data and prefer problem-solving and scientific and technical work. They are often described as curious, intellectual, and independent. They favor jobs that require abstract thinking, research, and analysis. Workers with high investigative interest are often found in the life and physical sciences, health and behavioral sciences, applied technologies, academics, research and development, and mathematics and engineering.

A—Artistic

Score: **15**
Persons interested in this area usually like to work with people, ideas, and things and prefer creative and self-expressive work. Artistic people are often described as imaginative, open, and original. They favor flexible and less predictable work environments. Workers with high artistic interest are often found in design, applied arts, architecture, culinary arts, performing arts, fine arts, education, communication and media, and fashion.

S—Social

Score: **17**

Persons interested in this area usually like to work with people and prefer helping, teaching, and healing work. Social types are often described as supportive, understanding, patient, and generous. They favor jobs that require listening, comforting, and advising. Workers with high social interest are often found in education, health and human services, recreation and fitness, safety and service, and religious vocations.

E—Enterprising

Score: **15**

Persons interested in this area usually like to work with people and prefer leading and persuading. Enterprising people are often described as confident, ambitious, and energetic. They generally favor jobs that involve selling and achieving set goals. Workers with high enterprising interest are often found in business and administration, marketing, finance and insurance, retail sales and wholesale, and law.

C—Conventional

Score: **15**

Persons interested in this area usually like to work with data, things, and people and prefer clerical and computational work. Conventional people are often described as organized, efficient, and careful. They generally favor jobs that involve working with numbers, machines, and computers to meet required goals. Workers with high conventional interest are often found in accounting, banking, financial analysis, office work, and the computer applications sector.

LIFE SKILLS

During the LSI, Mrs. Example was asked to explore her self-perception of abilities within the areas of communication skills, stress management skills, anger management skills, money management skills, time management skills, and career skills. Her performance on this test is listed as follows:

LIFE SKILLS CATEGORY	YOUR SCORE	SKILLS SCALE	
Communication	Effectiveness in communicating with other people	27	High
Stress Management	Effectiveness in managing stress	24	Average
Anger Management	Effectiveness in managing feelings of anger	27	High
Money Management	Effectiveness in managing your finances	29	High
Time Management	Effectiveness in managing your time	27	High
Career	Effectiveness in being productive in the workplace	28	High

The LSI has compiled your responses to the statements in Step 1 and ranked them according to six life skills categories to measure your level of development in each. The higher the score in a given category, the more advanced your life skills are in that area.

- **Scores from 24 to 30 are high** and indicate that you have developed many effective life skills in this category.

- **Scores from 17 to 23 are average** and indicate that you have developed some effective life skills in this category.

- **Scores from 10 to 16 are low** and indicate that you have not developed effective life skills in this category.

COMPUTER SKILLS

Typing Speed: A typing speed test was administered to assess Mrs. Example's typing speed and accuracy. Mrs. Example performed the test for 2 minutes and scored 24 words per minute with 87% accuracy and an adjusted score of 21 wpm, placing her in the **slow** category.
E-mail Access: Mrs. Example does have access to a computer at home and phone. During the evaluation, she was asked to access her phone and send the evaluator a brief e-mail about her vocational goals. She was able to complete that task.

MOTIVATION

The Self-Assessment of Motivation examination was used to determine Mrs. Example's self-report of interest and enthusiasm toward work and school. Mrs. Example performed with a total score of 90, suggesting many of her answers were positive. An example of her responses is as follows: "I wake up in a good mood: **almost always**." Her score on this test appears consistent with her demonstrated demeanor.

JOB OBSERVATION AND BEHAVIOR SCALE

The JOBS:OSD test was completed to assess Mrs. Example's Quality of Performance and Type of Support needed in the following three areas: Work-Related Daily Living Activities, Work-Related Behavior, and Work-Related Job Duties. Her scores are as follows:
Quality of Performance

Subscale: Points Earned:

Work-Related Daily Living Activities   37

Work-Related Behavior   23

Work-Related Job Duties   24

Total: **84**

Type of Support

Subscale: Points Earned:

Work-Related Daily Living Activities   38

Work-Related Behavior   24

Work-Related Job Duties   25

Total: **87**

These scores suggest that, if placed in work, Mrs. Example would be a competitive job placement, as opposed to supported or sheltered employment candidate.

TRANSFERABLE SKILLS

When assessing transferable skills, the vocational professional must incorporate the client's past relevant work experience (jobs held within the past 15 years). Mrs. Example has competitive and recent work experience as a cashier, order clerk, dispatcher, fork lifter operator, truck driver, operation supervisor, and housekeeper inspector. According to the occupational information network, the job tasks and skills required for order clerk and supervisor/administrative support worker are listed as follows:

Order clerk:

- Verify customer and order information for correctness, checking it against previously obtained information as necessary.
- Receive and respond to customer complaints.
- Review orders for completeness according to reporting procedures and forward incomplete orders for further processing.
- Inform customers by mail or telephone of order information, such as unit prices, shipping dates, and any anticipated delays.
- Obtain customers' names, addresses, billing information, product numbers, and specifications of items to be purchased and enter this information on order forms.
- Recommend merchandise or services that will meet customers' needs.
- Prepare invoices, shipping documents, and contracts.
- Confer with production, sales, shipping, warehouse, or common carrier personnel to expedite or trace shipments.
- Compute total charges for merchandise or services and shipping charges.
- Direct specified departments or units to prepare and ship orders to designated locations.

Supervisor and administrative support worker:

- Supervise the work of office, administrative, or customer service employees to ensure adherence to quality standards, deadlines, and proper procedures, correcting errors or problems.
- Resolve customer complaints or answer customers' questions regarding policies and procedures.
- Provide employees with guidance in handling difficult or complex problems or in resolving escalated complaints or disputes.
- Review records or reports pertaining to activities such as production, payroll, or shipping to verify details, monitor work activities, or evaluate performance.
- Discuss job performance problems with employees to identify causes and issues and to work on resolving problems.

■ SUMMARY

SUMMARY OF VOCATIONAL TESTING RESULTS

Strengths

- Access to a computer at home and phone
- JOBS:OSD for competitive employment
- Positive motivation score
- High motivation to achieve gainful employment
- Applied Math ability > 12.9 Grade Equivalent
- Reading ability > 12.4 Grade Equivalent
- High skill ability in all areas of Life Skills assessment

Weaknesses

- Slow typing speed

SUMMARY OF OTHER STRENGTHS AND WEAKNESS

Weaknesses

- Unemployed a year and a half
- Significant physical limitations and work restrictions

Strengths

- History of varied work experience
- Ability to drive a decent distance for work
- Access to a computer at home and phone
- High motivation to achieve gainful employment
- AS degree in Business Management

EMPLOYMENT RECOMMENDATIONS AND LABOR MARKET SURVEY

Job Title 1:
Dispatcher

Job Title 2:
Order Clerk Job

Job Title 3:
Receptionist

Job Title 4:
Call Center Representative

Job Title 5:
Customer Service Representative

*Job Openings Attached

LABOR MARKET INFORMATION (Taken From O*NET)

1. Dispatcher: Median wages (2017) $18.65 hourly, $38,790 annual
   Employment (2016)   202,000 employees
   Projected growth (2016–2026)   Little or no change (−1% to 1%)
   Projected job openings (2016–2026)   18,000

2. Order Clerk: Median wages (2017) $16.11 hourly, $33,510 annual
   Employment (2016)   179,000 employees
   Projected growth (2016–2026)   Decline (−2% or lower)
   Projected job openings (2016–2026)   19,400

3. Receptionist/Information Clerk:
   Median wages (2017) $13.65 hourly, $28,390 annual
   Employment (2016)   1,054,000 employees
   Projected growth (2016–2026)   Average (5%–9%)
   Projected job openings (2016–2026)   151,100

4. Call Center Representative/
   Telemarketer: Median wages (2017) $11.76 hourly, $24,460 annual
   Employment (2016)   217,000 employees
   Projected growth (2016–2026)   Little or no change (−1% to 1%)
   Projected job openings (2016–2026)   33,300

5. Customer Service Representative:
   Median wages (2017) $15.81 hourly, $32,890 annual
   Employment (2016)   2,785,000 employees
   Projected growth (2016–2026)   Average (5%–9%)
   Projected job openings (2016–2026)   373,500

GENERAL OBSERVATIONS, RECOMMENDATIONS, AND CONCLUSIONS

Summary of Client: Mrs. Client Example is a 60-year-old, married, Caucasian female who currently resides with her husband. She is independent in all activities. Mrs. Example reported that she is complying with taking her medications and should be able to sustain employment that offers accommodations.

Performance on Testing: Mrs. Example remained focused and calm throughout the evaluation. She had some limitations in areas of math computation, language, and the typing test. Overall, she scored slightly above average on the TABE. She performed well on the JOBS:OSD, motivation, and life skills. At the present time, Mrs. Example is not in need of supported employment services or additional counseling.

<u>Academic Recommendations:</u> Mrs. Example is not interested in furthering her education at this time nor does additional postsecondary education seem necessary in making her employable. Mrs. Example would benefit from exploration of local computer workshops to increase her familiarity with Microsoft Office and improve her typing speed.

<u>Employment Recommendations:</u> Mrs. Example presents with transferable skills and an ability to work part-time. She has the capabilities of working full-time with special accommodations (frequent breaks and transitional assignments). Mrs. Example is confident she can maintain employment with special accommodations. It is recommended that she continue to search for sedentary employment that matches her skill set. She reported a desire to earn $12.00 per hour and may need to adjust to a lower pay scale as a result of the local labor market and what jobs exist that she is capable of and willing to do.

<u>Medical/Psychological Recommendations:</u> Mrs. Example reported disliking taking tramadol and, therefore, she was recommended to see her primary care physician for pain management.

Respectfully Submitted,

Joe ABC, MC, CRC
Encl: Local Job Openings

WORKSITE EVALUATION AND SITUATIONAL ASSESSMENT TEMPLATE

WORKSITE EVALUATION/SITUATIONAL ASSESSMENT

DVR Client Name	
Date of Birth/Age	
Address	
Employment Status	
Primary Limitations	
Evaluation Date(s)	
Report Date	
Evaluator(s)	

PURPOSE AND SOURCE OF REFERRAL

_____
_____
_____
_____
_____
_____
_____
_____
_____
_____
_____

DOCUMENTS CONSIDERED

_____
_____
_____
_____
_____
_____

GENERAL INFORMATION

Current Living Situation: _____

_____

_____

Family History: _____

_____

Military Experience: _____

_____

Current Employment Status: _____

_____

Purpose for Entering Vocational Rehabilitation: _____

_____

Primary Diagnoses: _____

_____

Symptoms: _____

Functional Limitations in Work and School: _____

Health Insurance: _____

_____

_____

Current Treatment Regimen: _____

Current Medication: _____

Stability of Conditions: _____

_____

School History: _____

_____

_____

Status of High School Diploma or Other Degrees (Standard/Special): _____

_____

List All Certificates/Degrees: _____

Learning Accommodations: _____

Grade Point Average: _____

_____

_____

Educational Goals: _____

Job Goals: _____

Competitive Work Experience: _____

_____

Volunteer Work Experience: _____

_____

Hygiene: _____

Dressing: _____

Homemaking: _____

_____

Home Maintenance: _____

Community/Leisure: _____

_____

Self-Management: _____

▨ WORKSITE ASSESSMENT ACTIVITIES:

Day 1 Activities—Location 1

> **Location 2**

> **Location 3**

> **Location 4**

Day 2 Activities—Location 1

> **Location 2**

> **Location 3**

> **Location 4**

OVERVIEW OF GOALS OF SCHEDULED WORKSITE ACTIVITIES

_____
_____
_____
_____
_____
_____
_____
_____
_____
_____

WORKSITE ASSESSMENT DAY 1 ACTIVITIES:

1. Activity:

    Items:
    Tasks:

Physical Requirements:

Duration:

2.   Activity:

    Items:
    Tasks:

    Physical Requirements:

    Duration:

3.   Activity:

    Items:
    Tasks:

    Physical Requirements:

    Duration:

4.   Activity:

    Items:
    Tasks:

    Physical Requirements:

    Duration:

5. <u>Activity:</u>

    Items:
    Tasks:

    Physical Requirements:

    Duration:

6. <u>Activity:</u>

    Items:
    Tasks:

    Physical Requirements:

    Duration:

7. <u>Activity:</u>

    Items:
    Tasks:

    Physical Requirements:

    Duration:

8. <u>Activity:</u>

    Items:
    Tasks:

    Physical Requirements:

    Duration:

Summary of Day 1 Performance:

_____
_____
_____
_____
_____
_____
_____
_____

WORKSITE ASSESSMENT DAY 2 ACTIVITIES:

9. Activity:

Items:
Tasks:

Physical Requirements:

Duration:

10. Activity:

Items:
Tasks:

Physical Requirements:

Duration:

11. Activity:

Items:
Tasks:

Physical Requirements:

Duration:

12. <u>Activity:</u>

   Items:
   Tasks:

   Physical Requirements:

   Duration:

13. <u>Activity:</u>

   Items:
   Tasks:

   Physical Requirements:

   Duration:

14. <u>Activity:</u>

   Items:
   Tasks:

   Physical Requirements:

   Duration:

15. <u>Activity:</u>

   Items:

Tasks:

Physical Requirements:

Duration:

16. Activity:

   Items:
   Tasks:

   Physical Requirements:

   Duration:

Summary of Day 2 Performance:

_____
_____
_____
_____
_____
_____
_____
_____
_____
_____
_____
_____
_____

BEHAVIORAL AND VERBAL OBSERVATIONS:

Timeliness:

Physical Appearance:

Ability to Work with Others:

Concentration:

Breaks:

Other:

OVERALL DESCRIPTION OF CLIENT'S PERFORMANCE

1. Ability to arrive at work setting on time:
2. Ability to communicate effectively with staff:
3. Concentration and precision while working:
4. Engagement in activities:
5. Cooperation when directed to perform new tasks:
6. Accessibility and availability for scheduling via phone:
7. Professionalism in the workplace:
8. Ability to make changes/improvements in suggested areas:
9. Exerting diligence while working:
10. Overall performance in the simulated work setting:

SUMMARY OF VOCATIONAL ASSETS AND LIABILITIES:

Assets:

Liabilities:

GENERAL OBSERVATIONS, RECOMMENDATIONS, AND CONCLUSIONS

Summary of Client:

Performance on Testing:

Academic Recommendations:

Employment Recommendations:

Medical/Psychological Recommendations:

Additional Services:

APPENDIX 12.4

EXAMPLE WORKSITE EVALUATION AND SITUATIONAL ASSESSMENT

WORKSITE EVALUATION/SITUATIONAL ASSESSMENT

DVR Client Name	Client Example
Date of Birth/Age	22 years
Address	1234 Alphabet Ave, Naples, FL 34117
Employment Status	Unemployed
Primary Limitations	Diagnoses of attention deficit hyperactivity disorder (ADHD), Depression, Possible Tic Syndrome
Evaluation Locations	Golden Gate Library, Wendy's, Midas, Walmart, Michaels, Home Depot, Barnes & Noble
Evaluation Date(s)	November 18 and 19, 2017
Report Date	November 25, 2017
Evaluator(s)	Vocational Evaluator, MS, CRC

BACKGROUND

PURPOSE AND SOURCE OF REFERRAL

Mr. Client Example received a worksite evaluation to assist in determining his employability in competitive local employment. The worksite evaluation was conducted in his local community within simulated work settings. Mr. Example arrived early for the evaluation independently driving his vehicle. The initial meeting was held at Golden Gate Library on 2432 Lucerne Road, Naples, FL 34116. Information on the worksite evaluation and how long it would take was given to Mr. Example. There were questions asked of Mr. Example. Initially, Mr. Example was hesitant in answering the questions asked, but when the purpose of this evaluation was explained, and he had a better understanding of what was going to happen, Mr. Example was more cooperative with the assessment. He expressed his desire to obtain employment, but he hesitated because the last position as a mechanic did not work. Mr. Example further explained that his pace is slow, and he was expected to pick up his pace. Because he was not able to do that, they let him go. During the initial interviewing process, there were questions that Mr. Example could not answer, and he requested permission to talk to his mother and obtain the information requested for the assessment.

DOCUMENTS CONSIDERED

The following documentation was provided with the referral:

- Comprehensive Report from Dr. Adams, MD, Developmental Pediatrician from August 9, 2004

- Visit Reports from Dr. Smith, MD, Neurologist from NC Neuroscience and Spine Associates in 2013

- Psychological Evaluation by Dr. Luis, Ph.D., Clinical Psychologist in 2013

GENERAL INFORMATION

Mr. Client Example is a 22-year-old Caucasian man who was referred for vocational and worksite assessment. Mr. Example currently lives at home with his mother, her husband, and son. Mr. Example explained that his younger sister lives in the dormitory at Florida Gulf Coast University and comes home when it is convenient for her. Mr. Example explained that he was born and raised in Naples, his parents divorced when he was about 11 years old. Mr. Example does not have any military history or experience. Mr. Example is currently unemployed. For health insurance, he is currently covered under his mother's policy which he was not aware of.

Mr. Example has diagnoses of ADHD, depression, and low testosterone. Mr. Example is followed by Dr. Esert, family practice; Dr. Vickers, neurologist; and Dr. Daller, urologist. This evaluator spoke with Mr. Example's mother as he did not remember the medications he was taking. Mr. Example currently is on Topamax, paroxetine, and Adderall. Mr. Example's mother indicated that there is further follow-up needed with the neurologist to explore tic disorder. She explained that he has tremors and that the problem has been discussed with the neurologist but not explored. This information is not clear as the medical records from Dr. Vickers' office from October 7, 2013 show tic syndrome as a medical history. Mr. Example explained that when he was in high school, he played football and sustained an injury in 2010. Mr. Example did not elaborate about how bad the injury was or any details about it. Mr. Example graduated from high school and obtained an associate's degree in automotive mechanics. Mr. Example explained that he is qualified to work as an auto mechanic. He expressed his challenge at work, saying that it was very fast paced and he was not able to keep up with the schedule provided.

Mr. Example does not have volunteer experience. He has work history at McDonald's when he was in high school for about 6 months. He also worked for the Collier family for 6 months in their home, doing yard work, for example. Mr. Example explained that he was asked to work more hours but was not able to do so because he was going to school.

The purpose of the referral for a worksite evaluation was to set more realistic employment goals and see what type of job environment Mr. Example will feel comfortable in and enjoy going to daily.

(Independent, Assistance Needed, Depends on Others)
Hygiene: Independent
Dressing: Independent
Homemaking: Works together with his mother
Home Maintenance: Works together with his mother
Community/Leisure: Independent
Self-Management: Independent

Mr. Example arrived at the worksite early at 12 noon on Saturday, November 18, 2017. The worksite selected for this day was Golden Gate Public Library at 2432 Lucerne Rd., Naples, FL 34116. Mr. Example came to the library independently driving his vehicle. Mr. Example spoke of his interests and was cooperative with the assessment process upon arrival.

WORKSITE ASSESSMENT ACTIVITIES:

Day 1 Activities—11/18/2017 at 12 noon

Golden Gate Library
2432 Lucerne Rd., Naples,
FL. 34116

Midas
2111 Pine Ridge Rd., Naples,
FL 34109

Wendy's
10941 Airport Pulling Rd. N., Naples,
FL 34109

Walmart
5420 Juliet Blvd., Naples,
FL 34109

Day 2 Activities—9/24/2017 at 11 a.m.

Michaels
2255b Pine Ridge Rd., Naples,
FL 34109

Home Depot
2251 Pine Ridge Rd., Naples,
FL 34109
Barnes & Noble
5377 Tamiami Trail N., Naples, FL 34108

▧ WORKSITE ASSESSMENT DAY 1 ACTIVITIES:

1. <u>Activity:</u> Intake Interview
    The intake interview was conducted with Mr. Example. There were questions asked of Mr. Example for him to answer. Initially, Mr. Example had difficulty answering questions, and after reviewing the purpose of the assessment, he was more open to answering questions. First, background information was asked, and Mr. Example answered all the questions. When asked about his future and vocational plans, Mr. Example did not have any problems answering the questions. At the end of the intake interview, Mr. Example was open to the work assessment that was going to be held.

2. <u>Activity:</u> Typing, Using the Mouse, Taking PICS, LSI Test, Holland Code Quiz, and Institute of Psychometric Coaching (IPC) Aptitude Test
    <u>Items:</u> Using the computer with the mouse
    <u>Tasks:</u> Mr. Example was asked to use the computer with the mouse to take the PICS, LSI test, Holland Code Quiz, and IPC Aptitude Test.

Client's Performance: Mr. Example was able to follow directions for each of the tests given and answer the questions asked. He did not have any issues using the computer, typing, and using the mouse to maneuver through the system and the test requirements.

Client's Interest and Cooperation: Mr. Example was agreeable and cooperative with doing this activity. With every test and new instructions, he listened to each of the instructions and followed them well without any issues. He said he understood the activity and what needed to be done.

3.   Activity: Typing Test
Items: Mr. Example needed to use the laptop.
Task: Mr. Example was directed to www.typingtest.com to take a 1-minute typing test to assess his typing speed.
Client's Performance: Mr. Example performed the test for 1 minute and scored with 3% accuracy.
Client's Interest and Cooperation: Mr. Example was able to focus on his typing and was cooperative with his typing exercise. He typed with two fingers, typed 32 words, and had 31 errors.

4.   Activity: Card Sorting
Items: Picture Cards
Tasks: Mr. Example was directed to identify picture items on cards. Once picture items were identified, he was asked to alphabetize the picture cards to store into a card container.
Client's Performance: Mr. Example was able to identify all the items on the cards, and he was able to sort the cards accurately.
Client's Interest and Cooperation: Mr. Example was agreeable to doing the activity. He said he understood the activity and what needed to be done. He was able to identify the pictures on each of the cards. When Mr. Example was asked to alphabetize the cards and store them in the card storage container, he was able to sort the cards according to the items and place them in alphabetical order without any issues.

5.   Activity: Folding T-Shirts
Items: T-Shirts
Tasks: Mr. Example was asked to fold three T-shirts the way he found them initially.
Client's Performance: Mr. Example was able to fold the three T-Shirts without any issues or any assistance needed.
Client's Interest and Cooperation: Mr. Example was cooperative with conducting this activity and was able to keep his interest in the task.

6.   Activity: Asking Questions about Job Openings (Midas)
Items: No items needed at Midas.
Tasks: Mr. Example was asked to talk to the owner of the Midas shop regarding any job openings.
Client's Performance: Mr. Example refused to ask any questions to the owner, sharing that he was not interested after the activity was initiated. This evaluator talked to the owner and asked him about any job openings. The owner said there were no openings at this time as they were not busy enough at this time.
Client's Interest and Cooperation: Mr. Example shared that he was open and interested in the position, but did not want to ask any questions. Mr. Example explained that the interest is there but did not want to pursue with Midas at this time.

7. <u>Activity:</u> Ordering Food (Wendy's)
   <u>Items:</u> No items needed
   <u>Tasks:</u> Mr. Example was asked to order his food at Wendy's.
   <u>Client's Performance:</u> Mr. Example had no issues deciding what he wanted to eat at Wendy's and ordering it at the desk.
   <u>Client's Interest and Cooperation:</u> Mr. Example was interested in performing this task and he was cooperative with performing the task.

8. <u>Activity:</u> Cleaning Up the Table
   <u>Items:</u> Food tray and drinks after eating
   <u>Tasks:</u> Mr. Example was asked to pick up the trash and drink containers used during the meal so that the table would be clean afterward.
   <u>Client's Performance:</u> Mr. Example had no issues with the performance of this task and understood what was expected of him to complete the task.
   <u>Client's Interest and Cooperation:</u> Mr. Example showed interest in this task and was cooperative with this task.

9. <u>Activity:</u> Looking Up Information on the Computer
   <u>Items:</u> Computer/Laptop
   <u>Tasks:</u> Mr. Example was assigned to look up websites and education possibilities for himself.
   <u>Client's Performance:</u> Mr. Example was able to look up the website and at what was being said and what needed to be done to apply for the schooling. It was specifically on heavy equipment operation training.
   <u>Client's Interest and Cooperation:</u> Mr. Example was interested in this task and was very cooperative in performing this task.

10. <u>Activity:</u> Using Cell Phone for E-mail and Games
    <u>Items:</u> Cell phone
    <u>Tasks:</u> Mr. Example was asked to show if he is able to access his e-mail through his cell phone as well as pull up and play games on his cell phone.
    <u>Client's Performance:</u> Mr. Example was successful in sending e-mail and text messaging from his cell phone. He was able to demonstrate pulling up a game he plays (Hexa Block) and play a game.

11. <u>Activity:</u> Hanging Shirts and Sorting the Shirts by Size
    <u>Items:</u> Shirts of different sizes and hangers
    <u>Tasks:</u> Mr. Example was asked to sort shirts. He was asked to hang up the shirts to match the correctly labeled hangers, and then sort them by size when he places it back on the rack.
    <u>Client's Performance:</u> Mr. Example was able to perform the task requested by hanging up the shirt according to its size hanger and placing it back on the rack.
    <u>Client's Interest and Cooperation:</u> Mr. Example showed interest in completing this task and was cooperative.

12. <u>Activity:</u> Hanging Pants and Sorting the Pants
    <u>Items:</u> Pants of different sizes and hangers.
    <u>Tasks:</u> Mr. Example was asked to sort pants by hanging them up to match the correctly labeled hangers, then sort them by size when he places them back onto the rack.

Client's Performance: Mr. Example was able to perform this task as requested. He had some difficulty with hanging the pants where he had to clip the waist area onto the hanger because of his tremors. He took some time and was able to get them on, and he was able to sort the pants by size.

Client's Interest and Cooperation: Mr. Example held his interest in performing this task and was cooperative with getting this task completed.

13. Activity: Stocking Items in the Baby Section/Identifying the Items and Where They Belong

Items: Items taken off the shelves at Walmart.

Tasks: Mr. Example was asked to restock items taken off the shelves in the baby section to where the items belong.

Client's Performance: Mr. Example was able to perform the task and place all items back to where they belong.

Client's Interest and Cooperation: Mr. Example showed interest in completing this activity and was cooperative with getting this task completed.

14. Activity: Discuss/Share Knowledge of Video Games in the Video Game Section at Walmart.

Tasks: Mr. Example was asked to explain what video games are good for what age bracket.

Client's Performance: Mr. Example was able to answer the questions asked on what video games would be good for certain people.

Client's Interest and Cooperation: Mr. Example was able to maintain his interest and was cooperative with the evaluator to answer the questions asked.

15. Activity: Sorting Items in the Auto Section

Items: Items on the shelf in the auto section at Walmart.

Tasks: Mr. Example was asked to sort different items on the shelves according to where like items are placed in the auto section.

Client's Performance: Mr. Example was able to sort items in the auto section according to what was needed from a mechanic's point of view.

Client's Interest and Cooperation: Mr. Example showed interest in performing this task and was cooperative in getting the task completed.

Summary of Day 1 Performance:

Mr. Example arrived at the Golden Gate Library at 12 noon on Saturday, November 18th. He arrived independently in his own vehicle and arrived at the library about 15 minutes ahead of time. We spoke about the type of afternoon this will be. Mr. Example was initially hesitant to talk with the evaluator. The evaluator explained to him why the questions were being asked, and how that related to his work assignment and job placement. He was cooperative with the assessment process and did not hesitate with conducting any of the activities. Mr. Example did not show any mood changes during the afternoon. After all the activities were completed, we discussed how the Day 2 activities were going to be done. Mr. Example expressed that knowing where we were going to go for the Day 2 activities helped him prepare for the second day.

▨ WORKSITE ASSESSMENT DAY 2 ACTIVITIES:

16. Activity: Exploring Crafts at Michaels
    Items: Different craft items
    Tasks: Mr. Example was asked to identify what crafts he likes to do.
    Client's Performance: Mr. Example discussed different types of crafts and artistic things he likes to do. He was able to identify that he likes to paint, and if he is coloring, he likes to use color pencils.
    Client's Interest and Cooperation: Mr. Example was able to maintain his interest and was cooperative with his task.

17. Activity: Lifting Tools at Home Depot
    Items: Tools such as skill saw, chop saw, and other tools in the tool department at Home Depot.
    Tasks: Mr. Example was asked to lift five different tools in the tool department at Home Depot to see how heavy an item he can lift.
    Client's Performance: Every tool that was lifted and moved by this evaluator, Mr. Example was able to lift and place it back to where it was found.
    Client's Interest and Cooperation: Mr. Example maintained his interest in completing this activity and was cooperative.

18. Activity: Lifting Wood at Home Depot
    Items: Wood pieces of different sizes.
    Tasks: Mr. Example was asked to life different sizes of wood and put them back to where they were found. For example, he was asked to lift 4 × 4 treated posts that were 8 feet long.
    Client's Performance: Mr. Example was able to lift all the different sizes of wood, demonstrating his lifting abilities.
    Client's Interest and Cooperation: Mr. Example was able to maintain his interest and cooperation with completing this activity.

19. Activity: Coloring by Numbers
    Items: Coloring paper with a picture on it that was numbered.
    Tasks: Mr. Example was asked to color in areas that were numbered with reference to specific colors.
    Client's Performance: Mr. Example was able to color the areas numbered and not have an issue identifying the colors. This showed that he was able to identify what number goes with what color. When coloring Mr. Example was able to color within the lines, and keep his hands steady for accuracy in coloring.
    Client's Interest and Cooperation: Mr. Example was able to maintain his interest and concentration for a very short period of time, and did not want to finish the product. He was cooperative with doing the activity until he chose not to finish the product.

Summary of Day 2 Performance:

The appointment to meet with Mr. Example was at 10:30 a.m. on Sunday, November 19, 2017. Mr. Example arrived in his vehicle. Mr. Example was at Michael's, where he had agreed to meet, when the evaluator arrived mostly on time (arrived at 10:32 a.m.). Mr. Example traveled with the evaluator to the worksites and concluded the worksite evaluation at Michaels where we met. Mr. Example was very courteous, quiet, and professional. He was dressed casually in jeans, T-shirt, and comfortable shoes. His mood was stable during the day, no issues noted. He was diligent with the worksite activities and performed very well with all the tasks requested without any complaints and without asking for any breaks. Toward the end of the day, when he was doing the last activity, he showed some frustration, sharing that he did not want to finish this activity. During the second day of this worksite assessment, Mr. Example expressed his thought that he was very interested in being able to work part-time and go to school to learn to operate heavy machinery equipment.

BEHAVIORAL AND VERBAL OBSERVATIONS:

Timeliness: Mr. Example was prompt with time and arrived to the scheduled places on time both days.

Physical Appearance: Mr. Example was dressed casually on both days but was dressed nicely.

Ability to Work With Others: Mr. Example was very honest about his feeling of working with others. He shared that he does not feel comfortable working with others and holding any positions where he is required to interact with other people frequently, especially customers.

Concentration: Mr. Example was able to maintain his concentration during all activities and did not require breaks until the activity was completed.

Breaks: Mr. Example did not request for breaks and was able to perform the tasks requested without any difficulties.

Other: As Mr. Example spent more time with this evaluator, he showed that he was more comfortable and was more at ease when answering questions and performing the tasks requested.

OVERALL DESCRIPTION OF CLIENT'S PERFORMANCE

1. Mr. Example will have no issues arriving to the work setting on time as he arrived both days early and he has his own transportation.

2. After spending a few hours each for 2 days with Mr. Example, it showed that he may take a few moments to answer questions or to formulate answers, but he is able to communicate with staff members effectively.

3. During the worksite evaluations on both days, Mr. Example demonstrated his ability to concentrate and be precise with his actions. This showed his ability to concentrate on the job setting.

4. Mr. Example showed the ability to be engaged with all activities conducted. With some of the tasks, his facial expressions showed that the task was not enjoyable, but he still completed the tasks requested by this evaluator except for the last coloring activity.

5. Mr. Example was cooperative when performing the tasks without any hesitations.

6. Mr. Example has his own cell phone and has been accessible and available to schedule his own time via the phone.

7. Mr. Example demonstrated that he would act professionally in the workplace.

8. Mr. Example was open to making some changes and improvements such as working with people at times, but with hesitation. He was willing to further his education/training.

9. Mr. Example exerted diligence while working with this evaluator during the 2-day worksite assessment.

10. Mr. Example was able to follow directions well and was able to perform the tasks requested.

▮ SUMMARY OF VOCATIONAL ASSETS AND LIABILITIES:

Assets: Mr. Example prefers to work alone, is diligent with his work, and takes pride in the work he performs. He is quiet, very polite, and courteous toward others. Mr. Example is very precise when he is organizing things, and very particular with presentation.

Liabilities: Mr. Example does not like working with other people and prefers to work by himself without anyone around.

GENERAL OBSERVATIONS, RECOMMENDATIONS, AND CONCLUSIONS

Mr. Example is a 22-year-old single Caucasian man who presented to this evaluation after very little competitive work experience. He has worked at McDonald's for about 6 months during high school and worked for a family in Naples for a short period of time. He was asked to work longer hours, and when he shared that he was not able to do that because he was pursuing his associate's degree, he was let go. Mr. Example explained that after receiving his associate degree in automotive mechanics, he worked for an auto shop for a very short period of time. Mr. Example explained that he does not even talk about it as it was a very short time. He explained that he was not able to maintain the pace they wanted him to work, so he is not confident that he will be able to keep up as an auto mechanic.

Mr. Example graduated from high school and received a diploma. He pursued his education, attended technical school, and received an associate degree in automotive mechanics. Mr. Example expressed his interest in attending heavy equipment training. This information was reviewed and there was training available in the local Naples/Fort Myers area for 3 weeks. He was interested in looking at that.

During the worksite assessment, he was observed to have no difficulty with following directions, completing tasks, and maintaining focus that required concentration and attention to detail. Based on his performance, he demonstrated that he is able to perform in stocking items, and able to lift heavy items, showing that he has the strength to move things around as needed. Mr. Example showed signs of having tremors at times when doing fine motor skills work, such as when putting pants on the hangers or when he was coloring.

Employment Outcome and Recommendations

With his demonstrated abilities, it is recommended that he pursue competitive employment on a part-time basis. The results from the 2-day worksite assessment showed that for the short term, he would benefit from a workplace where he had minimal interactions with people. Based on his performance during the evaluation, he appears to be a suitable candidate for supported employment in entry-level settings such as at bookstores, stocking, merchandising, and other related occupations. Mr. Example explained that he has applied to different employment places for stocking positions. The places he said he applied to were Walmart, Target, Sears Automotive, GoodYear, and Costco. Mr. Example explained that he has not heard from any of the places, and he has not followed up as well. Mr. Example would benefit with assistance in following up with the places he has placed the applications. Mr. Example will benefit from some coaching in the areas of interviewing skills, independence, and practicing conversations involved with customer service as he was noted not to initiate conversations with anyone. This was noted even when he was talking with the evaluator.

Other than employment and training recommendations, the evaluator talked about some issues going on in his family with his siblings and the relationship he has with his father. Mr. Example explained that his parents separated when he was about 11 years old and he went and lived with his father for about 4 years and has been back with his mother for the last 10 years. He talked about some of the things going on with his father. As Mr. Example shared information, the evaluator noted some anger and frustration and not knowing how to channel them. Mr. Example would benefit from seeing a therapist to be able to process the changes going on in his life. The report the evaluator read from Dr. Smith showed that Mr. Example was diagnosed with tic syndrome. The evaluator spoke with his mother, Barbara, and Mr. Example confirmed that no one has addressed the tremors he has been having for a few years. Mr. Example's mother noted that they needed to follow up with Dr. Smith as the tremors continued and no further tests were run. This is definitely a follow-up that is needed to identify what triggers his conditions as they could interfere with work.

13

ASSESSMENT IN TRANSITION FROM SCHOOL TO WORK AND THE COMMUNITY

PAUL WEHMAN | WHITNEY HAM | HOLLY WHITTENBURG | LAUREN AVELLONE | JENNIFER TODD MCDONOUGH

LEARNING OBJECTIVES

After reviewing this chapter, the reader should be able to:

- Explain the importance of age-appropriate transition assessments and recent amendments to federal legislation that support the use of transition assessments.

- Identify various formal and informal academic assessments and appropriate uses of alternative assessments with students with significant disabilities.

- Describe essential assessment tools used in transition-to-work via supported and customized employment processes, including how to use situational assessments.

- Describe the various community assessment domains along with methods for mapping available community resources and assessing skills needed to use identified resources.

■ Transition From School to Work and the Community

Laura is a 19-year-old recent graduate of Lake Springs High School who has a significant cognitive disability. When the employment specialist first met Laura, it was apparent that she had a strong desire to work. Laura got extremely excited at the possibility that she could have a "real job" like her brother. Laura's previous employment experience at a local restaurant was positive, but ended abruptly when a new management staff came in. Approximately a year later, she was faced with obtaining a new job in her field of choice. She had taken a class in high school that had sparked her interest in office work, and she decided that she wanted a part-time clerical job, but she had many questions. Could she obtain a job in a field in which she had very little training? Would an employer expect her to do clerical work with reading and writing skills? Who would support her and help her at work when she needed it? Laura spoke to the employment specialist about possibilities in the clerical field. Would she be able to work around her school schedule? She preferred a position that involved filing and possibly computer work. Her teacher indicated that this type of position would be excellent for her. Laura's teacher and rehabilitation counselor both contributed information that could assist her in finding the right job. Within a short time, she successfully interviewed at a local law firm and was hired as a part-time file clerk.

On Laura's first day, the employment specialist helped her organize documents and determine a filing system. Laura needed verbal prompts to use the system consistently. She received support from her mentor and all of the office staff. The employment specialist was able to begin fading after 3 weeks of full-time job coaching. Relieving the receptionist during lunch became an everyday part of Laura's duties. She was responsible for checking her watch, and at 2 p.m. every day, she shredded documents that had been approved for disposal. She had been trained to use the photocopier and copied and correlated packages of information. She had also been asked to help the summer clerks with their work. These were all tasks that had been added to her work scope as she progressed there.

Laura's case is a good example of how a job can be designed and customized and how rehabilitation counselors and teachers can learn about her work capacity. Early jobs for young people are terrific sources of work assessment. This chapter is intended to help counselors, educators, parents, and students who are involved with planning transitions for students like Laura by providing concrete examples of transition assessments and interventions.

The Challenge of Transition

Entering adolescence and young adulthood presents many new challenges for all young people, especially those with autism (Wehman, 2013). When students with autism prepare for transition from school to the adult world, they must prepare for life without the daily structure of school. In short, these young people, their families, and educators must wonder, plan, and prepare for the time when the school bus no longer takes them to school. Whereas others without disabilities face the same eventuality, for persons with disabilities, the issue is complicated by the uneven provision of adult services to assist them. Transition-age youth with disabilities, under the Individuals with Disabilities Education Improvement Act of 2004 (IDEIA/IDEA, 2004), who have turned 22 or graduated from high school with the regular diploma no longer have the legal right to appropriate transition services, such as age-appropriate life skills training, vocational training, individual and family counseling, and transportation assistance. Yet, these are exactly the services young adults with disabilities need.

The Workforce Innovation and Opportunity Act (WIOA) can help to address these needs and help students like Laura. WIOA was signed into law in July 2014, reauthorizing the Workforce Investment Act of 1998 (WIA) and amending the Rehabilitation Act of 1973 (WIOA, 2014). This piece of legislation represents a renewed commitment to the workforce development system and is designed to strengthen our nation's workforce to address the needs of current employees, job seekers, and employers. The purpose of WIOA is to provide workforce activities to assist job seekers in accessing employment, education, training, and related supports; integrate and improve service delivery to assist workers in achieving a family-sustaining wage; and ensure the workforce meets the skill requirements of employers to compete in the global economy.

Title IV of the WIOA

The focus of Title IV of the WIOA legislation is specifically on transition-related regulations for youth and students with disabilities. This provision includes a requirement that vocational rehabilitation (VR) agencies must set aside 15% of their federal funds to provide Pre-Employment Transition Services (Pre-ETS) to students with disabilities who are eligible or potentially eligible to receive VR services (WIOA, 2014). Providing services to students who are potentially eligible to receive VR services is a shift from traditional VR practices. Table 13.1 outlines eligibility criteria for Pre-ETS along with required Pre-ETS activities under WIOA.

TABLE 13.1 Pre-Employment Transition Services (Pre-ETS) for Students With Disabilities Eligible to Receive Vocational Rehabilitation Services per the Workforce Innovation and Opportunity Act

ELIGIBLE STUDENTS UNDER PRE-ETS	FIVE REQUIRED PRE-ETS ACTIVITIES
■ Have a disability ■ Qualify for and receive special education or related services under an IEP or 504 Plan ■ Participate in secondary school ■ Aged 14–22 years	1. Job exploration counseling in a classroom or community setting 2. Work-based learning experiences that may include in-school and afterschool opportunities, experiences outside the traditional school setting, and/or internships 3. Counseling on opportunities for enrollment in comprehensive transition or postsecondary educational programs 4. Workplace readiness training to develop social skills and independent living 5. Instruction in self-advocacy

IEP, individualized education program.
SOURCE: Workforce Innovation and Opportunity Act. 29 U.S.C. § 2801, 105–220 (2004).

■ The Importance of Age-Appropriate Transition Assessment

Age-appropriate transition assessment is an important part of IDEA. We can divide this term into its three parts: *Age* simply refers to a student's chronological age, not his or her developmental age. *Appropriate* relates to the fact that the specific assessments should be both individualized and linked to specific postsecondary outcomes. And *transition assessment* is defined by the Division on Career Development and Transition (DCDT) "as the ongoing process of collecting data on the individual's needs, preferences, and interests as they relate to the demands of current and future working, educational, living, and personal and social environments" (Sitlington, Neubert, & Leconte, 1997, pp. 70–71). The information gleaned from the transition assessment process is the cornerstone of the transition planning process.

The Necessity of a Transition Assessment Goal

IDEA requires that students' postsecondary goals be based on age-appropriate transition assessments (IDEA § 300.320[b][1]). These assessments provide the information that leads to the development of a comprehensive and coordinated transition individualized education program (IEP), which, in turn, will lead to successful adult outcomes in the areas of employment, postsecondary education, training, and independent living. Each decision is important. The majority of transition planning decisions need to be made using assessment data. The fact that many students are making important decisions about their futures without the benefit of assessment data is very ineffective. Frequently, students do not understand their own strengths and needs, or they lack knowledge about how to use this information to make decisions. These students need guidance to understand how data can help them determine their readiness skills, progress toward a goal, and identify when goals need to change. The transition assessment process also provides an opportunity for teachers to improve rapport and build relationships with students. Therefore, this chapter reviews areas such as alternative education assessments, employment assessments, and community living assessments. Different techniques and strategies to glean data follow.

Academic Assessment

Well-conceived academic assessment provides valuable information in helping transition-age youth with disabilities become college, career, and community ready. Data gathered through this process can provide rich information for developing successful work experiences, and ensuring academic coursework aligns with the student's transition goals. The assessment information gathered informs, but does not dictate, the planning process. In other words, academic assessment should not be used to limit the aspirations of youth with disabilities, but rather to identify instructional supports and services they might need in order to achieve their goals. There are three main academic assessment categories: formal, informal, and alternative. Table 13.2 provides descriptions of each assessment category. The remainder of this section introduces each of these categories and describes how they can be used in transition.

Formal Academic Assessments

Several different types of formal academic assessments can be used to measure achievement, ability, aptitude, or adaptive skills (Thoma & Tamura, 2013). Academic achievement measures, such as the Woodcock-Johnson III Tests of Achievement, compare the test-taker performance in a specific area (e.g., math, reading, or writing) to a large, norm-referenced sample of his or her same-age peers. Other academic achievement assessments, such as statewide standards-based tests, evaluate students' understanding of a specific curriculum. In contrast, ability tests attempt to measure capacity (e.g., IQ tests). This is often done by evaluating a person's reasoning skills in a range of areas and then comparing those results to a norm-referenced sample. Aptitude tests, such as the SAT, seek to measure a person's potential (Thoma & Tamura, 2013).

TABLE 13.2 Categories of Academic Assessments

CATEGORY	DESCRIPTION	USES	EXAMPLES
Formal academic assessment	■ Measures achievement, ability, aptitude, or adaptive skills ■ Compares student's performance to peers or specific academic standards	■ Evaluates academic strengths and target areas for skill development ■ Identifies needed supports ■ Documents need for accommodations or services	■ Woodcock-Johnson III Tests of Achievement ■ Stanford-Binet Intelligence Scales ■ SAT ■ Vineland Adaptive Behavior Scales
Informal academic assessment	■ Individualized to student ■ Assesses academic skills (e.g., rote or soft skills) not measured by formal assessments	■ Identifies specific student strengths and needs ■ Evaluates individual progress over time	■ Interviews ■ Observations ■ Records review ■ Curriculum-based assessments ■ Checklists ■ Task analyses
Alternate academic assessment	■ Alternative measure to standards-based testing for students with most significant disabilities	■ Evaluates student mastery of modified or alternate curricular content	■ Student portfolios documenting mastery of specific curricular objectives

Finally, adaptive skills assessments, such as the Vineland Adaptive Behavior Scales, evaluate the everyday skills people need to know and use in order to be personally independent. Results from formal academic assessments can be analyzed and used during transition planning to identify areas of strength and areas for skill development. The transition team can then work together to connect youth with the learning experiences needed to build skills necessary for reaching life goals.

Teams might consider the following points when making decisions about formal academic assessments. First, in order to make informed decisions about using specific measures, planning teams should include credentialed professionals with expertise in selecting, administering, and interpreting results from formal assessments (Neubert & Leconte, 2013). Second, formal academic assessments by themselves may not provide sufficient information for identifying the supports and services needed for youth with disabilities to become college and career ready, especially youth with significant disabilities. For instance, recent research suggests that state-based alternate assessment measures for students with significant disabilities may not align with the skills identified as critical by transition experts in developing college and career readiness skills (Morningstar, Zagona, Uyanik, Xie, & Mahal, 2017). Other ways of assessing and developing these skills for students with significant disabilities may be needed (Morningstar et al., 2017), including informal academic assessment methods or alternative assessment methods.

Informal Academic Assessments

A wide range of informal assessment strategies are available, including interviews, observations, records review, portfolio development, curriculum-based assessments, use of checklists, and task analyses (Cook, Tankersley, & Landrum, 2015; Mazzotti et al., 2009, Neubert & Leconte, 2013). Table 13.3 provides a brief description of some informal assessments and how they can be utilized for different students. Informal assessments are more malleable and subjective than standardized assessments (Cook et al., 2015). Therefore, a major benefit of informal academic assessments is that they can be tailored to individual needs and can be used on an ongoing basis as additional areas of growth are identified. The flexibility of the assessment structure can also make it easier to link IEP goals to postsecondary goals. Informal methods may also be a more appropriate choice over formal methods, given student ability. For example, informal academic assessments are a useful strategy with students for which multiple choice or pen-and-paper tests could be difficult. In such cases, assessment teams may also want to consider the benefits of using alternative academic assessments.

Alternative Academic Assessments

Alternative academic assessments were developed to serve students with the most severe cognitive disabilities who, even with support, would not be able to achieve grade-level expectations (Kearns, Towles-Reeves, Kleinert, Kleinert, & Thomas, 2011). Students diagnosed with intellectual disability, autism, and multiple disabilities are most likely to participate in alternative assessments (Carter, Austin, & Trainor, 2012). Alternative assessments may entail compiling portfolios of student work or use of other performance-based measures, such as presentations, that are tailored to the student goals and the current curriculum.

Alternative assessment is extremely advantageous when evaluating the strengths and needs of students who are not the best candidates for more formal methods. However, it must be used appropriately. There is a significant drawback if the assessment strategies do not provide information needed to determine how to help the youth with a disability to reach his or her goals.

TABLE 13.3 Examples of Informal Academic Assessments

INFORMAL ACADEMIC ASSESSMENT	EXAMPLE OF USE
Questionnaire	Student: 18 years old, diagnosed with autism, wants to attend college, and get a degree in biology
	Example: VR counselor develops questionnaire to go home with parents and student to assess college interests, location, credits, transportation, and living arrangements
Interview	Student: 20 years old, diagnosed with emotional behavior disorder, reading level of a second-grade student
	Example: Meeting with parents, aunt, and counselor to explore academic interests and strengths to identify elective classes that will inform development of postsecondary goals
Observation	Student: 21 years old, diagnosed with autism, uses AAC device to communicate wants and needs
	Example: Employment specialist observes during community outing to get an idea of how or if student uses AAC device to interact socially with community members. Transition specialist observes student's use of AAC device during community work experience to ask employer questions when can't find work materials.

AAC, augmentative and alternative communication; VR, vocational rehabilitation.

Some research indicates that alternative assessment results are not always linked to a student's IEP goals nor do they show how to help youth with significant disabilities become college and career ready (Thoma & Tamura, 2013). When making decisions about using alternative assessments, the method selected must produce valuable information that can directly inform the transition team regarding interests, strengths, and needs.

It is likely that youth with disabilities will participate in all three academic assessment categories during the transition process. It is the responsibility of transition teams to work with youth and their families to identify individualized assessment strategies that align with a student's postsecondary goals. For instance, a student may have a goal of participating in postsecondary education. Although her SAT scores fall within the acceptance range for the college she wants to attend, observations of the student while shadowing at the local community college indicate that the student frequently becomes overwhelmed during group discussions—putting her head down or exiting the class. The team can use this information to develop support strategies for the student during discussions (e.g., identify a peer mentor, provide discussion questions ahead of time, teach self-advocacy skills). When used appropriately, academic assessments are a critical component of successful transition planning for youth with disabilities.

■ Supported and Customized Employment Assessment

As discussed earlier in the chapter, under federal legislation, transition-age students with disabilities must have measurable postsecondary goals. Proceeding from academic assessment, this section will now consider transition to employment assessment with a focus on supported employment (SE) and customized employment (CE). IDEA (2004) calls for students with disabilities to transition to integrated employment, which includes SE. Furthermore, Title IV of the WIOA places a specific focus on transition-age youth with disabilities transitioning into integrated employment. SE and CE, which are both recognized under federal legislation, focus on working with the student with a disability to make an employment match that not only meets employer needs but also builds on individual strengths. In order to do this, SE and CE focus on various assessment strategies that take place prior to making the actual job match. This way employment and support decisions can be made with the person that accurately reflect what she or he wants and needs. The most useful information for a person with a severe disability is obtained when the preliminary assessment strategies guide all aspects of the process, including the activities that are conducted, the methods that are used, and the manner in which they are interpreted.

Similar to academic assessments, employment assessments are not designed or performed to "screen out" a person from employment; rather, an assessment should be conducted to identify the type of support that the person will need in order to successfully reach independence in employment (Inge, Targett, & Armstrong, 2007). Employment assessments provide an opportunity to learn more about a person and develop a preferred employment placement. Employment assessment, like informal academic assessment, is characterized by a reliance on obtaining information from a variety of sources, focusing on actual behaviors in real environments where they occur, and documenting the information in behavioral terms without value judgments.

Looking at the abilities of the person in the context of what is required by the environment where the skill is to be performed allows an accurate assessment to be conducted under the natural circumstances and cues of the work environment where the skill will occur. Any gaps between what is required by the job site and what the worker is able to do can be lessened with the application of instructional techniques and individualized supports that meet the customer's specific needs. Often, many of the gaps are resolved through negotiations with the employer and specific job restructuring during job development that eliminate the need altogether. Other times, assistive technology, compensatory strategies, rehabilitation engineering, personal assistant services, or behavioral training techniques will reduce the difference between what is required and what the worker is able to do. Educators, transition specialists, and employment specialists are able to work with students with disabilities and employers to negotiate these accommodations and/or modifications.

The outcome of SE and CE service options is for a person with a disability to achieve competitive integrated employment (CIE) in the community. Defining features of CIE are making at least or more than minimum wage, interacting and working with persons without disabilities, and having opportunities for advancement. Similar to the benefits of informal academic assessments, SE and CE assessments provide an opportunity to adapt to the needs of the person and provide alternative methods for youth with significant disabilities to explore their likes and dislikes and to grow their pre-employment experiences. This is a great method to adequately support youth who may have a difficult time communicating their wants, needs, and preferences. A student may not be able to say that he or she doesn't like something, but a trained observer (i.e., transition or employment specialist) may be able to observe this during an assessment through body language or productivity rate. It also allows for the student to express preferences that may not be communicated owing to communication challenges or minimal experience for comparison.

SE models rely on a strategy called "situational assessments" that are typically funded through a VR agency. Usually, an employment specialist will work with a person with a disability to develop situational assessments in the community. As mentioned earlier, these assessments are valuable learning opportunities for the person with a disability and the employment specialist who will be working with him or her during job development. A brief description of situational assessments and their development follows.

Situational Assessments

Usually, a situational assessment is conducted for a 4-hour period in two to three different types of jobs in the community that are representative of the local labor market. However, a general guideline for the length of an assessment is that it should reflect the job seeker's future work-day. If the job seeker wants to work full time, then he or she should participate in assessments that reflect a full day of work. Any business can be a potential assessment site, identified from any number of experiences, contacts, or resources that the employment specialist is aware of (e.g., past employment, personal contacts, job development, previous SE setting, newspaper, social media). However, the sites selected for any specific job seeker depend on the choices of that person. For instance, one job seeker, during her initial meeting with her employment specialist, identified that she thought a job at a pet store or child-care center may be something that she would like. The employment specialist then set up two situational assessments in the community in two different businesses to give her the opportunity to see if these were possible career paths for her.

If the job seeker is unable to identify specific ideas about what type of employment he or she may enjoy, then situational assessments can be even more valuable to the person and the employment specialist. A variety of job types should be explored, and the job seeker's reaction to each recorded to compare which may be the most appropriate and most preferred job choice. It is important to note that it is not necessarily assumed that someone will choose to work in one of the types of businesses where the situational assessments occurred, but an opportunity is provided to assist the person with determining the career goal, work environment, job characteristics, or business that she or he might like.

For example, one person who chose to complete a landscaping assessment refused to hold the hose when asked to water the plants. The employment specialist asked whether he would like to help with loading bags of mulch and soil, which he quickly agreed to. He did a great job navigating to the mulch area, picking up the bags, and loading them onto carts. He chatted with the employees as he worked and was somewhat independent but took direction well from the employees and the employment specialist. At first glance, it would appear that he loved to move heavy items and may enjoy a job with similar responsibilities; however, he and his parents both confirmed that he hated doing hard physical labor. After spending more time together and performing additional assessment activities, it was discovered that he did not like the labor because it was hard work, hot outside, and he had low stamina. What he did enjoy was the comradery of the team and being able to chat with coworkers while he worked and feeling like he was helping someone. He also enjoyed the repetitive nature of the task and the limited decision making of the task. In addition to identifying some of the aspects of the job that the person would be interested in, and those he would not like, the use of compensatory strategies that would allow him to remember his job tasks without coworker prompting and which would give him the feeling of being part of a team were identified and put into place at his job. His job choice was ultimately an assistant to a handyman in a small business that dispatched carpenters and woodworkers to homes and businesses in the area to complete repairs. In this case, the situational assessments assisted the job seeker in making an informed job choice that best matched his skills, abilities, and interests.

Setting up Assessment Sites

Many employers are more than willing to participate in this type of activity. If an agency already has a relationship with the employer, then probably the employment specialist will have an idea of the employer's receptivity, the positions to be targeted, and the general logistical arrangements. If the employment specialist is contacting a business for the first time in order to arrange a situational assessment, much of the information gathering can be completed at the same time that the employment specialist is requesting the employer's participation.

When talking with the employer, it is very important to be clear about what the SE agency would like. Communicate in a professional manner using business terminology and avoid professional jargon. Most employers are not going to be familiar with situational or community-based assessment as this is not the typical practice when hiring most employees. However, employers understand the concept of hiring a good worker who can do the job, really wants to work there, and will be a loyal, reliable employee. Explaining that the best way to help someone find a job that she or he really wants and to know how to support the worker and employer is to "try out" some brief work experiences is typically well received. Tell the employer that the employment specialist would like to select one or more positions within the company, learn how to do them, and select times that the presence of two additional people wouldn't be disruptive to the regular workflow. Find out the business's needs, scheduling preferences, and capacity for conducting multiple assessments over time. Once agreement has been reached, several steps are suggested, which have been found to be helpful (Table 13.4).

Liability is a concern that business owners will mention while developing a situational assessment. Liability issues can be explained by describing the insurance that covers the customer and employment specialist and the responsibilities of all parties. For the employment specialist, the agency's worker's compensation insurance covers the person on the job site whether that is in the office or at an outside business for a situational assessment. The job seeker is covered either by the state VR agency (if they have an open case with VR) or by the student's private insurance or Medicaid/Medicare benefits. If it is a school situation and community-based training/assessments are included in the student's educational program, then the school's liability insurance covers the

TABLE 13.4 Suggestions for Setting Up a Situational Assessment in the Community

TASK	BENEFIT
Observe jobs performed in the business	Employment specialist can determine which tasks are characteristic of those in the community and offer variety in terms of work activities, environments, demands, and employees.
Discuss identified tasks/job with employer	Employment specialist has the opportunity to assess the employer's receptivity to the chosen task and negotiate from the option presented or available.
Observe the job that will be performed	This allows the employment specialist to understand exactly how the tasks are performed prior to teaching the job seeker, production standards, and expectations of employees of the business.
Verify knowledge of the job	Employment specialist is able to discuss observations with the business owner/department manager and ensures that all steps have been identified of the given tasks as well as any safety precautions that should be noted.

student at the business. Finally, if accident or injury occurs and is due to negligence of the employer or circumstances beyond her or his control, then the company's insurance would be liable as is the case for other employees, the public, or anyone else affected by the incident.

Supported to Customized Employment

With similar outcome goals and a focus on assessment strategies, it may appear difficult to differentiate between SE and CE. However, several defining features separate CE as a model from SE. CE evolved from the SE model and places a large emphasis on an assessment process called "discovery" to inform the job development process and secure a good match between the job seeker and the employer. *Discovery* is a process that is specifically focused on conducting in-depth analyses that consist of exploring and learning about a person with a disability and his or her needs, preferences, and interests. CE allows an individualized and customized match that addresses employer needs but capitalizes on the specific strengths of a person with a disability. In addition to the intense exploration phase of discovery, a large emphasis is placed on the negotiation that occurs between the job seeker and the employer to create a mutually beneficial employment contract that meets the specific needs of the employer while highlighting the unique assets that the worker with a disability brings to the employment space.

There are benefits to using CE as an employment model. CE breaks the traditional mold of applying to posted want ads and filling precreated job descriptions (Citron et al., 2008; Griffin, Hammis, Geary, & Sullivan, 2008; Riesen, Morgan, & Griffin, 2015). This change from tradition allows persons with disabilities to be placed in employment settings that are tailored to their skills and are outside traditional employment placements for those with disabilities (Griffin et al., 2008). In lieu of situational assessments, CE has a process called discovery whereby a person and support staff (teachers, transition specialists, or employment specialists) conduct various activities to find out more about that person's skills, interests, and needs. The discovery process is more flexible than situational assessments, and observation and skill assessment activities can be conducted in areas outside employment settings. For example, a student with a disability can be observed while on a community outing to a restaurant rather than while performing job tasks in a restaurant. This allows for the development of a consumer profile that highlights skills related to vocation while also identifying social needs and strengths. The discovery process can begin as early as middle school and can be conducted in conjunction with other assessment strategies to inform a student's transition plan. Table 13.5 presents a few examples of strategies for conducting the discovery process.

A lot of the assessment methods that are used during discovery can be used to develop targeted vocational assessments in the community that align with the identified interests of the student and provide hands-on employment experience. Following the discovery process and the situational assessment experiences, the CE model also places an emphasis on negotiations with the employer. An earlier part of this section discussed how negotiations with employers can help to remove environmental barriers, develop preferred schedules, and remove or add job tasks to facilitate a good job match between employer and person with a disability. CE provides a structured model for this negotiation, called the "employment proposal," which outlines the roles and expectations of the employer, employee, and the job coach. The proposal also clearly defines job tasks, hours, and how the employee will be supported to accomplish these tasks. Template 13.1 provides an example of an employment proposal form.

Based on this review of assessments used to guide SE and CE models, a brief case study of two transition-age youth transitioning to employment follows. The case study highlights similarities and differences between SE and CE models and how assessments can be used to inform which model a person will receive.

TABLE 13.5 Discovery Assessment Strategies and Examples

STRATEGY	EXAMPLE AND ASSESSMENT BENEFITS
Community outing	Talk with the student about favorite places to eat, observe the student order and pay for food, and observe personal hygiene needs. This can also provide an opportunity to observe the student's ability to utilize public transportation.
Observation at employment site	Identify areas of vocational strengths and areas in which increase skill instruction is needed. For example, the student can transition between tasks but requires prompting to go ask for help or additional materials.
Meeting	Meetings in discovery should be person centered, and the student's preferences should drive the planning process. Ask the student who important members of his or her support network are. Have a meeting to share strengths of the student and then brainstorm community and vocational activities that will best inform a plan to identify strengths, preferences, and needs.

Employment Proposal for: [   ]

Rationale:	
Benefit:	
Job Function:	
Proposed Employee:	
Employment Conditions:	
References:	

TEMPLATE 13.1 Sample employment proposal form.

Community Assessment

Community assessment is a critical part of the transition process. A full and satisfying life hinges on a person's ability to access preferred living situations, integrated employment, desirable leisure activities, and fulfilling friendships. Community life can vary widely depending on a number of factors, including geographical location, population, climate, and wealth of resources. Despite variations, participation within a community remains multidimensional. Therefore, community assessment should be comprehensive and include all aspects of life as an adult (Thoma & Tamura, 2013). The following list covers additional assessment domains that are essential to consider when planning for community life:

- *Legal representation/guardianship:* Assess level of guardianship needed. The Guardianship Alternative Assessment Template (GAAT) for young adults with disabilities is a tool to identify least restrictive guardianship alternatives (Millar, 2014).

- *Adaptive:* Evaluate general daily living skills that enable proper self-care and appropriate presentation in various situations, such as hygiene skills, laundering clothes, food preparation, budgeting or managing finances, and household chores.

- *Self-determination:* Assess level of autonomy via ability and opportunities to exercise self-determination, including self-advocacy, self-regulation, self-empowerment, self-awareness, self-efficacy, making personal choices, decision making, and goal setting.

- *Behavioral:* Identify challenging behaviors that may risk harm to self or others or result in legal ramifications, including self-injurious behavior, aggression, property destruction, inappropriate sexual behavior, and so on.

- *Social/communication:* Identify established forms of communication (verbal, speech communication device, etc.) most useful in the community and ability to establish and maintain interpersonal relationships.

- *Health/medical:* Assess medical conditions or physical mobility difficulties, needed frequency of doctor visits or treatments, and environmental restrictions due to existing health conditions.

- *Sensory:* Identify sensitivity to auditory, visual, tactile, or olfactory stimuli in the environment to consider when planning for housing and employment.

- *Assistive technology:* Evaluate need for assistive technology to aid in community participation, such as technology to create reminders or alarms, or visual schedules to complete daily activities in cooking, cleaning, or hygiene.

- *Leisure:* Identify resources needed to pursue personal hobbies or engage in preferred leisure activities to help determine appropriate community residencies.

- *Transportation/navigation:* Assess ability and availability of various forms of transportation, including driving, use of public transportation, bike, taxi, or peer-to-peer rideshare services.

Each area listed requires sufficient assessment during the transition process to ensure that youth with disabilities are provided with the opportunity to pursue a well-rounded future with the supports he or she needs for maximized quality of life. Community assessment is considered next and includes methods for assessing both community opportunities and community skills.

Community Assessment Methods

Community assessment is important to correctly guide transition goals and subsequent planning to ensure that each reflects the values and preferences of youth with disabilities and their families in relation to long-term life goals (Neubert & Leconte, 2013). There are two specific components of community assessment: (a) determining community opportunities and (b) evaluating skills needed to engage in community opportunities. For example, a student who chooses to live independently in an apartment that is located several miles from his or her place of work will need to make transportation arrangements. This will require the student and transition team to assess both the transportation options available within the community and then also to evaluate the skills of the youth with a disability to use those services. Assessing each of these components will enable the transition team to decide on the most appropriate transportation option in terms of safety, convenience, cost, and reliability and then plan for use by teaching the student the skills needed to utilize the transportation method.

CASE STUDY 13.1   SUPPORTED AND CUSTOMIZED EMPLOYMENT

Anna: Anna is a 20-year-old young woman with autism who is interested in stocking supplies. She is methodical in her work, very good at placing items in alphabetical and numerical order, takes care with her work tasks, and pays close attention to detail. Anna has challenges with communication, and her support team report a high level of anxiety when it comes to customer interactions. She uses short utterances when she does interact and tends to prefer to use her tablet as a communication device, she will open up more as she gets comfortable with you. Additionally, Anna has a high level of sensitivity to loud noises and bright lights. She tends to work better in calmer environments without a lot of background noise.

Cho: Cho is a 19-year-old young man with an intellectual disability who is interested in starting to work while beginning to attend classes part time at the local community college. In high school, he had work experiences at the local drugstore and a shoe store. He is interested in stocking, learning to fill customer orders, and enjoys interactions. He reads at a second-grade level and uses a calculator to complete math.

Situational Assessment(s): The transition specialist at the high school, Lory, has developed a strong working relationship with the manager at a chain of grocery stores who are currently expanding in the local community. Lory knows that a new store is opening up near the high school and is in need of stocking positions. She sets up to bring Cho and Anna by at separate times to try out stocking tasks. She brings Cho during the busiest time of the day and Anna after store hours. Both individuals excel with the stocking, and the manager expresses an interest in hiring Cho right away. The manager expresses concerns about Anna's ability to interact with coworkers and customers.

SE Solution: Lory lets Cho know about the manager's interest and sets up a time to work with Cho to fill out the application for an entry-level stocker. She attends the interview with Cho, and he is hired on the spot as a part-time stocker.

CE Solution: Lory sits down with the manager and explains Anna's additional skill sets in clerical tasks. While meeting with the manager, Lory noticed that the office area was very messy, with papers and employee files laying everywhere, and a huge pile of papers for shredding. Lory explained that Anna could also support the store with keeping track of filing and general clerical duties. The manager also shared with Lory that the store has a need for employees willing to work late or early morning hours to stock before customer volume is too high. Lory works with the manager to create a new job description based on the identified employer needs and that also matches the skills and strengths of Anna. She writes everything up and outlines each person's role in the employment contract. Anna was hired to work during off hours, stock on the floor, file, shred papers, and perform other clerical tasks on an ongoing basis.

Both Anna and Cho were successfully placed in integrated employment. Cho was able to perform a situational assessment and be placed into a generic stocker position. Anna's position required developing a new job description that addressed specific employer needs and also capitalized on her skills, strengths, and interests. Cho benefited from the SE model, whereas Anna benefited from the CE model.

Assessments are valuable tools to inform transition planning for students with disabilities, and their use can support schools and VR to adhere to standards put forth in legislation aimed at improving after-school outcomes for students with disabilities. Both SE and CE assessments are person centered and facilitate job matches, building on the unique skills that employees with disabilities can bring to the workplace. Securing and maintaining competitive employment enables youth with disabilities not only to achieve personal independence but also to contribute meaningfully to their community.

Assessing Community Opportunities

The first step in community assessment is understanding all available resources to which a youth with a disability has access. Charting all resources enables the most appropriate and most preferred method to be selected. One such method is called "community resource mapping," whereby an inventory of the community is established and analyzed by the transition team. A guide developed by the National Center of Secondary Education and Transition (NCSET) outlines each step (Hoover, 2016; NCSET, 2005):

- *Premapping*: A diverse set of stakeholders who have a vested interest in the success of the community mapping process is assembled.

- *Mapping*: The team collects information and resources related to high-priority goals by scanning the community and establishing contacts. The team will want to know where the student frequently visits, where the student would like to go in the future, and what resources are available to help the student get there.

- *Taking action*: Team members are assigned responsibility and timelines for obtaining the supports, services, and resources identified as necessary during the mapping stage.

- *Maintaining, sustaining, and evaluating*: Team members continually analyze progress and outcomes to ensure long-term success meeting goals (Hoover 2016, NCSET, 2005).

The benefit of community resource mapping hinges on the use of a comprehensive team. Teachers, parents, students, VR counselors, business representatives, and more will all be aware of different resources in which they can research and share with the collective group. Team members may also have personal connections that can be leveraged to develop work-based learning experiences or secure independent living opportunities for the student.

Assessing Community Skills

Once opportunities are identified, the skills needed to use those opportunities must be determined. A variety of methods can be used to assess knowledge, and performance has been discussed at length in previous sections of this chapter. Rather than reiterate, each method's application to community life will be presented instead.

Observation in community settings is a useful way to obtain information about a student's interests and skills in various settings and situations. Checklists, task analyses, and recordkeeping can be used to collect and document pertinent information about how a student interacts with unfamiliar community members, navigates familiar and unfamiliar places, handles personal safety, or makes purchases with or without support. Situational assessments in various community settings can also be used to assess skills (Neubert & Leconte, 2013). For example, if a student plans to live independently, participation in various domestic tasks such as washing clothes at a laundromat is an efficient way to determine support needs. *Interviewing* the student's inner support circle can help determine personal habits, such as reliability completing hygiene tasks, responsibility for locking the apartment door, safety awareness crossing the street, ability to evacuate independently during fire drills, or other aspects of community life that anyone would be expected to know. Finally, there are many *standardized assessments* that can be used to determine skill sets in all life domains. Qualifications for administering standardized assessments vary, so educators will want to be cognizant of this fact and work with appropriate sources (Kellems, Springer, Wilkins, & Anderson, 2016). A sample of standardized assessments appropriate for transition-age students is provided in Table 13.6.

TABLE 13.6 Examples of Standardized Assessments for Community Assessment Domains

AREA	STANDARDIZED ASSESSMENT	DESCRIPTION
Transition	Supports Intensity Scale – Adult (SIS-A)	Developed by the American Association on Intellectual and Developmental Disabilities (AAIDD), the SIS-A is an interview-style assessment that identifies the amount of support a student will need to accomplish community activities. It is appropriate for ages 16–64 years and takes approximately 2 hours to complete (Thompson et al., 2014).
	Transition Planning Inventory (TPI-2)	The TPI-2 is designed for students 14–22 years of age and takes under 30 minutes to administer. It assesses information from students, parents, and teachers to determine skills for independent living, health, leisure, money management, employment, interpersonal relationships, and self-determination (Clark & Patton, 2006).
Academic/aptitude	Life-Centered Education (LCE) Transition Curriculum and Assessments	Created by the Council for Exceptional Children (CEC), the LCE is a teaching curriculum accompanied by baseline and progress monitoring assessments to determine student knowledge/performance in three areas: daily living, self-determination and interpersonal skills, and employment. It is designed for students through age 26 years (CEC, 2018).
Adaptive	Adaptive Behavior Assessment System (ABAS-3)	The ABAS-3 offers a comprehensive assessment of adaptive skills, is appropriate for any age, and can be administered in under 20 minutes (Harrison & Oakland, 2015).
Social	Social Responsiveness Scale (SRS)	The SRS assesses social skills. It is appropriate for ages 4–18 years and takes approximately 20 minutes to administer (Constantino, 2005).
Health/medical	SF36v2 Health Survey	The Health Survey is appropriate for students aged 18 years and older and takes about 10 minutes to complete. The survey asks general health and well-being questions about changes in mood and physical health (Maruish & DeRosa, 2009).
Self-determination	Arc Self-Determination Scale	Self-determination is assessed for adolescents with disabilities in the areas of autonomy, self-regulation, psychological empowerment, and self-realization using a self-report style questionnaire (Wehmeyer, 1995).
	Self-Determination Inventory – Student Report (SDI-SR)	The SDI-SR is a recently developed self-report measure for youth with and without disabilities built upon psychometrically sound items from the Arc Self-Determination Scale (Shogren et al., 2017).
Employment	BRIGANCE Employability Skills Inventory	The BRIGANCE assesses basic employment skills for middle/high school students related to career awareness, job seeking, and postsecondary opportunities (Brigance, 1995).

Community life is dynamic, so assessment processes should holistically cover all aspects of adult living. Additionally, the assessment process should combine a variety of assessment methods and a variety of reporters in order to accrue the most accurate information concerning the youth's skill repertoire (Kellems et al., 2016). Choosing the best assessment requires knowledge of all (or most) available assessments. Community assessments, in particular, should account for cultural and religious factors that are central within the community or influential to the student. Ultimately, the assessment process should be guided by the student and the long-term goals he or she has for community living. Transition teams should keep in mind that students' personal goals and community interests are likely to change with age and experience. Therefore, encouraging them to take a central role in guiding their own transition process will help them build the skills they need to appropriately plan and advocate in the future when goals or support needs change.

CASE STUDY 13.2   A CONTINUATION OF LAURA'S STORY

Let's revisit the case discussed at the beginning of the chapter regarding Laura. To review, Laura is 19 years old, has a significant cognitive disability, and recently graduated from high school. Ultimately, she was hired for a clerical position at a law firm. To find a good job fit, her employment specialist considered her strengths, preferences, needs, and interests. Using a variety of assessments helped the employment specialist gain valuable information to guide the employment process. Let's review some of the assessments the employment specialist used to help Laura get a job she enjoys.

- **Record Review:** The employment specialist asked Laura's mother for access to her school records since she had recently left high school. This allowed the employment specialist to review the individualized education program (IEP) goals Laura had recently worked on, a summary of her progress meeting those goals, her overall academic progress, and scores on several standardized assessments. For example, the employment specialist was able to glean that most of her IEP goals were related to improving reading, writing, and communication skills. The employment specialist noted that Laura had a vocational IEP goal related to "increasing work stamina" and "asking a supervisor for help when needed." The employment specialist took inventory of these goals to later make sure they were addressed in the workplace. Laura's school record also included scores from the Supports Intensity Scale, completed by the school psychologist. Results from this standardized measure indicated that Laura was likely to need intensive support in the area of Employment and moderate support in two additional areas, Home Living and Health and Safety. This information, combined with other details from her file, gave the employment specialist an idea of how much support to anticipate providing in different areas related to work.

- **Interview:** The employment specialist spoke with Laura, her mother, an in-home aide who provided behavior support for Laura, and an adult sibling who often acted as a caregiver. This semistructured interview provided detailed information about Laura's general interests and support needs during the day. In particular, the employment specialist noted that most of Laura's caregivers shared safety concerns about her navigating large buildings on her own.

- **Situational Assessments:** Three different situational assessments were set up for Laura in the community. The locations were determined based on information the employment specialist had collected via previous interactions, interviews, and assessments. Laura seemed interested in being around an office, so the final sites included a human resources department at a local factory, the check-in/mail counter at a UPS store, and an administrative assistant office at a university. Although these were not potential job prospects, each allowed Laura to

(continued)

CASE STUDY 13.2   *(continued)*

try different types of clerical work. Each site also allowed the employment specialist to determine areas of strength and needs related to different types of work. The employment specialist collected data during each session, such as preparing a checklist of the job duties Laura completed independently, recording the duration of Laura's work stamina without prompting, and noting the number of times she independently asked for help when needed.

- **Job Analysis:** Once the employment specialist was ready to narrow down potential businesses for employment, a Job Analysis was completed. The employment specialist arranged to meet with a potential business to acquire some basic information and determine an appropriate fit for Laura. A completed job analysis for Laura is presented in Appendix 13.1

In conclusion, a combination of formal and informal assessments was used to find a good job fit and install appropriate supports to help Laura succeed at her new position as a clerical worker in a law firm. As mentioned, she has already become independent in making copies and preparing informational packets and is learning new skills every day. She continues to grow professionally the longer she is employed!

Conclusion

When used effectively, transition assessments for academics, employment, and community living inform transition planning. With a variety of assessment options available for all three domains, it can be difficult to confidently select the best options. For this reason, it is useful to keep the following points in mind when choosing assessment methods. First, it is beneficial to use more than one type and level of assessment when developing transition plans with youth with disabilities (Mazzotti et al., 2009). Because different types of information are obtained from different assessments, using a combination (e.g., interview, observation, standardized measures) will help capture an assortment of important data that can be analyzed comprehensively. Second, regardless of the type of assessment method, the quality of the information received is dependent upon the source. Be sure that interviewees are knowledgeable about the different domains in which they provide information and have frequent interaction with the student for whom they are reporting. Further, ensure that observers are well trained in how to record what is seen and that all standardized measures are completed and evaluated by qualified professionals. Information gleaned from existing assessments should be up to date or completed within the past school year. Lastly, the selection of assessment measures should be dependent on the student's goals and plans for the future. The ultimate goal should be to identify appropriate assessments that help youth with disabilities better understand their strengths, skills, and needs in order to achieve their own personal life goals.

References

Brigance, A. H. (1995). *Employability skills inventory: Brigance diagnostic.* North Billerica, MA: Curriculum Associates.

Carter, E. W., Austin, D., & Trainor, A. A. (2012). Predictors of postschool employment outcomes for young adults with severe disabilities. *Journal of Disability Policy Studies, 23*(1), 50–63. doi:10.1177/1044207311414680

Citron, T., Brooks-Lane, N., Crandell, D., Brady, K., Cooper, M., & Revell, G. (2008). A revolution in the employment process of individuals with disabilities: Customized employment as the catalyst for system change. *Journal of Vocational Rehabilitation, 28*(3), 169–179. Retrieved from https://content.iospress.com/articles/journal-of-vocational-rehabilitation/jvr00417

Clark, G. M., & Patton, J. R. (2006). *Transition planning inventory–Updated version: Administration and resource guide.* Austin, TX: Pro-Ed.

Constantino, J. N. (2005). *Social responsiveness scale.* Torrance, CA: WPS.

Cook, B. G., Tankersley, M., & Landrum, T. J. (2015). *Transition of youth and young adults, advances in learning and behavioral disabilities.* Bingley, UK: Emerald Group.

Council for Exceptional Children. (2018). *LCE assessment.* Retrieved from https://www.cec.sped.org/ Publications/LCE-Transition-Curriculum/Benefits-of-Using-LCE

Griffin, C., Hammis, D., Geary, T., & Sullivan, M. (2008). Customized employment: Where we are; where we're headed. *Journal of Vocational Rehabilitation, 28*(3), 135–139. Retrieved from https://content .iospress.com/articles/journal-of-vocational-rehabilitation/jvr00414

Harrison, P., & Oakland, T. (2015). *Adaptive behavior assessment system* (3rd ed.). Torrance, CA: WPS.

Hoover, A. (2016). The role of the community in transition to the adult world for students with disabilities. *American Secondary Education, 44*(2), 21–30. doi:10.4135/9781452275024.n3

Individuals with Disabilities Education Improvement Act. 20 U.S.C. § 1400 (2004).

Inge, K., Targett, P., & Armstrong, A. (2007). Person-centered planning. In P. Wehman, K. Inge, W. Revell, & V. Brooke (Eds.), *Real work for real pay* (pp. 57–74). Baltimore, MD: Paul H. Brookes.

Kearns, J., Towles-Reeves, E., Kleinert, H. L., Kleinert, J. O., & Thomas, M. K. K. (2011). Characteristics of and implications for students participating in alternate assessments based on alternate academic achievement standards. *The Journal of Special Education, 43*(1), 3–14. doi:10.1177/0022466909344223

Kellems, R. O., Springer, B., Wilkins, M. K., & Anderson, C. (2016). Collaboration in transition assessment: School psychologists and special educators working together to improve outcomes for students with disabilities. *Preventing School Failure: Alternative Education for Children and Youth, 60*(3), 215–221. doi:10.1080/1045988X.2015.1075465

Maruish, M. E., & DeRosa, M. A. (2009). *A guide to the integration of certified short form survey scoring and data quality evaluation capabilities.* Lincoln, RI: QualityMetric.

Mazzotti, V. L., Rowe, D. A., Kelley, K. R., Test, D. W., Fowler, C. H., Kohler, P. D., & Kortering, L. J. (2009). Linking transition assessment and postsecondary goals: Key elements in the secondary transition planning process. *Teaching Exceptional Children, 42*(2), 44–51. doi:10.1177/004005990904200205

Millar, D. S. (2014). Addition to transition assessment resources: A template for determining the use of guardianship alternatives for students who have intellectual disability. *Education and Training in Autism and Developmental Disabilities, 49*(2), 171–188.

Morningstar, M. E., Zagona, A. L., Uyanik, H., Xie, J., & Mahal, S. (2017). Implementing college and career readiness: Critical dimensions for youth with severe disabilities. *Research and Practice for Persons with Severe Disabilities, 42*(3), 187–204. doi:10.1177/1540796917711439

National Center for Secondary Education and Transition. (2005). *Essential tools: Improving secondary education and transition for youth with disabilities—Community resource mapping.* Retrieved from http:// www.ncset.org/Publications/essentialtools/mapping/NCSET_EssentialTools_ResourceMapping.pdf

Neubert, D. A., & Leconte, P. J. (2013). Age-appropriate transition assessment: The position of the Division on Career Development and Transition. *Career Development and Transition for Exceptional Individuals, 36*(2), 72–83. doi:10.1177/2165143413487768

Riesen, T., Morgan, R., & Griffin, C. (2015). Customized employment: A review of the literature. *Journal of Vocational Rehabilitation, 43*(3), 183–193. doi:10.3233/jvr-150768

Shogren, K. A., Wehmeyer, M. L., Little, T. D., Forber-Pratt, A. J., Palmer, S. B., & Seo, H. (2017). Preliminary validity and reliability of scores on the self-determination inventory: Student report version. *Career Development and Transition for Exceptional Individuals, 40*(2), 92–103. doi:10.1177/2165143415594335

Sitlington, P. L., Neubert, D. A., & Leconte, P. J. (1997). Transition assessment: The position of the division on career development and transition. *Career Development for Exceptional Individuals, 20*(1), 69–79. doi:10.1177/088572889702000106

Thoma, C. A., & Tamura, R. (2013). *Demystifying transition assessment.* Baltimore, MD: Paul H. Brookes.

Thompson, J. R., Bryant, B. R., Schalock, R. L., Shrogen, K. A., Tasse, M. J., Wehmeyer, M. L., & Rotholtz, D. A. (2014). *Supports intensity scale – Adult version, user's manual.* Washington, DC: American Association on Intellectual and Developmental Disabilities.

Wehman, P. (2013). *Life beyond the classroom: Transition strategies for young people with disabilities* (5th ed.). Baltimore, MD: Paul H. Brookes.

Wehmeyer, M. L. (1995). *The Arc's self-determination scale: Procedural guidelines.* Washington, DC: Arc.

Workforce Innovation and Opportunity Act. 29 U.S.C. § 2801, 105–220 (2004).

APPENDIX **13.1**

EXAMPLE JOB ANALYSIS FORM

Company Name: _____ Best Law Firm

Staff:_____ Date:_____ 3 /____ 12____ / 2018

                                                                    (month) (day) (year)

Address: _____ 345 Market Street _____ LA _____

                          (street)   (city)   (state) (zip)

Telephone Number: _____ 987-2167 _____ FAX Number: _____ 987-2168 _____

Contact Person: _____ Joe Kellog _____ Title: _____ Attorney _____

Job Title: _____ Clerical Staff _____

Current hourly wage (or wage at last date of employment in this position): _____ $10.50 _____

Did a wage change occur since the last Job Screening or Job Update? ☐Yes ☒No

If yes, complete this section: _____ _____ _____

         Hourly rate changed from: $ to $ on   /   /

         Hourly rate changed from: $ to $ _____ on ___ / /_____ _____

Number of Hours per week: __27_____ Months per year: ___12____

If <12 months per year, what months is the job not available:

Number of employees in this company at this location: ___10___

Number of employees without disabilities in immediate area (50 ft. radius): __10___

Number of other employees with disabilities: ____0____
In immediate area (50 ft. radius): ____0_____

Number of other employees in this position: ____0____
During the same hours: 0

General Directions: *PLEASE DO NOT LEAVE ANY ITEM UNANSWERED!*

Indicate the most appropriate response for each item based on observations of the job and interview with employers, supervisors, and coworkers. Record special instructions, regulations, or comments under each item for greater detail.

1. Schedule: (check Yes or No for each item)   Weekend work required: ☒Yes   ☐No
   Evening work required: ☐Yes   ☒No
   Part-time job: ☒Yes   ☐No
   Full-time job: ☐Yes   ☒No

   Specifics/Comments:_____

2. Travel Location: (check Yes or No for each item)   On public transportation route: ☒Yes ☐No
   On private transportation route: ☐Yes   ☒No

   Specifics/Comments:_____

3. Strength—Lifting and Carrying: |☐Very light work (<10 lb.)   ☐Average work (30–40 lb.)
   ☒Light work (10–20 lb.)   ☐Heavy work (>50 lb.)

   Specifics/Comments: _____Manipulation of bales onto dolly—average 30–40 lb._____

4. Endurance: (without breaks) ☒Work required for <2 hours ☐Work required for 3–4 hours
   ☐Work required for 2–3 hours ☐Work required for >4 hours

   Specifics/Comments: Typical break schedule, one 5-minute break in the a.m. and one
   5 minute break in the p.m.—Lunch is an hour.

5. Orienting: ☐Small area   ☐Building wide
   ☒One room   ☐Building and Grounds
   ☐Several rooms

   Specifics/Comments: _____

6. Accessibility: ☒Fully accessible site   ☐Accessibility issues

   Specifics/Comments: _____

7. Work Pace: ☐Slow pace   ☐Sometimes fast pace
   ☒Average steady pace   ☐Continual fast pace

   Specifics/Comments: _____

8. Appearance Requirements: ☐Grooming of little importance ☐Neat and clean required
   ☒Cleanliness only required   ☐Grooming very important

   Specifics/Comments:_____

9. Communication Required: ☐None/minimal   ☒Key words/signs needed
                             ☐Unclear speech accepted   ☐Clear speech in sentences/
                                                                 signs needed

   Specifics/Comments:_____

10. Social Interactions: ☒Social interactions not required ☐Social interactions required
                                                                   infrequently
                             ☐Social interactions required   ☐Appropriate responses
                                                                   required
   Specifics/Comments:_____

11. Attention to Task Perseverance: ☐Frequent prompts available
                                      ☐Intermittent prompts/high supervision
                                      ☐Intermittent prompts/low supervision available
                                      ☒Infrequent prompts/low supervision available
   Specifics/Comments:_____

12. Sequencing of Job Duties: ☐Only one task required   ☐4–6 tasks required in sequence
                                 ☒2–3 tasks required   ☐7 or more tasks
                                   in sequence   required in sequence
   Specifics/Comments:_____

13. Initiation of Work Motivation: ☒Initiation of work required
                                       ☐Volunteering helpful
                                       ☐Coworker support available
   Specifics/Comments:_____

14. Daily Changes in Routine: ☐7 or more changes   ☒2–3 task changes
                                 ☐4–6 task changes   ☐No task change
   Specifics/Comments:_____

15. Reinforcement Available: ☐Frequent reinforcement ☐Reinforcement
                                   available   infrequent (weekly)
                                 ☐Reinforcement   ☒Minimal
                                   intermittent (daily)   reinforcement (pay check)
   Specifics/Comments:_____

16. Coworker Supports Available: ☐None available   ☒Intermittent potential
                                   ☐Low to minimum potential   ☐High potential
   Specifics/Comments:_____

17. Supportive of Job Accommodations: ☒Very supportive   ☐Negative
                                         ☐Supportive w/reservations ☐Unknown
                                         ☐Indifferent
   Specifics/Comments:_____

18. Employer's Financial Requirements: ☒Financial incentives not necessary
                                          ☐Tax credit or incentive (e.g., TJTC or OJT)
                                          ☐Subminimum wage

   Specifics/Comments:_____

19. Opportunity for Career Advancement: ☐Low to minimum   ☐Procedures in place
                                          ☒Average   ☐No procedures in
                                                                  place
                                          ☐Most probable

   Specifics/Comments:_____

20. Object Discrimination: ☐Does not need to distinguish between work supplies
                             ☐Must distinguish between work supplies with an external cue
                             ☒Must distinguish between work supplies

   Specifics/Comments:_____

21. Time: ☐Time factors not important   ☐Must tell time to the hour
            ☒Must identify breaks/meals/etc. ☐Must tell time to the minute

   Specifics/Comments:_____

22. Functional Reading: ☐None   ☒Simple reading
                               ☐Sight words/symbols ☐Fluent reading

   Specifics/Comments:_____

23. Functional Math: ☒None   ☐Simple addition/subtraction
                       ☐Simple counting   ☐Complex computational skills

   Specifics/Comments:_____

24. Street Crossing: ☒None   ☐Must cross four lane street with light
                       ☐Must cross two lane   ☐Must cross four lane
                          street with light   street without light
                       ☐Must cross two lane street
                          without light

   Specifics/Comments:_____

25. Visibility to Public: ☐Employee not visible   ☒Regularly visible
                            ☐Occasionally visible   ☐Visible throughout the day/ongoing

   Specifics/Comments:_____

26. If individual known, is the job in accordance   ☐No
    with individual's vision, preference goals?   ☒Yes
                                                     ☐Close approximation (stepping stone)

27. Benefits of Job: 0 = None   ☐Yes ☒No
                       1 = Sick leave   ☒Yes ☐No
                       2 = Medical/health benefits   ☒Yes ☐No
                       3 = Paid vacation/annual leave ☒Yes ☐No
                       4 = Dental benefits   ☐Yes ☒No
                       5 = Employee discounts   ☐Yes ☒No
                       6 = Free or reduced meals   ☐Yes ☒No
                       7 = Other (specify): _____

28. Level of Social Contact: (check one)

☐ Employment in an integrated environment on a shift or position that is isolated. Contact with coworkers or supervisors is minimal. Example: Night Janitor.

☒ Employment in an integrated environment on a shift or position that is relatively isolated. Contact with coworkers or supervisors is available at lunch or break. Example: Data Entry Position.

☐ Employment in an integrated environment in a position requiring a moderate level of interdependent tasking and coworker interaction. Example: Office Service Aide – copying documents.

☐ Employment in an integrated environment in a position requiring a high degree of interdependent tasks and coworker interactions and/or high level of contact with business customers. Example: Wal-Mart Greeter.

29. List any job experience (skills) needed for this position:

Comments:

Rate of employee turnover (annual percentage): ____5____ Overall
____25____ This Position

Number of supervisors: __1__   Rate of supervisor turnover: __1__

Written job description available?   ☒Yes   ☐No

What are the absolute "don'ts" for an employee in this position? (Manager's pet peeves, reasons for dismissal, etc.)

Insubordination, excessive absences, disregard of safety and break of confidentiality.

Environmental characteristics (physical barriers, temperature extremes, etc.):

Minimal - Exposure to paper dust

Additional Comments:

SOURCE: Virginia Commonwealth University, Rehabilitation Research & Training Center on Supported Employment, 1997. Reprinted with permission.

14

ASSESSMENT IN PRIVATE-SECTOR REHABILITATION

TANYA RUTHERFORD OWEN | IRMO MARINI | DANIELLE LEIGH ANTOL | RIGEL MACARENA PINON

LEARNING OBJECTIVES

After reviewing this chapter, the reader should be able to:

- Differentiate between nonforensic versus forensic private-sector vocational assessment.

- Explain forensic life care planning and identify types of assessment used in the development of such reports.

- Identify the types of vocational assessment measures in non–private-sector versus private-sector vocational rehabilitation.

- Understand the various assessment measures and resources used in private-sector rehabilitation, including transferable skills analysis, labor market analysis, and functional capacity evaluations.

- Describe the various life care planning assessments, including activities of daily living, day-in-the-life videos, comprehensive intake interviews, and multidisciplinary expert consultant assessment.

Introduction

There are essentially three sectors of private rehabilitation counseling: the public sector, the private nonprofit sector, and the private for-profit sector (Brodwin, 2008, p. 503). Although graduate students in rehabilitation counseling have traditionally been well prepared to work in the public vocational rehabilitation sector, there has been less focus in academic institutions on training for private rehabilitation counselors. This is despite the fact that employment in private practice rehabilitation makes up the second largest segment of employment of certified rehabilitation counselors across the United States. Statistically, 12% of rehabilitation counselors are employed in this sector, compared with 36% of counselors who are employed in public rehabilitation agencies (Commission on Rehabilitation Counselor Certification [CRCC], 2007). Additionally, the Certified Rehabilitation Counselor (CRC) exam, which is required for all persons who seek the

CRC designation (despite their intent to work in either the private or public sector), also contains questions pertaining to private-sector rehabilitation practice (Commission on Rehabilitation Counselor Certification, 2018).

The private for-profit rehabilitation sector largely began in the 1970s with disability insurance, namely, workers' compensation, the Federal Employment Compensation Act, and the Longshore and Harbor Workers' Act. In these programs, contracted private rehabilitation counselors are assigned to vocationally (and in some settings medically) manage the cases of workers who have sustained disabilities (termed "injured workers"), with the goal of returning them, as efficiently as possible, to employment (Brodwin, 2008). Concomitantly in the 1970s, rehabilitation counselors began testifying as vocational experts in Social Security Disability adjudication hearings, and in the early 1980s, they began testifying as forensic life care planning experts (Deutsch & Raffa, 1982). In the next section, the nuances of private vocational rehabilitation, forensic vocational consulting, and forensic life care planning are differentiated.

Nonforensic Private Vocational Rehabilitation

The goal of vocational rehabilitation professionals in nonforensic rehabilitation is to assist injured workers (i.e., those who sustain on-the-job injuries) in returning to work as quickly and as medically safe as possible. In these capacities, private-sector vocational rehabilitation counselors, who are usually employed by case management companies or as contracted counselors with the U.S. Department of Veterans Affairs (VA) or the U.S. Department of Labor, meet with the affected workers to develop return-to-work plans (Brodwin, 2008; Shrey & Lacerte, 1995).

In these systems, evaluation and assessment may be very similar to those in public rehabilitation, for which the person's postdisability capacities are considered along with his or her age, education, past work, and available retraining options. Many rehabilitation counseling students receive a good foundation in their academic training to work in these capacities. Specific assessment procedures within nonforensic private vocational rehabilitation are discussed later in this chapter.

Forensic Vocational Rehabilitation Consulting

In nonforensic vocational rehabilitation, the parties involved are not typically represented by legal counsel. In contrast, within forensic vocational rehabilitation, the parties involved (both the injured worker and the employer) are represented by legal counsel, and both of them often involve themselves in the vocational rehabilitation process. In these roles, forensic vocational rehabilitation counselors provide opinions about the worker's future labor market access and/or earning capacity loss, following the onset of disability. Typically, the forensic vocational counselor (FVC) performs a one-time assessment without case follow-up.

The purpose of assessment in forensic vocational matters is to assist in educating the involved parties about the worker's postdisability earning capacity, through consideration of the evaluee's education, age, past earnings history (if relevant), and work experience. These evaluations are often requested to assist in determining the value of a legal matter that has arisen as a result of the worker's injury. This is a unique role for vocational rehabilitation counselors, as they are limited in their exposure to the evaluee and, in most cases, are not provided the opportunity to implement their recommendations for work with the employee. Because their exposure to the evaluee is often time-limited, conducting a quality assessment during their brief interaction is of utmost importance. The FVC is typically asked to provide opinions as to whether a worker has lost the ability to perform duties required for a segment of job titles as a result of functional limitations from an injury and/or to determine any future earning capacity loss.

Forensic Life Care Planning

The newest subspecialty of private rehabilitation, life care planning, emerged only 37 years ago in the book *Damages in Tort Actions* (Deutsch & Raffa, 1982). As indicated in the book title, life care plans are very often used in litigation, either through case resolution or in court proceedings, to assist in allocation of funds for future medical and disability-related care. Through what is typically a one-time assessment, the life care planner creates a detailed outline of disability-related future medical treatment, ongoing medications, durable medical equipment, aids for independent function, home healthcare needs, and so on, along with the monetary value of such items. In this role, the forensic life care planner, similar to the FVC, will serve in part as a damages expert who outlines in detail what an evaluee's recommended medical needs are and the cost of same.

Although the knowledge domain of life care planning was formerly included in the accreditation manual by the Council on Rehabilitation Education (CORE), many practicing life care planners have had little to no education in graduate school on this topic. Few rehabilitation programs in the United States prepare their students for forensic life care planning (Marini, Isom, & Reid, 2003). As Marini et al. found in their survey of 64 rehabilitation program educators, few educators have the background or experience necessary to introduce students to this subspecialty. Indeed, the authors found that only 35% of rehabilitation educators were knowledgeable enough to provide more than one lecture on the topic (Marini et al., 2003). The assessments performed by life care planners are outlined later in this chapter.

Overall, other than in private nonforensic vocational rehabilitation, which involves working with an affected person until return to work is accomplished, the FVC and life care planner typically perform one-time independent assessments that are very often used in litigation to mediate or try a case regarding future monetary damages related to loss of earning capacity and/or future medical care needs. As their assignments are often very different from those of vocational rehabilitation counselors involved in public rehabilitation systems, the goals and methods of their assessment are also unique. A discussion of the assessment methods used in these subspecialties follows.

▧ Goals and Methods of Private Rehabilitation Assessment

Although assessment in public rehabilitation is most often a mechanism for service provision, in private rehabilitation, this is not always the case. In forensic private rehabilitation, the assessment may be a component of a one-time-only meeting with the evaluee (clients in forensic rehabilitation are typically termed "evaluees," as the client–counselor relationship does not exist) or it may be a second-opinion evaluation after a prior vocational assessment has been completed by another FVC.

Skills typically required of all vocational rehabilitation counselors are required of private-sector rehabilitation professionals. These skills include case management, career/vocational counseling, counseling techniques, client advocacy, and assessment (Brodwin, 2008). Within both forensic and nonforensic private vocational rehabilitation, the rehabilitation counselor includes a vocational history usually taken from the worker, with an analysis of each job title according to the *O*Net* or *Dictionary of Occupational Titles* (DOT; Weed & Field, 2012). A determination of residual functional capacity must be considered by the rehabilitation counselor in order to determine the impact of injury or illness on the person's capacity to perform past and future work.

The next step for private vocational rehabilitation counselors in both forensic and nonforensic settings typically involves vocational assessment or evaluation. Robinson and Drew (2014) define vocational evaluation as "a time-limited, formal, standardized method of data collection that requires implementation by professionals schooled in test administration and interpretation" (p. 88). Although some have defined forensic vocational evaluation and forensic vocational assessment differently (Farnsworth et al., 2005), for purposes of this chapter, they will be used interchangeably. As indicated in the first part of this chapter, there can be significant differences among assessment-related tasks involved in nonforensic (e.g., not litigated) private rehabilitation, forensic vocational rehabilitation consulting, and forensic life care planning. Owing to the significant differences in these areas, assessment-related tasks are addressed separately for each area.

Nonforensic Private Rehabilitation

In the field of rehabilitation, private rehabilitation counselors are often asked to develop return-to-work plans for persons involved in various vocational rehabilitation programs. Examples of these types of programs include state and federal workers' compensation systems, long-term disability systems, vocational rehabilitation, and employment systems through the VA and others. These systems are typically nonlitigated systems, where the tasks assigned include client interview, vocational research, plan development, and/or job placement.

In these systems, a physician (or other healthcare professional) has issued injury-related work capacities that outline what the person is capable of performing in the world of work. Whereas in public rehabilitation, these assessments are conducted by an in-house or consulting physician, in private rehabilitation, they are often provided in the form of a functional capacity evaluation (FCE). A thorough discussion of FCEs can be found later in this chapter, but briefly, FCEs purport to project the amount of physical exertion (e.g., lifting, standing, kneeling) the worker can safely perform. These opinions often serve as the foundation for the rehabilitation counselor to develop a return-to-work plan. In most private-sector rehabilitation programs, a specific hierarchy of return-to-work services is used, outlined as follows:

1. Return the worker to work in the same job with the same employer.
2. Return to work with the same employer but in an alternate job.
3. Return to work in the same job but with a different employer.
4. Return the worker to a new job using skills acquired through past work (i.e., transferable skills).
5. Retrain the worker for a new occupation.
6. Explore self-employment.

The steps are usually followed sequentially, and the worker cannot move through the steps of the hierarchy without proving that each step was explored and eliminated as an alternative (Lynch & Lynch, 1998). This is in contrast to public vocational rehabilitation programs.

In these systems, the questions to be answered through a vocational assessment center on the return-to-work capacities of a worker typically following a mid-career injury. As these workers have recently been in the world of work, rather than involved in educational endeavors, a vocational evaluation is necessary to answer questions of the person's academic skills, vocational interests, intelligence, and aptitudes. The role of evaluation in this capacity will be very similar to that of the evaluation conducted within state and federal vocational rehabilitation programs.

Evaluation Instruments in Nonforensic Private Rehabilitation

Although the goals in both forensic and nonforensic rehabilitation can be different, when conducting vocational evaluation, many of the same evaluation instruments are utilized. Commonly used instruments include the Wide Range Achievement Test (WRAT), which measures math computation, word reading, sentence comprehension, and spelling; the Basic Achievement Skills Inventory (BASI), which measures reading and language skills; the Ohio Literacy Test, a measure of reading comprehension skills; the Kaufman Functional Academic Skills Test (K-FAST), a 15- to 20-minute measure of reading and mathematics as applied to daily life situations; the Nelson Denny, a measure of reading ability; and/or the Cognistat, formerly known as the Neurobehavioral Cognitive Status Examination (NCSE), a measure of language, construction, memory, calculation, and reasoning.

Again, akin to evaluations conducted by counselors in the public sector, private rehabilitation counselors use instruments that assess a person's area of occupational interest. Although, in private rehabilitation, a person's interest does not often guide rehabilitation plan development, it is but one element considered in the rehabilitation process. Commonly used interest inventories in private rehabilitation for the assessment of occupational interests include the Campbell Interest and Skill Survey (CISS); the Self-Directed Search (SDS), an instrument using John Holland's RIASEC theory to classify people according to six basic types: Realistic, Investigative, Artistic, Social, Enterprising, and Conventional; the Career Exploration Inventory; the Career Directions Inventory (CDI); and the Career Occupational Preference System (COPS).

Learning ability is another commonly assessed factor in rehabilitation. Instruments used in private rehabilitation to measure learning ability include the Beta III, which measures nonverbal intellectual ability; the Wechsler Adult Intelligence Scale (WAIS); the Shipley Institute of Living Scale; Raven's Progressive Matrices (RPM), another nonverbal measure of abstract reasoning and fluid intelligence; and the Slosson Intelligence Test–Revised Third Edition (SIT-R3), a quick index of intellectual ability, which can be used for those with visual impairments or for those with limited use of their hands, as answers are provided orally.

When assessing aptitude in private rehabilitation, a number of instruments may be considered. Instruments may be chosen by the counselor or examiner, based on the evaluee's limitations and work options. For example, the Revised Minnesota Paper Form Board Test is often chosen if education or work in mechanical, technical, engineering, and similar occupations is being considered. Another aptitude test to be considered when measuring spatial perception and mechanical reasoning is the Bennett Mechanical Test. For assessing clerical speed and accuracy, many private rehabilitation counselors choose the Minnesota Clerical Test. For some evaluees, the Therapists' Portable Assessment Lab (TPal), which measures cognitive and psychomotor abilities, is an option.

Personality instruments are often used to improve a person–environment fit in the rehabilitation process. Examples of commonly used personality instruments include the NEO Personality Inventory–Revised, the Personal Characteristics Inventory (PCI), the Myers-Briggs Type Indicator (MBTI), the 16PF, and the Career Orientation Placement and Evaluation Survey (COPES).

For some private rehabilitation counselors, measurements of body system function are occasionally included in their assessments. Commonly used measures of manual dexterity include the Purdue Pegboard and the Crawford Small Parts Dexterity Test (CSPDT).

Nonforensic Assessment Procedures

In nonforensic rehabilitation, many private vocational rehabilitation counselors are contracted to provide rehabilitation services. A component of such services is vocational assessment.

Assessments are completed by nonforensic private rehabilitation counselors in various systems, including the VA and workers' compensation systems, both state and federal. Although the purpose of these assessments may be very similar (i.e., to assist in development of a return-to-work plan), each program will likely have a slightly different approach to actual assessment procedures. As such, these programs will be discussed separately in the subsequent sections.

U.S. Department of Veterans Affairs Vocational Rehabilitation

Within the VA system, certain assessment instruments may require approval from the VA contracting officer, prior to administration. The regional officer may also require (or request) that when possible, assessments be administered in a group format. In these assessments, the veteran's personality traits, interest, academic skills, and aptitudes are assessed. The instruments used in the assessment battery are often agreed upon by the rehabilitation counselor and the VA contracting officer at the time of service provision or contract award.

Workers' Compensation Vocational Rehabilitation: State

Another area of practice for many private rehabilitation counselors is within the realm of workers' compensation. Workers' compensation systems are administered at the state level, but because of time constraints of the systems, often private rehabilitation counselors, rather than state and federal rehabilitation systems, are involved. It is not uncommon for a workers' compensation rehabilitation program to be limited to 1 to 2 years, to include assessment, retraining, and job placement activities. Depending on the state administrator, there may be specific time frames by which the private rehabilitation counselor must accomplish certain tasks. For example, from the time of referral until the time of plan development, the counselor may be limited to a period of 60 to 90 days. Within this time period, vocational assessment must be complete.

Unlike the VA system, many workers' compensation systems do not designate the types of instruments or specify acceptable instruments that the counselor can use. They may, however, limit the amount of time (or the total expense) that the counselor can spend in vocational assessment. Therefore, instruments may be chosen that can be administered within a brief period of time, typically 2 to 3 hours. Rates are typically not set by the states or insurance companies, but the counselor's bills are reviewed and paid by the insurance company that administers the workers' compensation claim.

Workers' Compensation Vocational Rehabilitation: Federal

In addition to state workers' compensation programs, the federal government administers a vocational rehabilitation program. The purpose of the Office of Workers' Compensation Programs (OWCP) rehabilitation program is to assist injured employees who are covered by the Federal Employees' Compensation Act (FECA) or the Longshore and Harbor Workers' Compensation Act (LHWCA) to minimize their disabilities and return to gainful work (U.S. Department of Labor, 2007). Persons covered under this program include federal employees injured in the course of their employment.

Rehabilitation counselors involved in this system are usually under contract with the U.S. Department of Labor's Office of Workers' Compensation for a designated period of time. These counselors complete training at the various regional offices, as required by the office, which covers the topic of vocational assessment. Within these systems, the government sets the rate of hourly pay for the counselor, and fees are paid by the U.S. Department of Labor to the counselor.

Within the OWCP system, there have historically been strict guidelines about the qualifications of counselors allowed to administer assessment devices. For example, the agency may require that the counselor assigned to the OWCP case refer the person with the injury to a second "qualified individual," who is not associated with the rehabilitation counselor's firm, for vocational testing. Typically, these qualified individuals are psychologists or certified vocational evaluators. In addition, OWCP requires preauthorization for requested testing. Although the OWCP program does not typically delineate the exact assessment instruments that the counselor can administer, it does require prior authorization for testing by an approved vendor. Additionally, it requires that the assessment report include information on raw scores, test norm groups, percentile scores, and grade equivalents (for educational achievement testing; U.S. Department of Labor, 2007).

Forensic Life Care Planning

Life care planning emerged as a rehabilitation-related subspecialty in the early 1980s, derived from the work of Dr. Paul Deutsch and Dr. Frederick Raffa. A life care plan is defined as follows:

A life care plan is a dynamic document based upon published standards of practice, comprehensive assessment, data analysis and research, which provides an organized, concise plan for current and future needs with associated costs, for individuals who have experienced catastrophic injury or have chronic health care needs (International Academy of Life Care Planners, 2015, p. 1).

Although some life care planners who are also providing forensic vocational rehabilitation opinions utilize many of the instruments outlined previously in this chapter, there are additional assessments unique to life care planning. These unique assessments include assessment of one's ability to perform instrumental activities of daily living (IADLs) and activities of daily living (ADLs) to determine where assistance is needed. In some cases, the life care planner may participate in the making of a "day-in-the-life" video. This video captures details about what is necessary for the person to accomplish daily functions (e.g., dressing, hygiene, eating, housekeeping), and it is used to educate the involved parties about the types of goods and services that are necessitated by disability. These assessment instruments are discussed in detail later in this chapter.

In order to determine what goods and services are needed, a life care planner conducts an assessment process involving multiple steps. For a detailed step-by-step process for developing a life care plan, the reader is referred to Berens and Weed (2010, p. 9), Weed and Berens (2018, pp. 9–13), Weed and Field (2012, p. 155), and Weed and Owen (2018, p. 17). In general, the first step in the assessment process involves a review of available medical and legal records, as well as medical billing records (Berens & Weed, 2010; Weed & Berens, 2018; Weed & Field, 2012; Weed & Owen, 2018). The legal records commonly reviewed include the deposition transcripts of the person with the disability, family members, and/or the healthcare professionals who provide care to the person.

After a review of records is performed, an interview with the evaluee and/or his or her family members is requested (Berens & Weed, 2010; Weed & Field, 2012; Weed & Owen, 2018). Very often, these evaluations occur in the home (Berens & Weed, 2010), both to ensure convenience for the person and to be able to tour the home and note the presence of or need for disability-related equipment, needed home modifications in cases of nonambulatory persons, medications, and supplies. Although the content of the interview varies depending on the evaluee's specific needs, these evaluations can take several hours to complete, as the interview involves collecting details not only about the person's current regimen but also the preinjury medical, psychological, and social history.

Following completion of these steps, the life care planner attempts consultation with the healthcare professionals involved in the person's care (Berens & Weed, 2010; Weed & Field, 2012; Weed & Owen, 2018) to identify necessary goods and services. Once items are identified, the cost of each item must be researched (Berens & Weed, 2010; Weed & Berens, 2018; Weed & Field, 2012; Weed & Owen, 2018). Ultimately, the life care planner has reviewed hundreds, sometimes thousands of pages of records, has interviewed the person and the family member often for hours, and has conducted additional hours of research to determine evidence-based research guidelines and reasonable cost determinations to culminate in one single life care plan.

As many life care planners are also qualified rehabilitation counselors, it is not uncommon for these professionals to develop a forensic vocational evaluation as a supplemental report to the life care plan (Berens & Weed, 2010; Weed & Field, 2012; Weed & Owen, 2018). In these cases, assessment procedures similar to those outlined in the "Forensic Vocational Rehabilitation" section are followed.

Forensic Vocational Rehabilitation

Within the world of forensic vocational rehabilitation, the types of actions taken by counselors may be very similar to the types of tasks performed by private rehabilitation counselors in non-litigated settings. For example, FVCs often review disability-related medical records to educate themselves about the person they are evaluating. Additionally, interviews with the person with the disability are typically conducted, during which the FVC will learn about the educational, medical, social, and vocational background of that person.

However, unlike in other settings, those persons involved in the forensic vocational rehabilitation process will have legal representatives who are involved in the process. In forensic vocational rehabilitation assessments, the question to be answered is most often how personal injury or disability onset has negatively impacted the affected person's ability to earn money. In this system, attorneys typically receive copies of any rehabilitation reports prepared and may advise the person with the disability throughout the process of plan development. Because the system can be adversarial, rehabilitation counselors may be required to provide sworn testimony, through deposition, hearing testimony, a bench trial (i.e., a trial without a jury), or a court appearance to testify in front of a live jury in either state or federal court.

Standardized Assessment Instruments in Forensic Rehabilitation

Robinson and Drew (2014) and Weed and Field (2012) note that forensic vocational rehabilitation reports cover the reason for referral; background identifying information; medical, educational, and/or psychological records and history; ADLs; review of vocational history; observations during the assessment process; transferable skills analysis (TSA; if applicable); earnings capacity evaluation (if applicable); assessment instruments; and results with recommendations. The goal of the report is to answer referral questions with recommendations for programming and services that are fair, useful, credible, and cost-effective (Robinson, 2014).

When counselors serve in a forensic capacity, test administration may play an important role, as it provides a source of standardized and objective data. Robinson and Drew (2014) note that the FVC must use valid and reliable methods and instruments, both to provide sound assessment services to the evaluee and to satisfy evidentiary standards imposed by the court. The vocational assessment instruments chosen by the FVC will likely be the same as or similar to those selected in nonlitigated areas. It is critical that counselors choose instruments that are reliable, valid, and within the scope of practice for them to administer and interpret, as not doing so is a violation of the CRCC *Code of Professional Ethics* (Robinson & Drew, 2014).

Most FVCs administer vocational assessments within their area of expertise. Specifically, graduate-level rehabilitation counselors are recognized as having the requisite qualifications to perform Category B assessment (graduate degree in social services or license/certification). Category C requires a doctoral degree in the related field and/or license/certification in the relevant state (Pearson, 2019). Typical assessment instruments include academic, achievement, career interest, and aptitudes. Specialized training would likely be required for IQ testing and abnormal personality testing.

Vocational assessment typically involves instruments within the following categories: intelligence, educational achievement, aptitude, interest, and personality (Weed & Field, 2012). In 2012, Robinson (Robinson & Drew, 2014) conducted a survey of 47 practicing FVCs to determine what instruments were commonly used in their forensic practice and with what frequency the instruments were used. The practitioners reported using 101 unique measurement instruments in domains including achievement and aptitude (termed "abilities"; 45%), body system function (15%), interest (13%), personality (12%), intelligence (10%), mental health (3%), effort (2%), and other specialized instruments (1%; Robinson & Drew, 2014; R. Robinson, personal communication, September 24, 2018). Within the area of abilities testing, 45 instruments were named. The most widely used abilities instruments included the Wide Range Achievement Test, Fourth Edition (WRAT-4), which was used by 78% of the survey respondents; the Career Ability Placement Survey (CAPS), with 49% of the sample reporting its use; and Purdue Pegboard, which was used by 23% of the respondents (Robinson, 2014). Fifteen body system function measures, including the Valpar Component Work Samples, Oswestry Neck and Low Back Pain Disability Questionnaire, and the Functional Capacities Checklist, were used by FVCs, each at 2% of the sample. For the 13 interest measures used by respondents, 45% reported using the COPS Interest Inventory, 26% reported using the Career Assessment Inventory (CAI), 19% used the SDS, and 17% used the Strong Interest Inventory. For the 12 personality measures, 19% of the sample used the COPES, followed by 17% of the sample who used the 16PF and 15% who used the MBTI. For the 10 intelligence instruments used in this sample, 21% of the respondents used the SIT, while 17% reported using Beta III. These findings are similar to those in prior reports by Weed & Field (2012), who noted that the commonly used intelligence instruments in vocational assessment were the WAIS, Stanford-Binet, SIT, and Revised Beta Examination (Weed & Field, 2012). In Robinson's 2012 survey of the three mental health measures used, the Beck Depression Inventory (BDI) was used the most by 11% of the respondents. Although measures of effort were not reported to be commonly utilized in forensic vocational evaluations, two instruments were named by FVCs. Measurement of effort may be unique to the vocational rehabilitation process in forensics, as some researchers have noted a higher risk of response bias in those involved in litigation-related matters (Robinson, 2014).

In addition to the many assessment instruments typically designed and published by large testing entities, private rehabilitation counselors often rely upon other assessment devices. Some of these same devices may be utilized in the public sector and have been written about in most vocational rehabilitation texts (Rubin, Roessler, & Rumrill, 2016). The need for these devices can be varied, based on the specialty practice of the rehabilitation counselor. Additional assessment measures commonly used in the forensic vocational rehabilitation process, including the TSA, labor market survey (LMS), and on-site job analysis (OSJA), are discussed in the next sections. A sample vocational analysis is included in Appendix 14.1.

Other Commonly Used Assessment Tools and Methods

Dictionary of Occupational Titles

The *Dictionary of Occupational Titles* (DOT; U.S. Employment Service, 1991) was developed in response to the demand for standardized occupational data to support the expanding public employment service. The DOT provides a brief single-paragraph description for each of the 12,741 job titles contained in it. Information includes what the job entails and the strength and specific vocational preparation required to perform the job. The DOT classifies each job title into five strength categories: sedentary, light, medium, heavy, and very heavy. The physical demand ranking is predominantly based on force, duration of material handling, intensity, and energy expenditure. The DOT is regularly utilized by vocational rehabilitation counselors in the private sector to classify a person's past work in terms of skill and exertion level, to conduct a TSA, and to determine a person's ability to perform work with work-related limitations.

The Classification of Jobs

The *Classification of Jobs* (COJ; J. E. Field & Field, 1992) contains an accumulation of data from the U.S. Department of Labor that provides additional details for the 12,741 jobs listed in the DOT. The COJ provides explicit job requirements for each job title, on each of seven criteria (termed the "Worker Trait Profile"): strength, physical demands, specific vocational preparation, environmental demands, aptitudes, general education development, and temperament. Forensic vocational counselors (FVCs) must be well familiarized with the seven areas and the criteria within each when testifying in forensic areas. When conducting a TSA, a loss of earnings capacity analysis, and/or an LMS, both the DOT and the COJ are indispensable sources of information (Sleister, 2000).

Neuropsychological Evaluations

A neuropsychological assessment is an instrument designed to evaluate cognitive functioning related to brain disease, mental illness, dementia, and other psychiatric conditions. In rehabilitation, the neuropsychological evaluation is used to collect diagnostic information and differential diagnostic information, assess treatment responses, and predict functional potential and recovery (Harvey, 2012). These assessments are conducted by a licensed psychologist specializing in neuropsychology who is trained to administer a battery of tests that examine one's cognitive abilities in areas such as memory, attention, processing speed, reasoning, judgment and problem-solving, and spatial and language functions. Commonly used neuropsychological tests include Beck Depression Inventory, Anxiety Inventory, and Hopelessness Scale Test of Variables of Attention (TOVA), Tower of London Test, Trail-Making Test (TMT) or Trails A & B, Validity Indicator Profile, verbal fluency tests, WAIS, Wechsler Intelligence Scale for Children (WISC-IV IQ test), Wechsler Memory Scale (WMS), Wechsler Test of Adult Reading, WRAT-4, Wisconsin Card Sorting Test (WCST), Wonderlic Personnel Test, Word Memory Test, Ammons Quick Test, Cambridge Neuropsychological Test Automated Battery (CANTAB), Dementia Rating Scale, Test of Memory Malingering (TOMM), and the Kaufman Short Neuropsychological Assessment (Rabin, Barr, & Burton, 2005).

In the forensic litigation field, these evaluations are commonly used in cases involving acquired or traumatic brain injury (TBI) to determine vocational options or capabilities and/or future life care needs, including the need for supervision and daily care. A neuropsychological evaluation report typically includes a detailed intake interview; observation opinions from caregivers or significant others regarding their loved one's behavioral, emotional, and cognitive functioning; and the results of test administration. Testing alone may last up to 8 hours and can be done over several days to limit fatigue factors. Evaluation results can reveal deficits in functioning with a differential diagnosis using the *Diagnostic and Statistical Manual of Mental Disorders, Fifth Edition* (American Psychiatric Association, 2013). In addition, reports include discussion of specific areas of cognitive deficits, how such deficits will likely affect a person's functioning, and treatment recommendations. Forensic rehabilitation consultants, including FVCs and life care planners, often consult with the neuropsychologist for more detailed opinions regarding work-related capacities as well as evaluees' capabilities to care for themselves at home and in the community.

Transferable Skills Analysis

In private vocational rehabilitation, a TSA is often performed in the evaluation of an adult who has sustained a mid-career disabling injury. Field (as cited in Farnsworth et al., 2005) defines a TSA as:

> The process by which similar, related or new jobs are identified for a person following injury or disability. These jobs are both consistent and compatible with previous work experience and fall within the range of residual post-injury functioning of the claimant (p. 104).

Transferable skills are applicable when they are valuable or marketable in the labor market in determining the affected person's vocational potential (Berens & Weed, 2010; Dunn & Growick, 2000). The U.S. Department of Labor's (n.d.) *Vocational Rehabilitation Counselor Handbook* notes that transferable skills can be acquired through various sources, including military experience, hobbies, parenting, volunteer activities, and education and training.

A TSA performed in forensic rehabilitation will be scrutinized by all parties involved in the litigation and ultimately may be reviewed by the jury when determining a claimant's wage earning capacity. Therefore, the FVC must be familiar with and able to effectively utilize TSAs (Sleister, 2000).

In a workers' compensation setting, the documented existence of transferable skills may strongly influence return-to-work efforts. As most workers' compensation systems strictly follow the hierarchy of return-to-work services (Lynch & Lynch, 1998), if a rehabilitation counselor determines that an evaluee has transferable skills, this may preclude a recommendation for retraining and direct the counselor and evaluee to explore only job placement efforts. In these roles, the rehabilitation counselor may be precluded from developing retraining plans, even if it is the desire of the employee, if there is documented existence of transferable skills occupations available to which the employee can return.

For a thorough discussion of the steps for conducting a TSA in private rehabilitation, the reader is referred to Weed and Field (2012). The DOT (U.S. Department of Labor, 1991) and the COJ (Field & Field, 1992) serve as foundational structures necessary to compile a TSA (Berens & Weed, 2010). In 2018, a TSA is typically performed via a computerized format. Decisions must be made by the private rehabilitation counselor about which TSA company to use, and these decisions often involve the element of price, as a self-employed private rehabilitation counselor often pays for the service (unlike a public rehabilitation counselor). Additional consideration must be given to the preference for reports generated by the TSA company. Like all TSA data, the resulting data are based on the DOT, last published in 1999. In order to determine the existence of these jobs in the local or regional labor market, the rehabilitation counselor often conducts a labor market survey.

Labor Market Surveys

Most forensic rehabilitation counselors who utilize a TSA in their assessments usually report the results alongside LMS data, based on the evaluee's geographic area of residence at the time of the evaluation. Once the results are obtained through a TSA, the next step taken by a private rehabilitation counselor is to survey the labor market to determine the actual existence of the jobs identified through the TSA in the evaluee's geographic area of residence, wages for the current jobs being considered, and current requirements for the jobs. This is typically accomplished through an LMS. Farnsworth et al. (2005) define an LMS as "a method or approach to gathering relevant and appropriate information about jobs in a specific labor market" (p. 52). The authors note critical questions such as "If these jobs exist, are they available locally?," "What do these jobs pay?," and "If available locally, are these jobs open to my client?" (Weed & Field, 2001, p. 131 as cited in Farnsworth et al., 2005, p. 52).

As an example, a TSA may identify registered nurse (DOT #075.364-010) as a transferable skill occupation. However, it is incumbent that the vocational counselor review the requirements from the evaluee's state Board of Nursing to determine the state-specific requirements for this occupation. Similarly, while the TSA may identify a transferable skill occupation of boat captain, an LMS may or may not substantiate the availability of these jobs based on the geographic requirements (i.e., availability of large bodies of water) where the evaluee resides.

According to Barros-Bailey & Heitzman (2014), LMSs serve as a collection of data from the domain of work that harmonizes with an evaluee's skills, abilities, needs, interests, and other variables. Labor market surveys are considered to be *important to extremely important* by those who use them in forensic practice (Barros-Bailey & Saunders, 2013a, 2013b). FVCs who apply LMS data are commonly considered be knowledgeable and have more clinical research experience than other professionals in their occupation (Barros-Bailey & Saunders, 2013a).

In general, the goal of the LMS is to identify evaluee-specific return-to-work options. That is, what jobs exist in the person's geographic area of residence, and what do these jobs require? (Brodwin, 2008). When working with an evaluee in nonforensic rehabilitation, the rehabilitation counselor may be assigned to develop a retraining plan. In this context, an LMS will demonstrate to the counselor and client what the requirements are for becoming employable in the field being considered for retraining. LMS data collection can be tailored to the evaluee's specific needs. For example, if the person has low vision, questions can be posed to potential employers about the vision requirements and availability of adaptive aids in the job.

For a thorough discussion of conducting an LMS in private rehabilitation, the reader is referred to Barros-Bailey and Heitzman (2014) and Weed and Field (2012). Data may be collected for an LMS through a variety of means. First, direct contact with local employers can be initiated. This may be done by telephone, via email, or in person. For small employers, contact may be made with the actual employer, whereas with larger employers, contact may be best made with the human resources department. Additionally, reviewing online job openings may provide a good deal of data about current job openings. For some occupations (e.g., electrician), contact with the local union may be the best place to obtain information about hiring practices of employers, requirements for employability, and demand for workers. Although there is not a "magic" number of contacts that are required in an LMS, most private rehabilitation counselors will agree that an LMS is complete when the questions posed in the LMS are answered, with Barros-Bailey and Heitzman (2014) noting that the sample size of the LMS "depends on the purpose of the LMS" (p. 180).

For FVCs, the results of both the TSA and the LMS will likely be presented to the judge and/or jury in a trial setting. During deposition, the details of both the TSA and LMS are often reviewed by attorneys on both sides, and the forensic rehabilitation counselor should be prepared to discuss not only the results of these assessments but also the underlying foundation for these methods. This type of information can be critical for a jury to consider when valuing earnings capacity. Therefore, the details of the TSA and LMS should be documented thoroughly and presented clearly and concisely for the trier of facts. The scrutiny under which the FVC's file is reviewed is something unique to the forensic rehabilitation practice, and the FVC must be prepared to conduct a detailed discussion of the methods, the purposes, and the outcomes of both the TSA and the LMS.

Private Rehabilitation: Specific Assessment Devices

In the previous section, assessment instruments such as the TSA, neuropsychological evaluation, and LMS were discussed. These, along with standardized instruments, are the types of instruments typically taught in most graduate-level rehabilitation programs (Rubin, Roessler, & Rumrill, 2016). However, it is not uncommon for private rehabilitation counselors to utilize assessment devices that may not be used in the realm of public rehabilitation. For example, for forensic life care planners, a day-in-the-life video is often presented as a part of the damages package that accompanies the life care plan, but this item would rarely be seen in the file of a rehabilitation counselor employed in the public sector. Other such assessment instruments including the OSJA, FCE, and ADL assessments are discussed in the following paragraphs.

Functional Capacity Evaluations

As in nonforensic rehabilitation, very often, a physician (or related specialist) provides an opinion of the evaluee's work-related capabilities. In cases in which there is a cognitive impairment such as a TBI, FVCs typically rely upon assessments of neurologists and/or neuropsychologists to determine a person's work capabilities. While public-sector rehabilitation counselors regularly rely upon medical opinions from physicians, in private rehabilitation, opinions about physical capacities also come from a FCE.

The FCE is an assessment that can provide information pertinent to an evaluee's functional abilities and prognosis regarding his or her ability to return to work after an injury. In Social Security Disability determination evaluations and in litigation, two types of assessments may be used: the Mental Functional Capacity Evaluation (MFCE) and the Physical Functional Capacity Evaluation (PFCE; Marini, 2016).

Although there are different versions of the PFCE, often items measured in the PFCE include how much an evaluee can lift/carry in an 8-hour day as well as how long the person can sit, stand, walk, climb, balance, stoop, kneel, crouch, crawl, reach, handle, finger, talk, hear, and see, based on the person's medical conditions. These exertional questions are based on whether an evaluee can functionally perform these actions up to one-third of the workday (occasionally), one-third to two-thirds of an 8-hour workday (frequently), or whether the person can perform the task constantly (i.e., 6 hours or more). In some cases, treating physicians will have an injured worker in their office and subjectively ask that person how well he or she might be able to perform these activities. Such assessments may have little utility because they are without concomitant objective measurement.

A lengthier (often 2–4 hours) and potentially more reliable PFCE is often completed by a physical or occupational therapist or chiropractor who utilizes various work systems to measure

TABLE 14.1 Mental Functional Capacity Evaluation Domains

MENTAL FUNCTION AREA	WORK-RELATED FUNCTION
Understanding and memory	The ability to understand and remember very short and simple instructions
Sustained concentration and persistence	The ability to maintain attention and concentration for extended periods
Social interaction	The ability to interact appropriately with the general public
Adaptation	The ability to respond appropriately to changes in the work setting

physical activities. Wind, Gouttebarge, Kuijer, Sluiter, and Frings-Dresen (2009) report that the top 10 systems on the market are the The Ergos Work Simulator and Ergo-Kit variation, The Blankenship, the Isernhagen Work System, Physical Work Performance Evaluation (Ergoscience), Hanoun Medical, Ergos, ARCON, WEST-EPIC, Key, and AssessAbility. These systems require the evaluee to lift certain weights from floor to waist, waist to shoulders, and above the shoulders. Other actions measured include stair-stepping, push/pull strength, grip strength, kneeling and crouching ability, and so on. These actions are recorded along with the evaluee's heart rate and subjective complaints of discomfort or pain. These assessments are conducted in a physical therapy type setting.

The result of the FCE is a multipage report describing what measured activities the person was able (or unable) to perform and the extent to which (i.e., frequency and duration) they could be performed. These measurements can be compared with the demands of various jobs to determine whether a person can meet the physical requirements to perform work at various physical demand levels. These systems generally link portions of the Worker Trait Profile in the government resource COJ (J. E. Field & Field, 1992) and its crosswalk resource DOT (U.S. Department of Labor, 1991).

The MFCE is most commonly used in Social Security Disability determinations. These evaluations are generally completed by a clinical psychologist or neuropsychologist who has often not evaluated the applicant in person, but rather has reviewed the available medical and psychological records. The evaluator then provides the administrative law judge an opinion of whether a Social Security Disability applicant has no impairments, slight impairments, moderate impairments, marked impairments, or extreme impairments in four different areas of function including: understanding and memory, sustained concentration and persistence, social interaction, and adaptation (Marini, 2016, p. 32). A description of each of the four psychological function criteria is outlined in Table 14.1.

In Social Security proceedings, the MFCE is then proffered to the vocational expert, who is asked whether a hypothetical person could perform the past work or any other work in the national economy based on these psychiatric/cognitive limitations. Depending on the range of severity of various impairments across each of the four criteria, a person may be deemed vocationally disabled by the administrative law judge.

We next turn our attention to two unique assessment measures used in forensic life care planning concerning the potential need for home healthcare and/or housekeeping assistance.

Activities of Daily Living Assessment

Activities of Daily Living (ADLs) are basic tasks performed in the course of a normal day that enable a person to function independently. In most cases, these activities can be classified into five categories: personal hygiene (i.e., bathing, grooming, oral, nail and hair care), maintaining continence (i.e., ability to use the bathroom mentally and physically including cleaning oneself), dressing (i.e., ability to dress independently), feeding (i.e., ability to eat independently but not necessarily prepare food), and transferring/ambulating (i.e., walking from one place to another independently and ability to transfer in/out of bed), all of which must be done autonomously. The skills are then typically coded as independent, standby supervision, limited assistance, and extensive assistance (Centers for Medicare & Medicaid Services, 2018).

In addition, IADLs encompass an essential yet complex extension of a person's ability to carry out daily life functions, including companionship and mental support, transportation and shopping, preparing meals, managing a person's household, managing medications, communicating with others, and managing finances (Centers for Medicare & Medicaid Services, 2018). These activities are dependent more on cognitive abilities; therefore, people with severe TBIs may be rated as requiring limited or extensive assistance in completing these daily tasks. In litigation cases involving severe injuries such as tetraplegia, cerebral palsy, amputation, and severe TBI, it becomes prudent for the life care planner to ascertain what the injured party can and cannot perform independently and in what areas the he or she requires assistance or supervision. This can be performed through consultation with the person's healthcare treatment team and through observation of the person in his or her residence.

A Day-in-the-Life Video

A day-in-the-life video is often used in litigation cases of persons who require some assistance accomplishing their ADLs and IADLs. It is a non-narrative demonstrative exhibit used to show jurors visually what specific impairments a person may have and what healthcare and/or homemaking needs are encountered in daily life following an injury. In a day-in-the-life video, the person is observed in various settings, carrying out various daily tasks, from different angles such as "the client eating, taking their meds, the architectural modifications, therapy, etc." (Hunt, 2010, p. 812).

There are also some specific parameters that need to remain intact in order to conserve the bounds of the legal process when creating a day-in-the-life video. These principles include preserving authentication by making sure the visuals delineate reality, ensuring relevance by connecting the baseline with the person's current circumstances, and maintaining an objective and accurate portrayal that accurately captures the person's present reality (Hunt, 2018, p. 693). In addition, maintaining chronological order is crucial when presenting a criterion for comparison of the life prior to the injury. Hunt (2018) reports such order includes the following: the baseline of the person's normal life prior to the event, the event that provides imagery and the progression to the client's present, the reality that portrays present-day life care visuals, and the conclusion that entails the final thoughts that encompass the effects of the event (p. 688). Ultimately, a day-in-the-life video objectively captures a person's day-to-day abilities and functional limitations that may or may not require the assistance of others to perform. These assessments are typically prepared by professionals with specialized training, such as a Certified Legal Video Specialist, who often confers with the life care planner in preparation of the video as the life care planner will have extensive information about the subject's level of independence in ADLs and IADLs.

On-Site Job Analysis

One assessment that FVCs regularly use is the on-site job analysis (OSJA). These analyses are utilized to evaluate the ability of a worker to return to work in a specific job with a specific employer. The results of the OSJA may also be presented in a legal proceeding, most often within workers' compensation settings.

A job analysis is designed to determine whether varying job traits coincide with the worker's traits (Berens & Weed, 2010). According to multiple sources (Blackwell, Conrad & Weed, 1992; Weed & Field, 2012), once a potential job is located, it may be suitable to conduct a job analysis. The *Revised Handbook for Analyzing Jobs* (*RHAJ*; U.S. Department of Labor, 1991) clarifies procedures and methods practiced in the public employment service to both analyze jobs and record said analyses. The *RHAJ* (U.S. Department of Labor, 1991) specifies that job analysis involves a systematic study of a specific job in terms of:

> *The worker's relationship to data, people, and things (worker functions);*
>
> *The methodologies and techniques employed (work fields);*
>
> *The machines, tools, equipment, and work aids used (MTEWA);*
>
> *The materials, products, subject matter, or services which result (MPSMS); and*
>
> *The worker attributes that contribute to successful job performance (worker characteristics; p. 1–1).*

Job analysis involves the process of identifying and determining particular job duties and requirements and the level of relative importance of these duties for a given job (Wilson, 2012). The physical demands of a job are demarcated in terms of 20 factors: strength, climbing, balancing, stooping, kneeling, crouching, crawling, reaching, handling, fingering, feeling, talking, hearing, tasting/smelling, near acuity, far acuity, depth perception, accommodation, color vision, and field of vision (U.S. Department of Labor, 1991). Forensic vocational counselors (FVCs) and other rehabilitation professionals use information gathered in a job analysis to determine whether the requirements for a job matches the evaluee's physical and mental capabilities (Paquette & Heitzman, 2014).

For a detailed Job Analysis Checklist, discussion of conducting a job analysis, and a sample job analysis narrative report, the reader is referred to Weed and Field (2012). To conduct the OSJA, the rehabilitation counselor reports to the worksite. The counselor typically brings various measurement tools to capture the various elements of the worksite. The items often include (but are not limited to) camera, video camera, tape measure, weight scale, and exertion scale, such as The Exertional Scale (Mihayl, n.d.). When on-site, the rehabilitation counselor often observes and documents the job tasks performed and the physical and/or mental exertion required of the job. These observations are documented in an OSJA report created by the counselor. Commonly used items at the worksite are weighed and measured, with their measurements recorded within the report. The heights of the various items at the worksite are also recorded. It is not uncommon for the employee to be present during the OSJA, as well as a representative of the employer. The assignment of the counselor in this role is to objectively observe and document the requirements of the job, typically to be transmitted to a medical professional for his or her opinion of the evaluee's capacity to perform this occupation. Once the OSJA is reviewed by such a professional and a decision is made about the evaluee's ability to perform the work, the rehabilitation counselor often works with the employee and the employer to assist the employee in return-to-work efforts, coordinating accommodations necessary to assist the employee in a successful return to work.

Issues Unique to Forensic Rehabilitation

In addition to utilizing unique assessment instruments, rehabilitation counselors engaged in forensic work often face situations and experiences not seen in the public vocational rehabilitation sector. In public rehabilitation, the counselor has a counselor–client relationship with the person being evaluated, and other than involved family members, there are rarely multiple parties involving themselves in the vocational rehabilitation process. This is not the case in private forensic rehabilitation, in which attorneys for the worker may be involved, as well as attorneys for the adverse party and a trier of fact (i.e., a judge and/or a jury). Whereas in public rehabilitation, there may not be caps on expenditures or statute-directed protocols to follow, such restrictions are commonplace in private forensic rehabilitation. Detailed in the following section are some unique aspects of assessment in private forensic vocational rehabilitation.

Vocational Evaluation as One-Time Evaluation

The role of a vocational rehabilitation counselor is to serve as a guide to assist people in reaching their vocational rehabilitation goals (Robinson, 2014). Vocational rehabilitation allots for ongoing services between a vocational rehabilitation counselor and an evaluee until a desired employment goal has been achieved (Robinson, 2014). According to Rubin, Roessler, and Rumrill (2016), four sequential phases are embedded within the vocational rehabilitation process: (a) evaluation, (b) planning, (c), treatment, and (d) termination.

However, in forensic rehabilitation, experts do not provide direct rehabilitation counseling services (American Board of Vocational Experts, 2007). The CRCC Code of Ethics states, "When employed to render an opinion for a forensic purpose, rehabilitation counselors do not have clients. In a forensic setting, the evaluee is the person who is being evaluated." (Commission on Rehabilitation Counselor Certification, 2017 p. 2). The client–counselor relationship is nonexistent in forensic rehabilitation, dismantling any expectations of future rehabilitation services (e.g., job placement, counseling, and job analysis; Strauser, 2014). According to Strauser (2014), an expert's function is that of an evaluator and not as a rehabilitation counselor, advocate, or case manager. Forensic rehabilitation professionals refrain from developing and implementing a plan or acting as a resource subsequent to the litigation. The task of FVCs is to provide an objective opinion regarding an injured person's future earning capacity. Additionally, life care planners are expected to determine the total cost of the injured person's care over a prolonged period of time and avoid dual roles.

Opposing Forensic Vocational Evaluators

Another unique feature of forensic vocational rehabilitation is that within the litigation realm, there may be a counselor hired by the attorney representing the injured party as well as a second counselor hired by the attorney representing the adverse party. When this occurs, one party may ask that the testing data conducted by either side's counselor be shared with the other side. This practice of examining data is to verify that testing protocols were properly followed, that the instruments were scored correctly, and/or that proper instruments were chosen for the purpose of the assignment.

Confidentiality

Various sectors within rehabilitation have their own section of the *Code of Ethics* that addresses confidentiality. Section F of the *Code of Professional Ethics for Rehabilitation Counselors*

(F.1.b) indicates clarification is required in advance given the nature of evaluative relationship and how the information will be shared (Barros-Bailey, Carlisle, & Blackwell, 2010; CRCC, 2017). Furthermore, members of the International Association of Rehabilitation Professionals (IARP, 2006), the national organization of private rehabilitation counselors and life care planners, abide by their own set of ethical standards regarding those who practice in a forensic setting. According to the 2007 Code of Ethics, subjects of such evaluations have the right to expect that confidentiality will be upheld and be provided with an explanation of limitations, service delivery, and disclosure of information to others (B1.a.). When circumstances require the disclosure of confidential information, experts should be expected to reveal only information that is relevant or essential (B1.b). Forensic rehabilitation consultants are required to maintain confidential records, but they may exchange relevant and necessary information without written consent (IARP, 2006).

Daubert Challenge

Prior to the *Daubert v. Merrill Dow Pharmaceuticals* (1993) decision, expert witnesses could essentially base their opinions on their education, training, and experience. These opinions could not only be vastly different from those of other experts in the field but also did not require a standardized methodology that was commonly accepted by the field (Isom & Marini, 2002). Based on the *Daubert v. Merrill Dow Pharmaceuticals* decision, a new set of criteria for the admissibility of scientific expert testimony was established, requiring that trial judges serve as gatekeepers to exclude unreliable expert testimony. Pursuant to the Federal Rules of Evidence, Rule 702, specific factors elucidated by the *Daubert* decision include:

a. Whether an expert's technique or theory can be challenged objectively or whether it is subjective and cannot be reasonably assessed for reliability;

b. Whether the testimony has been subject to peer review and publication;

c. The known or potential rate of error of the technique or theory when applied;

d. The existence and maintenance of standards and controls; and

e. Whether the technique or theory has been generally accepted in the scientific community.

Potential admissibility challenges may arise based on an expert's qualifications, methodology, and/or the empirical science that serves as foundation for the proposed expert testimony. Under federal rules, courts must evaluate an expert's qualifications, including the review of publications, confirmation of earned degrees, and relevant work in the expert's field (e.g., forensic rehabilitation, nursing, occupational medicine). Using a methodologically valid approach allows expert testimony to be forensically defensible (*Daubert* ruling as cited in T. F. Field, 2000; Schultz & Gatchel, 2008). When an expert's methodical approach is not of rigorous scientific principles through supported protocols and based on objective data, the opinion provided may result in a *Daubert* exclusion. It is important that the FVC utilizes standardized clinical assessments, as opposed to clinician-judgment–based assessments, when determining damages in order to effectively withstand court challenges and cross-examination (Beveridge & McDaniel, 2014; Schultz & Gatchel, 2008). The science relied upon should not be assumed, but should be empirically based and accepted by the profession and subjected to peer review and publication (Isom & Marini, 2002).

Conclusions

Although the work of rehabilitation professionals in both the public and the private sectors share many commonalities, private rehabilitation professionals have methods and tools that are unique to their profession. Most rehabilitation counselors have completed common academic training to acquire the skills necessary to conduct client interviews, review relevant disability-related records, and access community resources. For those who wish to pursue employment in the private-sector rehabilitation, however, additional training in one of the private rehabilitation subspecialties may be required.

Employment in private rehabilitation is a viable option for many academically trained rehabilitation counselors. In the most recent survey of rehabilitation counselors, 12% of rehabilitation counselors reported employment in private rehabilitation. Understanding the differences in private rehabilitation subspecialties will enhance the rehabilitation counselor's access to employment in these sectors.

Within each of the subspecialties of private rehabilitation (i.e., nonforensic, forensic, and life care planning), rehabilitation professionals utilize assessment devices that are commonly used in public rehabilitation, including LMSs and TSAs. In addition, however, most private rehabilitation professionals use devices specific only to their specialty area of practice. This chapter not only identifies these measures and explains their use but also educates the reader about how private rehabilitation practitioners employ these items in their specialty practices. Although traditional graduate training has focused on providing students the skills necessary to compete for work in public rehabilitation, information presented in this chapter can be critical in educating the aspiring private and forensic rehabilitation professional about the assessment skills necessary to work in this specialty practice of rehabilitation.

References

American Board of Vocational Experts. (2007). *Code of ethics*. Retrieved from http://www.abve.net/Assets/ABVE_Code_of_Ethics_2007_cover.pdf

American Psychiatric Association. (2013). *Diagnostic and statistical manual of mental disorders* (5th ed.). Arlington, VA: American Psychiatric Publishing.

Barros-Bailey, M., Carlisle, J., & Blackwell, T. L. (2010). Forensic ethics and indirect practice for the rehabilitation counselor. *Rehabilitation Counseling Bulletin, 53*(4), 237–242. doi:10.1177/0034355210368728

Barros-Bailey, M., & Heitzman, A. M. (2014). Labor market survey. In R. H. Robinson (Ed.), *Foundations of forensic vocational rehabilitation* (pp. 167–202). New York, NY: Springer Publishing Company.

Barros-Bailey, M., & Saunders, J. L. (2013a). Benchmarking the use of labor market surveys by certified rehabilitation counselors. *Rehabilitation Counseling Bulletin, 56*(3), 160–171. doi:10.1177/0034355212460590

Barros-Bailey, M., & Saunders, J. L. (2013b). Labor market surveys: Importance to the preparedness of certified rehabilitation counselors. *Rehabilitation Research, Policy, and Education, 27*(2). doi:10.1891/2168-6653.27.2.1

Berens, D. E., & Weed R. O. (2010). The role of the vocational rehabilitation counselor in life care planning. In R. O. Weed & D. E. Berens (Eds.), *Life care planning and case management handbook* (3rd ed., pp. 41–61). Boca Raton, FL: CRC Press.

Beveridge, S., & McDaniel, R. S. (2014). Private practice in vocational rehabilitation. In D. R. Strauser (Ed.), *Career development, employment, and disability in rehabilitation* (pp. 361–388). New York, NY: Springer Publishing Company.

Blackwell, T., Conrad, D., & Weed, R. (1992). *Job analysis and the ADA: A step-by-step guide*. Athens, GA: E&F Vocational Services.

Brodwin, M. (2008). Rehabilitation in the private-for-profit sector: Opportunities and challenges. In S. E. Rubin & R. T. Roessler (Eds.), *Foundations of the vocational rehabilitation process* (6th ed., pp. 503–523). Austin, TX: Pro-Ed.

Centers for Medicare & Medicaid Services. (2018). *Long-term care facility resident assessment manual 3.0 user's manual.* Washington, DC: Department of Health and Human Services. Retrieved from https://www.aanac.org/docs/mds-3.0-rai-users-manual/11122_mds_3-0_chapter_3_-_section_g_v1-12.pdf?sfvrsn=10

Commission on Rehabilitation Counselor Certification (2007). *2008 salary report: An update on salaries in the rehabilitation counseling profession.* Retrieved from https://www.uidaho.edu/-/media/UIdaho-Responsive/Files/coe/Leadership-and-Counseling/Academics/RCHS/CRCC-Salary-Report.pdf

Commission on Rehabilitation Counselor Certification. (2017). *Code of professional ethics for rehabilitation counselors.* Retrieved from https://www.crccertification.com/code-of-ethics-3

Commission on Rehabilitation Counselor Certification. (2018). *CRC certification guide.* Schaumburg, IL: Author.

Daubert v. Merrill Dow Pharmaceuticals, 509 U.S. 579 (1993)

Deutsch, P., & Raffa, F. (1982). *Damages in tort actions.* New York, NY: Matthew Bender.

Dunn, P. L., & Growick, B. S. (2000). Transferable skills analysis in vocational rehabilitation: Historical foundations, current status, and future trends. *Journal of Vocational Rehabilitation, 14*(2), 79–87.

Farnsworth, K., Field, J. E., Field, T. F., Griffin, S., Jayne, K . . . van de Bittner, S. (2005). *The quick desk reference for forensic rehabilitation consultants.* Athens, GA: Elliott & Fitzpatrick.

Field, J. E., & Field, T. F. (1992). *The classification of jobs* (4th rev.). Athens, GA: Elliott & Fitzpatrick.

Field, T. F. (2000). *A resource for the rehabilitation consultant on the Daubert and Kumho ruling.* Athens, GA: Elliott & Fitzpatrick.

Harvey, P. D. (2012). Clinical applications of neuropsychological assessment. *Dialogues in Clinical Neuroscience, 14*(1), 91–99.

Hunt, J. M. (2010). Day-in-the-life video production in life care planning. In R. O. Weed & D. E. Berens (Eds.), *Life care planning and case management handbook* (3rd ed., pp. 811–819). New York, NY: Routledge.

Hunt, J. M. (2018). Day-in-the-life video production in life care planning. In R. O. Weed & D. E. Berens (Eds.), *Life care planning and case management handbook* (4th ed., pp. 685–693). New York, NY: Routledge.

International Academy of Life Care Planners. (2015). *Standards of practice for life care planners* (3rd ed.). Glenview, IL: International Association of Rehabilitation Professionals.

International Association of Rehabilitation Professionals. (2006). *IARP Code of Ethics, Standards of Practice, and Competencies.* Retrieved from https://cdn.ymaws.com/rehabpro.org/resource/resmgr/IARP_Code_of_Ethics.pdf

Isom, R. N., & Marini, I. (2002). An educational curriculum for teaching life care planning. *Journal of Life Care Planning, 1*(4), 239–264.

Lynch, R. K., & Lynch, R. T. (1998). Rehabilitation counseling in the private sector. In R. M. Parker and E. M. Szymanski (Eds.), *Rehabilitation counseling: Basics and beyond* (3rd ed., pp. 71–86). Austin, TX: Pro-Ed.

Marini, I. (2016). Understanding mental and physical functional capacity evaluations. In I. Marini & M. Stebnicki (Eds.), *The professional counselor's desk reference* (2nd ed., pp. 321–328). New York, NY: Springer Publishing Company.

Marini, I., Isom, R. N., & Reid, C. (2003). Case management: Rehabilitation education curricula and faculty needs. *Journal of Life Care Planning, 2*(3), 171–174.

Paquette, S., & Heitzman, A. M. (2014). Job analysis. In R. H. Robinson (Ed.), *Foundations of forensic vocational rehabilitation* (pp. 145–166). New York, NY: Springer Publishing Company.

Pearson (2019). Qualifications. Retrieved from https://www.pearsonassessments.com/professional-assessments/ordering/how-to-order/qualifications.html

Rabin, L. A., Barr, W. A., & Burton, L. A. (2005). Assessment practices of clinical neuropsychologists in the United States and Canada: A survey of INS, NAN, and APA Division 40 members. *Archives of Clinical Psychology, 20*(1), 33–65. doi:10.1016/j.acn.2004.02.005

Robinson, R. (Ed.). (2014). *Foundations of forensic vocational rehabilitation*. New York, NY: Springer Publishing Company.

Robinson, R., & Drew, J. L. (2014). Psychometric assessment in forensic vocational rehabilitation. In R. H. Robinson (Ed.), *Foundations of forensic vocational rehabilitation* (pp. 87–132). New York, NY: Springer Publishing Company.

Rubin, S. E., Roessler, R. T., & Rumrill, P. D. (2016). The role and function of the rehabilitation counselor. In S. E. Rubin, R. T. Roessler, & P. D. Rumrill (Eds.), *Foundations of the vocational process* (7th ed., pp. 249–266). Austin, TX: Pro-Ed.

Schultz, I. Z., & Gatchel, R. J. (2008). Research and practice directions in risk for disability prediction and early intervention. In I. Z. Schultz & R. J. Gatchel (Eds.), *Handbook of complex occupational disability claims: Early risk identification, intervention, and prevention* (pp. 523–539). New York, NY: Springer.

Shrey, D. E., & Lacerte, M. (1995). Worksite disability management and industrial rehabilitation: An overview. In D. S. Shrey & M. Lacerte (Eds.), *Principles and practices of disability management and industry* (pp. 3–53). Grand Rapids, MI: Grand Rapids Press.

Sleister, S. L. (2000). Separating the wheat from the chaff: The role of the vocational expert in forensic vocational rehabilitation. *Journal of Vocational Rehabilitation, 14*(2), 119–129.

Strauser, D. R. (2014). Career Development, Employment and Disability in Rehabilitation: From Theory to Practice. *The Journal of Rehabilitation, 80*(1), 45.

U.S. Department of Labor. (1991). *Revised handbook of analyzing jobs*. Washington, DC: U.S. Government Printing Office. Retrieved from https://skilltran.com/rhaj/rhaj1_2.pdf#page=4

U.S. Department of Labor. (2007). *OWCP procedure manual—Part 3 rehabilitation*. Retrieved from https://www.dol.gov/owcp/procedure-manual/rehab.pdf

U.S. Department of Labor. (2007). *U.S. Department of Labor Employment Standards Administration OWCP training manual*. (n.p.).

U.S. Department of Labor. (n.d.). *Vocational rehabilitation counselor handbook*. Retrieved from https://www.dol.gov/owcp/dfec/procedure-manual.htm

U.S. Employment Service. (1991). *Dictionary of occupational titles* (4th ed.). Washington, DC: Author.

Weed R. O., & Berens, D. E. (Eds.) (2018). *Life care planning and case management handbook* (4th ed.). New York, NY: Routledge.

Weed, R. O., & Field, T. F. (2012). *Rehabilitation consultant's handbook* (4th ed.). Athens, GA: Elliott & Fitzpatrick.

Weed, R. O., & Owen, T. R. (2018). *Life care planning: A step by step guide* (2nd ed.). Athens, GA: Elliott & Fitzpatrick.

Wilson, M. A. (2012). Methodological decisions in work analysis: A theory of effective work analysis in organizations. In M. A. Wilson, W. Bennet, Jr., S. G. Gibson, & G. M. Alliger (Eds.), *The handbook on work analysis: Methods, systems, applications and science of work measurement in organizations* (pp. 3–21). New York, NY: Taylor & Francis.

Wind, H., Gouttebarge, V., Kuijer, P. P. F. M., Sluiter, J. K., & Frings-Dresen, M. H. W. (2009). Effect of functional capacity evaluation information on the judgment of physicians about physical work ability in the context of disability claims. *International Archives of Occupational and Environmental Health, 82*(9), 1087–1096. doi:10.1007/s00420-009-0423-8

APPENDIX 14.1

SAMPLE VOCATIONAL ANALYSIS

January 4, 2016

RE: Mr. Raymond James
       751 Park Avenue   *DOB:* 7/9/1987
       Russellville, AR 71054   *D/A:* 5/1/2015

■ VOCATIONAL ANALYSIS

BACKGROUND INFORMATION

Mr. Raymond James, a 31-year-old man, was referred for the purpose of a vocational analysis. The vocational analysis sought to answer the following questions:

1. What vocational options are available to Mr. James to return to work with his current work-related capacities?

2. What is the estimated rate of pay for the available occupations?

The analysis consisted of a January 2016 interview with Mr. James, a review of labor market data, a review of available medical records, a transferable skills analysis, and vocational assessment.

Mr. James states that he sustained an injury to his left knee in the course of his employment as an electrician. He reports that he stepped into a manhole and felt pain in his knee. He was initially seen at a walk-in clinic where he was treated and released. He attempted to continue work but had ongoing complaints of pain and limited range of motion. He was seen at St. Mary's Medical Center where he underwent magnetic resonance imaging (MRI) of his left knee and was referred to Dr. Pearce, who diagnosed a torn anterior cruciate ligament (ACL). Mr. James underwent surgery in June 2015, which was complicated by a postsurgical infection. Mr. James has not returned to work since that time.

He currently resides with his wife and two children in Russellville, Arkansas.

DAILY ACTIVITIES

Mr. James indicated that he wakes up at 8 a.m. and goes to bed at approximately 10 p.m. to 12 a.m. He reports difficulty going to sleep at night. During the day, he is at home alone as his wife works and his children are in school. He performs basic household tasks, including laundry and sweeping, but does so using a rest–work cycle to avoid prolonged standing.

Mr. James reports the following physical capacities:

Walk: Up to 45 minutes
Sit: Up to 1 hour and then must stand
Stand: Up to 2–3 hours, then must sit
Lift: Up to 75–100 pounds
Drives: Up to 1 hour at a time
Dominant hand: Right

Mr. James reports pain as follows:

Location: Left knee
Severity: 6 on scale of 1–10
Experience of pain: Throbbing, burning pain
Pain treatment: Applies ice, elevates leg

Mr. James reports additional pain in his right knee from a previous injury and pain in his elbows and feet bilaterally from a 1996 motor vehicle crash.

SOCIOECONOMIC FACTORS

Marital status: Married
Children: Two, ages 5 and 7, in good health
Residence: One-story single-family home on normal city lot
Family member employment status: Mrs. James is employed as a school teacher
Compensation: Workers' compensation payments of $1,400 biweekly
Social Security Disability status: Has not applied
Driver's license: Valid Arkansas license
Transportation status: Vehicle available for transportation
Felony convictions: None
Drug/alcohol difficulty: None
U.S. citizen: Yes

PRE-EVENT MEDICAL HISTORY

Mr. James's history is negative for previous chronic health conditions or head injuries, and he had never before applied for disability benefits. He is a former smoker. He takes medication for hypertension. He sustained orthopedic injuries in a motor vehicle crash in 1996 requiring surgery to his left ankle, right leg, and right arm. He continued to have pain in his elbows and feet bilaterally. This pain did not prevent his work as an electrician. He underwent a kidney stone surgery in 2004.

POST-EVENT MEDICAL HISTORY

Mr. James received treatment from the following physicians:
Dr. John Pearce, orthopedic surgeon

He underwent surgery as follows:
June 4, 2015: ACL repair (left)

Mr. James is currently taking the following medications:
Gabapentin 100 mg: 2 per day
Tylenol PRN
Enalapril

OTC Prilosec
Xanax .25 mg PRN
Diclofenac 10 mg: 1 per day

Side effects include: None

EDUCATION

In 2005, Mr. James completed the 12th grade at Central High School in Little Rock, Arkansas. He earned average grades. After high school, he participated in training as an electrician, earning a journeyman electrician license in 2010. Mr. James is able to use a computer to send and receive email. He is able to prepare word processing documents but indicates that his typing is slow.

EMPLOYMENT HISTORY

Mr. James previously worked for American Electric in Russellville, Arkansas, as an electrician (824.261-010 ELECTRICIAN M/7). He worked there from 2007 until 2015, first as an apprentice, then as a journeyman electrician. As an electrician, his duties included pulling pipe and running conduit, wiring, and making electrical repairs. Physically, the job involved standing, walking, climbing up and down ladders, and lifting items including construction-related panels and conduit, which could weigh up to 150 pounds.

From 2005 until 2007, Mr. James was in the U.S. Army, where he worked as an electronics technician (828.261-022 ELECTRONICS MECHANIC-M/7) prior to his honorable discharge. He denies having service-connected disabilities.

TEST RESULTS AND INTERPRETATION

Mr. James completed the following assessment instruments:

Wide Range Achievement Test, Fourth Edition (WRAT-4)

The test measures academic achievement and compares results nationally according to age.

Test Area	Raw Score	Standard Score	Percentile	Grade Score
Word reading	58	94	34th	11.6
Sentence comprehension	45	95	37th	12.0
Math computation	41	93	32nd	8.7
Reading composite	189	93	32nd	–

Raven Standard Progressive Matrices (Untimed)

The test is designed to measure abstract reasoning, spatial perception, and learning ability.
Norm group: 30- to 35-year-old   Age: 31
53 correct of 60 attempted of 60 available = 90–92nd percentiles

Minnesota Clerical Test

This test is designed to measure elements of perceptual speed and accuracy of the type required to perform various clerical activities. The test has two parts: Number Comparison and Name Comparison.

| Name Comparison Raw Score: | 94 | (25th percentile) |
| Number Comparison Raw Score: | 91 | (25–30th percentiles) |

Norms Used: *Male applicants to banks*

Job Search Attitude Inventory (JSAI)

The Job Search Attitude Inventory was developed to meet the need for a brief measure of attitudes related to the job search process. The purpose of the JSAI is to provide systematic identification of attitudes related to one's job search.

Luck vs. Planning (LP Scale):	30 – High
Uninvolved vs. Involved (UI Scale):	32 – High
Help from Others vs. Self-Help:	32 – High
Passive vs. Active (PA Scale):	21 – Average
Pessimistic vs. Optimistic Scale:	27 – High

Career Occupational Preference Systems (COPS) Interest Inventory

Mr. James completed the Career Occupational Preference Systems (COPS) Interest Inventory. The purpose of the COPS is to measure level of interest in different occupational fields.

Results were highest in occupational areas related to:

Area	**Percentile**
Business, Professional	92

Sample occupations: Store manager, Cost estimator, Property manager

| Business, Skilled | 92 |

Sample occupations: Title examiner, Sales agent, Department manager

| Clerical | 92 |

Sample occupations: License clerk, General office clerk, Payroll clerk

| Science, Skilled | 85 |

Sample occupations: Meter reader, Medical assistant, Surveyor

| Communication | 75 |

Sample occupations: Editor, Postsecondary teacher, Lawyer

RETURN TO PREVIOUS EMPLOYMENT

Based on results of a January 14, 2016, functional capacity evaluation, Mr. James demonstrated the following work-related capacities:
Mr. James demonstrated a maximum occasional lift/carry of up to 95 pounds. He also demonstrated the ability to perform lifting/carrying of up to 50 pounds on a frequent basis and up to 20 pounds on a constant basis. He can:

Frequent: *Walking, Stooping, Climbing stairs*
Constant: *Reaching, Reaching overhead, Handling, Fingering, Standing, Sitting*
Occasional: *Crouching, Kneeling*

Mr. James completed functional testing on this date with reliable results. Overall, Mr. James demonstrated the ability to perform work in the heavy classification of work as defined by the U.S. Department of Labor's guidelines over the course of a normal workday with limitations as noted earlier.

Mr. James's work history has consisted of medium-level work, according to the *Dictionary of Occupational Titles* (DOT; see attachment for definitions). Therefore, with the abovementioned capacities, Mr. James should be able to return to past work.

TRANSFERABLE SKILLS ANALYSIS: *The process by which similar, related, or new jobs are identified for a person following injury or disability. These jobs are both consistent and compatible with previous work experience and fall within the range of residual postinjury functioning of the claimant* (Farnsworth et al., 2005).

A review of transferable skills was not performed because Mr. James' has the capacities to return to work as an electrician, his usual and customary occupation.

LABOR MARKET SURVEY: *A labor market survey is a method or approach to gathering relevant and appropriate information about jobs in a specific labor market* (Farnsworth et al., 2005).

Mr. James's area of residence, Russellville, Arkansas (and surrounding approximately 50 miles), was reviewed to determine the jobs that exist and their impact on his potential to return to work. Data reviewed for Faulkner County reflect a civilian labor force of 61,695 with 59,810 employed and 1,885 unemployed and an unemployment rate of 3.1%. This information was obtained from the County Labor Force Statistics, Arkansas Counties (January 2016).

VOCATIONAL IMPLICATIONS

At this time, Mr. James has undergone surgery complicated by a surgical infection and has demonstrated the capacity to perform work within the heavy physical demand level, with postural limitations as outlined in the 2016 FCE. It appears that Mr. James's previous work is within his demonstrated capacities in 2016. It is recommended that a return-to-work process be started with his employer. As Mr. James describes his current job, there may be duties that require lifting greater than outlined in the DOT. On January 17, 2016, a job description from American Electric was reviewed and lifting beyond 75 pounds was noted as a "nonessential function." Contact was made with Jennifer Sharp, HR manager, who noted that Mr. James typically works with an electrician helper and lifting beyond his functional capacities can be delegated to the helper.

SUMMARY

Mr. James's prior work has been almost exclusively as an electrician, which is rated as medium-level work. Following his injury, surgery, and physical therapy, he has demonstrated in January 2016 the physical capacities to perform his prior work. Contact was made with the HR manager at his former employer, who has agreed that nonessential lifting greater than 75 pounds can be delegated to the electrician helper who is assigned to work with Mr. James. Therefore, I am recommending coordination of return to work commence with the goal of returning Mr. James to his prior occupation as an electrician.

If I can be of further assistance, please do not hesitate to contact me.

Sincerely,

Tanya Rutherford Owen, PhD, CRC, CLCP, CDMS, LPC

RECORD REVIEW

The following medical records were reviewed:

1/14/2016   FCE, Stuart Jones, PT, DPT, CDA, CFE
Mr. James demonstrated a maximal occasional lift/carry of up to 95 pounds. He also demonstrated the ability to perform lifting/carrying of up to 50 pounds on a frequent basis and up to 20 pounds on a constant basis. He can perform the following:

Frequent: Walking, Stooping, Climbing stairs
Constant: Reading, Reaching overhead, Handling, Fingering, Standing, Sitting
Occasional: Crouching, Kneeling

1/11/2016   John Pearce, MD
FCE

11/14/2015   Campbell Clinic, John Pearce, MD
Unable to work. Continue therapy × 6 weeks, then work hardening × 4 weeks. Then FCWE.

10/15/2015   Martha Parker, PT, DPT
It recommended that the client attend rehabilitative therapy for three visits a week with an expected duration of 8 weeks.

10/5/2015   Martha Parker, PT, DPT
Patient will continue to benefit from skilled physical therapy (PT) addressing his decreased strength, endurance, and return-to-work duty.

9/17/2015   Martha Parker, PT, DPT
Patient is a 30-year-old man who presents to PT with c/o left knee pain. The patient has functional limitations in walking, working, bathing, bathroom using, and independent dressing, with a functional scale score of Lower Extremity Functional Scale (LEFS) of 7/80.
Work status: Unable to work secondary to dysfunction
Plan: The patient was instructed in the independent performance of a home exercise program that addresses the problems and will achieve the goals outlined in the plan of care.

9/12/2015   Martha Parker, PT
Patient presents to PT after left knee surgery. He has been unable to work since his injury.

Occupation job title: Electrician current status
Work status: Unable to work secondary to dysfunction.
It is recommended that the client attend rehabilitative therapy for three visits a week with an expected duration of 6 weeks.

9/7/2015   Martha Parker, PT, DPT
Patient needs more PT to increase lower extremity (LE) strength and increase range of motion (ROM) to LE.

9/7/2015   John Pearce, MD
I am going to allow the patient to begin to weight bear as tolerated today.

8/22/2015   John Pearce, MD
Today, his incision is without signs of infection. I am going to plan to see him back in 2 weeks. At that point in time, we can go ahead with two view x-ray.

8/9/2015   Mark Adams, MD
No further specific treatment is indicated at this time. He will return to see me on an as-needed basis.
8/8/2015   John Pearce, MD

IV

ISSUES IN ASSESSMENT

TESTING ACCOMMODATIONS

MYKAL J. LESLIE | PHILLIP D. RUMRILL

LEARNING OBJECTIVES

After reviewing this chapter, the reader should be able to:

- Understand the nature and purpose of testing accommodations in educational, human services, and employment settings.
- Be aware of the legal, ethical, and procedural issues related to the provision of testing accommodations.
- Be familiar with the wide range of testing accommodations that are used with people with various disabilities.
- Identify reasonable testing accommodations based on practice setting and individual client needs.

▨ Introduction

The concept of accommodation for disability-related limitations is a central theme in all aspects of the rehabilitation counseling process (Job Accommodation Network [JAN], 2019; Rubin, Roessler, & Rumrill, 2016). Rehabilitation counselors assist people with disabilities in modifying their work environments, their educational programs, and their community activities in ways that allow them to achieve their goals. At times, the accommodation is implemented in an environmentally specific context (e.g., use of closed captioning during a television program or a movie), and at other times, the accommodation stays with the person across situations and activities (e.g., use of a wheelchair to facilitate mobility). With regard to employment, reasonable accommodations are defined under the Americans with Disabilities Act (ADA) as "any change to the application or hiring process, to the job, to the way the job is done, or the work environment that allows a person with a disability who is qualified for the job to perform the essential functions of that job and enjoy equal employment opportunities" (ADA National Network, 2018). For accommodations to qualify as "reasonable," they must not create an undue hardship to the employer or constitute a "direct threat" to the safety of the person using the accommodation or other people (ADA National Network, 2018).

This same expectation for reasonable accommodation applies within the context of testing and assessment. In fact, testing accommodations should be seen as a direct application of a rehabilitation counselor's duty to accommodate a person with a disability (Power, 2013; Rubin et al., 2016). Assessment can be an important component of the job acquisition process, as it may be necessary for obtaining needed educational credentials, entrance into college or technical school, licensing exams, driver's license exams, and typing tests. Assessment can also be vital in the vocational planning process through measuring vocational interests, values, and aptitudes in an effort to help consumers discern appropriate vocational goals.

According to U.S. Department of Justice (DoJ) regulations (U.S. Department of Justice, Civil Rights Division, Disability Right Section, 2015), testing accommodations are defined as "changes to the regular testing environment and auxiliary aids and services that allow individuals with disabilities to demonstrate their true aptitude or achievement level on standardized exams or other high-stakes tests." Perhaps most important within that definition is defining "true aptitude," that is, attempting to measure the person's skills and abilities, not her or his disability. Use of unaccommodated assessments that reveal disability-related limitations without reflecting the person's true aptitudes is known as construct-irrelevant variance. With the emphasis on high-stakes tests as gateways to both educational and employment opportunities, it is important to note that the definition of testing accommodations and corresponding legal mandates for such accommodations are not limited to assessments used in traditional academic settings. As rehabilitation counselors are increasingly working with consumers at both ends of the age spectrum (from age 14 and up and subsequently into and beyond retirement age), it is important to examine testing accommodations across the life span in educational, clinical, community, and employment settings.

Defining what a test accommodation is not is just as important as defining what one is. A test accommodation is not a test modification. Drawing yet another parallel between general rehabilitation counseling practice and accommodating tests, consider the example of accommodating a job task. Under the ADA, an accommodation cannot fundamentally alter the requirements of a job, but rather accommodations should reduce the functional limitations to completing a given job task that are a product of a person's disability and her or his work environment. Similarly, a valid testing accommodation does not change the content, format, constructs, or results of the assessment, but rather accommodates the test administration, environment, equipment, technology, or procedures (Salend, 2008). The difference between a test accommodation and a modification to the test itself can be subtle. For example, provision of a qualified reader for an elementary student on a reading test may change the nature of the test and what is being measured, whereas that same accommodation might be appropriate for that student on a mathematics test that is not designed to assess the student's reading abilities (Salend, 2008).

▨ Policy and Law

Testing accommodations have gained increased attention in recent years owing to an increased reliance on testing in educational and employment settings. This trend in reliance on standardized testing is reflected in the legislation that has served to increase access to equal assessment practices for persons with disabilities. In order to understand current guidelines and requirements in the United States for test accommodations, first we must examine the legislative foundations for today's practices.

Testing accommodations, as a form of reasonable accommodation, have been historically supported by constitutional and statutory law in the United States. Provision of testing accommodations was documented as early as the 1930s for persons with disabilities taking the Scholastic Aptitude Test (SAT). In 1946, the U.S. Civil Service Commission examined how to fairly test the job-related abilities of candidates with disabilities (Pitoniak & Royer, 2001). The Civil Service Commission would go on to investigate how to adapt tests for persons with visual impairments in the 1950s, recognizing the impact of disability on the validity of measurement instruments. However, it was not until the Rehabilitation Act of 1973 was enacted that these policies and practices were formalized and mandated by law. The Rehabilitation Act of 1973, the ADA of 1990, the ADA Amendments Act of 2008 (ADAAA), and the Individuals with Disabilities in Education Act (IDEA) are the core articles of legislation that have shaped assessment accommodation practice (Fuller & Wehman, 2003; Lovett, 2014; Niebling & Elliott, 2005; Pitoniak & Royer, 2001).

Rehabilitation Act of 1973

Testing accommodations have been mandated for persons with disabilities since the Rehabilitation Act of 1973, specifically Section 504 of the law. Section 504 requires that accommodations be made in any program or activity receiving federal financial assistance so that persons with disabilities are provided with equal access and opportunities to participate. Section 504 explicitly prohibits tests that discriminate against persons with disabilities who are otherwise qualified to participate in the programs for which the tests are given. Also prohibited under the Rehabilitation Act, the ADA, and the ADAAA are selection criteria that are used to screen job candidates with disabilities if the criteria are not directly job related. New research into how to provide valid testing accommodations, specifically for persons with hearing and motor impairments, was conducted in the wake of the passage of the Rehabilitation Act of 1973 (Fischer, 1994; Pitoniak & Royer, 2001).

Americans with Disabilities Act

Even though these accommodations had been mandated by the Rehabilitation Act of 1973, they were not widely used until the passage of the ADA of 1990 (Fuller & Wehman, 2003). Further, the ADA expanded the previous protections afforded to persons with disabilities in the public sector to the private sector (Pitoniak & Royer, 2001). Although the purpose of the ADA was protecting the civil rights of persons with disabilities as a whole, access to equal and equitable educational and employment opportunities was one of the main focal points. Owing to the critical nature of assessment in these realms, the ADA explicitly stated the following with regard to assessment:

> *a private entity offering an examination . . . is responsible for selecting and administering the examination in a place and manner that ensures that the examination accurately reflects an individual's aptitude or achievement level, or other factors that the examination purports to measure, rather than reflecting [an] individual's impaired sensory, manual, or speaking skills, except where those skills are the factors that the examination purports to measure.* (29 C.F.R. § 1630.10, 2018)

Under the ADA and the subsequent ADAAA, there are only four specific circumstances under which an entity is allowed to refuse to provide testing accommodations to a person with a disability. As noted by Fuller and Wehman (2003), those circumstances include cases in which the area of impairment is what is being measured by the assessment, the accommodation fundamentally alters the measurement of the targeted skill, the provision of the accommodation results in an undue hardship for the testing agency, or the person with the disability refuses the accommodation.

The other nuance to accommodation provision is that the person must have a disability as defined by the ADA. Critical to this definition was the passage of the ADAAA of 2008.

Dissatisfied with the narrow interpretation of disability by the court system under ADA, the Congress passed the ADAAA in order to broaden and expand its coverage to fulfill the original intent of the ADA (Lovett, 2014). The implications of ADAAA on test accommodations have been numerous, primarily stemming from the 2011 guidelines developed by the DoJ Civil Rights Division regarding implementation of the ADAAA. In a review of these DoJ guidelines (which carry the force of law), Lovett (2014) noted three main points that are directly related to the issue of testing accommodations. The regulations require:

1. that testing entities' requests for disability documentation be "reasonable and limited to the need for;"

2. that when testing entities consider applicants' requests for accommodations, the entities give "considerable weight to documentation of past" accommodations, including those from the individualized education programs (IEPs) used in special education; and

3. that testing entities respond "in a timely manner to requests" for accommodations (pp. 81–82).

In addition, the guidelines emphasize that the testing entities should place a high degree of trust in the diagnoses and recommendations made by applicants' clinical evaluators and should defer to applicants' past use of particular accommodations or aids, placing particularly high priority on the decisions made by K-12 within the IEPs and Section 504 Plans (Lovett, 2014).

Individuals with Disabilities Education Improvement Act

Nowhere has standardized assessment become more impactful than in education. The Individuals with Disabilities Education Improvement Act of 2004 (IDEA) is the guiding piece of legislation providing protections for the more than 6.7 million students with disabilities (13% of children aged 3–21 years) in the United States (National Center for Education Statistics [NCES], 2018). IDEA, originally the Education for All Handicapped Children Act of 1975, was first revised in 1991, and subsequently reauthorized and updated in 1997 and in 2004 (Lai & Berkeley, 2012; Pitoniak & Royer, 2001). IDEA requires that students with disabilities are afforded the same access to public education as those without disabilities. IDEA mandates that each student with a disability is entitled to an IEP that denotes a specialized plan of service based on her or his specific functional limitation(s). As assessments are an integral element of the U.S. educational system, IDEA explicitly mandates that students receive needed testing accommodations, specifically with large-scale assessments from which students with disabilities were often previously excluded (Pitoniak & Royer, 2001).

The exclusion of students with disabilities from statewide assessments was problematic on a number of levels. First and foremost, it reinforced low expectations for students with disabilities and increased referrals to special education, further segregating them from students without disabilities in important parts of the educational process. Second, it resulted in inaccurate school performance data that were not reflective of the schools' performance with special education programs (National Council on Disability [NCD], 2018). The 1997 reauthorization of IDEA was the first law to require that students with disabilities be included in state assessment systems, attempting to both raise expectations for students with disabilities and hold schools accountable for the academic outcomes of students with disabilities (NCD, 2018). Schools were able to create alternative assessments only for students whose disabilities were "too severe" for inclusion in the same large-scale assessments (NCD, 2018; Niebling & Elliott, 2005).

Every Student Succeeds Act

In 2001, the Congress reauthorized the Elementary and Secondary Schools Act of 1994 (ESEA), renaming it the No Child Left Behind Act (NCLB). NCLB, active from 2001 through 2015, further stipulated assessment requirements for students with disabilities. NCLB mandated that students with disabilities be held to the same standards as those without disabilities, that schools publicly report the performance of students with disabilities, and that schools be held accountable for their performance just as any other subgroup of students (NCD, 2018; Niebling & Elliott, 2005). The effort to include students with disabilities in testing programs was further bolstered by the language in the 2004 iteration of IDEA (Lai & Berkeley, 2012).

Through improvements in inclusion of students with disabilities through accommodations in these large-scale assessments, their dropout rates saw a sharp decrease from 33.6% in 2003 to 18.5% in 2014 (NCD, 2018). Still, the system was not without flaws and widespread criticism of schools "gaming the system" (e.g., using alternative assessments for some students with disabilities and counting their inflated scores on those assessments; NCD, 2018). In response to the shortcomings of NCLB, the Congress replaced NCLB with the Every Student Succeeds Act of 2015 (ESSA). With regard to testing accommodations, ESSA reinforces the mandates that states must provide accommodations to students with disabilities on the annual assessments and must list the accommodations within the students' IEPs and Section 504 Plans. ESSA only allows 1% of students with disabilities to take alternate tests, requiring that those tests are also accommodated accordingly (NCD, 2018).

Standards and Ethics

The ethical principle of justice is seen throughout these laws, evoking the foundations laid by the Equal Protection Clause of the 14th Amendment to the U.S. Constitution, which suggests that each member of society should be entitled to equal protection under the law (Fordham Law Review, 1963; Pitoniak & Royer, 2001). Although the various mandates within the laws reviewed in this chapter attempt to legislate this principle in various circumstances, standards and codes of ethics often go one step beyond, creating both minimum requirements and best practices that entities utilizing assessments should adhere to in order to ensure both validity and fairness within their assessment procedures. In this section, we review selected ethical guidelines and requirements pertaining to testing accommodations.

In an effort to emphasize the importance of providing testing accommodations to persons with disabilities, the American Educational Research Association (AERA), the American Psychological Association (APA), and the National Council on Measurement in Education (NCME) devoted an entire chapter to testing persons with disabilities within their 1985 *Standards for Educational and Psychological Testing* (also known as the *Joint Standards*). The chapter entitled "Testing People Who Have Handicapping Conditions" contained eight different standards specific to testing accommodations. It included examples of common accommodations for persons with specific limitations and provided details about frequent issues encountered in the provision of such accommodations (Pitoniak & Royer, 2001). The *Joint Standards* have since been revised (1999 and 2014), with the most recent 2014 edition placing increased emphasis on broadening the concept of accessibility of tests for all examinees (Plake & Wise, 2014).

In accordance with the *Joint Standards*, the *Code of Fair Testing Practices in Education* was released by the Joint Committee on Testing Practices (JCTP) in 1988 and then updated in 2004. The JCTP comprised seven organizations, including the three aforementioned organizations responsible for the standards (AERA, APA, and NCME) along with the American Counseling Association (ACA), American Speech-Language-Hearing Association (ASHA), National Association of School Psychologists (NASP), and National Association of Assessment Directors (NAAD). The code is meant to be a "guide for professionals in fulfilling their obligation to provide and use tests that are fair to all test takers regardless of age, gender, disability, race, ethnicity, national origin, religion, sexual orientation, linguistic background, or other personal characteristics" (JCTP, 2004, p. 2). It applies broadly to testing in education, but was not intended to apply to employment testing, licensure or certification testing, or other types of testing outside the field of education. The code generally includes recommendations for test developers and test users on how to develop and select appropriate tests, administer and score tests, report and interpret test results, and inform test-takers (JCTP, 2004). Accommodations are explicitly mentioned in Section A (developing and selecting appropriate tests) and Standard 8 for test users ("Select tests with appropriately modified forms or administration procedures for test takers with disabilities who need special accommodations," JCTP, 2004, p. 5).

For an in-depth examination of how an organization administers educational assessments on a large scale, we elected to review the standards set forth by the Educational Testing Service (ETS). ETS is a nonprofit educational testing organization that administers assessments such as the SAT, the Graduate Record Examination (GRE), the Praxis, and the Test of English as a Foreign Language (TOEFL; Educational Testing Service [ETS], 2019). ETS most recently published the *ETS Standards for Quality and Fairness* (SQF) in 2014. ETS described the purpose of SQF as "to help . . . design, develop, and deliver technically sound, fair, accessible, and useful products and services, and to help auditors evaluate those products and services" (ETS, 2014, p. 2). ETS noted that the SQF intentionally strives to be consistent with the *Joint Standards*; however, it is "far less redundant" and is intended for use by the ETS staff (ETS, 2014, p. 2). The SQF comprehensively outlines the responsibility and duties of ETS to develop, select, administer, score, and interpret assessments in a fair and accessible manner.

Of particular interest with regard to testing accommodations in the SQF is Chapter 5 (Fairness), Chapter 9 (Test Administration), and Chapter 13 (Test-Takers' Rights and Responsibilities; ETS, 2014). Chapter 5 addresses pervasive issues of fairness across the assessment process, and Standard 5:5 is specific to providing accommodations and modifications. Standard 5.5 states,

Tests and test delivery and response modes should be accessible to as many test takers as feasible. It will, however, sometimes be necessary to make accommodations or modifications to increase the accessibility of the test for some test takers. If relevant to the testing program, tell test takers how to request and document the need for the accommodation or modification. Provide the necessary accommodations or modifications at no additional cost to the test taker. The accommodations or modifications should be designed to ensure, to the extent possible, that the test measures the intended construct rather than irrelevant sources of variation. If feasible, and if sufficient sample sizes are available, use empirical information to help determine the accommodation or modification to be made (ETS, 2014, pp. 21–22).

In addition, Standard 9.3 explicitly addresses providing appropriate testing environments with focus on making locations reasonable accessible by means of appropriate temperature control, reasonable furniture, adequate lighting, and low noise levels. Finally, Standard 13.2 addresses the need to provide access and information to all test-takers with respectful and impartial treatment, which includes how to request appropriate accommodations (ETS, 2014).

Having reviewed common standards in the areas of educational and psychological testing, we now turn to examination of standards specifically relevant to assessment within employment settings. The two main guidelines of note in the employment arena include the assessment guide published by the U.S. Department of Labor Employment and Training Administration and the principles established by the Society for Industrial and Organizational Psychology (SIOP). We begin by examining the Department of Labor (DoL) guide, *Testing and Assessment: An Employer's Guide to Good Practices* (henceforth referred to as the Guide).

The Guide, developed in 2000, was designed to assist managers and human resource (HR) professionals in evaluating and selecting assessment tools and procedures, administering and scoring assessment tools, accurately interpreting assessment results, and understanding the professional and legal standards relevant to conducting personnel assessment (U.S. Department of Labor, Employment and Training Administration [DoL], 2000). It contains 13 principles of the assessment process throughout the Guide, covering a critical issue of assessment in each of its 9 chapters. The Guide begins by reviewing the purpose of personnel assessment and the laws and regulations governing assessment in employment, including the pieces of legislation previously reviewed in this chapter, such as the ADA and its implications for assessment practice. Chapter 6, Administering Assessment Instruments, is most relevant to this discussion of accommodations, as it devotes sections to ensuring suitable and uniform assessment conditions; how much help to offer test-takers, test anxiety, and alternative assessment methods for special cases; and providing reasonable accommodations in the assessment process to people with disabilities (DoL, 2000). Section 6.7 of the Guide, providing reasonable accommodations, states,

> Accommodation in the assessment process may involve ensuring physical accessibility to the test site, modifying test equipment or tests, or providing qualified assistance. Giving extra time on certain kinds of tests to test takers with dyslexia or other learning disability, and administering a larger print version of a test to a person who is visually impaired are examples of reasonable accommodation. Note, however, that providing a reader for a reading comprehension test, or extra time for a speeded test could invalidate the test results. You should become familiar with what accommodations can be made for different conditions or circumstances without invalidating the test. Provide all test takers with descriptive information about the test in advance, so that they will have ample opportunity to request needed accommodations. When the need for accommodation is not obvious, you may ask for reasonable documentation of the disability and functional limitations for which accommodation is needed... If an accommodation cannot be made without invalidating the test, alternative assessment strategies, such as a review of past job experience, a review of school records, or a brief job tryout, must be considered (DoL, 2000, pp. 6–4, 6–5).

In 2003, SIOP, a division of APA, released the fourth edition of the employment analogue to the *Joint Standards*, the *Principles for the Validation and Use of Personnel Selection Procedures* (the *Principles*; SIOP, 2003). The *Principles* were developed to "specify established scientific findings and generally accepted professional practice in the field of personnel selection psychology in the choice, development, evaluation, and use of personnel selection procedures designed to measure constructs related to work behavior with a focus on the accuracy of the inferences that underlie employment decisions" (SIOP, 2003, p. 1). The *Principles* are intended to be used as a decision-making tool, intentionally consistent with the *Joint Standards*.

The final section of the *Principles* is dedicated to assessment for candidates with disabilities. Subsections include responsibilities of the selection procedure, development and validation, documentation and communications regarding accommodations, selection procedure modifications, and maintaining consistency with assessments used in the organization (SIOP, 2003). With regard to rehabilitation consumers, the *Principles* indicate that

> *Assessing candidates with disabilities may require special accommodations that deviate from standardized procedures. Accommodations are made to minimize the impact of a known disability that is not relevant to the construct being assessed. For example, an individual's upper extremity motor impairment may affect a score on a measure of cognitive ability although the motor impairment is not related to the individual's cognitive ability. Accommodations may include, but are not limited to, modifications to the environment (e.g., high desks), medium (e.g., Braille, reader), time limit, or content. Combinations of accommodations may be required to make valid inferences regarding the candidate's ability on the construct(s) of interest* (SIOP, 2003, p. 59).

To conclude this section, we review the pertinent provisions of the code of ethics for certified rehabilitation counselors (CRCs). The Commission on Rehabilitation Counselor Certification (CRCC, 2017) maintains and enforces the CRCC Code of Ethics to ensure that CRCs provide quality services to persons with disabilities. Section G of the 2017 Code of Ethics, Assessment and Evaluation, provides a detailed explanation of the responsibilities of rehabilitation counselors in the comprehensive assessment process. Standard G.6.A (Test/Instrument Administration Conditions: Standard Conditions) specifically addresses the importance of accommodating persons with disabilities in the assessment process:

> *Rehabilitation counselors administer tests/instruments according to the parameters described in the publishers' manuals. When tests/instruments are not administered under standard conditions, as may be necessary to accommodate clients with disabilities or when unusual behavior or irregularities occur during the administration, those conditions are noted in the interpretation, and the results may be designated as invalid or of questionable validity* (CRCC, 2017, p. 21).

Psychometric Challenges

Although many professionals view the provision of testing accommodations from an ethical perspective as the "right" or "fair" way of conducting assessments, testing accommodations have also been rigorously evaluated for their psychometric impact. All assessment procedures strive to ensure the validity of their instruments, that the test is measuring the construct that it was designed to measure both accurately and reliably (Power, 2013). Specific populations such as persons with disabilities and non-native speakers of English can introduce confounds to the validity of assessments if the assessment was not properly designed and normed and if appropriate accommodations were not provided in the test-taking process (Lane & Leventhal, 2015). For the purpose of this chapter, we focus on the latter, accommodating persons with disabilities in the testing process.

Two frequently cited threats to validity for persons with disabilities along with English-Language Learners (ELLs) are construct underrepresentation and construct-irrelevant variance (Camara, 2009; Lane & Leventhal, 2015). That is, at times something is left out of an assessment that should be included (construct underrepresentation) and in other situations something that should have been excluded from the construct was included (construct-irrelevant variance). For example, a reading test administered orally to a student who is blind or a listening comprehension test administered in text to a student with a hearing impairment are both the examples of construct underrepresentation. Giving an ELL an assessment not in his or her dominant language is another example of construct underrepresentation. Construct-irrelevant variance is more commonly the issue that occurs when assessing persons with disabilities, often resulting from a lack of accommodations (Camara, 2009; Lane & Leventhal, 2015). Examples include not providing a qualified reader for a test-taker who has a specific learning disability such as dyslexia, or not providing a sign language interpreter to translate verbal instructions on an exam to a person who is deaf and uses American Sign Language (ASL). In both cases, the assessment would not be measuring what it was intended to directly measure, but rather would be heavily skewed by the presence of the aforementioned functional limitations (Lane & Leventhal, 2015).

On the other hand, some discussions regarding testing accommodations have centered on whether the presence of accommodations, in certain cases, invalidates the test results by fundamentally altering the measurement of the targeted skill, or by creating a situation wherein the area of impairment is what is being measured by the assessment. In the past, guidelines even instructed test administrators to document the accommodations given on an exam along with the score to denote the potential that the accommodations may have skewed the results. Although this is no longer recommended practice owing to the potential for bias and breach in confidentiality, there are still concerns about persons "cheating the system" through use of accommodations (Lai & Berkeley, 2012; Lane & Leventhal, 2015; Niebling & Elliott, 2005; Pitoniak & Royer, 2001). Measurement invariance is the idea that a test remains similar across all subgroups who are being assessed, measuring the same construct(s) across subgroups (Lane & Leventhal, 2015). The argument against accommodation or for more selective accommodation provision typically centers on accommodations being a threat to measurement invariance, therefore creating an "unfair advantage" for persons receiving accommodations. Commonly cited concerns include variability in the accommodations being provided, accommodations being provided in situations in which they were not needed, ease of feigning evidence needed to receive accommodations, and lack of supporting evidence in granting accommodations (Lovett, 2014; Lai & Berkeley, 2012; Niebling & Elliott, 2005).

The extant research supporting valid use of accommodations in assessment relies heavily on the interaction hypothesis and the presence of a "differential boost" (Lai & Berkeley, 2012; Niebling & Elliott, 2005; Sireci, Scarpati, & Li, 2005). Many controlled studies have demonstrated that, when administered appropriately, accommodations lead to much greater score improvements for persons with disabilities relative to those without disabilities (Lane & Leventhal, 2015, 2001; Sireci et al., 2005). In other words, accommodations can significantly positively impact the test scores of persons with disabilities, whereas the same accommodations often have little to no impact on the scores of persons without disabilities. This is the basis of the interaction hypothesis, and the phenomenon is often referred to in literature as a "differential boost" (Sireci et al., 2005). Often in controlled studies examining this phenomenon, both persons with and those without disabilities will be given an assessment without accommodations as a baseline measure; both groups will then be given the same assessment, this time with accommodations. The differential boost is documented if the accommodations significantly increase the scores of those with disabilities while simultaneously having no significant impact on those without disabilities (Lane & Leventhal, 2015, 2001; Sireci et al., 2005). It should be noted, however, that the Rehabilitation Act and the ADA and subsequent ADAAA do not afford people without disabilities the legal right to testing or other accommodations; those laws expressly stipulate that accommodations are warranted *only* if the applicant, student, employee, or examinee has a documented or documentable disability (Rubin et al., 2016).

■ Types of Test Accommodations

Accommodations are often categorized by type according to the strategy used in implementing the accommodation. The four accommodation categories most commonly cited are those pertaining to presentation, response, timing, and setting (Pitoniak & Royer, 2001). In the following paragraphs, we describe each category and provide examples.

Presentation

Accommodations in this category include those in which the presentation of the assessment material is modified to assist the person with any particular barrier she or he might have in accessing the material in the standard format. Some common examples of presentation accommodations include having the test administrator read the material aloud, having the instructions repeated, using enlarged print or braille for persons with visual impairment, listening to an audio version of the text, and using written or signed test directions in place of oral direction for persons with hearing impairments (Pitoniak & Royer, 2001). Other presentation-mode accommodations include listing directions in sequential order; highlighting any changes in directions; using closed-captioning or pictorially based tests; using reminders; highlighting key words or phrases; placing few items on a page; and using graphics, tactile and photo-enlarged materials, and color acetate overlays (Salend, 2008).

In a national meta-analysis of research on accommodations in high-stakes testing, Lai and Berkeley (2012) found multiple studies providing evidence that the use of reading aloud produces a differential boost in scores for students with disabilities. State policy across the United States was also examined, revealing that there were 23 different presentation accommodations mentioned in state testing manuals across the United States, with low-vision aids and colored overlays being the most frequently allowed. There was significant variability in policies on read-aloud accommodations, with 8 states allowing the accommodation without restriction and 21 states prohibiting reading aloud on the reading section (Lai & Berkeley, 2012).

Response

Response accommodations specifically adjust the manner in which the test-taker answers or responds to the assessment being administered. This can be done through use of technology or through use of an aid to assist in responding. These also include use of reference aids, such as a glossary or a calculator. For persons with functional limitations in written or oral communication, this may include use of a computer (with or without spell-check software), use of speech-to-text dictation software, or having a qualified aide acts as a scribe or notetaker (Pitoniak & Royer, 2001). Additional response-mode accommodations for consideration include providing extra space, using lined/grid paper, using enlarged answer bubbles/blocks, allowing writing answers on the test/test booklet, and embedding error minimization techniques (Salend, 2008). The limited research on response accommodations in high-stakes testing has demonstrated that, for persons with disabilities, speech recognition software had a moderately positive effect, whereas utilization of dictation through a scribe showed a larger positive impact (Lai & Berkeley, 2012). As for availability, most states allowed assistive technology (35), answers to be marked directly on the test booklet (30), and use of scribes without restrictions (37; Lai & Berkeley, 2012).

Timing

Modifications of timing are among the most widely debated types of testing accommodations (Spenceley & Wheeler, 2016). There are several different methods for providing test-takers with timing accommodations and a wide variety of reasons that a person may require such an accommodation. The most common types of timing adjustments include giving a person extended time to complete the assessment, allowing frequent breaks during the assessment process, and spreading the assessment across multiple days (Pitoniak & Royer, 2001). Other examples include shorter versions of tests, eliminating items/sections, or adjusting the test order (Salend, 2008). Lai and Berkeley (2012) found that timing accommodations such as extended time and spreading the test over multiple sessions demonstrated a differential boost in scores for students with disabilities. In addition, the researchers discovered that, although seven different timing accommodations were included across state manuals, extended time and frequent breaks were the accommodations used most frequently.

Setting

Setting or location accommodations are changes to the physical environment in which the assessment is administered in order to reduce the impact of a barrier or limitation. These include ensuring that the environment is physically accessible, for a person who uses a wheelchair, for example, but also include noise and temperature concerns (Pitoniak & Royer, 2001). Some specific examples of setting accommodations include access to noise-cancelling headphones, a quiet room, individual or small group administration, altering lighting or temperature, specific seating arrangements, adaptive furniture, and acoustics/sound amplification (Salend, 2008). For high-stakes tests, 16 different setting accommodations were found across all state testing manuals. Most states allow students with disabilities individualized or small group test administration (34), along with specific equipment such as adaptive furniture, study carrels, special lighting, and noise buffers (37; Lai & Berkeley, 2012).

Additional Accommodations

At times, test administrators will decide to use only parts of a test or use an alternate assessment, which can be seen as unique accommodation categories. The aforementioned categories also do not include linguistic-based accommodations that are commonly helpful for ELLs. An alternate categorization was proposed by Elliott, Kratochwill, and Schulte (1998) in their helpful resource, the Assessment Accommodation Checklist. The checklist further separates the accommodations categories to form eight types of accommodations that vary based on circumstance and the person. The eight categories include assistance prior to administering the test, motivational accommodations, scheduling accommodations, setting accommodations, assistance with test direction, assistance during the assessment, equipment or assistive technology, and test format accommodations (Elliott et al., 1998). Of note is the inclusion of motivational accommodations, which do not fit neatly into any of the four main accommodation types. These include providing treats/snacks/prizes to test-takers, providing verbal encouragement, encouraging a test-taker to sustain effort longer, and encouraging a test-taker to remain on task (Elliott et al., 1998).

◼ What Types of Tests Require Accommodations?

In general, a person with a disability may request an accommodation for any assessment (JAN, 2019). The DoJ technical assistance manual on ADA testing accommodations (DoJ, 2015) specifically denotes that "exams administered by any private, state, or local government entity related to applications, licensing, certification, or credentialing for secondary or postsecondary education, professional, or trade purposes are covered by the ADA and testing accommodations pursuant to the ADA, must be provided" (p. 2). Common examples of tests that meet these criteria include high school equivalency exams (e.g., General Equivalency Diploma [GED]), high school entrance exams (e.g., Secondary School Admission Test [SSAT] or Independent School Entrance Examination [ISEE]), college entrance exams (e.g., ACT or SAT), exams for admission to professional schools (e.g., Law School Admission Test [LSAT] or Medical College Admission Test [MCAT]), admissions exams for graduates schools (Graduate Record Examinations [GRE] or Graduate Management Admission Test [GMAT]), and licensing exams for trade purposes (e.g., cosmetology and electrician) or professional purposes (e.g., bar exams or medical licensing exams; DoJ, 2015). The caveat is that this guidance does not address how these requirements or protections apply to, or interact with, administration of statewide and district-wide assessments to students with disabilities in a public K-12 setting (DoJ, 2015).

Public K-12 Education

As previously discussed, IDEA is the preeminent federal legislation applying to students with disabilities in a public education setting. While IDEA mandates that test accommodations are provided to students, the amount and types of accommodations allowed are determined on a state level (Christensen, Braam, Scullin, & Thurlow, 2011; Lai & Berkeley, 2012). The passage of ESSA in 2015 returned more power to the states, as well as the individual school districts and parents in the aftermath of NCLB. ESSA requires states to accommodate students with disabilities on the annual assessments and to list those accommodations within the students' IEPs and Section 504 Plans (NCD, 2018). Of primary concern in this setting is how high-stakes tests are accommodated, given the substantial power given to these exams in subsequent educational decisions. These policies do not reflect how schools and teachers accommodate students for in-class exams given throughout a course, which are largely accommodated based upon student IEPs and Section 504 Plans. There tends to be substantial variability across states in how these accommodations are implemented. Examination of state accommodation policies revealed that there were states that allowed all students access to all available accommodations, some only allowed accommodations to students with specific qualifications (IEPs, 504 Plans, etc.), and some states allowed some access to accommodations to all students and access to all accommodations for students with disabilities (Christensen et al., 2011; Lai & Berkeley, 2012).

Entrance/Admission and Licensure Exams

As mentioned, the ADA requires that all high school entrance, college entrance, professional school admission, graduate school admission, and licensure exams be administered with accommodations, in accordance with ADA. The ADA Title III Technical Assistance Manual (ADA, 2010) specifies that "any private entity that offers examinations or courses related to applications, licensing, certification, or credentialing for secondary or postsecondary education, professional, or trade purposes shall offer such examinations or courses in a place and manner accessible to persons with disabilities or offer alternative accessible arrangements for such individuals" (§ 36.309). The test administration agencies are required to assure that the exams reflect the person's aptitude or achievement (rather than her or his disability), that exams designed for those with impairments are offered in a timely manner at equally convenient locations, that the facilities where the exams are offered are accessible, that any request for documentation is reasonable and limited to the need for accommodation, that considerable weight is given to past accommodations, and that the testing entity responds to requests for accommodations in a timely manner (ADA, 2010). The following three illustrations adapted from the Title III Technical Assistance Manual (ADA, 2010) provide insight into these regulations:

1. Jones Testing Service provides a reader for an applicant who is blind who is taking a bar examination, but the reader is unfamiliar with specific terminology used in the examination, mispronounces words, and, because he or she does not understand the questions, is unable to convey the information in the questions or to follow the applicant's instructions effectively. Because of the difficulty in communicating with the reader, the applicant is unable to complete the examination. Jones Testing Service is not in compliance with the ADA because the results of the examination will reflect the reader's lack of skill and familiarity with the material, rather than the applicant's knowledge.

2. A nurse licensing examination is administered in a warm, well-lit, second-floor classroom that is not accessible to a person who uses a wheelchair. The Nursing Board may allow that person to take the test in a classroom or office on the first floor that is accessible, but must ensure that the accessible room is also well-lit and has adequate heat.

3. A college entrance examination is offered by Pittman Testing Service in several cities in a large state, but only one location has either an accessible facility or an alternative accessible facility. David, a person who uses a wheelchair, lives near an inaccessible test location at which no alternative accessible facility is provided. The nearest test location with an accessible facility is 300 miles away. Pittman Testing Service has violated the ADA because David is required to travel a longer distance to take the examination than other people who can take the examination in the city that is most convenient for them (§ 36.309).

Fuller and Wehman (2003) noted the significant impact of ensuring that these types of exams are accommodated appropriately given the significant implications of potential lost educational and employment opportunities for persons with disabilities. To illustrate, the authors conducted an in-depth examination of accommodation policies of college entrance exams (i.e., the ACT and the SAT) for persons with disabilities. Owing to the competitive nature of college entrance, both organizations administering these exams have separate, but stringent policies on access to accommodations, especially extended time, which has been shown to provide a substantial differential boost for persons with disabilities (Fuller & Wehman, 2003). Traditionally, the question structure of the SAT and reliance on vocabulary, as well as the penalty for answering incorrectly (there is no such penalty on the ACT), has resulted in persons with disabilities having substantially lower mean scores on the SAT relative to the ACT. Fuller and Wehman (2003) suggested that preparation for these tests is more complicated for persons with disabilities and that professionals should be prepared to assist consumers with disabilities with these exams by understanding what accommodations are best, how to request them, and specific strategies to reduce test anxiety.

Employment Testing

Various types of employment tests might be administered to assist employers in different decision-making processes, such as hiring and promotion. Common examples of types of tests used in an employment setting include cognitive ability tests, skills tests, aptitude tests, physical ability tests, personality tests, substance abuse tests, and medical examinations (Dwoskin, Squire, & Patullo, 2013). An employer is permitted to use any kind of test to determine job qualifications, but there are two major requirements from the ADA in relation to employment tests. First, if a test tends to screen out persons with disabilities on the basis of disability, it must be job related and consistent with business necessity. Second, such employment tests given to persons with disabilities must not require them to use their skills that are impaired due to disability on that test unless the test is designed to measure that skill specifically (Equal Employment Opportunity Commission [EEOC], 2009). To clarify, the EEOC (2009) provides the following illustration:

> A person with dyslexia should be given an opportunity to take a written test orally, if the dyslexia seriously impairs the individual's ability to read. But if ability to read is a job-related function that the test is designed to measure, the employer could require that a person with dyslexia take the written test. However, even in this situation, reasonable accommodation should be considered. The person with dyslexia might be accommodated with a reader, unless the ability to read unaided is an essential job function, unless such an accommodation would not be possible on the job for which s/he is being tested, or would be an undue hardship. For example, the ability to read without help would be essential for a proofreader's job. Or, a firefighter applicant with dyslexia might be disqualified if s/he could not quickly read necessary instructions for dealing with specific toxic substances at the site of a fire when no reader would be available (p. V-19).

It is primarily the responsibility of the person with a disability to notify the employer if an accommodation will be needed during an employment test; however, there are some circumstances where an person with a disability may not realize the need for accommodation in advance, in which case the employer would be required to provide an "effective" accommodation. Consider the following example from the EEOC Technical Assistance Manual on Title I of the ADA (EEOC, 2009):

> A person with a visual impairment who knows that there will be a written test may not request an accommodation because she has her own specially designed lens that usually is effective for reading printed material. However, when the test is distributed, she finds that her lens is not sufficient, because of unusually low color contrast between the paper and the ink. Under these circumstances, she might request an accommodation and the employer would be obligated to provide one. The employer might provide the test in a higher contrast format at that time, reschedule the test, or make any other effective accommodation that would not impose an undue hardship (p. V-20).

Dwoskin and colleagues (2013) encouraged employers to exercise caution when conducting certain employment tests in which accommodations are not necessarily available because of the nature of the assessment. The researchers cited multiple recent EEOC cases in which medical exams that were given post-offer to candidates were used to justify rescinding job offers despite the candidates being capable of performing the essential functions of the jobs. The employers, in both cases, had discovered additional medical information about both candidates that the candidates had not disclosed; therefore, employers contended that they were justified in rescinding the offers because of failure to disclose/dishonesty on the candidates' parts. The EEOC ruled that this was a violation of ADA. In a related case, an employer used a positive test for tuberculosis, which was required of the healthcare facility, to justify keeping a person from working. In this case, the EEOC ruled that the ADA requires employers to conduct individualized assessments of the worker's circumstances, which was not done by this employer, who was thus in violation of ADA (Dwoskin et al., 2013). In addition, the EEOC is in the process of determining the legality of using personality assessments because of the influential nature of certain disabilities on personality tests. Dwoskin and colleagues (2013) warned that "any personality test that has an adverse impact based on disability and cannot be shown to be job related and consistent with business necessity can be found to be discriminatory" (p. 48).

▨ Selecting Accommodations

When considering the need for accommodation, two main decisions need to be made: Is provision of an accommodation appropriate, and if so, which accommodations should be provided based on that person's needs? We first examine how the decision of eligibility for accommodation is made, with an in-depth examination of each main type of functional impairment that requires accommodation. This is followed by a discussion of how to request accommodations, including necessary documentation and best practice in determining which accommodations should be used. To accomplish the former, we refer to the 2015 DoJ regulations for testing accommodations.

Who Needs Test Accommodations?

Generally, persons with disabilities, per the ADA definition, are eligible to receive necessary testing accommodations. Any person who has a physical or mental impairment that results in substantial limitation of a major life activity or a major bodily function is thus regarded as a person with a disability (DoJ, 2015). Especially for the purpose of testing accommodations, it is important to consider not just if a person is able to perform an activity, but the conditions under which the person performs the activity or the manner in which it is performed. Further, the length of time needed for the person to complete the task is a relevant concern when considering the need for testing accommodation (DoJ, 2015). It is important to remember that being successful at a particular activity does not preclude someone from being a person with a disability, as they still may experience difficulty with that task or may have a measure that reduces the impact of the disability (medication, mobility devices, low-vision devices, prosthetics, hearing aids, etc.). In the case of testing accommodations, having a history of academic success does not disqualify a person from receiving testing accommodations under the ADA. Per the DoJ (2015),

> For example, someone with a learning disability may achieve a high level of academic success, but may nevertheless be substantially limited in one or more of the major life activities of reading, writing, speaking, or learning, because of the additional time or effort he or she must spend to read, write, speak, or learn compared to most people in the general population (p. 3).

For the purpose of testing accommodations, it is most helpful to examine categories of limitations as opposed to categories of disability. There may be substantial overlap in the types of categories; in some circumstances, the same disability may create multiple different functional limitations for one person, or in other cases, the same condition may result in two totally different functional impairments for two different people. For these reasons, it is most useful to match the types of accommodations with the specific types of limitations. For the purposes of this chapter, we consider limitations in the areas of cognitive and neurological abilities, motor abilities, and sensory abilities. We also discuss issues of note in the "other limitations" category. For a complete list of specific testing accommodations based on each specific limitation within the following categories, visit the JAN online resource for testing accommodations at askjan.org/topics/test.cfm.

Cognitive and Neurological Limitations

A number of different disabling conditions can result in impairment of cognitive or neurological functioning. A few of these conditions that can affect people across the life span include learning disabilities (LDs), traumatic brain injuries (TBIs), attention deficit hyperactivity disorder (ADHD), intellectual disabilities, multiple sclerosis (MS), dementia, and developmental disabilities.

LD is one of the most commonly diagnosed conditions that result in cognitive and neurological limitations. Approximately 4.6 million children and adults in the United States have been identified as having LD, with about 2.4 million (5% of the total public school enrollment) of those persons currently in the American public education system (Rubin et al., 2016). This makes students with LD the largest category of persons receiving transition services in American public schools (Rumrill et al., 2017). Though persons with LD enroll in postsecondary education at similar rates as do their peers, only about 17% of those with LD enrolled at colleges/universities receive any type of classroom accommodations, including testing accommodations.

Owing to the varied and complex nature of cognitive and neurological limitations, it is not within the scope of this chapter to address each type of limitation that may occur at length, but a nonexhaustive list of limitations in these areas include memory loss, concentration issues, organization concerns, and lack of time management skills, along with specific deficits in reading, writing, or math. Table 15.1, adapted from JAN (2019) and the University of the State of New York (USNY; 2018), demonstrates common accommodations that may be helpful for each of these specific issues.

Motor Limitations

Impairment in motor functioning can be a result of both acquired and congenital conditions. Some of the more common causes of motor function include traumatic injuries (e.g., TBI, spinal cord injuries [SCIs], loss or damage of limbs), and various diseases and congenital conditions (e.g., cerebral palsy [CP]), muscular dystrophy [MD], MS, spina bifida, Parkinson's disease [PD], arthritis, various tremor conditions). Many of these conditions cause damage or malfunction in the motor cortex area of the brain that controls gross and fine motor movements (such as CP, TBI, or PD), while others can cause damage to nerve signal transmission in areas such as the spinal cord (such as SCI or spina bifida), and still others may cause damage directly to the muscle or limb (such as loss of limb or MD; Rubin et al., 2016).

Although impairment in motor functioning could pose a variety of complications to the assessment process across types of assessments and testing conditions, we focus on motor limitations that cause impairment in standardized testing environments, such as paper-and-pencil and computer-based assessments. Because of heavy reliance on seated, written, or typed assessments, the ability to sit for long periods of time, as well as the ability to manually manipulate objects with the hands and fingers, is of elevated significance in the assessment process. Testing

TABLE 15.1 Accommodations for Cognitive/Neurological Limitations

LIMITATION	TESTING ACCOMMODATION RECOMMENDATIONS
Memory loss	▪ Directions read more than standard number of times ▪ Directions provided for each page of questions ▪ Directions simplified
Concentration/organization	▪ Separate setting free from distractions ▪ On-task focusing prompts ▪ Provide breaks during exam period ▪ Extended time ▪ Study carrel ▪ Record answers directly in test booklet
Time management	▪ Extended time ▪ Multiple day administration ▪ Breaks ▪ On-task focusing prompts
Reading	▪ Oral reading of tests ▪ Text-to-speech software ▪ Extended time ▪ Present test reading passages in sections
Writing	▪ Extended time ▪ Speech-to-text software ▪ Use of computer/word processor or other writing aids ▪ Respond orally to scribe ▪ Record answers directly in test booklet ▪ Allow additional space for writing
Math	▪ Use of calculator ▪ Chart of basic math facts

SOURCE: University of the State of New York. (2018). *Testing accommodations for students with disabilities policy and tools to guide decision-making and implementation.* Retrieved from http://www.p12.nysed.gov/specialed/publications/documents/testing-accommodations-guide-february-2018.pdf

TABLE 15.2 Accommodations for Motor Limitations

LIMITATION	TESTING ACCOMMODATION RECOMMENDATIONS
Sitting	▪ Adaptive furniture ▪ Breaks ▪ Extended time
Fingering/grasping	▪ Use of adaptive writing utensils ▪ Speech-to-text software ▪ Respond orally to scribe (with separate setting) ▪ Papers taped/anchored to desk ▪ Adaptive keyboard/mouse ▪ Touch screen ▪ Switch interface ▪ Keyboard access features ▪ Word prediction software ▪ Extended time

SOURCE: University of the State of New York. (2018). *Testing accommodations for students with disabilities policy and tools to guide decision-making and implementation.* Retrieved from http://www.p12.nysed.gov/specialed/publications/documents/testing-accommodations-guide-february-2018.pdf

accommodation recommendations for limitations in sitting, grasping, and fingering can be found in Table 15.2 (JAN, 2019; USNY, 2018).

Sensory Limitations

The deficits caused by sensory limitations can often appear to be less complex to understand and accommodate than, for example, a brain injury that may have resulted in multiple functional limitations, yet knowledge of evidence-based practices for accommodating persons with sensory impairments is lacking (Bruce, Luckner, & Ferrell, 2018). Bruce and colleagues (2018) suggested that this could potentially be due to the low prevalence (less than 2% of all students with disabilities) and relatively even geographic distribution of sensory disabilities. For the purposes of this chapter, we include visual, hearing, and speech impairments in our review of appropriate testing accommodations. Within each type of impairment, there is a wide range of levels of impairment. For example, a person may have moderate hearing loss and require use of a hearing aid and preferential seating, while another person may have total deafness with no hearing capacity, relying strictly on signing and written forms of communication (Rubin et al., 2016).

Of primary concern when accommodating persons with sensory impairments is providing access to the content of the assessment in a preferred medium and ensuring that the person's ability to demonstrate performance or knowledge is not compromised (Bruce et al., 2018). It is important to remember, however, that persons with sensory impairments may also have other co-occurring disorders and conditions that require attention and accommodations in addition to the sensory limitation. For example, it is estimated that at least one-third of persons with hearing impairments also have additional disabilities (Bruce et al., 2018, Rubin et al., 2016). In Table 15.3, we present some of the more common testing accommodations used and recommended for persons with hearing, visual, and speech impairments (JAN, 2019; USNY, 2018).

Other Disability-Related Limitations That Require Test Accommodations

The list of disability-related limitations covered in this chapter, although comprehensive, is certainly not exhaustive. For reference, we have included an additional section covering some additional limitations that require testing accommodations (see Table 15.4). Stress intolerance, nausea, headaches, fatigue, temperature sensitivity, respiratory concerns, and test anxiety are all considered in this section. These limitations can be associated with a wide breadth of different disabling conditions. For example, fatigue may be directly related to a general medical condition/disease such as MS or cancer, or be associated with a psychological diagnosis such as depression or anxiety (Rubin et al., 2016). Test anxiety, a particularly controversial condition, can be related to a number of conditions and is considered, by some, to be a normal physiological response to high-stakes assessment. It was included in this discussion because of the growing concern for the impact of test anxiety on validity of outcomes (Lovett & Nelson, 2017).

Requesting Testing Accommodations

The initial step in requesting accommodations is disclosure of disability and providing supporting documentation of one's diagnosis and need for accommodation. The request for accommodation is ordinarily available in an accommodation form provided by the testing company. It is strictly

TABLE 15.3 Accommodations for Sensory Limitations

LIMITATION	TESTING ACCOMMODATION RECOMMENDATIONS
Deafness/hard of hearing	▪ Use of sign language interpreter ▪ Repeat listening section more than standard number of time (aloud or signed) ▪ Written directions provided ▪ Extended time ▪ Separate setting ▪ Amplification devices ▪ Preferential seating in front of interpreter ▪ Repeat directions more than standard number of times ▪ Directions simplified
Blindness/low vision	▪ Braille ▪ Tests read orally ▪ Recording device ▪ Large type ▪ Magnifier ▪ Digital text (manipulate font size or color) ▪ Special desk or book stand to hold materials for easier reading ▪ Extended time ▪ Increase spacing between test items ▪ Fewer items per page ▪ Use of calculator/talking calculator ▪ Speech-to-text software ▪ Templates to enlarge visible print ▪ Special lighting ▪ Oral description of graphs, charts, etc. ▪ Highlighting to increase contrast from color of page
Speech	▪ Augmentative and alternative communication devices ▪ Voice amplification ▪ Fluency devices ▪ Pointing to words/answers ▪ Voice synthesized computer ▪ Written alternative exams

SOURCE: University of the State of New York. (2018). *Testing accommodations for students with disabilities policy and tools to guide decision-making and implementation.* Retrieved from http://www.p12.nysed.gov/specialed/publications/documents/testing-accommodations-guide-february-2018.pdf

the responsibility of the person with a disability to provide necessary documentation of disability and to describe needed types of accommodations that will be effective. The test-taker is not, however, responsible for any additional financial cost beyond that of any other person taking the same test (JAN, 2019).

The DoJ (2015) has issued substantial guidance in this area as to what documentation is necessary and acceptable. The documentation that is needed will vary depending on the nature of the disability and the type of accommodation requested. Some examples of acceptable documentation include recommendations of qualified professionals, proof of past testing accommodations, observations by educators, results of psychoeducational or other professionals' evaluations, a history of diagnosis, and a statement of history regarding testing accommodations (DoJ, 2015).

TABLE 15.4 Accommodations for Other Limitations

LIMITATION	TESTING ACCOMMODATION RECOMMENDATIONS
Stress intolerance/text anxiety	▪ Extended time ▪ Breaks ▪ Separate location ▪ On-task focusing prompts ▪ Support animal/person
Nausea/headache/fatigue	▪ Extended time ▪ Breaks ▪ Multiple day administration ▪ Separate setting ▪ Noise reduction ▪ Special lighting ▪ Use of scribe when ability to write is affected ▪ Tests read when ability to read is affected ▪ Air cleaner or purifier
Temperature sensitivity	▪ Extended time ▪ Breaks ▪ Multiple day administration ▪ Separate location ▪ Temperature-controlled location ▪ Fans ▪ Heated/cooling clothing
Respiratory conditions	▪ Air cleaner or purifier ▪ Extended time ▪ Breaks ▪ Multiple day administration ▪ Separate setting

To protect the overall privacy of persons requesting test accommodations, the DoJ (2015) has emphasized that any documentation requested from a testing applicant must be "reasonable and limited to the need for the requested testing accommodations" (p. 5). With regard to past testing accommodations, the DoJ (2015) clarified that proof of past accommodations in similar test settings is generally sufficient to support the use of the same accommodations on future tests. For example, if a person received specific accommodations while taking the ACT, that should qualify her or him for the same accommodations when taking the GRE (DoJ, 2015).

Documentation of a history of public school accommodations, in the form of an IEP or a Section 504 Plan, is also adequate to justify need for accommodation in the assessment process. This includes testing accommodation in a private school setting as well, so long as the person certifies that she or he has a continuing need for those testing accommodations due to disability (DoJ, 2015). In the obverse, however, the DoJ (2015) was sure to highlight that "an absence of previous formal testing accommodations does not preclude a candidate from receiving testing accommodations" (pp. 6–7). Two examples were directly provided for clarification:

1.   A high school senior is in a car accident that results in a severe concussion. The report from the treating specialist says that the student has post-concussion syndrome that may take up to a year to resolve and that while his brain is healing, he will need extended time and a quiet room when taking exams. Although the student has never previously received testing accommodations, he may nevertheless be entitled to the

requested testing accommodations for standardized exams and high-stakes tests as long as the post-concussion syndrome persists.

2. A student with a diagnosis of ADHD and an anxiety disorder received informal, undocumented testing accommodations throughout high school, including time to complete tests after school or at lunchtime. In support of a request for extended time on a standardized exam, the student provides documentation of her diagnoses and their effects on test-taking in the form of a doctor's letter; provides a statement explaining her history of informal classroom accommodations for the stated disabilities; and certifies that she still needs extended time because of her disabilities. Although the student has never previously received testing accommodations through an IEP, Section 504 Plan, or a formal private school policy, she may nevertheless be entitled to extended time for the standardized exam (DoJ, 2015, p. 7).

The DoJ (2015) also issued guidance to testing entities to defer to qualified professionals who have assessed the person for accommodation need. Previously, some testing entities have attempted to review and reject requests for accommodations without an in-depth comprehensive assessment of the person. The guidelines are clear that this is not acceptable and that the decision should be deferred to a qualified professional, defined as someone who is licensed or credentialed with expertise in disability, who submits documentation (e.g., reports, evaluations, or letters) in favor of the person receiving accommodations (DoJ, 2015).

Once a request for an accommodation is submitted with corresponding documentation, the testing entity must respond to the applicant in a timely manner. This is important as it provides the person ample time to register and prepare for the test. If the testing entity has any additional requests for information, they should be made so that the candidate has reasonable opportunity to respond and still expect to take the assessment in the same testing cycle. Failure to follow these guidelines will put the testing entity in violation of the ADA.

Finally, once the exam is completed, scores for test-takers who received accommodations should be treated uniformly with all others who completed the assessment. The DoJ (2015) explicitly mandated that "testing entities should report accommodated scores in the same way they report scores generally" (p. 8). If a testing entity "flags" a score from a test-taker who received accommodations in any way that might result in discrimination and impede an educational or employment opportunity, it will be held in strict violation of the ADA (DoJ, 2015). These various regulations have prioritized protecting persons receiving accommodations and have further clarified the responsibilities of both the testing entity and the testing candidate with a disability.

■ Conclusions

Helping people with disabilities to identify, request, and implement reasonable accommodations in various educational, community, and employment settings is a hallmark of the rehabilitation counseling practice. The rehabilitation counseling process is guided by comprehensive assessments of the client's aptitudes, achievement, skills, interests, and values, and it is essential that clients who require accommodations to participate in valid assessments have access to those accommodations. Testing accommodations are legal, ethical, and best-practice imperatives for rehabilitation and healthcare professionals, and they are viewed as a fundamental right of participation in educational, human service, community, and vocational environments. By familiarizing themselves with the legal and ethical bases for testing accommodations, the psychometric implications of these accommodations, the nature and needs of examinees who require accommodations, and the specific strategies that are used to accommodate examinees with a wide variety of disability-related needs, readers will be equipped to ensure that client assessments are carried out in the most equitable, accessible, and valid manner possible.

■ References

ADA National Network. (2018). Reasonable accommodations in the workplace. Retrieved from https://adata.org/factsheet/reasonable-accommodations-workplace

Americans with Disabilities Act of 1990, Pub. L. No. 101-336, 104 Stat. 328 (1990).

Americans with Disabilities Act. (2010). *ADA title III technical assistance manual covering public accommodations and commercial facilities.* Retrieved from https://www.ada.gov/taman3.html

Bruce, S. M., Luckner, J. L., & Ferrell, K. A. (2018). Assessment of students with sensory disabilities: Evidence-based practices. *Assessment for Effective Intervention, 43*(2), 79–89. doi:10.1177/1534508417708311

Camara, W. (2009). Validity evidence in accommodations for English language learners and students with disabilities. *Journal of Applied Testing Technology, 10*(2), 1–23. Retrieved from http://www.jattjournal.com/index.php/atp/article/view/48357

Christensen, L. L., Braam, M., Scullin, S., & Thurlow, M. L. (2011). *2009 state policies on assessment participation and accommodations for students with disabilities* (Synthesis report 83). Minneapolis: University of Minnesota, National Center on Educational Outcomes.

Commission on Rehabilitation Counselor Certification. (2017). *CRCC code of ethics.* Retrieved from https://www.crccertification.com/filebin/pdf/ethics/CodeOfEthics_01-01-2017.pdf

Dwoskin, L. B., Squire, M. B., & Patullo, J. E. (2013). Welcome aboard! How to hire the right way. *Employee Relations Law Journal, 38*(4), 28–63.

Educational Testing Service. (2014). *ETS standards for quality and fairness.* Retrieved from https://www.ets.org/s/about/pdf/standards.pdf

Educational Testing Service. (2019). *ETS—Measuring the power of learning.* Retrieved from https://www.ets.org

Elliott, S. N., Kratochwill, T. R., & Schulte, A. G. (1998). The assessment accommodation checklist: Who, what, where, when, why, and how? *Teaching Exceptional Children, 31*(2), 10–14. doi:10.1177/004005999803100202

Equal Employment Opportunity Commission. (2009). *A technical assistance manual on the employment provisions (Title I) of the Americans with Disabilities Act.* Retrieved from https://files.eric.ed.gov/fulltext/ED352763.pdf

Fischer, R. J. (1994). The Americans with Disabilities Act: Implications for measurement. *Educational Measurement: Issues and Practice, 13*(3), 17–26. doi:10.1111/j.1745-3992.1994.tb00445.x

Fordham Law Review. (1963). Equal protection and discrimination in public accommodations. *Fordham Law Review, 32*, 327–338. Retrieved from http://ir.lawnet.fordham.edu/flr/vol32/iss2/6

Fuller, W. E., & Wehman, P. (2003). College entrance exams for students with disabilities: Accommodations and testing guidelines. *Journal of Vocational Rehabilitation, 18*(3), 191–197. Retrieved from https://content.iospress.com/articles/journal-of-vocational-rehabilitation/jvr00195

Job Accommodation Network. (2019). *Testing accommodations.* Retrieved from https://askjan.org/topics/test.cfm

Joint Committee on Testing Practices. (2004). *Code of fair testing practices in education.* Retrieved from https://www.apa.org/science/programs/testing/fair-testing.pdf

Lai, S. A., & Berkeley, S. (2012). High-stakes test accommodations: Research and practice. *Learning Disability Quarterly, 35*(3), 158–169. doi:10.1177/0731948711433874

Lane, S., & Leventhal, B. (2015). Psychometric challenges in assessing English language learners and students with disabilities. *Review of Research in Education, 39*(1), 165–214. doi:10.3102/0091732x14556073

Lovett, B. J. (2014). Testing accommodations under the amended Americans with Disabilities Act: The voice of empirical research. *Journal of Disability Policy Studies, 25*(2), 81–90. doi:10.1177/1044207312469830

Lovett, B. J., & Nelson, J. M. (2017). Test anxiety and the Americans with Disabilities Act. *Journal of Disability Policy Studies, 28*(2), 99–108. doi:10.1177/1044207317710699

National Center for Education Statistics. (2018). *Children and youth with disabilities.* Retrieved from https://nces.ed.gov/programs/coe/indicator_cgg.asp

National Council on Disability. (2018). *Every Student Succeeds Act and Students with Disabilities. IDEA Series.* Retrieved from https://ncd.gov/sites/default/files/NCD_ESSA-SWD_Accessible.pdf

Niebling, B. C., & Elliott, S. N. (2005). Testing accommodations and inclusive assessment practices. *Assessment for Effective Intervention, 31*(1), 1–6. doi:10.1177/073724770503100101

Pitoniak, M. J., & Royer, J. M. (2001). Testing accommodations for examinees with disabilities: A review of psychometric, legal, and social policy issues. *Review of Educational Research, 71*(1), 53–104. doi:10.3102/00346543071001053

Plake, B. S., & Wise, L. L. (2014). What is the role and importance of the revised AERA, APA, NCME standards for educational and psychological testing? *Educational Measurement: Issues & Practice, 33*(4), 4–12. doi:10.1111/emip.12045

Power, P. (2013). *A guide to vocational assessment* (5th ed.). Austin, TX: Pro-Ed.

Rubin, S., Roessler, R., & Rumrill, P. (2016). *Foundations of the vocational rehabilitation process* (7th ed.). Austin, TX: Pro-Ed.

Rumrill, P. D., Merchant, D., Kaya, C., Chan, F., Hartmane, E., & Tansey, T. (2017). Demographic and service-related correlates of competitive employment outcomes among state-federal vocational rehabilitation clients with learning disabilities: A purposeful selection logistic regression analysis. *Journal of Vocational Rehabilitation, 47*(2), 123–134. doi:10.3233/jvr-170889

Salend, S. J. (2008). Determining appropriate testing accommodations: Complying with NCLB and IDEA. *Teaching Exceptional Children, 40*(4), 14–22. doi:10.1177/004005990804000402

Sireci, S. G., Scarpati, S. E., & Li, S. (2005). Test accommodations for students with disabilities: An analysis of the interaction hypothesis. *Review of Educational Research, 75*(4), 457–490. doi:10.3102/00346543075004457

Society for Industrial and Organizational Psychology. (2003). *Principles for the validation and use of personnel selection procedures* (4th ed.). Bowling Green, OH: Author. Retrieved from http://www.siop.org/_principles/principles.pdf

Spenceley, L. M., & Wheeler, S. (2016). The use of extended time by college students with disabilities. *Journal of Postsecondary Education and Disability, 29*(2), 141–150. Retrieved from http://www.ahead-archive.org/uploads/publications/JPED/jped292/JPED%2029_2_FullDocument.pdf

University of the State of New York. (2018). *Testing accommodations for students with disabilities: Policy and tools to guide decision-making and implementation.* Retrieved from http://www.p12.nysed.gov/specialed/publications/documents/testing-accommodations-guide-february-2018.pdf

U.S. Department of Justice, Civil Rights Division, Disability Right Section. (2015). *Testing accommodations.* Retrieved from https://www.ada.gov/regs2014/testing_accommodations.pdf

U.S. Department of Labor, Employment and Training Administration. (2000). *Testing and assessment: An employer's guide to good practices.* Retrieved from https://www.onetcenter.org/dl_files/empTestAsse.pdf

TEST SCORE BIAS AND VALIDITY IN PERSON-ORIENTED HEALTHCARE

ELIAS MPOFU

LEARNING OBJECTIVES

After reviewing this chapter, the reader should be able to:

- Identify approaches to the development and use of scores from tests for healthcare quality improvement.
- Summarize concepts of test score bias and validity.
- Summarize the relationship between health behavior and other observed behaviors.
- Identify approaches to minimize test score bias and interpretation invalidity.
- Summarize characteristics of tests that can influence the reliability and validity of scores.

Introduction

The calibration of behavioral healthcare indicators associated with bias in person-oriented care is critically important for the design of interventions for quality improvement in healthcare systems in the United States. The significance of measures for person-oriented care is attested to by the fact that that federal agencies including the Agency for Healthcare Research and Quality (AHRQ), Health Resources and Services Administration, National Institute on Minority Health and Disparities (NIMHD), Patient-Centered Outcomes Research Institute (PCORI), and Substance Abuse and Mental Health Services Administration (SAMHSA) have open calls for studies on the development of measures for quality improvement care aimed to also address population health disparities.

The Institute of Medicine (IOM; 2001) defined patient-oriented care as "that which is respectful of and responsive to individual patient preferences, needs and values and ensuring that patient values guide all clinical decisions (p. 3)." Person-oriented healthcare is one in which the individual patient treatment and care support needs are the primary focus of the healthcare system rather than the needs of its administrative exigencies. Patient experience of care is a person-oriented healthcare measure that captures the ways in which patients transact the healthcare systems for health recovery, sustenance, and augmentation, inclusive of helping to derive the meaning as well as the importance the patients ascribe to the services they engage.

Self-reported patient experience of care is a widely used indicator of person-oriented care by healthcare systems for providing information on the qualities important to people with health conditions in their engagement with health service providers (Davies & Cleary, 2005; Davis, Schoenbaum, & Audet, 2005; Flott, Graham, Darzi, & Mayer, 2017; Institute of Health Improvement, 2006; Kowalski, Yeaton, Kuhr, & Pfaff, 2017; Swenson et al., 2004). The meanings that patients impute on their experience of care influence their health outcomes beyond those explained by objective functional limitations (Orbell, Johnston, Rowley, Davey, & Espley, 2001). Patients as partners in their healthcare planning and implementation add tremendous value to the success of healthcare systems in promoting the sustainable health of the communities they serve (Robert et al., 2015). Moreover, person-oriented healthcare and the evidence for its design, implementation, and evaluation empower people with health conditions to make choices to best recover and sustain their health and function. The case of Mr. Gregory in Box 16.1 is illustrative of the importance of participatory or person-oriented healthcare.

Person-oriented care data are also useful for determining whether there are race/ethnicity, gender, or other social identity disparities in patient experience of care (Asch et al., 2006; Black, 2013; Reeves, West, & Barron, 2013) and, if the data support this, what service qualities are associated with those disparities (Frost et al., 2007). Healthcare quality improvement initiatives for addressing population disparities in patient experience of care are premised on use of measures that yield true or unbiased scores to guide clinical care practices, health system administration, and related health policy decisions (Black, 2013; Flott et al., 2017). Unfortunately, the assumption may not be warranted or justified. The development of person-oriented healthcare measures is in its infancy (Teresi & Jones, 2016) and so is their use adoption (Davies, Materko, Charns, Seibert, & Cleary, 2011).

As evidence, in part, for the need to improve on test score reliability from measures of person-oriented healthcare, the literature is replete with contradictions as to whether disparities exist in patient experience of care and, if they exist, whether these differences are stable across patient characteristics and settings (see Clark & McMillan-Persaud, 2014; Dayton, Zhan, Sangl, Darby, &

BOX 16.1

MR. GREGORY: SIGNIFICANCE OF PATIENT EXPERIENCE OF CARE

Mr. Gregory was an inpatient in a rehabilitation ward following right leg transfemoral amputation for vascular disease. Incidentally, he was also diagnosed with throat cancer while in the rehabilitation hospital. Mr. Gregory went from perceiving himself to be a healthy, independent person to a patient with an amputation and malignancy within the space of a few weeks. Mr. Gregory's personality and coping style enabled him to remain optimistic toward the situation and open to new ideas, which, in turn, promoted continuing rehabilitation and eventual discharge home. Though a prosthesis was obtained, the vascular supply to his left foot was also vulnerable, and this prevented the use of the prosthesis. His home environment presented a substantial barrier, being a high-set house on a sloping block. It was important to Mr. Gregory and his partner that they remain in the family home. A wheelchair lift was installed, which allowed safe and easy access. Once inside, Mr. Gregory was able to participate in the running of the household by assisting with cleaning and food preparation tasks.

Moy, 2006; Fiscella & Sanders, 2016; Hicks et al., 2005; Krieger, Chen, Waterman, Rehkopf, & Subramanian, 2005; Smedley, Stith, & Nelson, 2003; Williams & Sternthal, 2010). For example, racial/ethnic disparities in patient experience of care were not significant when income, age, sex, self-reported health status, and insurance status were taken into account (Krieger at al., 2005; Smedley, et al., 2003). On the one hand, there is evidence to suggest that racial minority patients were less satisfied with their physicians (Clark & McMillan-Persaud, 2014; Harris et al., 2012; Hausmann, Kwoh, Hannon, & Ibrahim, 2013; Penner et al., 2009) and trusted them less than did White patients after controlling for socioeconomic status and health status (Blanchard & Lurie, 2004; Doeschler, Saver, Franks, & Fiscella, 2000; Dovidio et al., 2008; Hunt, Gaba, & Lavizzo-Mourey, 2005; Wagner et al., 2011; Weech-Maldonado et al., 2003). Hispanic and Asian patients were less satisfied with their interpersonal interactions with physicians than were White patients (Ngui & Flores, 2006). On the other hand, there is evidence to suggest that Hispanics assessed their interactions with physicians more positively than did non-Hispanic Whites (Dayton et al., 2006); White patients were more skeptical of medical care than Black patients (Kressin et al., 2002). Also, African American patients reported mixed ratings (higher/lower) in their satisfaction with physicians compared with White patients (Haviland, Morales, Dial, & Pincus, 2005). Arguably, the discrepancies in findings across studies are explained in part by the fact that the indicator items used were not constructed to measure the latent variable of patient experience of care similarly (Cooper, Hill, & Powe, 2002; Krieger et al., 2005). Thus, the question remains to consider the qualities of patient experience measures constructed to allow for clinical, administrative, and health policy advisement serving people with cultural diversity (Kowalski et al., 2017).

This chapter begins with a discussion of the approaches to the development and use of scores from tests for healthcare quality improvement that also would be useful for measuring population health disparities. As background for statistical applications, a brief overview of the concepts of test score bias and validity from the extant literature is provided. Test score reliability and validity issues also are considered, with the understanding that a health behavior is often part of a syndrome with other related behaviors that define it. The specifics of test score measurement approaches to minimize test score bias and interpretation invalidity are presented next, followed by a survey of the influences of demand characteristics of tests that would influence the reliability and validity of scores for intended purposes and, finally, issues for research in the development of unbiased measures in the context of person-oriented care.

Test Score Bias and Validity of Interpretation

A priority goal in the provision of assessment services is to support decision making for the participants of assessment and in areas of need for which assessment data would contribute important information (Bond & Fox, 2001; Hwang & Mpofu, 2010). In healthcare settings, the quality of decisions from assessment depend, in part, on the extent to which the measures and scores yield data usable for addressing the healthcare need (Dawson, Doll, Fitzpatrick, Jenkinson, & Carr, 2010; Dovidio & Fiske, 2012; Hwang & Mpofu, 2010; Madden, Fortune, Cheeseman, Mpofu, & Bundy, 2013). Scores from measures are reliable and valid for healthcare support decisions to the extent that the procedures are transparent to the patient and the outcomes manifestly address a present health and function need (Sanford, Rivers, Braun, Schultz, & Buchanan, 2018). These are matters of the consequential validity of test scores or the incremental difference knowledge of scores from a test makes to the practical decisions for which the test scores were needed. Consequential validity goes beyond construct validity, which is the extent to which a test measures what it proposes to measure based on the reliability of scores.

Clearly, a test can yield reliable scores that may also not be valid for use in making decisions for which other data may be appropriate. As explained in the next section, the decisional reliability of scores and their valid use for healthcare settings depend on the extent to which specific test indicators map the broad underlying healthcare construct for which the test is only one of many instruments. For instance, the construct of person-oriented care, as in patient-centric healthcare, is defined by a broad range of indicators subsumed under participatory interdisciplinary care practices for person-focused, quality healthcare (Madden et al., 2013; Mpofu & Mpofu, 2018; Reeves et al., 2013). These include measures of trust in physicians and treatment prescriptions, communication qualities, treatment alliance, experienced confusion, sources of health information, patient unmet healthcare needs, and patient satisfaction with healthcare and healthcare plans. In that regard, there is need for generic screening instruments that cut across healthcare service while also allowing for more focused or in-depth assessments within the more narrowly focused ones for better targeting of person-centric care. For instance, of 219 index measures of person-oriented healthcare qualities of integrative care, care continuity/comprehensive care, and care coordination/case management, considered separate from patient-centered care, none mapped to more than two domains (Bautista, Nurjono, Lim, Dessers, & Vrijhoef, 2016). Evidently, the test score use for quality-of-care improvements is yet to consider the spectrum that defines person-oriented healthcare service and indicators across the continuum.

Historically, the scholarly literature on bias in testing has been dominated by considerations on whether or not test score differences are associated with social groupings of race/ethnicity, gender, social class, education, and so on (Reynolds & Suzuki, 2013). Commonly cited indicators of probable test score bias include systematic differences "explained" by a grouping at the total score level so that membership of a prespecified social grouping would lead to a prediction to score higher or lower than a comparison group within a statistical confidence level interval (usually 95%). Other analysis has considered group membership-related differences in response at the test question level. Explanations for differences have been proposed encompassing genetic endowment, opportunity to learn, and fairness of the test content, procedures, and context. The Standards for Educational and Psychological Testing (American Educational Research Association, American Psychological Association, & National Council on Measurement in Education, 2014), known simply as "the Standards," denotes acceptable practices regarding use of test instruments to minimize bias or prejudicial, if not harmful, interpretations and decisions. Test score bias is often flagged by evidence of group-based differential item functioning (DIF).

Item and Test Score Bias

DIF analysis applied statistical techniques to determine whether respondents of matched ability (e.g., high, low) having the same ability have equal probability of getting an item correct, regardless of group (Reynolds & Suzuki, 2013; Rudner, Getson, & Knight, 1980). If examinees matched for ability have the same probability of success on the item, the item is functioning equivalently in both groupings in measuring the ability of trait of interest. Conversely, DIF is seen when respondents with equal ability, but from different groups, have an unequal probability of item success.

Two types of DIF are uniform DIF (see Figure 16.1A) and nonuniform DIF (see Figure 16.1B). Uniform DIF is seen when a test item is systematically more difficult for members of one group, even after matching respondents on ability. Uniform DIF alone might not indicate item bias, depending on the purposes of the testing and judgment applied to explain cases in which a subgroup is predicted to score differently on an item for some reason (Andrich, 2003). However, uniform DIF might indicate item bias in that respondents of one group of similar ability are less likely to

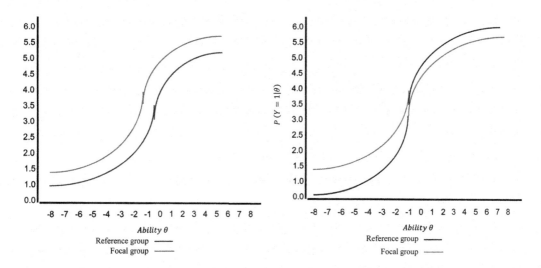

FIGURE 16.1 (A) Item characteristics curves for uniform differential item functioning. (B) Item characteristics curves for nonuniform differential item functioning.

answer an *item* correctly (or endorse an *item*) than respondents of another group because of some characteristic of the *test item* or *testing situation* that is not relevant to assessing the construct of interest. For instance, in the context of patient experience of care measures, evidence of uniform DIF between patients by racial or gender group with similar healthcare participation status may be explained by prior, unique care experiences for each of the groups (Dovidio et al., 2008).

Nonuniform DIF is seen when there is group interaction on the ability or trait continuum so that an increase or decrease in the probability for low-ability respondents to get an item correct is offset by the converse for respondents of high ability. For instance, in the context of patient experience of care, nonuniform DIF means that one group has an advantage on some proficiency-level item (e.g., instrumental ambulatory care), but is at a disadvantage at some other proficiency-level item (work hardening ambulatory care). In other words, differences in the probabilities of getting an item correct of respondents from different groups with the same ability level do not depend on the common ability or trait level (ambulatory competence). Nonuniform DIF might suggest misspecification of the item to the ability or trait assessed or a need for item revision or rewrite for better targeting of the ability or trait. In sum, DIF is necessary but not sufficient for item bias in the absence of explanation. Moreover, DIF in a few items may be of information value on the attribute measured by the item set. It might not have too much practical impact on the overall test score result.

Differential test functioning (DTF) is seen when group membership mirrors consistent differences in overall scores for members with matched ability or trait levels (Andrich, 1988; Lord, 1980), regardless of ability or trait levels. Test score bias is likely an explanation for DTF, unless there is a countervailing explanation. Most measures of person-oriented care are interpreted at the test score level. This might have the advantage of providing a global or summative indicator for cross-group comparisons (e.g., by race/ethnicity, gender) for documenting any disparities to be addressed through quality-of-care improvement efforts.

Historically, DIF analysis has been implemented more in high-stakes psychological and educational testing instruments and less so in healthcare service assessments (Teresi & Fleishman, 2007; Teresi & Jones, 2016). However, in the past two decades, more than 400 patient-oriented healthcare indicators have been identified as in need of study across patient populations and provider settings (Asch et al., 2006; Teresi & Jones, 2016). The transportability of DIF analysis to study test score bias and validity in healthcare settings is relatively recent (Teresi & Fleishman, 2007). Nonetheless, DIF analysis considerations and guidelines remain important and relevant. Moreover, the proliferation of patient-oriented measures has not taken into account that health behaviors are rarely discrete and tend to occur in a syndrome. The next section considers the syndromic nature of health conditions and implications for minimizing test score bias, while enhancing person-centric healthcare interpretation.

■ The Syndromic Nature of Health Behaviors

Health behaviors rarely exhibit in isolation and typically are defined by an underlying or latent construct and the indicators for it (Krueger & Markon, 2006; Mpofu et al., 2006). For instance, evidence is increasingly emerging regarding the presence of latent pathological processes that underlie the overt expression of a seemingly diverse range of symptoms (Kazdin, 2005; Krueger & Markon, 2006). Regrettably, most measures employed to assess person or patient outcomes in healthcare examine only a few of the health indicators, while the breadth of the health behavior syndrome associated with health conditions and care settings has yet to be fully explored.

Similarly, indicators of patient-centered care on current surveys are interpreted without regard of their equivalence in mapping the latent construct of patient-centered care (Frost et al., 2007). However, in reality, patients experiencing negative healthcare disparities on one indicator (e.g., "How difficult was it to get treatment information from a plan or managed behavioral healthcare organization?") may also experience access problems on another healthcare quality indicator (e.g., "How well did your clinician communicate?"). If these indicators of healthcare are not considered from a healthcare continuum perspective, valuable information for understanding drivers to committed patient partnership to the treatment care effort is lost.

In any healthcare setting, substantive characterization of the specific health behavior syndrome is important for a better understanding of the construct and its indicators at different levels of its characterization (Teresi & Jones, 2016). For example, although a general latent factor may be presumed for a person or patient experience of care in medical rehabilitation, the amount of variation of each behavior and extent of overlap among the behaviors is yet to be demonstrated (Hwang & Mpofu, 2010; Osterlind, Mpofu, & Oakland, 2010). Little is known about the relative contribution and efficiency of individual items or indicators in capturing the range of patient experience of care behaviors or about the response options for the indicators (Teresi et al., 2009; Teresi & Jones, 2016). The case of Mr. Alex in Box 16.2 illustrates how a health condition and response to it are framed by a syndrome, which influences the specific health behavior indicators.

To adequately model a health behavior syndrome, consideration needs to be given to a broad range of relevant indicators in the person that characterize the syndrome, the co-occurrence or overlap of the indicators, and their differentiation in people (Osterlind et al., 2010; Vickers, 2003). Few of the existing measures used in person-oriented care provide for these features (Teresi et al., 2009; Teresi & Jones, 2016). Furthermore, a majority of the behavioral health tests have a narrow bandwidth and do not sample the full range of a health construct from having a low ceiling and high floor design (Smith & Smith, 2004; Vickers, 2003).

BOX 16.2

THE CASE OF MR. ALEX: SYNDROMIC HEALTH BEHAVIOR

An 18-year-old man (Mr. Alex) experienced significant morbidity following a basal ganglia hemorrhage. His principal physical symptom was left-sided weakness, affecting both the upper and lower limbs, for which he underwent an intense inpatient rehabilitation program. Contextual factors played a significant role in his overall participation. Like many adolescents, Mr. Alex was highly self-conscious and was concerned with appearing physically different from his peers. This translated into a refusal to leave the hospital ward while wearing an ankle–foot orthosis (AFO) is case someone noticed it. While wearing an AFO, he was able to walk independently. Without the AFO, he required a wheelchair to walk for long distances. Strategies to hide the AFO were suggested, such as wearing it underneath jeans, but were not acceptable to Mr. Alex. He was extremely reluctant to attend social events or participate in recreational activities while wearing an AFO. He was granted leave from the hospital ward to attend several gatherings of friends and family, but declined on the basis that he would need to wear the AFO while in public.

Tests with a broad bandwidth have a high ceiling, meaning they include items that sample the upper end of the construct of interest (high-end abilities). Broad bandwidth tests also have a low floor, meaning they include items that test for more basic competencies on the abilities continuum. Measures of person-oriented care with a high ceiling and low floor would provide reliable scores across the healthcare quality improvement continuum. Existing measures of patient experience of care have serious ceiling and floor limitations so as to fail to provide meaningful discrimination across the continuum of care experiences. For example, 60% of patients reporting on their experience of care by physicians on the Consumer Assessment of Healthcare Providers and Systems (CAHPS, an AHRQ program) choose the top response option on the 4-point Likert-type scale, with less than 5% of the patients choosing the bottom option (Reise, Morizot, & Hays, 2007). Similarly, 70% of patients rated the quality of communication with physicians to a top response on the Communication Assessment Tool (CAT; Makoul, Krupat, & Chang, 2007). This indicates a ceiling effect limitation to use of data from these patient experience of care measures for discriminating levels of care for quality care improvement aimed at person-focused care. Measures are needed that yield scores for reliable distinctions between patients reporting marginally acceptable to very positive experiences of care. Yet, testing practices in healthcare research continue to prioritize measures developed, utilizing measurement approaches less likely to provide objective, person-centric care based on health function competencies rather than disability (Mpofu & Mpofu, 2018).

Measurement Approach and Test Score Bias and Validity in Person-Oriented Healthcare

Classical Test Theory (CTT) and Item Response Test (IRT) modeling are two major approaches to test development and use for consequential decisions for the participants (Bond & Fox, 2001). These models make different assumptions of how to address the variation in the contribution of the individual indicators of a behavioral syndrome, their overlap, and hierarchical positioning of the indicators for person-centric healthcare.

Contrasting CTT and IRT Approaches to Measure Development

Contrasting the two approaches to develop measures is useful to show why and how IRT approaches to construct measures of person-oriented care have greater merit for creating measures with transportability across settings or samples compared to the CTT approach. Three factors differentiate CTT- and IRT-based measures in regard to their healthcare construct: specification precision, sample-free measures, and interval scale qualities.

(Mis)specification of the Healthcare Construct Continuum

CTT is a measurement approach in which the meaning of scores from an instrument largely depends on the specific instrument used rather than the objective qualities of the attribute the instrument is designed to measure. For example, a person's health risk status on an instrument developed using a CTT approach depends, to a significant extent, on which instruments or scales the person used rather than on objective health risk. For example, depending on the samples on which these instruments were normed, a person could be high risk on one instrument and low-medium risk on a different instrument. With an instrument developed using CTT, it is difficult to determine the range of the construct that is tapped by the measure. To illustrate further, an instrument might address health-promotive lifestyle changes, but only with intensive carer help, while another instrument of health-promotive lifestyle changes may address the amount of lifestyle change (e.g., no change versus any involvement in health-promotive activity).

Many people with debilitating chronic health conditions with experimental use of lifestyle changes never get to regularly use a lifestyle behavior activity. Quite conceivably, a person might have a high score on the instrument that measures the amount of lifestyle change and a low score on the instrument that measures adherence to a lifestyle regimen. Use of any two instruments on lifestyle change without the ability to calibrate at the item level might lead one to make inaccurate or inappropriate comparisons from failure to take into account differences in the range of the construct measured by each instrument. The risks for bias in test scores and inferences based on them are immeasurably multiplied using CCT-based approaches to assessment.

IRT is a method to determine the utility of a test item (or group of items) by the information that the item (or group of items) contributes toward estimating a person's ability (e.g., likelihood of endorsing an item) on an underlying construct (or latent trait; Andrich, 1988; Gierl, Rasch 1980). This latent trait estimation is possible because with IRT, item characteristics (e.g., difficulty or endorsability) and person ability are placed on a common scale (or metric) using log-odd units or logits so that the distribution of the item parameters is removed during the estimation of the person measures and the distribution of the person parameter is removed during the estimation of the item measures. The concept of "ability," although more readily understandable within an educational framework, applies to measurement properties of items and not context. Hence, the concepts easily generalize to noneducational tests items, such as health assessments (Lord, 1980).

Person ability is an estimate of the person's endorsement of a set of items that measure a single trait (e.g., a measure of health-promotive behavior). A person who "passes" a particular item at a specified level of difficulty (e.g., endorses a clinician lifestyle behavior change treatment) can be reliably said to possess a certain level of competence on the underlying trait that the test item measures (e.g., health promotion). In the context of IRT modeling, the item difficulty parameter is a measure of the ability (or trait) level needed to endorse an item at a given level. The interaction between person ability and test item difficulty makes it possible to create a model that enables the prediction of the likelihood that a person with certain ability will answer a particular test item correctly (e.g., people with experimental lifestyle behavior change use are less likely to endorse items that measure high lifestyle change adherence behavior). IRT-based measures are also constructed to be equivalent measures of the domain of interest at the instrument level.

Sample-Free Measures

Unlike with instruments developed using CTT that are sample dependent, measures constructed using the IRT models enable a separation of a person's health risk status from the particular test items that are used to measure that person's health status or the performance of others who took the test (Cella & Chih-Hung, 2000; Reeve & Fayers, 2005). IRT modeling places the person and the items on the same axis so that the ability of the person and the difficulty of the items are probabilistically estimated. That is, a person at a specific health-promotive "ability" level (e.g., of adoption of a health-promotive lifestyle change) would have an estimated likelihood of endorsing lifestyle behavior change items at a given range of ability. The person's health-promotive lifestyle behavior use status can be reliably established even though he or she took different test items on different occasions and/or skipped some questions. Furthermore, a person's response to a lifestyle change item provides direct evidence of his or her health-promotive lifestyle behavior status independent of the sample on which the test was normed. This is possible because IRT-based measures place all these lifestyle change items on a continuum with each item maintaining its location on the hierarchy of lifestyle behavior items, regardless of the distributional properties of the respondents. Thus, IRT-based measures have comparability and transportability across samples because they are constructed to tap into the construct of interest and to yield comparable results for people of equal status on the target construct. This is a major strength in minimizing test score bias and the validity of interpretations based on those scores.

Interval Scale Properties

The CTT measurement approach mistakenly treats the concrete counts of indicators of health outcomes (e.g., response choices on health risk items) as abstract measures of amount. Items from surveys applied to health outcomes measurement are indicators rather than measures of health outcomes and only become measures after an IRT calibration procedure to interval measurement properties (Andrich, 2003). The summative indices from adding indicator values following a CTT approach are not valid for comparisons across settings or populations because they are not constructed on a common, interval metric. The lack of robustness of CTT instruments from their noninterval properties limits the generalizability of findings across studies or settings. IRT-based measurement models are useful for constructing measures that are invariant across samples and instruments to enable meaningful aggregation of data from multiple settings for analysis as well as for plotting people along the healthcare continuum of interest to reliably identity patient unmet needs at the individual person level.

With a CTT approach, there is an assumption that the respondent group uses every scale point and that there is a ratio (a score of "4" is twice the value of a score of "2" on a 4-point Likert-type scale) or an equal interval across the scale points. In real terms, when certain response options are not used for specific items in a scale, the scale is made up of items that essentially function on a different scale. This is because response categories and item scores are not necessarily the same thing; most conventional analyses make little or no use of this information.

IRT-based measures provide information on the frequency and monotonicity of response option use. IRT measures provide *step difficulty calibrations*, indicating how *difficult* it is to endorse *strongly agree* over *agree*. There is an assumption that step calibrations should increase monotonically. If not, the response options are considered disordered. Infrequent and inconsistently used response options are indications for revising the scale. Essentially, CTT assumes and treats responses as ratios or intervals when they are not; IRT provides estimates for each item and for each response option.

IRT analysis yields an information curve for each scale on the x- and y-axes. The x-axis for each curve shows the range of scores for people's experiences up to 4 standard deviations above and below the mean. The y-axis depicts the amount of patient experience care information that the scale provides for people reporting different levels of quality of care based on the number of items on the scale they endorsed and the ability of the items to discriminate among different levels of care needs (see Figure 16.2).

Scores from a test with reliability and validity have a widespread information curve indicating good discrimination across the full range of care experiences, adding value to quality care improvement efforts. One with a peaked and narrow information curve indicated good discrimination at the middle of the scale only, limiting utility for quality care improvements efforts across the spectrum of healthcare needs. For the purposes of developing measures of person-centric healthcare that are objective, usable across healthcare settings, and sensitive to prospective health, the use of an IRT probabilistic model is stronger and more valid than a CTT approach.

Test Response Demands

Tests and their items come with an implicit demand of the test questions or likelihood of expected responses to questions for the construct being assessed (Mpofu & Ortiz, 2009; Reynolds & Suzuki, 2013). These implicit test response demands, which would bias person response in unknown ways, may emanate from the language and content of the tests, the response format, and the situational or transactional context of the assessment situation.

Language Bias and Inappropriate Content

Tests written to mainstream white English-language phraseology may miscommunicate important patient experience of care understanding. As an example, questions that overly emphasize personal choice and control over treatment adherence may misrepresent the health management of Latino/Hispanic and African American patients who place a higher priority on the involvement of family and significant others in their health management (Mpofu, Beck, & Weinrach, 2004). Increasingly, family involvement is a pivotal resource in treatment care even with majority White culture patients, although less often asked about on person-oriented healthcare measures (Carman et al., 2013). The case of Mrs. Bradley in Box 16.3 is illustrative.

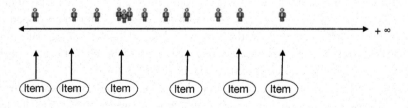

FIGURE 16.2 Line representing a trait continuum, with people and test stimuli scaled along it.

BOX 16.3

THE CASE OF MRS. BRADLEY: A PERSON-CENTRIC CARE EXEMPLAR

Mrs. Bradley was a rehabilitation inpatient following a diagnosis of neuromyelitis optica, which resulted in rapid loss of motor and sensory function in her lower limbs, along with incontinence of the bladder and bowel. She underwent intensive rehabilitation and pharmacological treatment for her demyelinating condition without any change in her degree of impairment. With assistance, she was able to transfer into and out of a motorized wheelchair. Major modifications, including ramp installation and bathroom remodeling, were made to her home to enable wheelchair access. Equipment, including a hoist and pressure relieving hospital bed, were obtained. Within her modified home environment, with the assistance of nurses and family, she was able to perform personal activities of daily living. Prior to the onset of illness, Mrs. Bradley was highly motivated to return to work. Unfortunately, traveling to and from work was very difficult, expensive, and time-consuming. Once at the office, she was able to perform the majority of her usual duties, and she reported significant personal satisfaction from returning to work. Much of her nursing care and home modifications were funded by Mrs. Bradley and her family. Mrs. Bradley's return to work helped her family financial situation. The lack of suitable public transportation was a major barrier to Mrs. Bradley's participation in paid employment.

Moreover, the language and content on person experience of care may be with a cultural loading on the meanings attached to states of wellness or ill-health significance, including the expectation for patients to lead their own treatment effort. Some racial/ethnic minority patients may prefer to defer to clinicians, taking a back seat in their treatment care (Mpofu, Chronister, Johnson, & Denham, 2012, Mpofu & Harley, 2015). They may also be less familiar with the language, instruments, and procedures for treatment uptake and adherence, which would reduce their sense of being the focus of the treatment effort.

Within domains of health and well-being, some tests may share considerable redundancy of items, in part from borrowing "good" items by authors from existing scales. Item redundancy between and within scales may also be explained by the need of researchers to maximize the likelihood that important behaviors of the health construct of interest are adequately sampled. However, when items are "borrowed" and used across settings (e.g., medical care settings, cultures), there is often the implicit assumption that they are measuring the same construct in both settings. If this assumption was in fact false (which often it is), then the substantive conclusions from using the data can be quite misleading (Leigh & Stall, 1993; van de Vijver & Leung, 1997).

As noted previously, traditionally, test development approaches have sought to privilege extant desk theories and peer review so that a test that was translated into many languages was perceived as a successful and culturally transportable test (Reynolds & Suzuki, 2013). In real terms, there is little evidence for this belief, which is in fact a myth. Person experience of care tests from desk theories and translations may miss out on lived experience of care understandings (or connotative meanings) not represented on the target test for healthcare provision (Robert et al., 2015). Furthermore, theory and peer-review approaches to developing frameworks for person-oriented care and without partnership with patient–provider networks may not reliably anticipate the response demands on people in care or others involved in treatment care.

Test Administration Procedure

Threats to test bias in person-oriented experience of care measures might also emanate from a lack of familiarity by participants with the test procedures and instructions (Mpofu, Oakland, Ntinda, Maree, & Seeco, 2015; Reynolds & Suzuki, 2013). Based on theory or peer review, tests may be developed for use in person-oriented care, including clinical and or administrative interventions, and management plans without the benefit on extensive prior study of response accessibility to patients with culturally diversity. Most test development and standardization efforts pay little attention to the possibility that persons with healthcare needs may have unique interpretations for the competence to exhibit for any specific question or the meaning of what may be transparently clear to the test designers (Gollust et al., 2018).

Most survey instruments use a Likert-type scale and provide polychotomous data. Of particular pertinence to this study is the fact that with Likert-type measures, respondents may differ in the extent to which they use item-choice categories by culture (Marquis, Keininger, Acquadro, & de la Loge, 2005; Snider & Styles, 2005; van Herk, Poortinga, & Verhallen, 2004). For example, Southern Europeans tended to use extreme ratings on a 5-point Likert scale more than did Northern Europeans (van Herk et al., 2004). Similarly, Latinos tended to choose extremes on a 5-point rating scale more than Anglo Americans (Azocar, Arean, Miranda, & Munoz, 2001). People with a cultural predisposition to endorse extreme choices with a polychotomously scored item may be more reliable with fewer choices (Wright & Masters, 1982). The utility of the response categories in differentiating patients in their experience of care has not been empirically investigated. For these reasons, instructions to test items may need to be checked with a sample of would-be responders for clarity to them, and practice items may need to be provided to ensure that the responses to the questions are appropriate. Moreover, trial test use is also important for troubleshooting any aspects of test administration that might pose problems for testing.

Situational or Transactional Context of the Assessment

Depending on their social grouping identity, patients or clients may perceive the demands of an experience of care differently from providers (Dovidio et al., 2008; Gollust et al., 2018; Nguyen et al., 2009; Wagner et al., 2011; Williams & Sterthal, 2010). For instance, if with a care provider assessor from a socioculturally privileged group and being appraised in the assessor's language, the demand characteristics from implicit self-perceptions of social disadvantage by the patient could supersede any objective aspects of experience of care settings (Clark & McMillan-Persaud, 2014; Gollust et al., 2018; Wagner et al., 2011), possibly resulting in lower patient experience of care scores than would be expected on the basis of actual quality of service received (Doividio & Fiske, 2012; Dovidio et al., 2008). Nonetheless, emotional invalidation in care is associated with poor health outcomes of emotional dysregulation, emotional distress, and decline in psychological health over time (Zielinski & Veilleux, 2018). This would be a case of people's perceptions being their reality. By contrast, if people perceived healthcare equity, scores in experience of care may be more reliable for clinical and administrative decisions (Nguyen et al., 2009). In summary, patients or clients in their self-reporting on experience of care may yield scores imputing the perceived demand characteristics of the care experience, regardless of the objective evidence that the care process and context were equitable (see also Beach et al., 2005; Dovidio et al., 2008; Flott et al., 2017; Jacobson, 2009).

▨ Issues for Research and Other Forms of Scholarship

Clinicians often rely on scores from tests for decisions about patient or client treatment choices, monitoring, and outcomes (First et al., 2004; Kendell & Jablensky, 2003; McFall, 2005). In the context of person-oriented care, improvements in service qualities are premised on the reliability and validity of scores from measures with a functional relationship to the enhanced provision and outcome of clinical services (Hunsley & Mash, 2007; Reeves et al., 2013). These observations are made with the important caveat that overreliance on scores from tests alone may result in underestimation of the patient's rehabilitation recovery potential (McGlynn, Adams, & Kerr, 2016). Research on test score reliability and validity in patient experience of care should seek to result in health syndrome-responsive measures, based on frameworks developed in partnership with patient–provider networks, with objective measurement qualities, and developed utilizing state-of-the-art measure equating approaches.

Syndrome-Responsive Measures

Patients or clients typically present with a primary and secondary health condition for which commonly used measures may not be designed to scale in the sense of a broadly scoped syndromic presentation (Kazdin, 2005; Krueger & Markon, 2006). In other words, scores from tests based on a poor estimation of the level and spread of the underlying latent health condition (e.g., with a small ceiling and floor range) are biased and unreliable for clinical decisions that require a syndromic understanding of the health condition. With use of scores from narrowly scoped measures, healthcare services run the risk of misallocating resources to provide for treatments that few clients would require. Moreover, mistargeted clinical and healthcare administrative services based on scores from narrow bandwidth tests that do not allow for reliable prognostic predictions risk unwanted costs from avoidable patient or client readmissions (Frost et al., 2007). Patients who perceive to be on a merry-go-round in their clinical and administration support likely will report experiencing poor satisfaction with services, with serious risk for avoidable death, in part from poor adherence to treatment services they find meaningless (Beach et al., 2005; Blanchard, Nayar, & Lurie, 2007).

Partnership for Framing Person-Centric Healthcare Measures

A majority of existing measures of person-oriented healthcare have been developed using a rational approach to item construction, whereby experts unilaterally derive test items that they administer to and norm on samples of patients (Asch et al., 2006, Teresi & Jones, 2016, Vickers, 2003). With these measures, experts may have derived items based on specific theories of person-centric care or simply on the need to cover important health status questions as adjudged by peer review. These are clearly defensible methods to develop measures and are very useful for epidemiological studies. The fact is that health behavior constructs are not necessarily universal and transportable across the provider and consumer divide, in the absence of use of active partnership-building procedures to minimize perceived demand level by patients (Flott et al., 2017; Gollust et al., 2018; Lim, Vardy, Oh, & Dhillon, 2017; William & Sternthal, 2010). Theoretical models were well represented in healthcare professionals training, whereas practical or functional models aligned well with patient demands (Lim et al., 2017).

For this reason, person-oriented care tests developed by patient–provider networks would be more serviceable for quality-of-care improvement compared to those constructed using rationalist or item bank sampling alone (Flott et al., 2017; Kowalski et al., 2017; Robert et al., 2015). Quality care improvement efforts aiming to address patient perceptions of equity in care should aim to result in patients reporting experiences of care closer to those of peers regardless of social grouping membership.

The initial pool of items to result with patient–provider networks partnerships should be over-inclusive to map the continuum of the construct exhaustively (Gehlbach & Brinkworth, 2011). Emphasis should be on retaining participants' own language for experience qualities rather than those primarily from the researcher's theoretical or technical orientation.

Objective Measures of Person-Oriented Care

The development of measures that objectively assess health status is a prerequisite for person-oriented healthcare premised on optimizing targeted health support interventions (Davies et al., 2011; Dawson et al., 2010; Reeves et al., 2013). Minimally, such measures in their use should enable a separation of a person's health ability or function from the particular test items that are used to measure that person's health ability (Cella & Chih-Hung, 2000). This means that a person's health ability can be reliably established from his or her responses to any set of questions that are equivalent in measuring the health ability construct of interest. That being the case, the person's health ability can be reliably established even though he or she took different test items on different occasions and/or skipped some questions. Moreover, scores from tests probabilistic estimation of a person's health ability can be used to plan for health promotion because they are futuristic in orientation (i.e., give a reliable indication of the chances of success with a health situation that may occur; Andrich, 1988; Rasch, 1980). These qualities are achievable when scores from tests are used for their value in enabling consequential health support decisions and studied for evidence of their ability to measure a person's current functioning, enabling estimation of the person's prospective health abilities.

Need for Measure Equating

The proliferation of person-oriented care measures calls for studies to applying IRT to co-calibrate the measures for efficiency and their transportability across population as well as service settings. The use of IRT to construct health status measures is relatively new to patient experience of care for quality improvement (Teresi &Jones, 2016, Vickers, 2003). However, there are large databases of patient experience of care indicators (Asch et al., 2006; Teresi et al., 2009; Teresi & Jones, 2016), including those from longitudinal population surveys (e.g., Community Tracking Study Household Survey [CTS]; Health Tracking Household Survey [HTHS], 2010) to allow for measure development using equating procedures.

Measure equating is a well-established and robust co-calibration procedure. *Measure equating* refers to the practice of linking different instruments to common metrics (McHorney & Cohen, 2000). Measures are linked to the extent that items common to the measures have stable parameter estimates across forms or have a good fit. A number of fit indices to examine the quality of the measure link, once parameters are estimated, (1) item within link, (2) item between links, (3) link within bank, and (4) form within bank (Wolfe, 2000). Item-within-link fit is the degree of fit of the link items within the respective link. Item-between-links fit is the extent to which the link items maintain their relative location between different measures. Link-within-bank fit is the agreement among links in relation to form difficulties. Specifically, it is a comparative index of the location shift between forms relative to the overall location shift for the combined set of items from the different forms. Form-within-bank fit is a measure of the fit of the link to the entire bank of items.

Two approaches to measure equating are anchor instrument design and simultaneous calibration (Kolen & Brennan, 1995; Linacre, 1998). Figure 16.3 shows a prospective measure equating strategy utilizing both anchor instrument design and simultaneous calibration of patient experience of care measures with publicly accessible data from the CTS data sets (succeeded by the HTHS): Patient Unmet Health Care Needs (PHCN), Satisfaction with Health Care and Health Care Plans (SHC), Patient Trust in Physicians (PTP), and Sources of Health Information (SIF).

Those data sets include a total of 46,587 patients (males = 21,541, females = 25,046), large race/ethnicity representation (white = 34,354; African American = 5,256; Hispanic = 4,711; and non-Hispanic Other = 2,266), and diversity in health conditions and treatment settings. The CTS data set also tracks up to four follow-up surveys, allowing examination of stability of measure parameters over time. These following research questions addressing test score bias can be addressed:

1. Can patient experience of care indicators from CTS data sets be constructed to yield comparable, equal interval measures?

2. Are response category functions for the patient experience of care used by patients in the projected direction and distribution? If not, could they be collapsed to yield reliable variables for measuring patient experience of care?

3. *Does nonuniform* DIF exist in the patient experience data by race/ethnicity to suggest atypical or group-specific experience on the indicator item? If DIF does exist for some items, would that necessitate the construction of group-specific patient experience of care variables?

Applying an *anchor instrument design,* linked or common items among instruments are identified and co-calibrated, and then the rest of the other items from related measures are aligned on a common scale with a single origin. The anchor instrument design is appropriate with samples from two populations, which took different measures (X, Y) for which data are available from a common measure (Z) for both samples. The data from the shared measure or items are used to link the items on the measures not shared by the samples (see Figure 16.3).

Simultaneous or concurrent measure calibration involves the equating of various aspects of items (difficulty, discrimination), rating scale (or distance between categories) with a study population, and adding to the efficiency with to create nonredundant measures of a health behavior construct (e.g., patient experience of care; see Figure 16.3). Using these approaches provides for a built-in replication procedure to establish the stability or comparability of parameter estimates both between and within measures. In the event that significant inconsistencies appear among the initial calibration (with random selection from among the study measures) and replications, anchor items with the most stable estimates are selected for the measure equating, and the simultaneous calibrations repeated to acceptable fit indices for the IRT measurement model.

Summary and Conclusion

Person-oriented healthcare services, their design, and the instruments for them are aspirational to health systems across the globe. Increasingly, healthcare systems seek to collect and use data on patient experience of care for their quality improvement changes. When healthcare systems prioritize primarily diagnostic medical needs and the instruments for them and less the person-focused care needs of the patients or clients, there is a tremendous loss to quality experience of care. Poor person-oriented care scores are associated with high financial costs from avoidable re-admissions,

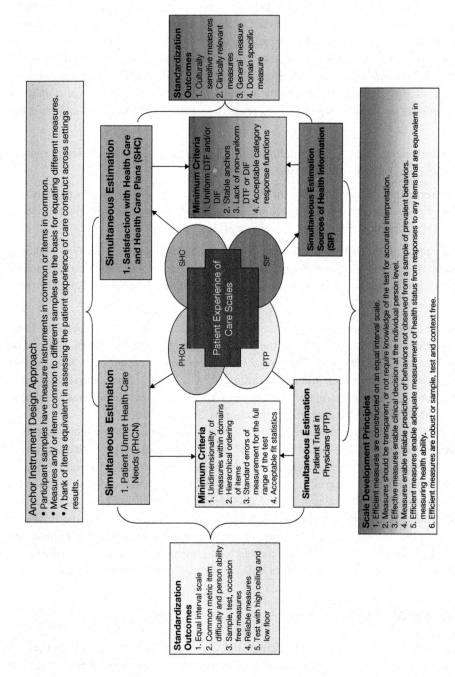

FIGURE 16.3 Patient experience measure standardization plan.

DIF, differential item functioning; DTF, differential test functioning.

morbidity, and mortality. Increasingly, healthcare services require use of instruments that yield scores usable for person-centric clinical, administrative, and policy decisions.

Scores from measures of person-oriented care provide important information for quality improvement care. The evidence is mixed on measures of patient experience of care by social groupings of race/ethnicity, gender, sexual orientation, and social class in the United States, yet the evidence is sorely lacking on the reliability and validity of scores across health populations and service settings. Also, healthcare providers increasingly use identical or similar self-report items from different instruments in assessing person-oriented care services and often with no proven cross-cultural population or setting comparability. Yet, health professionals are also keenly interested in achieving equivalence of care indicators across settings and cultures to enable comparative analysis for (a) a more complete understanding of health service utilization and (b) quality-of-care improvement interventions. Stakes are high for patients at risk for avoidable morbidity and mortality from use of instruments with little evidence for reliability of scores and valid interpretation for consequential care decisions. Considerations for test score bias and validity of interpretation require the use of measurement models for person-centric interpretation.

Test score bias and validity considerations in healthcare settings must take into account the presetting factors that patients may bring to care, understanding that these are likely explained by historical experiences and not the psychometric properties of the specific instruments. Moreover, what patients may be reporting on is likely influenced by latent or underlying beliefs about quality care in their service setting. Studies on test score bias and validity in patient experience of care have neglected the importance of presetting influences to observed scores and also consideration of malleable factors to which quality-of-care improvement efforts could be profitably directed. Moreover, there is need for equating measures of patient-oriented care indicators to allow the aggregation of evidence for best practices in quality care improvement. These quality-of-care improvement needs will likely be met with use of tests that yield comparable scores across patient populations and with an understanding of the syndromic nature of health conditions.

References

American Educational Research Association, American Psychological Association, & National Council on Measurement in Education. (2014). *Standards for educational and psychological testing*. Washington, DC: American Psychological Association.

Andrich, D. (2003). On the distribution of measurements in units that are not arbitrary. *Social Science Information, 42*, 557–589. doi:10.1177/0539018403424006

Asch, S. M., Kerr, E. A., Keesey, J., Adams, J. L., Setodji, C. M., Malik, S., & McGlynn, E. A. (2006). Who is at greatest risk of receiving poor-quality health care? *New England Journal of Medicine, 354*(11), 1147–1156. doi:10.1056/nejmsa044464

Azocar, F. Arean, P., Miranda, J., & Munoz, R. F. (2001). Differential item functioning in a Spanish translation of the Beck Depression Inventory. *Journal of Clinical Psychology, 57*, 355–365. doi:10.1002/jclp.1017

Bautista, M. A., Nurjono. M, Lim Y. W., Dessers, E., & Vrijhoef, H. J. (2016). Instruments measuring integrated care: A systematic review of measurement properties. *Mibank Quarterly, 94*(4), 862–917. doi:10.1111/1468-0009.12233

Beach, M. C., Sugarman, J., Johnson, R. L., Arbelaez, J. J., Duggan, P. S., & Cooper, L. A. (2005). Do patients treated with dignity report higher satisfaction, adherence, and receipt of preventive care? *The Annals of Family Medicine, 3*(4), 331–338. doi:10.1370/afm.328

Black, N. (2013). Patient reported outcome measures could help transform healthcare. *British Medical Journal, 346,* f167. doi:10.1136/bmj.f167

Blanchard, J., & Lurie, N. (2004). R-E-S-P-E-C-T: Patient reports of disrespect in the health care setting and its impact on care. *Journal of Family Practice, 53,* 721–730.

Blanchard, J., Nayar, S., & Lurie, N. (2007). Patient–provider and patient–staff racial concordance and perceptions of mistreatment in the health care setting. *Journal of General Internal Medicine, 22*(8), 1184–1189. doi:10.1007/s11606-007-0210-8

Bond, T. G, & Fox, C. M. (2001). *Applying the Rasch model: Fundamental measurement in the human sciences.* Mahwah, NJ: Lawrence Erlbaum.

Carman, K. L., Dardess, P., Maurer, M., Sofaer, S., Adams, K., Bechtel, C., & Sweeney, J. (2013). Patient and family engagement: A framework for understanding the elements and developing interventions and policies. *Health Affairs, 32*(2), 223–231. doi:10.1377/hlthaff.2012.1133

Clark, K. P., & McMillan-Persaud, B. (2014). Racial discordance in patient–physician relationships. *The American Journal of Medicine, 127*(3), e25. doi:10.1016/j.amjmed.2013.09.038

Community Tracking Study Household Survey (CTS) (1997–2003); Health Tracking Household Survey (HTHS) (2007+). (2010). Retrieved from https://dss.princeton.edu/catalog/resource447

Cooper, L. A., Hill, M. N., & Powe, N. R. (2002). Designing and evaluating interventions to eliminate racial and ethnic disparities in health care. *Journal of General Internal Medicine, 17,* 477–486. doi:10.1046/j.1525-1497.2002.10633.x

Davies, E., & Cleary, P. D. (2005). Hearing the patient's voice? Factors affecting the use of patient survey data in quality improvement. *Quality and Safety in Health Care, 14*(6), 428–432. doi:10.1136/qshc.2004.012955

Davies, E. A., Meterko, M. M., Charns, M. P., Seibert, M. E. N., & Cleary, P. D. (2011). Factors affecting the use of patient survey data for quality improvement in the Veterans Health Administration. *BMC Health Services Research, 11*(1), 334. doi:10.1186/1472-6963-11-334

Davis, K., Schoenbaum, S. C., & Audet, A. J. (2005). A 2020 vision of patient-centered primary care. *Journal of General Internal Medicine, 20*(10), 953–957. doi:10.1111/j.1525-1497.2005.0178.x

Dawson, J., Doll, H., Fitzpatrick, R., Jenkinson, C., & Carr, A. J. (2010). The routine use of patient reported outcome measures in healthcare settings. *British Medical Journal, 340,* c186. doi:10.1136/bmj.c186

Dayton, E., Zhan, C. L., Sangl, J., Darby, C., & Moy, E. (2006). Racial and ethnic differences in patient assessments of interactions with providers: Disparities or measurement biases? *American Journal of Medical Quality, 21,* 109–114. doi:10.1177/1062860605285164

Doeschler, M. P., Saver, B. G., Franks, P., & Fiscella, K. (2000). Racial and ethnic disparities in perceptions of physician style and trust. *Archives of Family Medicine, 9,* 1156–1163. doi:10.1001/archfami.9.10.1156

Dovidio, J. F., & Fiske, S. T. (2012). Under the radar: How unexamined biases in decision-making processes in clinical interactions can contribute to health care disparities. *American Journal of Public Health, 102*(5), 945–952. doi:10.2105/ajph.2011.300601

Dovidio, J. F., Penner, L. A., Albrecht, T. L., Norton, W. E., Gaertner, S. L., & Shelton, J. N. (2008). Disparities and distrust: The implications of psychological processes for understanding racial disparities in health and health care. *Social Science & Medicine, 67*(3), 478–486. doi:10.1016/j.socscimed.2008.03.019

First, M. B., Pincus, H. A., Levine, J. B., Williams, J. B., Ustun, B., & Peele, R. (2004). Clinical utility as a criterion for revising psychiatric diagnoses. *American Journal of Psychiatry, 161*(6), 946–954. doi:10.1016/j.measurement.2019.03.056

Fiscella, K., & Sanders, M. R. (2016). Racial and ethnic disparities in the quality of health care. *Annual Review of Public Health, 37,* 375–394. doi:10.1146/annurev-publhealth-032315-021439

Flott, K. M., Graham, C., Darzi, A., & Mayer, E. (2017). Can we use patient-reported feedback to drive change? The challenges of using patient-reported feedback and how they might be addressed. *BMJ Quality & Safety, 26*(6), 502–507. doi:10.1136/bmjqs-2016-005223

Frost, M. H., Reeve, B. B., Liepa, A. M., Stauffer, J. W., Hays, R. D., & Mayo/FDA Patient-Reported Outcomes Consensus Meeting Group. (2007). What is sufficient evidence for the reliability and validity of patient-reported outcome measures? *Value in Health, 10,* S94–S105. doi:10.1111/j.1524-4733.2007.00272.x

Gehlbach, H., & Brinkworth, M. E. (2011). Measure twice, cut down error: A process for enhancing the validity of survey scales. *Review of General Psychology, 15,* 380–387.

Gollust, S. E., Cunningham, B. A., Bokhour, B. G., Gordon, H. S., Pope, C., Saha, S. S., & Burgess, D. J. (2018). What causes racial health care disparities? A mixed-methods study reveals variability in how health care providers perceive causal attributions. *INQUIRY, 55,* 1–11. doi:10.1177/0046958018762840

Harris, R., Cormack, D., Tobias, M., Yeh, L. C., Talamaivao, N., Minster, J., & Timutimu, R. (2012). Self-reported experience of racial discrimination and health care use in New Zealand: Results from the 2006/07 New Zealand Health Survey. *American Journal of Public Health, 102*(5), 1012–1019. doi:10.2105/ajph.2011.300626

Hausmann, L. R., Kwoh, C. K., Hannon, M. J., & Ibrahim, S. A. (2013). Perceived racial discrimination in health care and race differences in physician trust. *Race and Social Problems, 5*(2), 113–120. doi:10.1007/s12552-013-9092-z

Haviland, M. G., Morales, L. S., Dial, T. H., & Pincus, H. A. (2005). Race/ethnicity socioeconomic status, and satisfaction with health care. *American Journal of Medical Quality, 20,* 195–203. doi:10.1177/1062860605275754

Health Tracking Household Survey. (2010). *U.S. version.* Retrieved from http://b2find.eudat.eu/dataset/dd4a9ad1-37b1-59f1-8ac0-4999a97c599d; doi:10.3886/ICPSR34141.v1

Hicks, L. S., Ayanian, J. Z., Orav, E. J., Soukup, J., McWilliams, J. M., Choi, S. S., & Johnson, P. A. (2005). Is hospital service associated with racial and ethnic disparities in experiences with hospital care? *American Journal of Medicine, 118,* 529–535. doi:10.1016/j.amjmed.2005.02.012

Hunsley, J., & Mash, E. J. (2007). Evidence-based assessment. *Annual Review of Clinical Psychology, 3,* 29–51. doi:10.1146/annurev.clinpsy.3.022806.091419

Hunt, K. A., Gaba, A., & Lavizzo-Mourey, R. (2005). Racial and ethnic disparities and perceptions of health care: Does health plan type matter? *Health Services Research, 40,* 551–576. doi:10.1111/j.1475-6773.2005.0z373.x

Hwang, K., & Mpofu, E. (2010). Health care quality assessments. In E. Mpofu & T. Oakland (Eds.), *Rehabilitation and health assessment: Applying ICF guidelines* (pp. 141–161). New York, NY: Springer.

Institute of Health Improvement. (2006). *Patient-centered care: General.* Retrieved from http://www.ihi.org/IHI/Topics/PatientCenteredCare/PatientCenteredCareGeneral

Institute of Medicine. (2001, March). *Crossing the quality chasm: A new health system for the 21st century.* Washington, DC: National Academies Press. Retrieved from http://www.nap.edu

Kendell, R., & Jablensky, A. (2003). Distinguishing between the validity and utility of psychiatric diagnoses. *American Journal of Psychiatry, 160*(1), 4–12. doi:10.1176/appi.ajp.160.1.4

Kolen, M. J., & Brennan, R. L. (1995). *Test equating: Methods and practices.* New York, NY: Springer-Verlag.

Kowalski, C., Yeaton, W. H., Kuhr, K., & Pfaff, H. (2017). Helping hospitals improve patient centeredness: Assessing the impact of feedback following a best practices workshop. *Evaluation & the Health Professions, 40*(2), 180–202. doi:10.1177/0163278716677321

Kressin, N. R., Clark, J. A., Whittle, J., East, M., Peterson, E. D., Chang, B.-H., . . . Petersen, L. A. (2002). Racial differences in health-related beliefs, attitudes, and experiences of VA cardiac patients—Scale development and application. *Medical Care, 40,* 72–85. doi:10.1097/00005650-200201001-00009

Krieger, N., Chen, J., Waterman, P. D, Rehkopf, D. H., & Subramanian, S. V. (2005). Painting a truer picture of US socioeconomic and racial/ethnic health inequalities: The public health disparities project geocoding project. *American Journal of Public Health, 95,* 312–323. doi:10.2105/ajph.2003.032482

Krueger, R. F., & Markon, K. E. (2006). Reinterpreting comorbidity: A model-based approach to understanding and classifying psychopathology. *Annual Review of Clinical Psychology, 2,* 111. doi:10.1146/annurev.clinpsy.2.022305.095213

Leigh, B. C., & Stall, R. (1993). Substance use and risky sexual behavior for exposure to HIV: Issues in methodology, interpretation, and prevention. *American Psychologist, 48*(10), 1035.

Lim, E. J., Vardy, J. L., Oh, B. S., & Dhillon, H. M. (2017). A scoping review on models of integrative medicine: What is known from the existing literature? *The Journal of Alternative and Complementary Medicine, 23*(1), 8–17. doi:10.1089/acm.2016.0263

Linacre, J. M. (1998). Detecting multidimensionality: Which residual data-type works best? *Journal of Outcome Measurement, 2*(3), 266–283.

Lord, F. M. (1980). *Application of Item Response Theory to practical testing problems*. Hillsdale, NJ: Lawrence Erlbaum.

Madden, R., Fortune, E., Cheeseman, D., Mpofu, E., Bundy, A. (2013). Fundamental questions before recording or measuring functioning and disability. *Disability and Rehabilitation, 35*(13), 1092–1096. doi:10.3109/09638288.2012.720350

Makoul, G., Krupat, E., & Chang, C. H. (2007). Measuring patient views of physician communication skills: Development and testing of the Communication Assessment Tool. *Patient Education and Counseling, 67*, 333–342. doi:10.1016/j.pec.2007.05.005

Marquis, P., Keininger, D., Acquadro, C., & de la Loge, C. (2005). Translating and evaluating questionnaires: Cultural issues for international research. In P. Fayers & R. Hays (Eds.), *Assessing quality of life in clinical trials: Method and practice* (pp. 95–112). Oxford, UK: Oxford University Press.

McFall, R. M. (2005). Theory and utility—Key themes in evidence-based assessment: Comment on the special section. *Psychological Assessment, 17*(3), 312–323. doi:10.1037/1040-3590.17.3.312

McGlynn, E. A., Adams, J. L., & Kerr, E. A. (2016). The quest to improve quality: Measurement is necessary but not sufficient. *JAMA Internal Medicine, 176*(12), 1790–1791. doi:10.1001/jamainternmed.2016.6233

Mpofu, E., Beck, R., & Weinrach, S. (2004). Multicultural rehabilitation counseling: Challenges and strategies. In K. R. Thomas, F. Chan & N. L. Berven (Eds.), *Counseling theories and techniques for rehabilitation professionals* (pp. 386–404). New York, NY: Springer Publishing Company.

Mpofu, E., Caldwell, L., Smith, E., Flisher, A. J., Mathews, C., Wegner, L., & Vergnani, T. (2006). Rasch modeling of the structure of health risk behavior in South African adolescents. *Journal of Applied Measurement, 7*, 323–334.

Mpofu, E., Chronister, J., Johnson, E., & Denham, G. (2012). Aspects of culture influencing rehabilitation and persons with disabilities. In P. Kennedy (Ed.), *The Oxford handbook of rehabilitation psychology* (pp. 543–553). New York, NY: Oxford University Press.

Mpofu, E., & Harley, D. A. (2015). Multicultural rehabilitation counseling: Optimizing success with diversity. In F. Chan, N. L. Berven, & K. R. Thomas (Eds.), *Counseling theories and techniques for rehabilitation and mental health professions* (2nd ed., pp. 417–441). New York, NY: Springer Publishing Company.

Mpofu, E., & Mpofu, N. (2018). Assessment. In V. Taryvidas & M. Hartley (Eds.), *Professional practice of rehabilitation counseling* (2nd ed., pp. 201–220). New York, NY: Springer Publishing Company.

Mpofu, E., Oakland, T., Ntinda, K., Maree, J. G., & Seeco, E. G. (2015). Locality, observability and community action (LOCUM) in test development and use in emerging education settings. *Handbook of international development and education* (pp. 326–342). Cheltenham, UK: Edward Elgar.

Mpofu, E., & Ortiz, J. (2009). Equitable assessment practices in diverse contexts. In E. Grigorenko (Ed.), *Multicultural psychoeducational assessment* (pp. 41–76). New York, NY: Springer.

Ngui, E. M., & Flores, G. (2006). Satisfaction with care and ease of using health care services among parents of children with special health care needs: The roles of race/ethnicity, insurance, language, and adequacy of family centered care. *Pediatrics, 117*, 1184–1196. doi:10.1542/peds.2005-1088

Nguyen, G. C., LaVeist, T. A., Harris, M. L., Datta, L. W., Bayless, T. M., & Brant, S. R. (2009). Patient trust-in-physician and race are predictors of adherence to medical management in inflammatory bowel disease. *Inflammatory Bowel Diseases, 15*(8), 1233–1239. doi:10.1002/ibd.20883

Orbell, S., Johnston, M., Rowley, D., Davey, P., Espley, A. (2001). Self-efficacy and goal importance in the prediction of physical disability in people following hospitalization: A prospective study. *British Journal of Health Psychology, 6*, 25–40. doi:10.1348/135910701169034

Osterlind, S., Mpofu, E., & Oakland, T. (2010). Item response theory and computer adaptive testing. In E. Mpofu & T. Oakland (Eds.), *Rehabilitation and health assessment: Applying ICF guidelines* (pp. 95–119). New York, NY: Springer.

Penner, L. A., Dovidio, J. F., Edmondson, D., Dailey, R. K., Markova, T., Albrecht, T. L., & Gaertner, S. L. (2009). The experience of discrimination and black-white health disparities in medical care. *Journal of Black Psychology, 35*(2), 180–203. doi:10.1177/0095798409333585

Rasch, G. (1980). *Probabilistic models for some intelligence and attainment tests*. Chicago, IL: University of Chicago Press.

Reeve, B., & Fayers, P. (2005). Applying item response theory modelling for evaluating questionnaire item and scale properties. In P. Fayers & R. Hays (Eds.), *Assessing quality of life in clinical trials: Method and practice* (pp. 95–112). Oxford, UK: Oxford University Press.

Reeves, R., West, E., & Barron, D. (2013). Facilitated patient experience feedback can improve nursing care: A pilot study for a phase III cluster randomised controlled trial. *BMC Health Services Research, 13*(1), 259. doi:10.1186/1472-6963-13-259

Reise, S. P., Morizot, L., & Hays, R. D. (2007). The role of the bifactor model in resolving dimensionality issues in health outcome measures. *Quality of Life Research, 16*(Suppl 1), 19–31. doi:10.1007/s11136-007-9183-7

Reynolds, C. R., & Suzuki, L. A. (2013). Bias in psychological assessment: An empirical review and recommendations. In J. R. Graham, J. A. Naglieri, I. B. Weiner, J. R. Graham, J. A. Naglieri, & I. B. Weiner (Eds.), *Handbook of psychology: Assessment psychology* (Vol. 10, 2nd ed., pp. 82–113). Hoboken, NJ: John Wiley & Sons.

Robert, G., Cornwell, J., Locock, L., Purushotham, A., Sturmey, G., & Gager, M. (2015). Patients and staff as codesigners of healthcare services. *British Medical Journal, 350*, g7714. doi:10.1136/bmj.g7714

Rudner, L., Getson, P., & Knight, D. (1980). Item bias detection techniques. *Journal of Educational Statistics, 5*, 213–233.

Sanford, K., Rivers, A. S., Braun, T. L., Schultz, K. P., Buchanan, E. P. (2018). Medical consultation experience questionnaire: Assessing perceived alliance and experiences confusion during medical consultation. *Psychological Assessment, 30*, 1499–1511. doi:10.1037/pas0000594

Smedley, B. D., Stith, A. Y., & Nelson, A. R. (2003). *Unequal treatments: Confronting racial and ethnic disparities in health care.* Washington, DC: National Academies Press.

Smith, E. V., Jr., & Smith, R. M. (2004). *Introduction to Rasch measurement.* Maple Grove, MN: JAM Press.

Snider, P. D., & Styles, I. (2005). Analysis of the collectivism and individualism scale using a Rasch measurement model. In R. F. Waugh (Ed.), *Frontiers in educational psychology* (pp. 311–332). Hauppauge, NY: Nova Science.

Swenson, S. L., Buell, S., Zettler, P., White, M., Ruston, D. C., & Lo, B. (2004). Patient-centered communication: Do patients really prefer it? *Journal of General Internal Medicine, 19*(11), 1069–1079. doi:10.1111/j.1525-1497.2004.30384.x

Teresi, J. A., & Fleishman, J. A. (2007). Differential item functioning and health assessment. *Quality of Life Research, 16*(1), 33–42. doi:10.1007/s11136-007-9184-6

Teresi, J. A., & Jones, R. N. (2016). Methodological issues in examining measurement equivalence in patient reported outcomes measures: Methods overview to the two-part series, "measurement equivalence of the Patient Reported Outcomes Measurement Information System*(PROMIS*) short forms". *Psychological Test and Assessment Modeling, 58*(1), 37–78.

Teresi, J. A., Ocepek-Welikson, K., Kleinman, M., Eimicke, J. P., Crane, P. K., Jones, R. N., & Reise, S. P. (2009). Analysis of differential item functioning in the depression item bank from the Patient Reported Outcome Measurement Information System (PROMIS): An item response theory approach. *Psychology Science Quarterly, 51*(2), 148.

van de Vijver, F. J. R., & Leung, K. (1997). *Methods and data analysis for cross-cultural research.* Newbury Park, CA: Sage.

van Herk, H., Poortinga, Y. H., & Verhallen, T. M. M. (2004). Response styles in rating scales: Evidence of method bias in data from six EU countries. *Journal of Cross-Cultural Psychology, 35*, 346–360. doi:10.1177/0022022104264126

Vickers, A. J. (2003). Statistical considerations for use of composite health-related quality-of-life scores in randomized trails. *Quality of Life Research, 13*, 717–723. doi:10.1023/b:qure.0000021686.47079.0d

Wagner, J. A., Osborn, C. Y., Mendenhall, E. A., Budris, L. M., Belay, S., & Tennen, H. A. (2011). Beliefs about racism and health among African American women with diabetes: A qualitative study. *Journal of the National Medical Association, 103*(3), 224. doi:10.1016/s0027-9684(15)30298-4

Williams, D. R., & Sternthal, M. (2010). Understanding racial-ethnic disparities in health: Sociological contributions. *Journal of Health and Social Behavior, 51*(1 Suppl), S15–S27. doi:10.1177/0022146510383838

Wolfe, E. W. (2000). Equating and item banking with the Rasch model. *Journal of Applied Measurement, 1*, 409–434.

Wright, B. D., & Masters, G. N. (1982). *Rating scale analysis.* Chicago, IL: MESA Press.

Zielinski, M. J., & Veilleux, J. C. (2018). The Perceived Invalidation of Emotion Scale (PIES): Development and psychometric properties of a novel measure of current emotion invalidation. *Psychological Assessment, 30*, 1454–1467. doi:10.1037/pas0000584

ETHICS AND ASSESSMENT IN REHABILITATION COUNSELING

MICHAEL T. HARTLEY | VILIA M. TARVYDAS

LEARNING OBJECTIVES

After reviewing this chapter, the reader should be able to:

- Identify the ethical issues related to assessment in rehabilitation counseling.
- Describe the ethical standards in the Commission on Rehabilitation Counselor Certification Code of Ethics.
- Explain the connection between the CRCC Code and related assessment standards.

Introduction

Assessment is an essential knowledge domain underlying rehabilitation counseling practice (Leahy, Muenzen, Saunders, & Strauser, 2009). Focused on optimal human development, mental health, and wellness, the American Counseling Association (ACA) has defined counseling as a "professional relationship that empowers diverse individuals, families, and groups to accomplish mental health, wellness, education, and career goals" (Kaplan, Tarvydas, & Gladding, 2014, p. 368). Recognized as an official specialization of the counseling profession, rehabilitation counselors have unique expertise in assisting "persons with physical, mental, developmental, cognitive, and emotional disabilities to achieve their personal, career, and independent living goals in the most integrated setting possible" (Commission on Rehabilitation Counselor Certification [CRCC], 2017, p. 1). With a history of collaboration with disability groups (Hartley, 2018), rehabilitation counselors have been "at the forefront in creating sustained positive change in the holistic wellbeing of persons with disabilities" (Myers, 2012, p. xvi), including advocacy for the professional and ethical use of assessment and diagnosis (Rubin, Roessler, & Rumrill, 2016; Tarvydas & Hartley, 2018).

In addition to administering tests and conducting evaluations, rehabilitation counselors interpret and apply a myriad of assessments and diagnostics for case management planning purposes (Leahy, Chan, Sung, & Kim, 2013). Stepping away from the outdated paradigm of "test-and-tell," rehabilitation counselors work with clients to make "mental connections between the assessment results and what they are doing or could be doing with their lives" (Burlew & Morrison, 1996, p. 163). Even though the primary ethical obligation of rehabilitation counselors is to their clients, assessment results are often used by institutions and agencies to determine client eligibility, service planning, and client outcomes, including "whether someone gets a job, custody, security clearance, declaration of disability, or release from involuntary hospitalization" (Pope & Vasquez, 2011, p. 189). Because assessment and diagnosis can have a profound effect on clients' lives, it is critical for rehabilitation counselors to adhere to best ethical practices.

Whether or not assessment is their predominant job function, all rehabilitation counselors are responsible for integrating assessment and diagnostic information in their work with clients. With this in mind, this chapter overviews the basic tenets of ethical practice related to assessment and evaluation, with specific consideration for disability and diversity. In reviewing processes for competence and informed consent as well as the selection, administration, and interpretation of instruments and tests, this chapter offers behavioral guidance for rehabilitation counselors.

▓ Professional Ethics

Ethics, for many of us, is a philosophy or set of beliefs about what we value. However, much more than morality and moral thinking, professional ethics in rehabilitation counseling is behaviorally orientated and focused on "acceptable or good practice according to agreed-upon rules or standards of practice established by a profession" (Cottone & Tarvydas, 2016, p. 7). To determine the most ethical course of action, Kitchener (1984) viewed professional ethics as the critical evaluation of *principle ethics*, specifically autonomy, nonmaleficence, beneficence, justice, and fidelity. As a complement to principle ethics, Meara, Schmidt, and Day (1996) claimed the importance of *virtue ethics* and its emphasis on character traits, such as being "motivated to do what is good" and respect for the "legitimacy of client diversity" (p. 28). Even more attentive to interpersonal relationships, Gilligan (1982) described an *ethic of care* as focused on compassion and empathy for oneself and others. Codified into ethical standards governing behavior, all of these ethical frames are fundamental to professional ethics. Rest (1984) thus argued the need for not only sensitivity and judgment but also the motivation and character to follow through with difficult ethical decisions. Taken together, rehabilitation counselors should understand professional ethics as much more than rote behavior, but rather, the blending of "personal moral sensitivities and philosophies of practice with clinical behavioral objectivity and the quest for efficient care of clients" (Tarvydas & Johnston, 2018, p. 313).

Merging complementary ethical frames, professional standards specific to rehabilitation counseling have evolved alongside their equivalents in general counseling (Tarvydas, Leahy, & Zanskas, 2009). As early as 1972, the National Rehabilitation Counseling Association (NRCA) developed and published its own ethical standards. Although a "milestone in the professional development of rehabilitation counseling" (Emener & Cottone, 1989, p. 578), the NRCA early standards were a "working document" rather than an enforceable code of ethics (Patterson, 2000, p. 186). In 1987, an enforceable code of ethics was developed so that the CRCC was formed to regulate the Certified Rehabilitation Counselor (CRC) credential (Tarvydas & Cottone, 2000). Revised in 2002 and 2010, and again in 2017, the CRCC *Code of Professional Ethics for Rehabilitation Counselors* (here in after referred to as the Code) has provided behavioral guidance for rehabilitation counselors to conduct themselves ethically. The CRCC Code has been a "living document" that has evolved in response to the expanding scope of practice for rehabilitation counselors over the years (Tarvydas, Cottone, & Saunders, 2010, p. 195). Rather than viewing the CRCC Code in isolation, it is important to understand how the CRCC Code overlaps with related professional and ethical standards in specific areas of practice, such as forensic rehabilitation and behavioral health.

One of the fastest growing areas of rehabilitation counseling practice is private and forensic rehabilitation, typically involving assessment for a legal reason, such as workers' compensation, personal injury, commercial liability, medical malpractice, and catastrophic injury (Barros-Bailey, Benshoff, & Fischer, 2009). Specifically, the CRCC (2017) Code has defined a forensic rehabilitation counselor as a professional who conducts "evaluations and/or reviews of records and conduct research for the purpose of providing unbiased and objective expert opinions via case consultation or testimony" (p. 38). Although the CRCC Code has a "stand-alone section to its code of ethics for forensic and indirect services" (Barros-Bailey, 2018, p. 307), rehabilitation counselors who practice in forensic rehabilitation may also adhere to the International Association of Rehabilitation Professionals (IARP, 2007) *Code of Ethics, Standards of Practice, and Competencies* (Barros-Bailey & Carlisle, 2013). IARP is a membership organization for vocational experts and life-care planners, and both the CRCC and IARP codes of ethics are particularly concerned with accurate assessments determining legal decisions, such as civil injury litigation, Social Security disability hearings, and workers' compensation cases (Barros-Bailey, 2018). Rehabilitation counselors who practice in forensic and private rehabilitation typically adhere to complementary ethical standards of the CRCC and IARP codes of ethics.

Behavioral health is another growing area of employment for rehabilitation counselors (Zanskas & Sherman, 2018), and the scope of practice for rehabilitation counselors who are "licensed as independent practitioners by counselor licensure laws includes the legal ability to diagnose and treat mental health and substance abuse disorders" (Tarvydas, Maki, & Hartley, 2018, p. 9). Although the diagnosis of mental health disorders is addressed in the CRCC (2017) Code, state counseling licensure laws have increasingly adopted the American Counseling Association (2014) *Code of Ethics* (Tarvydas, Hartley, & Gerald, 2016). Fortunately, the structure and content of the CRCC and ACA Codes complement one other, and rehabilitation counselors are often members of ACA regardless of whether or not they diagnose mental health disorders. To diagnose ethically, however, rehabilitation counselors need to stay within their own scope of practice based on their own unique "set of knowledge, skills, and abilities even though it must be drawn from the profession's overall scope of practice" (Tarvydas et al., 2016, p. 20). In addition to the CRCC Code, rehabilitation counselors who work in behavioral health must adhere to the ACA Code when it is written into their state counselor licensure law.

The larger point, it seems, is for rehabilitation counselors to adhere to multiple professional and ethical standards, such as the IARP (2007) and ACA (2014) codes of ethics, even though the CRCC (2017) Code is the primary certification body to define and govern the professional practice of rehabilitation counseling. The overlap across related codes of ethics is a reflection of the "changing needs of society and the individuals" whom rehabilitation counselors serve (Tarvydas et al., 2018, p. 8). With this in mind, it is critical for rehabilitation counselors to understand not only the ethical standards of the CRCC Code but also the connection to related ethical and professional standards that regulate assessment within particular practice settings.

▨ Ethics of Assessment

An understanding of Section G: Assessment and Evaluation in the CRCC (2017) Code will assist rehabilitation counselors to avoid common ethical violations and dilemmas in the assessment of persons with disabilities (Hartley & Cartwright, 2015; 2016). However, rather than viewing the ethics of assessment in isolation, rehabilitation counselors must contextualize the standards in "conjunction with other, related standards throughout the Code" and in the spirit of the six guiding ethical principles cited in the preamble (CRCC, p. 2–3):

- Autonomy: To respect the rights of clients to be self-governing within their social and cultural framework.

- Beneficence: To do good to others; to promote the well-being of clients.

- Fidelity: To be faithful; to keep promises and honor the trust placed in rehabilitation counselors.

- Justice: To be fair in the treatment of all clients; to provide appropriate services to all.

- Nonmaleficence: To do no harm to others.

- Veracity: To be honest.

However, ethical conduct is more complex than an abstract understanding of the abovementioned ethical principles would suggest. Indeed, rehabilitation counselors must consider how to apply ethical standards and principles in ways that account for the complexities of clinical situations (Tarvydas & Johnston, 2018). Rooted in a person–environment fit that accounts for the perspectives of virtue ethics (Meara et al., 1996) and an ethic of care (Gilligan, 1982), professional practice is highly contingent on the ability of rehabilitation counselors to account for the unique, but varied aspects of individual clients and their contexts. Furthermore, assessments vary considerably across practice settings; thus, rehabilitation counselors must be able to apply the information in this chapter to their particular practice setting. Organized around assessment processes, the present chapter overviews the following ethical issues: (a) primary obligation, (b) competence and appropriate use, (c) informed consent and disclosure, (d) selection and administration, (e) interpretation and application, (f) appropriate referral, (g) proper diagnosis of mental health disorders, and (h) forensic rehabilitation and indirect services.

Primary Obligation

Assessment and Evaluation, Section G of the CRCC (2017) Code, begins with a preamble intended to contextualize the role of assessment in rehabilitation counseling and the "ethical behavior and responsibility to which rehabilitation counselors aspire" (p. 3). Setting the tone for the enforceable ethical standards that follow, the primary ethical obligation for rehabilitation counselors is to "promote the well-being of clients or groups of clients by developing and using assessment and evaluation methods that take into account the client's personal and cultural context" (p. 20). Similar to Section E: Evaluation, Assessment, and Interpretation of the ACA (2014) Code, the CRCC (2017) Code notes that "while assessment is also associated with the administration of tests, it is a broader process that goes well beyond gathering quantitative data from assessment instruments," including the "collection of other qualitative data and information" (p. 20). Defining assessment broadly, the CRCC (2017) preamble goes on to explain that "rehabilitation counselors use a comprehensive assessment process as an integral component of providing individualized rehabilitation counseling services for their clients" (p. 20).

Rooted in a person–environment fit, rehabilitation counselors assess not only client characteristics but also the cultural and environmental contexts in which clients live, work, and function. Rather than limiting assessment to client interviews, observations, questionnaires, and rating forms (Mears, 2016; Sligar & Thomas, 2016), rehabilitation counselors often use a wide range of assessments, such as life design, functional capacity, and work samples (Marini, 2016;

Mpofu & Mpofu, 2018). Consistent with the historical values and perspectives of ethical and effective rehabilitation counseling services (Rubin et al., 2016; Tarvydas & Hartley, 2018), assessment in rehabilitation counseling is based on a multidimensional and "holistic approach to assessing clients and addressing their concerns," including a focus on disability rights, client strengths, and cultural factors (McCarthy, 2018, p. 76).

Competence and Appropriate Use

Competence is the ability to do something effectively and "cannot merely be asserted but must be demonstrable through formal education, training, and supervised experience" (Pope & Vasquez, 2011, p. 191). While the scope of practice for rehabilitation counselors has long involved conducting "assessment activities, such as selecting and administering standardized tests and conducting ecological assessments" (Leahy, Chan, & Saunders, 2003, p. 70), assessment standards have become increasingly specialized (Wheeler & Bertram, 2015). With this in mind, Standard G.4.a. Limits of Competence and Standard G.4.b. Appropriate Use restrict rehabilitation counselors to use only "tests/instruments they are qualified and competent to administer" and monitor the "appropriate applications, scoring, interpretations, and use of tests/instruments relevant to the needs of clients" (CRCC, 2017, p. 20). Also addressed in the ACA (2014) and IARP (2007) codes of ethics, it is imperative for rehabilitation counselors to know the limits of their training and expertise, referring clients to other professionals when particular assessments are beyond their scope of practice and competence, such as in the case of medical examinations conducted by physicians. Staying within one's scope of practice is an extension of the responsibility to "practice only within the boundaries of their competence, based on their education, training, supervised experience, professional credentials, and appropriate professional experience" per D.1.a. Boundaries of Competence (CRCC, 2017, p. 13).

Competence and appropriate use also refer to interpretation and application of assessments and diagnostics for case management and rehabilitation planning purposes (Chapin, Butler, & Perry, 2018). Without adequate training, rehabilitation counselors may not be competent to interpret assessments as part of the case management process or to explain the results to clients. Standard G.4.c. Decisions Based on Results, for instance, is the qualification that rehabilitation counselors who are "responsible for recommendations that are based on test results have a thorough understanding of psychometrics" (CRCC, 2017, p. 21). Psychometrics refers to "standardized tests such as interest, aptitude, intelligence, achievement" that are used to "compare the performance of the consumer with a norm group" (Sligar & Thomas, 2016, p. 338). Rehabilitation counselors may not have advanced training in psychometrics, and it is important to err on the side of caution when interpreting such tests, especially constructs that historically have had questionable validity, such as personality assessments (Cashel, 2016, p. 300).

With this in mind, Wheeler and Bertram (2014) identified a list of specialty standards and legal considerations, including standards developed by the Association for Assessment in Counseling and Education (AACE), an ACA division, and legal mandates and case law statutes. Wheeler and Bertram make the larger point that "different tests demand different levels of competence for their use" and thus "users must recognize the limits of their competence and make use only of instruments for which they have adequate preparation and training" (p. 49). Wheeler and Bertram went on to explain that test publishers often qualify competency requirements: Level A (no qualification needed), Level B (master's degree in psychology or related field), Level C (doctorate in psychology or related field), and Level Q (specific ethical training). Competence and appropriate use are dependent on training and supervision, and rehabilitation counselors must administer tests within their scope of practice.

Informed Consent and Disclosure

Regardless of practice setting, informed consent is an extension of the broader ethical obligation to ensure that clients are aware of the scope of services defined by the CRCC (2017) Standard A.3.a. Professional Disclosure Statement and Standard A.3.b. Informed Consent. Addressed in virtually all codes of ethics, the ACA (2014) defined informed consent as "information sharing associated with possible actions clients may choose to take, aimed at assisting clients in acquiring a full appreciation and understanding of the facts and implications of a given action or actions" (p. 20). Importantly, informed consent and disclosure statements are ongoing processes that rehabilitation counselors "review with clients, both orally and in writing," including the rights and responsibilities of both the rehabilitation counselor and the client (CRCC, 2017, p. 5). With consideration for the language and cognitive level of clients, scholars have "asserted that true autonomy is not possible unless the decision maker possesses the information necessary to make informed decisions" (Shaw & Tarvydas, 2001, p. 40). To be clear, it is critical for rehabilitation counselors to ensure clients understand the assessment procedures, including who will have access to the results.

Specific to assessment, Standard G.1.a. Explanation to Clients in the CRCC (2017) Code requires rehabilitation counselors to explain the "nature and purpose of the assessment and evaluation process," including the "potential use of the results" (p. 20). Rehabilitation counselors need to explain who will receive the assessment results, prioritizing "the welfare of clients, explicit understandings, and prior agreements in determining who receives the assessment or evaluation results" (CRCC, p. 20). According to the Joint Committee on Testing Practices (JCTP), "test takers have a right to know the purpose of testing, who will have access to their scores, how the tests will be used, and possible consequences of taking or not taking the test" (Wheeler & Bertram, 2014, p. 44), including reasonable accommodations for clients with disabilities. Because assessments may follow a client forever, the bottom line is rehabilitation counselors have a responsibility to inform clients about disability accommodations as well as the effects of the potential results on their lives and life decisions.

Selection and Administration

Prior to the selection and administration of assessments, rehabilitation counselors are expected to be knowledgeable about the "appropriateness, validity, reliability, and psychometric limitations" (CRCC, 2017, p. 21). Of particular concern are questions about the reliability and validity of assessments, especially administration procedures. While Standard G.6.a. Standard Condition requires rehabilitation counselors to "administer tests/instruments according to the parameters described in the publishers' manuals" (p. 21), it is also true that accommodations for persons with disabilities are often necessary. A client with visual impairment, for instance, who takes an aptitude test in small print may have a low score that does not accurately reflect cognitive ability (Dugger, 2016). It is similarly true that cultural bias can occur in intake interviews, such as the wording of questions as well as the interpretation of nonverbal communication, such as eye contact (Mears, 2016). To account for diversity and cultural factors, selection and administration of assessments must consider the client's "life stage, developmental history, context, and broader issues in assessment and treatment" (Chronister, Chou, & Chan, 2016, p. 9).

A consideration when selecting an assessment is how it was developed and constructed. Specifically, Standard G.8. Test/Instrument Security in the CRCC (2017) Code requires rehabilitation counselors to "maintain the integrity and security of tests/instruments consistent with legal and contractual obligations" and not to "appropriate, reproduce, or modify published tests/instruments" without permission from the publisher (p. 22). When rehabilitation counselors are engaged in developing, publishing, and utilizing testing procedures, Standard G.10. Test/Instrument Construction is the requirement to use "established scientific procedures, relevant standards, and current professional knowledge" (CRCC, 2017, p. 21). Finally, instruments can become outdated, and Standard G.9. Obsolete Test/Instruments and Outdated Results cautions rehabilitation counselors to not rely on "data or results" that are "obsolete or outdated for the current purpose," although an older version may be used "when necessary and due to specific, individual needs" (CRCC, 2017, p. 22). The protection of the integrity of psychometric instruments is critical to ensure that tests and instruments remain valid and reliable.

With more and more testing being conducted online, Standard G.6.b. Technological Administration requires rehabilitation counselors to "make reasonable efforts" to ensure tests are "accessible, function properly, and provide accurate results" (CRCC, 2017, p. 22). While online assessments offer many benefits, including the convenience of not traveling to a testing site, a disadvantage is that rehabilitation counselors are unsure of administration factors (Wheeler & Bertram, 2014). In particular, Standard G.6.c. Unsupervised Administration prohibits the "unsupervised or inadequately supervised use of tests/instruments unless they are designed for self-administration and/or scoring" as may be the case with online assessments (CRCC, 2017, p. 22). However, even when assessments are designed for online use, Mallen, Vogel, and Rochlen (2005) pointed out that many have no evidence of reliability or validity. Without behavioral observations about client reactions and testing conditions, limited reliability and validity have raised significant questions about the use of online assessments in professional practice, especially in relation to appropriate accommodations for persons with disabilities.

Interpretation and Application

When interpreting assessment results, rehabilitation counselors must "exercise caution and qualify any conclusions, diagnoses, or recommendations," as defined by Standard G.7.a. Psychometric Limitations (CRCC, 2017, p. 22). With careful consideration of "clients' personal and cultural background and the level of the clients' understanding," rehabilitation counselors must be sensitive to the fact that biased interpretations of tests and assessments may lead to misuse of assessments (CRCC, 2017, p. 22). Standard G.7.c. Reporting Standardized Scores directs rehabilitation counselors to include "standard scores when reporting results of a specific instrument" that is norm-referenced, such as in the case of intelligence and aptitude testing (CRCC, 2017, p. 22). In particular, the CRCC Code is concerned with the "interpretation of results normed on populations other than the client," including the "potential effects of disability, culture, or other factors that may result in potential bias and/or misinterpretation of data" (CRCC, 2017, p. 22). Contextualizing clients' personal and cultural backgrounds aligns with a social model understanding of disability that "strongly opposes the medical model's narrow and oppressive definition of disability as a problem within the person" (McCarthy, 2018, p. 85).

Concerned with raw data interpreted out of context, rehabilitation counselors must be careful about how data are shared with whom and for what purpose, especially raw data in which clients are identified. With this in mind, Standard G.2.a. Misuse of Results is the mandate that rehabilitation counselors do not "misuse assessment or evaluation results, including test results and interpretations, and take reasonable steps to prevent the misuse of such by others" (CRCC, 2017, p. 20). To prevent assessments interpreted out of context, Standard G.2.b. Release of Raw Data to Qualified Professionals limits rehabilitation counselors to release raw data only to "professionals recognized as qualified to interpret the data" (CRCC, 2017, p. 20). The most important point, it seems, is that rehabilitation counselors must be cautious in their interpretation of assessments, and failure to account for aspects of the client and the client's environment can lead to the misinterpretation and application of assessments in rehabilitation counseling. It is for this reason that rehabilitation counselors tend to rely on multiple assessment methods, rather than a single method of assessment that may be biased, especially for persons with disabilities.

Appropriate Referral

With high caseloads, rehabilitation counselors may not have time to conduct all of their own assessments. In addition, some assessments are beyond the rehabilitation counseling scope of practice. Regardless of the reason for the referral, it is critical for rehabilitation counselors to include sufficient referral information so that assessment procedures are appropriate to the needs of the client. In particular, Standard G.5.b. Referral Information in the CRCC (2017) Code directs rehabilitation counselors to "provide specific referral questions, furnish sufficient objective client data, and make reasonable efforts to ensure that appropriate tests/instruments are utilized" (p. 21). The concern is that failure to provide "relevant client data to third-party evaluators heighten the risk that inappropriate instruments will be used" (Barnett & Johnson, 2014, p. 88).

In addition to client information, rehabilitation counselors need to be knowledgeable about various assessment methods when making referrals. In rehabilitation counseling, the most useful assessments are mental functional capacity evaluations (MFCEs) and physical functional capacity evaluations (PFCEs). Used in Social Security disability determinations and guardianship hearings, MFCEs and PFCEs are comprehensive assessments that may determine service eligibility as well as residual functioning and transferable work skills (Marini, 2016). However, the usefulness of functional capacity evaluations is contingent upon the ability of the rehabilitation counselor to supply all relevant information necessary for an appropriate evaluation. With this in mind, it is critical for rehabilitation counselors to provide "adequate information when referring a client to a provider (e.g., contact, identification, medical, purpose, special instructions, payor, etc.)" (IARP, 2007, p. 12). When making referrals, rehabilitation counselors need to request the assessments and diagnostics necessary for case management and treatment planning decisions.

Proper Diagnosis of Mental Disorders

Standard G.3.a. Proper Diagnosis in the CRCC (2017) Code is the mandate to "take special care to provide diagnosis of mental disorders using the most current diagnostic criteria," including careful selection and use of assessment techniques to determine care of clients (p. 20). Because many mental health services depend on a diagnostic category to be covered by insurance companies, there can be a "temptation to substitute a fraudulent but covered diagnosis," referred to as the unethical practice of upcoding or downcoding (Pope & Vasquez, 2011, p. 199). In cases in which rehabilitation counselors are unsure of the accuracy of a diagnosis or are concerned with what will happen because of a potential diagnosis, Standard G.3.d. Refraining From Diagnosis allows rehabilitation counselors to "refrain from making and/or reporting a diagnosis if they believe that it would cause harm to the client" (CRCC, 2017, p. 21).

Proper assessment of mental health must be contextual to the client and his or her environment (Peterson, 2016). Rather than viewing mental health symptoms as a deficient, rehabilitation counseling has traditionally been grounded in a psychiatric rehabilitation emphasis on assessing "personal goals to develop a physically and psychologically healthy lifestyle characterized by hope, optimism, and a sense of purpose" (Easton & Corrigan, 2018, p. 383). Aligned with a holistic assessment of mental health, Mpofu and Mpofu (2018) argued for the functional approach of the World Health Organization (2001) International Classification of Functioning, Disability and Health (ICF) as a complement to the diagnostic criteria of the American Psychiatric Association (2013) *Diagnostic and Statistical Manual of Mental Disorders*, fifth edition. Concerned with the "historical and social prejudice in the misdiagnosis and pathologizing of certain individuals and groups," Standard G.3.b. Cultural Sensitivity and Standard G.3.c. Historical and Social Prejudices in the Diagnosis of Pathology "recognize that culture affects the manner in which a client's symptoms are defined and experienced" (CRCC, 2017, p. 21). The core issue is that ignoring cultural prejudice and bias may influence the diagnosis process and potentially perpetuate harm to clients by limiting their opportunities (Corrigan & Lam, 2007; Davidson, Tondora, Staeheli Lawless, O'Connell, & Rowe, 2009).

Forensic Rehabilitation and Indirect Services

Closely aligned with the IARP (2007) Code, the CRCC (2017) ethical standards addressing forensic and indirect services are "the most comprehensive in any counseling specialty" (Barros-Bailey, 2018, p. 308). A significant difference between Section F: Forensic Services and other sections of the CRCC Code is the term "evaluee," rather than "client" because services are often indirect in a forensic setting (i.e., no direct contact with the client). IARP defines an evaluee as the "person who is the subject of the objective and unbiased evaluation" (p. 15), capturing an important distinction that the person who is being evaluated may or may not be the person paying for the evaluation (Christenson, 2011). It is common for attorneys representing different legal parties to pay for the actual assessment.

Rather than the overall welfare of the evaluee, the primary obligation in forensic rehabilitation is "to produce unbiased, objective opinions and findings that can be substantiated by information and methodologies appropriate to the service being provided, which may include evaluation, research, and/or review of records" (CRCC, 2017, p. 18). In addition to general guidelines on assessment, forensic rehabilitation requires knowledge of the legal and systemic context, including "how courts are structured and the jurisdiction at various local, regional, and or national levels" (Barros-Bailey, 2018, p. 301). Focused on civil injury litigation, employment law, marital dissolution, Social Security disability, and workers' compensation, there are unique ethical concerns related to informed consent and role changes because forensic rehabilitation assessments often determine client eligibility for funding and services. While the assessment practices themselves are addressed within Section G: Assessment and Evaluation of the CRCC (2017) Code, the standalone Section F provides guidance on navigating the legal and systemic context within which private and forensic rehabilitation is practiced.

Conclusions

Although the CRCC (2017) Code provides a comprehensive set of assessment processes, it is important to contextualize these ethical standards, rather than viewing them as a static set of universal, impartial rules. From the perspective of virtue ethics and an ethic of care, ethical assessment includes an obligation to "assess and respect the client's worldview, refraining from imposing their worldview on the client" (Johnston & Hartley, 2018, p. 128). Because the application of ethical standards is complex, consultation is an important ethical practice to "engage in a process of information gathering, analyzing, reasoning, and planning to determine the most ethical course of action in a challenging situation" (Shaw & Lane, 2008, p. 170). Ongoing consultation with trusted colleagues and supervisors is a way to navigate potential ethical dilemmas and avoid ethical violations (Cartwright & Hartley, 2016). Given the increasingly specialized standards associated with diverse assessments, rehabilitation counselors need to realize that the expanding scope of rehabilitation counseling practice (Rumrill et al., 2016; Tarvydas & Hartley, 2018) will likely bring "news areas of specialization, each requiring its own set of competences" (Pope & Vasquez, 2011, p. 189).

References

American Counseling Association. (2014). *Code of ethics*. Retrieved from https://www.counseling.org/resources/aca-code-of-ethics.pdf

American Psychiatric Association (2013). *Diagnostic and statistical manual of mental disorders* (5th ed.). Arlington, VA: American Psychiatric Publishing.

Barnett, J., & Johnson, B. (2014). *Ethics desk reference for counselors*. New York, NY: Wiley.

Barros-Bailey, M., Benshoff, J. J., & Fischer, J. (2009). Rehabilitation counseling in the year 2011: Perceptions of certified rehabilitation counselors. *Rehabilitation Counseling Bulletin, 52*(2), 107–113. doi:10.1177/0034355208324262

Barros-Bailey, M., & Carlisle, J. (2013). Professional identity, standards, and ethical issues. In R. Robinson (Ed.), *Foundations of forensic vocational rehabilitation* (pp. 443–465). New York, NY: Springer Publishing Company.

Barros-Bailey, M. (2018). Forensic and indirect services. In V. M. Tarvydas & M. T. Hartley (Eds.), *The professional practice of rehabilitation counseling* (2nd ed., pp. 297–312). New York, NY: Springer Publishing Company.

Burlew, L. D., & Morrison, J. (1996). Enhancing the effectiveness of vocational assessment in promoting lifestyle change via specific change strategies. *Measurement & Evaluation in Counseling & Development, 29*, 163–175.

Cashel, M. L. (2016). What counselors should know about personality assessments. In M. Stebnicki & I. Marini (Eds.), *Professional counselors' desk reference* (2nd ed., 299–204). New York, NY: Springer Publishing Company.

Cartwright, B. Y., & Hartley, M. T. (2016). Ethics consultation in rehabilitation counseling: A content analysis of CRCC advisory opinions, 1996–2013. *Rehabilitation Counseling Bulletin, 59*, 84–93. doi:0034355215573537

Chapin, M. H., Butler, M. K., & Perry, V. M. (2018). Case management. In V. M. Tarvydas & M. T. Hartley (Eds.), *The professional practice of rehabilitation counseling* (2nd ed., pp. 241–256). New York, NY: Springer Publishing Company.

Christenson, J. (2011). The ethical implications for insurance rehabilitation practitioners. *The Rehabilitation Professional, 19*(4), 83–90.

Chronister, J. Chou, C., & Chan, F. (2016). The roles and functions of professional counselors. In M. Stebnicki & I. Marini (Eds.), *Professional counselors' desk reference* (2nd ed., pp. 9–16). New York, NY: Springer Publishing Company.

Commission on Rehabilitation Counselor Certification. (2017). *Code of professional ethics for rehabilitation counselors*. Schaumburg, IL: Author.

Corrigan, P. W., & Lam, C. (2007). Challenging the structural discrimination of psychiatric disabilities: Lessons learned from the American disability community. *Rehabilitation Education, 21*(1), 53–58. doi:10.1891/088970107805059869

Cottone, C. C., & Tarvydas, V. M. (Eds.). (2016). *Ethics and decision making in counseling and psychotherapy* (4th ed.). New York, NY: Springer Publishing Company.

Davidson, L., Tondora, J., Staeheli Lawless, M., O'Connell, M. J., & Rowe, M. (2009). *A practical guide to recovery-oriented practice.* New York, NY: Oxford University Press.

Dugger, S. M. (2016). Understanding the use of aptitude tests in counseling. In M. Stebnicki & I. Marini (Eds.), *Professional counselors' desk reference* (2nd ed., 305–310). New York, NY: Springer Publishing Company.

Easton, A. B., & Corrigan, P. (2018). Psychiatric rehabilitation. In V. M. Tarvydas and M. T. Hartley (Eds.), *The professional practice of rehabilitation counseling* (2nd ed., pp. 381–404). New York, NY: Springer Publishing Company.

Emener, W. G., & Cottone, C. C. (1989). Professionalization, deprofessionalization, and reprofessionalization of rehabilitation counseling according to criteria of professions. *Journal of Counseling & Development, 67,* 576–581. doi:0.1002/j.1556-6676.1989.tb01333.x

Gilligan, C. (1982). *In a different voice.* Boston, MA: Harvard University Press.

Hartley, M. T. (2018). Disability rights community. In V. M. Tarvydas & M. T. Hartley (Eds.), *The professional practice of rehabilitation counseling* (2nd ed., pp. 153–172). New York, NY: Springer Publishing Company.

Hartley, M. T., & Cartwright, B. Y. (2015). Analysis of the reported ethical complaints and violations to the Commission on Rehabilitation Counselor Certification, 2006–2013. *Rehabilitation Counseling Bulletin, 58*(3), 154–164. doi:10.1177/0034355214543565

Hartley, M. T., & Cartwright, B. Y. (2016). A survey of current and projected ethical dilemmas of rehabilitation counselors. *Rehabilitation Research, Policy and Education, 30,* 1–15. doi:10.1891/2168-6653.30.1.32

International Association of Rehabilitation Professionals. (2007). *Code of ethics, standards of practice, and competencies.* Glenview, IL: Author.

Johnston, S. J., & Hartley, M. T. (2018). Ethics and facilitating services for clients. In K. B. Wilson, C. L. Acklin, & S. Y. Chao (Eds.), *Case management for the health, human, and vocational rehabilitation services* (pp. 125–140). Linn Creek, MO: Aspen Professional Services.

Kaplan, D. M., Tarvydas, V. M., & Gladding, S. T. (2014). 20/20: A vision for the future of counseling: The new consensus definition of counseling. *Journal of Counseling & Development, 92*(3), 366–372. doi:10.1002/j.1556-6676.2014.00164.x

Kitchener, K. S. (1984). Intuition, critical evaluation, and ethical principles: The foundation for ethical decisions in counseling psychology. *The Counseling Psychologist, 12*(3), 43–55. doi:10.1177/0011000084123005

Leahy, M. J., Chan, F., & Saunders, J. L. (2003). Job functions and knowledge requirements of certified rehabilitation counselors in the 21st century. *Rehabilitation Counseling Bulletin, 46*(2), 66–81.

Leahy, M. J., Chan, F., Sung, C., & Kim, M. (2013). Empirically derived test specifications for the certified rehabilitation counselor examination. *Rehabilitation Counseling Bulletin, 56*(4), 199–214. doi:10.1177/0034355212469839

Leahy, M. J., Muenzen, P., Saunders, J. L., & Strauser, D. (2009). Essential knowledge domains underlying effective rehabilitation counseling practice. *Rehabilitation Counseling Bulletin, 52*(2), 95–106. doi:10.1177/0034355208323646

Mallen, M. J., Vogel, D. L., & Rochlen, A. B. (2005). The practical aspects of online counseling: Ethics, training, technology, and competency. *The Counseling Psychologist, 33*(6), 776–818. doi:10.1177/0011000005278625

Marini, I. (2016). Understanding mental and physical functional capacity evaluations. In M. Stebnicki and I. Marini (Eds.), *Professional counselors' desk reference* (2nd ed., 321–328). New York, NY: Springer Publishing Company.

Meara, N. M., Schmidt, L. D., & Day, J. D. (1996). Principles and virtues: A foundation for ethical decisions, policies, and character. *The Counseling Psychologist, 24*(1), 4–77. doi:10.1177/0011000096241002

Mears, G. (2016). Conducting an intake interview. In M. Stebnicki and I. Marini (Eds.), *Professional counselors' desk reference* (2nd ed., 83–86). New York, NY: Springer Publishing Company.

McCarthy, N. (2018). Concepts and models. In V. M. Tarvydas & M. T. Hartley (Eds.), *The professional practice of rehabilitation counseling* (2nd ed., pp. 73–94). New York, NY: Springer Publishing Company.

Mpofu, E., & Mpofu, N. (2018). Assessment. In V. M. Tarvydas & M. T. Hartley (Eds.), *The professional practice of rehabilitation counseling* (2nd ed., pp. 201–220). New York, NY: Springer Publishing Company.

Myers, J. (2012). Foreword. In D. R. Maki & V. M. Tarvydas (Eds.), *The professional practice of rehabilitation counseling* (pp. xv–xvii). New York, NY: Springer Publishing Company.

Patterson, J. B. (2000). Introduction to the special issue. *Rehabilitation Counseling Bulletin, 52*, 77–84. doi:10.1177/0034355208325077

Peterson, D. (2016). Diagnostic assessment in clinical counseling. In M. Stebnicki & I. Marini (Eds.), *Professional counselors' desk reference* (2nd ed., 311–320). New York, NY: Springer Publishing Company.

Pope, K. S., & Vasquez, M. (2011). *Ethics in therapy and counseling.* New York, NY: Wiley.

Rest, J. R. (1984). Research on moral development: Implications for training counseling psychologists. *The Counseling Psychologist, 12*(3), 19–29. doi:10.1177/0011000084123003

Rubin, S. E., Roessler, R., & Rumrill, P. D. (2016). *Foundations of the vocational rehabilitation process.* Pro-Ed: Austin, TX.

Shaw, L. R., & Lane, F. (2008). Ethical consultation: Content analysis of the advisory opinion archive of the Commission on Rehabilitation Counselor Certification. *Rehabilitation Counseling Bulletin, 51*, 170–176. doi:10.1177/0034355207311314

Shaw, L. R., & Tarvydas, V. M. (2001). The use of professional disclosure in rehabilitation counseling. *Rehabilitation Counseling Bulletin, 45*(1), 40–47. doi:10.1177/003435520104500106

Sligar, S. R., & Thomas, S. T. (2016). What counselors should know about vocational assessment and evaluation. In M. Stebnicki & I. Marini (Eds.), *Professional counselors' desk reference* (2nd ed., 337–341). New York, NY: Springer Publishing Company.

Tarvydas, V. M., & Cottone, R. R. (2000). The code of ethics for professional rehabilitation counselors: What we have and what we need. *Rehabilitation Counseling Bulletin, 43*, 188–196. doi:10.1177/003435520004300402

Tarvydas, V. M., Cottone, R. R., & Saunders, J. S. (2010). A new ethics code as a tool for innovations in ethical practice. *Rehabilitation Counseling Bulletin, 53*(4), 195–196. doi:10.1177/0034355210368726

Tarvydas, V. M., & Hartley, M. T. (2018). *The professional practice of rehabilitation counseling* (2nd ed.). New York, NY: Springer Publishing Company.

Tarvydas, V. M., Hartley, M. T., & Gerald, M. (2016). Professional credentialing. In M. Stebnicki & I. Marini (Eds.), *Professional counselors' desk reference* (2nd ed., 17–22). New York, NY: Springer Publishing Company.

Tarvydas, V. M., & Johnston, S. (2018). Ethics and ethical decision making. In V. M. Tarvydas & M. T. Hartley (Eds.), *The professional practice of rehabilitation counseling* (2nd ed., pp. 313–342). New York, NY: Springer Publishing Company.

Tarvydas, V. M., Leahy, M. J., & Zanskas, S. A. (2009). Judgment deferred: Reappraisal of rehabilitation counseling movement toward licensure parity. *Rehabilitation Counseling Bulletin, 52*(2), 85–94. doi:10.1177/0034355208323951

Tarvydas, V. M., Maki, D. R., & Hartley, M. T. (2018). Rehabilitation counseling: A specialty practice of the counseling profession. In V. M. Tarvydas & M. T. Hartley (Eds.), *The professional practice of rehabilitation counseling* (2nd ed., pp. 1–14). New York, NY: Springer Publishing Company.

Wheeler, A. M., & Bertram, B. (2015). *The counselor and the law: A guide to legal and ethical practice.* Alexandria, VA: American Counseling Association.

World Health Organization. (2001). *International classification of Functioning, Disability and Health: ICF.* Geneva, Switzerland: Author.

Zanskas, S. A., & Sherman, S. G. (2018). Professional credentialing. In V. M. Tarvydas & M. T. Hartley (Eds.), *The professional practice of rehabilitation counseling* (2nd ed., pp. 31–50). New York, NY: Springer Publishing Company.

18

BASIC PRINCIPLES OF PROGRAM EVALUATION

CATHERINE A. ANDERSON | TIMOTHY N. TANSEY |
TERESA ANN GRENAWALT | XIANGLI CHEN

LEARNING OBJECTIVES

After reviewing this chapter, the reader should be able to:

- Identify essential competencies for program evaluators.
- Apply logic models to structure program evaluation activities.
- Identify formative and summative evaluation components of program evaluation.
- Summarize measures and methods commonly used in program evaluation.

▩ Introduction

Program evaluation is systematic collection, analysis, interpretation, and presentation of findings to facilitate stakeholder decision-making regarding the efficacy and efficiency of programs, including, but not limited to, the needs of the organization, the impact of program on outcomes, the cost-effectiveness, and overall utility of a program (Leahy, Thielsen, Millington, Austin, & Fleming, 2009). Likewise, quality assurance, or the organized process designed to assess and reduce variations in services or outcomes, is emerging as an area of importance among state vocational rehabilitation (VR) agencies to achieve consistency in results across different providers (Leahy et al., 2009). To provide program evaluation and quality-assurance services to an evolving state VR system, a shift in practice that necessitates a thorough knowledge of contemporary program evaluation and quality-assurance methodologies and statistical techniques, stronger understanding of contemporary health and human services business models, related organizational and management practices, and effective VR service delivery practices is required. To perform effectively as evaluators in today's demanding health and human service delivery environments, Stevahn, King, Ghere, and Minnema (2005) developed a taxonomy of essential competencies for program evaluators that is consistent with the American Evaluation Association (AEA) guiding principles (see Table 18.1).

TABLE 18.1 Taxonomy of Essential Competencies for Program Evaluators

DOMAIN	CATEGORY
1.0 Professional Practice	1.1 Applies professional evaluation standards 1.2 Acts ethically and strives for integrity and honesty in conducting evaluations 1.3 Conveys personal evaluation approaches and skills to potential clients 1.4 Respects clients, respondents, program participants, and other stakeholders 1.5 Considers the general and public welfare in evaluation practice 1.6 Contributes to the knowledge base of evaluation
2.0 Systematic Inquiry	2.1 Understands the knowledge base of evaluation 2.2 Knowledgeable about quantitative, qualitative, and mixed methods 2.3 Conducts literature reviews, specifies program theory, and frames evaluation questions 2.4 Develops evaluation designs, identifies data sources, collects data, and assesses reliability and validity of data 2.5 Analyzes data 2.6 Interprets data, makes judgment, and develops recommendation 2.7 Provides rationales for decisions throughout the evaluation 2.8 Reports evaluation procedures and results 2.9 Notes strengths and limitations of the evaluation 2.10 Conducts meta-evaluations
3.0 Situational Analysis	3.1 Describes the program, determines program evaluability, and identifies the interests of relevant stakeholders 3.2 Serves the information needs of intended users, addresses conflicts, and examines the organizational context of the evaluation 3.3 Analyzes the political considerations relevant to the evaluation and attends to issues of evaluation use and organizational change 3.4 Respects the uniqueness of the evaluation site and client 3.5 Remains open to input from others 3.6 Modifies the study as needed
4.0 Project Management	4.1 Responds to requests for proposals and negotiates with clients before the evaluation begins 4.2 Writes formal agreements and communicates with clients throughout the evaluation process 4.3 Budgets an evaluation and justifies cost given information needs 4.4 Identifies needed resources for evaluation, such as information, expertise, personnel, and instruments 4.5 Uses appropriate technology 4.6 Supervises others involved in conducting the evaluation 4.7 Trains others involved in conducting the evaluation 4.8 Conducts the evaluation in a nondisruptive manner 4.9 Presents work in a timely manner
5.0 Reflective Practice	5.1 Aware of self as an evaluator (knowledge, skills, dispositions) 5.2 Reflects on personal evaluation practice (competencies and growth) 5.3 Pursues professional development in evaluation 5.4 Pursues professional development in relevant content area 5.5 Builds professional relationships to enhance evaluation
6.0 Interpersonal Competence	6.1 Uses verbal/listening and written communication skills 6.2 Uses negotiation and conflict resolution skills 6.3 Facilitates constructive interpersonal interaction (teamwork, group facilitation, processing) 6.4 Demonstrates cross-cultural competence

SOURCE: Stevahn, L., King, J. A., Ghere, G., & Minnema, J. (2005). Establishing essential competencies for program evaluators. *American Journal of Evaluation, 26*(1), 43–59. doi:10.1177/1098214004273180

In an era of empowerment, consumer choice, evidence-based practice, accountability, and constrained budgets, state agencies must revamp their approaches to provide efficacious and cost-effective services (Chan, Tarvydas, Blalock, Strauser, & Atkins, 2009; Rubin, Chan, & Thomas, 2003). Meeting and exceeding expected service outcome goals is one way to demonstrate the success and effectiveness of services provided and for justifying the continued funding of services (Rubin et al., 2003).

Similarly, the AEA recently updated their *Guiding Principles for Evaluators* that provides a framework to guide professional ethical conduct. The five primary principles address systematic inquiry, competence, integrity, respect for people, and common good and equity (see Table 18.2). Principles were originally adopted by the AEA membership in 1994 and are subsequently reviewed at least every 5 years to reflect contextual changes and evolution of the profession (AEA, 2018). The principles continue to align with the competencies noted by Stevahn and colleagues (2005).

TABLE 18.2 American Evaluation Association Guiding Principles for Evaluators

PRINCIPLE	DEFINITION AND PRINCIPLE SPECIFICS
A. Systematic Inquiry	**Evaluators conduct data-based inquiries that are thorough, methodical, and contextually relevant.** A1. Adhere to the highest technical standards appropriate to the methods being used while attending to the evaluation's scale and available resources. A2. Explore with primary stakeholders the limitations and strengths of the core evaluation questions and the approaches that might be used for answering those questions. A3. Communicate methods and approaches accurately, and in sufficient detail, to allow others to understand, interpret, and critique the work. A4. Make clear the limitations of the evaluation and its results. A5. Discuss in contextually appropriate ways the values, assumptions, theories, methods, results, and analyses that significantly affect the evaluator's interpretations of the findings. A6. Carefully consider the ethical implications of the use of emerging technologies in evaluation practice.
B. Competence	**Evaluators provide skilled professional services to stakeholders.** B1. Ensure that the evaluation team possesses the education, abilities, skills, and experiences required to complete the evaluation competently. B2. When the most ethical option is to proceed with a commission or request outside the boundaries of the evaluation team's professional preparation and competence, clearly communicate any significant limitations to the evaluation that might result. Make every effort to supplement missing or weak competencies directly or through the assistance of others. B3. Ensure that the evaluation team collectively possesses or seeks out the competencies necessary to work in the cultural context of the evaluation. B4. Continually undertake relevant education, training, or supervised practice to learn new concepts, techniques, skills, and services necessary for competent evaluation practice. Ongoing professional development might include formal coursework and workshops, self-study, self- or externally commissioned evaluations of one's own practice and working with other evaluators to learn and refine evaluative skills expertise.

(continued)

TABLE 18.2 American Evaluation Association Guiding Principles for Evaluators (*continued*)

PRINCIPLE	DEFINITION AND PRINCIPLE SPECIFICS
C. Integrity	**Evaluators behave with honesty and transparency in order to ensure the integrity of the evaluation.** C1. Communicate truthfully and openly with clients and relevant stakeholders concerning all aspects of the evaluation, including its limitations. C2. Disclose any conflicts of interest (or appearance of a conflict) prior to accepting an evaluation assignment and manage or mitigate any conflicts during the evaluation. C3. Record and promptly communicate any changes to the originally negotiated evaluation plans, that rationale for those changes, and the potential impacts on the evaluation's scope and results. C4. Assess and make explicit the stakeholders', clients', and evaluators' values, perspectives, and interests concerning the conduct and outcome of the evaluation. C5. Accurately and transparently represent evaluation procedures, data, and findings. C6. Clearly communicate, justify, and address concerns related to procedures or activities that are likely to produce misleading evaluative information or conclusions. Consult colleagues for suggestions on proper ways to proceed, if concerns cannot be resolved and decline the evaluation when necessary. C7. Disclose all sources of financial support for an evaluation and the source of the request for the evaluation.
D. Respect for People	**Evaluators honor the dignity, well-being, and self-worth of individuals and acknowledge the influence of culture within and across groups.** D1. Strive to gain an understanding of, and treat fairly, the range of perspectives and interests that individuals and groups bring to the evaluation, including those that are not usually included or are oppositional. D2. Abide by current professional ethics, standards, and regulations (including informed consent, confidentiality, and prevention of harm) pertaining to evaluation participants. D3. Strive to maximize the benefits and reduce unnecessary risks or harms for groups and individuals associated with the evaluation. D4. Ensure that those who contribute data and incur risks do so willingly and that they have knowledge of and opportunity to obtain benefits of the evaluation.
E. Common Good and Equity	**Evaluators strive to contribute to the common good and advancement of an equitable and just society.** E1. Recognize and balance the interests of the client, other stakeholders, and the common good while also protecting the integrity of the evaluation. E2. Identify and make efforts to address the evaluation's potential threats to the common good, especially when specific stakeholder interests' conflict with the goals of a democratic, equitable, and just society. E3. Identify and make efforts to address the evaluation's potential risks of exacerbating historic disadvantage or inequity. E4. Promote transparency and active sharing of data and findings with the goal of equitable access to information in forms that respect people and honor promises of confidentiality. E5. Mitigate the bias and potential power imbalances that can occur as a result of the evaluation's context. Self-assess one's own privilege and positioning within that context.

SOURCE: American Evaluation Association. (2018). *Guiding principles for evaluators.* Retrieved from https://www.eval.org/p/cm/ld/fid=51

Introduction to Logic Models

What are logic models, and why do they need to be considered within the context of program evaluation? These are important questions that are becoming more relevant as rehabilitation scholars and educators engage in evaluation efforts around public and private VR services, training and technical assistance, implementation research, and program management in an increasingly accountable environment. *Logic models* are defined as visual representations of how a program is intended to work (Centers for Disease Control and Prevention [CDC], n.d.; Mertens & Wilson, 2012; W.K. Kellogg Foundation [WKKF], 2004). They serve as a picture, connecting program resources and activities with outcomes in a comprehensible document intended to be accessed and used by all stakeholders involved. Logic models are typically one page in length but can be slightly longer depending on the complexity of the initiative.

The next reasonable question is, How do logic models fit with program evaluation? As the WKKF (2006) noted, good evaluation reflects clear thinking and responsible program management. Logic models help identify outcomes and anticipate ways to measure them, therefore providing a "road map" for all stakeholders to use in achieving the goals of the program. Effective evaluation should provide opportunities to continually learn and improve programs, not just to collect, analyze, and report data. It is intended to be a collaborative process facilitated by evaluators, involving multiple key stakeholders, with the logic model serving as a visual tool to systematically present shared understanding and responsibility. Ongoing communication among stakeholders, including evaluators, is necessary in ensuring the evaluation is on track. Logic models serve as a means for enhancing communication and common understanding during the evaluation process.

Participatory Nature of Logic Models

Ensuring that partners, including program staff, practitioners, and others, have a voice in the development of the logic model is important. Ideally, good logic models reflect a collaborative group process with combined input into the identification of program concepts, setting of priorities, and establishment of indicators used to measure success. The goal is to enhance shared understanding across partners through development of a relatively simple image. The logic model reflects how and why the program works, serves as a management and learning tool, enhances the participatory nature of the process, strengthens the evaluation as a whole, and builds evaluation capacity and commitment among stakeholders (Mertens & Wilson, 2012; WKKF, 2006).

Components of a Logic Model

Although numerous formats exist, all logic models use the same general domains to frame the *planned work*, including the resources needed to implement program activities, and *results* involving the outputs, outcomes, and impact the program intends to achieve. *Assumptions*, which form the theory used to develop the program or intervention, are important to document in the logic model, as are *contextual factors* describing the environment within which the program exists. Both assumptions and contextual factors are instrumental in understanding why and how programs succeed or fail and are important to document throughout the evaluation process. Unlike research that often controls for specific variables, program evaluation is a dynamic process conducted with multiple stakeholders, representing various organizations and roles, often resulting in actively changing contextual factors. Acknowledging this through the logic model

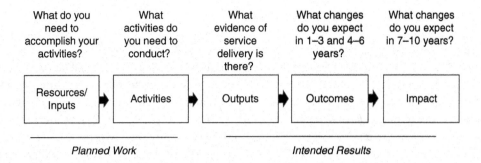

FIGURE 18.1 Basic components of a logic model.

process provides opportunity for program partners to discuss and proactively modify activities, as needed, to address the changing environmental aspects.

Logic models are constructed with a left to right flow, using a sequence of "If . . . then . . ." statements to connect the various parts of the program in a reasonable order. In addition to assumptions and contextual factors, the key components of a logic model include inputs, activities, outputs, short-term and longer term outcomes, and impact (see Figure 18.1).

Inputs

Inputs, or resources needed to implement the program, may include funding, potential partners, organizational or interpersonal networks, staff, community members, equipment, facilities, supplies, networks, and so on.

Activities

Activities involve the actions of the planned program intended to produce measurable results. Examples include development and implementation of training, processes, events, promotional materials, tools and curricula, and technology.

Outputs

Outputs are defined as the direct results flowing from program activities and are typically measured with quantitative data. Examples include the number of trainings conducted, materials produced or distributed, hours of service provided, participation rates, participant demographics, and more.

Outcomes

Program outcomes are delineated by short-term and longer term goals. They should be specific, measurable, action-oriented, realistic, and time-bound (SMART) and designed to measure specific changes in individual attitudes, behaviors, knowledge, skills, participation rates, and related outcomes resulting from program activities. *Short-term* outcomes are results expected within 1 to 3 years of implementing program activities. Short-term outcomes focus on formative evaluation or gathering information to help improve the program. Information can be analyzed and shared quickly using rapid cycle evaluation (RCE) techniques (www.mathematica-mpr.com/our -capabilities/rapid-cycle-evaluation). RCE is consistent with performance measurement and is ongoing, responsive, adaptive, and designed to use active data to answer questions and improve the program. The focus is on program activities, outputs, and short-term outcomes for the purpose of monitoring progress and making midcourse corrections when needed (WKKF, 2006). *Longer term* outcomes reflect results expected 4 to 6 years following the activities and typically build on the short-term outcomes. This summative information is used to demonstrate the results of the program to funders and other stakeholders. The focus is on the program's intermediate-term outcomes and impact to determine the value of the program based on results (WKKF, 2006).

Impact

Impact results are expected at least 7 to 10 years following implementation of a planned activity. They reflect the broader systems level changes within the organization and/or community that the program is working to achieve. Examples include improved performance through capacity building, policy changes, interagency collaboration, and funding commitment to support the change.

Developing a Logic Model

Theory-based logic models are commonly used with rehabilitation-focused evaluation efforts. They are designed using a "big picture" conceptualization of the program and link theoretical ideas together to help explain program assumptions, focusing on broad concepts and not necessarily on specifics (Mertens & Wilson, 2012; WKKF, 2006). See Figure 18.2 for an example logic model.

Engaging Stakeholders

Focusing discussion on the outcomes sections first is helpful with stakeholder involvement and useful in defining the program purpose and evaluation focus. Although conducting activities and producing outputs are important to measure, defining the results the program strives to achieve will help clarify how best to structure the other elements. Keep in mind that policymakers, administrators, practitioners, and community members often present a variety of interests. Gathering information across multiple stakeholder groups creates an opportunity to identify outcomes, and realistic measures, that are meaningful to all involved. Examples of stakeholder questions that can be adapted into evaluation questions include the following:

Rehabilitation counselors (practitioners): Are we reaching our target population? What are the time considerations involved in implementing a new service? In serving a different population?

Administrators: Are participants satisfied with our services? Is the program being run efficiently? What are the costs and benefits involved with the program? How can we improve our program?

Community members: Does the program fit with our needs? Does the program improve things in our community?

Policymakers: Who does the program serve? Has the program made a difference? What are the costs and benefits of the program? Is this an improvement to what we had before? What is the participants' perception of the program?

A well-designed logic model can be very useful in developing the evaluation strategy. The framework enhances the evaluation's effectiveness by focusing on questions that have real value for stakeholders and prioritizing where and how the investment will be the most useful (WKKF, 2006).

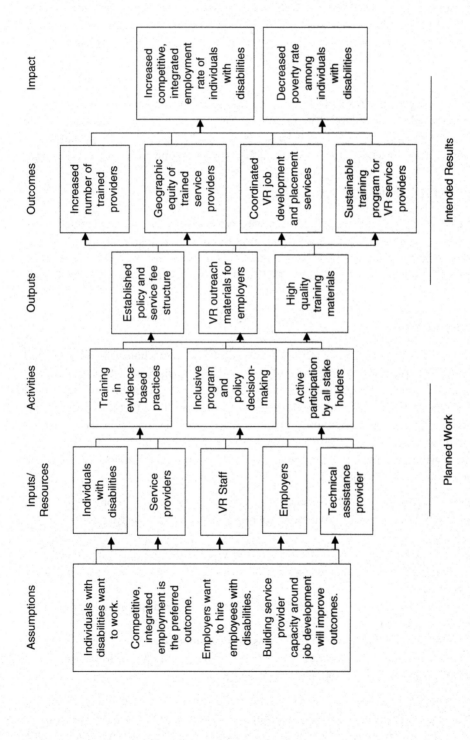

FIGURE 18.2 Example logic model for vocational rehabilitation services capacity building.

VR, vocational rehabilitation.

SOURCE: Adapted from W.K. Kellogg Foundation. (2004). *Logic model development guide.* Retrieved from https://www.wkkf.org/resource-directory/resource/2006/02/wk-kellogg-foundation-logic-model-development-guide

Context questions provide information about relationships and capacity (politics, funding, legislation, natural disaster, other) influencing implementation. Implementation questions assess the quality and quantity with which activities were performed as planned. And outcomes questions are designed to measure changes that occur as a result of the program, including effectiveness, magnitude, and satisfaction (WKKF, 2006). Keeping the logic model simple aids in supporting an effective evaluation strategy. In developing a logic model, evaluators must keep at the forefront the purpose and scope of the program evaluation. Consideration of the aims of the evaluation, what specific components are subject to the evaluation, how the evaluation will support the long-term vision of the organization, and the resources available to conduct the evaluation are just a few areas that program evaluators should consider in designing the logic model. Remember that the purpose of a logic model is to serve as a visual tool for stakeholders by illustrating the sequence of evaluation events, and desired results of the program, in a user-friendly format. They are intended to be flexible and serve as a communication instrument through which stakeholders can review, assess, and adjust as needed. Logic models support shared understanding and consensus around program goals, methodology, project management, responsibilities, reporting, and desired outcomes from design through implementation. This provides an important foundation in developing an evaluation plan that is meaningful and manageable (WKKF, 2006).

▨ Discrete Measures for Program Evaluation

Logic models provide an organizational and conceptual structure to the evaluation process. However, the benefits of the logic model can be muted without consideration of the measurement structure of outputs and outcomes. To support program evaluation efforts, metrics should be readily attainable and be relevant to the overall mission and goals of the agency. Subsequent to the development of a logic model to guide program evaluation efforts is the need to identify the type of evaluation. Differing types of evaluation call for different approaches and measures. *Formative evaluation*, also referred to as process evaluation, aims to learn how a program is designed and implemented. The primary objective is to use relevant data throughout the project to help improve implementation and ultimately improve the intended outcomes and impact. *Summative evaluation*, also referred to as impact evaluation, is typically conducted at the end of or following program implementation. The objective of summative evaluation is to learn how effectively a program achieved the outcomes identified in the logic model and to determine the program's influence in enacting the change (Tatian, 2016). Quantitative and qualitative data can be gathered and used with both the formative and summative evaluation phases. The evaluation questions identified by stakeholders play a key role in forming the nature of the evaluation and the methodologies used throughout the process.

Baseline Data

Regardless of whether you are conducting a formative (process) or summative (impact) evaluation or both, establishing baseline data is important in ascertaining a foundation. Baseline data provide the basis from which subsequent data will be compared and represent the environmental context prior to the implementation of program activities. Without baseline data, it is nearly impossible to determine whether the program interventions made a difference or resulted in any improvements or change.

Measures and Methods

The measures and indicators used are determined by the type of evaluation being conducted—formative or summative or both. Most evaluation efforts involve programs with a range of stakeholders. The evaluation questions identified by these groups, ideally through logic model development process, will guide and direct the methods best suited for the program and take contextual issues into consideration. The following methods are commonly applied in program evaluation efforts.

Review of Documentation

Review of documentation may often serve as a first step in program evaluation. As these data are available at the start of the evaluation process, they are often the first data available to the program evaluator. Although document review can be a cumbersome activity relative to other methods (e.g., survey), it provides a metric to assess the direction of the agency and the importance the organization has placed on certain activities by analyzing the development of policies and procedures to promote outcomes, increase efficiency, or promote quality assurance of services.

Surveys

Surveys ask a set of questions to collect data from stakeholders and can be administered online, over the telephone, or in person. It is a useful, lower cost method to gather data from a large sample of people. Common types of questions on surveys are multiple choice, ranking, and rating questions. Depending on the purpose of the survey, open-ended questions may also be included to allow stakeholders the opportunity to provide greater depth to their responses on the survey.

Interviews

Interviews are a method to gather information from a single stakeholder. They allow the program evaluator to collect detailed information on the area of interest. Interviews can be unstructured, semistructured, or structured qualitative. Depending on the level of structure, the facilitator asks group members a series of questions, ranging from predetermined to questions intended to promote conversation of points identified by focus group members.

Focus Groups

Focus groups consist of interviewing a small sample of stakeholders (8–12 people) who possess an insight into the functions of the agency, the services provided, or other effects the agency is having beyond its mission. These stakeholders can be the service recipients, members of their families, collaborating agencies, service providers, or any other group who is engaged in the mission of the agency being fulfilled. Focus groups use similar structures to interviews and are conducted as unstructured, semistructured, or structured qualitative interviews. Depending on the level of structure, the facilitator asks group members a series of questions, ranging from predetermined to questions intended to promote conversation of points identified by focus group members. Focus groups provide qualitative data that can be used to describe an effort or issue. Modern techniques in qualitative analysis also allow for the quantification of focus group data for use in quantitative analysis.

Public Forums and Listening Sessions

Public forums can be used to gather information from a group of people who may not have previously been identified as stakeholders but are interested in the aims of the agency. They are a good method for gathering information during the initial stages of a research project. Public forums provide a mechanism to evaluate the reach of agency initiatives to the general public, other agencies, local businesses, and members of the community.

Geographic Data and Community Mapping

Geographic information systems (GIS) are digital mapping methods that allow for closer examination of specific program variables based on defined geographic boundaries, such as zip codes. GIS maps are used frequently in evaluating public health and community-based programs and are becoming more common in public VR agencies. The maps, which are generated using GIS software packages, provide a visual representation of the program data to help illustrate patterns, scope, capacity, need, and participant characteristics, such as age, race and ethnicity, income level, and more (Center for Community Health and Development [CCHD], 2017). As an example, a program evaluator might be interested in better understanding the participant demographics within a particular rural county or perhaps the number and type of service providers present within a specific geographic area. GIS maps can be generated using baseline data and, subsequently, at various points of the formative and summative phases of evaluation to help illustrate change and outcomes over time. They provide an efficient method for creating maps and graphics that can be helpful in understanding the geographic and demographic aspects of a program and serve as effective tools in presentations to stakeholders.

Photovoice

Photovoice methods are intended to help evaluators and policymakers better understand the lives of marginalized and disadvantaged populations, including those based on poverty, language barriers, race, class, ethnicity, gender, culture, or other demographic factors. With this particular method, participants use photos and/or videos to document their experiences and environmental aspects, which are often identified as outcome areas the program is seeking to change. Photovoice is used as an empowerment strategy to help document the needs, resources, and experiences of a specific population or community (CCHD, 2017).

Public Records and Administrative Data

The use of public records and administrative data is an important component of both formative and summative evaluation of federal and state agencies. The data collected within the general operation of agencies, either for internal evaluation or for response to external queries, are often used as a broad metric of performance. For example, the Workforce Innovation and Opportunity Act (WIOA) was designed to support the employment, education, and training of the labor market in the United States. Under WIOA, state agencies are required to provide information on specific data points, identified as performance accountability indicators. These indicators are used to assess the effectiveness of state agencies and their local partners in the areas of employment, wages, educational attainment, skill development, and efforts to work with employers (see Table 18.3).

TABLE 18.3 Six Common Performance Indicators Required by the Workforce Innovation and Opportunity Act

PERFORMANCE INDICATOR	OVERVIEW
Employment Rate—Second Quarter After Exit	Percentage of participants who are in unsubsidized employment during the second quarter after exit from the program.
Employment Rate—Fourth Quarter After Exit	Percentage of participants who are in unsubsidized employment during the fourth quarter after exit from the program.
Median Earnings—Second Quarter After Exit	Median earnings of participants who are in unsubsidized employment during the second quarter after exit from the program.
Credential Attainment	Percentage of those participants enrolled in an education or training program who attain a recognized postsecondary credential or a secondary school diploma, or its recognized equivalent, during participation in or within 1 year after exit from the program.
Measurable Skill Gains	Percentage of program participants who are in an education or training program that leads to a recognized postsecondary credential or employment and who are achieving measurable skill gains, defined as documented academic, technical, occupational, or other forms of progress, toward such a credential or employment.
Effectiveness in Serving Employers	Requirement to establish a primary indicator of performance for effectiveness in serving employers.

SOURCE: U.S. Department of Labor. (2004). *WIOA performance indicators and program specific performance measures.* Retrieved from https://www.doleta.gov/performance/guidance/tools_commonmeasures.cfm

Conclusion

Ongoing evaluation is an important component of healthy program management and should be integrated throughout the design, implementation, and maintenance phases. Identifying fitting evaluation questions across multiple stakeholder groups, determining the most suitable means with which to gather data, and actively analyzing and using the data to inform continuous program improvement are essential. Ideally, this interactive process will lead to improved outcomes. Additionally, actively communicating formative and summative information with key partners is important in encouraging continuing engagement and support for the program. Ensuring competency in the field requires program evaluators to approach their work with curiosity and continuously learn with and from each other by participating in ongoing training and education opportunities.

References

American Evaluation Association. (2018). *Guiding principles for evaluators.* Retrieved from https://www.eval.org/p/cm/ld/fid=51

Center for Community Health and Development. (2017). *Chapter 3, Section 20: Implementing photovoice in your community* (Chapter 3, Section 20). Lawrence: University of Kansas, The Community Tool Box. Retrieved from http://ctb.ku.edu/en/table-of-contents/assessment/assessing-community-needs-and-resources/conduct-concerns-surveys/main

Centers for Disease Control and Prevention. (n.d.). *CDC evaluation documents, workbooks, and tools: Logic models.* Retrieved from https://www.cdc.gov/eval/tools/logic_models/index.html

Chan, F., Tarvydas, V., Blalock, K., Strauser, D., & Atkins, B. J. (2009). Unifying and elevating rehabilitation counseling through model-driven, diversity-sensitive evidence-based practice. *Rehabilitation Counseling Bulletin, 52,* 114–119. doi:10.1177/0034355208323947

Leahy, M. J., Thielsen, V. T., Millington, M. J., Austin, B., & Fleming, A. (2009). Quality assurance and program evaluation: Terms, models, and application in rehabilitation administration. *Journal of Rehabilitation Administration, 33,* 69–82.

Mertens, D. M., & Wilson, A. T. (2012). *Program evaluation theory and practice: A comprehensive guide.* New York, NY: Guilford Press.

Rubin, S. E., Chan, R., & Thomas, D. (2003). Assessing changes in life skills and quality of life resulting from rehabilitation services. *Journal of Rehabilitation, 69,* 4–9.

Stevahn, L., King, J. A., Ghere, G., & Minnema, J. (2005). Establishing essential competencies for program evaluators. *American Journal of Evaluation, 26*(1), 43–59. doi:10.1177/1098214004273180

Tatian, P. A. (2016). *Performance measurement to evaluation.* Washington, DC: Urban Institute. Retrieved from https://www.urban.org/sites/default/files/publication/78571/2000555-performance-measurement-to-evaluation-march-2016-update.pdf

U.S. Department of Labor. (2004). *WIOA performance indicators and program specific performance measures.* Retrieved from https://www.doleta.gov/performance/guidance/tools_commonmeasures.cfm

W.K. Kellogg Foundation. (2004). *Logic model development guide.* Retrieved from https://www.wkkf.org/resource-directory/resource/2006/02/wk-kellogg-foundation-logic-model-development-guide

INDEX